THE U.S. INTELLIGENCE
COMMUNITY

THE U.S. INTELLIGENCE COMMUNITY

Second Edition

JEFFREY RICHELSON

BALLINGER PUBLISHING COMPANY
Cambridge, Massachusetts
A Subsidiary of Harper & Row Publishers, Inc.

JK
468, 16
, I6
R53
1989

 # 18781564

International Standard Book Number: 0-88730-245-9
0-88730-226-2 (paperback)

Library of Congress Catalog Card Number: 88-8061

Printed in the United States of America

Library of Congress Cataloging-in-Publication Data

Richelson, Jeffrey.
  The U.S. intelligence community.

  Includes bibliographies and index.
  1. Intelligence service—United States. I. Title. II. Title:
United States intelligence community.
JK468.I6R53 1989   327.1'2'0973 88-8061
ISBN 0-88730-245-9
ISBN 0-88730-226-2 (pbk.)

CONTENTS

LIST OF FIGURES

LIST OF TABLES

LIST OF ABBREVIATIONS
AND ACRONYMS

ABMA	Army Ballistic Missile Agency
ACSI	Assistant Chief of Staff, Intelligence
ACOUSTINT	acoustic intelligence
AEDS	Atomic Energy Detection System
AFAR	Azores Fixed Acoustic Range
AFIA	Air Force Intelligence Agency
AFIS	Air Force Intelligence Service
AFMIC	Armed Forces Medical Intelligence Center
AFOSI	Air Force Office of Special Investigations
AFR	Air Force Regulation
AFSA	Armed Forces Security Agency
AFSAC	Air Force Special Activities Center
AFSA/IRC	Armed Forces Security Agency/Intelligence Requirements Committee
AFSG	Air Force Security Group
AFSS	Air Force Security Service
AFTAC	Air Force Technical Applications Center
AIA	Army Intelligence Agency
AIOD	Army Intelligence Operations Detachment
ALPA	Alaska Long Period Array
AMSIC	Army Missile and Space Intelligence Center
AOMC	Army Ordnance Missile Command
AR	Army Regulation
ARIA	Advanced Range Instrumentation Aircraft
ARIS	Advanced Range Instrumentation Ships

ASIS	Australian Secret Intelligence Service
ATGM	antitank guided missile
BBC	British Broadcasting Corporation
BMEWS	Ballistic Missile Early Warning System
BRUSA	British–United States Communications Intelligence Agreement
BSTIS	*Biweekly Scientific and Technical Intelligence Summary*
CAMS	COMIREX Automated Management System
CAPG	Covert Action Planning Group
CASPER	Contact Area Summary Position Report
CCD	charged couple devices
CCF	Collection Coordination Facility
CCP	Consolidated Cryptologic Program
CCPC	Critical Collection Problems Committee
CDAA	Circularly Disposed Antenna Array
CERP	Combined Economic Reporting Program
CFI	Committee on Foreign Intelligence
CIA	Central Intelligence Agency
CIG	Central Intelligence Group
CINCPACFLT	Commander in Chief Pacific Fleet
CINCSAC	Commander in Chief Strategic Air Command
CIPC	Critical Intelligence Problems Committee
CIRL	Current Intelligence Reporting List
CIS	Country Intelligence Study
CISR	Communications Intelligence Supplementary Regulations
COIC	Combat Operations Intelligence Center
COMINT	communications intelligence
COMIREX	Committee on Imagery Requirements and Exploitation
COMSEC	communications security
CORD	Current Operations and Readiness Department, NOIC
CSAW	Communications Supplementary Activity Washington
CSE	Communications Security Establishment (Canada)
CSS	Central Security Service
DARPA	Defense Advanced Research Projects Agency
DCI	Director of Central Intelligence
DCID	Director of Central Intelligence Directive
DCSI	Deputy Chief of Staff for Intelligence
DEA	Drug Enforcement Administration
DEFSMAC	Defense Special Missile and Astronautics Center
DEPLOC	Daily Estimated Position Locator
DGSE	Direccion General de Seguridad del Estado—Directorate General of State Security (Nicaragua)
DIA	Defense Intelligence Agency

DIE	Defense Intelligence Estimate
DIN	Defense Intelligence Notice
DIO	Defense Intelligence Officer
DIPPs	Defense Intelligence Projections for Planning
DISOB	Defense Intelligence Space Order of Battle
DISUM	Defense Intelligence Summary
DMSP	Defense Meteorological Satellite Program
DOD	Department of Defense
DOE	Department of Energy
DRSP	Defense Reconnaissance Support Program
DS&T	Directorate of Science and Technology, CIA
DSCS	Defense Satellite Communications System
DSD	Defense Signals Directorate (Australia)
DSSCS	Defense Special Security Communications System
DSP	Defense Support Program
DSPO	Defense Support Project Office
EAL	Economic Alert List
ELINT	electronic intelligence
ESAF	European Special Activities Facility
ESC	Electronic Security Command
EUCOM	European Command
EUDAC	European Defense Analysis Center
EXRAND	Exploitation Research and Development Subommittee (of COMIREX)
FAS	Foreign Agricultural Service
FBI	Federal Bureau of Investigation
FICEURLANT	Fleet Intelligence Center, Europe and Atlantic
FBIS	Foreign Broadcast Information Service
FDS	Fixed Distributed Surveillance System
FISINT	foreign instrumentation signals intelligence
FIST	Fleet Imagery Support Terminal
FLTSATCOM	Fleet Satellite Communications System
FMEP	Foreign Materiel Exploitation Program
FNLA	National Front for the Liberation of Angola
FOSIC	Fleet Ocean Surveillance Information Center
FOSIF	Fleet Ocean Surveillance Information Facility
FRD	Foreign Resources Division (Directorate of Operations, CIA)
FRD	Federal Research Division, Library of Congress
FSTC	Foreign Science and Technology Center
FTD	Foreign Technology Division
GATT	General Agreement on Tariffs and Trade
GCHQ	Government Communications Headquarters (U.K.)

GCSB	Government Communications Security Bureau (New Zealand)
GDIP	General Defense Intelligence Program
GEODSS	Ground Based Electro-Optical Deep Space Surveillance System
GIUK	Greenland–Iceland–United Kingdom
GMAIC	Guided Missile and Astronautics Intelligence Committee
GPS	Global Positioning System
GRU	Chief Intelligence Directorate, Soviet General Staff
HF	high frequency
HQ CSTC	Headquarters, Consolidated Space Test Center
HUMINT	human intelligence
ICBM	intercontinental ballistic missile
ICS	Intelligence Community Staff
IDC	Interagency Defector Committee
IG-CI	Interagency Group—Counterintelligence
IG-CM (P)	Interagency Group—Countermeasures (Policy)
IG-CM (T)	Interagency Group—Countermeasures (Technical)
IGCP	Intelligence Guidance for COMINT Production
IIM	Interagency Intelligence Memorandum
ILD	International Liaison Department (PRC)
INFOSEC	information security
INR	Bureau of Intelligence and Research, Department of State
INSCOM	Army Intelligence and Security Command
INTELSAT	International Telecommunications Satellite
IPAC	Intelligence Center Pacific
IPC	Intelligence Producers Council
IROL	Imagery Requirements Objectives List
IRAC	Intelligence Resources Advisory Committee
IRSIG	International Regulations on SIGINT
ISA	Intelligence Support Activity
ITAC	Intelligence and Threat Analysis Center
JAEIC	Joint Atomic Energy Intelligence Committee
JCS	Joint Chiefs of Staff
JRC	Joint Reconnaissance Center
JSTPS	Joint Strategic Target Planning Staff
KEYSCOM	Imagery Interpretation Keys Subcommittee (of COMIREX)
KGB	Soviet Committee for State Security
KH	Keyhole
KIQ	Key Intelligence Questions
LANTDAC	Atlantic Command Defense Analysis Center
LASINT	laser intelligence

MASINT	measurement and signature intelligence
MCL	McClellan Central Laboratory
MOTIF	Maui Optical Tracking and Identification Facility
MPLA	People's Movement for the Liberation of Angola
NASA	National Aeronautics and Space Administration
NATO	North Atlantic Treaty Organization
NAVFAC	Naval Facility
NAVSPASUR	Naval Space Surveillance System
NCD	National Collection Division, Directorate of Operations, CIA
NDS	Nuclear Detonation (NUDET) Detection System
NEACP	National Emergency Airborne Command Post
NETCAP	National Exploitation of Tactical Capabilities
NFAC	National Foreign Assessment Center
NFIB	National Foreign Intelligence Board
NFIC	National Foreign Intelligence Council
NFIP	National Foreign Intelligence Program
NFMP	Navy Foreign Materiel Program
NFOIO	Naval Field Operational Intelligence Office
NIAM	National Intelligence Analytical Memorandum
NIC	Naval Intelligence Command
NIC	National Intelligence Council
NID	*National Intelligence Daily*
NIE	National Intelligence Estimate
NIO	National Intelligence Officer
NIPSSA	Naval Intelligence Processing System Support Activity
NISC	Naval Intelligence Support Center
NISR	National Intelligence Situation Report
NISSTR	National Intelligence Systems for Support of Tactical Requirements
NITs	National Intelligence Topics
NITC	National Intelligence Tasking Center
NMCC	National Military Command Center
NMIC	National Military Intelligence Center
NOIC	Navy Operational Intelligence Center
NOO	Naval Oceanographic Office
NORSAR	Norwegian Seismic Array
NPIC	National Photographic Interpretation Center
NREC	National Reconnaissance Executive Committee
NRL	Naval Research Laboratory
NRO	National Reconnaissance Office
NRPC	Naval Regional Processing Center
NSA	National Security Agency
NSC	National Security Council

NSCIC	National Security Council Intelligence Committee
NSCID	National Security Council Intelligence Directive
NSDD	National Security Decision Directive
NSDM	National Security Decision Memorandum
NSGC	Naval Security Group Command
NSOC	National SIGINT Operations Center
NSRL	National SIGINT Requirements List
NSTL	National Strategic Target List
OACSI	Office of the Assistant Chief of Staff, Intelligence
OAG	Operations Advisory Group
OAS	Organization of American States
OASIS	Operational Applications of Special Intelligence Systems
OEE	Office of Export Enforcement
OIA	Office of Imagery Analysis, Directorate of Intelligence, CIA
OGI	Office of Global Issues, Directorate of Intelligence, CIA
OIR	Office of Information Resources, Directorate of Intelligence, CIA
OLA	Office of Leadership Analysis, Directorate of Intellience, CIA
OMB	Office of Management and Budget
ONI	Office of Naval Intelligence
OPEC	Organization of Petroleum Exporting Countries
OR&D	Office of Research and Development, Directorate of Science and Technology, CIA
OSI	Office of Strategic Information
OSO	Office of SIGINT Operations, Directorate of Science and Technology, CIA
OSS	Office of Strategic Services
OTS	Office of Technical Services, Directorate of Science and Technology, CIA
OSWR	Office of Scientific and Weapons Research, Directorate of Science and Technology, CIA
PACBAR	Pacific Radar Barrier
PACCS	Post-Attack Command and Control System
PACOM	Pacific Command
PARCS	Perimeter Acquisition Radar Characterization System
PCG	Planning and Coordination Group
PD	Presidential Directive
PDB	President's Daily Brief
PGW	precision guided weapons
PLO	Palestine Liberation Organization
PNET	Peaceful Nuclear Explosion Treaty
PRC	Policy Review Committee
QRT	Quick Reaction Team

RADINT	radar intelligence
RAF	Royal Air Force
RAW	Research and Analysis Wing (India)
RDSS	Rapidly Deployable Surveillance System
ROFA	Remote Operations Facility, Airborne
RTG	Reconnaissance Technical Group
RTS	Reconnaissance Technical Squadron
RWO	Ramstein Warning Office
SAC	Strategic Air Command
SAMOS	Satellite and Missile Observation System
SBSS	Space-Based Surveillance System
SCA	Service Cryptological Authority
SCC	Special Coordination Committee
SCI	Sensitive Compartmented Information
SDIE	Special Defense Intelligence Estimate
SDS	Satellite Data System
SECOM	Security Committee
SIG-I	Senior Interagency Group—Intelligence
SIGINT	signals intelligence
SIGSEC	signals security
SIOP	Single Integrated Operational Plan
SIRE	Space Infrared Experiments
SIRVES	SIGINT Requirements Validation and Evaluation Subcommittee
SIS	Secret Intelligence Service (United Kingdom)
SLBM	submarine launched ballistic missile
SNIE	Special National Intelligence Estimate
SORS	Space Operational Requirements Subcommittee
SOSUS	Sound Surveillance System
SOUTHCOM	Southern Command
SPADATS	Space Detection and Tracking System
SPINTCOM	Special Intelligence Communications
SPIREP	Spot Intelligence Report
SPOEM	Special Program Office for Exploitation Modernization
SPOER	Special Operational ELINT Requirements
SRC	Strategic Reconnaissance Center, SAC
SRBM	short-range ballistic missile
START	Strategic Arms Reduction Talks
STIC	Scientific and Technical Intelligence Committee
STS	Space Transportation System
SURTASS	Surface Towed Array Surveillance System
TAREX	target exploitation
TCP	Tactical Cryptologic Program
TDI	Target Data Inventory

TDI	Target Data Inventory
TELINT	telemetry intelligence
TENCAP	Tactical Exploitation of National Space Capabilities
TERCOM	Terrain Contour Matching
TFC	Tactical Fusion Center
TIARA	Tactical Intelligence and Related Activities
TIP	Travelers in Panama (file)
TK	Talent–Keyhole
TRANSCOM	Transportation Command
TSR	Time Sensitive Requirements
TTIC	Technology Transfer Intelligence Committee
UHF	ultra high frequency
UKUSA	United Kingdom–United States Security Agreement
UNITA	National Union for the Total Independence of Angola
USAFE	United States Air Forces, Europe
USAREUR	United States Army Europe
USCIB/IC	U.S. Communications Intelligence Board/Intelligence Committee
USIB	United States Intelligence Board
USNAVEUR	U.S. Naval Forces, Europe
USSID	United States Signals Intelligence Directive
USSS	United States SIGINT System
VHF	very high frequency
VKL	Communications Experience Facility (Finland)
VOD	Vertical Observation Data
WIS	*Weekly Intelligence Summary*
WISE	Warning Indications Systems, Europe
WSSIC	Weapons and Space Systems Intelligence Committee
WWR	*Weekly Watch Report*

PREFACE

This book represents an attempt to accomplish in one volume what requires several volumes. It attempts to provide a comprehensive and detailed order of battle of the U.S. intelligence community—to describe its collection and analysis organizations, their activities, and the management structure that is responsible for directing and supervising those organizations and activities.

Given the purpose of the book, I do not, up until the concluding chapter, seek to evaluate the intelligence community's effectiveness in performing its varied tasks or comment on the acceptability, wisdom, or morality of its activities. In the concluding chapter I address some of the issues facing the intelligence community and the general public.

The data used in this book comes from a variety of sources—interviews; official documents (many of which were acquired under the Freedom of Information Act); books written by former intelligence officers, journalists, and academics; trade and technical publications; newspapers; and magazines. The public literature on intelligence is vast and of varying quality, and I have done my best to sort out the wheat from the chaff. I have also sought to identify sources to the maximum extent possible while protecting those sources who wished to remain anonymous.

Two groups of individuals were instrumental in the writing of this book. The work of the Freedom of Information officers who responded to my many hundreds of requests is greatly appreciated. Some may have been frustrated to find that providing one set of requested documents only led to additional requests. Of course, there were a few organizations (U.S. Naval Forces Europe, the U.S. Southern Command, the Naval Security Group Command, and the Air Force Technical Applications Center) that avoided the problem by never acknowledging my requests or refusing to take any action on them.

In addition, various journalists, researchers, and others have provided information, documents, suggestions, corrections, assistance, and critiques of various chapters. Those who can be acknowledged publicly are: William Arkin, Scott Armstrong, Desmond Ball, Robert Bolin, William Burrows, Duncan Campbell, Seymour Hersh, Peter Kornbluh, Alan Krass, David Morison, Jay Peterzell, John Pike, Joseph Pittera, John Prados, Owen Wilkes, Marshall Windmiller, and Robert Windrem.

I am also happy to acknowledge the assistance of the National Security Archive in locating declassified documents.

I also would like to thank those at Ballinger Publishing Company who helped turn a manuscript into a book.

1 INTELLIGENCE

Informed policymaking and decisionmaking requires adequate information and analysis. Only if policymakers and decisionmakers are sufficiently informed about the state of the world and the likely consequences of policies and actions can they be expected to make intelligent decisions. If their responsibilities have foreign aspects, they will require the acquisition of foreign intelligence information.

The individuals with the most prominent need for foreign intelligence are those concerned with national security policymaking and decisionmaking. Hence, the President, National Security Council (NSC), the Secretary of State, and the Secretary of Defense are the most visible consumers of foreign intelligence.

However, there are many policymakers who have a need for foreign intelligence, just as there are ways other than political or military action that foreign governments or groups can effect the national security or public welfare of the United States. This became particularly evident due to the oil embargoes of the 1970s. While Chairman of the House Permanent Select Committee on Intelligence, Edward Boland noted that "many believe...that energy and related economic problems can threaten us more deeply and affect our national security more rapidly than any change in the military picture short of war itself."[1] Clearly, the availability of foreign energy resources, as well as the stability of the dollar, can be influenced by the actions of foreign governments or groups.

INTELLIGENCE

Strictly speaking, intelligence can be defined as the "product resulting from the collection, evaluation, analysis, integration and interpretation of all available information which concerns one or more aspects of foreign nations or of areas of operation which is immediately or potentially significant for planning."[2]

1

Collection can be defined as the purposeful acquisition of any information that might be desired by analyst, consumer, or operator. Collection activity can take any one of several overlapping forms: open source collection, clandestine collection, human source collection, or technical collection.

Open source collection includes the acquisition of material in the public domain: radio and television broadcasts, newspapers, magazines, technical and scholarly journals, books, government reports, and reports by foreign service officers and defense attachés concerning public activities. The extent to which open source collection yields valuable information will vary greatly with the nature of the targeted society and the subject involved. The information might be collected by human sources—individuals who buy books and journals or observe military parades—or by technical resources—recording television and radio programs.

Clandestine collection involves the acquisition of data that are not publicly available. As with open source collection, both human and technical resources may be employed for clandestine collection. The traditional human spy may be employed to provide sensitive political, military or economic information. Alternatively, technical collection systems can be used to photograph military installations or intercept a wide variety of communications and electronic signals.

Great secrecy and sensitivity are more characteristics of human-source clandestine collection. Although much technical collection is also clandestine, secrecy is not always as vital as in the case of human collection. The United States and Soviet Union are well aware of, if not totally informed of, each other's satellite reconnaissance programs. Even in the absence of an arms control agreement that prohibits concealment and deception measures with respect to certain activities, some of those activities would be extremely difficult, if not impossible, to conceal from technical collectors. In such cases, the ability to effectively collect the required data does not depend on its being done clandestinely. In contrast, a human "asset" in the Soviet establishment whose identity becomes known to the KGB (Soviet Committee for State Security) will soon be arrested or become the channel for disinformation.

Analysis involves the integration of collected information or raw intelligence from all sources into finished intelligence. The finished intelligence product might be a simple statement of facts, an estimate of the capabilities of another nation's military forces, or a projection of the likely course of political events in another nation.

Strictly speaking, intelligence activities involve only the collection and analysis of information and its transformation into intelligence; however, several other activities—counterintelligence and covert action—are intertwined with intelligence activity.

Counterintelligence is the acquisition of information or activity designed to assess foreign intelligence and security services and neutralize hostile services. These activities involve clandestine and open source collection, and analysis of information concerning the structure and operations of foreign services. Such collection and analysis, with respect to the technical collection activities of hostile services, can be employed to conduct "denial" operations. Counterintelligence may also involve the direct penetration and disruption of hostile services.

Covert action, also known as "special activities," can be defined as any operation or activity designed to influence foreign governments, persons, or events in support of the sponsoring government's foreign policy objectives while keeping the sponsoring government's *support* of the operation secret. While in the case of clandestine collection the emphasis is on keeping the activity secret, the emphasis in covert action is on keeping the sponsorship secret.

There are several distinct types of covert action: black propaganda (propaganda that purports to emanate from a source other than the true one); gray propaganda (in which true sponsorship is not acknowledged); paramilitary or political actions designed to overthrow or support a regime; support (aid, arms, training) of individuals and organizations (newspapers, labor unions, and political parties); economic operations; disinformation; and assassination.

THE INTELLIGENCE CYCLE

It is important to put the collection and analysis activities conducted by various intelligence units into proper perspective—one that relates those activities to the requirements and needs of the decisionmakers and the use made of the finished intelligence product. This is done through the concept of the "intelligence cycle."

The intelligence cycle is the process by which information is acquired, converted into finished intelligence, and made available to policymakers. Generally, the cycle comprises five steps: planning and direction, collection, processing, production and analysis, and dissemination.[3]

Planning and direction involves the management of the entire intelligence effort, from the identification of the need for data to the final delivery of an intelligence product to a consumer. The process may be initiated by requests or requirements for intelligence on certain subjects based on the needs of the consumers—the President, the Departments of State, Defense, and Treasury, or others. In some cases, the requests and requirements become institutionalized. Thus, the President does not need to remind the intelligence community to collect information on Soviet strategic forces.

Collection, as indicated above, involves the gathering of raw data from which finished intelligence will be produced. The collection process involves open sources, clandestine agents, and technical systems. Processing is concerned with the conversion of the vast amount of information coming into the system to a form more suitable for the production of finished intelligence. It involves language translation, decryption, and sorting by subject matters as well as data reduction—interpretation of the information stored on film and tape through the use of photographic and electronic processes.

Production and analysis refers to the conversion of basic information into finished intelligence. It includes the integration, evaluation, and analysis of all available data and the preparation of various intelligence products. The "raw intelligence" that is collected may often be fragmentary and at times contradictory, requiring specialists to give it meaning and significance.

The final step in the cycle is dissemination. This involves the distribution and handling of the finished intelligence to the consumers—the policymakers (and operators) whose needs triggered the intelligence-gathering process.

Like any model, this outline of the intelligence cycle is a simplification of the real world. As noted above, certain requirements become standing requirements. Similarly, policymakers will not specify, except in rare cases, specific items of information. Rather, they will indicate a desire for reports on, for example, Chinese strategic forces or the political situation in Egypt. The collectors are given the responsibility of determining how to obtain the information necessary to prepare such reports. Finally, the collection agencies will have a certain internal need to acquire information to provide for their continued operation—information related to counterintelligence and security and information that will be useful in potential future operations.

THE UTILITY OF INTELLIGENCE

The utility of intelligence activity, here narrowly construed to mean collection and analysis, depends on the extent to which it aids national, departmental, and military service decisionmakers. Two questions arise in this regard: in what ways does intelligence aid decisionmakers, and what attributes make intelligence useful? With respect to the first question, five distinct areas exist in which intelligence can be useful to national decisionmakers: policymaking, planning, conflict situations, warning, and treaty verification.

In their policymaking roles, national decisionmakers set the basic outlines of foreign, defense, and international economic policy. Their need for intelligence in order to make sound decisions is summed up in the report of the Rockefeller Commission:

> Intelligence is information gathered for policymakers which illuminates the range of choices available to them and enables them to exercise judgement. Good intelligence will not necessarily lead to wise policy choices. But without sound intelligence, national policy decisions and actions cannot effectively respond to actual conditions and reflect the best national interests or adequately protect . . . national security.[4]

In addition to its value in policymaking, intelligence is vital to the specific decisions needed to implement policy and decisions that might be labeled planning decisions. Some planning decisions may be concerned with the development and deployment of new weapons systems. It has been noted that: "(t)imely, accurate, and detailed Intelligence is a vital element in establishing requirements and priorities for new systems. Intelligence provides much of the rationale for planning and initiating RDT&E (Research, Development, Test & Evaluation) efforts and continues to impact these efforts throughout the development and system life cycle."[5]

One specific incident which illustrates the role of intelligence in weapons development occurred in 1968, when U.S. intelligence monitored a submarine belonging to the oldest class of Soviet nuclear submarines as moving at over 34 miles per hour, with apparent power to spare. That speed exceeded the speed the Central Intelligence Agency (CIA) estimated the submarine could reach, and led the CIA to order full scale revision of speed estimates for Soviet submarines. The revised estimates also provoked one of the largest construction programs in the history of the Navy—the construction of the SSN 688 attack submarine.[6]

Another set of planning decisions are those involved in the development of nuclear war plans—specifically, the Single Integrated Operational Plan (SIOP). Development of the SIOP requires a massive intelligence effort to locate potential targets, and determine their importance and vulnerability to destruction. The intelligence input to the development of the SIOP is illustrated by the titles of a variety of documents—the Nuclear Weapons Intelligence Support Plan, the SIOP Reconnaissance Plan, and the National Strategic Reconnaissance List (the latter based on the National Strategic Target List, from which the SIOP is drawn).

Other decisions aided by intelligence include the suspension or resumption of foreign aid and the employment of trade restrictions. Intelligence might be able to tell the decisionmaker(s) the likely effects of such actions, including the reactions of those nations toward which a particular decision is directed. President Carter's decision to embargo grain sales to the Soviet Union was based in part on the Agriculture Department's estimate that no other country could replace the United States as a major seller to the Soviet Union—"a conclusion which within days was shaken by Argentina's announcement that it would partially replace the United States grain shipments." In another case, the Carter Administration went ahead with the planned sale of planes to Saudi Arabia—partially on the basis of intelligence indicating that if the United States backed out of the deal the Saudis would simply buy French planes.[7]

Conflict situations in which intelligence is of value need not be exclusively of a military nature. Any situation where nations have at least partially conflicting interests, such as in arms control negotiations, trade negotiations or international conferences, would qualify. Intelligence can indicate how far the other negotiator can be pushed and the extent to which a position must be modified to be adopted. In 1969 the United States intercepted Japanese communications concerning the negotiations then taking place between the United States and Tokyo over the reversion of Okinawa to Japanese control.[8]

Warning is also a prime benefit of intelligence. Warning might concern military or other action to be taken against the decisionmaker's own government or nation, or against a country the fate of which concerns the decisionmaker. The warning mission requires, to the greatest extent possible, the monitoring of the armed forces of any potential adversaries. For the United States this means monitoring the status of the entire range of Soviet forces—knowing the numbers deployed, their locations and usual pattern of activity, and notifying the proper authorities in the event of major anomalies. Such anomalies include: (1) a major increase in the level of radio traffic to and from missile fields; (2) mass movements and increases in the level of readiness of combat troops; and (3) changes in codes and ciphers or a prolonged radio silence by key military units. It also means monitoring the activities of nations such as Iran, and terrorist groups. On the basis of advance notice, defenses can be prepared, responses considered and implemented, and preemptive actions (diplomatic or military) taken to forestall or negate action.

Intelligence is also necessary to assess whether other nations are in compliance with international obligations to which they and the United States are pledged to obey. The United States is concerned with whether the Soviet Union is complying with whatever arms control agreements are in force, and with Soviet and other nations' compliance with treaties limiting nuclear proliferation and nuclear testing. At times the United States may also be concerned with whether an allied nation is complying with terms of an economic agreement. One subject of contention in 1987 was whether Japan was violating the "Semiconductor Arrangement" made with the United States in 1986. The arrangement was intended to avoid the below-cost dumping of semiconductors and permit greater foreign semiconductor sales in the Japanese market.[9]

The overall utility of intelligence in regard to military matters was concisely summarized by the Eisenhower Administration's Technological Capabilities Panel:

> If intelligence can uncover a new military threat, we may take steps to meet it. If intelligence can reveal an opponent's specific weakness, we may prepare to exploit it. With good intelligence we can avoid wasting our resources by arming for the wrong danger at the wrong time. Beyond this, in the broadest sense, intelligence underlies our estimate of the enemy and thus helps guide our political strategy.[10]

The utility of intelligence, in addition to being dependent on whether it addresses relevant subjects, is also dependent on its quality and timeliness. Unless all relevant information is marshalled when assessing intelligence on a subject, the quality of the finished product might suffer. Intelligence obtained covertly should not be assessed in isolation from overtly obtained intelligence. As Professor H. Trevor Roper observed,

> Secret intelligence is the continuation of open intelligence by other means. So long as governments conceal a part of their activities, other governments, if they wish to base their policy on full and correct information, must seek to penetrate the veil. This inevitably entails varying methods. But, however the means may vary, the end must still be the same. It is to complement the results of what for convenience, we may call "public" intelligence: that is, the intelligence derived from the rational study of public or at least available sources. Intelligence, in fact, is indivisible.[11]

In addition to being based on all relevant information, the assessment process must be objective. As former Secretary of State Henry Kissinger told the U.S. Senate in 1973: "Anyone concerned with national policy must have a profound interest in making sure that intelligence guides and does not follow, national policy."[12]

Further, intelligence must reach decisionmakers in good time for them to act decisively. Intelligence as foreknowledge has always had particular relevance in military matters. It can give the military commander the great advantage of not being taken by surprise—an advantage the value of which was recognized by Sun

Tzu 2,500 years ago: "The reason the enlightened prince and the wise general conquer the enemy whenever they move and their achievements surpass those of ordinary men is foreknowledge."[13]

TYPES OF INTELLIGENCE

To understand how specific varieties of intelligence can be useful to government officials, one need only consider the components of intelligence. To begin, one might identify several categories of intelligence—political, military, scientific and technical, sociological, economic, and environmental.

Political intelligence will include intelligence about both a nation's foreign and domestic politics. Clearly, the foreign policies of other nations have an impact on the United States. A variety of issues might be involved: support of the United States on a U.N. issue, a nation's relations with the Soviet Union and Cuba, attitudes and policies concerning the Arab-Israeli conflict, the support of revolutionary groups, and leadership perceptions of the United States.

The domestic politics of other nations—whether those nations are friendly, neutral, or hostile—is also of significant concern to the United States, since the resolution of domestic political conflict—whether by coup, election, or civil war—can affect the orientation of that nation in the world, the regional balance of power, the accessibility of critical resources to the United States, or the continued presence of U.S. military bases.

Thus, the outcome of elections in Spain and Greece has threatened to affect those countries' continued participation in NATO (North Atlantic Treaty Organization) and the status of U.S. military bases. Likewise, the resolution of the internal conflict in Iran deprived the United States of several assets: oil, a military ally, and critical intelligence bases from which Soviet missile telemetry could be intercepted. Whether Mikhail Gorbachev or Deng Xiao Ping succeed in bringing significant domestic reforms to their countries may have a significant impact on the nature of their relations with the United States.

Military intelligence is useful and required in a wide variety of situations. The United States, in order to determine its own requirements in strategic weapons, must know the nature of Soviet strategic forces (numbers of delivery vehicles and warheads; their yield, accuracy, and reliability) as well as characteristics of the Soviet target base (numbers, blast resistance, locations). Much of this information is also vital to the negotiation and monitoring of arms limitation agreements. The same basic requirements exist with respect to conventional forces. The size and capabilities, as well as the location and readiness, of Warsaw Pact forces must be continually monitored—either as a guide to NATO planning requirements, as a means of warning against possible attack, or as a means of monitoring a Mutual and Balanced Force Reduction (MBFR) agreement.

The United States may also need to know the military capabilities and plans of friendlier countries—even the most friendly of countries. An Israeli decision to invade Lebanon, retaliate against Syria for some offense or destroy an Iraqi nuclear reactor can set in motion events that have a significant impact on the United States. The close U.S.-British alliance and British possession of an independent nuclear force means that the "United States could end up paying a horrendous price for an allied mistake, which makes it imperative that we learn more about the British command and control system and its susceptibilities to malfunction."[14]

Scientific and technical intelligence includes both civilian- and military-related scientific and technical development. A nation's ability to produce steel or oil may influence both that country's stability and U.S. fortunes. In many cases, technological developments that occur in the civilian sector have military applications. Areas such as computer technology, ball bearing production, mirrors and optical systems, and lasers all have significant military applications. Hence, intelligence concerning a nation's progress in those areas or its ability to absorb foreign-produced technology in those areas is relevant to its potential military capability.

One aspect of scientific and technological intelligence that has been a constant U.S. concern for over thirty years is atomic energy intelligence. Whether the announced purpose of a nation's atomic energy activities has been civilian or military, those activities have received a high intelligence priority. In addition to the obvious need to determine if a foreign government is developing nuclear weapons independent of U.S. government actions, there has also been a perceived need to acquire secret intelligence in support of decisionmaking concerning applications for nuclear technology exports. Thus, the first Director of Central Intelligence (DCI) noted in 1947 that the United States "cannot rely on information submitted by a licensee" and that is was necessary to the United States to "determine actual use, [to] endeavor to discover secondary diversions."[15]

Sociological intelligence concerns group relations within a particular nation. Such relations can have a significant impact on a nation's stability as well as the nature of its foreign policy. India has been subject on numerous occasions to the acts of Sikh terrorists, who seek to turn India's Punjab state into the independent Sikh nation of "Khalistan." Similarly, the extent of the nationality problem in the Soviet Union can have a significant effect on its Middle Eastern policy, as well as its ability to maintain high manpower levels in its armed forces.

Economic intelligence is also of great importance. The activities of, for example, OPEC (Organization of Petroleum Exporting Countries) and the Common Market are matters of concern to U.S. national security and economic policy officials. In 1975 the DCI noted that economic intelligence of value to U.S. policymakers includes "such topics as the activities of multinational corporations, international development programs, regional economic arrangements, and the workings of international commodity markets."[16] Specific areas of interest included:

- Rates of production, consumption, pricing of raw materials and energy sources, and international commodity arrangements as a means to share the burden of price fluctuation between producers and consumers of primary commodities.

- Price and nonprice restrictions on international trade.

- The international payments mechanism and the coordination of national fiscal monetary policies.[17]

Environmental intelligence is required both for decisions on the feasibility of and planning for military operations, and in support of intelligence operations. Aspects of the environment about which decisionmakers and planners must be informed include weather, the climate and prevalence of different types of diseases, surface and subsurface ocean conditions, terrain, and the effects of the earth's gravitational force.

With regard to any one country, U.S. officials may have a need for intelligence concerning all aspects of domestic and foreign affairs. In the case of the Soviet Union, intelligence of value would include (but not be limited to) intelligence concerning the forthcoming grain harvest, ethnic problems in the armed forces, strategic weapons systems (those deployed and under development), Soviet oil production, Gorbachev's consolidation of power, and Soviet negotiating strategy for the Strategic Arms Reduction Talks (START). With regard to the Middle East, U.S. officials need to know the health of the Israeli Prime Minister, Israeli plans for the West Bank, Arab government support for the Palestine Liberation Organization (PLO), the internal stability of the Egyptian and Saudi regimes, the willingness of various Arab governments to recognize Israel's right to exist, and the military capabilities of all nations in the region.

THE INTELLIGENCE COMMUNITY

The U.S. intelligence community has been precisely defined in a number of government directives and regulations. According to one of those regulations:

> The CIA, the NSA, the DIA, the Offices within the DOD for the collection of specialized national foreign intelligence through reconnaissance programs [a euphemism for the National Reconnaissance Office], the Bureau of Intelligence and Research of the Department of State, the intelligence elements of the Military Services, the FBI, the Department of the Treasury, the DOE, the Drug Enforcement Administration and the staff elements of the Director of Central Intelligence constitute the intelligence community.[18]

Also worthy of consideration are the intelligence elements of the Department of Commerce, the Defense Mapping Agency (DMA), the Armed Forces Medical Intelligence Center (AFMIC), the Federal Research Division (FRD) of the Library of Congress, and the intelligence components of the unified and specified commands. These intelligence elements, along with those mentioned directly above, can be grouped into five categories:

- National intelligence organizations,

- Department of Defense intelligence organizations,

- Military service intelligence organizations,
- The Intelligence components of the unified and specified commands, and
- Civilian intelligence organizations.

NOTES TO CHAPTER 1

1. U.S. Congress, House Permanent Select Committee on Intelligence, *Intelligence on the World Energy Future* (Washington, D.C.: U.S. Government Printing Office, 1979), p. 2.

2. *Dictionary of United States Military Terms for Joint Usage* (Washington, D.C.: Departments of the Army, Navy, and Air Force, May 1955), p. 53.

3. CIA, *Intelligence: The Acme of Skill* (Washington, D.C.: CIA, n.d.), pp. 6–7.

4. Commission on CIA Activities within the United States, *Report to the President* (Washington, D.C.: U.S. Government Printing Office, 1975), p. 6.

5. HQ USAF, ACS,I INOI 80-1, "The Intelligence Role in Research, Development, Test and Evaluation (RDT&E)," January 18, 1985.

6. Patrick Tyler, "The Rise and Fall of the SSN 688," *Washington Post,* September 21, 1986, pp. A1, A18.

7. Zbigniew Brzezinski, *Power and Principle: Memoirs of the National Security Adviser 1977–1981* (New York: Farrar, Straus and Giroux, 1983), pp. 248, 431.

8. Seymour Hersh, *The Price of Power: Kissinger in the Nixon White House* (New York: Summit, 1983), p. 103.

9. "Japan Counters Dumping Charges with Position Paper," *Defense Electronics* (June 1987): 18.

10. James J. Killian, Jr., *Sputnik, Scientists, and Eisenhower: A Memoir of the First Special Assistant to the President for Science and Technology* (Cambridge, Mass.: MIT Press, 1977), p. 80.

11. Hugh Trevor-Roper, *The Philby Affair—Espionage, Treason and Secret Services* (London: Kimber, 1968), p. 66.

12. U.S. Congress, Senate Committee on Foreign Relations, *Nomination of Henry A. Kissinger* (Washington, D.C.: U.S. Government Printing Office, 1973). For evidence that Kissinger did not always follow his own advice, see Hersh, *The Price of Power,* pp. 529–60.

13. Samuel Griffith, trans., *Sun Tzu, The Art of War* (London: Oxford Press, 1963), p. 144.

14. Ned Lebow, *Nuclear Crisis Management: A Dangerous Illusion* (Ithaca, N.Y.: Cornell University Press, 1986), p. 101.

15. Sidney Souers, "Atomic Energy Intelligence," *RG 218 Joint Chiefs of Staff, File 131,* July 1, 1947, Modern Military Branch, National Archives.

16. "Director of Central Intelligence: Perspectives for Intelligence 1976–1981," *Covert Action Information Bulletin* 6 (October 1979): 13–24 at 19.

17. Ibid., 20.

18. DIA Regulation 50-17, "Release of Classified DOD Intelligence to Non-NFIB U.S. Government Agencies," July 26, 1978.

2 NATIONAL INTELLIGENCE ORGANIZATIONS

The activities of the U.S. intelligence community are similar to those of many other nations—collection and analysis, counterintelligence, and covert action. However, the extent of those activities and the methods employed by the United States, especially with respect to technical collection, far surpass those of every other nation except the Soviet Union.

The United States collects information via reconnaissance satellites, aircraft, ships, signals and seismic ground stations, radar, and underseas surveillance as well as the traditional overt and clandestine human sources. The total cost of these activities is probably in excess of $20 billion per year.

Given this wide range of activity and the large number of intelligence consumers, it is not surprising that a plethora of organizations are involved in intelligence activities. Of these organizations, three are considered to be national intelligence organizations in that they perform intelligence functions for the entire government (rather than for just a department). Their activities provide intelligence for national level policymakers and they are responsive to direction by supra-departmental authority. The three organizations are: the Central Intelligence Agency (CIA), the National Security Agency (NSA), and the National Reconnaissance Office (NRO).

CENTRAL INTELLIGENCE AGENCY

In the aftermath of World War II, the U.S. central intelligence organization that had been created for the conflict—the Office of Strategic Services (OSS)—was disbanded. Several branches of the organization were distributed among other departments of the government. The X-2 (Counterintelligence) and Secret Intelligence

Branches were transferred to the War Department as the Strategic Services Unit, and the Research and Analysis Branch was relocated in the State Department.[1]

Shortly afterward, however, President Truman found himself deluged by intelligence reports from several government agencies, and set up the National Intelligence Authority and its operational element, the Central Intelligence Group (CIG), to coordinate and collate the reports. The CIG served as a coordinating mechanism and also had some responsibility for intelligence collection.[2]

As part of the general consideration of national security needs and organization, the question of intelligence organization was addressed in the National Security Act of 1947. The Act established the CIA as an independent agency within the Executive Office of the President to replace the CIG. According to the Act, the CIA was to have five functions:

1. to advise the National Security Council in matters concerning such intelligence activities of the government departments and agencies as relate to national security;
2. to make recommendations to the National Security Council for the coordination of such intelligence activities of the departments and agencies of the government as relate to the national security;
3. to correlate and evaluate the intelligence relating to the national security, and to provide for the appropriate dissemination of such intelligence within the Government using, where appropriate, existing agencies and facilities;
4. to perform for the benefit of the existing intelligence agencies such additional services of common concern as the National Security Council determines can be more effectively accomplished centrally; and
5. to perform other such functions and duties related to inelligence affecting the national security as the National Security Council may from time to time direct.[3]

The CIA was to have no role in domestic affairs or powers of arrest.

The provisions of the Act left a great deal of room for interpretation. Thus, the fifth and final provision above has been cited as authorizing covert action activities. In fact, the provision was intended only to authorize espionage.[4]

Whatever the intentions of Congress in 1947, the CIA developed in accord with a maximalist interpretation of the Act. Thus, the CIA has become the primary U.S. government agency for intelligence analysis, clandestine human intelligence collection, and covert action. It has also played a major role in the development of overhead reconnaissance systems—both aircraft and spacecraft—used to gather both imagery and signals intelligence. Additionally, the Director of the CIA is also the Director of Central Intelligence and is responsible for managing the activities of the entire intelligence community.

In addition, under President Reagan's 1981 Executive Order 12333, the CIA is permitted to collect "significant" foreign intelligence secretly within the United States, if that effort is not aimed at learning about the domestic activities of U.S. citizens and corporations. The order also gives the CIA authority to conduct, within

Figure 2–1. Organization of the Central Intelligence Agency.

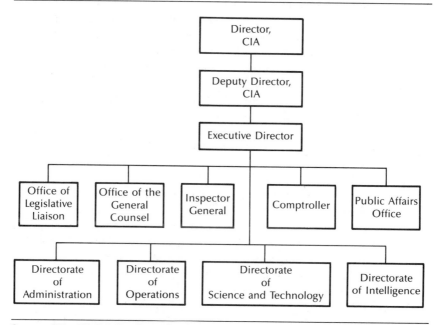

Source: CIA, *CIA Fact Book* (Washington, D.C.: U.S. Government Printing Office, 1983).

the United States, "special activities" or covert actions approved by the President that are not intended to influence U.S. political processes, public opinion or the media.[5]

Headquarters of the CIA are in Langley, Virginia, just south of Washington; other CIA offices and over 3,000 employees are scattered around the Washington area. Among its newer facilities may be a 2,500-square foot building complex in Reston, Virginia that appears to be connected with satellite reconnaissance operations. In 1988 the CIA has between 16,500 and 20,000 employees in the Washington area and budget of approximately $1.5 billion.[6]

The agency is divided into four major components, each headed by a Deputy Director, and five offices directly subordinate to the Director, Deputy Director and Executive Director. The major components are the Directorate of Administration, the Directorate of Operations, the Directorate of Science and Technology, and the Directorate of Intelligence. The offices are those of Legislative Liaison, General Counsel, Inspector General, Comptroller, and Public Affairs. The general structure of the CIA is depicted in Figure 2–1.

Day-to-day management of the agency is generally the responsibility of the Deputy Director and the Executive Director, with the DCI handling community-wide issues and representing the intelligence community to the President and the NSC.

Within the Directorate of Administration are nine offices which perform a wide variety of administrative services: the Office of Communications, the Office of Logistics, the Office of Security, the Office of Training and Education, the Office of Finance, the Office of Information Technology, the Office of Medical Services, the Office of Personnel, and the Office of Information Services.[7]

The Office of Communications, with over 2,000 employees as of 1973, maintains facilities for secret communications between CIA headquarters and overseas bases and agents. Presumably, this includes control over any CIA agent communications satellites. Its personnel install and maintain communications equipment (including transmitters and receivers that range from high-frequency to microwave), and install and operate high-speed data transmission equipment. The Office of Logistics operates weapons and other warehouses in the United States as well as supplying office equipment.[8]

The Office of Security is responsible for the physical protection of CIA installations at home and abroad. It also administers polygraph tests to CIA applicants and contract personnel. The Office of Finance is responsible for developing and maintaining accounting systems; establishing and supervising financial regulations and procedures; performing administrative, internal, and industrial audits; and disbursing funds. The Office maintains field units in Hong Kong, Buenos Aires, and Geneva with easy access to money markets.[9]

The Office of Medical Services plans and directs the CIA's medical programs. The Office is responsible for medical examinations and immunizations for employees and dependents going overseas, health education and emergency health care, and psychiatric services. It also helps develop the Psychological Assessment Program to determine which individuals are best suited for the Agency, as well as being involved in psychiatric and medical intelligence production on foreign targets. The Office of Personnel is responsible for recruitment and maintenance of personnel files. With the Office of Training and Education, Personnel operates CIA training facilities, including the main facility—"The Farm," at Camp Peary, Virginia. Along with the Office of Medical Services and Office of Security, Personnel shares responsibility for screening Agency applicants. In response to the statement of personnel needs from Agency components, the Office of Personnel prepares an Advanced Staffing Plan for the following fiscal year, listing the total personnel requirements by category of personnel and occupation job titles.[10]

The Office of Training and Education conducts courses on operations, intelligence analysis, management, languages, information science, and executive leadership. The Office of Information Technology operates the CIA's computer facilities. It is also responsible for the agency's domestic communications and computer security. The Office of Information Services is the CIA's records manager.[11]

The Directorate of Operations (formerly the Directorate of Plans) is in charge of clandestine collection and covert action (special activities). The Directorate is organized into various headquarters staffs, area divisions, and support divisions, as shown in Figure 2–2. The headquarters staffs, which perform supervisory,

Figure 2–2. Organization of the Directorate of Operations.

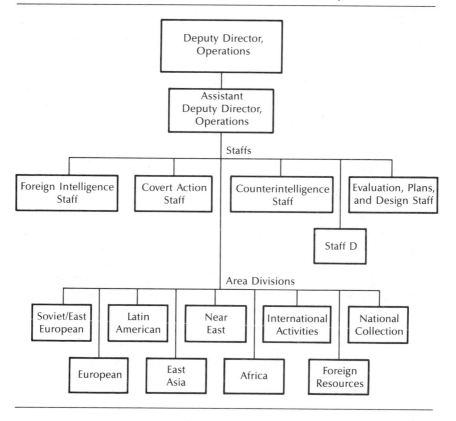

planning, and evaluative functions are the Foreign Intelligence Staff, Covert Action Staff, Counterintelligence Staff, Staff D, and the Evaluation, Plans, and Design Staff.

The Foreign Intelligence Staff is responsible for checking the authenticity of sources and information; screening clandestine collection requirements; and reviewing regional division projects, budget information, and operational cable traffic.[12] The responsibilities and authority of the Foreign Intelligence Staff were summarized by a former head of the Staff, Peer de Silva:

> The Foreign Intelligence Staff had a continuing responsibility for monitoring intelligence-collection projects and programs carried out abroad. These operations and collection programs were of course controlled and directed by the area divisions concerned; the FI Staff simply read the progress charts on the various projects (or the lack of progress) and played the role of determining which intelligence-collection programs should be continued, changed or terminated. With the exception of a few individual operations of special sensitivity, the FI Staff function was worldwide.[13]

The Covert Action Staff, in cooperation with area divisions, develops plans for covert action operations, considers plans proposed by area divisions, and evaluates the implementation of the plans. Covert action operations have included (1) political advice and counsel; (2) subsidies to individuals; (3) financial support and "technical assistance" to foreign political parties; (4) support to private organizations, including labor unions and business firms; (5) covert propaganda; (6) private training of individuals; (7) economic operations; (8) paramilitary or political action operations designed to overthrow or support a regime; and (9) attempted assassinations. Thus, during the presidency of Chile's Salvador Allende, the Covert Action Staff might have devised an article uncomplimentary to Allende in cooperation with the Chilean desk of the (at that time) Western Hemisphere Division. A CIA front such as Forum World Features in London would then be used to write and transmit the article.[14]

The Counterintelligence Staff is responsible for offensive counterintelligence—the collection and analysis of information concerning all foreign intelligence and security services, the penetration of hostile services, the debriefing of defectors, and the attempts to prevent the penetration of the U.S. intelligence community by hostile services. At the height of its influence, under James Jesus Angleton, this Staff had about 200 employees. After Angleton's dismissal in late 1975 the size of the staff was radically reduced (to 80) and assignment to the staff was made a temporary tour of duty. Operational counterintelligence responsibility was assigned to the geographical divisions of the directorate. In the wake of the penetrations and defections of 1985, the counterintelligence function was substantially upgraded by DCI William Webster in 1988.[15]

Staff D is in charge of bugging, wiretapping, and some COMINT (Communications Intelligence) activities—some in support of other government agencies. Thus, the U.S. Secret Service regularly tasks the CIA to provide real-time communications intelligence and close support to the Secret Service during foreign travel of the President. In 1973, at the request of the NSA, Staff D personnel monitored telephone conversations between the United States and Latin America for a period of three (or six) months in an effort to identify narcotics traffickers. On another occasion, Staff D apparently paid a code clerk working in the Washington embassy of a U.S. ally to supply information that assisted in breaking the ally's code.[16]

The Evaluation, Plans, and Design Staff does much of the bureaucratic planning and budgeting for the Directorate of Operations. It also has served as a home for unwanted elements of other CIA staffs and offices. The International Communism Branch of the Counterintelligence Staff was transferred to the evaluation staff as a result of the downgrading of the Counterintelligence Staff.[17]

Actual implementation of staff-planned activities are generally the responsibility of the nine area divisions: Soviet/East European, Latin American, European, East Asia, Africa, Near East, International Activities, Foreign Resources, and National Collection. Each regional area division has staffs for support, covert action, counterintelligence, and foreign intelligence. In addition, each regional area division is broken down into branches and desks representing ever more specific geographical areas.[18]

The International Activities Division, previously known as the Special Operations Division, handles paramilitary activities such as efforts directed against the Sandinista government of Nicaragua.[19]

The Foreign Resources Division was created in 1963 as the Domestic Operations Division and given the responsibility for "clandestine operational activities of the Clandestine Services conducted within the United States against foreign targets."[20] The present function of the Division is to locate and recruit foreign nationals who are of special interest and residing in the United States, to cooperate with the CIA abroad. As a means of identifying such individuals the Division has relationships with scores of individuals in U.S. academic institutions. These individuals do not attempt to recruit students but assist by providing background information and occasionally by "brokering" introductions.[21]

The National Collection Division (NCD), known previously as the Domestic Collection Division and the Domestic Contact Service, openly collects intelligence from U.S. residents who have traveled abroad; this includes scientists, technologists, economists, and energy experts returning from foreign locations of interest. Among those interviewed are academics—in 1982 the Division was in touch with approximately 900 individuals on 290 campuses in the United States.[22]

The Chief of the NCD (or the Foreign Resources Division) can approve the use of individuals who are employees or invitees of an organization within the United States to collect important foreign intelligence at fairs, workshops, symposia, and similar types of commercial or professional meetings sponsored by such an organization that are open only to those individuals in their overt roles and closed to the general public.[23]

In 1973 the Directorate had 6,000 employees and a budget of $440 million. About $260 million was spent on covert action, and 4,800 employees were located in the area divisions. Cutbacks by past CIA directors James Schlesinger and Stansfield Turner reduced personnel by about 2,000, but Director William J. Casey, appointed in 1981, restored many of the slots eliminated by Schlesinger and Turner. Present estimates of the covert action budget are in the area of $700 million.[24]

The Directorate of Science and Technology (DS&T), with over 8,000 employees in 1978, was created in 1962 as the Directorate for Research and renamed in 1963. At that time (1962), the various CIA offices dealing with technical intelligence collection were consolidated into one unit. The DS&T has undergone several reorganizations, and has gained and lost responsibilities in the twenty years since it was created. Both the Directorate of Intelligence and Directorate of Operations have at times disputed actual or planned DS&T control of various offices and divisions. Thus, at various times the DS&T has been assigned scientific intelligence analysis functions, to the dismay of the Directorate of Intelligence. At one time, the DS&T controlled the Office of Weapons Intelligence (which was formed by merging the Foreign Missile and Space Analysis Center with certain functions of the Office of Scientific Intelligence).[25]

In 1973 the National Photographic Interpretation Center (NPIC) was transferred to the DS&T from the Directorate of Intelligence. The NPIC is the successor to a series of CIA photographic interpretation units first established in 1953 as the Photographic Intelligence Division (PID) with thirteen interpreters. In 1958, the PID merged with a statistical analysis division of the Office of Current Intelligence to form the Photographic Interpretation Center. Under the provision of National Security Council Intelligence Directive (NSCID) 8 of 1961 and its successors, the NPIC is run by the CIA as a "service of common concern" for the entire intelligence community. It presently has over several thousand interpreters and is located in Building 213 of the Washington Navy Yard at 1st and M Streets.[26]

In addition to the NPIC, the components of the DS&T include the Office of Development and Engineering, the Office of SIGINT Operations, the Office of Research and Development, the Office of Technical Services, and the Foreign Broadcast Information Service (FBIS). The Office of Development and Engineering is the successor to a long line of CIA components involved in overhead reconnaissance-type R & D (Research and Development). The first such CIA component was created in 1954 to develop the U-2 and was named the Development Project Staff. It subsequently became known as the Office of Special Activities, the Office of Special Projects and, in 1973, the Office of Development and Engineering.[27]

The Office of Development and Engineering is involved in the development of major technical collection systems such as the KH-11 imaging satellite. The Office "provides total systems development for major systems—from requirements definition through design, engineering, and testing and evaluation, to implementation, operation and even support logistics and maintenance." Specific areas of research in developing such systems include laser communications, digital imagery processing, real-time data collection and processing, electro-optics, advanced signal collection, and advanced antenna design.[28]

The Office of SIGINT Operations (OSO) "develops, operates and maintains sophisticated equipment required to perform collection and analysis tasks with maximum efficiency." The OSO was heavily involved in the development of the RHYOLITE/AQUACADE series of signals intelligence satellites. Through its Special Collection Service, and in conjunction with the NSA, OSO operates covert listening posts in a large number of U.S. embassies. It has also been involved in the construction of SIGINT facilities operated by foreign nations (such as China), the training of their personnel, and the maintenance of the equipment on site.[29]

The Office of Research and Development (OR&D) conducts research in the areas of communications, sensors, semiconductors, artificial intelligence, image understanding, process modeling, database management, and high-speed computing. The OR&D conducts research for all directorates of the CIA, attempting to go beyond the state of the art, and anticipating and answering the future technology needs of the intelligence community. The OR&D's Advanced Concepts Staff provides a place for experienced researchers to conduct individual research projects aimed at identifying future intelligence issues and problems.[30]

The Office of Technical Services (OTS) was previously the Technical Services Division (TSD) of the Directorate of Operations. It was acquired by the DS&T in 1973—an acquisition that took over ten years. When the DS&T was formed, its leadership argued that the TSD should be brought under its control—a suggestion resisted by the leaders of the Operations (then Plans) Directorate, who argued that the division should be close to its consumers, the staff in Plans. The TSD was transferred to the DS&T as part of a series of transfers and changes initiated by CIA Director William Colby.[31]

The technical services provided by the OTS involve secret writing methods, bugging equipment, hidden cameras, coding and decoding devices, video and image enhancement, and chemical imagery.[32]

In addition to NPIC, the Directorate of Science and Technology operates a second service of common concern—the Foreign Broadcast Information Service (FBIS). The FBIS monitors the public radio and television broadcasts of foreign nations, as well as the broadcast of "black" or clandestine radio stations and prepares summaries and analyses of broadcasts of interest for use by intelligence analysts and officials. The FBIS dates back to 1941, when the Federal Communications Commission established, at the request of the State Department, the Foreign Broadcast Monitoring Service. From that point on the U.S. government had an organization to "record, translate, analyze and report to other agencies of the government on broadcasts of foreign origin."[33]

The Directorate of Intelligence, known from 1978 to 1981 as the National Foreign Assessment Center (NFAC), is the primary U.S. government organization for intelligence analysis. As such it has been the unit primarily responsible for preparing the various National Intelligence Estimates and Special National Intelligence Estimates. As shown in Figure 2–3, the present structure of the Directorate includes three staffs (Management and Analysis Support, Arms Control Intelligence, and Collection Requirements and Evaluation), five regional offices, and five functional offices.[34]

Prior to a 1981 reorganization, research offices were organized along purely functional lines, with offices for economic research, political analysis, geography and cartography, and strategic research. The regional offices—the Office of Soviet Analysis, the Office of African and Latin American Analysis, the Office of East Asian Analysis, the Office of European Analysis, the Office of Near Eastern and South Asian Analysis—were created by grouping analysts from all areas of research.[35]

The functional offices—the Office of Global Issues, the Office of Imagery Analysis, the Office of Production and Analytic Support, the Office of Information Resources, the Office of Leadership Analysis, and the Office of Scientific and Weapons Research—make up the remainder of the Directorate of Intelligence.[36]

The Office of Global Issues (OGI) is concerned with economic, geographic and technological issues on an international basis as well as narcotics, international terrorism, weapons transfers, and political instability.[37] The Office's Center for Insurgency, Instability and Terrorism produces analyses on those subjects.

Figure 2–3. Organization of the Directorate of Intelligence.

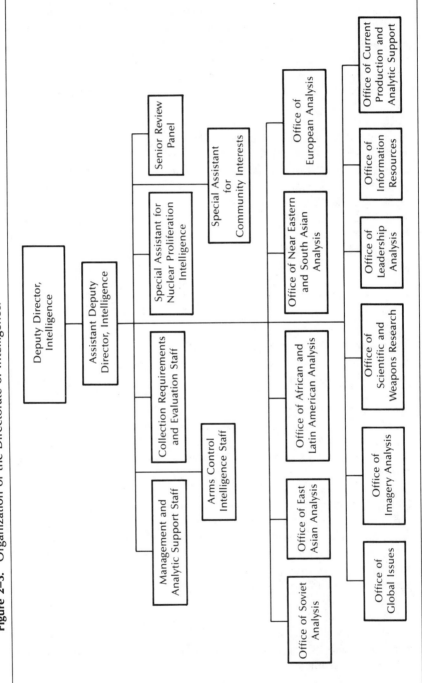

The Office of Imagery Analysis (OIA) was created in 1961 as the Imagery Analysis Service to give the CIA an imagery analysis capability apart from the CIA-run NPIC. OIA analysts examine satellite and aerial photography to extract information and prepare analyses on the deployment of military forces, industrial production, and the development of military forces, as well as the development, testing, and production of new foreign weapons systems.[38]

The Office of Current Production and Analytic Support publishes all reports from the Directorate of Intelligence and produces CIA maps, charts and specialized graphics for use in CIA reports and briefings for the President. It also manages the CIA's twenty-four hour Operations Center.[39] The Operations Center maintains watch over incoming data from a variety of collection assets and can inform higher authorities if incoming intelligence indicates a crisis situation is developing somewhere in the world.

In 1986, the Office of Central Reference was split into two new offices: the Office of Information Resources (OIR) and the Office of Leadership Analysis (OLA). The OIR provides library and reference support, computer-based applications development, and training and consulting in automated data processing. The OLA produces reports on foreign leaders and organizations for all levels of the U.S. government.[40]

The Office of Scientific and Weapons Research (OSWR) was formed by merging the Office of Scientific Intelligence and the Office of Weapons Research. The OSWR is responsible for determining the scope and nature of foreign scientific and technical activities and programs, as well as the performance characteristics of foreign weapons and space systems. The OSWR's analysts study science policy, the physical sciences, civilian and military technology, nuclear energy and weapons, nuclear proliferation, offensive and defensive weapons systems, general purpose weapons, antisubmarine warfare, and space systems.[41]

NATIONAL SECURITY AGENCY

The National Security Agency (NSA) is one of the most secret (and secretive) members of the U.S. intelligence community. The predecessor of the NSA, the Armed Forces Security Agency (AFSA), was established within the Department of Defense on May 20, 1949 by Secretary of Defense Louis Johnson. Johnson made the AFSA subordinate to the Joint Chiefs of Staff. The AFSA had little power to direct the activities of the military service SIGINT units, its functions being defined in terms of activities not performed by the service units.[42]

On or before October 24, 1952—the day that President Harry S. Truman sent a top secret, eight-page memorandum (now partially declassified) entitled "Communications Intelligence Activities," to the Secretary of State and the Secretary of Defense—Truman abolished the AFSA and transferred its personnel to the NSA. The creation of the NSA has its origins in a December 10, 1951 memo sent by DCI Walter Bedell Smith to National Security Council (NSC) Executive Secretary

James B. Lay stating that "control over, and coordination of, the collection and processing of Communications Intelligence have proved ineffective" and recommending a survey of communications intelligence activities. This proposal was approved on December 13, 1951; the study authorized on December 18, 1951; and the report completed by June 13, 1952. The report, known as the "Brownell Committee Report," surveyed the history of U.S. communications intelligence activities and suggested the need for a much greater degree of coordination and national level direction. As the change in the security agency's name indicated, the role of the NSA was to extend beyond the armed forces. The NSA is considered to be "within but not part of DOD."[43]

Although created in 1952, it was not until 1957 that the NSA's existence was officially acknowledged in the *U.S. Government Organization Manual* as a "separately organized agency within the Department of Defense (DOD)" that "performs highly specialized technical and coordinating functions relating to national security." Despite the lack of official acknowledgement, the NSA's existence was a matter of public knowledge from at least mid-1953. In that year, Washington newspapers ran several stories concerning the construction of the NSA's new headquarters at Ft. Meade, Maryland. In late 1954, the NSA was again in the news when an NSA employee was caught taking secret documents home.[44]

The charter for the NSA is National Security Council Intelligence Directive 6. In its most recently available form NSCID 6 (of January 17, 1972, "Signals Intelligence") directs the NSA to produce SIGINT "in accordance with objectives, requirements and priorities established by the Director of Central Intelligence Board." The directive also authorizes the Director of NSA "to issue directions to any operating elements engaged in SIGINT operations such instructions and assignments as are required" and states that "All instructions issued by the Director under the authority provided in this paragraph shall be mandatory, subject only to appeal to the Secretary of Defense."[45]

NSCID 6 defines the scope of SIGINT activities, which can be divided into Communications Intelligence (COMINT) and Electronics Intelligence (ELINT):

> COMINT activities shall be construed to mean those activities which produce COMINT by interception and processing of foreign communications by radio, wire, or other electronic means, with specific exception stated below and by the processing of foreign encrypted communications, however transmitted. Interception comprises range estimation, transmitter operator identification, signal analysis, traffic analysis, cryptanalysis, decryption, study of plain text, the fusion of those processes, and the reporting of the results.
>
> COMINT and COMINT activities as defined herein shall not include (a) any intercept and processing of unencrypted written communications, press and propaganda broadcasts, or (b) censorship.
>
> ELINT activities are defined as the collection (observation and recording) and the processing for subsequent intelligence purposes, or information derived from foreign non-communications electromagnetic radiations emanating from other than atomic detonation or radioactive sources. ELINT is the technical and intelligence information product of ELINT activities.[46]

Signals intercepted include diplomatic, military, scientific and commercial communications, as well as the electronic emanations of radar systems and the signals sent by weapons systems while being tested. The intercepted signals may be transmitted by telephone, radio telephone, radio, and cables.

NSCID 6 defines the extent of the NSA's SIGINT mission, but the NSA has another mission. Until recently that mission was known as Communictions Security (COMSEC) but has been broadened to Information Security (INFOSEC). In its INFOSEC role the NSA performs the same COMSEC functions as it did in the past—it creates, reviews, and authorizes the communications procedures and codes of a variety of government agencies, including the State Department, the DOD, the DIA, and the FBI. This role includes development of secure data and voice transmission links on such satellite systems as the Defense Satellite Communications System (DSCS) and the Satellite Data System (SDS). Likewise, for sensitive communications, FBI agents use a special scrambler telephone that requires a different code from the NSA each day. The NSA's COMSEC responsibilities also include ensuring communications security for strategic weapons systems such as the Minuteman and MX missiles, so as to prevent unauthorized instrusion, interference or jamming. In addition, the NSA is responsible for developing the codes by which the President must identify himself in order to authorize a nuclear strike. In fulfilling these responsibilities, the NSA produces documents such as the *National COMSEC Plan for Fixed Point and Strategic Communications* (1977), the *National COMSEC Plan for Space Systems and Nuclear Weapons Systems* (1982), and *Communications Security—The Warsaw Pact COMINT Threat* (1975).[47]

Another means of protecting communications is via the use of secure telephones. In 1984 the NSA launched an effort to provide 500,000 federal officials with secure telephones that would make eavesdropping virtually impossible.[48]

As part of its INFOSEC mission the NSA is also responsible for protecting data banks and computers, ensuring that unauthorized individuals or governments are not able to tap into such systems. The data banks to be protected include those with only unclassified information as well as those containing classified information. As a result of National Security Decision Directive (NSDD) 145, "National Policy on Telecommunications and Automated Information Systems Security," the NSA is concerned with the data processing activities of over 1,000 federal departments, agencies, boards, and commissions. Included are agencies such as the Department of Health and Human Services and the Internal Revenue Service.[49]

NSA headquarters at Ft. Meade houses somewhere between 20,000 and 24,000 employees housed in three buildings. As indicated in Figure 2–4, headquarters is divided into several offices/organizations, the three most prominent being the Office of Signals Intelligence Operations, the Office of Information Security, and the Office of Research and Engineering.

The Office of Signals Intelligence Operations, headed by the Deputy Director of Operations, has an executive staff (P Group) and three groups responsible for directing, collecting, and processing data for different geographical areas; as well as a unit for space and missile intercepts. The A Group is responsible for the Soviet

Figure 2–4. Organization of the National Security Agency.

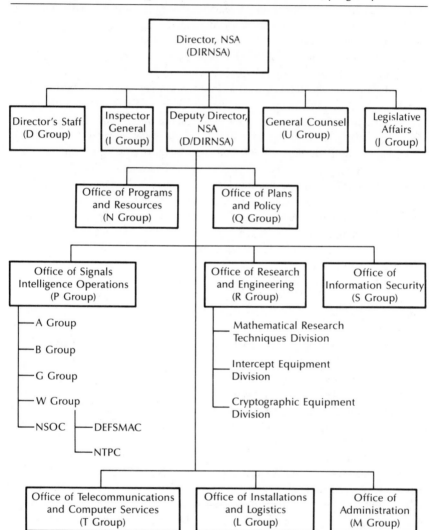

Union and Eastern European nations. Within the A Group, the A1 Office is the Executive Staff, the A2 Office is responsible for the Soviet Union, the A3 for East Europe, the A4 for Exploitation Management/Tasking, the A5 for Encrypted Communications, and the A6 for Transcription.[50]

The B Group is responsible for China, Korea, Vietnam, and the rest of Communist Asia. The G Group (formerly known as ALLO) is responsible for all other nations, both Third World and allied. Its G6 unit is responsible for the Middle

East and North Africa, while G92 (a subunit of G9) is responsible for SIGINT operations against "Insular Asia," including the Philippines.[51]

The W Group is responsible for space SIGINT—the interception and processing of all communictions and signals emitted by foreign spacecraft and missiles. The primary targets, or course, are Soviet space operations and missile tests. Subordinate to the W Group are the Defense Special Missile and Astronautics Center (DEFSMAC) and the National Telemetry Processing Center (NTPC).[52]

DEFSMAC was established as a joint NSA-DIA (Defense Intelligence Agency) operation by Department of Defense Directive S-5100.43, "Defense Special Missile and Astronautics Center" of April 27, 1964.[53] According to a former deputy director of the NSA, the DEFSMAC

> is a combination of the DIA with its military components and the NSA. It has all the inputs from all the assets and is a warning activity. They probably have a better feel for any worldwide threat to this country from missiles, aircraft or overt military activities, better and more timely, at instant fingertip availability than any group in the United States. So DEFSMAC is an input to NSA, but it also [is] an input to DIA and the CIA and the White House Situation Room and everybody else.[54]

The DEFSMAC receives data bearing on Soviet, Chinese, and other nations' space and missile launches. It, in turn, warns other assets that a launch or test is imminent and to prepare to monitor the event—such as U.S. COBRA BALL aircraft stationed in Alaska. DEFSMAC reports are transmitted in a special Top-Secret compartment known as SUGARBUSH.

The National Telemetry Processing Center processes the electronic signals radioed back to earth by Soviet, Chinese, and other nations' missiles during their test flights.

The Office of Signals Intelligence Operations also operates the National SIGINT Operations Center (NSOC). The NSOC's function is to oversee and direct the SIGINT coverage of any crisis event. It operates around the clock and is in instantaneous touch with every major NSA facility in the world. In the event that a facility intercepts signals indicating an event it believes should be reported immediately to the Director of the NSA, that facility files a CRITIC intelligence report with the NSOC. The NSOC may pass the message on or revoke its CRITIC status if it feels that the event is really not of sufficient importance.[55]

The Office of Information Security is responsible for INFOSEC with respect to the communications and signals discussed above. The Office of Research and Engineering has the responsibility for developing the techniques and equipment necessary for conducting intercept operations, breaking codes, and ensuring secure U.S. codes. The Office's Mathematical Research Techniques Division explores code-breaking possibilities. The Intercept Equipment Division concentrates on developing the equipment required for the NSA's COMINT and ELINT intercept programs. The Cryptographic Equipment Division seeks to develop secure coding machines.[56]

In addition to the three main offices there are several others of importance. The Office of Telecommunications and Computer Services is responsible for both computer support, computer security, and the functioning of the NSA's communication network, the Digital Network-Defense Special Security Communications System (DIN/DSSCS). Information transmitted on this system, via the Defense Satellite Communications System (DSCS), includes intercepts from overseas stations. The Office of Installations and Logistics is responsible for overseas housing, disposal of classified waste, construction of facilities at Ft. Meade, and procurement of computers. The Office of Administration has a variety of functions including personnel matters, training, employment, and security.[57]

The Office of Plans and Policy serves as a staff for the Director with the Deputy Director for Plans and Policy serving as a Chief of Staff. The Office of Programs and Resources is charged with the management and allocation of SIGINT/COMSEC resources, most specifically with the preparation of the Consolidated Cryptographic Program (discussed in Chapter 16).[58]

The NSA's headquarters budget is probably in the area of $3 billion. In addition to directing activities at NSA headquarters and the NSA's few overseas facilities, the Director of the NSA is responsible for supervising the SIGINT activities of the military's Service Cryptological Authorities (SCAs). In this role the Director serves as the head of the Central Security Service (CSS). The CSS function of the NSA, with the Director of the NSA serving simultaneously as Chief of the CSS, was established in 1971 in order "to provide a unified, more economical and more effective structure for executing cryptologic and related operations presently conducted under the Military Departments." There is, however, no separate CSS staff.[59]

NATIONAL RECONNAISSANCE OFFICE

The National Reconnaissance Office (NRO) manages satellite reconnaissance programs for the entire U.S. intelligence community. These programs involve the collection of photographic and signals intelligence via satellite.

The NRO has a broad range of functions. It has participated in various policy committees such as the NSAM (National Security Action Memorandum) 156 committee established by President Kennedy in 1962 to review the political aspects of U.S. policy on space reconnaissance.[60] It has played a significant role in drawing a curtain of secrecy around the reconnaissance program. Thus, in a memorandum to President Kennedy concerning the SAMOS II (Satellite and Missile Observation System, the Air Force's initial photographic reconnaissance satellite) launch, Assistant Secretary of Defense for Public Affairs Arthur Sylvester noted that the material to be made available to newsmen concerning the launch and the program "represents a severe reduction from what had been previously been issued." Sylvester further stated that "Dr. Charyk [Director of NRO] has reviewed those changes and is satisfied that they meet all his security requirements and those of his SAMOS

Project Director, Brigadier General Greer."[61] The NRO has also been heavily involved in developing security regulations for the release of information concerning military satellite payloads to be placed in orbit by the Space Transportation System (STS).

The NRO is also responsible for the routine operation of the satellites, including maneuvers such as turning them on and off and facing them toward or away from the sun.[62]

Although the NRO has existed under the "cover" of the Under Secretary of the Air Force and the Office of Space Systems, it is, as its name indicates, a national level organization. And, in fact, it is directly supervised by one of two executive committees, the National Reconaissance Executive Committee, chaired by the Director of Central Intelligence.[63]

The NRO came into existence on August 25, 1960 after several months of debate within and among the White House, Department of Defense, Air Force, and the CIA concerning the nature and duties of such an organization. Its creation was a response to various problems plaguing the early missile and satellite programs, as well as to the May 1, 1960 incident in which a U-2 was shot down over the Soviet Union. As a result of this latter event, the Office of the Secretary of Defense and the Air Force sought a revised program to exploit, as early as possible, any reconnaissance data that could be obtained from SAMOS test flights. On June 10, President Eisenhower asked Secretary of Defense Thomas S. Gates, Jr. to reevaluate the program and brief the National Security Council (NSC) on intelligence requirements, the technical feasibility of meeting those requirements, and the DOD's plans.[64]

Gates, in turn, appointed a panel of three—Dr. Joseph Charyk, Under Secretary of the Air Force; John J. Rubel, Deputy Director of the Defense Directorate of Research and Engineering; and Dr. George B. Kistiakowsky, the President's science adviser. The eventual product of their work was a briefing of August 25, followed, according to an official Air Force history, by a "key decision by the NSC and the President which, eliminating previous uncertainties, signaled the start of a highest priority program reminiscent of the wartime Manhattan Project efforts"—the creation of the NRO. The NRO superseded an office (the Directorate of Advanced Technology) that coordinated satellite development for the Air Force Chief of Staff.[65]

The national level character of the organization was a major point of importance to those involved in its formation. Thus, George Kistiakowsky noted that it was important "that the organization should have a clear line of authority and that on the top level direction be of a national character, including OSD [Office of the Secretary of Defense] and CIA and not the Air Force alone." One reason such a framework was desired was to be certain that the utilization of the photographic "take" not be left solely in the hands of the Air Force.[66]

The Air Force quickly moved to establish a cover organization for the NRO within the Office of the Secretary of the Air Force. On August 31, 1960, Secretary of the Air Force Dudley C. Sharp established via Order 115.1, the Office of Missile and Satellite Systems. The director of the office was to be responsible "for assisting the Secretary in discharging his responsibility for the direction, supervision and control of the SAMOS Project." On the same day, Order 116.1 established the Director of the SAMOS Project, located at El Segundo, California, directly responsible to the Secretary of the Air Force.[67]

As the entire reconnaissance program fell under a veil of secrecy, the connection of both offices with reconnaissance was obscured. The Office of Missile and Satellite Systems became the Office of Space Systems, with the present version of Order 115.1 making no mention of reconnaissance. The Office of the Director of the SAMOS Project became the more euphemistic Office of Special Projects, with the director and personnel being described only as a "field extension" of the Office of the Secretary of the Air Force.[68]

The first public revelation of the NRO's existence came in 1973 as the result of an error made in a Senate committee report. The name National Reconnaissance Office was, by mistake, not deleted from a list of intelligence agencies that the committee recommended should make their budgets public. The slip led to a fairly extensive article in the *Washington Post* a few months later in which the NRO's functions, budget, and cover were discussed. The following year the CIA lost its attempt to have a similar discussion deleted from Marchetti and Mark's *The CIA and the Cult of Intelligence*.

The NRO is still officially considered a secret or "black" institution, at least by the NRO and the DOD. References to the NRO in the *Department of Defense Annual Report* and Executive Orders are to offices charged with "the collection of specialized foreign intelligence through reconnaissance programs." The closest an executive branch document has come to admitting the existence of the NRO was the report of the Murphy Commission, which referred to a "semi-autonomous office within the Defense Department with the largest budget of any intelligence agency and that operates overhead reconnaissance programs for the entire intelligence community."[69] At the same time, the CIA's Publication Review Board cleared for publication two books by former high CIA officials, including former Director William Colby, that referred to the NRO. However, the board would not permit former DCI Stansfield Turner to refer to the NRO in his 1985 memoirs.[70]

Most often, the Under Secretary of the Air Force has served as the Director of the NRO—a custom that began with Joseph Charyk. There have been exceptions to the rule. Robert J. Hermann served as Director, NRO during the Carter Administration while he was Assistant Secretary of the Air Force for Research, Development, and Logistics—apparently because Antonia Chayes, the Under Secretary who replaced Hans Mark, knew little about reconnaissance satellites. During the Reagan Administration the Under Secretary once again served as NRO Director until Under Secretary Edward Aldridge was promoted to Secretary. Aldridge proceeded to take the NRO job with him.[71]

The Deputy Director of the NRO is also an Air Force civilian official. Day-to-day management of the office is the responsiblity of the Air Force officer (usually a Brigadier General) who serves as the NRO's staff director and is listed as the

Director of the Office of Space Systems. The office is located in the Pentagon, although the number of the office changes periodically—having changed from 4C1000 to 4C956 to 4C1052.[72]

Subordinate to the NRO top management are three programs. The Air Force component of the NRO is the El Segundo-based Special Projects Office. The Special Projects Office handles the Air Force's responsibility for satellite development and coordination with contractors.

The CIA component of the NRO is headed by the CIA's Deputy Director for Science and Technology. It has been responsible for the most significant advances in U.S. satellite development, such as the KH-11 and RHYOLITE satellites. This component exists more as a concept than as a physical entity—it is simply whatever work the CIA's DS&T is doing in the area of satellite reconnaissance that has been approved by the National Reconnaissance Executive Committee (NREC).

The naval component of NRO, responsible for the Navy's White Cloud ocean surveillance satellite, used to be the Navy Space Project of the Naval Electronics System Command (NAVALEX). Since the disestablishment of NAVALEX it is now part of the Space and Sensor Systems Program Directorate of the Naval Space and Warfare Command (NAVSPAWAR).

The NRO budget would appear to be in the area of $3 to 4 billion a year.[73]

NOTES TO CHAPTER 2

1. For a history of the OSS, see R. Harris Smith, *OSS: The Secret History of America's First Central Intelligence Agency* (Berkeley, Calif.: University of California Press, 1972); and Bradley F. Smith, *The Shadow Warriors: O.S.S. and the Origins of the C.I.A.* (New York: Basic Books, 1983).

2. U.S. Congress, Senate Select Committee to Study Governmental Operations with Respect to Intelligence Activities, *Supplementary Detailed Staff Reports on Foreign and Military Intelligence, Book IV* (Washington, D.C.: U.S. Government Printing Office, 1976), pp. 4–6.

3. U.S. Congress, House Permanent Select Committee on Intelligence, *Compilation of Intelligence Laws and Related Laws and Executive Orders of Interest to the National Intelligence Community* (Washington, D.C.: U.S. Government Printing Office, 1983), p. 7.

4. Lawrence Houston, "Memorandum for the Director, Subject: CIA Authority to Perform Propaganda and Commando Type Functions," September 25, 1947.

5. Ronald Reagan, "Executive Order 12333: United States Intelligence Activities," December 4, 1981 in the *Federal Register*, December 8, 1981, pp. 59941–54 at 59950.

6. Paul Hodge, "CIA Plans Major New Building," *Washington Post*, October 2, 1981, p. B1; Leah Y. Latimer, "Reston Mystery: Is the CIA Planning to Set Up Shop Downtown?" *Washington Post*, September 12, 1986, p. C5; Gregory Treverton, *Covert Action: The Limits of Intervention in the Postwar World* (New York: Basic Books, 1987) p. 14.

7. Central Intelligence Agency, *Fact Book on Intelligence* (Washington, D.C.: CIA, n.d.) p. 9.

8. Victor Marchetti and John Marks, *The CIA and the Cult of Intelligence* (New York: Knopf, 1974) p. 74; David Atlee Phillips, *Careers in Secret Operations: How to be a Federal Intelligence Officer* (Frederick, Md.: University Publications of America, 1984), p. 28; Jeffrey Lenorovitz, "CIA Satellite Data Link Study Revealed," *Aviation Week and Space Technology*, May 2, 1977, pp. 25–26; Arnaud de Borchgrave, "Space-Age Spies, *Newsweek*, March 6, 1978, p. 37.

9. Phillips, *Secret Operations*, p. 26; Marchetti and Marks, *Cult of Intelligence*, p. 73; Commission on CIA Activities in the United States, *Report to the President* (Washington, D.C.: U.S. Government Printing Office, 1975), p. 91.

10. *Directorate of Administration, Central Intelligence Agency* (Washington, D.C.: CIA, n.d.) unpaginated; Phillips, *Secret Operations*, p. 27; Marchetti and Marks, *Cult of Intelligence*, p. 74; U.S. Congress, House Permanent Select Committee on Intelligence, *Pre-Employment Security Procedures of the Intelligence Agencies* (Washington, D.C.: U.S. Government Printing Office, 1980), p. 31.

11. Commission on CIA Activities Within the United States, *Report to the President*, p. 92; *Directorate of Administration, Central Intelligence Agency.*

12. U.S. Congress, Senate Select Committee to Study Governmental Operations with Respect to Intelligence Activities, *Supplementary Detailed Staff Reports, Book IV*, p. 46. n. 4

13. Peer de Silva, *Sub Rosa: The CIA and the Uses of Intelligence* (New York: Times Books, 1978), p. 291.

14. Marchetti and Marks, *Cult of Intelligence*, p. 72.

15. Seymour Hersh, "The Angleton Story," *New York Times Magazine*, June 25, 1978, pp. 13ff; Henry Hurt, *Shadrin: The Spy Who Never Came Back* (New York: Reader's Digest, 1981), p. 147; David Binder, "Assessing Intelligence Breaches," *New York Times*, April 10, 1987, p. A18; Samuel T. Francis, "The Intelligence Community," in Charles L. Heatherly, ed., *Mandate for Leadership: Policy Management in a Conservative Administration* (Washington, D.C.: Heritage Foundation, 1980), pp. 903–53.

16. Department of Justice, *Report on CIA Related Electronic Surveillance Activities* (Washington, D.C.: Department of Justice, 1976), pp. 4, 13; James Bamford, *The Puzzle Palace: A Report on NSA, America's Most Secret Agency* (Boston, Mass.: Houghton Mifflin, 1982), p. 131.

17. Author's interview.

18. Marchetti and Marks, *Cult of Intelligence*, pp. 70–75; David Wise, *The American Police State* (New York: Vintage, 1976), pp. 188–92; "Aides Disciplined by CIA Are Irked," *New York Times*, November 15, 1984, pp. A1, A8; Robert Parry, "Latin Manual is Linked to 'Psy-War' Plan," *Washington Post*, December 3, 1984, p. A10; David Wise, *The Spy Who Got Away* (New York: Random House, 1988), p. 14.

19. Robert Parry, "CIA Manual Producers Say They're Scapegoats," *Washington Post*, November 15, 1984, p. A 28; "Aides Disciplined by CIA Are Irked;" Parry "Latin Manual is Linked to 'Psy-War' Plan."

20. Wise, *The American Police State*, p. 188.

21. U.S. Congress, Senate Select Committee to Study Governmental Operations With Respect to Intelligence Activities, *Foreign and Military Intelligence, Book I* (Washington, D.C., U.S. Government Printing Office, 1976), p. 439; Ralph E. Cook, "The CIA and Academe," *Studies in Intelligence* (Winter 1983), pp. 33–42 at 38–39.

22. U.S. Congress, Senate Select Committee, *Foreign and Military Intelligence, Book I*, p. 439; Cook, "The CIA and Academe," at p. 38; Wise, *The American Police State*, p. 189.

23. Central Intelligence Agency, *Appendices to Guidance for CIA Activities within the United States and Outside the United States*, (Washington, D.C.: CIA, November 30, 1982), p. 20.

24. Marchetti and Marks, *Cult of Intelligence*, pp. 70–75; "Casey's CIA: New Clout, New Danger," *U.S. News and World Report*, June 16, 1986, pp. 24–31.

25. U.S. Congress, Senate Select Committee, *Staff Reports, Book IV*, pp. 77–78.

26. U.S. Congress, House Select Committee on Intelligence, *U.S. Intelligence Agencies and Activities: Intelligence Costs and Procedures* (Washington, D.C.: U.S. Government Printing Office, 1976), p. 543; John Prados, *The Soviet Estimate: U.S. Intelligence Analysis and Russian Military Strength* (New York: Dial, 1982), p. 156; NSCID 8, "Photographic Interpretation," February 17, 1972, *Declassified Documents Reference System 1976–253G*; George Wilson, "N-PIC Technicians Ferret Out Secrets Behind Closed Windows," *Los Angeles Times*, January 12, 1975, p. 25; Curtis Peebles, "Satellite Photographic Interpretation," *Spaceflight* (October 1982), 161–63.

27. U.S. Congress, House Select Committee, *Intelligence Costs and Procedures*, pp. 537–44.

28. *Directorate of Science and Technology, Central Intelligence Agency* (Washington, D.C.: CIA, n.d.) unpaginated.

29. *Office of SIGINT Operations* (Washington, D.C.: CIA, n.d.), unpaginated; Desmond Ball, *A Suitable Piece of Real Estate: American Installations in Australia* (Sydney: Hale & Iremonger, 1980), p. 73; Bob Woodward, *Veil: The Secret Wars of the CIA 1981–1987* (New York: Simon & Schuster, 1987), pp. 313–14.

30. *Office of Research and Development* (Washington, D.C.: CIA, n.d.), unpaginated.

31. Thomas Powers, *The Man Who Kept the Secrets: Richard Helms and the CIA* (New York: Knopf, 1979), p. 340, n. 38.

32. *Directorate of Science and Technology, Central Intelligence Agency.*

33. Central Intelligence Agency, *Fact Book*, p. 9; Ray S. Cline, *Secrets, Spies and Scholars* (Washington, D.C.: Acropolis, 1976), pp. 11–12; U.S. Congress, Senate Select Committee to Study Governmental Operations with Respect to Intelligence Activities, *Supplementary Reports on Intelligence Activities, Book VI* (Washington, D.C.: U.S. Government Printing Office, 1976), p. 236.

34. Central Intelligence Agency, *Fact Book*, p. 9; private information.

35. "Shifting CIA Production From Topical to a Geographic Base," (Central Intelligence Agency Memo), April 1982.

36. Central Intelligence Agency, *Fact Book*, p. 9.

37. *Directorate of Intelligence, Central Intelligence Agency* (Washington, D.C.: CIA, n.d.), p. 4.

38. Ibid., p. 5; *Office of Imagery Analysis, Directorate of Intelligence, Central Intelligence Agency*, (Washington, D.C.: CIA, n.d.), unpaginated.

39. *Directorate of Intelligence, Central Intelligence Agency*, p. 4.

40. Ibid., p. 5.

41. Ibid.; Phillips, *Careers in Secret Operations*, p. 24.

42. The Brownell Committee, *The Origin and Development of the National Security Agency* (Laguna Hills, Calif.: Aegean Park Press, 1981), p. 30–31.

43. Walter Bedell Smith, "Proposed Survey of Communications Intelligence Activities," December 10, 1951; Brownell Committee, *National Security Agency*, pp. 1, 81; U.S Congress, Senate Select Committee to Study Governmental Operations with Respect to Intelligence Activities, *Foreign and Military Intelligence, Book III*, p. 736.

44. *United States Government Organization Manual 1957-1958* (Washington, D.C.: U.S. Government Printing Office, 1957), p. 137; "Washington Firm Will Install Ft. Meade Utilities," *Washington Post*, January 7, 1954, p. 7; "U.S. Security Aide Accused of Taking Secret Documents," *New York Times*, October 10, 1954. pp. 1, 33.

45. National Security Council Intelligence Directive 6, "Signals Intelligence," February 17, 1972. Sanitized version, *Declassified Documents Reference System 1976-168A*; Department of Justice, *Report on CIA Related Electronic Surveillance Activities* (Washington, D.C.: Department of Justice, 1976), pp. 77-78.

46. National Security Council Intelligence Directive 6.

47. U.S. Congress, Senate Select Committee, *Foreign and Military Intelligence, Book I* (Washington, D.C.: U.S. Government Printing Office, 1976), p. 354; U.S. Congress, House Committee on Appropriations, *Department of Defense Appropriations for 1983, Part 3* (Washington, D.C.: U.S. Government Printing Office, 1981), pp. 824-29; Leslie Maitland, "FBI Says New York is a 'Hub' of Spying in U.S.," *New York Times*, November 14, 1981, p. 12; Patrick E. Tyler and Bob Woodward, "FBI Held War Code of Reagan," *Washington Post*, December 13, 1981, pp. 1, 27.

48. David Burnham, "U.S. Agency Makes Vast Plan to Encode More Information," *New York Times*, December 29, 1985, pp. 1, 20.

49. National Security Decision Directive 145, "National Policy on Telecommunications and Automated Information Systems Security," September 17, 1984; Vic Mathurin, "NSA's New National Mission," *NSA Newsletter* (Feburary 1985): 4-5.

50. Private information. Within A3 Office the A31 (or Northern European Communist) Division is responsible for Poland, East Germany, Czechoslovakia, the A32 (South European Communist) Division for Hungary and Bulgaria (A-321), Yugoslavia and Albania (A-322), and Rumania (A-323).

51. Bamford, *The Puzzle Palace*, p. 91; *CINCPACFLT Intelligence Division Command History, 1985* (Pearl Harbor, Hawaii, CINCPACFLT, 1986), p. 8; private information.

52. Private information.

53. Department of Defense, *Defense Special Missile and Astronautics Center: Organization, Mission, Functions and Concept of Operations*, September 27, 1982, p. 1.

54. Raymond Tate, "Worldwide C³I and Telecommunications," Seminar on C³I, Harvard University, Center for Information Policy Resources, 1980, p. 30.

55. Seymour Hersh, *"The Target is Destroyed": What Really Happened to Flight 007 and What America Knew About It* (New York: Random House, 1986), pp. 52-53; 67-69.

56. Bamford, *The Puzzle Palace*, pp. 96-97.

57. Ibid., pp. 97-112.

58. Ibid., pp. 112-13.

59. Melvin Laird, *National Security Strategy of Realistic Deterrence: Secretary of Defense Melvin Laird's Annual Defense Department Report FY 1973* (Washington, D.C.: U.S. Government Printing Office, 1972), p. 135; Bamford, *The Puzzle Palace*, p. 157.

60. Raymond Garthoff, "Banning the Bomb in Outer Space," *International Security* 5, (1980/1981): 25-40 at 26.

61. Arthur Sylvester, "Memorandum for the President, White House; SAMOS II Launch," (Washington, D.C.: Office of the Assistant Secretary of Defense for Public Affairs, 1961), *Declassified Documents Reference System 1979–364B.*

62. Philip Taubman, "Secrecy of U.S. Reconnaissance Office is Challenged," *New York Times*, March 1, 1981, p. 10.

63. William Colby and Peter Forbath, *Honorable Men: My Life in the CIA* (New York: Simon & Schuster, 1978), p. 370.

64. George B. Kistiakowsky, *A Scientist in the White House: The Private Diary of President Eisenhower's Special Assistant for Science and Technology* (Cambridge, Mass.: Harvard University Press, 1976), pp. 378–79; Carl Berger, *The Air Force in Space Fiscal Year 1961* (Washington, D.C.: USAF Historical Liaison Office, April 1966), p. 34.

65. Berger, *The Air Force*, pp. 35, 42; and Larry Booda, "New Capsule to Be Developed for SAMOS," *Aviation Week*, September 12, 1960, pp. 26–27.

66. Kistiakowsky, *A Scientist in the White House*, pp. 382, 394.

67. Dudley C. Sharp, Secretary of the Air Force Order 115.1, "Organization and Functions of the Office of Missile and Satellite Systems," August 31, 1960; Dudley C. Sharp, Secretary of the Air Force Order 116.1, "The Director of the SAMOS Project," August 31, 1960.

68. Verne Orr, Secretary of the Air Force Order 115.1, Office of Space Systems, March 10, 1983; Verne Orr, Secretary of the Air Force Order 116.1, The Office of Special Projects, March 10, 1983.

69. U.S. Congress, Senate Special Select Committee on Secret and Confidential Documents, "Questions Related to Secret and Confidential Documents," (Washington, D.C.: U.S. Government Printing Office, 1973), p. 16; Laurence Stern, "$1.5 Billion Secret in the Sky," *Washington Post*, December 9, 1973, pp. 1, 9.

70. *Report of the Commission on the Organization of the Government for the Conduct of Foreign Policy*, (Washington, D.C.: U.S. Government Printing Office, 1975), p. 95; Colby and Forbath, *Honorable Men*, p. 370; Theodore Shackley, *The Third Option* (New York: McGraw-Hill, 1981); Stansfield Turner, *Secrecy and Democracy: The CIA in Transition* (Boston: Houghton Mifflin, 1985).

71. Bamford, *The Puzzle Palace*, pp. 191–92; James Canan, *War in Space* (New York: Harper and Row, 1982), pp. 110–11; "Aldridge Seeks Shift of USAF Space Program Responsibilities," *International Tech Trends*, May 19, 1986, p. 7.

72. James Bamford, "America's Secret Eyes in Space." *New York Times Magazine*, January 13, 1985, p. 38ff.

73. See the items for "Special Programs" and "Special Support Programs" in the Air Force budget in U.S. Congress, House Committee on Appropriations, *Department of Defense Appropriations for 1986, Part 6* (Washington, D.C.: U.S. Government Printing Office, 1985), p. 124; Department of the Air Force, *Budget Estimates, Aircraft Procurement, Missile Procurement and Research, Development, Test and Evaluation* (Washington, D.C.: Department of the Air Force, 1985), p. A-2.

3 DEFENSE DEPARTMENT INTELLIGENCE ORGANIZATIONS

In addition to the national intelligence organizations within the Department of Defense (DOD)—the National Reconnaissance Office (NRO) and the National Security Agency (NSA)—there are several agencies that are department level agencies, with primary functions to satisfy the intelligence requirements of the Secretary of Defense and DOD components.

Two of these agencies—the Defense Intelligence Agency and Defense Mapping Agency—can trace their origins to the centralization trend that began at the end of the Eisenhower Administration and continued through the early 1970s. Another agency is more recent—the Armed Forces Medical Intelligence Center.

DEFENSE INTELLIGENCE AGENCY

Creation of the Defense Intelligence Agency (DIA) was one manifestation of the trend toward centralization that began in the Eisenhower Administration and reached its peak in the Kennedy Administration. The Eisenhower Administration concluded in the late 1950s that a consolidation of the military services' general intelligence activities (defined as all non-SIGINT, non-overhead, non-organic intelligence activities) was needed.[1] According to one analyst, this belief was a byproduct of the missile gap controversy of the time:

> Faced with the disparate estimates of Soviet missile strength from each of the armed services which translated into what have been called self-serving budget requests for weapons for defense, the United States Intelligence Board created a Joint Study Group in 1959 to study the intelligence producing agencies.[2]

The Joint Study Group, chaired by Lyman Kirkpatrick, concluded that there was a considerable overlap and duplication in defense intelligence activities and a resulting maldistribution of resources. The consequence was that the

> overall direction and management of DOD's total intelligence effort becomes a very difficult if not impossible task. Indeed, the fragmentation of effort creates "barriers" to the free and complete interchange of intelligence information among the several components of the Department of Defense.[3]

The study group thus recommended that the Secretary of Defense should "bring the military intelligence organizations within the Department of Defense into full consonance with the concept of the Defense Reorganization Act of 1958."[4] How to do this was a subject of controversy. The Joint Chiefs of Staff were concerned with preserving the responsiveness of the service efforts to the military's tactical intelligence requirements. Thus, they preferred a "Joint Military Intelligence Agency" subordinate to them, within which the independence of the several military components, and hence their sensitivity to the needs of the parent service, would be retained. Robert McNamara, the future Secretary of Defense, wanted a much stronger bond—one that would allow for better utilization of service assets to support policymakers, and force structure planners as well as to achieve management economies.[5]

The agency that resulted was a compromise between those viewpoints. The DIA reports to the Secretary of Defense, but via the Joint Chiefs of Staff. As a result of the DIA's creation, the Joint Staff Director for Intelligence (J-2) was abolished, as was the Office of Special Operations, the small intelligence arm of the Secretary of Defense.[6]

The present responsibilities of the DIA are to:

1. satisfy or insure the satisfaction of the foreign intelligence requirements of the Secretary of Defense and DOD components;
2. participate in the Defense Systems Acquisition Review Council process by providing threat evaluations and validations based on information from coordinated intelligence;
3. coordinate all Defense intelligence collection and production requirements and validate, register, assign and recommend priorities for evaluating the satisfaction of DOD collection and production;
4. serve as Program Manager for the General Defense Intelligence Program and manage such other programs as may be designated by the Secretary of Defense;
5. manage all aspects of Defense intelligence production within the General Defense Intelligence Program;
6. manage and operate a facility for the timely and the interactive tasking of collection systems and capabilities in response to time-urgent needs of the Department of Defense;
7. manage the Defense Attaché system;

8. manage all DOD intelligence information systems except those dedicated to signals intelligence operations;

9. participate in joint national and Defense intelligence activities such as the National Photographic Interpretation Center, the Defense Special Missile and Astronautics Center and other such activities as may be developed by mutual interagency agreement and approved by the Secretary of Defense;

10. in coordination with other intelligence agencies concerned, recommend plans for intelligence operations and coordinate the execution of approved intelligence operations plans;

11. provide the focal point for relationships with foreign intelligence services;

12. review, coordinate and evaluate the effectiveness of career development for general military personnel; establish a DOD career development program for civilian general intelligence personnel;

13. recommend changes in the application of current and new collection systems or improvements in DOD intelligence systems and related collection systems;

14. operate the Defense Intelligence School;

15. supervise a DOD-wide intelligence dissemination program and provide centralized dissemination services in support of DOD and other authorized recipients;

16. establish, maintain and operate facilities for DOD imagery indexing, processing, duplication, evaluation, and central repository services in support of DOD and other authorized recipients;

17. provide guidance to DOD components concerning the release of Defense intelligence information to foreign governments, international organizations, and the public;

18. administer DOD security policies and programs to protect intelligence and intelligence sources and methods, including direction of the Defense Special Security System;

19. serve as the intelligence staff officer (J-2) of the Joint Chiefs of Staff;

20. . . . [coordinate] intelligence requirements and considerations for space, less C^3 systems. Collaborate with appropriate Joint Staff Directorates—with respect to intelligence activities, and procedures and development of intelligence requirements and considerations for space systems. Maintains cognizance over all space systems which have military intelligence utility;

21. in collaboration with J-3, JCS represent the OJCS (Office of the Joint Chiefs of Staff) and unified and specified commands in intelligence issues and efforts relating to the exploitation of current national capabilities.[7]

Since its creation the DIA has undergone numerous reorganizations (four between 1961 and 1970) and has been subjected to severe criticism. The criticism has been directed at the quality of DIA intelligence input as well as the agency's inability to effectively supervise and constrain the growth of the service components.[8]

Abolition of the DIA has often been suggested, most specifically by the 1975–76 House Select Committee on Intelligence (the Pike Committee). Such an outcome is not a likely prospect, and the DIA continues to be the prime intelligence component of the DOD with respect to strategic intelligence matters. Thus, the DIA takes part in the formulation of the National Intelligence Estimates and Special National Intelligence Estimates on such topics as Soviet strategic forces and terrorism. It also serves as the validating authority for much of the work done by the military services' scientific and technical intelligence centers. Additionally, it is responsible for the production of the Target Data Inventory (TDI), a 500,000-item data bank containing all Soviet facilities that U.S. strategic nuclear planners might desire to attack in the event of war. The TDI serves as the data base from which the National Strategic Target List (NSTL) and ultimately the Single Integrated Operational Plan (SIOP) is drawn.[9]

The DIA also engages in R & D (Research and Development) Test and Evaluation programs related to intelligence technology. In its Fiscal Year 1982 request, the DIA specified four areas of research: crisis management, scientific and technical intelligence, automated data processing capabilities, and collection management capabilities. Specifically, it requested funding to develop an automated system to "support timely analysis of Indicator and Warning Intelligence" as well as funding to "develop methodology and data bases to accommodate added intelligence requirements as a direct result of. . .U.S. policy regarding nuclear targeting in Presidential Decision # 59." The Agency also requested $700,000 to develop the Advanced Imagery Requirements and Exploitation System. In its request for the 1983 Fiscal Year it sought funds for a real-time technical data collection effort designated SUDDEN DAWN, as well as for an electro-optical collection program designated STEEL EYE.[10]

As shown in Figure 3-1, the DIA consists of seven units directly responsible to the Director and Deputy Director, and five major directorates. Among the units directly responsible to the Director and Deputy Director, three are particularly worthy of discussion.

The Director of the GDIP (General Defense Intelligence Program) Staff is responsible for preparing, with military service and Central Intelligence Agency collaboration, the budget estimates for the GDIP (discussed in Chapter 16). Further, the Director tasks organizations under GDIP direction to fulfill its objectives.[11]

The Directorate for Security and Counterintelligence (with Counterintelligence, Physical/TEMPEST, Security Programs, and Security Policy and Operations divisions) is responsible for providing counterintelligence and counterterrorist analyses and support to the OSD, the JCS, and the unified and specified commands as well as coordinating the counterintelligence production of the military departments. It is also responsible for administering the DIA's physical, TEMPEST, document, and personnel security programs. The compartmented Security Policy Branch of the Security Policy and Operations Division is responsible for establishing policy with regard to the three major categories of code word clearances relating to intelligence systems and their products—Special Intelligence (SI), Talent-Keyhole (TK), and Byeman (B).[12]

Figure 3–1. Organization of the Defense Intelligence Agency .

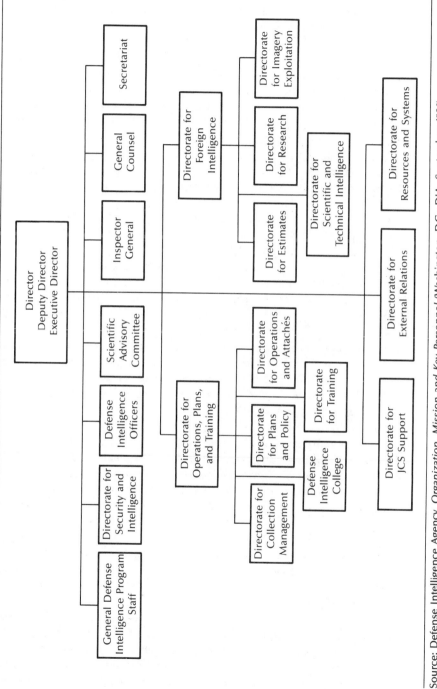

Source: Defense Intelligence Agency, *Organization, Mission and Key Personnel* (Washington, D.C.: DIA, September 1986).

The Defense Intelligence officers are responsible for directing the production of Defense Intelligence Estimates and Special Defense Intelligence Estimates in their areas of responsibility.[13]

Each of the DIA's five major directorates is headed by a Deputy Director. Within the Directorate of Operations, Plans, and Training are four directorates, including Collection Management, and Operations and Attaches. The Directorate of Collection Management (which consists of six divisions—Current Operations, Requirements and Evaluation, Human Resources, Imagery, MASINT (Measurement and Signature Intelligence) & DEFSMAC, and SIGINT) validates and prioritizes all Defense Department intelligence collection requirements levied on national collection systems. It also develops and collaborates in the development and review of plans, programs, and future requirements for Defense Department intelligence collection activities. In addition, the Directorate provides the DIA component for the DEFSMAC as well as operating the Collection Coordination Facility (CCF) for the interactive tasking of collection systems and operations.[14]

The Directorate of Attachés and Operations (with Defense Plans, Policy and Programs; DAS Programs, Service, Systems, and Current Operations divisions) develops and issues the DOD Human Intelligence (HUMINT) Program and DOD HUMINT planning guidance for the military services, the DIA and the unified and specified commands. It manages and conducts DOD HUMINT collection activities and the tasking of DOD HUMINT collection.[15]

DOD HUMINT collection activities are primarily conducted from the ninety-five Defense Attaché offices throughout the world. The mission of the attachés are to observe and report military and political-military information, represent the Department of Defense and the military services, administer military assistance programs and foreign military sales, and advise the U.S. Ambassador on military and political-military matters.[16]

Within the Directorate of Foreign Intelligence are four directorates: Estimates, Scientific and Technical Intelligence, Research, and Imagery Exploitation. The Directorate for Estimates develops and produces DIA contributions to the National Intelligence Estimates, Special National Intelligence Estimates, and other national intelligence estimative papers that are the responsibility of the National Foreign Intelligence Board. It also develops and produces Defense Intelligence Estimates, Special Defense Intelligence Estimates, Defense Intelligence Estimative Memoranda, and Defense Estimative Briefs. Finally, it provides intelligence support to the Office of the Secretary of Defense, the JCS, and the Defense Systems Acquisition Review Council as well as developing and providing all-source, military related, intelligence publications specifically designed for senior level Executive Branch and DOD officials.[17]

The Directorate for Scientific and Technical Intelligence (with five divisions: Nuclear Energy; Weapons and Systems; Production Control, Resources, and Technical Data Support; Strategic Defense, Command, and Control, and Space; and Research and Technologies) provides all-source, finished, scientific intelligence for the entire Defense establishment—either through direct production or delegation to the military services' scientific and technical intelligence units. It reviews and validates requirements and priorities for scientific and technical intelligence production, and reviews and approves finished scientific and technical intelligence production at both the DIA and military service intelligence level. It also maintains liaison with other elements of the DIA, other DOD agencies, the CIA, and other government elements to coordinate scientific and technical intelligence activities.[18]

The Directorate for Research produces all-source, finished military intelligence and maintains data bases on order of battle, military doctrine, strategy and tactics, C^3, equipment and logistics, biographies, economics, material production and assistance programs, terrorism, and narcotics trafficking. Its biographies focus on military and civilian defense leaders in allied, neutral, and hostile nations. The Directorate also provides intelligence support for national level studies, current intelligence, indications and warning intelligence, and special studies. Its Operational and Target Intelligence Support Division formulates target intelligence policies and plans.[19]

The Directorate for Imagery Exploitation (with seven divisions: Imagery Exploitation; Priority Exploitation; Exploitation Systems, Support and Management; Soviet/Warsaw Pact; Regional Analysis; Current Imagery Intelligence; and Systems, Technology and Resources) provides imagery analysis on foreign military capabilities including order of battle, transportation and logistics, and force dispositions. It also provides imagery-derived intelligence to support special operations, unconventional warfare planning, counterterrorism, and some activities related to narcotics. Lastly, it exercises administrative management over DIA personnel assigned to the imagery exploitation elements of the NPIC.[20]

The Directorate of Foreign Intelligence also is responsible for the five defense liaison offices—DL1 (London), DL2 (Ottawa), DL3 (Canberra), DL4 (Wellington) and DL5 (Bonn).[21]

The Directorate for JCS Support consists of four directorates—the Directorate for OJCS Intelligence Support, the Directorate for Current Intelligence, the Directorate for Indications and Warning, and the Directorate for NMIC Operations—as well as the Central American Joint Intelligence Team. The Directorate for OJCS Intelligence Support has primary responsibility for all actions (within the Directorate's capabilities) assigned to the DIA by the JCS/OJCS and assigns action responsibilities to appropriate directorates, when required, to satisfy JCS requirements. It also provides support personnel to the National Military Command Center and the National Emergency Airborne Command Post (NEACP).[22]

The Directorate for Current Intelligence (with four regional and two functional divisions) assesses, coordinates, produces, and integrates all-source current and indications and warning intelligence. It provides daily briefings on current intelligence to the Secretary of Defense; the Chairman, JCS; and other DOD officials. It produces a Morning Summary, daily Defense Intelligence Notices, Warning Reports, and Intelligence Appraisals and contributes to the National Intelligence Daily. In addition, it provides analytical support to the National Military Intelligence Center (NMIC) and National Military Command Center (NMCC) on a twenty-four-hour basis.[23]

The Directorate for Indications and Warning (with Operations, Development and Implementation and ELINT divisions) administers the Worldwide Warning Indicator Monitoring System. Whereas the Directorate for Current Intelligence focuses on producing indications and warning related to finished intelligence, the I&W Directorate is concerned with the methods of producing raw I&W data. The Directorate for NMIC Operations manages and operates the National Military Intelligence Center.[24]

The Directorate for External Relations (with Executive Management and Research, Director's Staff Group, Legislative and Public Affairs, Foreign Liaison, International Negotiations Support, Military Operational Support, and Foreign Exchanges and Disclosures divisions) serves as the DIA focal point for providing tailored, anticipatory defense intelligence support to the Secretary of Defense and others in the OSD and on the NSC Staff. It also is tasked with ensuring that the defense intelligence requirements of the House and Senate are fully supported by the DIA. A third function of the Directorate is to provide intelligence support to U.S. policy offices and delegations involved in international negotiations— START, INF, MBFR. Finally, it conducts foreign intelligence liaison activities, manages foreign disclosures, and serves as the primary point of contact for foreign representatives conducting business with the Department of Defense.[25]

The Directorate for Resources and Systems is divided into six directorates: Procurement, Human Resources, Information Systems, DODIIS Planning Management, and DODIIS Engineering.[26] The Directorate of Human Resources is the personnel office, while the Directorate of Communications provides overall management of the worldwide Special Intelligence Communications (SPINTCOMM) portion of the DSSCS. The Directorate for Technical Services and Support provides central reference, photo processing, and presentation support to other branches of the DIA.[27]

As of 1978 the DIA had 4,300 to 5,500 employees (including 1,000 attaches) and a budget in the $200 to $250 million range. It is presently estimated to have 6,500 employees and a budget of $450 million.[28]

Main headquarters for the DIA is the Defense Intelligence Analysis Center at Bolling AFB, District of Columbia. It also conducts some of its operations from other locations—the Pentagon, the Washington Navy Yard, and the Plaza West.

DEFENSE MAPPING AGENCY

The Defense Mapping Agency (DMA) was created in 1972 to consolidate the mapping, charting, and geodesy (MC&G) functions of the various military services. The primary mission of the DMA is to support the military services by providing mapping, charting, and geodetic products and services that are critical to successful military operations. Specifically, the DMA is responsible for producing strategic and tactical maps, charts, geodetic information, data bases, and specialized products to support current and advanced weapons and navigation systems. It is also responsible for establishing DOD mapping, charting, and geodetic requirements and providing them to the Assistant Secretary of Defense (C³I).[29]

In many instances, DMA operations involve the processing of data acquired by technical intelligence systems, indicated by the fact that 80 percent of the DMA's 9,500 employees hold Sensitive Compartmented Information (SCI) clearances. SCI data enables targeting of cruise missiles by Terrain Contour Matching (TERCOM). Such data is also required for precise specification of target location in the SIOP and accurate targeting of U.S. warheads on those targets. This is particularly important since "on all geographic maps published in the U.S.S.R. not one Soviet city or town is shown in its current position with relation to its lines of latitude and longitude."[30]

The DMA maintains a headquarters operation and two principal production facilities. The headquarters organization, as shown in Figure 3–2, consists of ten offices, four directorates and the Special Program Office for Exploitation Modernization. The Directorate of Plans and Requirements establishes DMA mapping, charting, and geodetic objectives, prepares plans, and develops policy to provide MC&G products throughout the government. The Directorate's Weapons System Division serves as the focal point for defining all aspects of MC&G requirements for DOD advanced weapons systems, cruise missile systems, and for support systems requiring MC&G products.[31]

The Directorate for Programs, Production, and Operations programs resources and assigns tasks to subordinate DMA elements. It reviews and evaluates utilization of resources and execution of production and support task assignments. It also establishes policy for DOD participation in national, interagency, and international MC&G activities as well as MC&G data collection requirements and priorities. The Directorate's Land Combat Division, among other functions, oversaw production on Digital Terrain Elevation Data and Digital Feature Analysis Data in support of Pershing II missile targeting.[32]

The Hydrographic Division provides program guidance and policies for the development and maintenance of MC&G products and services for a variety of programs—hydrographic chart production, hydrographic survey and data collection, nautical publications, and special purpose hydrographic products. The latter includes a variety of antisubmarine, undersea, and mine warfare planning charts. The Aerospace Division is responsible for overseeing the production of MC&G data in support of military aerospace forces, weapon systems, and programs; this includes the TERCOM data, Vertical Observation Data (VOD), and several other products.[33]

In 1982 the DMA established a new component, the Special Program Office for Exploitation Modernization (SPOEM), with a mission "to develop the capability to produce DMA products by digital/softcopy techniques from advanced acquisition systems and enhance production capabilities to utilize hard copy source material from a new collection system."[34] In plainer language, the SPOEM gives the DMA

Figure 3–2.   Organization of the Defense Mapping Agency.

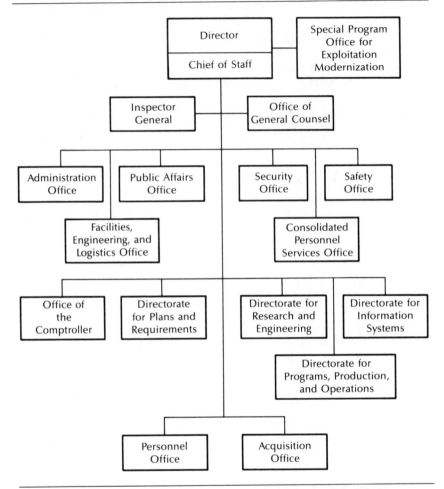

Source: *Department of Defense Telephone Directory* (Washington, D.C.: U.S. Government Printing Office, August 1987), p. 0–24; Defense Mapping Agency, *FY85–89 Joint Manpower Program: Headquarters and Headquarters Support Activity*, Part I (Washington, D.C.: DMA, 1985) n.p..

the capability to receive and utilize the digital readout from KH-11 and KH-12 imaging satellites, as well as improving DMA capability to use such data when transformed into a photograph.

The DMA has two principal production facilities providing mapping, charting, and geodetic products. Among its functions, the DMA Aerospace Center in St. Louis, Missouri is to

1. produce, distribute and maintain aeronautical, extraterrestrial, and aeronautical charts, air target materials, and special products in support of aerospace and missile systems;
2. operate and maintain the Department of Defense centralized libraries for aeronautical charts, free world air facilities and flight information, point positioning data bases, gravity data and installation/positional data;
3. produce and maintain flight information publications, flight control aids and evaluated information on air facilities to satisfy the daily operational requirements of the Armed Forces;
4. provide geodetic and geophysical studies and data in support of various weapons systems;
5. produce and maintain digital and point positioning data base in support of aerospace weapons delivery systems;
6. produce cultural and terrain information for use in radar simulators, terminal guidance, enroute navigation, and SAC penetration routes.[35]

The geodetic and geophysical studies (Item 4), partially based on data acquired by military and civilian geodetic satellites (SEASAT-1, GEOSAT, GOES), allow compensation for force fields that might throw missiles off their intended path. These studies are crucial to the accuracy for U.S. missiles such as MX and Trident.[36]

The DMA Hydrographic/Topographic Center at Brookmont, Maryland produces topographic and hydrographic charts (including bottom contour maps) and related material for surface and subsurface navigation, topographic maps for land forces, Digital Terrain Evaluation Data for cruise missiles, as well as some products for air operations. The Hydrographic/Topographic Center produces Precise Bathyspheric Naval Zone Charts, required by submarines to obtain location fixes without surfacing. The Special Navy Support Branch (of the Navigation Publications Division of the Center's Navigation Department) is responsible for overseeing the production of "Special Graphics" in support of submarine intelligence missions—missions that often take submarines within or near Soviet territorial waters.[37]

ARMED FORCES MEDICAL INTELLIGENCE CENTER

In 1982, the Armed Forces Medical Intelligence Center (AFMIC) was established, replacing the Army's Medical Intelligence and Information Agency (MIIA) which provided medical intelligence for the entire defense community. The AFMIC was possibly formed as the result of dissatisfaction with the medical intelligence efforts of the MIIA. Discussions between the Defense Audit Service personnel and the Director of the General Defense Intelligence Program Staff in 1981 indicated the intelligence community's concern about a lack of adequate medical intelligence in Southwest Asian and Third World countries, "where casualties from unusual diseases and environmental conditions could occur."[38]

Figure 3–3. Organization of the Armed Forces Medical Intelligence Center.

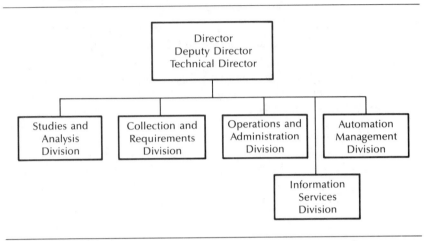

Medical intelligence is particularly vital in planning for combat operations, particularly in areas significantly different from the United States in terms of the environment and prevalence of disease.

One aspect of AFMIC activities consists of producing general medical intelligence—intelligence on health and sanitation, epidemiology, environmental factors, and military and civilian medical care capabilities—as in the AFMIC's "Medical Capabilities Study: Democratic People's Republic of Korea." A second aspect of its activities is the production of medical, scientific, and technical intelligence concerning all basic and applied biomedical phenomena of military importance, including biological, chemical, psychological, and biophysical areas. The AFMIC report "Medical Effects of Non-Ionizing Electromagnetic Radiation—LASER" is one example.[39]

The AFMIC is also certainly responsible for assessing foreign biomedical R & D and its impact on physiological effectiveness of medical forces, as well as the exploitation of foreign medical materiel obtained under the DOD Foreign Materiel Exploitation Program (FMEP).[40]

There are five divisions in the AFMIC, subordinate to the Director, Deputy Director, and Technical Director, as shown in Figure 3–3. The Studies and Analysis Division produces all foreign medical intelligence for the AFMIC. The Collection and Requirements Division coordinates all aspects of medical intelligence collection and the acquisition and exploitation of medical materiel for the DOD. The Operations and Administration Division is responsible for budgeting, fiscal reporting, personnel, and security. The Automation Management Division provides data processing services, while the Information Services Division provides translation support; develops user-interest profiles; and acquires, controls, and disseminates intelligence documents.[41]

Management of the AFMIC is the responsibility of the Secretary of the Army via the Army Deputy Chief of Staff for Intelligence and the Army Surgeon General. AFMIC's link to the military services, the DOD, and the Secretary of the Army is provided by an Interdepartmental Advisory Panel. The panel consists of representatives from the Assistant Secretary of Defense (Health Affairs); the Surgeons General of the Army and Air Force; and representatives of the intelligence chiefs of the Army, Navy and Air Force, and Defense Intelligence Agency. The panel provides recommendations to the Secretary of the Army and the Center on medical intelligence requirements for the DOD and military services.[42]

NOTES TO CHAPTER 3

1. U.S. Congress, Senate Select Committee to Study Governmental Operations with Respect to Intelligence Activities, *Foreign and Military Intelligence, Book I* (Washington, D.C.: U.S. Government Printing Office, 1976), p. 325.
2. U.S. Congress, Senate Select Committee to Study Governmental Operations with Respect to Intelligence Activities, *Supplementary Reports on Intelligence Activities, Book VI* (Washington, D.C.: U.S. Government Printing Office, 1976), p. 266.
3. Secretary of Defense Robert S. McNamara, "Memorandum for the President, Subject: The Establishment of a Defense Intelligence Agency," July 6, 1961 Declassified Documents Reference System *1986-000085*.
4. Ibid.
5. U.S. Congress, Senate Select Committee, *Foreign and Military Intelligence, Book I*, p. 325.
6. Ibid.
7. Joint Chiefs of Staff, *JCS Pub 4: Organization and Functions of the Joint Chiefs of Staff* (Washington, D.C.: JCS, August 1, 1985), pp. VII-3-3 to VII-3-5.
8. "Defense Intelligence Organization Criticized," *Aviation Week and Space Technology*, August 3, 1970, p. 17; Patrick McGarvey, *The CIA: The Myth and the Madness* (Baltimore: Penguin Books, 1972), p. 148–59.
9. The Pike Committee, *CIA: The Pike Report* (Nottingham, England: Spokesman, 1977), p. 261; Desmond Ball, *Deja Vu: The Return to Counterforce in the Nixon Administration* (Santa Monica, Calif.: California Seminar on Arms Control and Foreign Policy, 1974), pp. 10–11; Desmond Ball, *Targeting for Strategic Deterrence* (London: International Institute for Strategic Studies, 1983).
10. U.S. Congress, House Committee on Armed Services. *Hearings on Military Posture and HR 2970, Part 4* (Washington, D.C.: U.S. Government Printing Office, 1981), pp. 1143–45; U.S. Congress, House Committee on Armed Services, *Hearings on Military Posture and HR 5968, Part 5* (Washington, D.C.: U.S. Government Printing Office, 1982), p. 1189.
11. Defense Intelligence Agency, *Organization, Mission and Key Personnel* (Washington, D.C.: DIA, September 1986), p. 8.
12. Ibid., pp. 16–17.
13. Ibid., pp. 12, 13.
14. Ibid., p. 18, 19, 21.

15.   Ibid., pp. 22–23; *Department of Defense Telephone Directory* (Washington, D.C.: U.S. Government Printing Office, August 1987), p. O-18.

16.   U.S. Congress, House Committee on Armed Services, *Hearings on H.R. 4181 to Authorize Certain Construction at Military Installations for Fiscal Year 1987, and Other Purposes*, (Washington, D.C.: U.S. Government Printing Office, 1986), pp. 199–200.

17.   Defense Intelligence Agency, *Organization, Mission and Key Personnel*, p. 31–33.

18.   Ibid., pp. 38–39.

19.   Ibid., pp. 34–35.

20.   Ibid., p. 36.

21.   Ibid., p. 31.

22.   Ibid., pp. 41–42.

23.   Ibid., pp. 44–45.

24.   Ibid., pp. 46–48.

25.   Ibid., pp. 50–51.

26.   Ibid., pp. 54–55; *Department of Defense Telephone Directory*, pp. O-19 to O-20.

27.   Defense Intelligence Agency, *Organization, Mission and Key Personnel*, p. 62.

28.   "Shaping Tomorrow's CIA," *Time*, February 6, 1978, pp. 10ff and "Pruning the Pentagon's Spreading Tree," *National Journal*, October 31, 1987, p. 2737.

29.   U.S. Congress, House Committee on Armed Services, "Written Statement of Maj. Gen. Richard N. Wells," *Hearings on Military Posture and HR 5968, Part 5* (Washington, D.C.: U.S. Government Printing Office, 1982), pp. 1231–34; DOD Directive 5105.40, "Defense Mapping Agency," April 23, 1986.

30.   David C. Morrison, "You Are Here," *National Journal*, October 31, 1987, pp. 2735–38; Leonid Vladimirov, *The Russian Space Bluff* (New York: Dial, 1973), p. 49.

31.   Defense Mapping Agency, *FY 85–89–Joint Manpower Program–Headquarters and Headquarters Support Activity, Part I* (Washington, D.C.: DMA, 1985), pp. 29, 34.

32.   Ibid., pp. 36, 43.

33.   Ibid., pp. 46–47, 53–54.

34.   Department of Defense, *Department of Defense Justification of Estimates for Fiscal Year 1984* (Washington, D.C.: U.S. Government Printing Office, 1983), p. 5; also see, Defense Mapping Agency, *FY 85–89–Joint Manpower Program—Special Program Office for Exploitation Modernization* (Washington, D.C.: U.S. Government Printing Office, 1985).

35.   Defense Mapping Agency, *FY 85–89–Joint Manpower Program—DMA Aerospace Center, Part I* (Washington, D.C.: DMA, 1985), p. 2.

36.   U.S. Congress, Senate Committee on Appropriations. "Prepared Statement of Brigadier General Donald O. Aldridge," *Department of Defense Appropriations for 1982, Part 5* (Washington, D.C.: U.S. Government Printing Office, 1981), p. 262.

37.   Ibid.

38.   Defense Audit Service, *Semiannual Audit Plan First Half, Fiscal Year 1982* (Washington, D.C.: DAS, 1981), p. 32.

39.   Armed Forces Medical Intelligence Center, *Organization and Functions of the Medical Intelligence Center* (Fort Detrick, Md.: AFMIC, April 1986), p. vi; and Defense Audit Service, *Semiannual Audit Plan First Half, Fiscal Year 1982*, p. 32.

40.   Defense Audit Service, *Semiannual Audit Plan First Half, Fiscal Year 1982*, p. 32.

41.   Armed Forces Medical Intelligence Center, *Organization and Functions of the Armed Forces Medical Intelligence Center*, p. 1–3.
42.   DOD Directive 6240.1, "Armed Forces Medical Intelligence Center," December 9, 1982, p. 2.

4 MILITARY SERVICE INTELLIGENCE ORGANIZATIONS

Unlike the United Kingdom and Canada, which abolished their military service intelligence organizations with the creation of defense intelligence organizations, or Australia, which restricts its service intelligence organizations to the production of low-level tactical intelligence, the United States has maintained elaborate service intelligence organizations. Further, these organizations have grown substantially in budget, personnel, and importance over the last several years.

Part of the explanation of the continued major role of U.S. service intelligence organizations may be found in bureaucratic politics, but is more significantly a function of U.S. military requirements. A military force with large service components, each with wide-ranging functional and geographic responsibilities, may be better served in terms of intelligence support by organizations that are closely aligned with the service components. Additionally, some strategic intelligence and collection functions may be best performed by service organizations. Thus, given the Air Force's obvious requirement to be informed on foreign aerospace technology or the Navy's need to be informed on foreign submarine technology, assignment of such intelligence production tasks to the Air Force and Navy may allow for the most efficient production of such intelligence for all concerned.

ARMY INTELLIGENCE ORGANIZATIONS

The U.S. Army intelligence community, as depicted in Figure 4–1, is directed by the Office of the Deputy Chief of Staff for Intelligence. The major operational agency is the Army Intelligence and Security Command (INSCOM), which is charged with human intelligence, counterintelligence, and SIGINT/COMSEC.

51

Figure 4–1. Organization of the Army Intelligence Community.

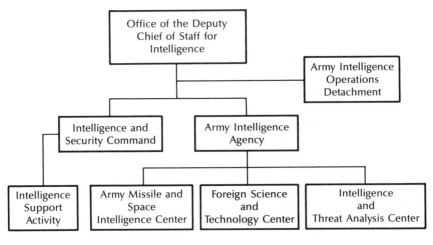

Other members of the Army intelligence community are the Army Intelligence Agency (AIA), the Army Missile and Space Intelligence Center (AMSIC), the Foreign Science and Technology Center (FSTC), the Intelligence and Threat Analysis Center (ITAC) and the Intelligence Support Activity (ISA).

The Office of the Deputy Chief of Staff for Intelligence, shown in Figure 4–2, consists of a Plans, Program, and Budget Office; Intelligence Automation Management Office; and four Directorates—Foreign Liaison, Foreign Intelligence, Counterintelligence and Security Countermeasures, and Intelligence Systems.[1]

The Foreign Liaison Directorate conducts liaison with other Army intelligence organizations such as Australia's Military Intelligence Directorate. It also coordinates the activities of the Foreign Liaison Office of the U.S. Army Intelligence Operations Detachment (AIOD), with its Attache Coordination, Tours, and Protocol branches representing elements of the AIOD. In addition the Directorate develops and coordinates the Foreign Intelligence Assistance Program.[2]

The Foreign Intelligence Directorate is concerned with current intelligence, long-term assessment, scientific and technical intelligence, and the establishment of requirements. Its Current Intelligence Division, DCSI Watch Office, Scientific and Technical Branch, and Exploitation and Applications Branch constitute elements of the AIOD.[3]

The Directorate of Counterintelligence and Security Countermeasures is concerned with counterintelligence operations, signals security, and operations security as well as personnel, physical, and information security. It formulates the policy for the Army's cryptologic effort, including Communications Intelligence Security Standards. Its Technology Transfer Division is simultaneously an element of the

Figure 4-2. Organization of the Office of the Deputy Chief of Staff, Intelligence.

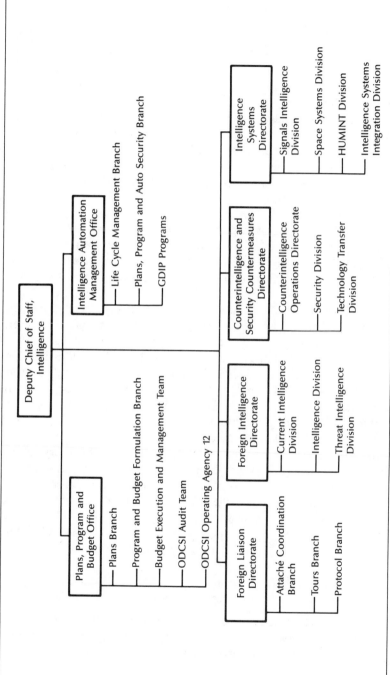

Source: *Department of Defense Telephone Directory* (Washington, D.C.: U.S. Government Printing Office, August, 1987), p O-41.

AIOD. The Directorate represents the Army on several interagency counterintelligence and security committees, including the Defense Counterintelligence Board and the NSC's interagency groups on counterintelligence and countermeasures.[4]

The Intelligence Systems Directorate is concerned with intelligence collection by space systems, signals intelligence platforms, human resources, and the integration of the collection methods.[5]

The Army Intelligence Operations Detachment is a field-operating agency under the supervision and control of the DCSI. Each element of the Detachment is authorized to communicate directly with the Office of the Secretary of Defense, Office of the JCS, and the headquarters of the Department of the Army.[6]

The Detachment's Office of Foreign Liaison administers foreign military attaché tours, Army VIP tours, and visits of foreign counterparts. It also processes identification and applications for foreign attachés. The Intelligence Command and Control Office monitors and inspects all Army-wide intelligence activities to ensure compliance with Executive Orders and DOD and Army directives. The Detachment's Watch Office monitors global situations to provide I&W support to the Army's Operations Center and provides I&W briefings to members of the Army staff. The Current Intelligence Division provides a daily written current intelligence "Black Book" for distribution to the Army Secretariat or Army staff.[7]

In 1984, the Office of the Assistant Chief of Staff for Intelligence (OACSI) established an Army Intelligence Agency to direct the production of scientific, technical, and general intelligence (except medical). Establishment of the AIA was followed by several other changes. In June 1984, the AIA assumed operational control of the ITAC, the FSTC and the MIA, which had been under the control of the INSCOM, the Army Material Command, and the Army Missile Command, respectively. In 1985 it assumed direct control of those organizations. On August 1, 1985, the Army Missile Intelligence Agency was redesignated the U.S. Army Missile and Space Intelligence Center.[8]

The AIA, located in the Pentagon, is organized into a Management Support Division, Resource Management Division, Plans and Operations Division, and Research, Development, and Analysis Division. The AIA is responsible for managing the overall production activities of the three major intelligence production centers, as well as Army counterintelligence production. The AIA also validates Army requests for U.S. SIGINT System (USSS) products and medical intelligence products to be provided by the Armed Forces Medical Intelligence Center.[9]

The U.S. Army Intelligence and Threat Analysis Center, with about 300 employees, located in the Washington Navy Yard, is responsible for

- providing intelligence assessments of near-term to twenty-year projected capabilities and vulnerabilities of those foreign forces that represent either potential threats to, or potential allies in support of, U.S. operations;

- providing intelligence assessments of current military capabilities and vulnerabilities as well as military aspects of the political, economic, sociologic, demographic, and geographic environment of those non-allied, non-Warsaw Pact countries in which the U.S. Army may operate;
- producing intelligence assessments (current and projected) of a foreign force's doctrinal, organizational, operational, and tactical concepts;
- producing counterintelligence and international assessments of the current projected organizations, capabilities, and methods of foreign intelligence and security services, and terrorist groups;
- producing imagery intelligence on foreign ground force equipment and weapons systems, according to the National Tasking Plan and providing national-level imagery exploitation support to the U.S. Army; and
- providing direct analytic exchange between the Army Intelligence Agency and the National Security Agency in support of Army requirements for SIGINT.[10]

As indicated in Figure 4-3, the ITAC is organized into several management units (Administrative Office, Resource Management and Program Office, Automation Management Office, Production Support Division, Special Security Detachment) and four substantive divisions (Warsaw Pact, Regional, Imagery, Counterintelligence and Terrorism.)

The Warsaw Pact Division forecasts doctrinal, operational, strategic, tactical, and organizational trends of Warsaw Pact armies and models/simulates Warsaw Pact combat support and decision processes. In addition, it explores Soviet C^3 systems and their impact on the planning and execution of military operations at or below the theater level. It also examines the roles of the MVD (Soviet Ministry of Internal Affairs) and KGB in the maintenance of government control and Spetznaz combat operations and capabilities.[11]

The Regional Division produces comprehensive studies on the military capabilities, and the political, sociologic, economic, demographic, cultural, and military geographic aspects of selected countries in which the Army may be deployed. It also produces near-, mid- (ten year) and long-term (twenty year) forecasts of conflict environments, military capabilities, and vulnerabilities of selected countries.[12]

The Imagery Division produces imagery and photogrammetric analysis of ground force weapons, electronic systems (e.g., radars), support systems (e.g., remotely piloted vehicles, river crossing equipment, mine warfare equipment) and installations (e.g., nuclear weapons depots). Its Geographic Analysis Branch conducts imagery exploitation in support of contingency planning, military operations, special operations, training and exercises—identifying geographical features that can provide cover for special operations infiltrators or impediments to the advance of a brigade.[13]

The Counterintelligence and Terrorism Division produces assessments of the organization and functions of foreign intelligence and security services, of worldwide terrorist activity, international technology transfer, and the efficiency of Army Special Access Programs.[14]

Figure 4–3. Organization of the Intelligence and Threat Analysis Center (ITAC).

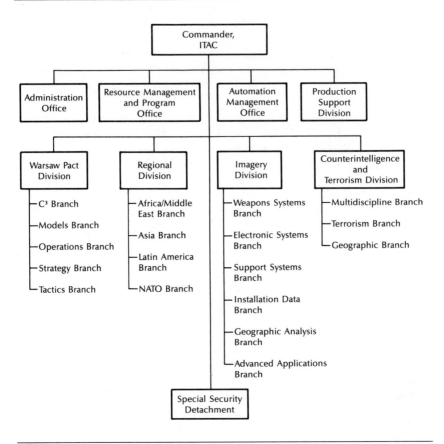

Source: *Department of Defense Telephone Directory* (Washington, D.C.: U.S. Government Printing Office, August 1987), p. O-62

Two-thirds of ITAC production concentrates on the Soviet Union and Warsaw Pact developments, while the remaining one-third focuses on areas such as the Caribbean, Central America, Africa, Middle East/Persia, and the Far East, where Army contingency missions might exist. One, circa 1985, ITAC initiative was the Army Intelligence Survey, intended to produce a six-volume study on each of the thirty-one countries in those areas. The AIS will provide operational commanders with basic planning data to use in contingency planning. An earlier ITAC effort, *Combat Elements of the North Korean Army,* was credited by the ITAC with influencing President Carter's decision to halt the withdrawal of U.S. troops from South Korea.[15]

Figure 4–4. Organization of the Foreign Science and Technology Center (FSTC).

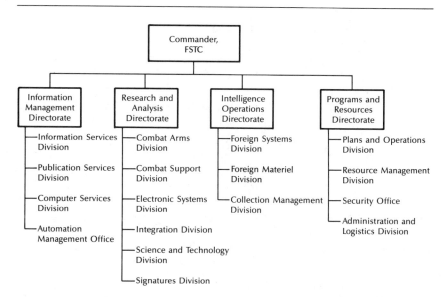

Source: FSTC Regulation 10-1, "Organization and Functions: U.S. Army Foreign Science and Technology Center," April 1, 1986.

The Foreign Science and Technology Center (FSTC), established in 1962 by consolidation of the intelligence offices of the individual army technical services (among them Signal, Ordnance, Quartermaster, Engineer, and Chemical services) is located in Charlottesville, Virginia.[16] As of 1982, it had a total of 570 personnel and a budget of over $20 million. The FSTC's mission is to "produce scientific and technical intelligence concerning sciences, ground force weapon systems, and technologies (less medical and missiles) in response to valid intelligence production requirements."[17] Its specific functions include:

- identifying and projecting the scientific and technical threat to the U.S. Army;
- forecasting foreign military research, development, and acquisition trends;
- producing and disseminating all-source scientific and technical intelligence products;
- managing the Army Foreign Materiel Program (FMP) to include the acquisition and exploitation of foreign materiel and the dissemination of the resulting data; and
- producing Foreign Target Signatures data.[18]

As shown in Figure 4–4, subordinate to the Commander, FSTC are four directorates—Information Management, Research and Analysis, Intelligence Operations, and Programs and Resources. The Research and Analysis Directorate, through its Combat Arms and Combat Support Divisions, is responsible for analysis of the characteristics, components, deployment, and employment of all combat arms and support systems. The Directorate's Electronic Systems Division is responsible for similar information on all operational electronic systems and advanced electronic technologies, while the Science and Technology Division is responsible for assessing foreign science and technology and their potential impact on future ground force weapons systems. The Integration Division assesses foreign chemical warfare capabilities, and research and development activities, as well as processing current intelligence products. The Signatures Division is responsible for providing intelligence on the signatures of foreign military systems.[19]

The main function of the Intelligence Operations Directorate involves foreign materiel. The Directorate's Foreign Materiel Division develops and executes activities related to the acquisition and exploitation of foreign materiel. The Foreign Systems Division maintains the Army's inventory of foreign systems, as well as acquired materiel, which it refurbishes as required and exploits to provide technical data reports. The Directorate's Collection Management Division registers, validates, prioritizes, and levies information collection requirements as well as monitoring the extent to which they are fulfilled.[20]

The U.S. Army Missile and Space Intelligence Center, with about 400 personnel in 1982, is located at Redstone Arsenal, Alabama. In June 1956 the Special Security Office of the Army Ballistic Missile Agency (ABMA) was established to procure missile and space intelligence data for the Commander of the ABMA. To analyze the data, a Technical Intelligence Division, subordinate to the Assistant Chief of Staff for Research and Development, ABMA, was established. Subsequent to the March 1958 consolidation of all Army activities at Redstone Arsenal into the Army Ordnance Missile Command (AOMC), the fifty-person intelligence activity was redesignated the Office of the Assistant Chief of Staff for Missile Intelligence. When the AOMC was absorbed in 1962 by the Army Missile Command (itself subordinate to the U.S. Army Materiel Command) the AOMC was redesignated the Directorate of Missile Intelligence and in September 1970 became the Missile Intelligence Agency. As noted above, on August 1, 1985, it was redesignated the U.S. Army Missile and Space Intelligence Center.[21]

The Center's mission is to

acquire, produce, maintain, and disseminate scientific and technological intelligence pertaining to missile and space weapons systems, subsystems, components, and activities; related sciences and technologies representing state-of-the-art to support [Department of the Army] and DOD requirements.[22]

The structure of the AMSIC is shown as Figure 4–5. The Systems Simulations and Scientific Applications Directorate provides data processing and scientific and technical computations to all units of the AMSIC, as well as the development and use of computational models, simulations, and data processing systems. The Advanced Sensors Directorate acquires and analyzes imagery, signals intelligence,

Figure 4–5. Organization of the Army Missile and Space Intelligence Center.

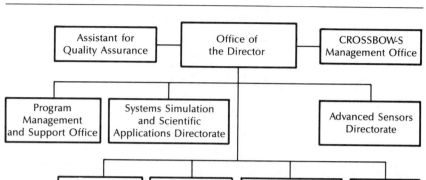

Source: Organizations and Functions, U.S. Army Missile and Space Intelligence Center (Redstone Arsenal, Ala.: AMSIC, June 9, 1986).

and human intelligence data in support of the AMSIC's scientific and technical intelligence production effort.[23]

The Land Combat Missile Systems Directorate produces scientific and technical intelligence concerning single and integrated short-range ballistic missile (SRBM) and antitank guided missile (ATGM) weapon systems, as well as providing threat support to the Department of the Army for projected intercontinental ballistic missiles (ICBMs) and precision guided weapons (PGWs) systems. The Tactical Air Defense Missile Systems Directorate produces the same intelligence for single and integrated Tactical Air Defense weapons systems, including projected systems and modifications. This Directorate also determines the state-of-the-art in foreign tactical weapons systems technologies; command, control, and communications; R & D organizations; personalities; capabilities; and programs which can effect present or projected systems needed by U.S. tactical air defense forces. The Strategic Defense Directorate is responsible for determining the foreign state-of-the-art in strategic ballistic missile defense; strategic air defense; space defense; command, control, and communications; as well as examining R & D organizations and personalities.[24]

The Army Intelligence and Security Command, headquartered at Arlington Hall Station (until it moves into new headquarters at Ft. Belvoir, Virginia), was established on January 1, 1977 when the U.S. Army Security Agency (ASA) was redesignated as the Intelligence and Security Command and absorbed the (then) U.S. Army Intelligence Agency, the Forces Command Intelligence Group, the Intelligence Threat Analysis Detachment, and the Imagery Interpretation Center.

Figure 4–6. Organization of INSCOM.

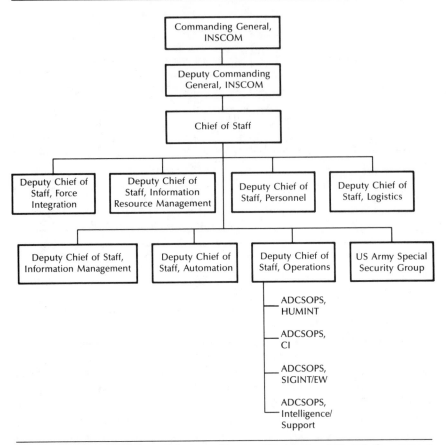

Source: *Department of Defense Telephone Directory* (Washington, D.C.: U.S. Government Printing Office, August 1987, pp. O-59 to O-60.

The latter three had been field operating activities of the Assistant Chief of Staff for Intelligence.[25] The ASA was the successor to the variously named Army signals intelligence agencies of World War II. The Commanding General of INSCOM is therefore responsible both to the Army's DCSI and to the Chief, Central Security Service (i.e., DIRNSA). INSCOM personnel operate SIGINT collection facilities at numerous overseas bases, including several in Turkey. In addition, the INSCOM conducts clandestine human intelligence and counterintelligence operations. With the transfer of the ITAC to the AIA, INSCOM lost its analytical role.

The organizational structure of the INSCOM is based on a number of Deputy Chiefs of Staff (DCS) responsible for different areas of activity. Thus, as illustrated in Figure 4-6, in addition to the Chief of Staff there are DCSs for: Force Integration, Information Resource Management, Personnel, Logistics, Information

Management, Automation, and Operations. The later DCS is responsible for INSCOM intelligence collection and counterintelligence activities.

Subordinate to the DCS for Operations are Assistant Deputy Chiefs of Operations (ADCSOPS) for HUMINT, Counterintelligence, SIGINT/EW (electronic warfare), and Intelligence/Support. Reporting to the ADCSOPS (HUMINT) are the five divisions and two offices that manage the HUMINT collection program. The Collection Management Division (with its Requirements and Reports, Concepts and Targets, and Biographies Branches) prepares the INSCOM HUMINT Plan; maintains the HUMINT target system; oversees the preparation of Mission Target Analysis for HUMINT collection units; and provides guidance on collection emphasis, changing priorities, and new collection objectives. The Field Activities Division (through its Controlled Collection, Overt Collection, and Sources Management branches) directs both clandestine and overt HUMINT collection activities, including the Emigré Exploitation Program. The Special Actions Office conducts "specialized intelligence collection operations in response to INSCOM, departmental and national intelligence needs." Other units are the TAREX (Target Exploitation) Division, Programs and Policy Division, Plans Division, the Project Coordination Office, and the FMA Office. Actual collection activities are performed by groups such as the 66th Military Intelligence Group in Munich and Augsburg, West Germany.[26]

The ADCSOPS, Counterintelligence supervises both technical and human counterintelligence through the Technical, SIGSEC (Signals Security), and Counter-HUMINT divisions. The ADCSOPS, SIGINT/EW directs the activities of the U.S. Army Field Stations involved in the collection of signals intelligence. Present field stations are located at Sinop, Turkey; Augsburg, West Germany; West Berlin; Key West, Florida; San Antonio, Texas; Panama; Kunia, Hawaii; Pyong Taek, South Korea; Misawa, Japan; and Okinawa, Japan. The ADCSOPS, SIGINT/EW is also responsible for measurement and signature intelligence and imagery intelligence. In the later capacity the Assistant Deputy exercises staff responsibility for national imagery collection and exploitation operations in support of intelligence requirements, as well as representing the Army and/or INSCOM on boards involving Army imagery activities, including the National Foreign Intelligence Board's Committee on Imagery Requirements and Exploitation (COMIREX).[27]

As of December 31, 1985, the INSCOM had a little over 15,000 personnel. Of this total, 2,220 were stationed at INSCOM headquarters, 2,756 at Ft. Meade, 1,555 at Vint Hills Farm, Ft. Bragg, Ft. Shafter, and Ft. Monmouth, 4,897 at field stations, and 3,521 at collection, counterintelligence, and operations security (OPSEC) units overseas. The personnel breakdown for INSCOM units is shown in Table 4–1.

The most covert Army intelligence unit is the Intelligence Support Activity (ISA), headquartered at Ft. Belvoir, Virginia. The ISA is the successor to the Foreign Operating Group (FOG) that was established on an *ad hoc* basis to aid in the attempted rescue of the hostages in the U.S. Embassy in Tehran in 1979. The FOG infiltrated four Special Forces soldiers posing as civilians into Tehran to

Table 4–1. Personnel Assigned to INSCOM Units.

Unit	Station	Manpower Military	Civilian
HQ INSCOM	AHS	283	300
USA Garrison AHS	AHS	161	79
USA Automated Systems Activity	AHS	97	72
Finance & Accounting Activity	AHS	15	39
Maintenance & Assistance Team	AHS	16	0
Administrative/AV Activity	AHS	19	32
USAISC INSCOM Detachment	AHS	23	29
USAISC AHS Detachment	AHS	53	9
Intelligence Threat Analysis Center	AHS	301	276
Intelligence Exchange/Support Center	AHS	72	38
USA Programs Analysis Group	FGGM	1	16
CONUS MI Group (SIGINT)	FGGM	1142	4
USA Element NSA	FGGM	20	0
Admin Survey Detachment	FGGM	316	330
Security Support Detachment	FGGM	161	39
USA Operational Group	FGGM	115	32
Admin Support Detachment	FGGM	25	20
USA Central Security Facility	FGGM	161	39
USA Foreign Area Officer Detachment	FGGM	13	1
USA Foreign CI Activity	FGGM	34	11
USA Systems Exploitation Detachment	FGGM	18	4
USA Garrison VHFS	VHFS	136	132
INSCOM Mission Support Activity	VHFS	63	18
USA Theater Intelligence Center	Ft. Shafter, HI	55	4
INSCOM Field Exploitation Detachment	Ft. Monmouth, NJ	0	0
Field Station Sinop	Sinop, TK	290	0
Field Station Key West	Key West, FL	62	0
Field Station Okinawa	Okinawa, JP	182	2
Field Station Berlin	Berlin, FRG	769	26
Field Station Augsburg	Augsburg, FRG	1681	133
Field Station Misawa	Misawa, JP	124	1
Field Station Korea	Pyong'taek, ROK	252	2
Field Station San Antonio	San Antonio, TX	272	3
Field Station Kunia	Kunia, HI	964	17
Field Station Panama	Galeta Island, PM	117	0
66 MI Group (CI), HHC	Munich, FRG	182	0
66 MI Group (CI), Aug	Munich, FRG	84	45
502 I&S Battalion, HHC	Augsburg, FRG	108	0
502 I&S Battalion, Aug	Wobeck, FRG	47	3
409 EW Co. (Rear)	Augsburg, FRG	182	0
328 Co. (Cont & Proc)	Augsburg, FRG	132	0
18 MI Battalion (Collection)	Munich, FRG	137	0
18 MI Battalion (Collection), Aug	Munich, FRG	10	70
5 MI Co. (Interrogation)	Munich, FRG	54	0
5 MI Co. (Interrogation), Aug	Munich, FRG	0	6
430 MI Detachment (Collection)	Munich, FRG	59	0
430 MI Detachment (Collection), Aug	Munich, FRG	0	6
766 MI Detachment (CI)	Berlin, FRG	30	0
766 MI Detachment (CI), Aug	Berlin, FRG	4	5
527 MI Battalion (CI/OPSEC), HHC	Kaiserslautern	120	0
527 MI Battalion (CI/OPSEC), Aug	Kaiserslautern	64	81
527 MI Battalion (CI/OPSEC), Co. A	Kaiserslautern	101	0

Table 4–1. continued

Unit	Station	Manpower Military	Civilian
527 MI Battalion (CI/OPSEC), Co. B	Stuttgart, FRG	96	0
581 MI Detachment (II)	Zweibrucken, FRG	44	0
582 MI Detachment (II)	Alconbury, UK	34	0
583 MI Detachment (II)	Wiesbaden, FRG	45	0
584 MI Detachment (CI) & Aug	Vicenza, IT	23	1
Institute for Adv USSR/EEur Studies	Garmisch, FRG	11	29
INSCOM For Lng Tng Center Europe	Munich, FRG	12	9
USA Crypt Support Activity	Heidelberg, FRG	17	0
500 MI Group (Collection), HHC	Camp Zama, JP	59	0
500 MI Group (Collection), Aug	Camp Zama, JP	21	60
USA Asian Studies Detachment	Camp Zama, JP	9	83
181 MI Detachment (Collection)	Camp Zama, JP	17	0
181 MI Detachment (Collection), Aug	Camp Zama, JP	2	7
149 MI Detachment (Collection)	Camp Zama, JP	22	0
149 MI Detachment (Collection), Aug	Camp Zama, JP	0	8
470 MI Group (CI)	Ft. Clayton, PM	108	0
470 MI Group (CI), Aug	Ft. Clayton, PM	25	13
501 MI Group (CI), HHC	Cp. Coiner, ROK	243	0
501 MI Group (CI), Aug	Cp. Coiner, ROK	23	20
3 CEWI Battalion (AE)	Cp. Humphrey, ROK	406	0
524 MI Battalion (Collection)	Cp. Coiner, ROK	147	0
524 MI Battalion (Collection), Aug	Cp. Coiner, ROK	0	22
332 Co. (EW)	Cp. Page, ROK	245	0
209 MI Co. (OPSEC)	Cp. Coiner, ROK	166	0
209 Mi Co. (OPSEC), Aug	Cp. Coiner, ROK	0	20
513 MI Group, HHC	Ft. Monmouth, NJ	105	0
513 MI Group, Aug	Ft. Monmouth, NJ	39	2
201 MI Battalion, HHC	Ft. Monmouth, NJ	62	0
17 MI Co.	Ft. Bragg, NC	146	0
174 MI Co. (Ops)	Ft. Monmouth, NJ	219	0
202 MI Battalion (Collection Exploitation)	Ft. Monmouth, NJ	141	0
164 MI Co. (CI/OPSEC)	Ft. Monmouth, NJ	115	0
166 MI Co. (Rear)	VHFS, VA	201	0
219 MI Co. (Interrogation)	Ft. Monmouth, NJ	79	0
203 MI Battalion	APG, MD	50	0
11 MI Co. (Tech Intelligence)	APG, MD	112	0
11 MI Co. (TI), Aug	APG, MD	109	0
585 MI Detachment (II)	Ft. Bragg, NC	38	0
USA EW Avn Intelligence Detachment	Lakehurst, NJ	103	3
USA Special Security Group	AHS	286	20
902 MI Group (CI), HHC	FGGM	56	0
902 MI Group (CI), Aug	FGGM	4	14
USA CI/SIGSEC Spt Battalion	FGGM	142	38
USA Detachment Pentagon (902 MIG)	Pentagon	18	14
USA Detachment SF (902 MIG)	Pres of SF, CA	213	7
INSCOM CI Detachment DNA (902 MIG)	Alexandria, VA	18	14

Total INSCOM Manpower as of December 31, 1985 was as follows: 1,599 officers, 766 warrant officers, 10,890 enlisted men and 2,134 civilian employees, for a total of 15,389 men and women.

Source: Office of the Deputy Chief of Staff, Operations, *Department of the Army Force Accounting System, Active Army Troop Strength* (Washington, D.C.: Department of the Army, 1985).

collect information about the type of locks on the gates of the American embassy compound, where the hostages were held. They also rented trucks in Tehran for the ill-fated rescue team that was to arrive in Tehran.[28]

Since that time the ISA has been involved in a variety of intelligence gathering and covert operations in North Africa and Latin America. At its peak it had agents in Morocco, Nigeria, Somalia, Sudan, and approximately ten Latin American countries. In 1981 the ISA conducted a joint operation with the CIA to slip Phalangist leader Bashir Gemayel back into Lebanon after a secret visit to the United States, circumventing a suspected Syrian plot to assassinate Gemayel. In late 1981/early 1982 the ISA arranged a deal, which later collapsed, to obtain the most modern version of the T-72 battle tank from Iraq in return for self-propelled artillery weapons for the Iraqi army. It has also been active in Lebanon, where it had one officer stationed in 1986.[29]

In 1982, the ISA, along with a CIA-Army unit known as Seaspray, worked on a mission (code named QUEENS HUNTER), to locate leftist guerilla forces in El Salvador by monitoring their radio transmissions. Seaspray pilots flew planes from Honduras to track the transmitters electronically while ISA agents rode along to operate the airborne radio equipment. In Panama, the ISA operated a refrigeration company that served as a front for its agents. Among the agents' activities was monitoring of General Manuel Noriega.[30]

ISA agents have been employed to map out the routes U.S. rescue teams would use to reach American embassies likely to be seized by terrorists. The ISA was also reported to have played a role in the January 1982 rescue of Brigadier General James Dozier from Italian terrorists. Other reported ISA intelligence missions have included the provision of military equipment to foreign forces and the deployment of servicemen using false identities. In one nation with which the United States has no diplomatic relations, arms and bulletproof vests were provided to cooperative persons for information about that country's military deployments.[31]

In a 1982 memo then Deputy Secretary of Defense Frank Carlucci ordered that ISA be disbanded. In the memo Carlucci wrote that "We seem to have created our own CIA, but like Topsy, uncoordinated and uncontrolled . . . we have created an organization that is unaccountable" and ordered termination of all ISA operations within 30 days. However, he left open the option for an appeal, if supported by an adequate plan for ISA activities.[32]

As of December 31, 1985, the ISA had 287 employees. It is organized at the headquarters level into divisions for Administration, Operations, Training, and SIGINT. When originally established it was placed under the Army's Deputy Chief of Staff for Operations rather than the Army's Intelligence Chief. In 1981, it became subordinate to the Commanding General, INSCOM.[33]

NAVAL INTELLIGENCE ORGANIZATIONS

At the apex of the naval intelligence community is the Office of Naval Intelligence (ONI). The ONI is primarily a supervisory organization that directs the activities of the various naval organizations that collect and produce intelligence.

Directly subordinate to the ONI's Director are fourteen Assistant DNIs who cover a wide range of matters. As shown in Figure 4–7, among them are the Assistant DNIs for Current Intelligence, Foreign Liaison, Plans and Policy, Special Programs, Counterintelligence, and Analysis. The Assistant DNI for Foreign Liaison is responsible for foreign attachés and foreign VIP tours. The Assistant DNI for Plans and Policy is responsible for, among other things, technical collection requirements. The Assistant DNI for Special Projects is concerned with electromagnetic, electro-optical, and acoustic collection projects. The Assistant DNI for Counterintelligence is responsible for security review and education, and classification management as well as assessing and directing actions against hostile intelligence services. The Assistant DNI for Analysis directs two analytical branches, the Political/Military Analysis Branch and the Soviet Systems Branch.[34]

Subordinate to the DNI are two Deputy DNIs, each of whom heads an intelligence organization: the Naval Intelligence Command (NIC) and Naval Security Group Command (NSGC).

The NIC is headquartered at 4600 Silver Hill Road, Washington, D.C. The functions of the Command include the direction and coordination of intelligence collection, production, and dissemination to satisfy Navy and national requirements. Specifically, the NIC is responsible for

1. directing and coordinating intelligence collection, production, dissemination, and other activities necessary to satisfy Department of the Navy and DIA tasks;
2. supporting overt fleet intelligence collection planning, implementation, and evaluation, and producing time-sensitive collection guidance, specialized equipment, and qualified personnel;
3. managing overt collection of information from human and other open sources directly accessible to Navy intelligence collectors;
4. ensuring that the Navy's information requirements are introduced into the intelligence community requirements mechanism, and monitoring fulfillment of those requirements;
5. managing intelligence production within the NIC to satisfy Navy R & D, Department of Defense, and national requirements;
6. managing the dissemination of intelligence products to ensure their adequacy and timeliness in meeting national and Department of Defense requirements;
7. promoting effective naval intelligence cooperation and exchange programs with foreign navies, and approving release of intelligence to foreign government nationals and intelligence organizations;
8. managing budget and financial requirements; and
9. developing plans for monitoring the R & D and procurement of intelligence systems and equipment in order to satisfy intelligence requirements.[35]

At the top of the NIC organization, as shown in Figure 4–8, is the Commander. Directly subordinate to the Commander are several Staff Assistants. The remaining functions of the NIC are divided among five Assistant Commanders for Manpower,

Figure 4-7. Organization of the Office of Naval Intelligence.

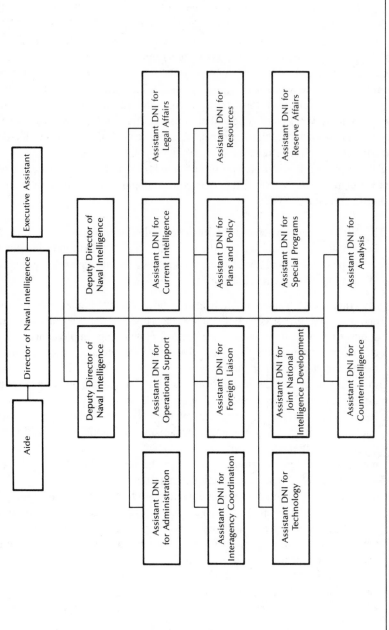

Source: *Department of Defense Telephone Directory* (Washington, D.C.: U.S. Government Printing Office, August 1987), p. O-83.

Figure 4–8. Organization of the Naval Intelligence Command.

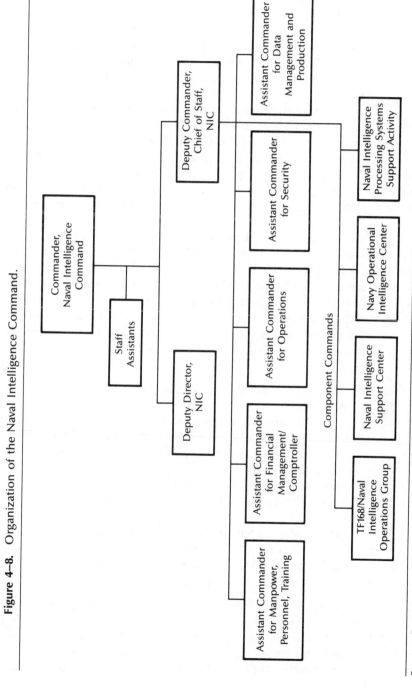

Source: *Department of Defense Telephone Directory* (Washington, D.C.: U.S. Government Printing Office, August 1987), p. O-128.

Personnel and Training; Financial Management; Operations; Security and Data Management; and Production.

The Assistant Commander for Operations coordinates the formation, assignment, and evaluation of collection requirements; and supervises naval intelligence liaison and exchange programs, including policy matters related to the acquisition of foreign materiel. In addition, he exercises release and denial authority concerning the disclosure of military intelligence to foreign governments and international organizations.[36]

The Production Tasking Divison under the Assistant Commander for Data Management and Production serves as the central coordination point for the receipt, validation, prioritization, and assignment of scheduled intelligence production requirements and unscheduled requests for intelligence production support. The division is also responsible for ensuring that intelligence production requirements for threat support intelligence and weapons systems development and acquisition are properly submitted and that threat support is provided in a timely manner.[37]

The Assistant Commander for Operations is also simultaneously head of a component command of the NIC—Task Force 168/Naval Intelligence Operations Group, whose organizational structure is shown in Figure 4–9. Task Force 168 performs both management and collection functions. It coordinates the formulation, tasking, and evaluation of collection requirements generated by or levied on the naval shore establishment; provides guidance to Navy collectors on the administration of intelligence collection and reporting; and manages a Collection Advisory Center to allow direct communication with Fleet Commands.[38]

Task Force 168 also

- collects scientific, technical, and general intelligence in Europe, the Far East, and the United States;
- collects maritime intelligence on worldwide merchant shipping, and foreign naval combatants that transit the Panama Canal or visit associated port facilities;
- conducts bilateral intelligence collection operations with selected foreign navies against Soviet naval targets;
- conducts intelligence exchange with friendly foreign navies;
- seeks to identify Soviet naval and merchant ships with nuclear weapons or materials on board;
- collects biographic data on foreign naval officers attending Navy and Marine Corps schools in the United States; and
- acquires intelligence across the entire spectrum of naval interests from the debriefing of foreign sources in Europe and the United States.[39]

The Task Force's Collection Guidance and Requirements Department manages collection, guidance, requirements, and reporting in support of the fleet, naval shore establishments, and the intelligence community. The Collection Support Department is responsible for providing personnel, equipment, and analysis in support of collection activities. The International Programs Department is responsible

Figure 4–9. Organization of Task Force 168.

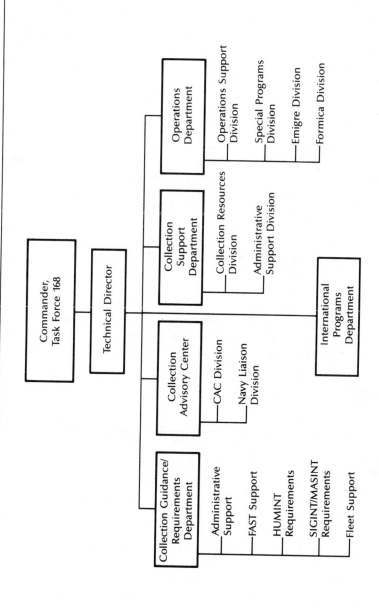

Source: *Department of Defense Telephone Directory* (Washington, D.C.: U.S. Government Printing Office, August 1987), p. O-128.

for conducting and monitoring liaison and exchange programs with foreign naval intelligence authorities. In 1986, the Department exchanged naval intelligence with forty-six friendly navies. It is the Operations Department that (1) collects information from individuals ("designated by higher authority") who, because of their travel or contact with foreign nationals, may have information of intelligence value to the Navy; (2) collects biographic data on the foreign naval intelligence officers attending Navy and Marine Corps schools in the United States; (3) collects information of interest to the Navy from emigres and defectors; and (4) directs the clandestine collection tasks assigned to Task Force 168.[40]

Task Force 168 operates in the United States, Europe, Asia, and the Pacific. Task Group 168.1 constitutes the Pacific Forward Area Support Team (PACFAST). The seventeen-person unit, with headquarters at Pearl Harbor, Hawaii, three detachments (Kamiseya, Japan; Subic Bay, Philippines; San Diego, California), and representatives at Moffet Field, California; Misawa, Japan; and Ford Island, Pearl Harbor, has expertise in fleet intelligence collection, photography, and acoustic intelligence. Among its specific responsibilities are monitoring Pacific Fleet photographic intelligence resources, as well as managing the Acoustic Characteristics Analysis Program, the Portable Acoustic Collection Equipment (CLUSTER PACE), and SUNFLYER collection programs for the Commander in Chief, Pacific Fleet (CINCPACFLT).[41]

The Naval Intelligence Support Center (NISC), located at Suitland, Maryland, is the scientific and technical intelligence organization for the Navy. Its mission is to process, analyze, produce, and disseminate scientific and technical intelligence on foreign naval systems to support national and naval strategic plans and R & D objectives and programs. Specifically, it

- develops and produces scientific and technical intelligence on the current and future technical characteristics and warfare capabilities of foreign navies concerning surface, subsurface, air and space systems; including weapons systems; command, control and communications; ocean surveillance systems; electromagnetics; and research and development;
- provides naval intelligence threat support to the U.S. naval weapons systems planning, development, and acquisition process by: producing long-range threat assessment and projections; producing threat/capabilities projections; developing threat assessments and threat support plans in support of specific programs and projects; and maintaining liaison with program sponsors, project managers, and other participants in the naval weapons system planning, development, and acquisition process;
- conducts imagery analysis in support of the Navy's technical and current intelligence programs. Exploits imagery obtained by special Navy and national collection systems;
- develops and maintains the Navy's intelligence data base including data from acoustic, non-acoustic, electronics, imagery, electro-optical, and other sensors for technical intelligence production;

- provides technical support for intelligence exploitation systems, processes, and techniques to include acoustic, non-acoustic, electronic, imagery, and electro-optical sensor collection systems; and
- acts as the CNO's Executive Agent for acquisition and exploitation of foreign materiel within the Navy Foreign Materiel Program.[42]

As a result of a 1986 study of the NISC, a major command-wide reorganization took place in which previously independent departments were subordinated to one of four directorates: Analysis, Exploitation, Technology, and Services.[43] The present structure of the NISC is shown in Figure 4–10.

The Analysis Directorate focuses on foreign capabilities in specific areas of naval warfare—surface, subsurface, and air. Thus, the Undersea Warfare Technology Department is concerned with, among other things, the acoustic vulnerabilities of foreign submarines and surface ships as well as producing intelligence on foreign operational and RDT&E acoustic and non-acoustic antisubmarine warfare (ASW) sensors.[44]

The NISC's Exploitation Directorate is concerned with the extraction of information from the two major forms of technical collection: imagery and signals intelligence. For example, NISC imagery interpreters study KH-11 photos of Soviet aircraft carriers and other vessels to determine their characteristics and capabilities, while signals intelligence experts might examine the emissions of Soviet shipborne radars to determine their characteristics and vulnerabilities.

The Technology Directorate's Naval Technical Assessment Department focuses on: the application, by foreign nations, of science and technology (e.g., electro-optics, microelectronics, computers, nuclear reactors, ocean sciences) to naval systems development; foreign naval research, development, test, and evaluation facilities and activities; and foreign technical literature. The Foreign Materiel Department manages and coordinates the acquisition, funding, and exploitation of all foreign materiel of naval interest to determine the characteristics, capabilities, and vulnerabilities of foreign systems and equipment.[45]

The Navy Operational Intelligence Center (NOIC), formerly the Navy Field Operational Intelligence Office (NFOIO), is headquartered at Suitland, Maryland and maintains detachments at Newport, Rhode Island; New London, Connecticut; and Ft. Meade, Maryland. NOIC's functions are to:

1. provide current operational intelligence and ocean surveillance information on a continuous watch basis;
2. provide current locating information on and operational histories of selected foreign merchant and fishing fleets;
3. provide control data base and intelligence interface for the Navy Ocean Surveillance Information System (OSIS);
4. publish all-source intelligence articles and studies on the organization, tactics, doctrine, and operational patterns of selected foreign naval/air forces and merchant/fishing fleets;

Figure 4–10. Organization of the Naval Intelligence Support Center.

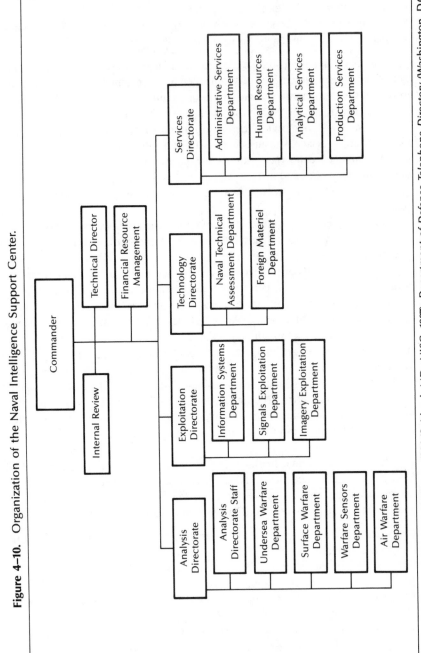

Sources: NISC, *NISC Command History 1986* (Suitland, MD.: NISC, 1987); *Department of Defense Telephone Directory* (Washington, D.C.: U.S. Government Printing Office, August 1987), p. O-128.

5. provide timely analytical support and feedback to special collection resources;
6. provide direct support to the Commander, NIC on matters relating to foreign antisubmarine warfare threats to the U.S. Navy's strategic deterrent force; and
7. provide specialized operational intelligence for the U.S. Navy's underseas warfare operations.[46]

As shown in Figure 4–11, the NOIC is organized into nine departments: Resource Management, Current Operations and Readiness, Naval Analysis, World Navies, Submarine Warfare Operations Research, Special Projects, Intelligence Systems, Merchant Operations and Analysis, and Strike Projection Evaluation and Anti-air Warfare Research.

The key department is the Current Operations and Readiness Department (CORD), formerly the Naval Ocean Surveillance Information Center (NOSIC). In 1978, the NOSIC was officially designated a member of the DOD Indications and Warning Network. In conjunction with a worldwide network of intelligence correlation centers, the CORD maintains an accounting of the location of foreign military aircraft, surface ships, and submarines as well as foreign merchant/fishing fleets operating in the world's oceans. It also prepares operational intelligence reports and ocean surveillance information for the Joint Chiefs of Staff (JCS), the Department of the Navy, the Defense Intelligence Agency, and other government organizations.[47]

In addition the CORD prepares studies on the Soviet Navy's current readiness status, readiness doctrine (as indicated by Soviet writings), exercise activities, in-port procedures, and deployment and patrol practices.[48]

The Naval Analysis Department studies Soviet naval and combined arms exercises and Soviet naval strategy and tactics, and employment doctrine of non-Soviet bloc naval and maritime-associated air forces. The Submarine Warfare Operations Research Department advises the Commanding Officer, NOIC on matters involving the collection, processing, evaluation, and dissemination of all-source information for use by U.S. submarine forces during peacetime and wartime operations; included is information on Soviet military operations and tactics against U.S. submarine forces, as well as Soviet oceanographic research operations and use of ocean sensor devices directed against U.S. submarine forces.[49]

The Special Projects Department analyzes foreign naval antisubmarine warfare operations of interest to the Navy. It also provides "in-depth analyses of certain selected Soviet activities," probably including Soviet intrusions in Swedish territorial waters. In addition, it provides "threat analyses, area studies, and intelligence support for special U.S. defense programs at the direction of higher authorities," undoubtedly special submarine intelligence collection operations. The Merchant Operations and Analysis Department examines the operations, characteristics, capabilities, and inventories of all-flag merchant, fishing, shipping, and research vessels.[50]

The Naval Security Group Command (NSGC), with headquarters at 3801 Nebraska Avenue, N.W., Washington, D.C. is headed by a Deputy Director of Naval

Figure 4–11. Organization of the Navy Operational Intelligence Center (NOIC).

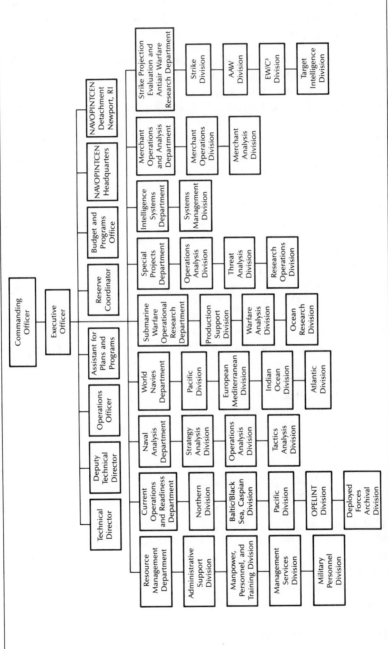

Source: Navy Operational Intelligence Center, *Navy Operational Intelligence Center, 1986* (Suitland, MD.: NOIC, 1987), p. 29.

Table 4–2. NSGC Activities and Detachments.

NSGC Activities	NSGC Detachments
Adak, Alaska	Atsugi, Japan
Anchorage, Alaska	Barbers Pont, Hawaii
Athens, Greece	Brunswick, Maine
Augsburg, West Germany	Crane, Indiana
Charleston, South Carolina	London, United Kingdom
Edzell, United Kingdom	Mayport, Florida
Fort Meade, Maryland	Monterey, California
Galeta Island, Panama	Norfolk, Virginia
Groton, Connecticut	Subic Bay, Philippines
Guantanamo Bay, Cuba	Sugar Grove, W. Virginia
Hanza, Japan	Yokosuka, Japan
Homestead, Florida	
Kamiseya, Japan	
Keflavik, Iceland	
Key West, Florida	
Kunia, Hawaii	
Misawa, Japan	
Naples, Italy	
Northwest, Virginia	
Pearl Harbor, Hawaii	
Clark AFB, Philippines	
Pyong Taek, Republic of Korea	
Sabana Seca, Puerto Rico	
San Vito, Italy	
Skaggs Island, California	
Terceira, Portugal	
Winter Harbor, Maine	

Intelligence. The NSGC began its existence as OP-20-G-G Section of the 20th Division (Office of Naval Communications) of the Office of the Chief of Naval Operations. During World War II it was known by the cover name Communications Supplementary Activity Washington (CSAW).[51]

The NSGC has two basic responsibilities: signals intelligence and communications security. As a result of these responsibilities, NSGC personnel perform a variety of tasks. They staff the land-based HF-DF CLASSIC BULLSEYE collection sites, run sea-based collection equipment, install SIGINT or COMSEC equipment on ships and submarines, staff the downlinks for the Navy's CLASSIC WIZARD ocean surveillance satellites, and conduct COMSEC monitoring operations.

The most important NSGC units are the twenty-seven Naval Security Group activities spread over the world. The location of these units is listed in Table 4–2. In addition there are five NSG Departments, eleven NSG Detachments and four NSG Field Offices in the United States and abroad.[52]

As indicated in Figure 4-12, there are, subordinate to the Commander, NSGC, several Assistants and eight Assistant Commanders, for: Special Operations (i.e., SIGINT); Signals Security; Technical Development; Space and Technology; Personnel and Training; Telecommunications and Automatic Data Processing Systems; Logistics and Material; and Plans, Programs, Budget, and Resource Management.

Also of significance is the Naval Oceanographic Office (NOO), at Bay St. Louis, shown in Figure 4-13. The mission of the NOO is to

plan, organize and execute survey operations to acquire global oceanographic, hydrographic and geophysical data using assigned ships, aircraft and platforms, including spacecraft; engage in data acquisition efforts with other DOD and government activities, contractors and foreign nations.[53]

The Oceanographic Intelligence Group of the Management and Support Services Department monitors and assesses the operations, capabilities, and intentions of foreign oceanographic programs and conducts liaison with the intelligence and scientific community to obtain information on the progress of foreign nations' oceanography. The Special Projects Branch of the Information Systems Department: (1) plans and conducts special surveys in support of submarine trial areas, missile launch and impact sites, and special search missions; (2) maintains the capability to conduct detailed surveys and searches of the ocean floor to aid in the implantation of sea-floor positioning systems; (3) provides analytical support to several projects, including Project CAESAR (see Chapter 9); and (4) maintains visible and ocean bottom photographic data banks. The Hydrographic Department reviews, edits, and/or prepares a variety of navigation charts and listings.[54]

AIR FORCE INTELLIGENCE ORGANIZATIONS

Five Air Force organizations perform intelligence missions: the Office of the Assistant Chief of Staff, Intelligence (OACSI); the Air Force Intelligence Agency (AFIA); the Air Force Electronic Security Command (ESC); the Foreign Technology Division (FTD) of the Air Force Systems Command; and the Air Force Technical Applications Center (AFTAC).

The Office of the Assistant Chief of Staff Intelligence (OACSI) is the premiere organization of the Air Force intelligence community. Subordinate to the OACSI and his deputy are, as shown in Figure 4-14, an Assistant for Administrative Support Matters, an Assistant for Joint and NSC Matters, and four directorates—Targets; Force Management; Security and Communications Management; and Policy, Plans, and Programs.

The Directorate of Targets consists of two divisions: the Concepts and Applications Division; and the Mapping, Charting, and Geodesy Division. The Directorate of Force Management develops total force personnel, policy, programs, and implementation plans for the development, training, and utilization of personnel to support Air Force intelligence activities.[55]

Figure 4–12. Organization of the Naval Security Group Command.

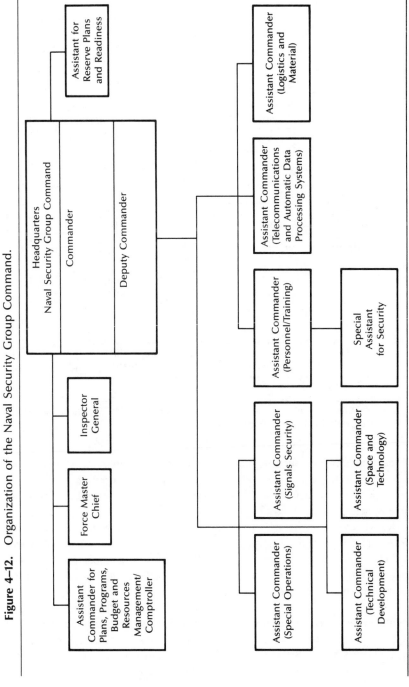

Source: *Department of Defense Telephone Directory* (Washington, D.C.: U.S. Government Printing Office, April 1988), p. O-129.

Figure 4–13. Organization of the Naval Oceanographic Office.

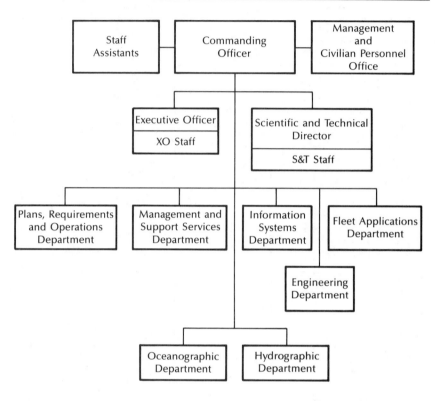

Source: Naval Oceanographic Office, NAVOCEANO Instruction, 5450.1A, Change Transmittal 6, "NAVOCEANO Organization Manual," May 6, 1987, p. 0940-2.

The Directorate of Security and Communications Management manages the Air Force Sensitive Compartmented Information (SCI) Security Program, the Air Force Special Security Office (SSO) System, and coordinates SCI support to Air Force Special Access Programs.[56]

The Directorate of Policy, Plans, and Programs: (1) evaluates, validates, and prioritizes intelligence requirements levied on the Air Force and national HUMINT, SIGINT and imagery collections systems; (2) validates requirements for developing, acquiring, integrating, and applying intelligence collection systems; and (3) manages special reconnaissance and collection operations.[57]

The OACSI is primarily a management organization, directing the work of the Air Force intelligence community with respect to collection and analysis, with the Assistant Chief of Staff, Intelligence representing the Air Force in dealings with the rest of the U.S. intelligence community. This framework was dictated

Figure 4–14. Organization of the Assistant Chief of Staff, Intelligence, U.S. Air Force.

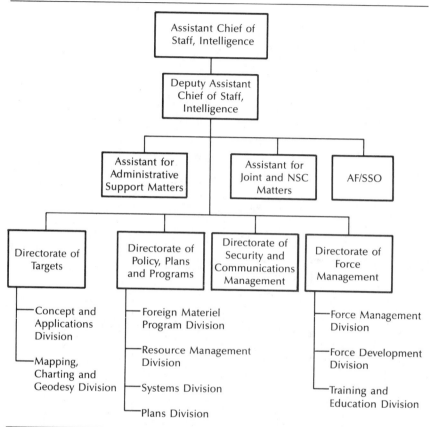

Source: *Department of Defense Telephone Directory* (Washington, D.C.: U.S. Government Printing Office, August 1988), pp. O-152 to O-153.

by a 1971 directive by the Secretary of the Air Force that mandated reassignment of Air Staff operating and support functions to other organizations. In response to this directive the Air Force Intelligence Service was established on June 27, 1972.[58]

In early 1988 the AFIS became the Air Force Intelligence Agency (AFIA). The AFIA, which has about 2,200 employees, consists (as shown in Figure 4–15) of several administration and support offices, nine Directorates and a Special Activities Center.[59]

The Directorate of Security and Communications runs the Air Force Special Security Office, which is responsible for ensuring the security of signals intelligence, as well as handling personnel security matters. The Directorate of Intelligence Data Management plans, coordinates, and exercises management control of

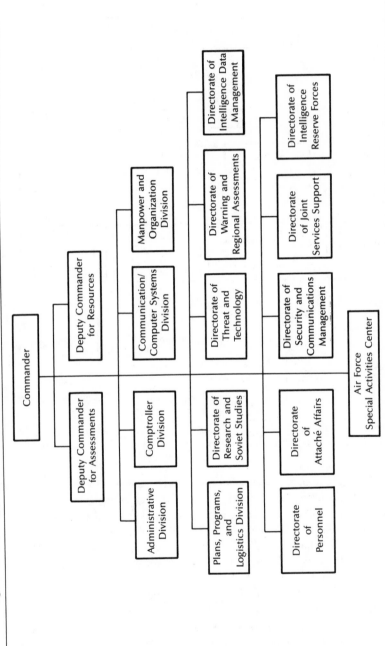

Figure 4-15. Organization of the Air Force Intelligence Agency.

Source: *Department of Defense Telephone Directory* (Washington, D.C.: U.S. Government Printing Office, April 1988), pp. O-163 to O-164.

worldwide Air Force systems for the handling of intelligence data. The Directorate of Attaché Affairs supports the Defense Attaché System and monitors all matters concerning Air Force participation in that program.[60]

The Directorate of Intelligence Reserve Forces manages the AFIA Intelligence Reserve Program. The Directorate's responsibilities include recruitment, administration, readiness, training, and operational utilization of more than 1,200 assigned reserve personnel.[61]

The Directorate of Joint Services Support is responsible for Air Force prisoner of war matters, serves as the action office in the DOD for Code of Conduct training, manages the Hostage Survival Program, and provides escape and evasion intelligence support for U.S. airmen shot down behind enemy lines. The information collected for escape and evasion may come from satellite photography, open sources and human sources—satellite photography to give a broad view of the terrain, open source collection on regulations and customs, and human sources concerning likely U.S. sympathizers.

The Directorate of Research and Soviet Affairs (through its Soviet Awareness Division) carries out the Soviet Awareness Program. Under this Program the Directorate produces the "Soviet Military Thought" series, the "Studies in Communist Affairs" book series, the *Soviet Press Selected Translations* and *Soviet Military Concepts* periodicals, internal publications, and runs other aspects of the program—Soviet Military Power Week, the Soviet Awareness Team, and the Soviet Literature Research Facility.[62] The other divisions of the Directorate of Research and Soviet Studies include the Special Studies, Military Research, and Strategic Studies Divisions. The Special Studies Division (with Denial and Deception and Imagery Analysis branches) is located in the NPIC building at the Washington Navy Yard. The Division is responsible for intelligence production on foreign denial and deception, and imagery exploitation in support of the U.S. intelligence community and policymakers. In 1985 the Division also continued to fund research projects on denial and deception. One of those studies, performed by the Federal Research Division of the Library of Congress, focused on Soviet concepts of camouflage, concealment, and deception. A second study, carried out by the Arnold Engineering Development Center, analyzed camouflage, concealment, and deception activity at a classified facility in the Soviet Union.[63]

The Military Research Division, with its Aircraft, C^3I and Missiles and Space branches, exploits signals intelligence in analyzing (1) air, missile, space, and nuclear force development, doctrine, and strategy; (2) force exercises, deployment, and employment; (3) force command, control, and communications and counter-C^3; (4) force tactics; and (5) encroachment, interference, or expansion beyond national boundaries.[64]

The Strategic Studies Division provides intelligence, summaries, studies and briefings on Soviet and Chinese strategic offensive and defensive systems and doctrine. The Directorate of Threat and Technology studies advanced R & D weapons, defensive systems, and strategic and tactical offensive weapons systems.

The Directorate of Warning and Regional Assessments focuses on actual and potential regional conflicts.

The Directorate of Targets is responsible for weaponeering, target analysis, force application, mission planning, target material, and mapping, charting, and geodesy. Its wartime mission would include providing bomb damage assessment and target analysis to support retargeting.[65]

The Air Force Special Activities Center at Ft. Belvoir, Virginia provides centralized management of all Air Force activities involved in the collection of information from human sources. These activities include clandestine collection as well as the debriefing of defectors. The Center was previously known as the 7612th Air Intelligence Group and prior to that, the 1127th Field Activities Group. The 1127th was described as "an oddball unit, a composite of special intelligence groups who 'conducted worldwide operations to collect intelligence from human sources.' The men of the 1127th were con artists. Their job was to get people to talk— Russian defectors, North Vietnamese soldiers taken prisoner."[66]

The AFSAC mission remains the debriefing of emigres, refugees, and defectors and the collection of intelligence through clandestine HUMINT operations. In wartime its additional mission would be the debriefing of U.S. escapees and enemy prisoners of war. AFSAC field units and augmentation teams may also assist in the acquisition of foreign materiel and exploitation of captured enemy documents.[67]

Headquartered at Ft. Belvoir, the AFSAC, with about 350 personnel, is organized as shown in Figure 4–16, with the Operations Division being the key component of the headquarters organization. In addition to twelve operating locations the Division has three detachments in the United States—Detachments 21 and 23 at Ft. Belvoir, as well as Detachment 22 at Wright-Patterson AFB, Ohio. Detachment 21's forty personnel are involved in the Defense Liaison Program, Project SHOTGUN, and Projects SEEK/LADEN.[68]

Overseas activities are conducted via two Special Activities Areas. The European Special Activities Area is headquartered at Lindsey Air Station, West Germany and has four detachments, all located in Germany (11 at Munich, 12 at Nierrod, 13 at Bitburg and 14 at Lindsey Air Station). The Pacific Special Activities Area is headquartered at Hickam AFB, Hawaii and has a staff of eight. Its two detachments are the 31-person Detachment 31 at Yokota Air Base, Japan (with a staffed operating location at Camp Zama, Tokyo) and Detachment 32 at Yongsan Army Garrison, Seoul, Korea.[69]

The Air Force Electronic Security Command (ESC), headquartered at San Antonio, Texas, was first established informally as the Air Force Security Group (AFSG) in May 1948 and then formally on July 1, 1948 with the same title. In October 1948 it became the Air Force Security Service (AFSS), headquartered at Arlington Hall Station, Arlington, Virginia. The AFSG of May 1948 consisted of eleven officers and some enlisted clerical personnel on loan from the Army Security Agency. Today the ESC employs almost 14,000 individuals.[70]

Figure 4–16. Organization of the Air Force Special Activities Center.

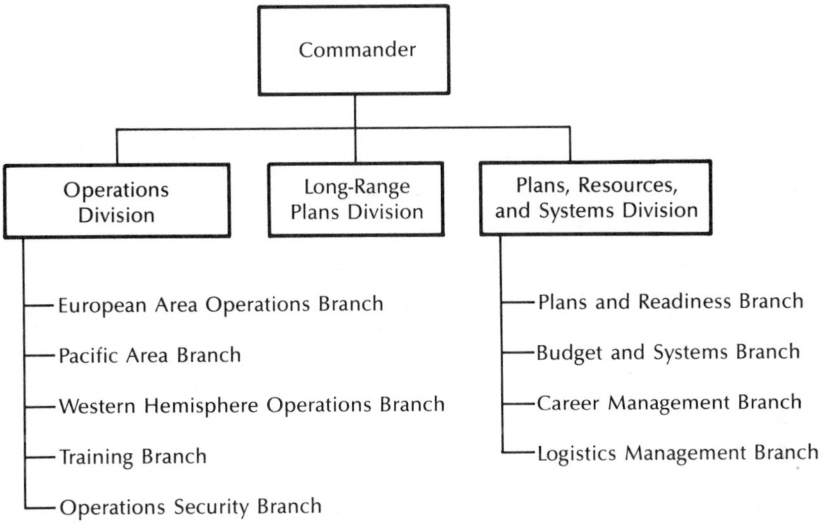

Source: *Department of Defense Telephone Directory* (Washington, D.C.: U.S. Government Printing Office, April 1988), pp. O-163 to O-164.

The ESC performs cryptographic, cryptanalytic, and electronic warfare functions for the Air Force as well as operating under NSA/CSS direction. In the latter capacity it provides personnel for overseas and domestic intelligence collection sites and airborne collection programs.

As indicated in Figure 4-17, the ESC's main activities are managed by seven Deputy Chiefs of Staffs, the most important being the DCS/Intelligence and the DCS/Operations, the latter directing the overall collection operations of the ESC.

To manage its field units involved in SIGINT and COMSEC, the ESC has established as set of geographic divisions each based in their region of operations: the European Electronic Security Division (at Ramstein AFB, West Germany), the Pacific Electronic Security Division (at Hickam AFB, Hawaii), the Continental Electronic Security Division (at San Antonio, Texas), and the Space Electronic Security Division (at Peterson AFB, Colorado).[71]

The Foreign Technology Division of the Air Force Systems Command is located at Wright-Patterson AFB. First established in 1917 as the Foreign Data Section of the Airplane Engineering Department, it was soon transferred from Washington, D.C. to Dayton, Ohio. It was subsequently renamed the Technical Data Section (1927), Technical Data Laboratory (1942), T-2 (Intelligence) of the Air Technical Service Command (1945), the Air Technical Intelligence Center (1951), and the FTD.[72]

Figure 4–17. Organization of the Air Force Electronic Security Command.

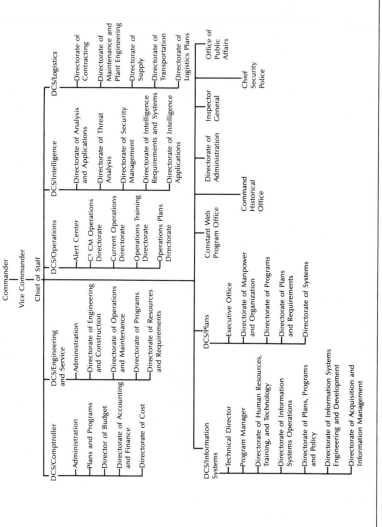

Source: Electronic Security Command.

In 1947 all nonintelligence functions were removed from the FTD's mission statement. Today, the FTD is one of the largest and most important U.S. intelligence units. Its major areas of technical intelligence activity include the prevention of technological surprise, advancement of U.S. technology by use of foreign technology, identification of weaknesses in foreign weapons systems, and use of certain design traits of foreign weapons systems as indicators of strategic intent.[73]

As indicated in Figure 4–18, the main body of the FTD consists of six directorates: Administration and Support, Information Systems, Plans and Operations, Systems, Sensor Data, and Technology and Threat.

The Directorate of Plans and Operations publishes a variety of FTD intelligence reports, manages selected Air Force sensor collection programs, consolidates and submits all formal scientific and technical intelligence collection requirements to Air Force and national authorities, acquires and processes foreign materiel for Air Force organizations, and manages the testing and exploitation of materiel acquired.[74]

The Directorate of Systems plans, directs, and manages the production of scientific and technical intelligence on the characteristics, capabilities, limitations, and vulnerabilities of space systems, ballistic missiles, and electronic defense systems, including radars, defensive missiles, and countermeasure systems. The directorate's Low Observables Office is responsible for determining the threat to the USAF's stealth programs and assesssing the performance of characteristics of foreign stealth aircraft.[75]

The Directorate of Sensor Data, via its Data Exploitation Division, processes and analyzes sensor data from foreign aerospace weapon system R & D tests, as well as providing technical support and guidance for the design and operation of new technical collection systems and the modification and improvement of existing systems. The Directorate's Imagery Exploitation Division analyzes imagery relating to foreign aerospace weapons systems and associated facilities, and prepares detailed engineering drawings, briefings, and photo analysis reports from imagery exploitation and the application of intelligence methods. The Signal Exploitation Division analyzes foreign non-communication signals from radars, IFF (Identification Friend or Foe), navigation systems, directed energy weapons, and foreign command systems to produce technical analysis reports, while the Telemetry Exploitation Division analyzes and reports on telemetry and acoustic data from foreign aerospace systems.[76]

The Directorate of Technology and Threat provides for scientific and technical intelligence support to USAF operational commands, AFSC commands and laboratories, and USAF and DOD headquarters in the following areas: technology and technology transfer assessments, future aerospace weapons systems, C^3 studies, tailored threat information products, simulator validation, and electronic warfare.[77]

The Air Force Technical Applications Center was first established in 1948 as the Special Weapons Squadron, and subsequently became known as AFOAT-1 (the 1st Section of the Office of Assistant Secretary of the Air Force for Atomic Energy). It received its present name in 1958. Until the 1970s its mission was classified and was described in sanitized congressional hearings only as "Project Clear Sky."[78]

Figure 4-18. Organization of the Foreign Technology Division.

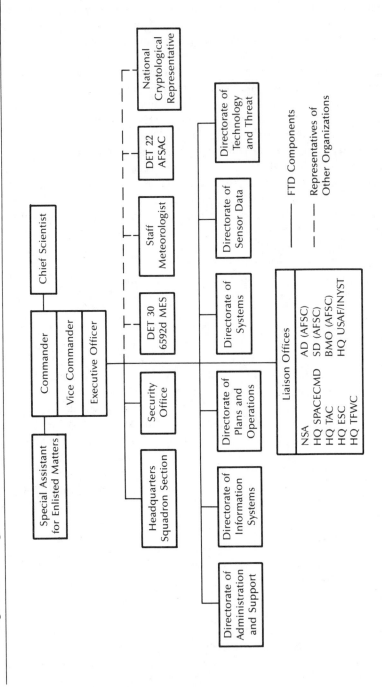

Source: Foreign Technology Division, *FTD: Mission, Organization, Key Personnel* (Wright-Patterson AFB, Ohio: FTD, December 1986), p. 1.

With 1,400 personnel and headquarters at Patrick AFB, Florida, the AFTAC operates the U.S. Atomic Energy Detection System (AEDS). The AEDS is a world-wide system with operations in more than thirty-five countries. The System uses scientific means to obtain and evaluate technical data on the nuclear energy activities of foreign powers, especially those activities covered by the Limited Test Ban Treaty, Non-Proliferation Treaty, Threshold Test Ban Treaty of 1974 (which limits the yield of underground tests to 150 kilotons), and the Peaceful Nuclear Explosion Treaty of 1976. The AFTAC was responsible for tracking debris from the Chernobyl disaster of 1986.[79]

In pursuit of its mission the AFTAC has an extensive network of U.S. and foreign sites: over twenty manned detachments, five operating locations and seventy un-manned equipment locations.[80] In addition to those seismic and hydroacoustic sites, the AFTAC collects data via airborne and space operations.

AFTAC worldwide operations (the structure of which is shown in Figure 4–19) are managed through its headquarters organization, (shown in Figure 4–20), Direct Reporting Units and two Operations Areas—the Headquarters Pacific Technical Operations Area (at Wheeler AFB, Hawaii) and Headquarters European Technical Operations Area (at Lindsey Air Station, Germany). In addition, at McClellan Air Force Base is the McClellan Central Laboratory (MCL), which is divided into three different laboratories:

- Applied Physics Laboratory: responsible for sample preparation, optical characterization, instrumental analysis, identification of samples, and precision isotopic measurement of samples.
- Radiation Analysis Laboratory: responsible for managing the flow of samples through chemical processing techniques and the measurement of chemically separated radioactive samples using alpha, beta, and gamma detection systems.
- Gas Analysis Laboratory; performs separation, purification, and measurement of all radioactive gases of interest to the AFTAC.[81]

MARINE CORPS INTELLIGENCE

Management of Marine Corps intelligence activities is the responsibility of the Director of the Intelligence Division, Marine Corps headquarters. The Director supervises the activities of five branches: Counterintelligence, Intelligence Plans and Estimates, Intelligence Management, Signals Intelligence and Electronic Warfare, and National Intelligence Activity.

The Counterintelligence Branch prepares counterintelligence plans, policies, and directives; provides representation to national level counterintelligence and security committees; and reviews reports of Marine Corps security violations. The Intelligence Plans and Estimates Branch researches and prepares intelligence studies in support of Marine Corps contingency plans, produces threat assessments, maintains files on "Marine Corps" of the world, and conducts liaison with the Navy

Figure 4–19. Air Force Technical Applications Center, Worldwide Organization.

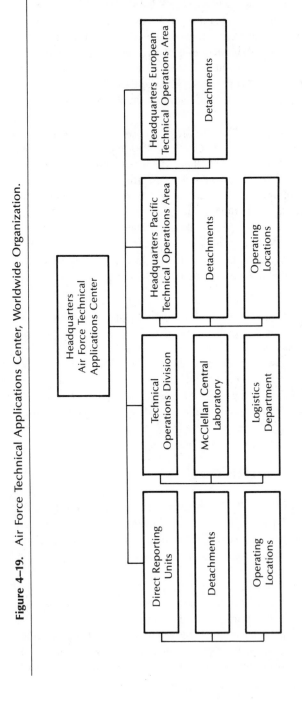

Source: Air Force Technical Applications Center.

Figure 4-20. Organization of Headquarters Air Force Technical Applications Center.

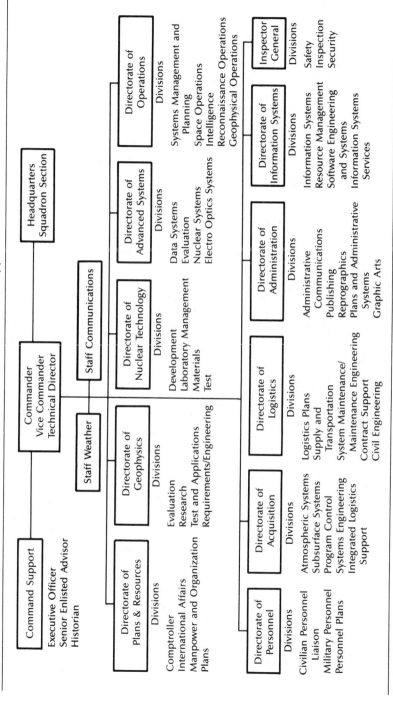

Source: Air Force Technical Applications Center.

Foreign Materiel Exploitation Committee. The Intelligence Management Branch formulates, coordinates, and monitors intelligence research and development requirements. The Signals Intelligence and Electronic Warfare Branch manages Marine Corps participation in Navy SIGINT and COMSEC activities. The National Intelligence Activity Branch develops and implements the Marine Corps Tactical Exploitation of National Space Capabilities (TENCAP) program as well as representing the Marine Corps in the implementation, coordination, and integration of national level intelligence plans, programs, and policies.[82]

The Marine Support Battallion provides for Marine Corps participation in Naval Security Group activities. The Batallion is headquartered in Washington, D.C. with lettered companies assigned to NSG field sites throughout the world.[83]

NOTES TO CHAPTER 4

1. *Department of Defense Telephone Directory* (Washington, D.C.: U.S. Government Printing Office, August 1987), p. O-41.
2. AR 10-5, "Department of the Army," November 1978, pp. 2-29 to 2-31; Chief of Staff Regulation No. 10-27, "Department of the Army, Office of the Chief of Staff, Organization and Functions, Office of the Assistant Chief of Staff for Intelligence," September 11, 1986, p. 21.
3. AR 10-5, "Department of the Army," pp. 2-29 to 2-31; Chief of Staff Regulation No. 10-27, "Department of the Army, Office of the Chief of Staff, Organization and Functions, Office of the Assisant Chief of Staff for Intelligence," p. 21.
4. AR 10-5, "Department of the Army," pp. 2-29 to 2-31; *Department of Defense Telephone Directory*, p. O-41; Chief of Staff Regulation No. 10-27, "Department of the Army, Office of the Chief of Staff, Organization and Functions, Office of the Assistant Chief of Staff for Intelligence," p. 6.
5. *Department of Defense Telephone Directory*, p. O-41.
6. AR 10-61, "Organization and Functions, United States Army Intelligence Operations Detachment," March 1, 1983, p. 3.
7. Ibid., pp. 2–3.
8. HQ, Department of the Army, General Order No. 20, "U.S. Army Intelligence Agency," August 30, 1985; General Order No. 13, "U.S. Army Intelligence Agency," June 23, 1985; General Order No. 18, "U.S. Army Intelligence Agency," June 15, 1984; and *U.S. Army Foreign Science and Technology Center* (Charlottesville, Va.: FSTC, n.d.), p. 7.
9. *Department of Defense Telephone Directory*, p. O-61; AR 10-86, "United States Army Intelligence Agency," February 27, 1986, pp. 3–4.
10. USAITAC Regulation 10-1, "Organization and Functions Manual," October 15, 1986, p. 2-1.
11. Ibid., pp. 4-2 to 4-5.
12. Ibid., p. 4-5.
13. Ibid., pp 4-10 to 4-12.
14. Ibid., pp. 4-8 to 4-9.

15. Captain John Arbeeny, "ITAC: The Unique Organization," *INSCOM Journal* (February 1982): 3–4.

16. *U.S. Army Foreign Science and Technology Center Unit History*, FY 63–FY 77, (Charlottesville, Va.: FSTC, n.d.), p. 3; Donald B. Dinger, "U.S. Army Foreign Science and Technology Center," *Army Research, Development and Acquisition Magazine* (July–August 1982): 40.

17. AR 10-86, "United States Army Intelligence Agency," p. 3.

18. FSTC Regulation No. 10-1, "Organization and Functions of U.S. Army Foreign Science and Technology Center," April 1, 1986, p. 3.

19. *U.S. Army Foreign Science and Technology Center*, pp. 10–11.

20. FSTC Regulation 10-1, "Organization and Functions, U.S. Army Foreign Science and Technology Center," pp. G-3, G-5, G-7.

21. *Organization, Mission and Functions, U.S. Army Missile and Space Intelligence Center, Redstone Arsenal, Alabama*, (Redstone Arsenal, Al.: USAMSIC, June 9, 1986). pp. II-1 to II-3; *U.S. Army Missile Intelligence Agency, Redstone Arsenal, Alabama* (Redstone Arsenal, Al.: USAMIA, n.d.), pp. 4–6.

22. AR 10-86, "United States Army Intelligence Agency," p. 3.

23. *Organizations, Mission and Functions, U.S. Army Missile and Space Intelligence Center*, pp. 8–13.

24. Ibid., pp. 14–20.

25. Memorandum to correspondents, undated.

26. INSCOM Regulation 10-2, "Organizations and Functions, United States Army Intelligence and Security Command," April 1, 1982, pp. 5-21 to 5-25.

27. Ibid., pp. 5-11 to 5-18; *Department of Defense Telephone Directory*, p. O-59.

28. Caryle Murphy and Charles R. Babcock, "Army's Covert Role Scrutinized," *Washington Post*, November 29, 1985, pp. A1, A8–A9; "The Secret Army," *Time*, August 31, 1987, pp. 12–14.

29. "The Secret Army"; *The Tower Commission Report* (New York: Times Books, 1987), p. 352.

30. "The Secret Army"; Seymour M. Hersh, "Who's In Charge Here?," *New York Times Magazine*, November 22, 1987, pp. 34ff.

31. Jay Peterzell, "Can Congress Really Check the CIA?" and "What Is the Army's ISA Up To?" *Washington Post*, April 24, 1983, pp. C1, C4; Raymond Bonner, "Secret Pentagon Intelligence Unit is Disclosed," *New York Times*, May 11, 1983, p. A13; Robert Toth, "White House to Put Limits on Army's Secret Spy Unit," *Los Angeles Times*, May 15, 1983, pp. 1, 10.

32. Frank C. Carlucci, Memorandum to the Deputy Under Secretary for Policy, May 26, 1982.

33. "The Secret Army"; Hersh, "Who's in Charge Here"; "INSCOM Permanent Orders 8-1," March 3, 1981.

34. *Department of Defense Telephone Directory*, p. O-83.

35. Charles David Taylor, *An Alternative Method of Information Handling Within the Naval Intelligence Community* (Monterey, Calif.: Naval Postgraduate School, 1980), pp. 148–49.

36. NAVINTCOMINST 5450.9, "Naval Intelligence Command Organization," September 15, 1986, p. 1-44.

37. Ibid., p. 1-55.

38. Ibid., p. 1-61.

39. Private information.
40. *Task Force 168 Command History* (Suitland, Md.: Task Force 168, 1987), p. 6; NAVINTCOMINST 5450.8A, "Naval Intelligence Command Organization," September 30 1981, p. 61; CTF 168, Instruction 5450.1, "Task Force 168 Headquarters Organization," November 9, 1984, p. 10.
41. CINCPACFLT C3880.4F, "Letter of Instruction for Commander, Task Group 168.1/ Pacific Forward Area Support Team (PACFAST)," August 8, 1986, p. 1 and Enclosure 1: Pacific Area Support Team Functions.
42. NISC Instruction 3120.1A, "NISC Organization and Regulations Manual (NORM)," November 15, 1985, p. 1-1.
43. *Naval Intelligence Support Center Command History 1986*, (Suitland, Md.: NISC, 1987), p. 2.
44. NISC Instruction 3120.1A, "NISC Organization and Regulations Manual," p. 2-18.
45. Ibid., pp. 2-12, 2-14.
46. Taylor, *An Alternative Method of Information Handling*, pp. 152–55.
47. NOIC, "Naval Intelligence and Ocean Surveillance," undated; NAVOPINTCEN Instruction 5450.1C, "NAVOPINTCEN Organization with mission and functions statements," February 7, 1986, unpaginated.
48. NAVOPINTCEN Instruction 5450.1C, "NAVOPINTCEN Organization with mission and functions statements."
49. Ibid.
50. Ibid.
51. David Kahn, *The Codebreakers* (New York: Macmillan, 1967), pp. 11–12; The Brownell Committee, *The Origin and Development of the National Security Agency* (Laguna Hills, Calif.: Aegean Park Press, 1982), p. 90.
52. USN PLAD-1, pp. 88–89 in United States Military Communications Electronics Board, *Message Address Directory* (USMCEB Publication No. 6), July 25, 1986.
53. Department of the Navy, Naval Oceanographic Office, NAVOCEANO Instruction 5450.1A, Change Transmittal 6, *NAVOCEANO Organization Manual*, May 6, 1985, p. 0940-3.
54. Ibid., pp. 4000-15, 7000-4, 7000-5, 8000-2, 8000-5.
55. U.S. Air Force, *Headquarters Publication 21-1*, March 1986, p. 6-17.
56. Ibid., p. 6-7.
57. Ibid., pp. 6-22 to 6-24.
58. "Air Force Intelligence Service," *Air Force Magazine* (May 1982): 126.
59. "Air Force Intelligence Service," *Air Force Magazine* (May 1987): 145; *Department of Defense Telephone Directory*, pp. O-162 to O-163.
60. AFISR 23-1, "Organization and Functions: Air Force Intelligence Service," February 15, 1984 (Change 9 November 1984), pp. L-1, M-1, N-1; "Air Force Intelligence Service," May 1987, p. 145.
61. "Air Force Intelligence Service," May 1987, p. 145; AFISR 23-1, "Organizations and Functions: Air Force Intelligence Service," p. Q-1.
62. "Air Force Intelligence Service," May 1987, p. 145; AFISR 23-1, "Organization and Functions: Air Force Intelligence Service," p. Q-1.
63. Diane T. Putney, *History of the Air Force Intelligence Service*, 1 Jan.–31 Dec. 1984, Volume I—Narrative and Appendices, (Ft. Belvoir, Va.: AFIS, n.d.), pp. 38, 44.
64. AFISR 23-1, "Organization and Functions: Air Force Intelligence Service," pp. S-3 to S-4.

65. AFISR 23-1, "Organization and Functions: Air Force Intelligence Service," p. T-1.

66. Benjamin Schemmer, *The Raid* (New York: Harper & Row, 1975), pp. 26–27.

67. AFISR 23-2, "Organization and Functions, Air Force Special Activities Center," December 20, 1984, p. 2.

68. Ibid., p. 7; AFR 10-4, *Air Force Address Directory* (Washington, D.C.: Department of the Air Force, June 10, 1986), p. 43; Putney, *History of the Air Force Intelligence Service*, pp. 250–52.

69. AFR 10-4, *Air Force Address Directory*, pp. 53, 64; Putney, *History of the Air Force Intelligence Service*, pp. 260, 269–270.

70. *Electronic Security Command: Master of the Electronic Battlefield* (San Antonio, Tx.: ESC, n.d.), p. 1; USAF Personnel Strength by Commands, SOAs and DRUs," *Air Force Magazine* (May 1987): 81.

71. "Electronic Security Command," *Air Force Magazine* (May 1987): 111.

72. *FTD 1917–1967* (Dayton, Ohio: FTD, 1967), pp. 8, 10, 12, 22, 26.

73. Colonel Robert B. Kalisch, "Air Technical Intelligence," *Air University Review* 12 (July–August 1971): 2–11 at 7, 9.

74. FTD Pamphlet 23-4, *FTD: Mission, Organization, Key Personnel*, (Dayton, Ohio: FTD, December 1986), pp. 15, 17, 18, 20.

75. Ibid., pp. 21–25.

76. Ibid., pp. 28–33.

77. Ibid. p. 34.

78. U.S. Congress, Senate Committee on Appropriations, *Department Defense Appropriations FY 1973, Part 4* (Washington, D.C.: U.S. Government Printing Office, 1972), pp. 364–65; "Air Force Technical Applications Center," *Air Force Magazine* (May 1987): 165–66.

79. "Air Force Technical Applications Center," pp. 165–66.

80. Ibid.

81. 3400 Technical Training Wing, *Introduction to Detection Systems*, (Lowry AFB, CO.: 3400 TTW, October 18, 1984), p. 16.

82. *Marine Corps Organization Manual* (Washington, D.C.: U.S. Marine Corps, n.d.), pp. 15-7 to 15-14.

83. "Marine Corps Intelligence," *Military Intelligence* (July–September 1983): 12ff.

5 INTELLIGENCE COMPONENTS OF THE UNIFIED AND SPECIFIED COMMANDS

In addition to the large number of intelligence units subordinate to the Department of Defense (DOD) and the military services, there are a significant number of intelligence units subordinate to the unified and specified commands of the armed forces.

The unified commands consist of forces drawn from all the military services, generally from a specific region of the world. Thus, among the unified commands are the Atlantic Command, Pacific Command, European Command, Southern Command, and Central Command. Unified commands not based on specific regions are the Special Operations Command, Space Command, and Transportation Command.

A specified command is drawn from a single service, although it performs a mission of national importance. At present the only operational specified command is the Strategic Air Command (SAC), whose primary mission is to maintain the ability to deliver several thousand nuclear warheads, via missile and bomber, to their designated targets in the Soviet Union and Eastern Europe. An additional SAC mission is performing strategic reconnaissance, employing SR-71, U-2, and RC-135 aircraft. In 1986 the Aerospace Defense Command (a specified command) was disestablished, while the Military Air Command (also a specified command) was subordinated to the Transportation Command.

Both unified and specified commands have significant intelligence requirements. Many of those requirements will be satisfied by the CIA, the DIA, the NSA or military service intelligence organizations. In such cases the intelligence units of the commands will serve as conduits through which material is passed and as a channel through which the command can make its intelligence requirements known to the appropriate collectors and analysts.

In other cases, command intelligence organizations may provide additional intelligence support, especially analysis, geared to command operations. Command intelligence organizations may also provide finished intelligence to DOD and military service headquarters organizations. Additionally, components of the commands may be assigned management responsibilities for the on-scene aspects of national reconnaissance and other sensitive collection operations.

The present unified and specified command structure is shown in Figure 5-1. The geographic responsibilities of the relevant unified commands are shown in Figure 5-2.

PACIFIC COMMAND

The responsibility of the Pacific Command (PACOM) extends from 100°E to 95°W in the north and 17°E to 92°W in the south. This area covers the Indian Ocean, parts of Africa, India, Australia, Japan, China, Alaska, and portions of Canada and the United States.

As illustrated in Figure 5-3, the PACOM contains a number of significant intelligence units either directly subordinate to PACOM or subordinate to PACOM components. Directly subordinate to the Commander in Chief PACOM (CINCPACOM) are the Director for Intelligence and the Director for Operations. As shown in Figure 5-4 the Director of Intelligence manages four divisions (Intelligence Planning and Systems, Management, Collection Management, and Special Security) and various branches. The Target Branch of the Management Division coordinates target intelligence matters with national agencies, CINCPACOM elements and other unified and specified commands. It also provides guidance and assistance to subordinate PACOM commands on target intelligence concepts, policies, programs, and plans.[1]

The Imagery Intelligence Branch of the Collection Management Division performs advisory, validation, and management functions. The branch serves as principal adviser to the CINCPACOM Joint Reconnaissance Center on imagery reconnaissance sensor systems and aerial imagery reconnaissance collection requirements. It validates PACOM high-priority imagery collection, processing, and exploitation requirements for collection by national platforms (that is, reconnaissance satellites). It manages imagery collection programs in the PACOM, including the processing, exploitation, and distribution of aerial imagery reconnaissance products.[2]

The Collection Management Division's Signals Intelligence Branch validates signals intelligence requirements proposed by PACOM components, as well as initiating, researching, processing, and managing PACOM signal intelligence collection requirements and monitoring SIGINT system performance to satisfy those requirements. The Human Intelligence Branch manages HUMINT collection activities by units assigned to the PACOM and "manages all aspects of the intelligence

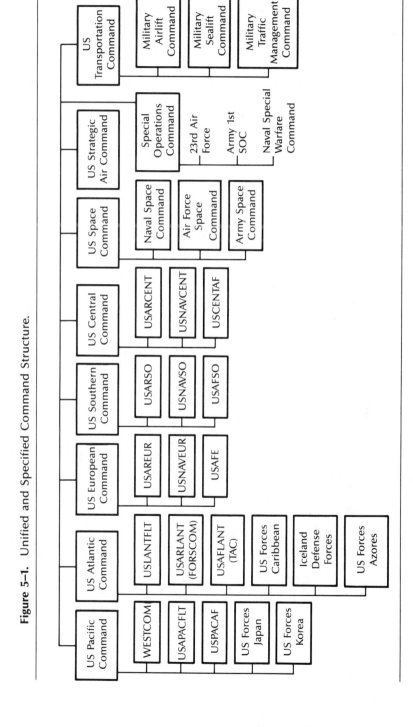

Figure 5-1. Unified and Specified Command Structure.

Figure 5-2. Unified Commands Areas of Responsibility.

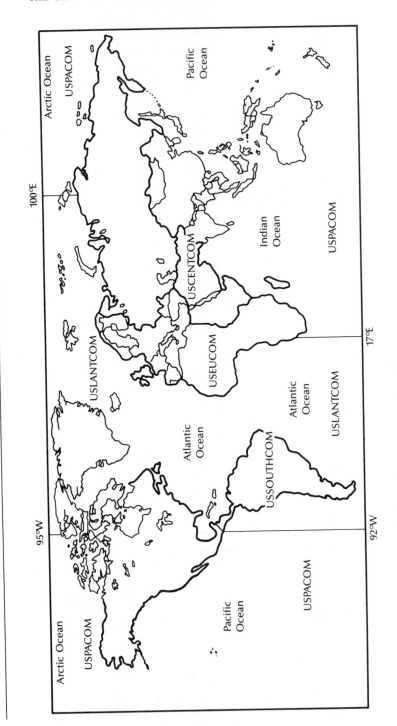

Alaska, Antarctica, Canada, Conus, and Mexico are not assigned for normal operations; JCS has cognizance over USSR.

Figure 5–3.   PACOM Intelligence Structure.

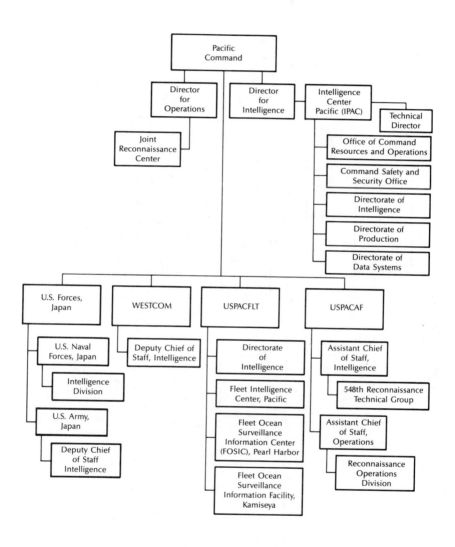

Figure 5–4. Organization of the Directorate of Intelligence, PACOM.

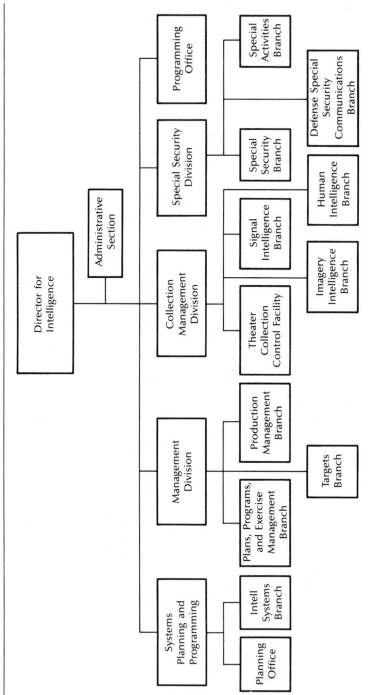

Source: CINCPAC, Organization and Functions Manual, FY 86/87 (Pearl Harbor, HI: CINCPAC, 1986). p. 49.

exploitation of foreign human sources, to include POWs, refugees, repatriates, escapees, defectors or other foreign personnel who become available for interrogation or exploitation on military subjects.[3]

Also subordinate to the Directorate of Intelligence is the Intelligence Center Pacific (IPAC), which is responsible for intelligence production in six areas. The IPAC provides all-source indications and warning and intelligence analysis. Additionally, the IPAC identifies target systems and installations whose destruction is required to satisfy the Command's objectives. It also analyzes the capabilities of nuclear and conventional weapons against those targets. The IPAC also produces all-source air defense intelligence analysis concerning air operational tactics, weapons systems, aircraft equipment and capabilities, and surface-to-air missile (SAM) and anti-aircraft artillery (AAA) orders of battle.[4]

A fourth IPAC function is producing Ground Order of Battle files, with information on changes in combat unit dispositions, personnel, weapons systems and equipment strengths, and combat unit tactics. The IPAC also produces electronic intelligence by maintaining an Electronic Order of Battle for the countries in its domain as well as conducting operational ELINT exploitation in crisis situations and imagery interpretation.[5] In addition, it produces "all-source intelligence pertaining to the. . . internal security, political, economic, sociological and scientific and technological situations in all PACOM countries."[6]

The Reconnaissance Operations Branch, Current Operations Division, Directorate of Operations manages the PACOM element of the Peacetime Aerial Reconnaissance Program (PARPRO), PONY EXPRESS, and space reconnaissance operations. The Branch also conducts coordination and liaison activities with components of the PACOM as well as with other commands (U.S. and allied) and national agencies on PARPRO and related matters.[7]

Subordinate to CINCPACFLT, in addition to the Directorate of Intelligence, are several organizations producing intelligence for both the Pacific Fleet and higher level organizations. The Commander in Chief, Pacific Fleet (CINCPACFLT) is responsible, via the Directorate of Intelligence, for managing national intelligence collection activities in the area of ocean surveillance. Thus, CINCPACFLT Instruction S-3271.1, "Narrowband Assignment and Reporting Instruction for the Pacific High Frequency Direction Finding Net" instructs stations in the net to report one fix every thirty minutes for priority ONE targets, to report one fix every four hours for priority TWO targets, and to report one fix every day for priority THREE targets. A related instruction is CINCPACFLT Instruction C3431.1C, "Rainform Formatted Message Reporting System," which defines a series of message types for reporting encounters on the high seas with shipping vessels. Included are OSIS WHITE for periodic reporting of movements or locations of all merchant and friendly naval shipping (excluding those of special interest) and OSIS RED for reporting the arrival, departure, or routine movement of Communist-flag merchant and fishing ships.[8]

Located at Pearl Harbor is the Fleet Ocean Surveillance Information Center (FOSIC), Pacific. The FOSIC, Pacific is one of six such facilities—others are located at Rota, Spain; Norfolk, Virginia; London; San Francisco; and Kamiseya, Japan.[9] The FOSICs receive data from underwater sensors, satellites, ships, land stations, and ocean surveillance aircraft. They process the data to obtain a picture of naval movements in their area of responsibility. Of particular interest is any indication of buildups in activity of Soviet or other hostile navies. The data are then transmitted to both the Navy Operational Intelligence Center (NOIC) and the area Commander in Chief.

The FOSIC, Pacific is responsible for the analysis of the navies of China, North Korea, and allied and neutral countries in the PACOM region. The intellience produced concerns the mission, organization, personnel, tactics, training, weapons, equipment, naval facilities, and seaborne infiltration activities of those navies. The Soviet Navy Branch provides intelligence on Soviet naval facilities, ports and harbors, logistics, and training; maintains files and historical records on Soviet submarine trends, developments, operations, and weapons; reviews, evaluates, and maintains records and files on Soviet naval aviation, naval missiles and missile control systems, space systems of interest, naval forces and naval electronic systems; and collects, analyzes, and maintains files on intelligence material pertaining to Soviet navy surface ship operations, especially of ships in the Soviet Pacific Ocean Fleet.[10]

Among the products provided by the FOSIC located at Pearl Harbor are two types of reports concerning foreign shipping activities relevant to naval operations. The Contact Area Summary Position Report (CASPER) provides information on shipping that is passing through an area of operations, in the vicinity of a ship or aircraft, or that can provide medical assistance. CASPERs come in four varieties. One variety gives such information in a circular area within a maximum 9,999 nautical mile radius, while a second consists of a series of circular patterns with radii as requested. A third variety of CASPER is a polygon with a minimum of three and a maximum of twenty-three points defined by latitude and longitude; the fourth variety is a rectangular corridor defined by two endpoints and a corridor width in nautical miles. Figure 5–5 illustrates these different patterns. The Daily Estimated Position Locator (DEPLOC) provides detailed underway and in-port shipping information on specified geographic areas over an extended period of time.[11]

The Fleet Intelligence Center, Pacific (FICPAC)—also located at Pearl Harbor—is organized as shown in Figure 5–6. The mission of the FICPAC is to "develop and maintain an intelligence exploitation, processing and production capability which is immediately available to support U.S. Naval Forces in the Pacific and Indian Ocean areas assigned to the U.S. Pacific Command."[12]

The Intelligence Production Department's Naval Analysis Division produces Naval Order of Battle intelligence on non-Soviet Pacific, Indian Ocean and designated Middle East and African navies, including Communist and Third World navies. The Strike Warfare Support Division supervises the production and dissemination of intelligence related to both conventional and nuclear weapons mission planning, while the Amphibious Support Division is responsible for the development and distribution of amphibious warfare intelligence materials, including

Figure 5–5. Available CASPER Patterns.

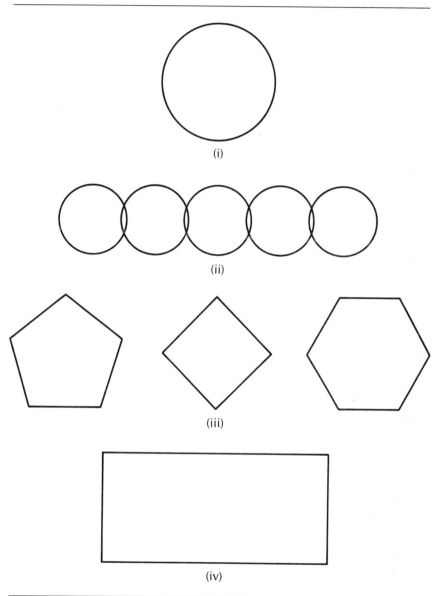

(i)

(ii)

(iii)

(iv)

Figure 5–6. Organization of the Fleet Intelligence Center, Pacific.

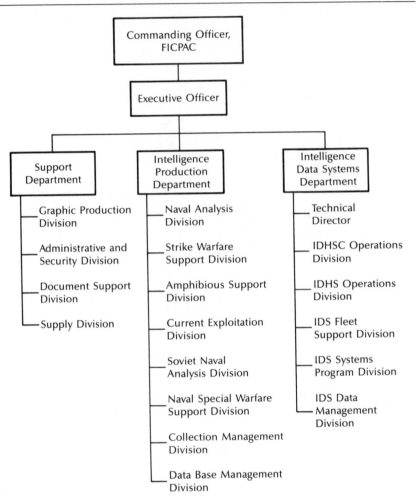

Transportation, Ports and Harbors, Coastal Landing Beaches and Helicopter Landing area studies, Amphibious Contingency Support Briefs, and Pacific Ocean and Indian Port directories.[13]

The Current Exploitation Division supervises the exploitation and dissemination of imagery reports. The Soviet Naval Analysis Division supervises the preliminary and second-phase imagery analysis of all Soviet Pacific Fleet (SOVPACFLT) bases and deployment locations as well as supervising studies on SOVPACFLT capabilities, operations, and related matters of intelligence interest. The Naval Special Warfare Support Division produces studies such as the Naval Special Warfare Target

Intelligence Studies, in support of the PACOM's naval special warfare forces. The Collection Management Division manages and maintains all the FICPAC's standing imagery collection requirements and submits all FICPAC ad hoc imagery collection requirements. The Data Base Management Division supervises production and maintenance of the Naval Order of Battle data base for the Pacific, Indian Ocean, and designated Middle Eastern and African countries.[14]

In the case of U.S. Naval Forces, Japan, the N2 (Intelligence Division) performs functions to support both local forces and national collection and liaison programs. The N2 is headed by the Assistant Chief of Staff, Intelligence (ACSI). Subordinate to the ACSI are the Force Investigation and Counterintelligence Adviser, the Special Security Office, the Special Intelligence Communications Section, Intelligence Liaison and Production Section, Special Fleet Support Section, and the Scientific Advisor.[15]

The Special Fleet Support Section provides local coordination and administration of U.S. Navy intelligence collection programs such as SOSUS and BARNACLE. The Intelligence Liaison and Production Section coordinates the intelligence activities of the CINCPACFLT and Commander, U.S. Naval Forces, Japan with the Chief of the Intelligence Division of the Japanese Maritime Staff Office and the Intelligence Officer, Commander in Chief of the Japanese Self-Defense Forces Fleet.[16]

Within the Pacific's Air Force intelligence activities are the responsibility of the Assistant Deputy Chief of Staff, Intelligence (ADCSI), subordinate to the Deputy Chief of Staff for Operations and Intelligence. In addition to supervising the Directorate of Intelligence Systems and Directorate of Intelligence Applications, the ADCSI also supervises the activities of the 548th Reconnaissance Technical Group, although the 548th is under the direct authority of USAF headquarters. Located at Hickam AFB, Hawaii and with subordinate Reconnaissance Technical Squadrons at Yokota Air Base, Japan (and possibly at Yongsan AB, Korea), the 548th interprets photographs for PACOM, Pacific Air Forces, and national agencies. The Yokota squadron serves as a primary site for interpretation of SR-71 photos provided by flight from Kadena AB, Japan.[17]

ATLANTIC COMMAND

The Atlantic Command is primarily responsible for U.S. naval activities in the Atlantic Ocean, making the Atlantic Fleet the Command's key component.

Subordinate to the Commander in Chief, Atlantic (CINCLANT) is the J2 or Intelligence Directorate for the Command, managed by the Assistant Chief of Staff, Intelligence. The organization of J2 is shown in Figure 5-7. Of particular interest is the Target Intelligence Division, which is responsible for handling nuclear and conventional targeting materials and coordinating, with CINCLANT representatives to the Joint Strategic Target Planning Staff, concerning matters of targeting and reconnaissance planning. The Collection Management Division supervises the planning, management, and administration of Atlantic Command/Fleet intelligence collection programs and maintains liaison with other intelligence organizations.

Figure 5–7. Organization of the Atlantic Command Intelligence Directorate.

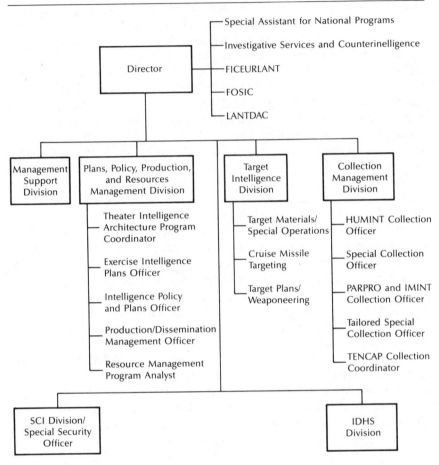

Source: USCINCLANT/CINCLANTFLT/CINCWESTLANT/COMOCEANLANT Staff Instruction 5200.1Q, Promulgation of Commander in Chief, U.S. Atlantic Fleet, Commander in Chief Western Atlantic Area and Commander Ocean Sub-Area Staff Organization and Regulations Manual, February 8, 1985, pp. 2-2-1 to 2-2-49.

The Division operates through a set of collection officers, each responsible for a different aspect of collection. The Human Intelligence Collection Officer supervises the Human Intelligence Tasking Program, while the Special Collection Officer is concerned with submarine intelligence collection missions. The PARPRO and IMINT (Imagery Intelligence) Collection Officer manages the development of intelligence collection requirements for the PARPRO system, providing feedback to tasked PARPRO collectors on the success and shortfalls of collections and providing recommendations for improvement. This Officer also supervises the maintenance of submission of the Atlantic Command's Imagery Requirements Objectives List (IROL). The Tailored Special Collection Officer receives, collates, and initiates collection tasking for national level SIGINT collection systems through Standing Operational ELINT Requirements (SOERs) and Time-Sensitive Requirements (TSRs) for COMINT and ELINT.[18]

Also subordinate to the Director of the Atlantic Command Intelligence Directorate is the Atlantic Command Defense Analysis Center (LANTDAC), the Fleet Intelligence Center, Europe and Atlantic (FICEURLANT) and the Norfolk Fleet Ocean Surveillance Information Center. On May 1, 1986 the Atlantic Command Electronic Intelligence Center became LANTDAC, which then absorbed the I&W and Current Intelligence sections of the USCINCLANT staff. In addition to I&W and current intelligence, LANTDAC responsibilities include intelligence support to joint planning, theater-technical ELINT and operational ELINT production, and support to the Navy's Electronic Warfare Reprogrammable Library Program.[19] The organization of the LANTDAC is shown in Figure 5-8.

The FICEURLANT, manned by 388 full-time personnel, is

> responsible for gathering and analyzing a wide variety of intelligence data. Aircraft and satellite photographic data are studied, ship and aircraft transmissions are recorded and analyzed, and all other inputs from a wide variety of human and electronic sources are gathered and studied. This information is used by Atlantic Fleet and Naval Forces, Europe planners in developing tactics and strategies for a range of potential enemies and contingencies. The information produced by FICEURLANT is [employed by] the fleet and many other national intelligence organizations in keeping track of potential enemy activities, weapons development, and information regarding submarines, ships and electronic transmissions.[20]

The Fleet Ocean Surveillance Information Center Detachment at Norfolk, created on January 1, 1972 as the Ocean Surveillance Information Processing Center, supervises the analysis and near real-time (i.e., almost immediate) reporting of Soviet, Warsaw Pact, and Cuban naval, air, and aerospace activity to CINCLANT and CINCLANTFLT consumers. The Center's task also includes the maintenance of a current plot of Soviet/Warsaw Pact activities in the CINCLANTFLT area of responsibility, and conducting all-source analysis of Soviet and other Communist surface and submarine operations in the CINCLANT area of responsibility. The Center also analyzes Soviet aerospace operations for inclusion in the daily "Soviet Satellite Activity Message."[21]

The Operations Directorate under the Commander in Chief, Atlantic Command (CINCLANTCOM) is responsible for active intelligence collection that employs submarines, surface ships, fixed array, and aircraft. Management responsibility is assigned to the Director of Special Surveillance Operations. The Assistant Director is responsible for reviewing USCINCLANT/CINCLANTFLT operational policy/directives concerning: (1) ocean surveillance, (2) antisubmarine warfare, (3) installation and repair of SOSUS, and (4) special submarine operations.[22]

Figure 5–8.   Organization of LANTDAC.

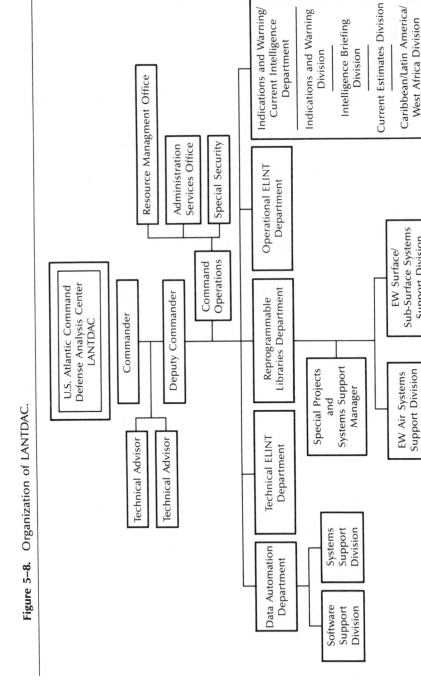

Source: U.S. Atlantic Command.

Figure 5–9. Intelligence Structure, EUCOM.

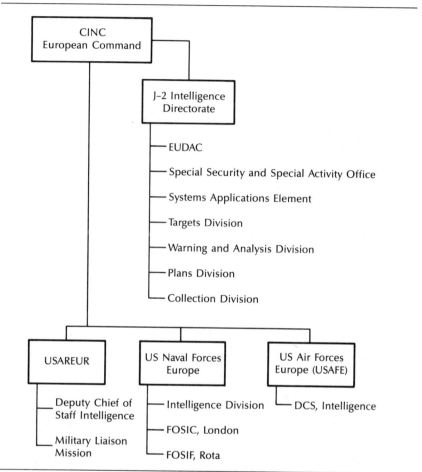

EUROPEAN COMMAND

The European Command's geographic area of responsibility includes all of Europe, excluding the Soviet Union.* Component commands are U.S. Army Europe (USAREUR), U.S. Naval Forces Europe (NAVEUR) and U.S. Air Forces Europe (USAFE), each of which has important intelligence responsibilities.

Directly subordinate to the Commander in Chief European Command (CINCEUCOM) is the Directorate of Intelligence (J-2), as shown in Figure 5-9.

*Responsibility for the Soviet Union is assigned to the Joint Chiefs of Staff.

Figure 5–10. Organization of the European Defense Analysis Center.

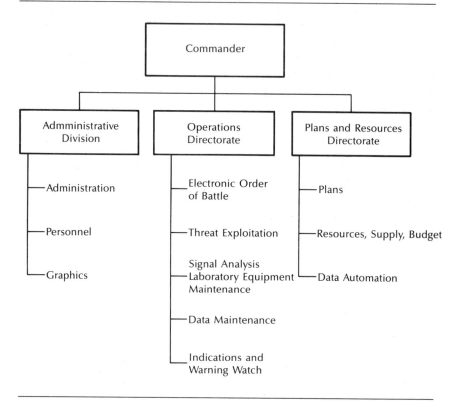

Source: United States Military Communications Electronics Board, USMCEB Publication No. 6, *Message Address Directory* (Washington, D.C. USMCEB, July 25 1986), p. 59.

The intelligence functions carried out by the Directorate include the collection, processing, analysis, and dissemination of intelligence necessary for strategic indications and warning; the development of plans, policies, and requirements for Command intelligence activities; the initiation and direction of measures to identify and counter the action of enemy agents and supporters or terrorists who might penetrate the Command's forces; and operation of the European Collection Management Office and Regional Joint Collection Management Office. The two offices manage theater collection assets, and validate and levy collection requirements for all-source collection by national activities.[23]

A second responsibility of the J-2 is electronic intelligence analyses, performed by the European Defense Analysis Center (EUDAC), located at Vaihingen, West Germany. The EUDAC, shown in Figure 5–10, prepares studies on Warsaw Pact electronic intelligence aircraft, Electronic Order of Battle studies, and indications and warning intelligence derived from ELINT.

The subordinate commands of the EUCOM are also significant. The USAREUR Deputy Chief of Staff, Intelligence is responsible for monitoring foreign ground force threats to USAREUR security or mission capability, and operates the USAREUR Indications and Warning Center on a twenty-four–hour basis as part of the Warning Indications Systems, Europe (WISE) and the DOD Worldwide I&W System. The DCSI supervises the USAREUR Intelligence Collection Program, which includes tasking theater, subordinate, and national HUMINT and technical collection activities, and reports the information obtained to the appropriate consumers. The USAREUR is also responsible for managing the U.S. Military Liaison Mission to Germany.[24]

The NAVEUR Intelligence Division (with Intelligence Support, Intelligence Operations, Administration and Security, Geopolitical Intelligence, and Special Projects branches) collects, produces, and disseminates the Command's maritime intelligence and provides quality control comments and recommendations concerning naval forces intelligence produced for the NAVEUR by external agencies. The NAVEUR is also responsible for directing the activities of the Fleet Ocean Surveillance Information Center at London and the Fleet Ocean Surveillance Information Facility at Rota, Spain.[25]

The intelligence responsibilities of the USAFE are extensive, as indicated by the organization of the Office of the Deputy Chief of Staff, Intelligence shown in Figure 5–11. USAFE intelligence objectives include:

- indications and warning of a potential or executed enemy attack or other hostile act
- intelligence on foreign military capabilities and intentions required by US and allied commanders and staffs for making decisions
- intelligence to support training, mission planning, and survival, evasion, resistance, and escape (SERE)
- intelligence to support requirements of national authorities.[26]

Subordinate to the DCSI are seven directorates: Intelligence Plans and Programs, Intelligence Systems, Intelligence Research, Intelligence Applications, Intelligence Operations, Intelligence Requirements and Reconnaissance, and Intelligence Collection. The Applications, Operations, and Requirements and Reconnaissance directorates constitute the 7450 Tactical Intelligence Squadron.[27]

The Directorate of Intelligence Plans and Programs is responsible for USAFE intelligence resource actions, including planning, programming, budgeting, and staffing allocations. The Operations Divison of the Intelligence Systems Directorate manages programs designed to enhance USAFE Intelligence capabilities, including the Operational Applications of Special Intelligence System (OASIS) program for the Tactical Fusion Center (TFC) and programs to enhance the capabilities of the Combat Operations Intelligence Center (COIC), which is discussed below.[28]

The Directorate of Intelligence Research is responsible for the processing and analysis of intelligence collected by human and technical resources. This responsibility includes management of the 300-person 497th Reconnaissance Technical

Figure 5–11. Organization of USAFE Intelligence.

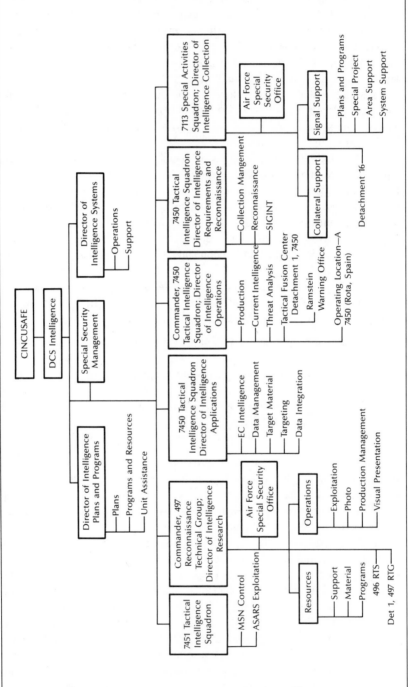

Source: USAFE Regulation 200-2, USAFE Intelligence Mission Objectives, Functions, Activities and Policy, April 17, 1987, Attachment 1.

Group (497 RTG). The 497 RTG, at Schierstein Compound outside Wiesbaden, West Germany, is the main imagery, processing, and analysis unit for the European theater. The Group was first activated in 1951 to provide photoprocessing and photo interpretation services for theater operations. It presently consists of seventy to seventy-five enlisted men and officers from the Air Force, Army, and Marine Corps who are divided into groups by country.[29]

In addition to directing the activities of its headquarters organization, the 497th RTG directs the European Special Activities Facility (ESAF), which conducts joint exploitation of reconnaissance imagery in support of requirements for the USAREUR, USAFE, and EUCOM. It also maintains Detachment 1 at Ramstein and the subordinate 496th Reconnaissance Technical Squadron at Alconbury, United Kingdom.[30]

The Directorate of Intelligence Applications is primarily concerned with targeting matters. Based on signals intelligence and overhead photography from both tactical and national systems, the Directorate keeps updated folders on potential targets (for both nuclear and conventional systems) and identifies gaps in intelligence information. Located at Ramstein AB, the Directorate is co-located with the COIC. The COIC operates in a multistory concrete and underground bunker across the street from the headquarters building of the USAFE. The primary function of the COIC is to provide photographic interpretation support to the Directorate's targeting operations.[31]

The Directorate of Intelligence Operations is the current intelligence/indications and warning unit of USAFE intelligence. In addition to current intelligence and threat analysis branches, the Directorate operates the Tactical Fusion Center at Boerfink, an underground complex for all-source intelligence analysis designed to provide near real-time warning. At Directorate headquarters is the Ramstein Warning Office (RWO), which provides an extension from Boerfink to the USAFE Commander in Chief and staff. Finally, the Directorate is also responsible for the I&W activities conducted at Operating Location-A (OL-A), the Fleet Ocean Surveillance Information Facility at Rota, Spain.[32]

The Directorate of Intelligence Requirements and Reconnaissance has three branches: Collection Management, Reconnaissance, and SIGINT. Among its functions is the management of the CREEK MISTY and CREEK FLUSH overflights of the Berlin Corridor. The Director of Intelligence Collection is simultaneously the Commander of the 7113 Special Activities Squadron. As noted in Chapter 4, the Squadron is responsible for human intelligence collection activities, involving the handling of defectors and collecting intelligence for escape and evasion plans for U.S. fliers in the event of war, as well as support of targeting and combat forces.[33]

CENTRAL COMMAND

The Central Command was formed on January 1, 1983 as a successor to the Rapid Deployment Force, with responsibility for the general southwest Asia region. Included in this area are the countries of the Middle East and Persian Gulf (Iran,

Iraq, Jordan, Saudi Arabia, and Kuwait), Northeast Africa (Egypt, Somalia, Kenya, Ethiopia, and Sudan) and Southwest Asia (Pakistan and Afghanistan).[34]

As indicated in Figure 5–12, the Central Command Intelligence Directorate consists of five divisions—Intelligence Operations, Resource Management, Targets, Production/Collection, and Intelligence Assessments. The Intelligence Operations Division is responsible for directing, coordinating, and accomplishing specific planning and actions necessary to ensure the provision of intelligence support during the development and execution of command operations plans, contingency operations, and command exercises. The Targets Division is responsible for target guidance and development for nuclear, conventional, and special operations forces as well as the provision of aeronautical topographic, and hydrographic maps and charts. The Production/Collection Division is responsible for collection management and tailored intelligence support for indications and warning, imagery exploitation, nuclear-war fighting, and short-term decision making. The Intelligence Assessments Division is responsible for indications and warning intelligence; analyses of political, social, economic, and military activities and events in the CENTCOM area; and production of the Daily Intelligence Briefing for the Commander in Chief, CENTCOM.[35]

SOUTHERN COMMAND

The U.S. Southern Command (SOUTHCOM) is responsible for Central and South America. The J2 is divided into four sections—Collection Management, Indications and Analysis, Plans and Security, and the Contingency Production Support Division—and directs intelligence production as well as managing the SOUTHCOM Automatic Ground Order of Battle System for Panama.[36]

The Collection Management Division is responsible for determining and delegating intelligence requirements throughout the Command. It also serves as liaison with national agencies and the Joint Reconnaissance Center. The Division also provides collection planning guidance, and develops and reviews plans and programs in support of local, national, and DOD intelligence collection activities.[37]

The Indications and Analysis Division produces a variety of SOUTHCOM products—Special Intelligence Briefs, Annual Intelligence Briefs, and the Country Intelligence Study (CIS), Panama. It maintains the Travelers in Panama (TIP) file as well as operating the Indications and Warning Center. The Plans and Security Division manages Command walk-in and defector programs and publishes the *SOUTHCOM Intelligence Plan*.[38]

To provide a significant photographic interpretation capability, the Tactical Air Command's 480th Reconnaissance Technical Group is tasked by SOUTHCOM. According to 1987 Congressional testimony, the "tasking of the 480 RTG has changed significantly, new programs have been assigned and others expanded; the geographic area of responsibility was expanded and numerous state-of-the-art equipment/systems added."[39]

Figure 5-12. Organization of Central Command Intelligence Directorate.

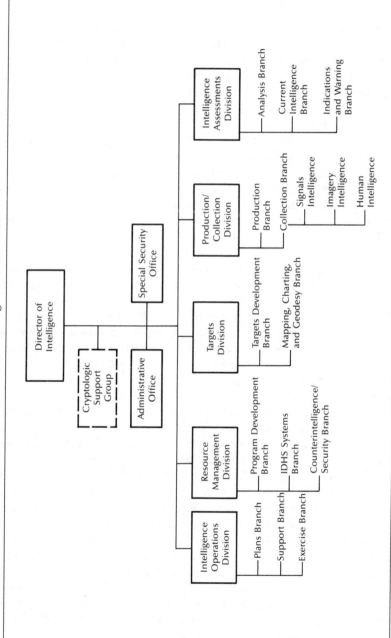

Source: U.S. Central Command R10-2, "Organization and Functions," 1 February 1985; *Central Command 1985 Command History* (MacDill AFB, Fla.: Central Command, 1987), p. 11-14.

STRATEGIC AIR COMMAND

The Commander in Chief, SAC (CINCSAC) is in fact, Commander of three organizations. Located with the SAC at Offutt AFB, Nebraska are the Joint Strategic Connectivity Staff and the Joint Strategic Target Planning Staff (JSTPS). The former is responsible for developing and implementing programs that are designed to ensure that in the event of nuclear war, an adequate C^3 system will continue to operate through the trans- and post-attack periods. The JSTPS is responsible for developing the National Strategic Target List and, from that list, in response to guidance from the President, Secretary of Defense, and Joint Chiefs of Staff (JCS), the Single Integrated Operational Plan (SIOP).

The SAC itself is responsible for the operation and maintenance of two-thirds of the triad of forces that would be used to execute the SIOP in the event of war: land-based ICBMs (intercontinental ballistic missiles) and bombers. It is also responsible for the operation of strategic reconnaissance aircraft—the U-2, SR-71, and RC-135.

The DCSI is responsible for providing the SAC with the intelligence required to accomplish its mission, and the JSTPS with the intelligence support directed by the JCS. The DCSI has, as illustrated in Figure 5-13, three subordinate directorates and a Special Security Office.

The Directorate of Plans is responsible for all planning, programming, and budget activities required to fulfill the SAC's intelligence mission. It formulates and evaluates intelligence policy, concepts, and objectives. As part of its responsibility, it promulgates the *SAC Intelligence Plan*, which outlines objectives for intelligence acquisition and production.[40]

Subordinate to the Directorate are three divisions: Systems, Plans and Policy, and Unit Support. The Systems Division formulates policy and develops plans for the development and integration of intelligence collection, processing, data handling, and dissemination systems used by the SAC for intelligence purposes. Along with the DCS, Data Systems the Division oversees the design and operation of the SAC Intelligence Data Handling System.[41]

The Plans and Policy Division develops and seeks to ensure the implementation of SAC intelligence policies, concepts, objectives, and plans. In pursuit of that goal, it directs and coordinates the development of intelligence annexes and other intelligence involvement in SAC military capabilities planning. It also represents the SAC with regard to the General Defense Intelligence Program. The Unit Support Division coordinates staff support to intelligence elements at SAC units.[42]

The Directorate of Assessments, with its Offensive, Defensive, and Space Divisions, is responsible for the acquisition and production of intelligence on the capabilities, strength, vulnerabilities, and operational activities of offensive, defensive, and space systems; and the development of intelligence on foreign strategic doctrine, employment concepts, and tactics. It also assesses scientific and technological factors that influence foreign military capabilities, planning and force structure.[43]

Figure 5–13. Strategic Air Command Deputy Chief of Staff/Intelligence Organization.

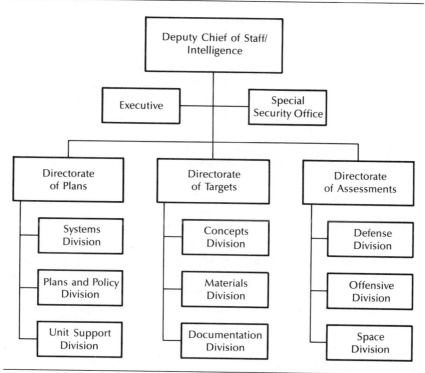

Source: SAC Regulation 23-6, "Organization and Functions—Headquarters Strategic Air Command," August 22, 1983, p. 30.

The Directorate of Targets develops and implements targeting concepts and target weaponry policy based on national and Command guidance. It is responsible for the development and maintenance of target intelligence data bases and for SAC inputs to national target files, as well as tasking subordinate SAC units for targeting, and mapping, charting, and geodesy support.[44]

The Directorate's Concepts Division develops and validates concepts, requirements, and plans associated with targeting methodologies, procedures, and policies for non-SIOP and conventional targeting of SAC forces. In collaboration with the Strategic Targeting Intelligence Center, it provides for the acquisition and application of targeting intelligence for SAC military planning activities. The Materials Division directs and manages aircraft and missile target material. The Documentation Division manages the documentation of the targeting aspects of operations plans and orders related to the SAC Post Attack Command and Control System (PACCS) and other command and control assets. It also identifies and coordinates support for PACCS intelligence requirements.[45]

In addition, the DCSI, via the SAC's Strategic Reconnaissance Center (SRC), manages the operation of the U-2, SR-71, and RC-135 aircraft of the 9th Strategic Reconnaissance Wing at Beale AFB, California, 55th Strategic Reconnaissance Wing at Offutt AFB, Nebraska and their detachments.

The SRC is responsible for planning, coordinating and executing all SAC reconnaissance operations. It monitors and follows worldwide SAC reconnaissance missions on a near real-time basis, as well as conducting liaison with the JCS, national agencies, and other Commands on all matters relating to SAC reconnaissance. Subordinate to the Center are four divisions—Reconnaissance Control, Reconnaissance Special Operations, Reconnaissance Plans, and Reconnaissance Operations. The Reconnaissance Control Division is responsible for flight schedule coordination, flight following, and active control of all reconnaissance missions for the SAC. It also monitors reconnaissance schedules of other commands to insure compatability with SAC operations. The Reconnaissance Special Operations Division is responsible for planning, directing and monitoring SR-71, U-2, and TR-1 reconnaissance aircraft.[46]

The Reconnaissance Plans Division is responsible for developing reconnaissance plans for all stages of conflict from contingency planning to conventional war, to nuclear and post-SIOP planning. It develops SAC's NUWEP reconnaissance plan as well as developing employment concepts and provides technical assistance to the JSTPS relative to the JCS's SIOP Reconnaissance Plan. The Reconnaissance Operations Division manages and directs all special purpose (SIGINT) collection by RC-135 aircraft.[47]

U.S. SPACE COMMAND

The U.S. Air Force Space Command was established on September 1, 1982 to bring under one managerial roof the responsibility for the Air Force's space-related research, development, and acquisition and operational activities. The deputy head of the Space Command (SPACECOM) is the head of the Space Division—the Air Force space research, development, and acquisition organization at El Segundo, California.[48] Since then the Navy followed suit by establishing a Naval Space Command in 1983. The Army established a Space Command in 1988. To provide overall direction of U.S. and military service space activities, a U.S. Space Command was established. All perform intelligence functions.

Subordinate to the Commander in Chief USSPACECOM is the Directorate of Intelligence, with its Deputy Directorate for Plans and Programs, and Deputy Directorate for Intelligence Operations. The Deputy Directorate for Plans and Programs is responsible for intelligence plans and programs supporting the missions of the USSPACECOM, while the Deputy Directorate for Intelligence Operations prepares intelligence estimates and related command inputs to national intelligence documents relating to any strategic threat to North America. It also reviews threat estimates prepared by national and theater intelligence agencies that affect the strategic defense mission.[49]

The Deputy Directorate for Intelligence Operations also manages the Space Operational Intelligence Center, which is intended to provide the Space Command, intelligence community, and other commands and agencies with intelligence and assessments on foreign space activities and the operational status of all foreign space systems. In addition, the Deputy Directorate coordinates production of the *Defense Intelligence Space Order of Battle* (DISOB) for the DOD as well as coordinating and managing intelligence support to the U.S. anti-satellite program.[50]

The primary intelligence functions managed by the Air Force Space Command relate to space surveillance; nuclear detection monitoring and weather reconnaissance functions also fall under its purview. The 1st Space Wing of the Command is responsible for the operation of two satellite systems—the Defense Support Program (DSP) and the Defense Meteorological Satellite Program (DMSP) systems—as well as a network of twenty-four radar and optical sensor sites for space surveillance.[51]

The DSP satellites have a primary mission of early warning detection of the launch of Soviet or Chinese ICBMs and SLBMs. The DMSP satellites also provide militarily useful weather information, including the existence of cloud cover.

The ground-based sensors run by the 1st Space Wing provide information to the Space Defense Operations Center, which is responsible for

- detecting, tracking, and providing information on space objects by employing all source input data
- providing real-time coordination for status and alert of U.S. and allied space assets to owners, operators and users of interference, attack, malfunctions and damage assessment
- providing space object identification data for all satellites
- generating alert, warning and verification of potentially hostile space-related events that affect space systems survivability, by employing all source data[52]

Real-time operational control of the Space Surveillance Center (SSC), which was integrated into the Space Defense Operations Center (SPADOC) in December 1985, is the responsibility of the Deputy Director of Space Control, Directorate of Operations of the USSPACECOM. The SSC also tasks and alerts sensors for tracking support of routine catalog maintenance, space object identification support, space launches and maneuvers, decays, and deorbits. Finally, it maintains a catalog of orbital characteristics of all observable man-made space objects to predict their positions. This involves more than 20,000 daily space observations to monitor the status of more than 5,400 man-made space objects.[53]

The Naval Space Command also operates a space surveillance network, the Naval Space Surveillance (NAVSPASUR) Network, discussed in detail in Chapter 9. Using information collected by the NAVSPASUR and other sources, the Naval Space Command's Intelligence Division (with its Space Intelligence, Cryptology, and Intelligence Analysis branches) is repsonsible for

- providing space intelligence support and expertise to the headquarters staff;
- providing rapid accessibility to the foreign space order of battle and maintaining first-hand, in-depth knowledge of foreign space systems' functions and capabilities;
- providing indications and warning support to the Commander and Operations Division of foreign threats arrayed against the naval space segment, the ground segment and satellite systems uplinks/downlinks;
- providing long term threat assessments and intelligence support data and assistance as required to the Operations and Space Plans Division;
- monitoring fleet space intelligence requirements and, through coordination with fleet users and external intelligence organizations, assessing the adequacy and effectiveness of space intelligence in meeting those requirements.[54]

U.S. SPECIAL OPERATIONS COMMAND

On April 16, 1987, the U.S. Special Operations Command (USSOC) was established to supervise the activities of the military service special operations units, which became component commands of the USSOC. The Command began operations on June 1, 1987.[55]

Intelligence responsibilities in the U.S. Special Operations Command are located in the Directorate of Intelligence. Subordinate to the Directorate's Director and Deputy Director are three divisions—Intelligence Management; Intelligence Architecture, Programs, and Systems; and Operational Intelligence, with branches as shown in Figure 5–14.[56]

Subordinate commands are the Army's 1st Special Operations Command at Ft. Bragg, N.C.; the Navy's Special Warfare Command; and the Air Force's 23rd Air Force.

The 1st Special Operations Command's Assistant Chief of Staff (ACS), G-2 is the official responsible for satisfying the Command's intelligence requirements. Subordinate to the ACS, G-2 are a Special Security Office and three divisions—Security; Plans, Production, and Dissemination; and Operations and Training. Figure 5–15 shows the organization of the Office of the ACS, G-2.

The key production element of that Office is the Plans, Production, and Dissemination Division. The Division's Strategic Industrial Target Analysis Systems Branch develops strategic industrial targeting studies for use by special operations forces, and conducts training on how to neutralize or destroy strategic industrial units. The Regional Intelligence Teams are responsible for intelligence support planning for the 1st SOCOM units as specified in unified command operations plans. The teams also prepare special intelligence studies, summaries, and the *Weekly All Source Intelligence Summary.*[57]

Figure 5–14. Organization of the Directorate of Intelligence, U.S. Special Operations Command.

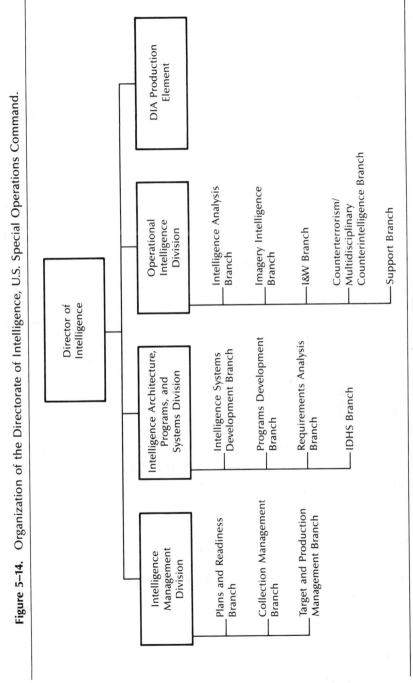

Source: U.S. Special Operations Command Staff Directory, September 1, 1987.

Figure 5–15. Organization of the Office of the Assistant Chief of Staff, G2, 1st Special Operations Command.

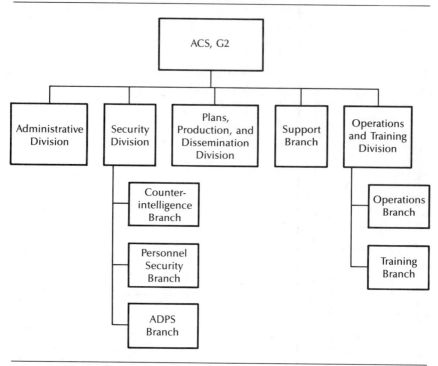

Source: 1st SOCOM Regulation 10-1, "1st Special Operations Command: Organization and Functions," September 15, 1986, p. 2-1.

In the 23rd Air Force, intelligence functions are supervised by the Deputy Chief of Staff, Intelligence. Subordinate to the DCSI are components for: Plans and Programs, Unit Support, Operational Intelligence, and Intelligence Resource and Security.[58]

TRANSPORTATION COMMAND

On October 1, 1987 the U.S. Transportation Command (TRANSCOM) was activated at Scott AFB, Illinois. The TRANSCOM is responsible for consolidating all U.S. strategic air, sea, and land transportation during war or a buildup to war, and for exercising centralized control over military transportation. TRANSCOM components are the Navy's Military Sealift Command, the Army's Military Traffic Management Command, and the Air Force Military Airlift Command.[59] As of early 1988 no intelligence component had yet been established for the TRANSCOM.

NOTES TO CHAPTER 5

1. Commander in Chief U.S. Pacific Command, *Organization and Functions Manual FY 86/87* (Pearl Harbor, Hawaii: PACOM, 1986), pp. 52, 56, 58–59.

2. Ibid., pp. 62–63.

3. Ibid., pp. 63–65.

4. Enclosure (1) to CINCPAC Instruction 5400.22, "Intelligence Center Pacific (IPAC) Augmentation Support," July 23, 1979.

5. Ibid.

6. Information provided by Pacific Command.

7. Commander in Chief U.S. Pacific Command, *Organization and Functions Manual FY 86/87*, pp. 81–82.

8. CINCPACFLT Instruction S3271.1A, "Narrowband Assignment and Reporting Instructions for the Pacific High Frequency Direction Finding Net," n.d.; CINCPACFLT Instruction C3431.1C, "RAINFORM Formatted Message Reporting System," May 18, 1981.

9. U.S. Congress, Senate Committee on Appropriations, *Department of Defense Appropriations FY 1972, Part 3* (Washington, D.C.: U.S. Government Printing Office, 1971), p. 487; U.S. Congress Senate Committee on Appropriations, *Department of Defense Appropriations FY 1973, Part 3* (Washington, D.C.: U.S. Government Printing Office, 1972), p. 475; Paul Bracken, *The Command and Control of Nuclear Forces* (New Haven, Conn.: Yale University Press, 1983), p. 38.

10. CINCPACFLT Instruction 5400.3M, Ch-5, March 9, 1984, pp. A 2-13 to A 2-14; A 2-18 to A 2-21.

11. CINCPACFLT Instruction 3130.6F, "Pacific Area Ocean Surveillance Report Serces," November 8, 1982, pp. 1–2.

12. FICPAC Instruction 5400.1P, Fleet Intelligence Center (FICPAC) Organization and Regulations Manual, February 7, 1986, p. 1-2.

13. Ibid., pp. 2-36, 2-37, 2-39.

14. Ibid., pp. 2-41, 2-43, 2-45.

15. Commander, U.S. Naval Forces, Japan, Staff Instruction 5450.1G, *Staff Manual*, May 13, 1983, p. iii.

16. Ibid., pp. V-4, V-6.

17. PACAF Regulation 23-4, "Organization and Functions—Headquarters Pacific Air Forces," September 24, 1986, p. 62; PACAF Regultion 23-17, "548th Reconnaissance Technical Group," June 8, 1987; Benjamin Schemmer, *The Raid* (New York: Harper & Row, 1975), p. 254.

18. USCINCLANT/CINCLANTFLT/CINCWESTLANT/COMOCEANLANT Staff Instruction 5200.1Q, "Promulgation of Commander in Chief, U.S. Atlantic Command, Commander in Chief, U.S. Atlantic Fleet, Commander in Chief, Western Atlantic Area, and Commander Ocean Sub-Area Staff Organization and Regulations Manual," February 8, 1985. pp. 2-2-12, 2-2-22 to 2-2-27; USCINCLANT, *Staff Organization Chart*, n.d.

19. LANTDAC Message 25205 OZ April 1986 Subj: Establishment of Atlantic Command Defense Analysis Center, (LANTDAC) (n.d.).

20. U.S. Congress, House Committee on Appropriations, *Military Construction Appropriations for 1987, Part 2* (Washington, D.C.: U.S. Government Printing Office, 1986), pp. 261–62.

21. CINCLANT Instruction C5450.75, "Fleet Ocean Surveillance Information Center, Detachment (FOSIC DET), CINCLANTFLT," May 7, 1986, Enclosure (1): Missions, Tasks and Functions Assigned to Fleet Ocean Surveillance Information Center Detachment, CINCLANTFLT.

22. USCINCLANT/CINCLANTFLT/CINCWESTLANT/COMOCEANLANT Staff Instruction 5200.1Q, "Promulgation of Commander in Chief, U.S. Atlantic Command, Commander in Chief, U.S. Atlantic Fleet, Commander in Chief Western Atlantic Area, and Commander Ocean Sub-Area Staff Organization and Regulations Manual," pp. 2-3-41 to 2-3-42.

23. HQ EUCOM Directive No. 40-1, "Intelligence Mission and Responsibilities," January 4, 1987, pp. 2–3.

24. USAREUR Regulation 10-5, "Organization and Functions, United States Army, Europe," September 27, 1984. pp. 16–18.

25. Headquarters U.S. Naval Forces Europe, *Staff Organization Chart*, (n.d.); U.S. Naval Forces Europe, *Mission Statement, Intelligence Division*, (n.d.).

26. USAFER 200-2, "USAFE Intelligence Mission Objectives, Functions, Activities and Policy," April 19, 1985, pp. 1–2.

27. Ibid., Attachment 1.

28. Ibid.

29. Ibid., *497th Reconnaissance Technical Group* (Weisbaden, West Germany: 497th RTG, 1976), unpaginated.

30. USAFER 23-9, "497th Reconnaissance Technical Group," March 13, 1980, pp. 1–2; USAFER 23-51, "496th Reconnaissance Technical Squadron," November 15, 1984; USAFER 200-2, "USAFE Intelligence Mission, Objectives, Functions, Activities and Policy," Attachment 1.

31. USAFER 200-2, "USAFE Intelligence Mission, Objectives, Functions, Activities and Policy," Attachment 1; private information.

32. USAFER 200-2, "USAFE Intelligence Mission, Objectives, Functions, Activities and Policy," Attachment 1; private information.

33. USAFER 200-2, "USAFE Intelligence Mission, Objectives, Functions, Activities and Policy," Attachment 1.

34. U.S. Congress, House Committee on Armed Services, *Hearings on HR 1816* (Washington, D.C.: U.S. Government Printing Office, 1983), p. 955.

35. USCENTCOM Regulation 10-2, "U.S. Central Command: Organization and Functions," n.d., pp. N-11, N-19; *Central Command 1985 Command History* (MacDill AFB, Fla.: Central Command, 1987), pp. 11–14, 25.

36. Headquarters U.S. Southern Command Regulation 10-1, "Organization and Functions Manual," October 1, 1983, p. 7-1.

37. Ibid., p. 7-3.

38. Ibid., p. 7-4.

39. U.S. Congress, House Committee on Appropriations, *Military Construction Appropriations for 1988, Part 2* (Washington, D.C.: U.S. Government Printing Office, 1987), p. 510.

40. Strategic Air Command Regulation 23-6, "Organization and Functions—Headquarters Strategic Air Command," August 22, 1983, p. 30.
41. Ibid., pp. 30–31.
42. Ibid.
43. Ibid.
44. Ibid.
45. Ibid., pp. 31–32.
46. Strategic Air Command Regulation 23-10, November 27, 1984, p. 7; Letter from R.L. Herron, SAC FOIA Officer to Kathleen Clark, December 31, 1985.
47. Strategic Air Command Regulation 23-10, November 27, 1984, p. 7.
48. "Space Command," *Air Force Magazine* (May 1983), 96–97.
49. Headquarters, United States Space Command, *Initial Manning Document, FY 1986/87 Part I*, n.d., unpaginated.
50. Ibid.; U.S. Congress, House Committee on Appropriations, *Military Construction Appropriations for 1987, Part 5* (Washington, D.C.: U.S. Government Printing Office, 1986), pp. 409–10.
51. "Space Command."
52. Headquarters United Space Command, *Initial Manning Document FY 1986/87*, n.d.
53. Ibid.: "Space Defense Operations Center Upgrades Assessment Capabilities," *Aviation Week and Space Technology*, December 9, 1985, pp. 67–73.
54. Naval Space Command, "Mission of NAVSPACECOM," (Dahlgren, Va.: NAVSPACECOM, n.d.), pp. 1-14 to 1-15.
55. Kenneth Brooten, Jr., "The U.S. Special Operations Command," *Journal of Defense and Diplomacy* (1987), pp. 21–23.
56. *United States Special Operations Command Staff Directory, September 1, 1987* (MacDill AFB, Fla.: USSOC, 1987).
57. 1st SOCOM Regulation 10-1, *1st Special Operations Command [Airborne], Organization and Functions* (Ft. Bragg, N.C.: 1st SOCOM, September 15, 1986), pp. 7-1, 7-8 to 7-10.
58. *Headquarters 23rd Air Force Staff Directory*, October 15, 1987.
59. James W. Canan, "Can TRANSCOM Deliver?," *Air Force Magazine* (October 1987), 40–46.

6 CIVILIAN INTELLIGENCE ORGANIZATIONS

The bulk of U.S. intelligence resources, whether in terms of personnel or dollars, lies in the hands of the national and military intelligence organizations. At the same time, several civilian executive departments have offices that collect and analyze intelligence on foreign political and military affairs, economic affairs, or narcotics.

Such offices are to be found in the Departments of State, Commerce, Treasury, Justice, and Agriculture. In addition, a component of the Library of Congress provides analytical services to the intelligence community.

STATE DEPARTMENT INTELLIGENCE

With the dissolution of the Office of Strategic Services (OSS), its research and analysis functions were transfered to the State Department. Those functions were carried out in State by the Interim Research and Intelligence Service. Since then the organization's name has changed twice. It has been designated the Bureau of Intelligence and Research (INR) since 1957.[1]

The Bureau does not collect intelligence beyond reporting through normal diplomatic channels and open source collection. However, it performs a variety of functions concerning operational matters in the liaison area between the Department of State and the intelligence community to ensure that the actions of other intelligence agencies, such as the Central Intelligence Agency, are in accord with U.S. foreign policy.[2]

In terms of production, the INR faces in two directions. One direction is outward, where it is involved in interagency intelligence production efforts such as

Figure 6–1.   Organization of the Bureau of Intelligence and Research.

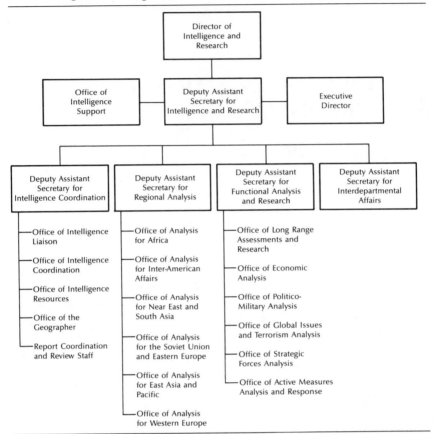

Source: U.S. Congress, House Committee on Appropriations, *Departments of Commerce, Justice, and State, the Judiciary and Related Agencies Appropriations for 1987, Part 6* (Washington, D.C.: U.S. Government Printing Office, 1986), p. 351.

the National Intelligence Estimates (NIEs) and Special National Intelligence Estimates (SNIEs). The second direction is inward, toward the State Department internal organization. *The Morning Summary* is prepared in collaboration with the Department's Executive Secretariat and is designed to inform the Secretary of State and principal deputies of current events and current intelligence. INR also prepares regional and functional summaries, as well as single subject reports under three different titles.[3]

The Director of the INR holds a rank equivalent to an Assistant Secretary and, as shown in Figure 6–1, is assisted by four Deputy Assistant Secretaries who directly supervise the INR's twenty offices and staffs. The Deputy Assistant Secretary for Intelligence and Research is the second-ranking individual in the Bureau and supervises the Office of the Executive Director and the Office of Intelligence Support.

The Office of the Executive Director handles personnel, budget and finance, and general administrative support for the Bureau. The Office of Intelligence Support is the State Department's center for the receipt of intelligence information, in whatever form, and for processing and disseminating that information under security safeguards. The Office of Intelligence Support contains both the INR Watch Office and the Current Intelligence Staff.[4]

The Deputy Assistant Secretary for Regional Analysis supervises six geographic offices of Analysis: for Africa, Inter-American Republics, East Asia and the Pacific, the Near East and South Asia, the Soviet Union and Eastern Europe, and Western Europe. The primary function of the Regional Analysis offices is to produce analyses of developments and issues that are, or will be, of concern to the policymaker. The offices are responsible for preparing regional and other special summaries, and for INR contributions to intelligence community estimates and assessments. An analyst for the Office of Analysis for West European Affairs might be asked to examine the direction of the Greek government under Georges Papandreou, the future of democracy in Turkey, and/or the situation in Cyprus. An East Asian and Pacific analyst might be concerned with the role of the Chinese People's Liberation Army in domestic politics.[5]

The Deputy Assistant Secretary for Functional Analysis and Research has the primary responsibility for the Bureau's long-range analytical studies. He/she is responsible for the Office of Politico-Military Analysis, the Office of Strategic Forces Analysis, the Office of Active Measures Analysis and Response, the Office of Long Range Assessments and Research, the Office of Economic Analysis, and the Office of Terrorism and Narcotics Analysis.

The Office of Politico-Military Analysis is primarily concerned with theater and regional military forces. The Office of Strategic Forces Analysis focuses on the strategic force capabilities, vulnerabilities, and planning of the Soviet Union, China, Britain, and France. The Office of Active Measures Analysis and Response maintains a data base on Soviet active measures activities and attempts to devise the most effective responses to them. The Office of Long Range Assessments and Research prepares its own long-range assessments on selected topics, contributes on occasion to assessments prepared elsewhere in the Bureau, and commissions those projects that cannot be done in the INR. The Office of Economic Analysis produces reports for policymakers on current and longer range issues involving international economic policies, business cycles, trade, financial affairs, food, population and energy, and economic relations between the industrialized countries and the developing nations and between Communist nations.[6]

The Deputy Assistant Secretary for Intelligence Coordination supervises the Office of the Geographer, the Office of Intelligence Liaison, the Office of Intelligence Coordination, the Office of Intelligence Resources, and the Report Coordination and Review Staff. The Office of the Geographer prepares studies of policy issues associated with physical, cultural, economic, and political geography, emphasizing the law of the sea, U.S. maritime issues, and international boundaries and jurisdictional problems.[7]

The Office of Intelligence Liaison works with other intelligence agencies, primarily the CIA, on human collection efforts and coordinates proposals for covert actions. Its basic responsibility in connection with such programs is to ensure "thorough consideration of their support of and implications for U.S. foreign policy." The Office also handles defector cases and requests for biographic data and other intelligence agency documents, and conducts briefings on intelligence matters for State Department officers going to and returning from overseas posts. It also handles liaison with designated foreign intelligence representatives. The Reports and Coordination Review Staff is responsible for the final production of the INR's formal reports. It is responsible for editorial review, format, printing, and distribution.[8]

The Office of Intelligence Resources provides staff support, representation, and coordination of the Department's interests in the National Foreign Intelligence Program, and budget. It works with other intelligence community agencies, concerned areas of the department, and overseas missions in planning, tasking, deploying, and evaluating technical collection activities. It also advises State Department officers on the use of intelligence produced by major technical collections systems.[9]

The INR employs approximately 330 individuals.[10]

DEPARTMENT OF COMMERCE INTELLIGENCE

Department of Commerce participation in intelligence activities has been heightened in recent years by many factors—most recently, the concern over technology transfer. Intelligence is required concerning (1) those who wish to acquire such technology, (2) those who may attempt or are attempting to provide it, and (3) its accessibility to foreign sources.

Neither the concern over technology transfer nor an intelligence role for the Department of Commerce in that area are new. For a brief period in the 1950s, U.S. efforts to regulate the flow of information and goods to the Soviet Union and other potential adversary nations involved the Commerce Department in an intelligence role. At the urging of the National Security Council, the Office of Strategic Information (OSI) was established within the Department of Commerce in 1954.[11]

The OSI was not authorized by legislation. It was created by Presidential directive on November 1, 1954 in response to the NSC recommendation—a recommendation that resulted from concern about Soviet efforts to obtain U.S. industrial and military information. The OSI tried to create "prepublication awareness" concerning the danger resulting from the availability of certain unclassified scientific and technical information. Particular concern focused on aerial photography, resulting in creation of an OSI Task Force on Aerial Photography. The Task Force recommended a specific educational program through government and industry "to alert producers and users of the strategic intelligence value of aerial photographs."[12] The OSI clashed with the DOD and Congress—the DOD considered the OSI's security role redundant; Congress was concerned about the OSI's negative impact on scientific projects. As a result, the OSI was disestablished in June 1957.[13]

At present, the Department of Commerce has three units with intelligence functions, including the Office of Intelligence Liaison, and the Intelligence Division of the Office of Export Enforcement (OEE). The Office of Intelligence Liaison, which is subordinate to the Office of the General Counsel, serves as the liaison office between the Department of Commerce and the intelligence community, particularly for technology transfer issues. The Office receives all information transmitted from the intelligence community to the Department of Commerce and then distributes the information to the appropriate components.[14]

The Office also provides day-to-day intelligence support to key Department of Commerce officials with international policy or program responsibilities. This support includes preparation of a daily departmental foreign intelligence summary covering major international developments. Support also includes intelligence information for key Department officials traveling abroad.[15]

Additionally, the Office is responsible for reviewing and assessing Department of Commerce intelligence requirements. Based on the results of such assessments, it tasks the intelligence commmunity to provide the necessary data.[16]

The OEE, formerly the Compliance Division of the Office of Export Administration, is subordinate to the Assistant Secretary for Trade Administration. Its function is to ensure that the proper approvals have been obtained for the export of sensitive technology and to prevent unauthorized shipments of such technology. The functions of the OEE's Intelligence Division include:

- receiving, interpreting, and analyzing intelligence and trade data to determine whether preventive, deterrent, or other type of enforcement action [is] required or appropriate;
- providing leads for ongoing investigations and assisting investigative personnel in the conduct of investigations;
- disseminating intelligence information and analysis to agents of the OEE and other appropriate Federal agencies;
- applying qualitative and quantitative methodologies to establish patterns and profiles of diversion and acquistion; and
- collecting intelligence to assist in the conduct of pre-license checks and post-shipment verifications.[17]

In 1984, a Foreign Availability Assessment Division, subsequently renamed the Foreign Availability Division and then the Office of Foreign Availability (OFA), was established under the Office of Export Administration (which is, in turn, subordinate to the Assistant Secretary for Trade Administration). The OFA was established to assess the foreign availability of high technology products to the Soviet Bloc and the People's Republic of China. Foreign availability for a national security item exists when an item of non-U.S. origin and comparable quality is available

Table 6–1. Activities and Impact of the Office of Foreign Availability.

	FY 86	FY 87	FY 88
Classified Reports Reviewed	55,000	65,000	65,000
Foreign Availability Studies Completed	26	28	28
Decontrol Actions Initiated	4	10	10

Note: FY 87 and FY 88 figures are estimated.
Source: U.S. Congress, House Committee on Appropriations, *Departments of Commerce, Justice and State, the Judiciary and Related Agencies Appropriations for 1988, Part 6* (Washington, D.C.: U.S. Government Printing Office, 1987) p. 695.

to controlled countries in quantities sufficient to satisfy their needs, so that U.S. exports of this item would not contribute significantly to the military potential of such countries. Such assessments could influence U.S. decisions concerning the export of U.S. high technology products or lead to discussions with allied governments in an attempt to eliminate that availability.[18]

The Office consists of three branches: Technical Data Collection, Comparative Capabilities Assessment, and Information Analysis. The Technical Data Collection Branch collects data on comparable goods and technologies from a variety of sources—including the U.S. and Foreign Commercial Service, national labs, government scientists and engineers, foreign commercial groups and data bases, and the U.S. intelligence community. The Comparative Capabilities Assessment Branch assesses the capabilities of non-U.S. sources to provide controlled goods and technology and prepares reports on such capabilities which examine technical comparability in quantity and quality, the extent to which a good or technology is freely available to controlled countries, and other aspects of comparability required by law. The Information Analysis Branch collects and screens intelligence reports and studies to determine technologies and commodities available to Soviet Bloc nations from uncontrolled sources. It also identifies producers, production capabilities, and marketing efforts of non-U.S. producers to the Soviet Bloc and monitors non-COCOM export control agreements and systems.[19]

Several foreign availability studies have led to the decontrol of assorted technologies. Among the thirteen foreign availability studies conducted between May and November 1986, one indicated that automatic wafering saws for cutting computer chip blanks out of silicon stock were available from firms in Switzerland. As a result the White House ordered decontrol of the wafering saws.[20] In other cases, OFA studies resulted in decisions not to control a technology. Included in this category are step-and-repeat mask alignment systems, Winchester disk drives, aerial film, and a digitally controlled office switching system. Table 6–1 gives some indications of OFA activities and their impact.

DEPARTMENT OF THE TREASURY INTELLIGENCE

The Office of Intelligence Support overtly collects foreign economic, financial, and monetary data, in cooperation with the Department of State. It also disseminates foreign intelligence relating to U.S. economic policy as required by the Secretary of the Treasury and other Treasury officials. Additionally, it develops intelligence requirements and informs the remainder of the intelligence community as well as generally representing the Department in intelligence community deliberations.[21]

The Office is subordinate to the Executive Secretary of the Department of the Treasury and consists of eighteen individuals: a Special Assistant to the Secretary (National Security), a Senior National Intelligence Adviser, four National Intelligence Advisers, four support personnel, and a nine-person Watch Office. The National Intelligence Advisers are responsible for: (1) Latin America, Africa, and Narcotics; (2) the Soviet Union, Eastern Europe, Middle East, East Asia, and Energy; (3) Western Europe, Japan, Trade, and Monetary Affairs, National Foreign Intelligence Board support; and (4) National Security Agency support.[22]

DEPARTMENT OF ENERGY INTELLIGENCE

The Department of Energy participates with the Department of State in the overt collection of information on foreign energy matters, produces and disseminates foreign intelligence necessary for Energy Department operations, participates in formulating intelligence collection and analysis requirements, and provides technical, analytical, and research capability to other agencies of the intelligence community.[23] Most importantly, Energy Department analysts are heavily involved in the analysis of civilian and military Soviet nuclear energy activities, including weapons-testing activities and warhead characteristics.

As shown in Figure 6–2, these responsibilities are assigned to the Office of the Deputy Assistant Secretary for Intelligence and two subordinate offices—the Office of Foreign Intelligence and the Office of Threat Assessment.

The Department is also responsible for the Lawrence Livermore Laboratory's Proliferation Intelligence Program, which seeks to provide

- National capability assessments of potential proliferant countries;
- analyses of the state-of-the-art fuel cycle technologies such as enrichment and reprocessing, that proliferants could use to acquire fissile material;
- assessments of worldwide availability of nuclear weapons technology that could enable a proliferant to build the physics package of a weapon;
- assessments of worldwide availability of related but non-nuclear weapon technology such as safety, arming, firing, and fusing systems; and
- assessments of the activities and behavior of nuclear supplier states and international organizations involved in nuclear commerce, safeguards, and physical security.[24]

Figure 6–2. Organization of the Office of the Deputy Assistant
Secretary for Intelligence, Department of Energy.

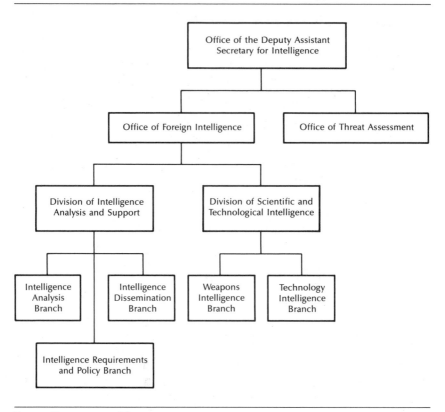

Source: Department of Energy.

DEPARTMENT OF AGRICULTURE INTELLIGENCE

The Department of Agriculture's intelligence consumers are, in general, more likely
to be U.S. farmers than national security officials. However, in certain circumstances, such as proposed grain sales to the Soviet Union, the Department's Foreign
Agriculture Service (FAS) might contribute to the production of intelligence relevant
to foreign policy decisionmaking.

The FAS maintains a worldwide agricultural intelligence and reporting system,
consisting of approximately 100 professional agriculturists posted as agricultural
attaches at approximately seventy U.S. embassies. Attache reporting includes information and data on foreign government policies, analysis of supply and demand
conditions, commercial trade relationships, and market opportunities. In Washington, part of the FAS staff analyzes the activities of international trade conducted
under the General Agreement on Tariffs and Trade (GATT).[25]

DRUG ENFORCEMENT ADMINISTRATION INTELLIGENCE

The Drug Enforcement Administration (DEA) operates in the United States and abroad. DEA intelligence operations are the responsibility of the Assistant Administrator for Intelligence, who heads the Office of Intelligence of the DEA Operations Division. The Office, (which until 1985 was divided into an Operational Intelligence Section, Strategic Intelligence Section and El Paso Intelligence Center) is responsible for

- providing technical and operational intelligence products and services which identify the structure and members of international and domestic drug trafficking organizations and exploitable areas for enforcement operations;
- preparing strategic intelligence assessments, estimates, and probes focusing on trafficking patterns, source country production, and domestic production and consumption trends;
- developing intelligence that focuses on the financial aspects of drug investigations such as money laundering techniques, drug-related asset discovery and forfeiture, and macroeconomic impact assessments of the illegal drug trade; and
- provides interagency intelligence support to other Federal, state, and local law enforcement organizations, and a variety of state and foreign drug intelligence clearinghouses, and participates in the National Narcotics Interdiction System.[26]

In 1985 the DEA also established the U.S. Southwest Border Intelligence Task Force, which supports DEA intelligence operations along the U.S.–Mexican border. The Task Force provides strategic assessments of all aspects of drug trafficking from Mexico to the United States and in conjunction with DEA field offices, collates, analyzes, and disseminates intelligence on major Mexican drug traffickers and their organizations.[27]

The Office's Special Field Intelligence Program provides funding "to exploit highly specialized or unique collection opportunities against a wide variety of intelligence problems in foreign areas." The target of such activities is the collection of data on the entire raw material production process, smuggling routes and methods, trafficking, and terrorist or financial matters relating to narcotics activities.[28]

According to the DEA's 1984 congressional budget submission, its major activities and accomplishments included:

- development of sources of information knowledgeable of illicit cultivation, production, and transportation activities;
- undercover penetration of trafficking organizations in support of host country operations;
- surveillance assistance and development of evidence against major traffickers of drugs destined for the United States; and
- intelligence support to governments in Mexico and Central America in eradicating marijuana and poppy fields.[29]

Additionally, the DEA reported that intelligence probes in West Germany have identified a sizeable number of Turkish and Pakistani traffickers transporting Southwest Asian heroin into Western Europe. Likewise, inelligence probes in Pakistan, Turkey, and Mexico are reported to have pinponted illicit laboratory locations, identified the operators, and assessed the potential output of a number of sophisticated morphine, heroin, and opium production operations.[30]

Among the DEA's forty-one overseas offices is one in the U.S. Embassy in Cyprus. This Office collects intelligence on Lebanon's Bekaa Valley, one of the world's fastest growing heroin and hashish production centers. Apparently, some of Lebanon's most prominent families, as well as Palestinian guerillas and other militia forces that control illegal ports, are deeply involved in the drug trade and use its revenues to finance their organizations.[31]

In the course of its activities the DEA interacts with several major intelligence agencies. Detection of drug trafficking operations can involve human agents, both DEA and CIA, as well as a variety of technical collection systems. Hence, the DEA has contacts with the CIA, the NSA, the NRO and Naval intelligence. The Administrator of the DEA stated, in 1981 congressional testimony, that he

> met with Deputy Director of CIA, Admiral Inman for quite some time at their headquarters and discussed our narcotics problem. I've worked with him in the past, both at NSA and on other matters, and we are expecting increased attention from that agency, and we need it desperately. Because without intelligence, the enforcement effort is immediately limited.[32]

The CIA has provided the DEA with international narcotics intelligence derived from both human and electronic surveillance operations overseas.[33]

FEDERAL BUREAU OF INVESTIGATION

The responsibilities of the Federal Bureau of Investigation (FBI) are predominantly in the criminal law enforcement, domestic counterterrorism and domestic counterintelligence areas, the later responsibilities being performed by the Bureau's Intelligence Division. The Intelligence Division also does have some present responsibility with regard to collection of foreign intelligence in the United States.

Over the years the FBI has tried to expand its role in foreign intelligence collection. In 1939, President Roosevelt gave the FBI responsibility for collection of intelligence in the Western Hemisphere, which created a Special Intelligence Service (SIS) for this function. The SIS had approximately 360 agents, mostly in Mexico, Argentina, and Brazil. Although it was stripped of this function after the war, the Bureau maintained representatives as Legal Attaches in ten embassies as of 1970. The attaches' official function was to be liaison with national police forces on matters of common concern and to deal with Americans who found themselves in trouble with the law. In 1970 the Bureau increased from ten to twenty the number of embassies with FBI representation and instructed agents to collect foreign intelligence, particularly interesting intelligence being slugged with the designation HILEV (High Level) by overseas agents. Some such material was distributed to high officials—for example, to Henry Kissinger—outside normal channels. In the aftermath of J. Edgar Hoover's death and FBI revelations, the program was terminated and FBI representation abroad was reduced to fifteen embassies.[34]

At least two instances of FBI attempts to engage in foreign clandestine collection have come to light. During the investigation of the murder of former Chilean Defense Minister Orlando Letelier, the FBI had an undercover agent in Chile. The agent told the FBI that the right-wing Patria y Libertad had contracted with Chilean narcotics traffickers to murder Letelier. The FBI's agent turned out to be a DEA informant who had been terminated and blacklisted years earlier for double dealing, misinterpretation, and moral turpitude. A more successful operation involved the FBI placement of a young woman informant among one of the first groups of American leftists to visit China in the early 1970s.[35]

Despite its failure to acquire a significant *overseas* role in the collection of foreign intelligence, the FBI is involved in domestic activities to generate such intelligence. Thus, Executive Order 12333 allows the FBI to

> conduct within the United States, when requested by the officials of the intelligence community designated by the President, activities undertaken to collect foreign intelligence or support foreign intelligence collection requirements of other agencies within the intelligence community.[36]

In the past such activities have included wiretapping and break-ins. The FBI has operated wiretaps against numerous foreign embassies in Washington. FBI agents regularly monitored the phones in the offices of all Communist governments represented in Washington. Additionally, the telephones in the offices of non-Communist governments are tapped, especially when those nations are engaged in negotiations with the United States or when significant developments are taking place in those countries. This type of bugging has included the phones of an ally's Trade Mission in San Francisco. In addition, the FBI has conducted break-ins at foreign embassies to obtain cryptanalytical and other foreign intelligence.[37]

FEDERAL RESEARCH DIVISION, LIBRARY OF CONGRESS

The Federal Research Division was created in 1948 as the Air Research Division, with responsibility for using the resources of the Library of Congress to identify targets in the Soviet Union.[38]

Today, the Federal Research Division (FRD) conducts special research and bibliographic and abstracting services in support of various agencies of the U.S. government, employing the collections of the Library of Congress and other materials available through the Library's resources. At one time the FRD had an exclusive relationship with the Defense Intelligence Agency, participating along with DIA and the military service intelligence units in the General Intelligence Career Development Program. Since then it has broadened its sponsors, who provide the funding, to include the Department of Commerce, the NASA, the National Science Foundation, and the Environmental Protection Administration.[39]

FRD studies have focused on Soviet elites and propaganda, Middle Eastern cultural dynamics, laser technology, insurgencies in Central America, defense and military capabilities, technology and arms transfers, African instability, Warsaw Pact economies, strategic mineral production, and foreign medical facilities.[40] As noted earlier, in 1984 the FRD performed studies for the Air Force Intelligence Service on Soviet denial and deception activities.

The FRD operates under the Director for General Reference, Research Services and is divided into six sections: Research Support, Western Europe/Latin America, Middle East/Africa, Asia, USSR/Eastern Europe (Military, Political, Economic) and USSR/Eastern Europe (S&T, Industrial).[41] While technically part of the Library of Congress, the FRD's offices are located in the Washington Navy Yard, well away from the Library, in large part due to the Library's sensitivity over the FRD's intelligence connection.

NOTES TO CHAPTER 6

1. U.S. Congress, Senate Select Committee to Study Governmental Operations with Respect to Intelligence Activities, *Supplementary Reports on Intelligence Activities* (Washington, D.C.: U.S. Government Printing Office, 1976), pp. 271–76.

2. U.S. Congress, House Committee on Foreign Affairs, *The Role of Intelligence in the Foreign Policy Process* (Washington, D.C.: U.S. Government Printing Office, 1980), p. 57.

3. *INR* (Washington, D.C.: Department of State, 1983), pp. 6–8.

4. Ibid., pp. 10, 15–16; *United States Department of State Organizational Directory* (Washington, D.C.: U.S. Government Printing Office, March 1987), p. 28.

5. *INR*, pp. 11–12; *United States Department of State Organizational Directory*, p. 29; U.S. Congress, House Committee on Appropriations, *Departments of Commerce, Justice, and State, the Judiciary and Related Agencies Appropriations for FY 1986, Part 6* (Washington, D.C.: U.S. Government Printing Office, 1985), pp. 370, 374; U.S. Congress, House Committee on Appropriations, *Departments of Commerce, Justice, and State, the Judiciary and Related Agencies Appropriations for FY 1986, Part 6* (Washington, D.C.: U.S. Government Printing Office, 1986) p. 351.

6. Ibid., pp. 12–13; *United States Department of State Organizational Directory*, pp. 29–31; David B. Ottaway, "State Dept. Unit to Monitor Soviet Disinformation," *Washington Post*, October 7, 1986, p. A12; U.S. Congress, House Committee on Appropriations, *Departments of Commerce, Justice, and State, the Judiciary and Related Agencies Appropriations for FY 1987, Part 6*, p. 351.

7. *INR*, p. 13.

8. Ibid., p. 14.

9. Ibid., p. 15.

10. U.S. Congress, House Committee on Appropriations, *Departments of Commerce, Justice, and State, the Judiciary and Related Agencies Appropriations for FY 1986, Part 6,* p. 361.
11. National Academy of Sciences, *Scientific Communication and National Security* (Washington, D.C.: National Academy Press, 1982), pp. 99.
12. U.S. Congress, House Committee on Government Operations, *Availability of Information from Federal Departments and Agencies, Part 6* (Washington, D.C.: U.S. Government Printing Office, 1956), pp. 1671–72.
13. National Academy of Sciences, *Scientific Communication and National Security,* p. 99.
14. Department of Commerce, "Department Organization Order Series 10-6, Appendix A," June 10, 1981, p. 2.
15. Ibid.
16. Ibid.
17. Department of Commerce, "Organization and Function Order 41-4, Assistant Secretary for Trade Administration," May 8, 1985, pp. 21, 22.
18. Ibid., U.S. Congress, House Committee on Appropriations, *Departments of Commerce, Justice and State, the Judiciary and Related Agencies Appropriations for 1988, Part 6* (Washington, D.C.: U.S. Government Printing Office, 1987), p. 695.
19. Department of Commerce, "Organization and Function Order 41-4," pp. 17–18.
20. James K. Gordon, "Commerce Decontrols Technology Because of Foreign Availability," *Aviation Week and Space Technology,* November 24, 1986, p. 63; U.S. Congress, General Accounting Office, *Commerce's Assessment of the Foreign Availability of Controlled Items Can Be More Effective* (Washington, D.C.: GAO, 1988), p. 11.
21. Ronald Reagan, "United States Intelligence Activities," Executive Order 12333 *Federal Register* 46, no. 235 (December 5, 1981): 59941–54 at 59946; "Foreign Intelligence—It's More than the CIA," *U.S. News and World Report,* May 1, 1981, pp. 35–37; Department of the Treasury Order 100-3, "Functions of the Executive Secretariat," January 13, 1987, p. 2.
22. Department of the Treasury, "OIS Organization Structure," undated.
23. Reagan, "United States Intelligence Activities," at p. 59949.
24. U.S. Congress, House Committee on Armed Services, *Department of Energy: National Security and Military Applications of Nuclear Energy Authorization Act of 1984* (Washington, D.C.: U.S. Government Printing Office, 1983), p. 394.
25. Department of Agriculture, *FAS USA: The Farmer's Export Arm* (Washington, D.C.: Department of Agriculture, 1980), unpaginated.
26. Drug Enforcement Administration, *Annual Report Fiscal Year 1986* (Washington, D.C.: DEA, 1986), pp. 9–10.
27. Ibid., p. 6.
28. U.S. Congress, House Committee on Appropriations, *Department of Commerce, Justice, and State, the Judiciary and Related Agencies Appropriations for FY 1984, Part 6—Department of Justice* (Washington, D.C.: U.S. Government Printing Office, 1983), pp. 3, 21.
29. Ibid., p. 22.
30. Ibid., pp. 22–23.
31. Patrick E. Tyler, "Smugglers, Gun Runners, Spies Cross Paths in Cyprus," *Washington Post,* March 12, 1986, pp. A1, A30.

32. U.S. Congress, Senate Committee on the Judiciary, *Oversight of the Drug Enforcement Administration* (Washington, D.C.: U.S. Government Printing Office, 1981), p. 9.

33. Department of Justice, *Report on Inquiry into CIA-Related Electronic Surveillance Activities* (Washington, D.C.: Department of Justice, 1976), p. 20.

34. Sanford J. Ungar, *The FBI* (Boston: Little Brown, 1976), pp. 225–26, 242.

35. Taylor Branch and Eugene M. Proper, *Labyrinth* (New York: Viking, 1982), pp. 231, 350, 358; Ungar, *The FBI*, pp. 240–41.

36. Reagan, "United States Intelligence Activities," Section 1.14, provision c. at p. 59949.

37. Victor Marchetti and John Marks, *The CIA and the Cult of Intelligence* (New York: Knopf, 1974), p. 204; "Mole Tunnels Under a Soviet Consulate," *Newsweek*, August 15, 1983, p. 21; Douglas Watson, "Huston Says NSA Urged Break-Ins," *Washington Post*, March 3, 1975, pp. 1, 6.

38. See Jeffrey Richelson, *American Espionage and the Soviet Target* (New York: William Morrow 1987), pp. 252–53.

39. Defense Intelligence Agency, *Defense Intelligence Agency Review and Analysis of the General Intelligence Career Development Program (ICDP) Annual Status Report for FY 1980 and FY 1981* (Washington, D.C.: DIA, 1983), p. III–12; *Federal Research Division* (Washington, D.C.: FRD, n.d.); Library of Congress Regulation 214-10, "Functions and Organization of the Federal Research Division, Research Services," May 10, 1985.

40. *Federal Research Division*.

41. Library of Congress Regulation 214-10, "Functions and Organization of the Federal Research Division, Research Services."

CIA Headquarters, Langley, Virginia.

Photo Credit: Central Intelligence Agency.

CIA's Blue U at 1000 North Glebe Road, Arlington, Virginia. Courses in Photography, Clandestine Letter Opening, and Lock Picking are Given at the "Blue U."

National Security Agency Headquarters, Ft. George G. Meade, Maryland.

Photo Credit: Department of Defense.

The Locked Doors to the National Reconnaissance Office.

Defense Intelligence Analysis Center, Bolling AFB, Washington, D.C.

Photo Credit: Department of Defense.

Headquarters, U.S. Army Intelligence and Security Command, Arlington, Virginia.

Headquarters, U.S. Army, Foreign Science and Technology Center, Charlottesville, Virginia.

Photo Credit: INSCOM

Photo Credit: FSTC

Headquarters, Naval Intelligence Command, Suitland, Maryland.

Headquarters, Naval Intelligence Support Center, Suitland, Maryland.

Photo Credit: NIC

Photo Credit: NISC

7 IMAGERY COLLECTION AND PROCESSING

The concept of using overhead platforms to observe events on the earth can be traced to the time of the French Revolutionary War, when France organized a company of *aerostiers* in April 1794. One of the company's balloons is said to have been kept in the air for nine hours while the groups' commander made continuous observations during the battle of Fleurus in Belgium.[1]

The United States made similar use of balloons during the Civil War, although not much valuable intelligence was obtained. By the latter part of the 19th century Britain was conducting experiments using balloons as platforms from which to obtain "overhead photography." In January 1911, the San Diego waterfront became the first subject of airplane-carried cameras. In the same year the U.S. Army Signal Corps put aerial photography on the curriculum at its flight training school. Between 1913 and 1915 visual and photographic reconnaissance missions were flown by the U.S. Army in the Philippines and along the Mexican border.[2]

During World War II the United States made extensive use of airplane photography, using remodeled B-17 (Flying Fortress) and B-24 (Liberator) aircraft. The remodeled B-24, known as the F-7, carried six cameras internally—all were triggered via remote control by an operator placed over the sealed rear bomb-bay doors. After the war ended and a hostile relationship with the Soviet Union emerged the United States conducted photographic missions along the Soviet periphery, sending planes to fly outside Soviet territory. The planes, however, were equipped with cameras capable of looking into Soviet territory for a limited number of miles.[3]

Realizing that it was imperative to obtain photographic coverage not just of the periphery but of the Soviet interior, in the late 1940s and early 1950s, the United States began exploring means to obtain such coverage. The result has been the development, production, and employment of a variety of spacecraft and aircraft that allow the United States to monitor events in the Soviet Union and other nations by overflight or peripheral missions.

In the years since the United States began operating such systems, their capabilities have improved in numerous ways. Satellites now have longer lifetimes, produce more detailed images, and transmit their imagery almost instantly. Some aircraft fly at supersonic speed and at higher ceilings, and have advanced sensor systems.

In addition, aircraft have—and spacecraft will soon have—the capability to produce high-quality imagery in situations that do not allow the production of standard visible-light photography. The basic difference between alternative means of obtaining imagery is that they rely on different portions of the electromagnetic spectrum to produce images. Photographic equipment is sensitive to electromagnetic radiation that has a wavelength between 0.0004 and 0.00075 mm, the visible light portion of the spectrum.[4]

Photographic equipment can be either film-based or television type. A conventional camera records, on film, the varying light levels reflected from a scene by all of the separate objects in that scene. On the other hand, an electro-optical camera converts the varying light levels into electronic signals. A numerical value is assigned to each of the signals, which are called picture elements or pixels. The process transforms a picture (analog) image into a digital image, which can be transmitted electronically to distant points. The signal can be reconstructed from the digital to the analog format and finally the analog signal can be displayed on a video screen or made into a photograph.[5]

Imagery can be obtained using both visible light and near-infrared portions of the electromagnetic spectrum. Unlike the portion of the spectrum used by visible light photography, the near-infrared portion is not visible to the human eye. At the same time, infrared, like visible light photography, depends on the reflective properties of objects rather than their emission of radiation. As a result, such imagery can only be produced in daylight and in the absence of substantial cloud cover.[6]

Thermal infrared imagery, obtained from the mid- and far-infrared portion of the electromagnetic spectrum, produces imagery purely by detecting the heat produced by objects. Such devices can detect buried structures such as missile silos, or underground construction, by measuring temperature differences between targets and the earth's surface. Since thermal infrared imagery does not require visible light, it can be obtained under conditions of darkness (however, the sky must be free of cloud cover).[7]

A means of producing imagery in the presence of cloud cover is imaging radar (an acronym for radio detection and ranging). Radar imagery is produced by bouncing radio waves off an area or object. The returning waves allow formation of a picture of that object. Since radio waves are not attenuated by the water vapor in the atmosphere, they are able to penetrate cloud cover.[8]

COLLECTION

The most important means of producing imagery, particularly of the Soviet Union, is through satellite photography. For several years the United States relied on several different varieties of satellite systems. Some, such as the KH-8, took highly detailed pictures of specific targets. Others, such as the KH-9, produced images of broader areas, allowing photo interpreters to examine a large area and select targets for more detailed inspection. In 1976, the KH-8 and KH-9 were joined by the KEYHOLE-11 (KH-11), which has been the sole type of military imaging satellite operated by the United States since October 18, 1984 (when the last KH-9 was deorbited) and will be until the launch of the first KH-12.

The origins of the KH-11 (which is also known by the codename KENNAN) go back to the 1967 Arab-Israeli Six Day War. As a result of that conflict the CIA convened a panel to study the question of what kind of imaging system was needed under the circumstances. The KH-11 system that emerged was less capable than a KH-X system, which would have involved sufficient orbiting spacecraft to permit daily coverage of every point on earth. When the immensity of the data to be collected, processed, and analyzed became clear, plans for the KH-X were dropped. On the other hand, the KH-11 was more complex than another system proposed by the Air Force. Richard Helms, then DCI, fought for the system designed by his Directorate of Science and Technology over the less complex system, successfully taking his case to the President. As a result, the KH-11 was born.[9]

On December 19, 1976, a single KH-11 was launched on a Titan 3D rocket from Vandenberg AFB into an orbit of 164 by 329 miles. The craft itself is sixty-four feet long and weighs 30,000 pounds.[10] The satellites fly lengthwise, with the axis of the camera parallel to the earth. A downward-looking mirror in the front of the camera can be rotated to look from side to side, causing a periscope effect in which the camera view can change from moment to moment. Two benefits result from that capability: the same location can be viewed more frequently than if the camera could only look straight down, and the satellite can generate a stereoscopic image.

Only a very select set of government officials was permitted to know of the KH-11's existence or even see its products. The KH-11 was treated with an even greater degree of secrecy than usual in the black world of reconnaissance satellites. The photographs and data derived from them were not incorporated with those of the other operational imaging satellites of the time (the KH-8 and KH-9). The decision to restrict the data to a very small group of individuals was taken at the urging of senior CIA officials, but opposed by military officers who wanted information to be more widely distributed throughout the armed forces. It was only when it was discovered that a disgruntled CIA employee, William Kampiles, had sold the KH-11 technical manual to the KGB that the restrictive policy was changed.

The KH-11, in contrast to the KH-8 and KH-9, does not return imagery via film canisters. Instead, to permit instant transmission, its optical system employs

Table 7–1. KH-11 Lifetimes.

Launch Date	Deorbited On	Lifetime (Days)
December 19, 1976	January 28, 1979	770
June 14, 1978	August 23, 1981	1,166
February 7, 1980	October 30, 1982	993
September 3, 1981	November 23, 1984	1,175
November 17, 1982	August 13, 1985	987
December 4, 1984	—	—
October 27, 1987	—	—

an array of light-sensitive silicone diodes. The charge from the diodes is read by an amplifier and converted from analog to digital signals for transmission. The signals then are transmitted to Satellite Data System (SDS) spacecraft while they slowly pass over the Soviet Union. The SDS satellite then transmits the signals for initial processing to a ground station at Ft. Belvoir, Virginia, about twenty miles south of Washington. The Mission Ground Site—a large, windowless, two-story concrete building—is officially known as the Defense Communications Electronics Evaluation and Testing Activity.[11]

Partially as a result of its electronic method of transmitting data, a KH-11 satellite can stay in orbit for a much longer period than either a KH-8 or KH-9, since a KH-11 cannot run out of film. An additional positive factor of the KH-11 is its higher orbit (approximately 150 by 250 miles) which reduces atmospheric drag on the spacecraft. Thus, the lifetime of the first KH-11 was 770 days, almost 500 days longer than the lifetime of the longest-lived KH-9. The lifetimes of the subsequent KH-11s, shown in Table 7–1, give it an average lifetime of 1,018 days—almost three years.

Between the time the second KH-11 was deorbited on August 23, 1981, and August 28, 1985 (when an attempted KH-11 launch failed), a particular pattern had been established. Two KH-11s were kept in orbit at all times, and when one was deorbited it was replaced shortly thereafter by a new satellite. Thus, the KH-11 deorbited on August 23, 1981 was replaced by one put into orbit on September 3, 1981, while the satellite launched on February 7, 1980 and deorbited on October 30, 1982 was replaced by a KH-11 launched on November 17, 1982. By the time one satellite was ready to be deorbited, both were circling the earth at a faster speed—every ninety minutes—than usual. After one satellite was removed from orbit the other made a major maneuver several days later, which increased its period to 92.5 minutes. The satellite replacing the deorbited satellite then was launched and made a few maneuvers to get the same period and desired plane spacing with the other, after which joint operations began. As shown in Figure 7–1, the satellite pairs divided the work of providing late morning and early afternoon coverage. The combination of viewing angles produced is a substantial aid in interpreting the satellite images.[12]

Figure 7-1. KH-11 Coverage.

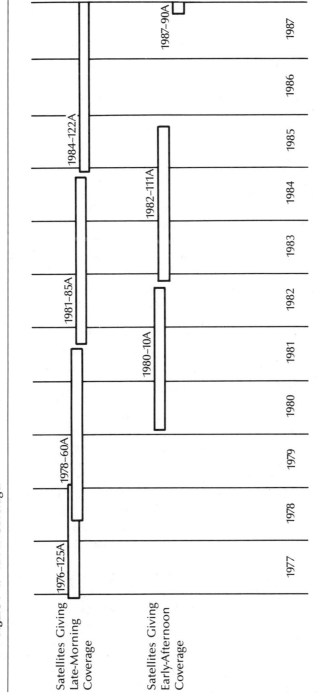

Source: Anthony Kenden.

Beyond its longer lifetime, the KH-11 has an even more significant advantage over the film-return satellites. Its ability to provide data instantly allows it to be used in a crisis-monitoring and an early-warning role. Whereas film-return satellites could take days or even weeks to provide data, the KH-11 can return the data instantly. It is only a matter of an hour before the data can be processed at Mission Ground Site, analyzed at the CIA's National Photographic Interpretation Center, and then put in the hands of decisionmakers. According to one person familiar with the system, "You can call up the KH-11 and when it comes up on its geometry to the target area, you can get a photo and have it back down here, printed out, in an hour, and have it over to the White House."[13] In 1985, Richard Evan Hineman, CIA Deputy Director for Science and Technology, testified that the KH-11 is used "against active military targets for early-warning purposes."[14]

Several examples of KH-11 photographic production have been exposed to public view. Among the data carried to the Desert One site in Iran during the April 1980 hostage rescue mission was KH-11 photography, which was left behind when an EC-130 and a helicopter crashed during the aborted mission. Photographs left behind, which later appeared in a book published by Iranian students, included overhead views of a sports stadium and the U.S. Embassy compound. Among other uses, the data were employed to determine the location of the personnel in the compound and to scout the route the rescue team would take.[15]

In December 1981, a KH-11 photograph of a future Soviet bomber—the BLACK-JACK—appeared in *Aviation Week and Space Technology*. The photograph was taken on November 25, 1981, while the plane sat on the tarmac at Ramenskoye Airfield, a strategic test center. The photograph also showed two TU-144 Charger transports, similar to the Concorde. Distinguishable features included the passenger windows on the side of the aircraft. The picture was taken by the KH-11 launched on September 3, 1981, on a southbound pass across the Soviet Union during the late morning, local time. The picture, which was taken at quite a steep slant or oblique angle, indicated a KH-11 capability to obtain a resolution between 5.46 and 17.7 inches, depending on the satellite's distance from the target.[16]

In 1984, there appeared in *Jane's Defence Weekly*, three KH-11 photos of a Kiev-class carrier under construction, a carrier code-named BLACK COM II (for Black Sea Combatant II) by the United States and KREMLIN by the Soviet Navy. The photos were taken at an oblique angle, although not as oblique as the angle for the BLACKJACK photo. In one case the slant angle was such that the photo was taken from 504 miles away.[17]

One computer-enhanced photograph, taken at an oblique angle, shows the general layout of the Nikolaiev 444 yard on the Black Sea, with what would appear to be a foundry in the foreground and assembly shops behind. Buildings that housed the technical staff are shown to lie alongside the dry dock where the 75,000 ton nuclear carrier was under construction. The photograph also shows the stern section of the KHARKOV, the fourth Kiev-class carrier, in the process of being fitted out. Nearby, an amphibious landing ship, apparently of the 13,000 ton Ivan Rogov class, is shown under construction. The photography is distinct enought to identify objects such as ladders and windows. A second photo gives a more detailed view of the CVN dry dock. It also indicates the position of vertical silo-launched SAMs forward of the superstructure.[18]

More recently, in the summer of 1985, the KH-11 showed that Soviet personnel had cut off the tail sections of fifteen Bison bombers, as part of its SALT II obligation to destroy old bombers to compensate for the deployment of new Bear H bombers. The bombers were placed in plain view at an airfield to facilitate monitoring by the KH-11.[19]

In April and May 1986 the KH-11 monitored the situation at the Chernobyl nuclear power plant, where a disastrous nuclear accident took place on April 26. Before the accident, the last KH-11 photograph was taken on April 16. After the Soviet news agency TASS announced the accident on April 28, the KH-11 was instructed to take a photograph that very afternoon on its next pass. However, the photography was conducted at a considerable distance, and subsequent computer enhancement did not produce a photograph that provided much information. The following morning another photograph was obtained, also from a considerable distance. However, by that afternoon the satellite was in a good position and obtained the first high-quality photograph of the damaged plant.[20]

In addition, KH-11 imagery reportedly revealed that the Soviet Union was constructing an advanced submarine and a new mini-aircraft carrier, and disproved reports of a new Soviet chemical-biological warfare (CBW) center by showing it was actually a reserve arms storage facility, KH-11 imagery also apparently led to the discovery of a SS-20 ballistic missile in its canister alongside an encapsulated ICMB. It has been suggested that the Soviets were seeking to have Soviet reconnaissance spacecraft compare the two so steps could be taken to increase the similarity and the chances of successful disguise. The KH-11 also has been used to monitor directed-energy-related construction activities at Sary Shagan. According to one report, a number of experts knowledgeable on Soviet charged particle-beam physics were convinced by KH-11 photographs that a particle-beam device was being constructed at Sary Shagan.[21]

In 1985, the KH-11 program suffered its worst setback since the sale of the *KH-11 Technical Manual* to the KGB. On August 13, 1985, the KH-11 launched on November 17, 1982 was deorbited after a lifetime of 987 days. On August 28, the sixth KH-11 was to be placed in orbit, using a Titan 34D booster. However, a launch failure occurred when one of the Titan's two Aerojet engines shut down, resulting in the booster and payload splashing down in the Pacific Ocean.[22]

The loss was more serious than it might have been otherwise for two reasons. There were no remaining KH-11s intended for launch, as the first KH-12 was expected to be launched on board the space shuttle in September 1986. All that was left was a KH-11 demonstration or "floor model" that had been used for flight qualification trials and other tests but was never meant to be placed in orbit. When the space shuttle *Challenger* exploded on January 28, 1986, the space shuttle program itself suffered a major setback. It was clear that the first KH-12 flight would be delayed by a substantial number of months, since there were no expendable launch vehicles presently in the U.S. arsenal that could handle the 40,000-pound KH-12. The new Titan 4 vehicles that could perform the mission would not be available until at least 1988. As a result, plans were made to refurbish the ground demonstration model for launch around May 1986.[23]

Unfortunately, disaster struck again, on April 18, 1986, when a Titan 34D booster exploded shortly after launch, 800 feet above the launch pad at Vandenberg AFB. It appears that the payload was the final KH-9. The explosion also put the launch of the KH-11 ground demonstration model on hold until confidence in the 34D booster could be restored. Finally, on October 26, 1987, a Titan 34D, apparently carrying the KH-11 floor model, was successfully launched.[24]

A successor to the KH-11 has been in the works for many years. Originally, the KH-12 was scheduled to be launched in September 1986, on the second shuttle launch from Vandenberg AFB. The KH-12, as the satellite has commonly been referred to, is expected to be a 40,000 pound satellite with greater capabilities than the KH-11. As with the KH-11, it will transmit its data in real time—via the SDS and the elliptically orbiting MILSTAR satellites that will replace the SDS. One reported improvement for the KH-12 will be a thermal imaging capability to allow photography at night.[25]

Additionally, the KH-12 will be equipped with a greater fuel supply, totaling about 10,000 to 15,000 pounds, giving it greater maneuverability. Thus it will be able to move from a high altitude of 560 miles to a low of 80 miles, although generally it will operate in a 150-nautical mile, circular orbit. It will be able to provide both high-resolution imagery of small areas and lower resolution imagery of wider areas. Further, its maneuvering capability could be employed in attempts to evade Soviet ASAT weapons or to defeat Soviet denial and deception activities. For further protection the satellite will also be hardened against nuclear effects, contain a variety of protection devices to prevent damage from Soviet laser weapons, and have a radar detector to alert it when it is being chased.[26]

If the Vandenberg space shuttle facility begins operations in the early 1990s, as originally planned, the space shuttle will be able to retrieve fuel-depleted KH-12s and bring them back to earth. After being refueled, repaired, or refurbished on earth, the KH-12 can then be returned to orbit. Thus, the KH-12 could have an eight-year lifetime.[27]

Sometime after the KH-12 becomes part of the U.S. space reconnaissance fleet, another satellite system, first known as INDIGO and now as LACROSSE, will be added. LACROSSE, a radar imagery satellite, will close a major gap in U.S. satellite imagery capabilities. Its ability to penetrate cloud cover is a capability absent from both the KH-11 and KH-12.[28]

Cloud cover is a serious impediment in monitoring the USSR, where some areas are covered by clouds for at least 70 percent of the year. In some cases, a particular installation—for example, the Kharkov tank factory—may be under cloud cover for the entire year. In other cases, the cloud cover requires imaging a particular area or target over several years; possibly, a complete picture will be formed only by constructing a photographic montage of an area with pictures taken on several orbital passes. Thus, in 1983, the United States was "surprised" at the discovery of a Pechora-class, large phased-array radar in central Siberia at Krasnoyarsk. The early warning radar, which had not yet been completed but was substantially along in construction, represented an apparent violation of the ABM Treaty due to its inland location, a location banned by the treaty to prevent use of such radars for ABM "battle management."[29]

LACROSSE, built by Martin Marietta at a cost of about $1 billion, is a CIA project with a launch date in the late 1980s. The first LACROSSE was completed in October 1987, but requires the space shuttle as a delivery vehicle. Its prime target will be Soviet and Warsaw Pact armor. Orbiting at about 300 miles above the earth and powered by a small nuclear reactor, LACROSSE will have a resolution in the area of five to ten feet. Data acquired by such a satellite would be relayed back to a ground station at White Sands, New Mexico, by the Tracking and Data Relay Satellite. In the event of a European crisis either within Eastern Europe or between the East and West, the satellite will be able to keep watch regardless of weather conditions.[30]

Satellites are the most productive of U.S. imaging collection systems—able to overfly without hindrance, and in the case of the KH-11, to provide imagery almost instantly. However, satellites have their own limitations. Even if already in orbit, they cannot be dispatched to cover events on short notice. They also fly on a well-known path, which can be predicted. The Soviet Union or any other nation that seeks to hide activities from the satellite's view may be able to do so. Further, such systems are extraordinarily expensive and their uses must be prioritized. Aircraft reconnaissance systems can supplement satellite coverage, however, as well as provide quick reaction capability.

The United States has relied for many years on two aircraft for strategic imagery reconnaissance: the (Strategic Reconnaissance) SR-71, and the U-2. The SR-71A has been nicknamed "Blackbird" for its black epoxy surface and was code-named OXCART in its days as a classified project. Both names are deceptive to varying degrees. The color of the SR-71A, which was chosen after heat emissions tests, becomes blue as temperatures increase at high speed and altitude. OXCART, the name of a slow-moving body, was selected from a list of deliberately deceptive code names.[31]

The SR-71A is 107.4 feet long with a wingspan of 55.6 feet and a fuselage of 5 feet, 4 inches in diameter. The height at the twin vertical stabilizers is 18.5 feet.[32] What a SR-71A looks like depends on the vantage point, since to "look at a three-view drawing of the SR-71 is to see three totally different aircraft—one like an arrow, another like a flying saucer, and a third like an enormous bat."[33]

As with the plane's body, both the engines and fuel employed are new. The engines are Pratt and Whitney J-58 turbojets, and rather than pointing straight ahead, the jets' intake spikes point down and in at an acute angle. When the plane is operating at extreme speed and altitude, the airframe distortion that is created straightens the spikes. The JT-7 fuel, unique to the SR-71, is especially nonvolatile—

so much so that the engines have to be started chemically, with a substance known as polyethyl bromide (PEB).[34]

The shape, engines, and fuel of the SR-71A make it a viable strategic reconnaissance aircraft—one that can fly at over Mach 3 (2,100 miles per hour) and at an altitude of over 80,000 feet, putting it out of range of both the SAMs and MiG fighters possessed by countries such as North Korea. With aerial refueling, the SR-71 has global range.[35]

The exact speed limit and operational ceiling of the SR-71 have been matters of speculation for years. In a public demonstration on July 27, 1976, Captain Robert Holt and Major Larry Elliot established flying records of 85,069 feet in height and 2,193.17 miles per hours. It is thought, however, that the plane can do much better—while even secret documents only specify the SR-71 speed as over Mach 3 and a ceiling over 80,000 feet, it may in fact be able to travel faster and higher than those figures seem to imply. Its speed may be Mach 4. Its operational ceiling, according to its designer Kelly Johnson, exceeds 100,000 feet. In any case, its combination of height and speed allow the SR-71A to photograph 100,000 square miles of territory in a single hour.[36]

The plane is not flown manually on a reconnaissance mission since a human operator could not fly it precisely enough to allow its sensors to perform effectively. The plane's inertial navigation system is up to the task. According to Kelly Johnson, "The inertial navigation system is so good that you can take off, put in sixteen different checkpoints, and on autopilot fly at speed, altitude, and direction desired."[37]

The sensors that are placed in the nose or underbelly of an SR-71, including imaging equipment, can vary from mission to mission. Thus, SR-71s can be equipped with two Technical Objective Framing Cameras capable of producing high-resolution (nine inch) imagery of the terrain below and to each side of the flight path. These cameras are, in general, operated automatically and respond to in-flight instructions from the on board navigation system to image specific, preselected geographic coordinates. Likewise, an Optical Bar Camera can be fitted in the nose and is capable of providing black and white and/or color infrared imagery, in mono or stereo, of the terrain below and to each side of the flight path. Its resolution is approximately twelve inches. A third option is the High Resolution Radar System, which can produce imagery day or night, under all weather conditions. The resolution is, however, less than that of camera systems, so this radar system is most valuable when it supplements satellite and aircraft systems that have been neutralized by cloud cover or darkness.[38]

For the last several years, the United States has maintained nine operational SR-71s out of the twenty that remain from the thirty-one originally produced. For budgetary reasons that number may be cut to six in the 1989 Fiscal Year, and the entire fleet may be eliminated shortly thereafter.

In addition to those at Beale AFB, California there are presently two overseas SR-71 detachments—one at Kadena AB on Okinawa, and the other at RAF Mildenhall in the United Kingdom. Each detachment has up to two SR-71s. The first such plane arrived at Mildenhall in early 1982 and was augmented by a second late that year to support both USAFE and national intelligence requirements. The second plane was painted with the U.S. Air Force's new low-visibility markings, with all national insignia removed. By now all SR-71As probably are painted in this fashion.[39]

From Beale, SR-71As may be used to provide intelligence to Britain, as they were during the Falklands War or employed to overfly Nicaragua and Cuba. Cuba has been a frequent target of SR-71 flights, although in the large majority of cases the flights have been conducted along the periphery rather than directly over Cuban territory. Given the small width of the island, SR-71 cameras can see a substantial distance into the Cuban interior. In addition, President Carter halted overflights in 1977, in an attempt to facilitate better relations between the United States and Fidel Castro.

Flights against Cuban targets, whether they be peripheral or overflights, have been conducted from Beale AFB under the code name GIANT PLATE, and take between three and one-half and four hours. Overflights were conducted in November 1978 in response to data produced by satellite reconnaissance which indicated that a Soviet freighter had unloaded crates which appeared to hold MiG-23s. The question was whether the MiG-23s were of the interceptor or the ground attack variety; the latter is capable of delivering nuclear weapons and their presence in Cuba would represent a violation of a 1962 pledge by the Soviets not to deploy "offensive" weapons to Cuba. SR-71 photography was able to confirm that the MiG-23s were of the interceptor variety. In late September 1979; a SR-71 overflew Cuba to determine the size and presence of the Soviet "combat" brigade in Cuba that had been the cause of great controversy in the United States.[40]

On October 31, 1985, a SR-71 photographed the Cuban port of Mariel, showing military equipment being unloaded from Soviet ships. According to intelligence analysts, the deliveries included at least two batteries of SA-2 or SA-3 surface-to-air missiles as well as Mi-8 troop transports and six Mi-24D attack helicopters.[41]

In the fall of 1984, cargo on a Soviet freighter that had docked in Nicaragua interested intelligence analysts. Photographs taken by a reconnaissance satellite showed what appeared to be MiG-21 crates. Nicaragua denied this; saying the crates contained Mi-8 helicopters. With White House approval, four or five SR-71 missions were flown over Nicaragua from Beale, the first sortie taking place on November 7, 1984, and the final one on November 11. The ultimate result was that the issue faded away.[42]

From the Kadena base, SR-71s have been used against a variety of Asian targets. Until 1971, SR-71s overflew China (indeed, a SR-71 photographed the entire first Chinese nuclear test). Other prominent Asian targets have included North Korea, Vietnam, and Laos. The SR-71 was used to gather photographic intelligence concerning the Sontay POW (prisoner of war) camp in Vietnam in preparation for the raid that was designed to rescue POWs. In 1986, SR-71 photos of Cam Ranh Bay showed five TU-95 Bear and fifteen TU-16 Badger aircraft—illustrating a Soviet presence. North Korea has claimed that SR-71s made 170 intrusions into North Korean airspace in 1986.[43]

The Middle East is also a major target of SR-71 operations. A SR-71 overflew the Negev Desert during the 1973 Arab-Israeli War on the basis of information that Israel was preparing to arm its Jericho missiles with nuclear warheads. Today, SR-71s fly over the Middle East from Akrotiri Air Base in Cyprus, and some missions monitor the disengagement lines resulting from the 1973 Yom Kippur War. Libya is another Middle Eastern target for the SR-71. Damage assessment photographs of the destruction caused by U.S. Navy aircraft on Benina Airfield were taken on April 15, 1986 by a SR-71 from Mildenhall.[44]

To avoid detection and destruction, the SR-71 is equipped with both a radar detector and an infrared sensor, so, not only the presence but intensity of the tracking can be detected. Further, the radar detector and infrared sensor are linked, so when a SAM is launched it can be detected and then tracked by following the missile's heat trail as it moves up the radar track. Together the detectors can pick up approaching planes or missiles that are 100 miles or more away. Such a detector warned a SR-71 pilot of a North Korean SAM launched on August 26, 1981. That launch represented only one of about a thousand attempts to shoot down an SR-71— all unsuccessful. Other countermeasures include a "range gate system that literally projects the plane's image several miles away when viewed on enemy radar," a means of electronically deflecting approaching missiles, and a powerful radar jammer.[45]

Another aid to its survivability are the SR-71s stealth characteristics. Indeed, the SR-71 was the first stealth aircraft, with a shape that gives a very small radar cross section. Additionally, its black epoxy paint both absorbs hostile radar emissions and limits the emitted heat that could be picked up by an infrared tracking system.[46]

Despite the radar detector, its stealth characteristics, and its operational ceiling of over 80,000 feet, the SR-71 does not overfly the Soviet Union in peacetime. (In peacetime it does fly along the Soviet periphery in both the Far East and Europe for ELINT and imagery-collection purposes.) In the event of a nuclear war, however, the SR-71 would be employed for "post-attack strategic reconnaissance missions," according to an Air Force fact sheet.[47]

From bases at Mildenhall and Kadena, the SR-71As fly a variety of different "tracks"—North Norway/Kola Peninsula, the Baltic, the Mediterranean/Black Sea, and the Sea of Japan/Kamchatka. The Baltic track apparently involves runs made from Mildenhall over Denmark and then over the Baltic parallel to the borders of East Germany, Poland, and the USSR, turning back when the plane reaches the southern tip of Finland.[48]

In its imagery role the plane can photograph installations such as airfields, ports, naval bases, and radar installations on the Soviet periphery. In particular, its high-resolution radar is employed to obtain imagery of Soviet submarine port facilities.[49]

In conducting their peripheral missions on the Siberian coast, the SR-71s often have visitors—MiG-25s. Soviet defector Viktor Belenko explained that the MiG-25s were ineffective in intercepting the SR-71s:

First of all, the SR-71 flies too high and too fast. The MiG-25 cannot reach it or catch it. Secondly . . . the missiles are useless above 27,000 meters [88,582 feet], and as you know, the SR-71 cruises much higher. But even if we could reach, our missiles lack the velocity to overtake the SR-71 if they are fired in a tail chase. And if they are head-on, their guidance systems cannot adjust quickly enought to the high closing speed.[50]

The SR-71 is the second strategic reconnaissance aircraft built by Lockheed. Prior to the 1966 deployment of the SR-71, the only U.S. strategic reconnaissance aircraft was the U-2, code named IDEALIST. More than fifty-five U-2s in various versions are believed to have been built. In 1984 there were eight U-2s in the U.S. arsenal, with Lockheed under contract to build two more in the following two years.[51]

Development of the U-2 by the CIA and Lockheed began in 1954 at the urging of the Eisenhower Administration's Surprise Attack Panel. The U-2 became operational in 1956 and began overflying the Soviet Union that year. The U-2s brought back significant intelligence on airfields, aircraft, missile testing and training, nuclear weapons storage, submarine production, atomic production, and aircraft deployment. The center of U-2 operations against the Soviet Union was Adana, Turkey, where U-2 operations were conducted by the 10-10 Detachment under the cover of the Second Weather Observational Squadron (Provisional).[52]

It was the flight of May 1, 1960, that began in Peshawar, Pakistan and was to conclude 3,788 miles later in Bodo, Norway that brought the U-2 to world attention. The plane was shot down over Sverdlovsk, but its pilot, Francis Gary Powers, survived to stand trial. Powers' plane contained a camera with a rotating 944.6-mm lens which peered out through seven holes in the belly of the plane. It would take 4,000 paired pictures of a 125-2,174 mile strip of the Soviet Union.[53]

The U-2R, the version now used, has a wingspan of 103 feet, a height of 16 feet, and a length of 63 feet. It has a range of over 3,000 miles, a maximum speed of 528 knots at an altitude of 40,000 feet, and an operational ceiling of more than 70,000 feet. As with the SR-71, the U-2R can be equipped with a variety of sensors. The U-2Rs H Camera system, with an electro-optical relay capability, can provide six-inch resolution at its nadir and twelve- to eighteen-inch resolution at a distance of 35 to 40 nm (nautical miles). The Optical Bar Camera is a thirty-inch, focal-length panoramic camera capable of providing six-inch resolution. The Advanced Synthetic Aperture Radar System (ASARS) developed for the U-2R is an all-weather, day-night, standoff imaging system designed to detect, locate, classify, and, in some cases, identify enemy ground targets. The ASARS was developed to collect and process radar imagery in near real-time at ten-foot resolution. U-2Rs are capable of slant photography—looking in the target area at an angle. Thus, one can be flying along the borders of a region and still get pictures inside those borders.[54]

U-2s have been flown from bases in Cyprus, Turkey, Pakistan, Japan, Formosa, Okinawa, the Philippines, Alaska, West Germany, and England. The flights provided photographic intelligence coverage of not only the Soviet Union but the People's Republic of China, North Korea, and the Middle East. With the advent of satellite coverage and the SR-71, reliance on the U-2 was reduced. However, U-2s still provide coverage of some areas.

The U-2s photographic capabilities have been used to document the buildup of military forces in Nicaragua, regularly taking pictures of military construction and arms depots. These flights have operated (most probably) from bases in Texas and from Patrick AFB, Florida. U-2s are also used for overhead reconnaissance directed against other targets in the Caribbean and Central America—for example, Cuba and Grenada. At present, U-2s fly from bases in the United States, Europe (RAF Akrotiri on Cyprus, RAF Mildenhall in the United Kingdom) and Asia (Osan, Korea and Kadena, Okinawa).[55]

In 1988 a new plane was added to the strategic imaging arsenal. The plane, a modified C-135, is known as the RC-135X, or COBRA EYE. It is flown as part of the Optical Aircraft Measurement Program, jointly managed by the Strategic Defense Initiative Organization and the Army. Equipped with a large optical telescope, it flies BURNING VISION missions to observe Soviet ballistic missile tests off Kamchatka.[56]

Several other aircraft are considered tactical reconnaissance planes, although the line between strategic and tactical is not always clear. Just as there is a TENCAP (Tactical Exploitation of National Space Capabilities) program to provide tactical forces with data from national collection systems, there is a NETCAP (National Exploitation of Tactical Capabilities) program to provide national intelligence using tactical systems.

One tactical system is the TR-1. The TR-1 is a copy of the U-2R, and is a single-engine, single-place, fixed-wing aircraft that supports NATO theater intelligence requirements. The TR-1 operates at above 60,000 feet and at 430 miles per hour (mph) and has a range of over 3,000 miles. It is in service with the 17th Reconnaissance Wing, RAF Alconbury, United Kingdom.[57]

The RF-4C, an unarmed version of the F-4C fighter, was designed to collect tactical intelligence by penetrating through enemy defenses during day or night and below the weather. Operated by a two-person crew, it normally carries optical cameras and an infrared sensor. Some RF-4Cs are equipped with side-looking airborne radar. Its KS-87 framing camera can be carried in either a forward oblique, side oblique, or vertical configuration. In addition, the KA-56 panoramic camera provides low-altitude horizon-to-horizon coverage. Its maximum speed is Mach 2.2. Six RF-4Cs are wired to carry a sixty-six-inch Long Range Oblique Photography system. Targets include surface-to-air missile/anti-aircraft artillery sites, vehicles, air fields, assembly areas, personnel, and bridges. At present there are eleven operational squadrons—five active duty and six Air National Guard. The squadrons operate in the Tactical Air Command, USAFE, Pacific Air Forces (PACAF), and the Air National Guard.[58]

Tactical overhead imagery for the Navy is obtained by specially equipped F-14s fitted with the Tactical Air Reconnaissance Pod System (TARPS). The TARPS contains two day-only optical imagery sensors (the KS-87B serial frame camera and KA-99 panoramic camera) and a day-night high resolution infrared imagery

Table 7–2. Defense Attaché Offices with Assigned Aircraft.

Argentina, Buenos Aires	Zaire, Kinshasa
Honduras, Tegucigalpa	Liberia, Monrovia
Egypt, Cairo	Morocco, Rabat
Thailand, Bangkok	Turkey, Ankara
Philippines, Manila	Venezuela, Caracas
Greece, Athens	Pakistan, Islamabad
Indonesia, Jakarta	Ecuador, Quito
Brazil, Brasilia	Bolivia, La Paz
Saudi Arabia, Riyadih	Somalia, Mogadishu
South Africa, Pretoria	Mexico, Mexico City

Source: U.S. Congress, House Committee on Appropriations, *Department of Defense Appropriations for 1987, Part 1* (Washington, D.C.: U.S. Government Printing Office, 1986) p. 655.

sensor. The KS-87B has high-resolution forward oblique or vertical film. The KS-99 has high-resolution panoramic film. There is no data link that would allow the real-time transmission of data.[59]

Three TARPS-equipped F-14s are assigned to one of two F-14 squadrons on each carrier air wing. The plane can operate between 500 and 50,000 feet, has a 500-nm range, and can operate for 2 hours. A total of forty-eight TARPS-equipped F-14s were envisioned in 1983. Targets include land-based installations such as coastal defenses, lines of communications, and foreign ships.[60]

U.S. Defense Attachés also produce intelligence through imagery. Attachés in twenty countries, listed in Table 7–2, have Cessna aircraft to allow them to travel freely by air and often, sensitive cameras are attached.

PROCESSING AND INTERPRETATION

Imagery can be obtained from the visible light portion of the electromagnetic spectrum using either film-based or television type photographic equipment, as described previously.

Even if imagery is not obtained via a digital imaging system, conventional camera signals can be converted into digital signals. The signals can then be computer processed to improve the quantity and quality of information that can be extracted from the imagery. Specifically, computers disassemble a picture into millions of electronic Morse code pulses, and then use mathematical formulas to manipulate the color contrast and intensity of each spot. Each image can be reassembled in various ways to highlight special features and objects that were hidden in the original image.[61] Such processing allows

- building multicolored single images out of several pictures taken in different bands of the spectrum, making the patterns more obvious;
- restoring the shapes of objects by adjusting for the angle of view and lens distortion;

Table 7–3. Joint Imagery Interpretation Keys.

World Tanks and Self-Propelled Artillery	Major Surface Combatants
World Towed Artillery	Minor Surface Combatants
General Transportation Equipment	Mine Warfare Types
World Tactical Vehicles	Amphibious Warfare Types
Combat Engineer Equipment	Naval Auxilliaries
World Mobile Gap and River Crossing Equipment	Intelligence Research Vessels
Coke, Iron, and Steel Industries	Shipborne Electronics
Chemical Industries	Shipborne Weapons
World Electronics	Airfield Installation
World Missiles and Rockets	Petroleum Industries
Miltiary Aircraft of the World	Atomic Energy Facilities
Submarines	

Source: Defense Intelligence Agency Regulation 0-2, "Index of DIA Administrative Publications," December 10, 1982, pp. 35–36.

- changing the amount of contrast between objects and backgrounds;
- sharpening out-of-focus images;
- restoring ground details largely obscured by clouds;
- electro-optical subtraction, in which earlier pictures are subtracted from later ones—making unchanged buildings in a scene disappear while new objects such as missile silos under construction remain;
- enhancing shadows; and
- surpressing glint.[62]

Such processing plays a crucial role in easing the burden on photogrammetrists and photo interpreters. Photogrammetrists are responsible for determining the size of objects from overhead photographs using, along with other data, the shadows cast by objects. Photo interpreters are trained to provide information about the nature of the objects in photographs—based on what type of crates carry MiG-21s, what a Soviet IRBM site or a Soviet fiber optics factory looks like from 150 miles in space. Such information is provided in interpretation keys such as those listed in Table 7-3. Thus, an

> interpreter might see a picture with excavations, mine headframes, derricks, piles of waste, conveyor belts, bulldozers and power shovels, but with just a few buildings. His key would suggest that this is a mine. Special kinds of equipment, the tone or color of the waste piles and the ore piles, as well a knowledge of local geology, might further indicate that this was a uranium mine.[63]

The ultimate utility of any imaging system is a function of several factors, the most prominent being resolution. Resolution can be defined as the minimum size of an object for it to be measurable and identifiable by photo analysts. The higher the resolution, the greater the detail that can be extracted from a photo. It should be noted that resolution is a product of several factors—the optical or imaging system, atmospheric conditions, and orbital parameters, for example.[64]

Table 7–4. Resolution Required for Different Levels of Interpretation.

Target	Detection	General Identification	Precise Identification	Description	Technical Intelligence
Bridge	20 ft.	15 ft.	5 ft.	3 ft.	1 ft.
Communications radar/radio	10 ft./10 ft.	3 ft./5 ft.	1 ft./1 ft.	6 in./6 in.	1.5 in./6 in.
Supply dump	5 ft.	2 ft.	1 ft.	1 in.	1 in.
Troop units (bivouac, road)	20 ft.	7 ft.	4 ft.	1 ft.	3 in.
Airfield facilities	20 ft.	15 ft.	10 ft.	1 ft.	6 in.
Rockets and artillery	3 ft.	2 ft.	6 in.	2 in.	.4 in.
Aircraft	15 ft.	5 ft.	3 ft.	6 in.	1 in.
Command and control hq.	10 ft.	5 ft.	3 ft.	6 in.	1 in.
Missile sites (SSM/SAM)	10 ft.	5 ft.	2 ft.	1 ft.	3 in.
Surface ships	25 ft.	15 ft.	2 ft.	1 ft.	3 in.
Nuclear weapons components	8 ft.	5 ft.	1 ft.	1 in.	.4 in.
Vehicles	5 ft.	2 ft.	1 ft.	2 in.	1 in.
Land minefields	30 ft.	20 ft.	3 ft.	1 in.	—
Ports and harbors	100 ft.	50 ft.	20 ft.	10 ft.	1 ft.
Coasts and landing beaches	100 ft.	15 ft.	10 ft.	5 ft.	3 in.
Railroad yards and shops	100 ft.	50 ft.	20 ft.	5 ft.	2 ft.
Roads	30 ft.	20 ft.	6 ft.	2 ft.	6 in.
Urban area	200 ft.	100 ft.	10 ft.	10 ft.	1 ft.
Terrain	—	300 ft.	15 ft.	5 ft.	6 in.
Surfaced submarines	100 ft.	20 ft.	5 ft.	3 ft.	1 in.

Source: Adapted from U.S. Congress, Senate Committee on Commerce, Science, and Transportation, *NASA Authorization for Fiscal Year 1978, Part 3* (Washington, D.C.: U.S. Government Printing Office, 1977), pp. 1642–43; and Bhupendra Jasani, ed., *Outer Space—A New Dimension in the Arms Race* Cambridge, Mass.: Oelgeschlager, Gunn & Hain, 1982), p. 47.

The degree of resolution required depends on the specificity of the intelligence desired. Five different interpretation tasks have been differentiated—*Detection* involves the location of a class of units, objects, or activity of military interests. *General identification* involves the determination of general target type while *precise identification* involves discrimination within target type of known types. *Description* involves specification of the size-dimension, configuration-layout, components-construction, and number of units. *Technical intelligence* involves determination of the specific characteristics and performance capabilities of weapons and equipment.[65] Table 7-4 gives estimates of the resolution required for interpretation tasks.

Factors other than resolution that are considered significant in evaluating the utility of an imaging system include coverage speed, readout speed, analysis speed, reliability, and enhancement capability. Coverage speed is the area that can be surveyed in a given time, readout speed is the speed with which the information is processed into a form that is meaningful to photo interpreters, and reliability is the fraction of time the system produces useful data. Enhancement capability refers to whether the initial images can be enhanced to draw out more useful data.[66]

NOTES TO CHAPTER 7

1. William E. Burrows, *Deep Black: Space Espionage and National Security* (New York: Random House, 1987), p. 28.
2. Ibid., p. 32.
3. See Jeffrey T. Richelson, *American Espionage and the Soviet Target* (New York: William Morrow, 1987), p. 16.
4. Bhupendra Jasani, *Outer Space—Battlefield of the Future?* (New York: Crane, Russak, 1978), p. 12.
5. Farouk el-Baz, "EO Imaging Will Replace Film in Reconnaissance," *Defense Systems Review* (October 1983): 48–52.
6. Richard D. Hudson Jr. and Jacqueline W. Hudson, "The Military Applications of Remote Sensing by Infrared," *Proceedings of the IEEE* 63, no. 1 (1975): 104–28.
7. Hudson and Hudson, "The Military Applications of Remote Sensing by Infrared"; Bruce G. Blair and Garry D. Brewer, "Verifying SALT," in William Potter, ed., *Verification and SALT: The Challenge of Strategic Deception* (Boulder, Colo.: Westview, 1980), pp. 7–48.
8. Homer Jensen, L.C. Graham, Leonard J. Porcello, and Emmet N. Leith, "Side-looking Airborne Radar," *Scientific American* 237 (October 1977): 84–95.
9. Author's interview.
10. D.C. King-Hele, et al., *The RAE Table of Earth Satellites 1957–1980* (New York: Facts on File, 1982), p. 474.
11. John Pike, "Reagan Prepares for War in Outer Space," *Counterspy* 7, no. 1 (1982): 17–22; James Bamford, "America's Supersecret Eyes in Space," *The New York Times Magazine*, January 13, 1985, pp. 39ff.
12. Correspondence from Anthony Kenden (May 23, 1985).
13. Bamford, "America's Supersecret Eyes in Space."
14. George Lardner, Jr., "Satellite Unchanged from Manual Bought By Soviets, U.S. Official Says," *Washington Post*, October 10, 1985, p. A20.
15. "Inside the Rescue Mission," *Newsweek*, July 12, 1982, p. 19.
16. "Soviet Strategic Bomber Photographed at Ramenskoye," *Aviation Week and Space Technology*, December 14, 1981, p. 17; Max White, "U.S. Satellite Reconnaissance During the Falklands Conflict," Earth Satellite Research Unit, Department of Mathematics, University of Aston, Birmingham, England, n.d.
17. "Satellite Pictures Show Soviet CVN Towering Above Nikolaiev Shipyard," *Jane's Defence Weekly*, August 11, 1984, pp. 171–73; Lardner, "Satellite Unchanged from Manual Bought by Soviets, U.S. Officials Say."
18. "Satellite Pictures Show Soviet CVN Towering Above Nikolaiev Shipyard."
19. Michael Gordon, "U.S. Says Soviet Complies on Some Arms Issues," *New York Times*, November 24, 1985, p. 18.
20. Private information.
21. "How Satellites May Help to Sell SALT," *U.S. News and World Report*, May 21, 1979, pp. 25–26; "Missile Disguise," *Aviation Week and Space Technology*, September 29, 1980, p. 17; "Soviets Build Directed Energy Weapon," *Aviation Week and Space Technology*, July 28, 1980, pp. 47–50.

22. "Industry Observer," *Aviation Week and Space Technology*, September 9, 1985, p. 150;
     "Titan 34D Booster Failed Following Premature Shutdown of Aerojet Engine," *Aviation Week and Space Technology*, November 18, 1985, p. 26.
23. Jack Cushman, "Space Shuttle Explosion Throws Military Programs Into Disarray,"
     Defense Week, February 3, 1986, pp. 2–4.
24. "Titan Explosion Cripples U.S. Launch, Surveillance Capability," *Aviation Week and Space Technology*, April 28, 1986, pp. 16–19; William J. Broad, "2 Years of Failure
     End as U.S. Lofts Big Titan Rocket," *New York Times*, October 27, 1987, pp. A1, C4.
25. "KH-11 Overruns Said to Slow Development of Follow-On Spacecraft," *Aerospace Daily*, January 23, 1984, pp. 16–17.
26. Deborah G. Meyer, "DOD Likely to Spend $250 Billion on C^{3}I Through 1990,"
     Armed Forces Journal International (February 1985): 72–84; Pat Ohlendorf, "The
     New Breed of High-Tech Peacekeeper," *Maclean's*, January 23, 1984, pp. 52–53;
     Walter Pincus, "Hill Conferees Propose Test of Space Arms," *Washington Post*, July
     11, 1984, pp. A1, A13; Edward Welles, "The New Right Stuff," *San Jose Mercury News*, January 8, 1984, p. 13.
27. "New Payload Could Boost Shuttle Cost," *Aviation Week and Space Technology*,
     August 14, 1978, pp. 16–17.
28. Bob Woodward, *Veil: The Secret Wars of the CIA 1981–1987* (New York: Simon & Schuster, 1987), p. 221.
29. Andrew Cockburn, *The Threat: Inside the Soviet Military Machine* (New York: Random House, 1983), p. 19; Paul E. Sherr, Arnold H. Glasser, James C. Barnes,
     and James H. Williand, *Worldwide Cloud Cover Distributions for Use in Computer Simulations* (Concord, Mass.: Allied Research Associates, 1968), p. 5; Philip Klass,
     "U.S. Scrutinizing New Radar," *Aviation Week and Space Technology*, August 22, 1983, pp. 19–20.
30. "Space Reconnaissance Dwindles," *Aviation Week and Space Technology*, October 6,
     1980, pp. 18–20; "Navy Will Develop All-Weather Ocean Monitor Satellite," *Aviation Week and Space Technology*, August 28, 1978, p. 50; Craig Covault, "USAF, NASA
     Discuss Shuttle Use for Satellite Maintenance," *Aviation Week and Space Technology*,
     December 17, 1984, pp. 14–16; "Washington Roundup," *Aviation Week and Space Technology*, June 4, 1979, p. 11; Robert C. Toth, "Anaheim Firm May Have Sought
     Spy Satellite Data," *Los Angeles Times*, October 10, 1982, pp. 1, 32; Bill Gertz,
     "New Spy Satellite, Needed to Monitor Treaty, Sits on Ground," *Washington Times*,
     October 20, 1987, p. A5; Woodward, *Veil*, p. 221; Bill Gertz, "Senate Panel Asks
     For Radar Funds," *Washington Times*, April 5, 1988, p. A4.
31. Clarence L. "Kelly" Johnson with Maggie Smith, *More than My Share of it All*
     (Washington, D.C.: Smithsonian Institution Press, 1985), pp. 136, 144.
32. Donald E. Fink, "U-2s, SR-71s Merged in One Wing," *Aviation Week and Space Technology*, May 10, 1976, p. 83; Jay Miller, *Lockheed SR-71* (Austin, Tex.: Aerofax,
     1983), p. 5.
33. Bill Yenne, *SAC: A Primer of Modern Strategic Airpower* (Novato, Calif.: Presidio Press, 1985), p. 34.
34. Ibid.
35. Ibid.
36. Miller, *Lockheed SR-71*, p. 3; Burrows, *Deep Black*, p. 160; Johnson with Smith,
     More than My Share of it All, p. 195; Fink, "U-2s, SR-71s Merged in One Wing."

37. Johnson with Smith, *More than My Share of it All*, p. 144.
38. Burrows, *Deep Black*, pp. 164–65.
39. Martin Streetly, "U.S. Airborne ELINT Systems, Part 4: The Lockheed SR-71A," *Jane's Defence Weekly*, April 13, 1985, pp. 634–35; Joint Chiefs of Staff, *JCS 1982 Posture Statement* (Washington, D.C.: U.S. Government Printing Office, 1981), p. 198; "Second SR-71 Deployed to England," *Aviation Week and Space Technology*, January 31, 1983, p. 59.
40. Paul F. Crickmore, *Lockheed SR-71 Blackbird* (London: Osprey, 1986), pp. 164, 166; "Friends in Need, Friends Indeed," *Time*, November 18, 1985, p. 65; "News in Brief," *Jane's Defence Weekly*, January 17, 1987, p. 58.
41. "Friends in Need, Friend Indeed."
42. Crickmore, *Lockheed SR-71 Blackbird*, p. 166.
43. Colonel Asa Bates, "National Technical Means of Verification," *Royal United Services Institute Journal* 123, no. 2 (June 1978): 64–73; Benjamin Schemmer, *The Raid* (New York: Harper & Row, 1975), p. 69; "Pentagon Confirms Soviet Presence at Cam Ranh Bay," *Aviation Week and Space Technology*, February 16, 1987, pp. 26–27; "News in Brief," *Jane's Defence Weekly*, January 17, 1987, p. 58.
44. Colonel William V. Kennedy, *Intelligence Warfare* (New York: Crescent, 1983), p. 105; Crickmore, *Lockheed SR-71 Blackbird*, p. 188.
45. David Binder, "Radar Detector Aboard SR-71 Alerted Pilot to Missile's Attack," *New York Times*, August 29, 1981, p. 3; Burrows, *Deep Black*, p. 161.
46. Burrows, *Deep Black*, p. 161.
47. U.S. Air Force Fact Sheet 82-36, "SR-71," Secretary of the Air Force, Office of Public Affairs, 1982.
48. William Arkin, "Current Intelligence Collection: Its Effect on Crisis Mangement and Policy Formulation," Paper presented at International Studies Association, Washington, D.C., March 5–9, 1985; Dick Van der Art, *Aerial Espionage: Secret Intelligence Flights by East and West* (New York: Arco/Prentice Hall, 1984), p. 71.
49. Burrows, *Deep Black*, p. 165.
50. John Barron, *MiG Pilot: The Final Escape of Lt. Belenko* (New York: Avon, 1980), p. 174.
51. "U-2 Facts and Figures," *Air Force Magazine*, January 1976, p. 45; Joint Chiefs of Staff, *JCS Posture Statement 1982*; "Lockheed Back into U-2 Spy Plane Business," *Defense Week*, February 22, 1983, p. 16.
52. David Wise and Thomas B. Ross, *The U-2 Affair* (New York: Random House, 1962), p. 56.
53. Ibid., p. 11.
54. Bates, "National Technical Means of Verification"; United States Air Force Fact Sheet, 83-5, "U-2," Secretary of the Air Force, Office of Public Affairs; Private information.
55. Wise and Ross, "The U-2 Affair"; Howard Silber, "SAC U-2s Provided Nicaraguan Pictures," *Omaha World Herald*, March 10, 1982, p. 2; Brian Bennett, Tony Powell, and John Adams, *The USAF Today*, (London: West London Aviation Group, 1981), p. 135.
56. Craig Covault, "Alaskan Tanker, Reconnaissance Mission Capabilities Expanded," *Aviation Week and Space Technology*, June 6, 1988, pp. 70–72.

57. Office of Legislative Liaison, Secretary of the Air Force *Systems Information Briefs for Members of Congress*, (Washington, D.C.: Department of the Air Force, 1987), p. 45.
58. Ibid., p. 46.
59. Private information.
60. Private information.
61. Paul Bennett, *Strategic Surveillance* (Cambridge, Mass.: Union of Concerned Scientists, 1979), p. 5.
62. Richard A. Scribner, Theodore J. Ralston, and William D. Mertz, *The Verification Challenge: Problems and Promise of Strategic Nuclear Arms Control Verification* (Boston: Birkhauser, 1985), p. 70; John F. Ebersole and James C. Wyant, "Real-Time Optical Subtraction of Photographic Imagery for Difference Detection," *Applied Optics* 15, no. 4 (1976): 871-76.
63. Scribner, et al., *The Verification Challenge*, p. 69.
64. James Fusca, "Space Surveillance," *Space/Aeronautics* (June 1964): 92-103.
65. U.S. Congress, Senate Committee on Commerce, Science, and Transportation, *NASA Authorization for Fiscal Year 1978, Part 3* (Washington, D.C.: U.S. Government Printing Office, 1977), pp. 1642-43.
66. Ibid.; National Photographic Interpretation Center, "Problems of Photographic Imagery Analysis," *Declassified Documents Reference System 1981-13B.*

8 SIGNALS INTELLIGENCE

Signals intelligence (SIGINT) is traditionally considered to be one of the most important and sensitive forms of intelligence. The interception of foreign signals can provide data on a nation's diplomatic, scientific, and economic plans or events as well as the characteristics of radars, spacecraft and weapons systems.

SIGINT can be broken down into five components:

- communications intelligence (COMINT)
- electronics intelligence (ELINT)
- radar intelligence (RADINT)
- laser intelligence (LASINT)
- non-imaging infrared.

As its name indicates, COMINT is intelligence obtained by the interception, processing, and analysis of the communications of foreign governments or groups, excluding radio and television broadcasts. The communications may take a variety of forms—voice, Morse code, radioteletype or facsimile. The communications may be encrypted, or transmitted in the clear.

The targets of COMINT operations are varied. The most traditional COMINT target is diplomatic communications—the communications from each nation's capital to its diplomatic establishments around the world. The United States has intercepted and deciphered the diplomatic communications of a variety of nations—Britain during the 1956 Suez Crisis, Libya's communications to its East Berlin People's Bureau prior to the bombing of a nightclub in West Berlin in 1985, Iraq's communications to its embassy in Japan in the 1970s.

The United States also targets the communications between different components of a large number of governments. On some occasions both components are located

167

within the country, on other occasions at least one is located outside national boundaries. Communications that may be targeted include those between government officials, different ministries, a ministry or agency and subordinate units throughout the country and abroad, arms factories, military units during exercises and operations, and police and security forces and their headquarters. More specifically, the United States intercepts communications between the Soviet Ministry of Defense and Military District headquarters, and between Military District headquarters and units in the field; between transmitter stations and Soviet submarines; between the President of Egypt and his subordinates (including the time when Egypt was holding the hijackers of the *Achille Lauro*); and between military units at all levels in the Philippines.

In 1980, U.S. intercepts of Soviet communications generated a fear that the Soviets were about to invade Iran. In 1983 intercepts allowed the United States to piece together the details concerning the sinking of a Soviet submarine in the North Pacific.[1]

At times, entire sets of targets may be dropped or have their coverage dramatically increased. In the early 1970s the United States dropped COMINT coverage of the Soviet civil defense network (coverage was later resumed). In 1983 it began an all-source intelligence program (that included COMINT) to improve intelligence on the Soviet prison camp system, with the specific intent of issuing a study that would embarrass the Soviets. The intelligence was intended to determine the location of the camps, existing conditions, and the number of political prisoners.

Governmental communications do not exhaust the set of COMINT targets. The communications of political parties or guerilla movements may also be targeted. The communications of the African National Congress in South Africa, the El Salvadoran rebels, and the Greek Socialist Party are all likely targets of COMINT activities. In addition, the communications of terrorist groups can also be COMINT targets—both to permit understanding of how the group functions and the personalities of its leaders, and to allow prediction of where and how the groups will strike next.

Another major set of COMINT targets are associated with economic activity (of both the legal and illegal variety)—for example, the communications of multinational corporations and narcotics traffickers. In 1970, the predecessor to the Drug Enforcement Administration informed the NSA that it had "a requirement for any and all COMINT information which reflects illicit traffic in narcotics and dangerous drugs." Specific areas of interest included organizations and individuals engaged in such activities, the distribution of narcotics, narcotic cultivation and production centers, efforts to control the traffic in narcotics, and all violations of U.S. laws concerning narcotics and dangerous drugs.[2]

Electronic intercept operations are intended to produce electronic intelligence (ELINT) by intercepting the non-communication signals of military and civilian hardware, excluding those signals resulting from atomic detonations. Under NSA project KILTING, all ELINT signals are stored in computerized reference files containing the most up-to-date technical information about the signals.

The earliest of ELINT targets were World War II air defense radar systems. The objective was to gather emanations that would allow the identification of the presence and operating characteristics of the radars—information that could be used to circumvent or neutralize the radars (through direct attack or electronic countermeasures) during bombing raids. Information desired included frequencies, signal strengths, pulse lengths and rates, and other specifications. Since that time, intelligence, space tracking, and ballistic missile early-warning radars have joined the list of ELINT targets.

In the early 1950s the primary targets were Soviet Bloc (including PRC) radars. Soviet radars remain a prime ELINT target. Monitoring Soviet radars also has an arms control verification aspect, since the 1972 ABM Treaty restricts the use of radars in an "ABM mode." During the Vietnam war, North Vietnamese radars were also major targets. Libyan and Iranian radars are clearly prime targets in the late 1980s.

A subcategory of ELINT is Foreign Instrumentation Signals Intelligence (FISINT). Foreign instrumentation signals are electromagnetic emissions associated with the testing and operational deployment of aerospace, surface, and subsurface systems that have military or civilian applications. Such signals include, but are not limited to, signals from telemetry, beaconing, electronic interrogators, tracking-fusing-aiming/command systems, and video data links.[3]

A subcategory of FISINT is Telemetry Intelligence (TELINT). Telemetry is the set of signals by which a missile, missile stage, or missile warhead sends, back to earth, data about its performance during a test flight. The data relate to structural stress, rocket motor thrust, fuel consumption, guidance system performance, and the physical conditions of the ambient environment. Intercepted telemetry can provide data to estimate the number of warheads carried by a given missile, its payload and throw-weight, the probable size of its warheads, and the accuracy with which the warheads are guided at the point of release from the missile's post-boost vehicles.[4]

Radar intelligence—the intelligence obtained from the use of non-imaging radar—is similar to ELINT in that no intercepted communications are involved. However, RADINT does not depend on the interception of another object's electronic emanations. It is the radar which emanates electronic signals—radio waves—and the deflection of those signals allows for intelligence to be derived. Information that can be obtained from RADINT includes flight paths, velocity, maneuvering, trajectory, and angle of descent.

Two further categories of SIGINT were listed in the proposed National Security Agency charter of 1980—information derived from the collection and processing of (1) non-imaging infrared, and (2) coherent light signals. The former involves sensors that can detect the absence/presence and movement of an object via temperature. The term "coherent light signal" refers to lasers, and hence this category includes the interception of laser communications, as well as the emissions from Soviet laser research and development activities.[5]

The ease with which signals (whether communications or electronic signals) can be intercepted and understood depends on three factors: the method of transmission, the frequencies employed, and the encipherment system (or lack of) used to conceal the signals meaning form unauthorized personnel.

The most secure form of transmission is that sent by cables, either land lines or underwater cables. Communications or other signals transmitted through such cables cannot be snatched out of the air. Interception of cable traffic has involved physically tapping into the cables or using "induction" devices that are placed in the proximity of the cables and maintenance of equipment at the point of access. This might be unobtainable with respect to hardened and protected internal land-lines, the type of landline that carries much high-priority, secret command and control communications. Undersea cables are most vulnerable since the messages transmitted by them are then transmitted by microwave relay once the cable reaches land.

A tremendous volume of communications is sent via satellite systems. Domestic and international telephone messages, and military and business communications are among those regularly transmitted via satellite using ultra, very, super, and extremely high frequencies (UHF, VHF, SHF and EHF). Thus, the United States has established major programs for the interception of Soviet and international commercial satellite messages. By locating satellite dishes at the proper locations, an enormous volume of traffic can be intercepted. Ground stations that send messages to satellites have antennas that direct the signals to the satellite with great accuracy; satellite antennas, on the other hand, are smaller and the signals they send back to earth are less narrowly focused—perhaps covering several thousand square miles.[6]

Often, communications that are transmitted through part of their path by satellite are sent via microwave towers through the rest of their path. In other cases, particularly telephone calls within a country, microwave towers serve as the entire means of transmission and reception. For example, in Canada, the majority of telephone calls are transmitted via microwave. As one observer has written with regard to microwave relay towers:

> With modern communications, "target" messages travel not simply over individually tappable wires like those that connect the ordinary telephone, but as part of entire message streams, which can contain up to 970 individual message circuits, and have voice, telegram, telex and high speed data bunched together.[7]

Microwave signals can be intercepted by two means—(1) ground stations near the invisible line connecting the two microwave towers, or (2) by space collection systems, if the area of transmission is within the footprint of the system.

Radio is the most traditional means to transmit signals—including communications, missile telemetry, and foreign instrumentation signals. The accessibility of radio signals to interception will often depend on the frequencies upon which the signal is transmitted and the signal's geographic location. Messages transmitted at lower frequencies (ELF, VLF, LF, HF) travel for long distances since they bounce off the atmosphere and come down in locations far from the transmitting and intended receiving locations. On the other hand, data sent at higher frequencies will pass through the atmosphere and out into space. To intercept such higher frequency signals, intercept stations must be within line of sight of the radio communications. The curvature of the earth can therefore make monitoring from ground-based sites impossible. Former CIA Deputy Director for Intelligence Sayre Stevens has written of the Soviet ballistic missile defense test center at Sary Shagan that:

> It lies deeply enough within the USSR to make it difficult to monitor from peripheral intelligence-gathering sites along the border. Because flight test operations at Sary Shagan can be conducted well below the radio-horizon from such external monitoring locations, the Soviet Union has been able to conceal the details of its activities at Sary Shagan for many years.[8]

Under such conditions, geosynchronous space collection systems may be necessary to collect such signals.

Two additional methods of communication that are targets of interception operations are walkie-talkie and radio-telephone communications. Walkie-talkie communications are employed during military exercises as well as during emergency situations such as Chernobyl. Radio-telephone communications are used by government officials as they travel in their limousines. Since walkie-talkie traffic, particularly in the Soviet Union and China, may occur over areas not accessible to ground stations, satellite interception may be required. On the other hand, radio-telephone traffic is particularly large and significant in national capital areas, where embassy-based listening posts are often found.

Once intercepted, signals have to be processed. If communications are sent without encipherment or scrambling, then the only processing needed may be translation. Communications may be sent in the clear either because they are considered too low level to justify the time and expense for protection, or because the method of transmission (e.g., cable) is believed immune to interception.

Electronic signals sent in the clear still need to be interpreted. Thus, telemetry signals on all channels may be transmitted as numbers. The variables being measured and the units of measurement must be inferred by correlating data on missile maneuvers with the intercepted telemetry. For example, measurement may be made concerning different types of events: one-time events (e.g., the firing of explosive bolts or separation of RVs from the post-boost bus), discontinuous events (e.g., adjustments to the guidance system during flight), and continuous events (e.g., fuel flow, motor burn, or acceleration of the missile during the boost phase). These events can be expressed in terms of absolute values, arbitrary values (a one to ten scale), relative values (percentages) or inferential values. It will not necessarily be evident what the particular characteristic to which an intercepted reading refers or the particular values used. A fuel tank reading may be given as "30," which could refer either to a tank that is 30 percent full or 30 percent empty. The temperature in the rocket motor combustion chamber can be measured from the temperature of another part known to have a specific temperature relative to that in the chamber.

Communications or electronic signals may be either encrypted or scrambled, complicating the translation process. Diplomatic communications are traditionally enciphered. The sophistication of the encipherment and the quality of the operators determines whether such ciphers can be broken. Conversations via radio and radiotelephone can be scrambled and unscrambled. Non-communications signals may also be encrypted, as are a large portion of Soviet missile telemetry signals.

Interception of signals involves a massive effort, employing space and airborne collectors, ground stations, embassy listening posts, ships and submarines.

SPACE COLLECTION

The United States operates three basic types of satellite systems to collect foreign signals. Since 1962 the United States has been operating low-earth orbiting satellites whose mission has been to intercept the signals emitted by Soviet, Chinese, and other nations' air defense, ABM, and early-warning radars. The satellites, known as "ferrets" in the popular literature, are actually referred to as "balls" within the U.S. intelligence community.

The first ferret was launched by a Thor-Agena B on May 15, 1962, into an orbit with a 190-mile perigee and 392-mile apogee. Between the first launch and July 16, 1971, seventeen satellites of the initial type were launched, about one to three satellites being launched each year. The inclination of the earlier ferrets was approximately eighty-two degrees, while the inclination of the later satellites was seventy-five degrees. Likewise, the orbit changed after the first several launches to a more circular orbit, with about 300 miles separating the satellite from the earth. Switches to new boosters in June 1963 and October 1968 may have indicated new generations of ferrets coming into operation.[9]

A second class of ferret satellites was put into operation beginning in August 1963. Unlike the first class, which were launched as the only payload on the rocket, the new class served as the secondary payload to imaging satellites. As with the first class, elliptical orbits of 180 by 250 miles gave way to more circular orbits, in the vicinity of 300 miles above the earth.[10] By 1972, launches no longer placed just ferret satellites in orbit. From 1972 to the present only ferret subsatellites have been launched. In general, the satellites were launched as the secondary payload on launches of the KH-9 imaging satellite. The final KH-9 was orbited in 1984. If subsatellite launches are to continue once the presently operational ferrets expire, they will have to be piggybacked with a different primary payload. It is possible that the KH-11 satellite also has a ferret capability.

The exact number of ferrets within each class is not publicly known. What is known is that the code names for the satellites have had a common theme—they were all named after female sex symbols. Two of the satellites operating in the late 1970s were code-named RAQUEL and FARRAH, while earlier satellites had been code-named BRIDGET and MARILYN.[11]

In addition to ferret satellites, the United States is presently using two or three types of geosynchronous satellites. In the early 1970s the United States began operating a set of geosynchronous satellites which were given the code name RHYOLITE. According to the most recent account, a total of five RHYOLITE spacecraft were placed into orbit, with one launch failure. RHYOLITEs were launched on June 19, 1970, December 20, 1972 (a failure), March 6, 1973, May 23, 1977, December 11, 1977, and April 7, 1978; all were launched from Cape Canaveral, Florida using an Atlas-Agena D booster.[12]

By the time the fourth satellite was in orbit, a two-station arrangement had emerged. Two of the satellites apparently were stationed near the Horn of Africa, at 45 degrees east, to receive telemetry signals transmitted from liquid-fueled ICBMs launched from Tyuratam in a northeasterly direction toward the Kamchatka Peninsula impact zone. Another two spacecraft were stationed farther east, over Borneo, at 115 degrees east, to monitor Soviet solid-propellant missiles such as the SS-16 and the SS-20 IRBM, launched from the Soviet Union's northern space launch facility at Plesetsk.[13] The respective satellite footprints provided coverage of almost all the USSR and Africa, Europe, Asia, and the Middle East.

In addition to the telemetry signals from Soviet and Chinese missile tests, RHYOLITE satellites reportedly also engaged in a variety of COMINT activities. The satellites apparently were used to intercept Soviet and Chinese telephone and radio communications across the VHF, UHF, and microwave frequency bands. Robert Lindsey has written that the satellites "could monitor Communist microwave radio and long-distance telephone traffic over much of the European landmass, eavesdropping on a Soviet commissar in Moscow talking to his mistress in Yalta or on a general talking to his lieutenants across the great continent."[14]

Walkie-talkie traffic generated by Soviet military exercises, which fall in the VHF-UHF range, also were regularly monitored by RHYOLITE satellites. Beyond the Soviet Union, RHYOLITE satellites intercepted communications from China, Vietnam, Indonesia, Pakistan, and Lebanon.[15]

The RHYOLITE project was described by former CIA official Victor Marchetti as

a very interesting project, a very much advanced project in terms of technology, and a very desirable project because getting information of the type that we wanted and needed on Soviet ICBM testing, antiballistic missile programs, anti-satellite programs, and the like, much of this activity of course takes place in eastern Siberia and central Asia, getting information on the Chinese ICBM program.[16]

The RHYOLITE program suffered a serious setback in 1975 when a TRW employee, Christopher Boyce, and his boyhood friend, Andrew Daulton Lee, sold the KGB technical details about RHYOLITE. In accordance with standard security practice, the NRO changed RHYOLITE's code name to AQUACADE.[17] At this time it is probable that none of the compromised satellites are operational.

The first satellite of a follow-on generation, code-named MAGNUM, was launched from the space shuttle *Discovery* on January 25, 1985. The satellite is reported to have two huge parabolic antennas, one of which is intended to intercept communications and telemetry signals. According to one account, MAGNUM is stationed over the western Soviet Union and its second antenna is to be used to relay the intercepted data to another satellite (possibly the SDS) for transmission to the Pine Gap, Australia ground control station.[18] MAGNUM may, in fact, be stationed over Borneo, in which case its second antenna would transmit the data directly to Pine Gap.

Exactly how much MAGNUM is an improvement over RHYOLITE/AQUA-CADE is not known publicly. One possibility is that MAGNUM will be able to pick up lower powered signals than RHYOLITE, such as "turned-down" telemetry. MAGNUM's increased power might come from bigger antennas, and the satellite's potential is suggested by a project being undertaken for the NASA by Lockheed's Missile and Space Company. The project involves unfurling an antenna in space from the space shuttle's cargo bay. The antenna, resembling an umbrella, will be nearly twice the size of a football field, and so sensitive to low-powered signals from earth that it would pick up broadcasts from radios the size of a wristwatch.[19]

In addition, MAGNUM may have some stealth or spoofing capabilities that make it harder for the Soviet Union to find and jam its signals—as has been alleged they were doing to AQUACADE in recent years. In 1984, Richard Perle, Assistant Secretary of Defense for International Security Policy charged in testimony before the House Foreign Affairs Committee that the USSR had begun jamming telemetry-monitoring satellites to prevent collection of even the encrypted data. The jamming was alleged to be electronically precise, to have begun sometime after the Soviets shot down Korean Airlines Flight 007 in 1983, and to occur only during missile testing. The distinctive visual and radar image of MAGNUM will ordinarily allow the Soviets to know its location and mission.[20] Hence, some sort of stealth technology would be required to hide the satellite from Soviet detection.

On June 10, 1978, the first of another class of geosynchronous SIGINT satellites was launched. Originally code-named CHALET, it was renamed VORTEX after its original code name was revealed in the press.[21]

VORTEX's original mission was strictly COMINT-related. However, after the loss of Iranian ground stations and the discovery of the sale of RHYOLITE documents to the KGB, VORTEX was modified to intercept Soviet telemetry. The first modified VORTEX was launched on October 1, 1979; subsequent launches occurred on October 31, 1981 and in 1984.[22]

The primary targets of VORTEX are in the Soviet Union. At the height of VORTEX operations at least three VORTEX satellites were operational. One covered Eastern Europe and the Western USSR, the other the central USSR, and the third the eastern portion of the Soviet Union, as well as non-Soviet targets in their footprints. During the Chernobyl incident the VORTEX responsible for monitoring the western USSR was employed to intercept all communications within several hundred miles of the accident site, including those of the military, party, government and security forces.

Unlike AQUACADE, MAGNUM, or VORTEX, the other class of SIGINT satellites are neither in geosynchronous orbit nor are launched from Cape Canaveral. Rather, this class—known as JUMPSEAT—has been launched into sixty-three-degree inclined, highly elliptical orbits (200 by 24,000 miles) with Titan 3B-Agena D boosters from Vandenberg AFB, California. Approximately four JUMPSEATs have been launched since the first launch on March 5, 1975. In its highly elliptical orbit, JUMPSEAT "hovers" over the Soviet Union for eight to nine hours at a time. Its primary mission is to monitor Soviet ABM radars.[23]

There appears to be several new generations of SIGINT satellites in development, probably including JUMPSEAT and VORTEX follow-ons. One of those satellites will monitor Soviet laser activities.

Satellite operations are supported by a worldwide network of ground control stations, stations that conduct housekeeping operations as well as receive information from the satellites. A key element in the network is the HQ Consolidated Space Test Center (HQ CSTC), formerly the Air Force Satellite Control Facility at Onizuka AFS (Sunnyvale). The HQ CSTC has ground stations across the globe—Vandenberg AFB; New Boston, New Hampshire; Kaena Point, Hawaii; Thule (AB), Greenland; Mahe, the Seychelles; Andersen AFB, Guam; Oakhanger, England. The stations perform basic housekeeping functions—communicating commands to the satellites, altering orbits, checking the equipment on board. The stations also receive ELINT data from the JUMPSEAT and ferret satellites.[24]

In addition to the HQ CSTC, several more specialized stations exist to control and receive signals from SIGINT satellites. Ft. Meade (NSA headquarters) is itself able to receive data from the satellites, but three overseas ground stations are backbone of the network: Pine Gap, Australia; Menwith Hill, United Kingdom; and Bad Aibling, Germany.[25]

RHYOLITE/AQUACADE and MAGNUM satellites have been controlled since the beginning of their respective programs from a facility in Alice Springs, Australia, commonly known as Pine Gap. Officially, the facility is the Joint Defence Space Research Facility and is code-named MERINO. The facility consists of seven large radomes, a huge computer room, and about twenty other support buildings. The radomes (which resemble golf balls with one end sliced off and then mounted on a pedestal) are made of Perspex and mounted on a concrete structure. The radomes are intended to protect the enclosed antennas against dust, wind, and rain and to hide some of the operational elements of the antennas from unfriendly observation, such as from Soviet imaging satellites.[26]

The first two radomes at Pine Gap were installed in 1968 and remain the facility's largest. The first appears to be about 100 feet in diameter and the second about 70 feet in diameter. They now form the western line of the antenna complex. The third and fourth radomes were fully installed by mid-1969. The third radome is about 55 feet in diameter and some 196 feet east of the largest radome, while the fourth is under 20 feet in diameter and just north of the second radome. In 1973 the antenna originally installed inside the third radome was dismantled and replaced by a thirty-three-foot communications terminal. The fifth radome is less than forty feet in diameter and was installed in 1971. The sixth dish is about the same size as the fifth and was installed in 1977. The seventh radome, which was built in 1980, houses a second communications terminal.[27]

On the northern edge of the complex is a high-frequency antenna that provides a direct communications link with Clark AB in the Philippines. It is the only non-satellite communications system linking Pine Gap with terminals outside Australia, and before installation of the 1973 antenna was the primary communications link between Pine Gap and the United States.[28]

Originally, the main computer room was about 210 feet square, but it was expanded twice in the 1970s to its present size, about 60,000 square feet. Its immense size requires that operators at each end of the room communicate with each other via headphones. The room is divided into three principal sections. The Station-Keeping Section is responsible for maintaining the satellites in geosynchronous orbit and for correctly aligning them towards targets of interest. The Signals Processing Office receives the signals transmitted from the satellites and transforms them into a form that can be used by the analysts. The Signals Analysis Section is staffed solely by CIA personnel—no Australian citizens or contractor personnel are included. Many individuals in the section are linguists who monitor the voice intercepts.[29]

As of January 1986, there were 557 people employed at Pine Gap—273 Australians and 284 Americans. While in theory Pine Gap is a joint facility, the 50-50 relationship holds only with respect to the gross number of personnel. This relationship is achieved by counting Australian housemaids, cooks, and gardeners who work at the base as "equal" to the CIA personnel who conduct the actual operations.[30]

The two other major control stations for SIGINT satellites are located in Europe—Bad Aibling and Menwith Hill. Information received at either location can be transmitted directly via DSCS satellite to Ft. Meade.[31]

AIRBORNE COLLECTION

At present, the single most important airborne platform involved in the collection of signals intelligence is the RC-135, of which there have been twelve versions. The first RC-135, a RC-135B, entered the SAC reconnaissance inventory in December 1965. This began the replacement of thirty obsolescent RB-47Hs and ERB-47Hs that were then "performing the ELINT portion of the Global Peacetime Airborne Reconnaissance Program."[32]

At present there are eighteen RC-135s in the U.S. inventory. Fourteen are modernized RC-135V and RC-135M (RIVET CARD) models, code-named RIVET JOINT (Block III). These and the other models of the RC-135 have an overall length of 129 feet, a wingspan of 131 feet, and an overall height of 42 feet. At its operational altitude, 34,990 feet, it cruises at 460 miles per hour.[33]

RIVET JOINT planes fly their missions (known as BURNING WIND missions) from bases in Alaska (Eielson AFB), Nebraska (Offutt AFB), Panama (Howard AB), England (RAF Mildenhall), Greece (Hellenikon AB), and Japan (Kadena AB,

Okinawa). RIVET JOINT/BURNING WIND missions average about seventy flights a month in Western Europe and the Far East and about twelve a month in Central America.[34]

The RC-135V carries a crew of seventeen and flies at 35,000 feet for up to ten hours before it requires refueling. Its COMINT capability can be expanded from a minimum of six positions to thirteen depending on the requirements of the mission. The RIVET JOINT-ELINT system is comprised of three collection positions—an Automatic ELINT Emitter Location System position supplemented by two manual operator positions. From Alaska the aircraft can patrol along the Kamchatka and Chukotski peninsulas, intercepting short-range tactical signals from Soviet naval and ground forces. The Japanese-based RC-135s patrol along the coasts of Vietnam, China, North Vietnam, and the USSR, including the Sea of Okhotsk.[35]

British-based RIVET JOINT planes fly along the Baltic Sea, and over the Barents Sea just off the Kola Peninsula, possibly intercepting signals from the three naval bases in the Murmansk area or the Severodvinsk submarine construction yard. The pilots are under orders not to get within 40 nautical miles of the Soviet coastline, and generally loiter 100 miles or more out over the Barents Sea until they intercept signals of interest. The planes based at Hellenikon have Libya, Egypt, Israel, and Syria and to a lesser extent the USSR among their targets. Planes from Hellenikon periodically deploy to Saudi Arabia to operate against Iraq and Iran. In the past they have also deployed to Egypt and the Sudan.[36]

From Eielson AFB, RIVET JOINT/BURINING WIND missions target the Soviet Far East. The missions proceed around the southern tip of Kamchatka and into the Sea of Okhotsk, a projected deployment area for Soviet missile submarines. If not assigned to patrol the Sea of Okhotsk, they slide down the coast toward Sakhalin Island. The missions monitor the alert status of Soviet air squadrons on Sakhalin as well as Soviet Air Force exercises. In the latter case the planes track Soviet fighters in flight.[37]

RIVET JOINT/BURNING WIND missions flown from Nebraska and Panama are directed against Spanish and Russian-language targets in Cuba and Central America. Central American flights have been conducted in support of the El Salvador military and the contra rebels.[38]

The remaining four RC-135 aircraft are evenly divided between the RC-135U and RC-135S models. The RC-135Us (modified RC-135Cs) bear the nickname COMBAT SENT. COMBAT SENT missions are flown along the periphery of the Soviet Union and other Warsaw Pact countries, with specific routes, tactics, and even aircraft configurations varying with the tasking requirements.[39]

As with the RIVET JOINT planes, the COMBAT SENT aircraft fly at 35,000 feet and can fly for ten hours without refueling if necessary. Among their targets have been Soviet ODD PAIR, SIDE NET, and TOP STEER radar systems. The primary sensor for COMBAT SENT planes is the Precision Power Measurement System, which determines the absolute power, pattern, and polarization of selected target emitters. In addition there is a high-resolution camera and television and radar sensors in the tail that are used when the occasion permits. One of the

COMBAT SENT planes is equipped with a system known as COMPASS ERA, a system containing infrared thermal imaging, interferometer-spectrometer, and spectral radiometer sensors.[40]

The RC-135S planes, based at Eielson AFB, Alaska and operating on occasion from Shemya, are nicknamed COBRA BALL and are the result of a late 1960s modification of two C-135Bs. The missions they conduct, known as BURNING STAR missions, involve the monitoring of the reentry phase of Soviet and Chinese ICBM, SLBM (submarine launched ballistic missile), and IRBM (intermediate range ballistic missile) research and development tests. The reentry phase of Soviet ICBM tests from Plesetsk and Tyuratam takes place either at Kamchatka Peninsulsa or into the expanses of the Pacific. For example, in 1974, three Soviet ICBM-test reentry phases occurred in the Pacific. In 1987 one test concluded in the vicinity of Hawaii.[41]

Because COBRA BALL missions are dictated by Soviet decisions to conduct missile tests, missions cannot be planned on any regular basis. Only some of these tests—specifically, multiple tests or those tests with reentry phases outside Soviet territory—need to be announced in advance. Thus, the COBRA BALL aircraft must be ready to fly on a moment's notice, in response to notification by the Defense Special Missile and Astronautics Center (DEFSMAC) that a Soviet test is about to occur. Immediate launches are "announced by the sounding of a Klaxon horn" at Eielson.[42]

The planes operate at 35,000 feet and up to ten hours unrefueled and eighteen hours refueled. Each COBRA BALL carries three sensor systems—one ELINT system and two photographic systems. The ELINT system is the Advanced Telemetry System (ATS), which automatically searches a portion of the frequency band and makes a digital record of all signals present. The operator of the ATS system allocates its collection resources to Soviet reentry vehicle links and records all telemetry detected.[43]

The Ballistic Framing Camera System images all the objects of interest in the reentry phase, while the Medium Resolution Camera (MRC) System photographs individual reentry vehicles.[44] The images produced by the MRC System are used to determine the reentry vehicle size. In turn, size estimates are used to produce estimates of the explosive yield of the warheads.

During its orbit the RC-135S records and cross-checks its position coordinates at least once every twenty minutes. It is also called on to provide a variety of information—including air speed, altitude, estimated time of arrival, orbit point, adjustments in timing or track, track length (in minutes), the status of the equipment, wind direction, and time remaining on the track.[45]

As a supplement to the COBRA BALL aircraft, the NSA and the SAC have employed another version of the C-135 to collect intelligence during Soviet missile tests. This variant is the EC-135N, a plane with a ten-foot radome built into its nose. This "droop snoot" radome carries an antenna seven feet in diameter that allows the eight-person crew to intercept voice communications, plus telemetered or radioed data on speed, temperature, and other characteristics of the object being tracked. The plane also has a probe antenna on each wingtip for high-frequency radio transmission and reception, and high-frequency trailing wire beneath the fuselage.[46]

The EC-135N has had, as its primary mission, tracking U.S. missiles during flight tests as well as keeping tabs on unmanned satellites. They perform these missions, according to the Air Force, "over land where tracking stations are limited by geographical constraints and over water where ships cannot move quickly enough to cover different portions during launch."[47] However, as a secondary mission, the EC-135Ns—known as Advanced Range Instrumentation Aircraft or ARIAs—have been used to monitor the end phase of Soviet missile tests, flying opposite Siberia or over the Pacific.

The EC-135Ns have been augmented by a new set of ARIA aircraft, which resulted in an increase in 1985 flying time of 300 percent. Three EC-135Ns have been equipped with new engines. They have been redesignated EC-135Es and will continue to be part of the ARIA program through the late 1990s. The replacement aircraft are EC-18B—American Airlines 707-313—modified into the ARIA configuration by the Air Force System Command's Aeronautical Systems Division. The first two EC-18Bs became operational in 1985, and by 1988 all four were in operation.[48]

Much of the equipment on the EC-18B airplanes will be recycled from the retired EC-135Ns. The recycled equipment includes radomes, antennas, and on-board mission equipment such as receivers, data processors, and recorders. Additions to the internal portion of the craft include a navigation station, a new flight director, a modified electrical system, and an improved environmental control system.[49]

Additions to the forward portion of the aircraft include a large, drooped radome housing the seven-foot steerable antenna, high-frequency (HF) probe antennas on each wingtip, and a trailing wire, HF antenna on the bottom of the fuselage. Antennas for post-mission data transmission and satellite transmission also have been added. As with the EC-135Ns, the EC-18Bs will have as their primary mission monitoring U.S. space and missile launches, including unmanned space launches, cruise and ballistic missiles tests, and space shuttle launches.[50]

Also employed for signals intelligence purposes are eight EC-130 aircraft, which are flown by the U.S. Air National Guard's 193rd Tactical Electronic Combat Group (headquartered at Harrisburg International Airport, Pennsylvania). The planes are deployed to Central America to fly missions against rebel targets in El Salvador and government targets in Nicaragua.[51]

Also employed for SIGINT collection are the SR-71, U-2, and TR-1. In its SIGINT role, the SR-71 is used to fly "peripheral intelligence missions. . .to pinpoint locations and characteristics of potentially hostile signal emitters."[52] Thus, the SR-71s SIGINT role continues the peripheral electronic reconnaissance that has been part of U.S. intelligence activities since the late 1940s. The SR-71 apparently also continues the tradition of inducing the Soviet air defense system to "turn on" critical radar systems. The Commander of the Strategic Air Command in 1978, speaking of the SR-71 and RC-135, stated that "it is possible to operate these systems in a way that tells us things we want to know. This can't be done with satellites."[53]

There are three SIGINT collection systems designed for the U-2/TR-1: SENIOR RUBY, SENIOR STRETCH, and SENIOR SPEAR. SENIOR RUBY is a near real-time ELINT collection, processing, and reporting system that provides information (including type and location) on radar emitters within line of sight of the U2-R. The SENIOR RUBY system can handle a large number of emitters simultaneously and send its data to a Ground Control Processor that is colocated with the Transportable Ground Intercept Facility (TGIF), used in conjunction with real-time U-2 missions.[54]

SENIOR STRETCH is a near real-time COMINT collection, processing, and reporting system. The airborne receiver subsystem consists of a multichannel microwave receiver, remotely controlled via satellite link from the Remote Operations Facility, Airborne (ROFA) at Ft. Meade. The data collected is transmitted via DSCS satellite back to the ROFA.[55]

SENIOR SPEAR is also a near real-time collection, processing, and reporting system that provides a line-of-sight collection capability—out to 300 nm—from the aircraft. Under development, as of 1983, was SENIOR SPAN. SENIOR SPAN, to be installed in the U-2R, is a near real-time SIGINT collection, processing, and reporting system—with the airborne receiver subsystem consisting of HF, VHF, UHF, and microwave receivers. The receiver is remotely controlled via a satellite from the ROFA or a TGIF, with the collected data transmitted via satellite back to the control site.[56]

U-2/TR-1 missions are flown from several bases against a variety of targets. From Patrick AFB, Florida, Detachment 5 of the 99th Strategic Reconnaissance Wing flies SENIOR JUMP U-2Rs in collection missions against Cuba and Central America. The main Cuban targets are Cuban army, air force, and navy communications, with the intercepts being transmitted to Key West Naval Air Station, Florida. Data collected during Central American missions has been downlinked to installations in Honduras at Tiger Island or Cerro la Mole.[57]

SENIOR STRETCH U-2Rs fly from RAF Akrotiri (Operating Location OLIVE HARVEST) to intercept signals from several Middle Eastern states. The data are then uplinked to DSCS satellites for transmission to the ROFA. From Osan AB, South Korea, SENIOR SPEAR U-2Rs fly OLYMPIC GAME missions against the communications of Chinese and North Korean activities, with the intercepted communications being downlinked to an Electronic Security Command unit at Osan.[58]

TR-1/CREEK SPECTRE aircraft conduct COMINT/ELINT missions from RAF Alconbury, United Kingdom during missions along the border with East Germany and Czechoslovakia. The data are downlinked to an ESC unit in West Germany.[59]

Two additonal airborne SIGINT systems are Army systems: GUARDRAIL V and Improved GUARDRAIL V. GUARDRAIL is a remotely controlled airborne and ground-based intercept and radio-direction finding system, designed to exploit HF-VHF-UHF voice communications, mounted on RU-21H/GUARDRAIL V and RC-12D (Improved Guardrail V) aircraft. Both aircraft operate at between 10,000 and 20,000 feet, and can spend up to four hours on station. The RC-12D aircraft allow a wider range of frequencies to be targeted for intercept or DF (direction finding) purposes. The targets of both sets of aircraft include mobile forces, missile units, aviation elements, air defense units, and artillery regiments. Each system consists of six aircraft—two RU-21Hs and four RC-12Ds.[60]

GROUND STATIONS

Beginning in the late 1940s, the United States began establishing ground stations to monitor the Soviet Union and Eastern Europe. This network changed composition over the years and has grown to include stations directed against China, Vietnam, North Korea, the Middle East, Central America, and other areas. Today, the network, largely run by the NSA, comprises approximately sixty stations in twenty countries. Included are heavily manned stations (employing about 30,000 personnel) and unmanned locations whose "take" is remoted to other locations and then to Ft. Meade. In addition, several radar stations, operated by the Air Force Space Command, are involved in detecting and tracking Soviet missile tests and space launches. The stations collectively conduct intercept operations across the VHF-UHF-HF bands. Approximately thirty stations collect HF, strategic COMINT while others focus on VHF-UHF tactical communications. Other stations target various forms of electronic emanations.

The biggest and most important set of stations remain those directed at the Soviet Union and Warsaw Pact countries. Several facilities in Alaska are among those monitoring the Soviet Union. At Shemya Island, Alaska—which is approximately 400 miles across the Bering Sea from the Soviet eastern seaboard—is the Anders facility. Run by the Bendix Field Engineering Corporation for the NSA, the facility's Pusher HF antenna monitors Soviet communications in the Far East.[61]

Also located on Shemya is the COBRA DANE phased-array radar. The primary purpose of COBRA DANE is "to acquire precise radar metric and signature data on developing Soviet ballistic missile weapons systems for weapons system characterization determination. The Soviet developmental test to Kamchatka and the Pacific Ocean provided the United States with the primary source for collection of these data early in the Soviet developmental programs." Secondary missions are early warning and tracking of space objects.[62]

The COBRA DANE system consists of a AN/FPS-108 radar facility, measuring 87 by 107 feet at its base and approximately six stories or 100 feet in height, plus an attached one-story Precision Measurement Equipment Laboratory (PMEL) measuring 87 square feet. Both structures are located on a 230-foot-high bluff in the northwestern section of Shemya, where it overlooks the Bering Sea.[63]

The most important characteristic of COBRA DANE is that it is a phased-array radar. To an observer depending only on eyes or using binoculars, a phased-array radar is simply a dormant structure, sort of an electronic pyramid. This is in sharp contrast to the older, more traditional radar dish "sweeping its beam of microwave

Figure 8–1.   Range of COBRA DANE Coverage.

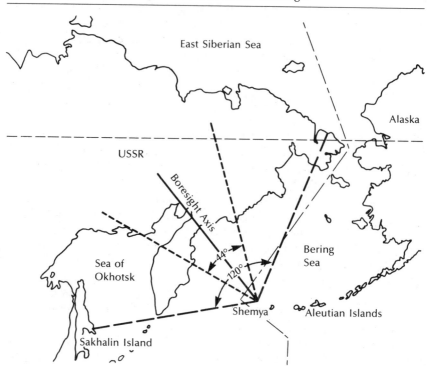

radiation along the horizon in search of distant objects." Rather, COBRA DANE consists of 15,360 radiating elements occupying ninety-five feet in diameter on the radar's face. Each element emits a signal that travels in all directions. When the signals are emitted at the same time, only targets in the immediate vicinity of the array's perpendicular axis are detectable. However, by successively delaying by a fraction of a wavelength, one can "steer" the beam to detect objects away from the perpendicular axis.[64]

COBRA DANE, which achieved initial operating capability on July 13, 1977, can detect (with a 99 percent probability) and track a basketball-sized object at a range of 2,000 miles with a 120-degree field of view extending from the northern half of Sakhalin Island to just short of the easternmost tip of the Soviet Union nearing the Bering Strait. However, its ability to provide information on the size and shape is available only over a forty-four-degree range centered on the upper portion of Kamchatka, as indicated in Figure 8–1. COBRA DANE can simultaneously track up to 100 warheads when operating in an intelligence collection mode. It can also be employed for early warning and space surveillance; in those modes it can track up to 300 incoming warheads and up to 200 satellites.[65]

The major limitation of COBRA DANE is that the final, near earth trajectory of Soviet reentry vehicles is not visible due to the line-of-sight constraints imposed by the curvature of the earth.[66]

Elmendorf AFB, located in Anchorage, is home of Naval Security Group Command and Electronic Security Command contingents, and an AN/FLR-9 "Elephant Cage" antenna. The AN/FLR-9 consists of three circular arrays, each made up of antenna elements around a circular reflecting screen. In the middle of the triple array is a central building, which contains the electronic equipment that forms the directional beams for monitoring and direction finding. The entire system is about 900 feet in diameter. The ESC contingent monitors USSR-Far Eastern military activity through voice, Morse Code, and printer intercepts.[67]

Also targeted on the Soviet Far East is a major base at Misawa AB in Japan. Four miles northwest of Misawa is the "Hill." On the hill is a 100-foot AN/FLR-9 antenna system. The base and its antenna lie at the northern tip of Honshu Island, about 500 miles west of Vladivostok and 400 miles south of Sakhalin Island. Misawa's importance is testified to by the presence of representatives of all four services' cryptological authorities. There is a 900-person detachment from the Electronic Security Command, a 700-person detachment from the Naval Security Group Command, 200 representatives of the Army's Intelligence and Security Command, and 80 representatives of Company E, Marine Support Batallion.[68]

According to one account, Misawa's AN/FLR-9 "can pick up a Russian television broadcast in Sakhalin or an exchange of insults between Chinese and Soviet soldiers on the Sino-Soviet border."[69] The INSCOM contingent focuses its attention on Soviet army and General Staff activity, as well as on Afghanistan. The NSGC contingent monitored the Soviet Navy's search and rescue activity after the Soviets shot down Korean Airlines Flight 007 in 1983.[70]

Misawa is also the site of Project LADYLOVE, which involves the interception of the communications transmitted via several Soviet satellite systems—Molniya, Raduga, and Gorizont.[71]

Also involved in the satellite communications interception project are three additional stations, all run by the NSA. Rosman Research Station was transferred from the NASA to the Department of Defense on February 1, 1981 for use as a "Communications Research Station" and became operational on July 1, 1985 with 250 employees. At present it has four satellite dishes pointed straight up and four in radomes. Also involved is the NSA's Menwith Hill station, located eight miles west of Harrogate in Yorkshire, England. The 562-acre station consists of a large array of satellite tracking aerials. Under Project MOONPENNY, a variety of Soviet satellite communications are intercepted by Menwith Hill's antennas. In addition, Menwith Hill is also the home of Project SILKWORTH, a high-frequency, wideband communications interception program. Finally, the Bad Aibling station in Germany represents the fourth component of the satellite communications (SATCOM) intercept project.[72]

Another station located in the United Kingdom that is heavily involved in the interception of Soviet communications is RAF Chicksands, near Bedford, home of an 800-person ESC contingent. Among the Soviet communications targeted are those of the air defense network.[73]

Over the years, the Chicksands mission has expanded to also focus on the military and diplomatic signals of Western European nations, particularly France. Inside the Chicksands facility are rooms and compartments with interception and direction finding allocated to different mission targets. Signs used to hang above the heads of coordinating "mission supervisors" which included, in the early 1970s, "France," "Czechoslovakia," and "Civil Navigation." On each of 3 daily shifts, over 100 operators staff interception positions. With over 1,750 military staff alone, Chicksands is the USAF's largest non-flying base in Britain.[74]

Outside of Britain, important European ground stations involved in the monitoring of Soviet Bloc activities are located in Italy, Germany, and Turkey. At San Vito dei Normanni, Italy is a 700-person contingent of the Electronic Security Command. Employing the AN/FLR-9, the unit intercepts selected Soviet, East European, and Middle East communications.[75]

In Turkey there are two important facilities, one run by the NSA and its SCAs, the other by the Air Force Space Command. Sinop, nicknamed "Diogenes Station," began operating in the mid-1950s and is now home to the 290-person Army Field Station Sinop and the 97-person Naval Security Group Activity Sinop. Sinop is a fishing port and farm center with a population of just over 18,000 persons. The station is 2 miles west of the town and is a 300-acre facility on a bleak 700-foot hill at the end of a peninsula. The INSCOM contingent and Turkish civilians at the base are involved in monitoring Soviet activity in the Black Sea area as well as Soviet missile testing activities. A major aspect of monitoring Soviet missile telemetry from Sinop is the interception of electronic emanations and telemetry connected with Soviet missile and space rocket launches from Kapustin Yar and other locations in the southern USSR. The monitoring of Soviet air activity can be a rather "boring job. . .a morse operator, for instance, just sits there in front of a radio receiver with headphones, and a typewriter copying morse signals."[76]

The single most important U.S. intelligence facility in Turkey is the one at Pirinclik Air Base, a satellite operation of Diyarbakir Air Station. Located on a rocky plateau in southeastern Turkey, Pirinclik had its operations suspended from 1974 to 1978. During that time U.S. housekeeping personnel rotated one radar dish to prevent roller-bearing damage while the Turks locked up a key piece of radar equipment to make sure the radar was inoperative.[77]

The base resumed operations on November 3, 1979, with its 2 radar antenna fixed permanently toward the northeast, where the Soviet border lies 180 miles away. The electronic beams of the radar operate through a natural "duct" in the mountains around the plateau, picking up Soviet missiles and space launches as they rise above the horizon. An AN/FPS-17 detection radar is used which can detect an object 1 meter in diameter up to 5,000 miles away. After the AN/FPS-17 indicates that a missile launch or space shot has taken place, the AN/FPS-79 "swings its white, round face in a noiseless arc in the same direction, ready to track missiles along their course."[78]

The radars are operated largely by civilian technicians from the contractor, General Electric. In addition to the 70 contractor personnel there are about 145 Air Force personnel, mostly enlisted personnel. Few of them are permitted in the top-secret radar control rooms. Rather, they are more likely to operate the communications facilities that transmit the data via DSCS satellite to Washington.[79]

As might be expected, Germany is home for several strategic and tactical SIGINT stations targeted on the Soviet Union and Eastern Europe. The two most important are located at Augsburg and Bad Aibling. Augsburg hosts units from INSCOM (Field Station Augsburg), the Electronic Security Command, and the Naval Security Group Command. With 1,814 personnel, Augsburg covers selected communications in East Germany, Poland, Czechoslovakia, Hungary, and the western USSR, employing an AN/FLR-9 antenna.[80]

As already noted, the Bad Aibling station serves as a downlink for satellite SIGINT data and as part of a four-station network involved in intercepting Soviet satellite communications. In addition, Bad Aibling has two other functions. Employing Rhombic and Pusher antennas, the Bad Aibling station conducts HFDF (high-frequency, direction finding) and communications intercept coverage of Eastern Europe and the Soviet Union, in support of Augsburg. It also serves as the initial reception site for data from two unmanned locations on Cyprus and Oman. The Cyprus stations consists of a Pusher HF antenna set up by the NSA at the Episkopi Sovereign Base Area to cover targets in the Middle East and southern USSR. The Abut Sovereign Base Area, home for a British SIGINT operation, is also home for NSA equipment that monitors military activity in the Near East and the southern USSR.[81]

A second set of stations are directed primarily against the activities of Asian Communist nations. The major targets are the PRC, Vietnam, and Korea, with Cambodia and Laos being secondary targets.

The two stations farthest from their targets are at Clark AB in the Philippines and Kunia, Hawaii. Clark AB is host to an AN/FLR-9 antenna and a 180-person contingent of the Electronic Security Command which intercepts a variety of Vietnamese and Chinese communications, both air and ground based, as well as diplomatic communications.[82]

Kunia is host to the NSA-run "Defense Research Facility," INSCOM (Field Station Kunia), NSGC, and ESC contingents. Kunia serves as the NSA's B-Group Remote Operations Facility, receiving data from two remote facilities at Taegu, South Korea and Khon Kean, Thailand.

The Khon Kean facility was apparently set up in the fall of 1979. The absence of such a facility apparently resulted in a shortfall of intelligence during the Chinese-Vietnam War earlier that year.[83]

The Taegu facility, run for the NSA by the Bendix Field Engineering Group, is equipped with a Pusher HF antenna and targeted against communications in China, North Korea, and Vietnam.[84]

Located at Pyong' Taek, Korea is U.S. Army Field Station, Korea (also known as Zoeckler Station), with a 304-person contingent and three operating locations:

Detachment J (at Koryo-Son Mountain on the island of Kangwna), Detachment K (at Kanak-San Mountain, six miles from the demilitarized zone), and Detachment L (on Yawol-San Mountain, within 1,500 meters of the DMZ). Collectively, the installations focus on a variety of North Korean COMINT and ELINT targets.[85]

A third set of ground stations are those targeted on the Middle East and North Africa, Latin America, and international satellite traffic. Among the stations with Middle East intercept functions is the previously mentioned San Vito facility, which in addition to its Soviet Bloc intercept mission is responsible for the interception of diplomatic messages in the Mediterranean, South European, and North African regions. In addition, the remote facility at Episkopi Sovereign Base Area, Cyprus covers targets in the Middle East in addition to the southern USSR. Finally, a 400-person contingent of the ESC is stationed at Iraklion, Greece and engages in the interception of Arabic language communications originating from countries in North Africa and the Middle East.[86]

The Iraklion station employs a rhombic/dipole antenna field to conduct its intercept operations. A rhombic array is a highly directional antenna system. Each element or antenna of that array consists of a wire several feet off the ground and attached to four posts spaced in the shape of a diamond, each side being approximately ten feet long. At one end the wire is connected to a coaxial cable that runs underground to a centrally located operations building. The entire array consists of between thirty and forty structures over several hundred acres.[87]

Latin America, and particularly Central America, has obviously become a target of increased importance. At Lackland AFB, Medina Annex, San Antonio is a 272-person contingent from INSCOM (U.S. Army Field Station, San Antonio) and one from the ESC which receive intercepted, Spanish language communications remoted from Tiger Island and Cerro la Mole in Honduras. Homestead AFB, Florida is the headquarters of Naval Security Group Activity Homestead, with its main operations center at Card Sound (known as Site Alpha or Seminole Station), which engages in the monitoring of Cuban military communications as well as Soviet activity in Cuba. It also monitors all communications involving Cuban and Soviet air activity originating in or destined for Cuba. Intercept operations are conducted using an AN/FRD-10 antenna system. Also targeted on Cuba are the antennas of the U.S. Army Field Station, Key West.[88]

Outside of the continental United States, two stations on U.S. territory contribute to SIGINT operations directed against Latin America. At Guantanamo Bay, Cuba are more than 100 members of the Guantanamo Naval Security Group Activity. Employing an AN/FRD-10 antenna system, the unit intercepts Cuban and Soviet military communications in and around Cuba and the Caribbean Basin. The 430-person Naval Security Group Activity at Sabana Seca, Puerto Rico employs an AN/FRD-10 to target internationally leased carrier and diplomatic communications for all of Central and South America.[89]

Two stations target INTELSAT/COMSAT satellite communications. An NSA facility at Sugar Grove, West Virginia with 30, 60, 105, and 150 foot satellite antennas intercepts the signals being sent by the INTELSAT/COMSAT satellite over the

Atlantic and intended for the INTELSAT/COMSAT ground station at Etam, West Virginia. A second installation at the Yakima Research Station in Yakima, Washington targets the Pacific INTELSAT/COMSAT satellite.[90]

COVERT LISTENING POSTS

In addition to the ground-based listening posts such as those described above, there is a second set of such posts. However, rather than using large areas of land they are surreptitiously hidden in U.S. embassies and consulates. Such listening posts allow the United States to target the internal military, political, police, and economic communications of the nation in which the embassy is located.

Such listening posts are joint CIA-NSA operations, formally known as Special Collection Elements, and exist in approximately forty-five U.S. embassies and consulates.

The best known of the listening posts is the one in the U.S. Embassy in Moscow. In the late 1960s and early 1970s the Embassy listening post was used to intercept the radio-telephone conversations of Soviet Politburo members, including General Secretary Leonid Brezhnev, President Nikolai Podgorny, and Premier Alexsei Kosygin as they drove around Moscow.[91]

Traffic from the interception operation was transmitted back to a special CIA facility a few miles from the agency's Langley, Virginia headquarters. Originally, the conversations simply needed to be translated, since no attempt had been made to scramble or encipher the conversations.[92]

After a 1971 disclosure in the press concerning the operation, code-named GAMMA GUPY, the Soviets began enciphering their limousine telephone calls to plug leaks. Despite that effort, the United States was able to intercept and decode a conversation between General Secretary Brezhnev and Field Marshal Grechko that took place shortly before the signing of the SALT I treaty. Grechko assured Brezhnev that the heavy Soviet SS-19 missiles under construction would fit inside the launch tubes of lighter SS-11 missiles, making the missiles permissible under the SALT I treaty.[93]

In general, however, the intelligence obtained was less than earthshaking. According to a former intelligence official involved in GAMMA GUPY, the CIA "didn't find out about, say, the invasion of Czechoslovakia. It was very gossipy—Brezhnev's health and maybe Podgorny's sex life." At the same time the official said that the operation "gave us extremely valuable information on the personalities and health of top Soviet leaders."[94]

Other covert listening posts are located in the U.S. embassies in TelAviv and Buenos Aires. The Tel Aviv outpost is targeted on Israeli military and national police communications. The latter gives the United States the capability to follow very closely the activities of the police in suppressing Palestinian demonstrators. The presence of a U.S. listening post has not gone unnoticed by Israeli officials due to the large number of antennas on the roof of the Tel Aviv embassy.[95]

The Buenos Aires post was used to target the communications of the Argentine General Staff during the Falklands crisis—information that would be quickly passed to the British.[96]

SURFACE SHIPS

At one time, the United States placed great reliance on signals intelligence gathered by ship-based sensors. The United States began using combat ships in this role. Destroyers and destroyer escorts often carried mobile vans packed with antennas as well as special detachments to operate the equipment. Use of destroyers and destroyer escorts, however, degraded fighting capabilities as combat ships were assigned to intelligence missions. Further, some Navy officials felt the stationing of a destroyer off a foreign shore, especially that of a hostile nation, to be provocative.[97]

Two alternatives were deployed—Auxiliary General Technical Research (AGTR) and Auxiliary General Environmental Research (AGER) ships in 1961 and 1965, respectively. The AGTRs were converted World War II Liberty ships—each 458 feet long and 10,860 tons. The AGERs were old World War II vintage, converted, diesel-driven light-cargo ships approximately 170 feet in length, with a maximum speed of thirteen knots and a cruising speed of ten knots. Each had an estimated range of 4,000 nautical miles. AGER collection capability was more restricted than AGTR capability, being concerned with SIGINT and hydrographic information. Elimination of the AGER and AGTR collection ships resulted from events in 1967 and 1969. The AGTR U.S.S. Liberty was bombed by Israeli aircraft in the midst of the 1967 Six Day War, resulting in severe damage and the death of thirty-four crew members. It was alleged by the Israeli government that the ship was mistaken for an Egyptian vessel; others have alleged the attack was deliberate and intended to prevent the United States from learning of Israeli military gains that would lead the United States to pressure Israel into a "premature" cease-fire.[98]

In 1969, the AGER U.S.S. Pueblo was captured by the North Koreans and its crew held hostage. Shortly after the Pueblo was seized, the U.S.S. Sergeant Joseph P. Muller almost drifted into Cuban waters. After several attempts she was finally towed to safety by the escorting destroyer. Subsequently, the AGERs and AGTRs were decommissioned.[99]

More recently, the United States has employed Spruance-class destroyers and frigates to collect intelligence concerning Nicaragua and El Salvador. The 7,800-ton destroyer Deyo, as well as her sister ship Caron, were stationed in the Gulf of Fonzeca. The ships could monitor suspected shipping, intercept communications and encrypted messages, and probe the shore surveillance and defense capabilities of the other nations. With regard to the latter use, they can induce nations to switch on shore-to-sea, ship-to-ship, and air-to-air radar.[100]

In addition to being in the Gulf of Fonzeca, the Caron has been present in the Baltic, the Northern Sea, and off the Libyan coast. During the birth of Solidarity in Poland in August 1980, the Caron cruised fourteen miles off the coast of Gdansk, and in the summer of 1981 she was among the ships that constituted the task force that was on an exercise off the Libyan coast in the Gulf of Sidra. During a North Atlantic cruise, she came as close to the Soviet naval base at Murmansk as the Chesapeake Bay Bridge is to the U.S. Naval Base at Norfolk, Virginia.[101]

The *Caron* was again employed in an intelligence collection mission against a Soviet target in 1986. Along with another warship, the *U.S.S. Yorktown*, the *Caron* entered Soviet-claimed territorial waters in the Black Sea on March 10 and remained there a week, coming as close as six miles to the Soviet coast. While a Pentagon official claimed that intelligence collection was not the primary rationale of the exercise—which had been ordered by the Joint Chiefs of Staff in the name of Secretary of Defense Weinberger—it was at the very least an important secondary mission.[102]

In addition to helicopters to gather information, the *Yorktown* is also outfitted with electronic equipment that can monitor voice communications and radar signals. It has been normal procedure to use such systems to determine if new radars have been deployed onshore and to check the readiness of Soviet forces. Additionally, with the headquarters of the Soviet Union's Black Sea Fleet at Sevastopol, communications monitoring would be certain. In a previous expedition, the *Yorktown's* equipment was used in part to monitor aircraft movements within the Soviet Union.[103]

The Soviets responded to the *Yorktown/Caron* mission both militarily and diplomatically. A destroyer was used to trail both ships, while military aircraft overflew them. In addition, a Soviet protest note said the episode "was of a demonstrative, defiant nature and pursued clearly provocative aims."[104]

In February 1988, the *Yorktown* and *Caron* again entered the Black Sea with the same objectives as in 1986—to assert the right to free passage in waters outside the U.S.-recognized three-mile limit and to collect intelligence. When the ships came closer than the twelve-mile limit claimed by the Soviets, destroyers were sent to nudge the ships as a means of indicating Soviet displeasure.[105]

Two Navy frigates stationed in the Pacific have also been used against targets in Nicaragua, El Salvador, and Honduras. One ship—the 3,990-ton *Blakely*—is a Knox-class frigate commissioned in 1970; the other—the 3,400-ton *Julius A. Furei*—is a Brooke-class guided-missile frigate. The missions involved homing and recording voice and signals communcations, locating transmitting stations, logging ships' movements, and studying their waterlines to help determine if they were riding low in the water when entering port and high when exiting—indicating the unloading of cargo.[106]

Frigates have also been used to monitor Soviet missile telemetry. It was reported in 1979 that "American ships equipped with sensitive listening gear . . . patrol the North Atlantic, where they collect telemetry broadcast by the new Soviet submarine-launched missiles tested in the White Sea, northeast of Finland." Likewise, on the night of August 31, 1983, when the United States was expecting the Soviet Union to test a SS-X-24 missile, the frigate *Badger* was stationed in the Sea of Okhotsk.[107]

The *Badger* and the rest of the forty-six Knox-class frigates have dimensions of 438 by 46.8 by 24.8 feet, can travel at 27 knots and carry 275 personnel. In addition to ASROC (antisubmarine rocket) weapons, search radar, and sonar, they are fitted with satellite communications antennas for both transmission and reception.[108]

In August 1985, the Navy commissioned its first ship dedicated solely to intelligence collection since the decommissioning of the AGTR and AGER ships in 1969. The ship, the ARL-24 *Sphinx*, is a former repair ship converted to its present role. The 328 by 50 foot ship can travel at 11.6 knots. With a home port at Little Creek, Virginia, it spends most of its time off the coast of Nicaragua intercepting Sandinista military communications.[109]

The most important ship-based system for monitoring Soviet missile tests is a phased-array radar designated COBRA JUDY, which resides on the U.S.N.S. *Observation Island*. Emplaced on the 563-foot ship is a 4-story turret on the aft deck that houses the major components of COBRA JUDY. The turret is essentially a thirty-foot cube with one face tilted slightly inward. An antenna array 22.5 feet in diameter occupies an octagonal, raised area on the cube's slanting face. In addition, on top of the superstructure there are two, thirty-two-foot diameter geodesic radomes containing a complex of passive receiving antennas funded by the NSA.[110]

The deployment of COBRA JUDY was designed to allow the monitoring of the final near-earth trajectories of Soviet reentry vehicles during the portion of their flight not "visible" to COBRA DANE because of the earth's line-of-sight constraints. In particular, the sensors provide information on the radar signatures of reentry vehicles and warheads. To enhance that capability, an X-band radar with parabolic dish antennas was added in 1985 to further improve COBRA JUDY's capability. Because of the higher degree of resolution and target separation, the radar may be able to distinguish between multiple warheads and penetration aids such as decoys and chaff.[111]

SUBMARINES

A program that had its genesis in the later years of the Eisenhower Administration but is still operational today involves not surface ships but submarines. Known by a variety of code names, the best known of which is HOLYSTONE, the program is one of the most sensitive intelligence operations of the United States.

HOLYSTONE, which also has been known as PINNACLE, BOLLARD, and most recently as BARNACLE, began in 1959 and has involved the use of special electronically equipped submarines to collect electronic communications and photographic intelligence. The primary target has always been the Soviet Union, but at times countries such as Vietnam and China have been targets of the operations, which sometimes involved penetration of the Soviet, Chinese, and Vietnamese three-mile territorial limits.[112]

The missions lasted about ninety days. Crews were given cover stories such as being on an undersea geodetic survey project that was using sonar to study ocean water temperatures in support of data collected by satellites. The crews were forbidden to use any active electronic or sonar gear while on a HOLYSTONE mission so as to avoid detection by Soviet antisubmarine warfare devices. In addition, hatches were tied down to prevent rattling.[113]

By 1975, the program apparently had provided vital information on the Soviet submarine fleet—its configuration, capabilities, noise patterns, missiles, and missile firing capabilities. One mission involved obtaining the "voice autographs" of Soviet submarines. Using detailed tape recordings of noise made by submarine engines and other equipment, analysts of the Naval Scientific and Technical Intelligence Center (now the Naval Intelligence Support Center) were able to develop a methodology to identify individual Soviet submarines, even those tracked at long range under the ocean. The analysts could then follow the submarine from its initial operations to its decommissioning.[114]

HOLYSTONE operations also provided information about theater and strategic sea-based missiles. Some Soviet sea-based missiles were tested against inland targets to reduce U.S. observation. On occasion, HOLYSTONE submarines would penetrate close enough to Soviet territory to observe the missile launchings, providing information on the early stages of the flight. According to one government official, the most significant information provided by the missions was a readout of the computer calculations and signals put into effect by Soviet technicians before launching the missiles. Beyond that the U.S. submarines also provided intelligence by tracking the flight and eventual landing of the missiles, providing continuous information on guidance and electronic systems.[115]

In addition to providing acoustic and telemetry intelligence, the HOLYSTONE submarines also tapped into Soviet communictaions cables on the ocean floor. The tapping operation allowed the United States to intercept higher level military messages and other communications considered too sensitive to be entrusted to insecure means of communication such as radio and microwave.[116]

Beyond signals intelligence, the submarines also were able to bring back valuable photographs, many of which were taken through the submarine's periscope. In the mid-1960s, photographs were taken of the underside of an E Class submarine that appeared to be taken inside Vladivostok harbor.[117]

As was the case when the program was code-named HOLYSTONE, today's BARNACLE operations employ thirty-eight nuclear-powered Sturgeon-class submarines such as the SSN-637. The submarines have dimensions of 292 by 31.7 by 26 feet and carry SUBROC (submarine rocket) and antisubmarine torpedos as well as Harpoon and Tomahawk missiles. With their 107-person complement (twelve officers and ninety-five enlisted personnel), the ships can travel at speeds at over twenty knots when surfaced and at over thirty knots underwater and can reach a depth of 1,320 feet. Their standard electronic equipment includes a search radar and both active and passive sonar systems.[118]

The special equipment placed on submarines for HOLYSTONE/BARNACLE missions has included the WLR-6 Waterboy Signals Intelligence System. The WLR-6 is in the process of being replaced by a more advanced system known as SEA

NYMPH, described in one document as "an advanced, automatic, modular signals exploitation system designed for continuous acquisition, identification, recording, analysis and exploitation of electromagnetic signals." All the Sturgeon submarines will carry a basic skeletal system that can be upgraded to full capacity when authorized.[119]

Another reconnaissance project involving submarines that began later than the HOLYSTONE program was code-named IVY BELLS. This project involved implanting a device to intercept the signals transmitted along a Soviet underwater cable in the Sea of Okhotsk, between the Kamchatka Peninsula and the eastern Soviet coastline. A combined Navy-NSA team, operating from a submarine, installed a miniaturized waterproof eavesdropping device—a large tape pod that fit over the Soviet cable, through which key Soviet military and other communications flowed. The pod had a wraparound attachment that intercepted the cable traffic by "induction"—it could intercept the signals being transmitted along the cable without physically tapping into the cable. In addition, if the cable were raised by the Soviets for maintenance, the pod would break away and remain on the ocean floor. Tapes in the pod recorded messages and signals on various channels or communications links for four to six weeks, with the pod being installed for only two recording sessions a year.[120]

The Sea of Okhotsk operation continued until 1981, when former NSA employee Ronald Pelton sold the Soviets information about the operation.

NOTES TO CHAPTER 8

1. George C. Wilson, "Soviet Nuclear Sub Reported Sunk," *Washington Post*, August 11, 1983, p. A9.
2. John E. Ingersoll, "Request for COMINT of Interest to Bureau of Narcotics and Dangerous Drugs," in U.S. Congress, Senate Select Committee to Study Governmental Operations with Respect to Intelligence Activities, *The National Security Agency and Fourth Amendment Rights* (Washington, D.C.: U.S. Government Printing Office, 1976), pp. 152–55.
3. U.S. Congress, House Permanent Select Committee on Intelligence, *Annual Report* (Washington, D.C.: U.S. Government Printing Office, 1978), p. 38.
4. John Prados, *The Soviet Estimate: U.S. Intelligence Analysis and Russian Military Strength* (New York: Dial Press, 1982), p. 203; Farooq Hussain, *The Future of Arms Control Part IV, The Impact of Weapons Test Restrictions* (London: International Institute for Strategic Studies, 1980), p. 44; Robert Kaiser, "Verification of SALT II: Art and Science," *Washington Post*, June 15, 1979, p. 1.
5. U.S. Congress, House Permanent Select Committee on Intelligence, *HR 6588, The National Intelligence Act of 1980* (Washington, D.C.: U.S. Government Printing Office, 1980), p. 521.
6. Deborah Shapley, "Who's Listening?: How NSA Tunes In On America's Overseas Phone Calls and Messages," *Washington Post*, October 7, 1977, pp. C1, C4.
7. Ibid.

8. Sayre Stevens, "The Soviet BMD Program," in Ashton B. Carter and David N. Schwartz, eds., *Ballistic Missile Defense* (Washington, D.C.: Brookings Institution, 1984), pp. 182–221 at p. 192.

9. Anthony Kenden, "U.S. Reconnaissance Satellite Programs," *Spaceflight*, 20, pp. 7 (1978): 243ff.

10. Philip Klass, *Secret Sentries in Space* (New York: Random House, 1971), p. 194.

11. Seymour M. Hersh, *"The Target is Destroyed: What Really Happened to Flight 007 and What America Knew About It* (New York: Random House, 1986), p. 38; Private information.

12. Des Ball, *Pine Gap: Australia and the US Geostationary Signals Intelligence Satellite Program* (Sydney: Allen & Unwin Australia, 1988), pp. 14–15.

13. Philip Klass, "U.S. Monitoring Capability Impaired," *Aviation Week and Space Technology*, May 14, 1979, p. 18.

14. Robert Lindsey, *The Falcon and the Snowman: A True Story of Friendship and Espionage* (New York: Simon and Schuster, 1979), p. 111.

15. Ball, *Pine Gap*, p. 54.

16. Victor Marchetti, *Allies* (A Grand Bay film directed by Marian Wilkinson and produced by Sylvia Le Clezio, Syndey, 1983).

17. See Lindsey, *Falcon and the Snowman*, for a full-length account; on the renaming of RHYOLITE, see William E. Burrows, *Deep Black: Space Espionage and National Security* (New York: Random House, 1987), p. 192; Glenn Zorpette, "Monitoring the Tests," *IEEE Spectrum* (July 1986), 57–66 at 60.

18. James Gerstenzang, "Shuttle Lifts Off with Spy Cargo," *Los Angeles Times*, January 25, 1985, pp. 1, 11.

19. William J. Broad, "Experts Say Satellite Can Detect Soviet War Steps," *New York Times*, January 25, 1985, p. A12.

20. Walter Andrews, "Defense Aide Confirms U.S. Satellites Jammed," *Washington Times*, June 21, 1984, p. 1.

21. Richard Burt, "U.S. Plans New Way to Check Soviet Missile Tests, *New York Times*, June 29, 1979, p. A3; Burrows, *Deep Black*, p. 192.

22. Hussain, *The Future of Arms Control Part IV*, p. 42; Ball, *Pine Gap*, pp. 14–15.

23. Hersh, *"The Target is Destroyed,"* p. 4; Burrows, *Deep Black*, p. 223.

24. James B. Schultz, "Inside the Blue Cube," *Defense Electronics* (April 1983) 52–59; *Organization and Functions Chartbook* (Onizuka AFS, Calif.: Air Force Satelllite Control Facility, December 1, 1986), p. 61; Space Division Regulation 23-3, "Air Force Satellite Control Facility," December 16, 1983.

25. Paul Stares, *Space and National Security* (Washington, D.C.: Brookings Institution, 1987), p. 188; Private information.

26. Desmond Ball, *A Suitable Piece of Real Estate: American Installations in Australia* (Sydney: Hale & Iremonger, 1980), p. 59.

27. Ball, *Pine Gap*, p. 61.

28. Ibid., p. 70.

29. Ibid., pp. 67, 80.

30. Ibid., p. 77.

31. Ibid., pp. 27–28; Private information; Defense Communications Agency, *Facilities Handbook (Areas 1, 2, and 9)* (Scott AFB, Ill,: DCAOC, January 1985), p. 5A.

32. Untitled memo, *Declassified Documents Reference System 1982-001583.*

33.   U.S. Congress, House Committee on Appropriations, *Department of Defense Appropriations for 1984, Part 8* (Washington, D.C.: U.S. Government Printing Office, 1983), p. 384; Martin Streetly, "U.S. Airborne ELINT Systems, Part 3: The Boeing RC-135 Family," *Jane's Defence Weekly*, March 16, 1985, pp. 460–65.

34.   Hersh, *"The Target is Destroyed,"* p. 9.

35.   Burrows, *Deep Black*, p. 171; Private information.

36.   Hersh, *"The Target is Destroyed,"* pp. 9–10; Burrows, *Deep Black*, p. 171; Private information.

37.   George C. Wilson, "U.S. RC-135 Was Assessing Soviet Air Defenses," *Washington Post*, September 7, 1983, p. A-12; Philip Taubman, "U.S. Says Intelligence Plane Was On A Routine Mission," *New York Times*, September 5, 1983, p. 4; Hersh, *"The Target is Destroyed,"* p. 220.

38.   Hersh, *"The Target is Destroyed,"* p. 9

39.   Private information.

40.   Private information; References to the COMBAT SENT missions against the mentioned radars were found in the documents catalog of the Office of Air Force History.

41.   Streetly, "U.S. Airborne ELINT Systems, Part 3"; Bill Gertz, "Soviets Test-Fire ICBM Just North of Hawaii," *Washington Times*, October 1, 1987, pp. A1, A10.

42.   6th Strategic Wing Regulation 55-2, "Operations, Aircrew and Staff Procedures," September 30, 1983, pp. 4–11.

43.   Private information; Burrows, *Deep Black*, p. 172.

44.   Private information; Burrows, *Deep Black*, p. 172.

45.   6th Strategic Wing Regulation, "Operations, Aircrew and Staff Procedures," pp. 3–5.

46.   Charles W. Corddry and Albert Sehlstedt, Jr., "Plane's Covert Role is to Monitor Soviet Space Flights, Missile Tests," *Baltimore Sun*, May 1, 1981, p. 1.

47.   Ibid.

48.   U.S. Congress, House Committee on Appropriations, *Military Construction Appropriations for 1985, Part 3* (Washington, D.C.: U.S. Government Printing Office, 1984), pp. 105–6; Brendan M. Greeley, Jr., "USAF Readies Range Instrumentation Aircraft for First Flight," *Aviation Week and Space Technology*, February 25, 1985, pp. 23–4; "Aerospace World," *Air Force Magazine*, December 1987, p. 33.

49.   Greeley, "USAF Readies Range Instrumentation Aircraft for First Flight."

50.   Ibid.

51.   Martin Streetly, "Hercules C-130 Electronic Missions," *Jane's Defence Weekly*, November 16, 1985, pp. 1092–96; Private information.

52.   "Electronic Environment Sampled Regularly," *Aviation Week and Space Technology*, May 10, 1976, pp. 90–92.

53.   Duncan Campbell, "Spy in the Sky," *New Statesman*, September 9, 1983, pp. 8–9.

54.   Private information.

55.   Ibid.

56.   Ibid.

57.   Ibid.

58.   Ibid.

59.   Ibid.

60.   Ibid.

61.   Ibid.

62. Dr. Michael E. del Papa, *Meeting the Challenge: ESD and the Cobra Dane Construction Effort on Shemya Island* (Bedford, Mass.: Electronic Systems Division, Air Force Systems Command, 1979), pp. 1–2.

63. Ibid., p. 2–3.

64. Eli Brookner, "Phased-Array Radars," *Scientific American* (April 1985) 94–102.

65. Philip J. Klass, "USAF Tracking Radar Details Disclosed," *Aviation Week and Space Technology*, October 25, 1976, pp. 41–46; del Papa, *Meeting the Challenge*, p. 38.

66. Klass, "USAF Tracking Radar Details Disclosed."

67. Duncan Campbell, *The Unsinkable Aircraft Carrier: American Military Power in Britain* (London: Michael Joseph, 1984), p. 155; "British MP Accuses U.S. of Electronic Spying," *New Scientist*, August 5, 1976, p. 268; Private information.

68. Hersh, *"The Target is Destroyed,"* p. 47.

69. Keyes Beech, "Secret U.S. Base Keeps Eye on Far East," *Los Angeles Times*, January 20, 1980, p. 17.

70. Hersh, *"The Target is Destroyed,"* pp. 47–48.

71. U.S. Congress, House Committee on Appropriations, *Military Construction Appropriations for 1981, Part 2* (Washington, D.C.: U.S. Government Printing Office, 1980), p. 875; Hersh, *"The Target is Destroyed,"* p. 49; David Morison, "Sites Unseen," *National Journal*, June 4, 1988, pp. 1468–72.

72. Duncan Campbell and Linda Melvern, "America's Big Ear on Europe," *New Statesman*, July 18, 1980, pp. 10–14; Stella Trapp, "Rosman Research Center is a 'Vital Part of the Security'," *Transylvania Times*, August 21, 1986, pp. 1A, 16A; Morison, "Sites Unseen"; Private information.

73. Hersh, *"The Target is Destroyed,"* p. 4.

74. Campbell, *The Unsinkable Aircraft Carrier*, p. 155.

75. Hersh, *"The Target is Destroyed,"* p. 47n.; Private information.

76. Marvine Howe, "U.S. and Turks Monitor Soviet at Isolated Post," *New York Times*, January 4, 1981, p. 7; Michael Getler, "U.S. Intelligence Facilities in Turkey Get New Attention After Iran Turmoil," *Washington Post*, February 9, 1979, p. A15; U.S. Congress, Senate Committee on Foreign Relations, *Fiscal Year 1980 International Security Assistance Authorization* (Washington, D.C.: U.S. Government Printing Office, 1979), p. 365; U.S. Congress, House Committee on International Relations, *United States Military Installations and Objectives in the Mediterranean* (Washington, D.C.: U.S. Government Printing Office, 1977), pp. 43–44; Michael K. Burns, "U.S. Reactivating Bases in Turkey," *Baltimore Sun*, October 21, 1978, pp. 1, 23; TUSLOG Detachment 28, *Command History, 1 January–30 September 1977*; "U.S. Electronic Espionage: A Memoir," *Ramparts* (August 1972) pp. 35–50 at 40.

77. Burns, "U.S. Reactivating Bases in Turkey."

78. Getler, "U.S. Intelligence Facilities in Turkey Get New Attention After Iran Turmoil."

79. Ibid.

80. Private information.

81. Ibid.

82. Hersh, *"The Target is Destroyed,"* p. 47; Private information.

83. Brian Toohey and Marian Wilkinson, *The Book of Leaks: Exposes in Defence of the Public's Right to Know* (North Ryde, Australia: Angus & Robertson, 1987), p. 135; Private information.

84. Private information.
85. United States Army Field Station Korea, *Fiscal Year 1986 Annual Historical Report*, 1987, p. 2; Private information.
86. Private information.
87. Ibid.
88. Ibid.
89. U.S. Congress, House Committee on Appropriations, *Military Construction Appropriations for 1987, Part 2* (Washington, D.C.: U.S. Government Printing Office, 1986), p. 682; Private information.
90. James Bamford, *The Puzzle Palace: A Report on NSA, America's Most Secret Agency* (Boston, Mass.: Houghton Mifflin, 1982), pp. 172–72; Private information.
91. Laurence Stern, "U.S. Tapped Top Russian's Car Phones," *Washington Post*, December 5, 1973, pp. A1, A16; Ernest Volkman, "U.S. Spies Lend an Ear to Soviets," *Newsday*, July 12, 1977, p. 7.
92. Stern, "U.S. Tapped Top Russians Car Phones."
93. Ibid.; Bill Gertz, "CIA Upset Because Perle Detailed Eavesdropping," *Washington Times*, April 15, 1987. p. 2A.
94. Jack Anderson, "CIA Eavesdrops on Kremlin Chiefs," *Washington Post*, September 16, 1971, p. F7.
95. Howard Kurtz, "Pollard: Top Israelis Backed Spy Ring," *Washington Post*, February 28, 1987, p. A8.
96. Arthur Gavshon and Desmond Rice, *The Sinking of the Belgrano* (London: Secker & Warburg, 1984), p. 205 n.5.
97. Trevor Armbrister, *A Matter of Accountability* (New York: Coward McCann, 1970), p. 87.
98. Ibid.; U.S. Congress, House Committee on Armed Services, *Inquiry into the U.S.S. Pueblo and EC-121 Incidents* (Washington, D.C.: U.S. Government Printing Office, 1969), pp. 1632, 1634; James Ennes, *Assault on the Liberty* (New York: Random House, 1980).
99. Paul Backus, "ESM and SIGINT Problems at the Interface," *Journal of Electronic Defense* (July–August 1981) 23ff.
100. Richard Halloran, "U.S. Navy Surveillance Ship is Stationed Off Central America," *New York Times*, February 25, 1982, pp. 1, 6; Private information.
101. Private information.
102. Richard Halloran, "2 U.S. Ships Enter Soviet Waters Off Crimea to Gather Intelligence," *New York Times*, March 19, 1986, pp. A1, A11; George C. Wilson, "Soviet Ships Shadowed U.S. Vessels' Transit," *Washington Post*, March 20, 1986, p. A33.
103. Halloran, "2 U.S. Ships Enter Soviet Waters Off Crimea to Gather Intelligence"; Private information.
104. Halloran, "2 U.S. Ships Enter Soviet Waters Off Crimea to Gather Intelligence"; Private information.
105. Philip Taubman, "Moscow Blames U.S. for Incident Between Warships," *New York Times*, February 14, 1988, pp. 1, 19; John H. Cushman, Jr., "2 Soviet Warships Reportedly Nudged U.S. Navy Vessel," *New York Times*, February 13, 1988, pp. 1, 6.
106. George C. Wilson, "U.S. Detects Slowdown in Shipments of Weapons to El Salvador," *Washington Post*, April 29, 1983, p. A13.

107. Richard Burt, "Technology is Essential to Arms Verification," *New York Times*, August 14, 1979, pp. C1, C2; Murray Sayle, "KE 007: A Conspiracy of Circumstance," *The New York Review of Books*, April 25, 1985, pp. 44–54.

108. *Jane's Fighting Ships 1983–1984* (London: Jane's Publishing, 1983), p. 681.

109. Norman Polmar, *The Ships and Aircraft of the U.S. Fleet*, 14th ed., (Annapolis, Md.: Naval Institute Press, 1987), p. 317.

110. Kenneth J. Stein, "Cobra Judy Phased Array Radar Tested," *Aviation Week and Space Technology*, August 10, 1981, pp. 70–73.

111. Ibid.; "X-Band Expands Cobra Judy's Repertoire," *Defense Electronics* (January 1985) 43–44.

112. Seymour Hersh, "Submarines of U.S. Stage Spy Missions Inside Soviet Waters," *New York Times*, May 25, 1975, pp. 1, 42.

113. Seymour Hersh, "A False Navy Report Alleged in Sub Crash," *New York Times*, July 6, 1975, pp. 1, 26.

114. Hersh, "Submarines of U.S. Stage Spy Missions Inside Soviet Waters."

115. Ibid.

116. Ibid.

117. Ibid.

118. *Jane's Fighting Ships 1983–1984*, p. 639.

119. Private information.

120. Bob Woodward, *Veil: The Secret Wars of the CIA 1981–1987* (New York: Simon & Schuster, 1987), pp. 448–449.

9 OCEAN SURVEILLANCE/ SPACE SURVEILLANCE/ NUCLEAR MONITORING

Whereas imagery and signals intelligence are particular varieties of technical collection that are used to gather information on a wide variety of targets, there are some targets about which information is gathered largely by a specialized set of collection systems.

Thus, some information about foreign naval activities, particularly in-port activities, is gathered by imaging and signals intelligence systems. KH-11s will periodically produce imagery of Murmansk, Petropavlovsk, and other major Soviet port areas as well as naval yards such as Nikolaev, while VORTEX satellites may intercept some of the communications from port areas. But a separate set of technical collectors perform the vast majority of the naval monitoring missions. Foreign space activities are partially monitored by KH-11s and SIGINT systems monitoring launch areas. However, detecting and tracking satellites in space is the function of a set of radar and optical systems, many designed specifically for the purpose. Likewise, while imagery and SIGINT make important contributions to the monitoring of foreign nuclear activities, the various systems that perform a unique nuclear monitoring mission are the crux of the U.S. ability to monitor Soviet and other nations' nuclear detonations.

OCEAN SURVEILLANCE

Twenty-five years ago, the Soviet Navy was predominantly concerned with coastal defense. Since then it has expanded dramatically to become a well-equipped "blue-water" Navy. As of 1987, the Soviet Union possessed six aircraft carriers, 283 other major surface combatants (e.g., destroyers), 77 ballistic missile submarines

(63 nuclear powered), 269 attack and cruise missile submarines (121 nuclear powered), and a large number of intelligence, oceanographic, and space support ships. Deployment of the Akula-class SSN and the Typhoon SSBN (with six to nine warheads on each of its twenty SLBMs) have further increased Soviet naval capabilities.[1] Thus, the Soviet fleet represents a major target of U.S. intelligence activities.

Additionally, the naval activities of numerous other nations, both hostile and friendly, are of interest to the U.S. intelligence community and policymakers. The ability of allied nations to fulfill alliance commitments or contribute to the protection of ships in the Persian Gulf is one concern. The naval capabilities and intentions of hostile nations such as Iran or North Korea can be an object of even greater concern. The ships of drug smugglers and arms traffickers are also often intelligence targets. Further, any naval activity in sensitive political, military or economic areas— for example, the Suez Canal, Sea of Japan, Panama Canal, Persian Gulf or Hawaiian Islands—is an intelligence target.

Systems employed to monitor such activities operate in space, in the air, on the ground, on the surface of the world's oceans, and underneath those oceans.

Until 1976, the U.S. Navy did not have a dedicated overhead reconnaissance system for ocean surveillance. Ocean surveillance data were obtained from U.S. imaging satellites, with the Air Force and Navy cooperating on reconnaissance matters. Thus, the April 18, 1975 launch of a high-resolution KH-8 satellite was intended to acquire data on the massive Soviet naval exercise then taking place.[2]

Initial studies for a dedicated ocean surveillance satellite system began in 1968. In 1970, the Chief of Naval Operations ordered a study of overall ocean surveillance requirements, which resulted in a five-volume *Ocean Surveillance Requirements Study* by the Naval Research Laboratory (NRL). Such studies were initiated by the Navy in response to the buildup in Soviet naval forces and capabilities. Designated as Program 749, the ocean surveillance satellite study focused on the development of high-resolution, phased-array radars that would allow all-weather ocean surveillance monitoring as well as detection of low-trajectory sea-launched missiles. The possibility of equipping the satellites with infrared scanners was also explored. Experimental phased-array radars were developed by Hughes Aircraft and Westinghouse Electric.[3]

Despite the emphasis of these initial studies, the ocean surveillance satellite system that resulted, CLASSIC WIZARD, lacks any radar capability. WHITE CLOUD, the spacecraft portion of the system, is a passive interceptor—it is apparently equipped with a passive infrared scanner and millimeter wave radiometers, as well as radio-frequency antennas capable of monitoring radio communications and radar emissions from Soviet submarines and ships. Passive interferometry (interferometry being the use of interference phenomena to make precise measurements) techniques are used to determine the location of Soviet vessels: the craft computes a ship's position from data provided by several antennas that measure the direction from which a vessel's radar or radio signals arrive.[4]

The satellite system consists of a mother ship and three subsatellites. The basic techniques involved in using multiple spacecraft for eavesdropping and direction finding on Soviet surface vessels and submarines were first demonstrated using three NRL spacecraft launched on December 14, 1971. The launch vehicle was a McDonnell-Douglas Thorad; a Lockheed Agena was used as the satellite dispenser to place the spacecraft in appropriate orbits.[5]

Present ocean surveillance satellites are launched from the Western Test Range—Vandenberg Air Force Base—into a near circular sixty-three-degree inclined orbit at an altitude of approximately 700 miles, employing Titan II boosters. The three spacecraft are dispersed from the main vehicle into three parallel orbits with latitude separation as well as time/distance separation along their orbital paths. There is a displacement of approximately 1,866 miles between passes.[6] At the 700-mile altitude, the spacecraft can receive signals from surface vessels more than 2,000 miles away, providing overlapping coverage on successive passes.

In addition to the 1971 test, there was apparently a test of a subsatellite on June 8, 1975, in which the subsatellite was ejected from the payload carrying a KH-9 satellite. Subsequently, there have been nine operational clusters placed in orbit on: April 30, 1976; December 8, 1977; March 3, 1980; February 9, 1983; June 9, 1983; February 6, 1984; February 9, 1986; May 15, 1987; and September 5, 1988.[7] Given the increased launch rate in recent years, the Navy requested and received funds for antenna upgrades at all CLASSIC WIZARD ground stations.

The subsatellites are relatively small, measuring approximately three by eight by one foot. The largest surface area on one side is covered by solar cells; four spherical objects that are deployed on the end of metal booms are believed to be sensors.[8]

The ground segment of the CLASSIC WIZARD system includes five ground stations, managed by the Naval Security Group Command, located at Diego Garcia; Guam; Adak, Alaska; Winter Harbor, Maine; and Edzell, Scotland. Several tracking domes have been built at Edzell to control and receive information from these satellites. Information received at the stations can be quickly transmitted to regional ocean surveillance centers and via satellite to a main downlink at Blossom Point, Maryland.[9]

As with imagery and signals intelligence activities directed at land-based targets, the United States employs several aircraft in an ocean surveillance role. Included are the P-3, EP-3E, and EA-3B (Skywarrior).

The most important component of the U.S. ocean surveillance program is the P-3C Orion. The P-3C is the third generation of the P-3 antisubmarine warfare aircraft that succeeded the Neptune P2V in the late 1950s. A typical P-3C mission, which can last up to fourteen hours, has three main objectives: selecting the area in which to search for a submarine, finding the submarine, and determining its identity.[10]

The first generation of the P-3, the P-3A, was produced by converting an Electra airliner—shortening its airframe by twelve feet, equipping it with weapons, and giving it an increased fuel capacity. The P-3B version has a fourfold increase in acoustic processing capability over the P-3A, and in 1981 infrared detection and HARPOON missile systems were added. Four P-3Bs have been reconfigured for multisensor surveillance, two assigned to the Pacific Fleet and two to the Atlantic Fleet. The aircraft are then deployed from their parent command to various areas of Soviet naval activity. They have communications intelligence, electronic intelligence, photographic, nuclear, acoustic, and infrared sensors installed. The information collected is forwarded to processing centers. Operating at between 200 and 25,000 feet, the plane has a range of 4,000 nm and an endurance time of ten hours. In early 1987, a P-3B photographed the Soviet guided missile destroyer *Osmotritenny* as the vessel crossed the Indian Ocean en route to join the Soviet Pacific Fleet.[11]

The P-3C itself has undergone three updates and is scheduled to undergo a fourth in 1989 to increase its capability to counter quieter Soviet submarines. In it present configuration it stands 33.7 feet high, is 1,168 feet long, and has a 99.7-foot wingspan. Its maximum speed is 410 knots an hour, while it has a service ceiling of 28,300 feet. Its sixteen hours endurance capability and speed give it a range of 4,500 nautical miles; it can search up to 95,000 square nautical miles in one hour.[12]

The P-3C can carry up to eighty-four sonobuoys. Once deployed, the sonobuoys, which are dropped in patterns along the ocean's surface, lower small, highly sensitive hydrophones (or sensors) which listen for sounds emitted from submarines. Forty-eight of the sonobuoys are preset and loaded in external launch chutes prior to takeoff. The remaining thirty-six are carried internally and their operating channels can be chosen during the mission. It is possible to select operating depth and length of transmission time for many of the sonobuoys. The acoustic operators on the P-3C can monitor up to sixteen sonobuoys simultaneously. A sonar-type recorder stores all acoustic data for reference to reconstruct the missions in detail.[13]

In addition to the sonobuoys, there are several non-acoustic detection systems on the P-3C. Its magnetic anomaly detector (MAD) is used in concert with the submarine anomaly detector to determine if known, submarine magnetic profiles are present. To get a good MAD reading, the plane must fly 200 to 300 feet above the water. Under the base of the plane are automatic cameras. The Infrared Detection System converts infrared energy into visible light and provides an image of the target. An airborne search radar, designated AN/APS-115, is used to detect radar returns from ships or submarines on the surface and pick out periscopes at the waterline.[14]

P-3Cs, of which there were 232 on January 1, 1985 (with 16 funded but not delivered and another 18 requested for Fiscal Years 1986 and 1987), make up 21 active P-3C squadrons. These squadrons are based at various locations throughout the world, including: Clark AB in the Philippines; Misawa and Kadena in Japan; Adak, Alaska; Keflavik, Iceland; Hawaii; Anderson AFB, Guam; Rota, Spain; Italy; Ascension Island; Diego Garcia; Lejes Air Base on Terciera Island in the Azores; California; Canada; Bermuda; and Puerto Rico. Since 1983, P-3Cs have also operated from Pakistani air bases, most commonly from Mauripaur Air Base, near Karachi.[15]

The Navy has requested $69.1 million in Fiscal Year 1989 for research and development for a follow-on to the P-3C: a Long-Range Air Antisubmarine Warfare Capability Aircraft (LRAACA).[16]

Two modifications of the P-3 are used for intelligence collection. Five P-3C airframes have been specifically configured for the collection, analysis, and recording of high-quality acoustic data on Soviet submarines, sonars, and underwater communications. These aircraft, known by the code name BEARTRAP, have a 4,000-nautical-mile range, an operational altitude of 200 to 10,000 feet, and twelve hours endurance. They operate from Patrol Squadron Special Project Units One (Brunswick, Maine) and Two (Barbers Pt., Hawaii).[17]

Another modification of the P-3A is the EP-3, which has been specifically altered for signals intelligence collection. The plane is distinguished from the Orion by a flat circular radome under the fuselage and lacks the long, thin MAD boom at the tail. The plane is a four engine, land-based aircraft with a 3,400-nautical-mile range, an operational altitude of 18,000 to 25,000 feet, and an endurance capability of twelve hours.[18]

The twelve EP-3Es are assigned (six each) to the Atlantic and Pacific Fleet Air Reconnaissance Squadrons, VQ-1 PR and VQ-2JQ, and are headquartered at Rota, Spain and Agana, Guam. The Rota-based planes operate over the Mediterranean and Baltic seas and the Atlantic Ocean. Detachments are located at Naval Air Station, Sigonella, Italy; Hellenikon Air Station, Greece; and Stuttgart, West Germany. Planes also are periodically deployed to RAF Wyton and RAF Akrotiri, Cyprus. From those locations the planes fly missions over the Mediterranean, Baltic, Caribbean, North Atlantic and Norwegian seas. COMINT missions are code named FLOOR DOOR, while ELINT missions are code named FLOOR LEADER.[19]

The planes subordinate to the Guam headquarters operate over all of the Pacific (especially the Sea of Japan and the South China Sea, from the Sea of Okhotsk to the west coast of Africa) and the Indian Ocean. Detachments from Guam are found at Atsugi, Japan, and Cubi Point in the Philippines, while there is an operating location at Diego Garcia. The SIGINT missions flown in the Far East are designated BEGGAR HAWK, BEGGAR SHADOW, and BEGGAR WATCH.[20]

The targets of the EP-3E may be land-based radars and UHF-VHF communications systems. Thus, a Soviet ship leaving its construction site for a trial in the open ocean may be visited by an EP-3E. For example, the Soviet nuclear-powered cruiser *Kirov* is weighted down with a variety of radar systems—Top Pair and Top Steer 360-degree search radars, Palm Frond navigational radars, Top Dome missile-guidance systems for the SA-N-6 antiaircraft missiles, Pop Group radars for SA-N-4 aircraft missiles, Eye Bowl guidance radars for SS-N-14 antisubmarine missiles, a Kite search fire-control radar for the two 110-mm cannon, Bass Tilt fire-control radars for the eight 30-mm-rotating machine guns, and two Round House and one Fly Screen navigational aids for the helicopters carried on board.[21]

Twelve EA-3Bs are also employed for intelligence purposes. The EA-3B is often employed on aircraft carriers for periods ranging from days to months to extend the range of coverage. The EA-3B is primarily targeted against communications and non-communications emitters in VHF-UHF frequency range. Its targets may be air, surface, subsurface, or land-based. The aircraft has a recording capability for ground processing of collected signals. Perishable information can be transmitted directly from the aircraft via secure UHF communications. The aircraft operates at 20,000 to 35,000 feet with a range of less than 2,000 nm and can operate for 5.5 hours.[22]

Two U-2s also serve in an ocean surveillance role. These are U-2 variants with a longer loiter capability and specially equipped with a Westinghouse high-resolution radar, infrared scanner, and ELINT and COMINT receivers designed for ocean surveillance purposes.[23]

The Naval Security Group Command operates a network of land-based stations directed at HFDF monitoring of naval activity. The stations generally use the AN/FRD-10 circularly disposed antenna array, which has a nominal range of 3,200 nm. The network, known as CLASSIC BULLSEYE, monitors the Caribbean Sea, Atlantic Ocean, Mediterranean Sea, Indian, and Pacific oceans. A total of twenty-two stations are configured in three operating nodes (Atlantic Fleet, Pacific Fleet, Naval Forces Europe). The bearings produced by individual stations are used by a net control station for automated fix production.[24]

A 378-person Naval Security Group Activity, headquartered at Homestead, Florida and operating out of Card Sound, employs an AN/FRD-10 and is part of the North Atlantic–Caribbean–South Atlantic HFDF net, and monitors air and naval activity in the Atlantic and Caribbean. Farther up the eastern coast is an 82-person NSG Detachment at Sugar Grove, West Virginia and a 593-person NSG Activity at Northwest, Virginia. Both use AN/FRD-10s to monitor Soviet and other naval traffic in the Middle Atlantic. Farther north, the 365-person NSG Activity at Winter Harbor, Maine employs an AN/FRD-10 to monitor naval activity in the North Atlantic.[25]

Three European stations involved in naval monitoring are located at Edzell, United Kingdom; Keflavik, Iceland and Terceira, Portugal. Edzell is home to a 1000-person NSG Activity and 79-person Marine Support Batallion, Company B. Employing its AN/FRD-10 antenna, with its eighty vertical supports, each ninety feet in height, it conducts high-frequency intercepts of Soviet Northern Fleet activity, with secondary coverage of Soviet/Warsaw Pact naval activity in the Baltic and Mediterranean Seas. The 132-person NSG Activity at Keflavik, Iceland operates an AN/FRD-10 as part of the NSGC's North Atlantic HFDF net. Terceira, Portugal is home to an 87-person NSG Activity which conducts intercept operations against Soviet naval/shipping HF communications in the North Atlantic, as well as some diplomatic traffic.[26]

Foreign-based stations in the Pacific/Indian Ocean HFDF nets are located at Diego Garcia, British Indian Ocean Territory; Clark Air Base, Philippines; and

Torri Station, Okinawa. The Diego Garcia station hosts a 124-person NSG Department that operates a Pusher HF antenna directed at monitoring naval activity in the Indian Ocean. The Air Force's AN/FLR-9 antenna at Clark is also employed by the Naval Security Group Activity for HFDF operations against naval traffic in the area and off the coast of Vietnam. The NSG Activity at Hanza, Okinawa employs an AN/FRD-10 to intercept Soviet, Chinese and Vietnamese naval communications.[27]

Stations in Guam and along the West Coast of the United States also play a substantial role in the monitoring of naval activity in the Pacific. The 361-person NSG Activity at Adak, Alaska along with the 26-person Company I, Marine Support Batallion, monitors Soviet naval communications in the Northern Pacific region. The 336-person Naval Security Detachment at Guam, employing an AN/FRD-10, is responsible for high-frequency coverage of USSR, PRC and Vietnamese naval activity in the Western Pacific. At Wahiawa, Hawaii, a 257-person NSG unit also employs an AN/FRD-10 antenna to monitor naval traffic around the Hawaiian Islands, as well as collecting internationally leased carrier and other communications for the Pacific region. At Imperial Beach, California, 60 members of the NSG Activity from San Diego operate an AN/FRD-10, as does the 278-person NSG Activity at Skaggs Island, California.[28]

Ocean surveillance operations are also conducted from surface ship-based platforms. Thirty USN surface combatants are outfitted with equipment code named CLASSIC OUTBOARD that allows the detection, classification, and location of hostile ships, aircraft, and submarines by exploitation of their command and control communications. The data collected, like that from ground stations, are transmitted to Net Control Centers for correlation, as well as being analyzed on board.[29]

In addition to CLASSIC OUTBOARD ships, four ships (two Atlantic/European, two Pacific) are outfitted with Operational Intelligence Collection System Vans, with both COMINT and ELINT capabilities. Selected surface combatants also carry an AN/SSQ-80 communications intercept system, capable of intercepting HF and VHF tactical communications. The system is capable of detecting communications activity and classifying the emitter. All 215 surface combatants are equipped with the AN/WLR-1/WLR-11 system, capable of passively intercepting electromagnetic emissions and determining the bearing of the emitter source from the sensor platform by means of direction finding. The equipment can detect and measure parameters to permit identification of missile, airborne, and shipborne radars.[30]

Some surface ships have a portable system known as CLUSTER PACE (Portable Acoustic Collection Equipment). Among the capabilities of the CLUSTER PACE system are a tape recording capability, which allows post-mission retrieval of underwater signals for intelligence exploitation.[31]

As important as intelligence concerning surface naval activities is, intelligence concerning underseas activities is even more important. The Soviet Union has placed the preponderance of its strategic nuclear weapons capability on land, but it also maintains sixty-two submarines armed with SLBMs and has begun to deploy the modern Typhoon SSBN armed with multiwarhead SS-N-20 missiles.

Additionally, Soviet attack submarines represent a threat to the U.S. SSBN fleet. In the midst of the transition from Poseidon to Trident submarines, the U.S. SSBN fleet represents only half of the number of Soviet SSBNs, although they are qualitatively superior. Since the submarines play a more significant role in U.S. nuclear strategy than Soviet SSBNs in Soviet strategy, it is imperative to detect and track any possible threats to U.S. SSBNs.

Much of the data gathered fall under the heading of acoustic intelligence (ACOUSTINT)—intelligence information derived from the analysis of acoustic waves radiated either intentionally or unintentionally by the submarine into the surrounding ocean. This includes the underwater acoustic waves from submarines that can be used to determine the "signature" of those vehicles, much in the same manner as voice autographs can be developed of individuals.

The most important submarine detection and tracking system is a global network of large, fixed, sea-bottom hydrophones that passively listen for the sounds generated by submarines. These arrays are collectively known as SOSUS (Sound Surveillance System), although only about two-thirds of the arrays are part of the SOSUS network proper, the other one-third being allied systems. The SOSUS system was described by one U.S. admiral in 1979 as the "backbone of our ASW [Antisubmarine Warfare] detection capability."[32]

SOSUS was described by the Stockholm International Peace Research Institute (SIPRI):

> Each SOSUS installation consists of an array of hundreds of hydrophones laid out on the sea floor, or moored at depths most conducive to sound propagation, and connected by submarine cables for transmission of telemetry. In such an array a sound wave arriving from a distant submarine will be successively detected by different hydrophones according to their geometric relationship to the direction from which the wave arrives. This direction can be determined by noting the order in which the wave is detected at different hydrophones. In practice the sensitivity of the array is enhanced many times by adding the signals from several individual hydrophones after introducing appropriate time delays between them. The result is a listening "beam" that can be "steered" in various sectors of the ocean by varying the pattern of time delays. The distance from the array to the sound source can be calculated by measuring the divergence of the sound rays within the array or by triangulating from adjacent arrays.[33]

Development work on the SOSUS began in 1950, at which time the hydrophone arrays were code named CAESAR. Installation of the first SOSUS/CAESAR array was completed on the continental shelf off the East Coast of the United States in 1954. Subsequent SOSUS arrays were installed elsewhere on the East Coast, at Brawdy in Wales, and at other locations as well. The CAESAR arrays have been progressively updated and the technology is now in its fifth generation of development.[34]

The CAESAR arrays proved extremely effective during the Cuban missile crisis of October 1962, when every Soviet submarine in the area was detected and closely trailed, and it was decided to expand and upgrade the network. Variants, code-named COLOSSUS, were constructed along the Pacific coast of the United States. Another array was established covering the Greenland–Iceland–United Kingdom (GIUK) Gap, the Gap being the portion of the Atlantic through which Soviet submarines stationed at the Polyarnyy submarine base in the northwestern Soviet Union must pass to head toward the United States. Even earlier warning is provided by an array strung between Andoya, Norway and Bear Island.[35]

By the late 1960s several more arrays had been established. An upgraded variant of CAESAR, COLOSSUS, was deployed along the Pacific coast of the United States and extends from the top of Alaska to the Baja Peninsula. COLOSSUS employed a more advanced form of sonar than CAESAR. Farther out in the Pacific a circular array 1,300 miles long and code-named SEA SPIDER surrounds the Hawaiian Islands. Reportedly it was this array that monitored and localized the breakup of the Soviet submarine that sank north of Hawaii in March 1968. Another Pacific array extends from Alaska and runs parallel to the Aleutian Islands. An array that runs down the western side of the Kuril Islands allows detection of Soviet submarines exiting the naval base at Petropavlovsk or the Sea of Okhotsk.[36]

Construction began on an array, known as the Azores Fixed Acoustic Range (AFAR), in September 1968 off the island of Santa Maria, the southernmost of the Azores group. In May 1972 the system was commissioned by NATO with a dual mission—to track Soviet submarines either approaching the Strait of Gibraltar or on passage around the Cape of Good Hope. An array in the Bosphorous between Yugoslavia and Turkey can detect submarines exiting the Soviet Black Sea port of Sevastopol. Yet another array is placed next to the coast of Taiwan and the Philippines, and there is an Indian Ocean array in the vicinity of Diego Garcia. Other arrays are located off Turkey (in addition to the Bosphorous array), Japan, Puerto Rico, Barbados, Canada (Argentia, Newfoundland), Italy, Denmark, Gibraltar, Galeta Island (in Panama), and Guam.[37]

The hydrophones are sealed in tanks, approximately twenty-four to a tank, with cables transmitting the data to shore facilities. The first step in converting the data collected by the hydrophones to finished intelligence are the Naval Facilities (NAVFACs) and Naval Regional Processing Centers (NRPCs), which are the initial recipients of the data. There were, in 1983, seventeen Naval Facilities (down from twenty-two a few years before)—eight Pacific Fleet and nine Atlantic Fleet facilities. Among the NAVFACs still operating are those at Adak, Alaska; Argentia, New-foundland; Bermuda; Brawdy, Wales; Centerville Beach, California; Whidbey Island, Washington; Keflavik, Iceland; Point Sur, Big Sur California; Naval Air Station, Barbers Point, Oahu; and Ritidian Point, Guam. The Whidbey Island facility, with a staff of 200, will receive remote data from unmanned relay centers at Coos Bay and Pacific Beach and provide signal analysis and processing of underwater signals, with the data transmitted twenty-four hours a day to the Pacific Fleet.[38]

From the NAVFACs and the NRPCs the data are sent by landline or FLTSATCOM (Fleet Satellite Communications) satellite to Naval Ocean Processing Facilities at Damn Neck, Virginia and Ford Island, Hawaii. Those facilities are responsible for centralized reporting, correlation, localization, and tracking of submarine targets. The FLTSATCOM system has a variety of missions in addition to transmitting SOSUS data, especially providing a communications link between command and communication centers and ships and submarines at sea.[39]

The data collected about each submarine detected—its sonar echo and the noises made by its engine, cooling system, and the movement of its propellers—can be translated into a recognition signal. A distinctive pattern can be determined that indicates not only a particular type of submarine—an Alfa-class attack submarine versus Typhoon-class ballistic missile carrying submarine—but also the individual submarine. Thus the data, when analyzed, operate much like fingerprints or voiceprints do in identifying different individuals.

In regard to SOSUS' identification capabilities, a Massachusetts Institute of Technology (MIT) study concluded that location of older and noisier Soviet submarines to within 10 miles of their actual position from a distance of 10,000 miles was possible under the best circumstances, while a localization to within 25 miles from several thousand miles was feasible in most cases. However, its capability against more modern Soviet submarines is probably considerably less.[40]

While SOSUS capabilities are excellent in some regards, the system can be vulnerable and fallible. The cables laid by the Navy's underwater construction teams can be and have been cut by Soviet ships. Soviet trawlers have attempted to hook the cables, while undersea midget submarines patrol to locate and identify the location of the hydrophone arrays. According to one account, when it can be made to appear accidental, the cables are cut and recovered for examination. To deal with damage to the cables the United States has a fleet of cable repair ships, designated T-ARC, operated by the Military Sealift Command.[41]

Of particular concern has been the fact that in 1980 a Soviet Alfa attack submarine slipped past the SOSUS in the North Atlantic, and would have gone undetected had it not broken radio silence. The Alfa class is the second smallest (in length) of the Soviet attack submarines. To attempt to prevent such incidents, a SOSUS update was planned in early 1984.[42]

However, irrespective of the race between Soviet quieting programs and SOSUS enhancement programs, a fundamental change in Soviet submarine capabilities over the years has reduced the value of the SOSUS. The first three generations of Soviet sea-based ballistic missiles—the SS-N-4 Snark, the SS-N-5 Serb, and the SS-N-6 Sawfly—had ranges between 350 and 1,600 nautical miles. Beginning in 1973, with the operation of the SS-N-8, with a range of 4,200 nautical miles, Soviet subs did not have to exit Soviet home waters to hit targets in the United States. Soviet capability in this regard has grown over the years with the deployment of the SS-N-8 Mod 2, with a 4,900 nautical mile range, and the SS-N-18 and SS-N-20, with ranges of from 3,500 to 4,500 nautical miles.[43]

An advanced version of the SOSUS that is under development is the Fixed Distributed Surveillance (FDS) system, which is intended to counter quieter Soviet submarines. The FDS will integrate large-scale, sea-bottom-mounted acoustic sensor arrays on a single fiber-optic cable system.[44]

Additionally two other sonar surveillance systems have been developed—the Rapidly Deployable Surveillance System (RDSS) and the Surface Towed Array Surveillance System (SURTASS). Together with the SOSUS they form the Integrated Undersea Surveillance System.

The RDSS is designed to operate in areas where fixed or manned systems cannot operate safely or reliably. The system consists of large sonobuoys that can be remotely deployed by aircraft and ships (from frigates on up) or launched through submarine torpedo tubes, and moor themselves automatically to the ocean bottom. The RDSS would be particularly useful in monitoring "such high interest areas as the Dardanelles, Baltic approaches, Straits of Gibraltar, and the [GIUK] gap."[45]

The SURTASS is designed to provide a mobile backup to the SOSUS network. It will be used in areas where the SOSUS is unavailable or inoperative, or can be used to enhance coverage within SOSUS regions. The program involves the acquisition of twelve 217-foot ships, designated T-AGOS, designed to tow the 1,220-meter-long aperture hydrophone array by a 2,000-meter cable. Data from the hydrophone array will be processed on board ship and sent via FLTSATCOM and DSCS satellites to the ocean processing facilities at Damn Neck and Ford Island.[46]

SPACE SURVEILLANCE

In addition to being concerned with events on land and sea, the U.S. intelligence community is also concerned with events in space. An accurate understanding of the capabilities of foreign space systems is required for assessing military capabilities, operational security, intelligence, and ASAT targeting.

The nation whose space systems are of primary concern for the U.S. intelligence community is, of course, the Soviet Union. The capabilities of Soviet navigation, communications, meteorological, and other military support satellites can have a significant effect on the overall capabilities of Soviet military forces. The capabilities of Soviet reconnaissance satellites have to be factored into plans to provide operational security to U.S. military forces and research and development activities. The vulnerabilities of the satellites, if known, can be employed in developing plans to negate such satellites, via ASAT weapons or other means, in the event of war.

The space systems of other nations, whether civilian or military, are also of interest. As other nations, such as China or France, develop an increasing variety of space systems for military support purposes, their impact on military capabilities will grow. Intelligence about civilian communications satellites will be used to develop plans to intercept the communications passing through those satellites.

The space surveillance network is faced with a formidable task. It makes an average of 45,000 sightings of orbiting objects each day. Twenty percent of the objects and debris cannot be reliably tracked. About 7,000 orbiting objects from the size of a baseball or larger are tracked. According to the Commander in Chief of the U.S. Space Command, the network is a predictive rather than a constant surveillance system and is especially deficient beyond 3,000 nm.[47]

The means of detecting, tracking, and investigating foreign satellites are primarily ground based, although research and development is underway which may give the United States a dedicated space-to-space reconnaissance capability. The Defense Advanced Research Projects Agency (DARPA) has conducted Space Infrared Experiments (SIRE) as part of its Space Infrared Surveillance Program to develop an infrared system to detect hostile satellites. The system has been successfully tested on the ground.[48]

Development of a space-based surveillance system in the far term was described in 1983, by the Air Force Deputy Chief of Staff for Research, Development, and Acquisition as the "primary thrust of the Space Surveillance Technology Program." The system was to provide full-earth orbit coverage, reduce overseas basing of sensors, and provide near real-time "operationally responsive coverage of objects and events in space."[49] Thus, the Air Force requested $22.6 million for Fiscal Year 1984 for research, development, testing, and evaluation of a Space-Based Surveillance System (SBSS) with a deployment goal in the early 1990s. The system was envisaged as consisting of four satellites in low-altitude equatorial orbit. The long-wave, infrared mosaic-staring sensor on each satellite would have viewed the volume of space from approximately sixty nautical miles to geosynchronous altitude.[50]

Subsequently the SBSS program was absorbed into the SDI program and renamed the Space Surveillance and Tracking System (SSTS). As of Fall 1986 it was projected that an SSTS system, would be able to monitor satellites in space as well as characterize ICBM signatures against the earth's background radiation.[51]

The overall ground-based military space surveillance system is known as the Space Detection and Tracking System (SPADATS); the Air Force portion of the system is SPACETRACK. SPADATS consists of three types of sensors: dedicated, collateral, and contributing. Dedicated sensors are Strategic Air Command (SAC) and Navy sensors, with a primary mission of space surveillance. Collateral sensors are SAC sensors with a secondary space surveillance role. Contributing sensors are non-SAC sensors with a secondary space surveillance mission.[52] Sensors can also be differentiated, based on whether they employ radar, electro-optics or some other means of detection.

Until the mid-1980s, a major space surveillance system was a series of Baker-Nunn telescope/cameras at five locations. The role of the Baker-Nunn cameras has been taken by the Ground-Based Electro-Optical Deep Space Surveillance System (GEODSS), which consists of electro-optical systems at five locations—White Sands, New Mexico; Maui, Hawaii; Taegu, South Korea; Diego Garcia; and (in 1989) the southern coast of Portugal.[53]

The GEODSS provides the capability to track objects optically from above 3,000 nautical miles out to 22,000 miles. It is also able to search up to 17,400 square degrees per hour. Further, GEODSS installations are close enough together to provide overlapping coverage to overcome poor weather at any one site.[54]

As with the Baker-Nunn system, the GEODSS depends on the collection of light reflected by the objects under investigation and is operational only at night during clear weather. Additionally, sensitivity and resolution is downgraded by adverse atmospheric conditions. On the other hand, GEODSS is able to provide real-time data, with a computer-managed instant video display of surveillance data. Further, the computer automatically filters stars from the night sky backdrop, and then uses its memory of known space objects to determine the existence of new or unknown space objects, alerting the user when such objects are found.[55]

The GEODSS consists of three telescopes at each site which work together under computer control. Two forty-inch telescopes, designed primarily for high-altitude object observation, are capable of examining up to 2,400 square degrees of the night sky each hour. A fifteen-inch telescope is employed mainly for low-altitude observations, searching up to 15,000 square degrees per hour. Each telescope has a sensitive Ebiscon tube which will register the image of an object for real-time processing, as well as a radiometer for optical signature characterization and identification.[56]

According to one account,

In a typical operational scenario the small telescope will be conducting a low-altitude, high-speed search, one of the large telescopes will be tracking an object at high altitude and the other large telescope will be tracking an object—at either high or low altitudes and collecting radiometric data.[57]

To locate an object, the system computes an object's position from information on its orbit and points the telescope to the required position. The operator may then pick out the spacecraft by locating a stationary object in a moving star field. The operator may also fix the telescope on the moving star background and collect camera frames that show a satellite streak building up.[58]

GEODSS cameras can reach to a geosynchronous altitude—as demonstrated in 1985, when a GEODSS site photographed a FLTSATCOM satellite at geosynchronous altitude. At that altitude the cameras can detect a reflective object the size of a soccer ball.[59]

The present sensor capability of the GEODSS is scheduled to be improved by the replacement of the Ebiscon by charged couple devices (CCDs). The CCDs will allow for higher quality images of space objects.[60]

A second set of dedicated sensors are those that constitute the Naval Space Surveillance (NAVSPASUR) system. The NAVSPASUR system detects and tracks satellites that pass through an electronic fence that consists of a fan-shaped radar beam with a 7,500-mile range, extending in an east-west direction from San Diego, California to Ft. Stewart, Georgia. The beam cannot be steered. Detection results when the satellite passing through the beam deflects the beam energy back to earth, where it is detected by several arrays of dipole antennas—"a form of cheap, unsophisticated antenna not unlike a television receiving aerial."[61]

The central transmitter for the beam is located at Lake Kicapoo, Texas with two smaller transmitting stations at Gila River, Arizona and Jordan Lake, Alabama.

The six receiver stations—at San Diego, California; Elephant Butte, New Mexico; Red River, Arkansas; Silver Lake, Mississippi; Hawkinsville, Georgia; and Ft. Stewart, Georgia—are all located, as are the transmitting stations, across the southern part of the United States along a great circle inclined about thirty-three degrees to the equator. The data obtained are then transmitted to the NAVSPASUR Headquarters and Computation Center at Dahlgren, Virginia.[62]

On October 1, 1984, the NAVSPASUR became the Alternate NORAD Space Surveillance Center (ANSSC) responsible for tasking space sensors and space catalog maintenance backup to the Cheyenne Mountain Complex.[63]

Two mechanically steered AN/GPS-10 model radars, with 60-foot dishes and ranges of 23,000 miles, constitute two-thirds of the Pacific Radar Barrier (PACBAR). One radar, operated by 17th Surveillance Squadron, 1st Space Wing, is located at San Miguel in the Philippines. The second GPS-10 site is located at Saipan, North Mariana Islands. Also part of the PACBAR system is the ALTAIR radar at Kwajalein Atoll. Along with the San Miguel radar, ALTAIR provides radar coverage in their area of the Pacific. The Saipan radar provides coverage of the portion of the Pacific corridor not covered by the other two radars.[64]

Two additional dedicated sensors are the electro-optical telescopes located at Haleakala, Maui, Hawaii and Malabar, Florida. The telescopes at the Maui Optical Tracking and Identification Facility (MOTIF), code-named TEAL BLUE, are two co-mounted forty-eight-inch Cassegrain telescopes capable of both near-earth and deep space satellite tracking and space object identification, using visual light and long-wave infrared imaging.[65]

Along with the similar Malabar telescopes, code-named TEAL AMBER, the two sites provide computer enhanced high-resolution, close-up photographs of Soviet and Chinese spacecraft. It has been reported that the system has been used to photograph cosmonauts during one of the space walks conducted from the Soviet SALYUT 6 space laboratory. Such photography implies a resolution of less than forty inches.[66]

Collateral sensors include the mechanically steered Ballistic Missile Early Warning System (BMEWS) radars, radars at Shemya Island, Alaska; Cavalier, North Dakota; Pirinclik, Turkey; and the PAVE PAWS, SLBM Early Warning radars.[67]

The main function of the BMEWS is to track missiles, determining the number launched and their intended targets. The system consists of three-sites—Clear, Alaska; Thule, Greenland; and Fylingdales, Moor (Great Britain)—each with a pair of radars. The Thule and Fylingdales sites are each equipped with AN/FPS-49 tracking and AN/FPS-50 detection radars while the Clear site is equipped with an AN/FPS-92 tracking radar in addition to its AN/FPS-50. The AN/FPS-50 antennas direct a fan of radio energy for detection purposes; the steerable AN/FPS-49 consists of dish antennas within their radomes to track targets acquired by the AN/FPS-50. Together the radars provide a 3,000-mile detection and tracking range. It is planned to convert all the radars to phased-array radars.[68]

The PAVE PAWS system consists of AN/FPS-115 large phased-array radars at three sites—Beale AFB, California; Otis AFB, Massachusetts; and Goodfellow

AFB, Texas—and an AN/FPS-123 (V)3 radar at Robins AFB, Georgia. Each radar has two arrays, providing a total of 240 degrees of coverage out to 3,100 miles. The site at Robins also provides surveillance and tracking of space objects and will also take over the mission of the AN/FPS-85 radar at Eglin AFB, Florida.[69]

The AN/FPS-85 phased array at Eglin was constructed in 1967. The radar, thirteen stories high and as long as a city block, has its principal axis aligned due south across the Gulf of Mexico and is capable of receiving and transmitting over an arc extending sixty degrees on either side. Most satellites pass through its beam, which has a range of 2,500 miles, twice a day.[70]

As with COBRA DANE, the AN/FPS-85 "consists of several thousand individual transmitters, the power outputs of which are added together by controlling their phases to form a single beam which can be electronically swept across the sky in millionths of a second."[71] The radar can search for unknown objects across 120 degrees of azimuth, from horizon to zenith, while simultaneously tracking several already acquired targets. In a typical 24-hour period, it makes 10,000 observations.[72]

When first established, the radar was the main U.S.-based active sensor of the Spacetrack system. Thirty percent of its operating time was devoted to search and surveillance, 50 percent to tracking specific satellite targets requested by NORAD, and 20 percent to SLBM early warning. Today, one-third of its operating time is devoted to space surveillance; its remaining time is occupied by SLBM detection and other tasks.[73]

The Perimeter Acquisition Radar Characterization System (PARCS), run by the 10th Missile Warning Squadron at Cavalier, North Dakota, is a vestige of the U.S. ABM system that was dismantled in 1975. With a 3,100-mile range, the PARCS provides early warning and "also provides surveillance, tracking, reporting, and space object identification (SOI) support for space surveillance and intelligence operations."[74]

Strategic verification radars also used in a space surveillance role are the phased-array COBRA DANE (AN/FPS-108) and the mechanically steered AN/FPS-79 radar at Pirinclik, Turkey, which have been discussed. The COBRA DANE has a 28,000-mile range, while the AN/FPS-79 has a 24,000-mile range. With its coverage extending northward over an arc from Kamchatka to the Bering Straits, COBRA DANE can be used for tracking satellites in polar and near-polar orbits.[75]

Contributing sensors provide inputs to the SPADATS data base on the basis of contracts or agreements with their governmental or non-governmental operators. Thus, the FPQ-14 and FPQ-15 mechanically steered radars at Antigua Island and Ascension Island, whose primary mission is to provide launch support to the Eastern Test Range, are also employed for space surveillance. Similarly, the FPS-16 radar at Onizuka AFS, California, the FPQ-14 radar at Kaena Point, Hawaii, and the ALCOR and ALTAIR radars at Kwajalein Atoll are all employed for space surveillance purposes in addition to their primary launch support missions.[76]

The MIT Lincoln Laboratory's Milstone and Haystack radars at Westford, Massachusetts are mechanically steered radars whose primary mission is satellite tracking. The Haystack radar can resolve down to one foot objects in low-earth orbit and has been described in congressional hearings as providing "images of orbiting satellites that we can get from no other location. [It is a] long-range, high-altitude capable radar which provides extremely good intelligence data and now has a real-time operational reporting capability."[77]

In addition, the AMOS (Maui Optical Station) electro-optical telescope at Halea-kala, Maui has satellite tracking as its primary mission. Recently, SPACECOM has plugged the National Science Foundation UHF radar developed by Lincoln Laboratory's Electro-Optical Test Site at Socorro, New Mexico into its network of deep-space sensors.[78]

Figure 9-1 shows the location of U.S. ground-based space surveillance sites.

NUCLEAR DETONATION MONITORING

As noted in Chapter 1, a subject of considerable interest to the U.S. intelligence community is the nuclear energy programs of foreign nations. Of greatest priority are the nuclear weapons aspects of these programs, particularly when actual nuclear detonations are involved.

Detection of such detonations is important in several respects. It allows the United States to monitor compliance with several international agreements and treaties concerning such activity. The United States is a signatory to the 1963 Partial Test Ban Treaty which banned atmospheric testing and testing in space; the 1974 Threshold Test Ban Treaty barring underground nuclear testing of devices with a yield greater than 150 kilotons; and the Peaceful Nuclear Explosion (PNE) Treaty of 1976.[79] Of the 603 Soviet nuclear explosions that have taken place since 1949, over 400 have taken place under one or more treaty regime.

The same collection systems that can be employed for treaty verification purposes obviously can also be employed to monitor the nuclear detonation activities of nonsignatories such as France, China, South Africa, and Israel. Whether a country is a treaty signatory or not, the United States is concerned with the sophistication and likely future development of nuclear weapons. Nuclear monitoring can provide, at least, some clues in this regard. Additionally, nuclear detonation monitoring can provide data on the characteristics of detonated devices that can be employed to develop countermeasures. Thus, it has been noted in Congressional testimony,

> another aspect [of the U.S. worldwide nuclear test detection system] is devoted to the general area of nuclear weapon diagnostics. As a general rule, the assessment of the sophistication of a foreign weapons development program and the estimation of the probable intent of the developing nation in the application of nuclear weapons require some knowledge of the internal details of the device.
>
> Such questions as yield, nuclear materials employed and the construction characteristics that determine size, weight, and output of the device are all-important to determine the type of delivery system that might be required and the vulnerability of U.S. systems

Figure 9–1. Sites of U.S. Ground-Based Space Surveillance Sensors.

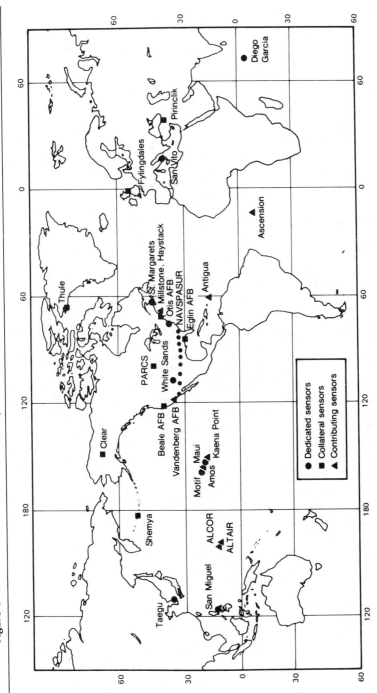

Source: Capt. Dennis K. Harden, "Current Capabilities and Future Requirements of the Air Force Space Surveillance Network," in U.S. Department of the Air Force, *Proceedings of the Tenth Aerospace Power Symposium: The Impact of Space on Aerospace Doctrine* (Maxwell AFB, Ala.: Air War College, 1986), p. 6.

to the output of such devices. In other words, in order to determine the response of the United States to a foreign nuclear weapons development program, more information than the mere existence of a nuclear explosion is required.[80]

Thus, the Atomic Energy Commission was able to announce a few days after China's first nuclear explosion on October 16, 1964, that the bomb used uranium 235 rather than plutonium, based on examination of the radioactive cloud.[81]

An additional factor appeared in the late 1970s. Revisions in U.S. nuclear strategy, as expressed in President Carter's Presidential Directive (PD)/NSC-59, and President Reagan's National Security Decision Directive (NSDD)-13, both titled "Nuclear Weapons Employment Policy," require the United States to possess the capability to fight a prolonged nuclear war—one that could last up to six months. Such a strategy requires the U.S. leadership to determine the precise location of nuclear detonations and assess the damage that results.[82]

The means that the United States employs to monitor foreign detonations include space platforms, airborne platforms, ground sites, and hydroacoustic (undersea) systems.

Detection of nuclear detonations is the secondary function of at least two satellite systems. Since the Defense Support Program (DSP) satellites' initial launch in 1971, their secondary function has been the detection of nuclear explosions in space or the atmosphere.

The principal mission of DSP satellites is to provide early warning of a Soviet missile attack. Hence, they also provide notification of Soviet, Chinese, and other nations' missile tests. The satellites are cylindrical and about 23 feet long and 9 feet in diameter, weighing up to 22,000 pounds. The means of detection is a twelve-foot-long Schmidt infrared telescope that is thirty-nine inches in diameter. The telescope has a two dimensional array of lead sulfide detectors at its focus to sense energy emitted by ballistic missile exhausts during the powered stages of their flights.[83]

DSP satellites are launched into a geosynchronous orbit from the Eastern Test Range (Cape Canaveral). At 22,300 miles over any point on the equator, the orbit of the satellite matches the rotation of the earth. Hence, the satellites "hover" over the same point continuously. One satellite is maintained on station over the Indian Ocean (70 degrees East) to provide first warning of a Soviet or Chinese ICBM launch, and two are maintained on station over the Western Hemisphere (over Brazil, 70 degrees West and the eastern Central Pacific, 135 degrees West) to monitor SLBM launchings off the East and West Coasts of the United States. An additional two satellites are maintained as spares.[84]

Subsequent to the unsuccessful attempt to launch a DSP in 1970, over fourteen DSP satellites have been placed in orbit. As with other satellites, modifications have improved the capability of the DSP sensors, the most recent improvement being the installation of the Advanced Atmospheric Burst Locator (AABL). The capability of such a system is multidimensional. The information provided by the

Figure 9–2. Approximate Earth Coverage of U.S. Defense Support Program Early Warning Satellites.

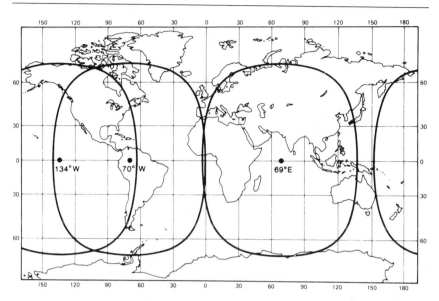

Source: Anthony Kenden, "U.S. Military Satellites, 1983," *Journal of the British Interplanetary Society*, 38 (February 1985) p. 63. Reprinted by permission.

AABL allows estimates of yield, location, height of burst, frequency of detonations, and timing. Its improved capability is a reflection of its allowing estimates with a smaller range of uncertainty than previous sensors, as well as its ability to detect events below a certain threshold.[85] A final measure of its capability is its range of coverage as shown in Figure 9–2.

The ground segment of the DSP includes two dedicated ground stations—also known as Large Processing Stations—a Simplified Processing Station and a main operating base for six mobile ground terminals (MGTs) at Holloman AFB in New Mexico and a DSP multipurpose facility at Lowry AFB, Colorado.[86]

The dedicated ground stations include the CONUS Ground Station at Buckley Air National Guard Base in Colorado, and the Overseas Ground Station at Woomera Air Station, Australia (also known as Nurrungar). The latter is code-named CASINO, bears the official cover title of Joint Defense Space Communications Facility, and is operated by the 5th Defense Space Communications Squadron of the 1st Space Wing of the Space Command. Data from Nurrungar to the United States is transmitted via both submarine cable and the Defense Satellite Communications System (DSCS) satellite stationed over the Western Pacific.[87]

The CONUS Ground Station, formally known as the Aerospace Data Facility, and operated by the 2nd Defense Space Communications Squadron, receives data from Nurrungar as well as from the DSP West satellites. Buckley is also Operating Location BN (OL-BN) of AFTAC. The AFTAC personnel stationed at Buckley are responsible for processing any nuclear detonation data provided by the nuclear detonation sensors aboard DSP spacecraft. The Kapuan and Lowry facilities provide backup capabilities to Nurrungar and Buckley, respectively.[88]

The prime means for providing trans- and post-attack nuclear detonation monitoring will be the Nuclear Detonation (NUDET) Detection System (NDS), carried on board the NAVSTAR Global Positioning System (GPS) satellites. The primary function of the GPS is to provide accurate locational data for targeting and navigational purposes; the NDS will represent a major secondary function. The GPS satellite constellation will consist of eighteen operational satellites plus three active spares in near-circular 10,900-mile orbits with an inclination of sixty-three degrees. The eighteen satellites will be deployed in three or more planes, each plane containing no more than six equally spaced satellites. The arrangement will guarantee that at least four to six satellites are in view at all times from any point on or near the earth.[89] The GPS constellation is shown in Figure 9–3.

The entire GPS constellation was intended to be operational in 1988, but the *Challenger* disaster of 1986 delayed that goal until the early 1990s. Seven developmental satellites were launched between 1978 and the end of 1982, six of which attained orbit. Beginning with the launch of GPS-8 in 1983, the NDS has been carried (and will continue to be carried) on all GPS satellites.[90] Table 9–1 shows the launch dates, orbital parameters, and lifetimes of the GPS-8 through GPS-11 satellites as of April 1987.

The two NDS packages will include x-ray and optical sensors, Bhangmeters, EMP (electromagnetic pulse) sensors, and a data processing capability that will allow the detection of nuclear weapons detonations "anywhere in the world at any time and get its location down to less than a [100 meters]." Data will be reported on a real-time basis—either directly to ground stations located at Diego Garcia; Kwajalein Atoll; Ascension Island; Kaena Point, Hawaii; Andersen Air Base, Guam; Adak, Alaska—or first to airborne terminals or other GPS satellites for subsequent downlink transmissions. All principal U.S. command posts, including E-4B and EC-135 aircraft, will receive NDS sensor data directly.[91]

Besides the nuclear detonation packages on DSP and GPS satellites, there also appear to be NUDET packages on at least one other satellite system, the NUDET role of which is classified. This might be the previously discussed Satellite Data System (SDS) satellites (which apparently have a classified early warning capability) or the Defense Meteorological Satellite Program satellites. The latter are acknowledged to have "classified sensors" in addition to their meteorological sensors.[92]

In addition to space-based detection systems, aerial sampling is used to detect the atomic particles that would be emitted by an above-ground nuclear explosion and might be "vented" by an underground test. Aircraft employed in aerial sampling operations include the U-2, P-3, WC-135, and B-52. Aerial sampling operations are conducted over the United States, Southern Hemisphere, and other areas under

Figure 9–3. The NAVSTAR GPS Operational Constellation.

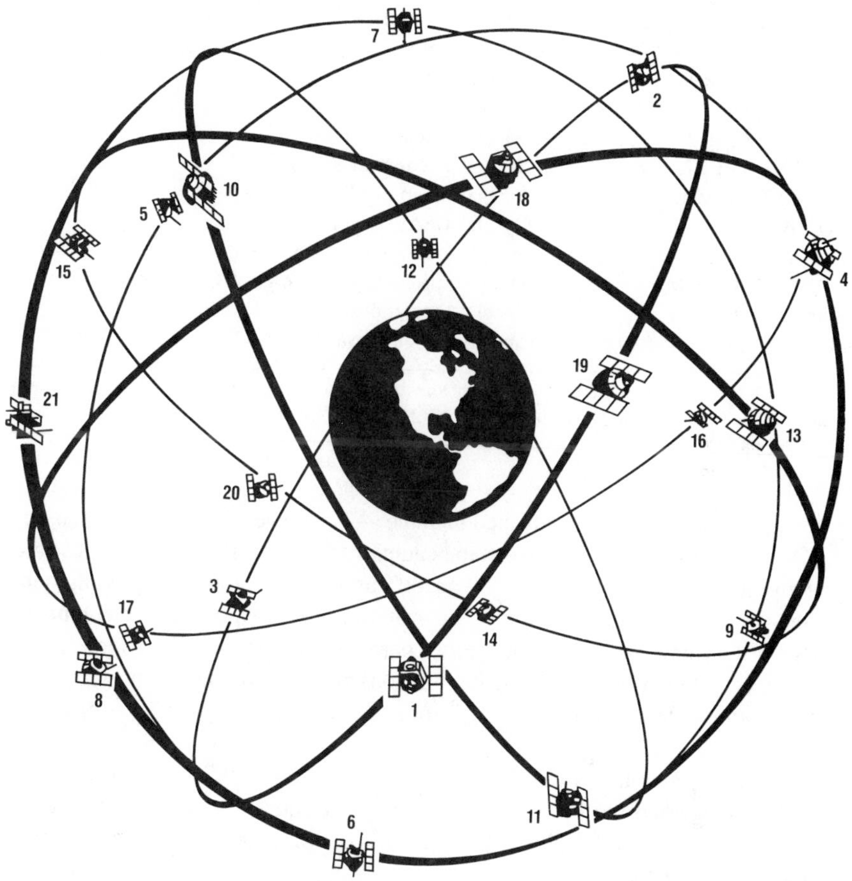

Source: General Accounting Office, *Global Positioning System Acquisition Changes After Challenger's Accident* (Washington, D.C.: GAO, 1987), p. 12.

Table 9–1. Launch Data for GPS Satellite with NDS Packages.

Satellite	Launch Date	Inclin.	Perigee (km)	Apogee
8	7-14-83	62.8	19,952	20,798
9	6-13-84	62.5	20,318	20,620
10	9-8-84	63.2	20,271	20,713
11	10-9-85	63.4	19,822	20,541

Source: Royal Aircraft Establishment, *The RAE Table of Earth Satellites 1983–1986* (Farnborough, Hants, England: RAE, 1987), pp. 745, 787, 803, 848.

Table 9–2.   Varieties of Aerial Sampling Operations.

Code name	Type of Operation
VOLANT CHUCK	Southern Hemisphere Reconnaissance for HQ, USAF
VOLANT CURRY	Special Weather Reconnaissance
VOLANT DOME	Domestic Reconnaissance for HQ, USAF
VOLANT FISH	Water Sampler
VOLANT SPECK	Special Reconnaissance for HQ, USAF
VOLANT TRACK	Special Sampling Requirement
COMBAT CATCH	Special USAF Reconnaissance
CONSTANT GLOBE	Worldwide Sampling Operations
CONSTANT DOME	Domestic Reconnaissance for HQ, USAF
CONSTANT FISH	Special Operations for HQ USAF[a]
PONY EXPRESS	Special Reconnaissance for JCS

a. Special Operations are sorties flown against foreign nuclear atmospheric and underground tests.
Source: Air Force Technical Applications Center CENR 55-3, "Aerial Sampling Operations," October 22, 1982, pp. 2-2 to 2-3.

a variety of code names, as indicated in Table 9–2. One version of the C-130 used, the HC-130, is outfitted with a sea water sampler for sorties flown against possible foreign underwater nuclear tests.[93] Aircraft carrying aerial sampling equipment (filters which would absorb any nuclear material) are flown under the command of the military units for whom the aircraft perform their primary functions. Thus, a significant number of aerial sampling missions are flown by ASW (antisubmarine warfare) and weather reconnaissance units, flying P-3 and WC-135 aircraft.

Given the adherence of the United States and the Soviet Union to the Limited Test Ban Treaty and the French and Chinese restriction to underground testing, monitoring underground explosions is the major aspect of the U.S. nuclear detonation monitoring program.

Detection of underground explosions depends on distinguishing between the seismic waves generated by a nuclear explosion and those created by an earthquake. In most cases, determining the location of seismic events eliminates the large majority of earthquakes from consideration as possible nuclear detonations. Otherwise, analysts may be able to distinguish earthquakes from detonations by the differing nature of the signals produced by each phenomenon—detonations being a point source, earthquakes the result of two bodies of rock slipping past each other. At distances of less than 625 miles from an event, explosions greater than a few kilotons can easily be distinguished from earthquakes. At greater distances, such distinctions become far more difficult. Moreover, the actual recording of a seismic signal is disturbed by both instrumental and natural background noise, the latter setting a threshold of detectability.[94]

These limitations place a premium on placing monitoring stations or equipment in suitable locations and developing techniques to enhance the signal-to-noise ratio obtained at any location. The simplest form of earth-based monitoring equipment is the seismometer, which is basically composed of a magnet fixed to the ground and a spring-suspended mass with an electric coil. According to the SIPRI, "when seismic waves move the ground and the magnet attached to it, they leave the mass with the coil relatively unaffected. The relative motion of the magnet and coil generates a current in the coil which is proportional to their relative velocity."[95]

One means of enhancing the signal-to-noise ratio is the use of several seismometers in an array. Arrays increase the data set available for analysis in several ways, including provision of different arrival times of the seismic waves at the different seismometers. The major non-AFTAC arrays are located in Montana, Alaska, and Norway. The largest and most modern is the Large Aperture Seismic Array (LASA) in Montana. It consists of thirteen subarrays, each made up of twenty-five short period instruments and a three-component set of long-period seismometers. The Alaska Long Period Array (ALPA) originally consisted of nineteen long-period seismometers. It has been refitted with newly developed long-period borehole seismometers and now consists of seven three-component seismometers with an aperture of twenty-five miles. The Norwegian Seismic Array (NORSAR) consists of seven subarrays, each with forty-nine short- and seven long-period seismometers, extending over a distance of thirty-two miles.[96]

The seismic arrays and seismometers operated by the Air Force Technical Applications Center (AFTAC) are distributed throughout the world. Each detachment possesses broadband seismic detection capabilities, which are operated on a twenty-four-hour a day basis, with each detachment responsible for detecting, recording, and analyzing all of the seismic activity that occurs.[97]

In addition to seismic monitoring, some stations are equipped with four types of devices to monitor the atmosphere for signs of nuclear detonations. One type, the Ground Filter Unit, is an electrically powered, ground-based, air filtering unit. The unit draws free air into a transition cone, which flows through a filter paper and is then emitted back into the atmosphere. The filter paper containing airborne particles is then removed and forwarded for analysis and classification.[98]

The second type of atmospheric device, the Ground Moisture Unit, is a whole-air sampling device that employs two traps. The first contains a molecular sieve that removes water vapor from free air. The second contains a molecular sieve coated with polladium, which acts as a catalyst to oxidize gaseous hydrogen and form water vapor that is absorbed. The traps are changed daily and forwarded to AFTAC's McClellan Central Laboratory for analyses and classification.[99]

Another unit, the B-20-5, is an automated cryogenic distillation device that employs very low tempertures to isolate rare elements (gases) contained in the atmosphere. The unit is designed to operate continuously over any preset sample run of twenty-four hours (or multiple thereof) for periods up to seven days. Samples are collected in 800-cc metal containers that are forwarded to the MCL.[100]

The fourth non-seismic system is the Electromagnetic Pulse System (EMP) which is employed for detecting, locating, and identifying the source of electromagnetic pulse signals in the VLF and HF range occurring in the atmosphere. The

Table 9-3. AFTAC Manned Detachments.

Detachment	Location
045	Buckley ANGB, Colorado
046	Falcon AFS, Colorado
057	Lowry AFB, Colorado
301	Belbasi Seismic Research Station, Turkey
313	Sonseca, Spain
315	Iraklion AS, Greece
360	Keflavik, Iceland
370	RAF Edzell, United Kingdom
372	Ascension Island
377	Bad Aibling, Germany
401	Clark AFB, Philippines
407	Yokota AB, Japan
415	Chiang Mai Apt, Thailand
421	Alice Springs, Australia
422	Misawa AS, Japan
423	Delmonte Plantation, Cagayande Oro, Mindanao, Philippines
428	Anderson AFB, Guam
452	Camp Long Wonju, South Korea
459	Pindedale, Wyoming
460	Eielson AFB, Alaska
471	Elmendorf, AFB, Alaska

system is comprised of J Field Sets (JFS) that are linked via dedicated lines to the Central Data Terminal (CDT) located at AFTAC headquarters. Data from EMP signals that satisfies priority criterion at The JFS are transmitted in real time to the CDT via a synchronous communications circuit. The CDT is a continuously operating terminal with the capability to receive EMP signal data from all JFS sites via dedicated communications lines and to perform real-time data processing of incoming data.[101]

Altogether, the AFTAC operates ninety-two sites capable of detecting nuclear events—included are approximately twenty manned detachments (some of whose presence in a country is not acknowledged) and over fifty unmanned "equipment locations" and covert stations located within embassies and consulates.[102]

The AFTAC's detachments are located in the United States, Europe, and Asia as indicated in Table 9-3. The installation at Alice Springs, Australia, code-named OAK TREE, is operated by Detachment 421. An underground seismic array located about 1.5 miles northeast of the detachment consists of nineteen seismometers arranged in a circular pattern over 7.25 miles. Thirteen of the seismometers are buried approximately 200 feet in the ground and designed to pick up the long-period waves that pass through the surface layer of the earth. The remaining six seismometers are buried 1.1 miles deep and tuned to detect the short-period waves that pass through the mantle and core of the earth.[103]

Table 9–4. AFTAC Equipment Locations.

EL Number	Location
79	Hay River, NT, Canada
105	Goodfellow AFB, Texas
206	Pt. Barrow, Alaska
208	NAS Adak, Alaska
223	Juneau, Alaska
300	NAS Bermuda
307	Mahe Island, Seychelles
329	Bremerhaven, West Germany
334	Sinop, Turkey
372	Ascension Island
421	Hickam AFB, Hawaii
432	Kadena AB, Japan
461	Shemya AFB, Japan
462	Kotzebue, Alaska
465	Bangkok, Thailand
466	Naval Ordnance Facility, Sasebo Japan
468	Anderson AFB, Guam
476	Osan AB, South Korea
	Burnt Mountain Research Site, Alaska
	Attu Research Site, Alaska
	Beaver Creek Research Site, Alaska
	Chena River Research Site, Alaska
	Eielson ALPA Research Site, Alaska
	Indian Mountain Research Site, Alaska

The seismometers are linked by cables to a central recording station where the signals are processed to provide an indication of the direction and speed at which they are traveling and the amplitude of the ground motion.[104]

Unmanned equipment locations are even more extensive and spread over all continents except Antarctica, as indicated in Table 9–4. These sites are exclusively involved in seismic and electromagnetic pulse detection. While some are located in open territory as manned ground stations, others are more covert, located in embassies.[105]

One area where there will apparently be an expansion of seismic detection stations is in the Southern Hemisphere. In 1986, the AFTAC requested funds for the construction of a central equipment facility, drilling two boreholes at five overseas locations. According to the request:

there are insufficient seismic detection systems in the Southern Hemisphere, seismic surveillance capable of detecting long-period and short-period data is required to detect, identify and monitor seismic disturbances, both natural and man-made, occurring on or within the earth's surface. This project will provide an improved capability to detect and identify these disturbances in the Southern Hemisphere.[106]

One focus of research concerns nonseismic detection, specifically, ionospheric and infrasonic monitoring. The shock waves created by nuclear detonations produce perturbations in certain levels of the ionosphere which can be detected by over-the-horizon (OTH) radar. Infrasonic monitoring involves use of a microphone array for long-range monitoring of VLF sound waves generated by nuclear explosions that propagate in the upper levels of the atmosphere.[107]

The same system employed by the Navy to detect Soviet submarines is also employed for hydroacoustic detection of nuclear detonations. These equipment locations (ELs) transmit, in digital form, recorded hydroacoustic data (sound waves in water) to a central analysis terminal located within AFTAC headquarters. Operated on a twenty-four-hour a day basis, the hydroacoustic data terminal is tasked to identify the source of each recorded wave.[108]

The hydroacoustic or Digital "O" System (DOS) is comprised of two separate systems that are interrelated—the Acquisition and Analysis Systems. The Acquisition System presently consists of up to nine "O" Field Set (OFS). The OFS is a real-time data acquisition system designed to collect raw data, perform frequency filtering, data processing, and data transmissions. The Analysis System is more commonly referred to as the Hydroacoustic Recorder and Processor (HRP). Hydroacoustic equipment locations are shown in Table 9–5.[109]

Table 9–5. AFTAC Equipment Locations for Hydroacoustic Detection.

EL Number	Location
70	NAVFAC Adak, Alaska
72	NAVFAC Bermuda
73	NAVFAC Argentia, Canada
74	NAVFAC Midway
135	NAVFAC Centerville Beach, California
145	NAVFAC St. Nicholas Island, Pt. Mugu, California
360	NAVFAC Keflavik, Iceland
423	NAVFAC Guam

NOTES TO CHAPTER 9

1. Warren Strobel and James S. Doresey, "Soviet Navy Now a World Class Power," *Washington Times*, November 2, 1987, p. A6; Department of Defense, *Soviet Military Power 1987* (Washington, D.C.: U.S. Government Printing Office, 1987), pp. 31–35, 80–86.

2. "U.S. Launches Recon Satellite Soviet Fleet Maneuvers May Be Target," *Aerospace Daily*, April 22, 1975, pp. 290–91.

3. Anthony Kenden, "U.S. Reconnaissance Satellite Programs," *Spaceflight*, July 20, 1973, pp. 243ff, at p. 257; Janko Jackson, "A Methodology for Ocean Surveillance Analysis," *Naval War College Review* 27, no. 2 (September/October 1974): 71–89; "Navy Plans Ocean Surveillance Satellite," *Aviation Week and Space Technology*, August 30, 1971, p. 13; "Industry Observer," *Aviation Week and Space Technology*, February 28, 1972, p. 9.

4. "Navy Ocean Surveillance Satellite Depicted," *Aviation Week and Space Technology*, May 24, 1976, p. 22; "Expanded Ocean Surveillance Effort Set," *Aviation Week and Space Technology*, June 10, 1978, pp. 22–23; Mark Hewlish, "Satellites Show Their Warlike Face," *New Scientist*, October 1, 1981, pp. 36–40.

5. "Expanded Ocean Surveillance Effort Set"; Hewlish, "Satellites Show Their Warlike Face."

6. "Expanded Ocean Surveillance Effort Set"; Hewlish, "Satellites Show Their Warlike Face."

7. D.C. King-Hele, *The RAE Table of Earth Satellites 1957–1980* (New York: Facts on File, 1981), pp. 444, 512, 600–601; *The RAE Table of Earth Satellites 1983–1986* (Farnborough, Hants, England: RAE, 1987), pp. 721, 738, 769–70, 863; "Air Force Launches Secret Satellite for Military," *Washington Post*, May 16, 1987, p. A16.

8. "Expanded Ocean Surveillance Effort Set."

9. Paul Stares, *Space and National Security* (Washington, D.C.: Brookings Institution, 1987), p. 188.

10. Lori A. McClelland, "Versatile P-3C Orion Meeting Growing ASW Challenge," *Defense Electronics* (April 1985): 132–41.

11. David Miller, *An Illustrated Guide to Modern Sub Hunters* (New York: Arco, 1984), p. 125; George A. Wilmoth, "Lockheed's Antisubmarine Warfare Aircraft; Watching the Threat," *Defense Systems Review* 3 no; 6 (1985) 18–25; Private information; Brendan M. Greeley, Jr., "Soviets Extend Air, Sea Power with Buildup at Cam Ranh Bay," *Aviation Week and Space Technology*, March 2, 1987, pp. 76–77.

12. Miller, *An Illustrated Guide to Modern Sub Hunters*, p. 124; Wilmoth, "Lockheed's Antisubmarine Warfare Aircraft"; U.S. Congress, Senate Committee on Armed Services, *Department of Defense Authorization for Appropriations for Fiscal Year 1986, Part 8* (Washington, D.C.: U.S. Government Printing Office, 1985), p. 4510.

13. McClelland, "Versatile P-3C Orion Meeting Growing ASW Challenge"; Miller, *An Illustrated Guide to Modern Sub Hunters*, p. 124; *P-3C Orion Update Weapon System* (Burbank, Calif.: Lockheed, n.d.), p. 17; Timothy J. Christmann, "The Multimission Orion," *Air Progress Review*: 38–45.

14. *P-3C Orion Update Weapon System*, p. 18; McClelland, "Versatile P-3C Orion Meeting Growing ASW Challenge"; Nicholas M. Horrock, "The Submarine Hunters," *Newsweek*, January 23, 1984, p. 38.

15. Jeffrey T. Richelson and Desmond Ball, *The Ties that Bind: Intelligence Cooperation Between the UKUSA Countries* (London: Allen & Unwin, 1985), p. 220; U.S. Congress, House Committee on Appropriations, *Department of Defense Appropriations for 1986, Part 4* (Washington, D.C.: U.S. Government Printing Office, 1985), p. 133; U.S. Congress, Senate Committee on Armed Services, *Department of Defense Authorization for Appropriations for Fiscal Year 1986, Part 8*, pp. 4503, 4510; Lawrence Lifschultz, "New U.S. Spy Flights from Pakistan," *The Nation*, November 29, 1986, pp. 593, 606, 608, 610.

16. "Boeing, Lockheed and Douglas Bid on Navy P-3 Follow-On," *Aviation Week and Space Technology*, February 22, 1988, p. 31.

17. Private information.

18. Dick Van der Art, *Aerial Espionage: Secret Intelligence Flights by East and West* (New York: Arco/Prentice Hall, 1986), pp. 53–54; Private information.

19. Private information.

20. Ibid.

21. Van der Art, *Aerial Espionage*, pp. 53–54.

22. L.T. Peacock, *U.S. Naval Aviation Today* (Uxbridge, England: Cheney Press, 1977), p. 25; Private information.

23. Defense Marketing Service, "Program 749," *DMS Market Intelligence Report* (Greenwich, Conn.: DMS, 1977), pp. 1, 2.

24. Private information.

25. Ibid.

26. U.S. Congress, House Committee on Appropriations, *Military Construction Appropriations for 1981* (Washington, D.C.: U.S. Government Printing Office, 1980), p. 1123; Private information.

27. U.S. Congress, House Committee on Appropriations, *Military Construction Appropriations for 1981* p. 1123; Private information.

28. Private information; U.S. Congress, House Committee on Appropriations, *Military Construction Appropriations for 1987, Part 2* (Washington, D.C.: U.S. Government Printing Office, 1986), p. 463.

29. Private information.

30. Ibid.

31. CINCPACFLT Instruction S3824.1A, "Portable Acoustic Collection Equipment," October 16, 1985.

32. Testimony of Admiral Metzel, U.S. Congress, Senate Committee on Armed Services, *Department of Defense Authorization for Appropriations for Fiscal Year 1980, Part 6* (Washington, D.C.: U.S. Government Printing Office, 1979), p. 2925.

33. Owen Wilkes, "Strategic Anti-Submarine Warfare and Its Implications for a Counterforce First Strike," in *World Armaments and Disarmament, SIPRI Yearbook 1979*, (London: Taylor & Francis Ltd., 1979), p. 430.

34. U.S. Congress, House Committee on Appropriations, *Department of Defense Appropriations for Fiscal Year 1977, Part 5* (Washington, D.C.: U.S. Government Printing Office, 1976), p. 1255; Drew Middleton, "Expert Predicts a Big U.S. Gain in Sub Warfare," *New York Times*, July 18, 1979, p. A5; Chapman Pincher, "U.S. to Set

Up Sub Spy Station," *Daily Express*, January 6, 1973; Harvey B. Silverstein, "Caesar, SOSUS and Submarines: Economic and Institutional Implications of ASW Technologies," *Ocean '78*, Proceedings of the Fourth Annual Combined Conference, sponsored by the Marine Technology Society and the Institute of Electrical and Electronics Engineers, Washington, D.C., September 6–8, 1978, p. 407.

35. U.S. Congress, House Committee on Appropriations, *Department of Defense Appropriations for Fiscal Year 1977, Part 5*, p. 1255; Middleton, "Expert Predicts Big U.S. Gain in Sub Warfare."

36. Defense Market Survey, "Sonar-Sub-Surface-Caesar," *DMS Market Intelligence Report* (Greenwich, Conn.: DMS, 1980), p. 1; Clyde W. Burleson, *The Jennifer Project* (Englewood Cliffs, N.J.: Prentice-Hall, 1977), p. 18; Joel S. Wit, "Advances in Antisubmarine Warfare," *Scientific American* (February 1981): 36ff; Burleson, *The Jennifer Project*, pp. 17–19, 24–25; Silverstein, "Caesar, SOSUS and Submarines."

37. Howard B. Dratch, "High Stakes in the Azores," *The Nation*, November 8, 1975, pp. 455–56; "NATO Fixed Sonar Range Commissioned," *Armed Forces Journal International* (August 1972): 29; "Atlantic Islands: NATO Seeks Wider Facilities," *International Herald Tribune*, June 1981, p. 75; Richard Timsar, "Portugal Bargains for U.S. Military Aid with Strategic Mid-Atlantic Base," *The Christian Science Monitor*, March 24, 1981, p. 9; Wit, "Advances in Antisubmarine Warfare."

38. William Arkin and Richard Fieldhouse, *Nuclear Battlefields: Global Links in the Arms Race* (Cambridge, Mass.: Ballinger, 1986), Appendix A; Ed Offley, "Turning the Tide: Soviets Score a Coup with Sub Progress," *Seattle Post-Intelligencer*, April 8, 1987, p. A5.

39. William Burrows, *Deep Black: Space Espionage and National Security* (New York: Random House, 1987), p. 180n.; USN-PLAD pp. 28, 33 in U.S. Military Communications Electronics Board, USMCEB Publication 6, *Message Address Directory*, (Washington, D.C.: U.S. Government Printing Office, July 25, 1986); CINCPACFLT Instruction 5450.76, "Mission and Functions of Naval Ocean Processing Facility, Ford Island, Pearl Harbor, Hawaii," February 22, 1985.

40. Walter Sullivan, "Can Submarines Stay Hidden?" *New York Times*, December 11, 1984, pp. C1, C9.

41. Thomas S. Burns, *The Secret War for the Ocean Depths: Soviet-American Rivalry for Mastery of the Seas* (New York: Rawson, 1978), p. 156; Robert C. Aldridge, *First Strike: The Pentagon's Strategy for Nuclear War* (Boston, Mass.: South End Press, 1983), p. 165n.

42. Melinda C. Beck with David C. Martin, "The War Beneath the Seas," *Newsweek*, February 8, 1982, pp. 37–8; Department of Defense, *Soviet Military Power 1985* (Washington, D.C.: U.S. Government Printing Office, 1985), p. 96; A. Preston, "SOSUS Update Aims to Keep Track of Alfa," *Jane's Defence Weekly*, January 21, 1984, p. 60.

43. Robert P. Berman and John C. Baker, *Soviet Strategic Forces: Requirements and Responses* (Washington, D.C.: Brookings Institution, 1982), pp. 106–7.

44. "Stray Voltage," *Armed Forces Journal International* (April 1987): 94.

45. U.S. Congress, House Committee on International Relations, *Evaluation of Fiscal Year 1979 Arms Control Impact Statements* (Washington, D.C.: U.S. Government Printing Office, 1978), pp. 111–12.

46.   Ibid.; James Shultz, "Anti-Sub Warfare Escalates," *Defense Electronics* (June 1983): 76–89; U.S. Congress, Senate Committee on Armed Services, *Department of Defense Authorization for Appropriations for Fiscal Year 1980, Part 6*, pp. 1147–49; Larry L. Booda, "SURTASS, RDSS Augment Ocean Surveillance," *Sea Technology* (November 1981): 19–29; Norman Polmar, "SURTASS and T-AGOS," *U.S. Naval Institute Proceedings*, March 1980, pp. 120–24; U.S. Congress, House Committee on Foreign Affairs and Senate Committee on Foreign Relations, *Fiscal Year 1981 Arms Control Impact Statement* (Washington, D.C.: U.S. Government Printing Office, 1980), p. 342.

47.   William J. Broad, "New Space Challenge: Monitoring Weapons," *New York Times* December 8, 1987, pp. C1, C6.

48.   "Washington-Roundup," *Aviation Week and Space Technology*, April 18, 1983, p. 17.

49.   U.S. Congress, House Committee on Appropriations, *Department of Defense Appropriations for 1984, Part 4* (Washington, D.C.: U.S. Government Printing Office, 1983), pp. 618–19.

50.   U.S. Congress, House Committee on Appropriations, *Department of Defense Appropriations for 1984, Part 8*, pp. 506–8.

51.   Craig Covault, "SDI Delta Space Experiment to Aid Kill-Vehicle Design," *Aviation Week and Space Technology*, September 15, 1986, pp. 18–19.

52.   U.S. Air Force, "SAC Fact Sheet," August 1981, p. 81-001.

53.   Paul Stares, *Space and National Security*, (Washington, D.C.: Brookings Institution, 1987), p. 204; AFSPACECOM Regulation 23-42, "Detachment 1, Space Wing," June 30, 1986; "Industry Observer," *Aviation Week and Space Technology*, February 12, 1987, p. 13; U.S. Congress, Senate Committee on Armed Services, *Department of Defense Authorization for Appropriations for Fiscal Year 1980, Part 6*, p. 3022; "U.S. Upgrading Ground-Based Sensors," *Aviation Week and Space Technology*, June 16, 1980, pp. 239–42; David M. Russell, "NORAD Adds Radar, Optics to Increase Space Defense," *Defense Electronics* (July 1982): 82–86.

54.   Russell, "NORAD Adds Radar, Optics to Increase Space Defense"; Lt. Colonel William C. Jeas and Robert Anctil, "The Ground-Based Electro-Optical Deep Space Surveillance (GEODSS) System," *Military Electronics/Countermeasures* (November 1981): 47–51.

55.   "U.S. Upgrading Ground-Based Sensors"; Russell, "NORAD Adds Radar Optics to Increase Space Defense."

56.   "U.S. Upgrading Ground-Based Sensors."

57.   Ibid., at p. 239.

58.   "GEODSS Photographs Orbiting Satellite," *Aviation Week and Space Technology*, December 5, 1983, pp. 146–47.

59.   Ibid.; *Anti-Satellite Weapons, Countermeasures and Arms Control* (Washington, D.C.: Office of Technology Assessment, 1985), p. 55.

60.   "Focus," *Defense Electronics* (November 1983): 30; Department of the Air Force, *Justification of Estimates for Fiscal Year 1984 Submitted to Congress January 1983* (Springfield, Va.: National Technical Information Service, 1983), pp. 137–38.

61.   "Spacetrack," *Jane's Weapons Systems 1982–1983*, (London: Jane's Publishing, 1982), pp. 233–34; Russell, "NORAD Adds Radar"; "The Arms Race in Space," *SIPRI Yearbook 1978 World Armaments and Disarmaments* (New York: Crane,

Russak, 1978), pp. 104–30; Brendan M. Greeley, Jr., "Navy Expanding Its Space Command to Bolster Readiness," *Aviation Week and Space Technology*, February 3, 1986, pp. 54–47.

62.   "Spacetrack."

63.   U.S. Congress, Senate Committee on Armed Services, *Department of Defense Authorization for Appropriations for Fiscal Year 1986, Part 7* (Washington, D.C.: U.S. Government Printing Office, 1985), p. 4342.

64.   AFSPACECOM Regulation 23-34, "17 Surveillance Squadron," June 30, 1986; Stares, *Space and National Security*, p. 204; U.S. Congress, Senate Committee on Armed Services, *Department of Defense Authorization for Appropriations for Fiscal Year 1980, Part 6*, p. 3021; Covault, "USAF Awaits Space Defense Guidance," *Aviation Week and Space Technology*, February 22, 1982, p. 65; U.S. Congress, House Committee on Appropriations, *Department of Defense Appropriations for 1981, Part 8* (Washington, D.C.: U.S. Government Printing Office, 1980), p. 240; U.S. Congress, House Committee on Appropriations, *Military Construction Appropriations for 1987, Part 3*, (Washington, D.C.: U.S. Government Printing Office, 1986), p. 812.

65.   Stares, *Space and National Security*, p. 204; John L. Piotrowski, "C³I for Space Control," *Signal* (June 1987): 23–33; AFSPACECOM Regulation 23-44, "Detachment 3, 1 Space Wing," August 18, 1986.

66.   Joel W. Powell, "Photography of Orbiting Satellites," *Spaceflight* (February 1983): 82–83; Stares, *Space and National Security*, p. 204.

67.   Stares, *Space and National Security*, p. 204.

68.   "U.S. Upgrading Ground-Based Sensors"; Stares, *Space and National Security*, p. 204; "The Arms Race in Space," p. 116; "Improved U.S. Warning Net Spurred," *Aviation Week and Space Technology*, June 23, 1980, pp. 38ff.

69.   "PAVE PAWS Radar," *Jane's Weapons Systems 1982–1983*, p. 501; "U.S. Upgrading Ground-Based Sensors"; Stares, *Space and National Security*, p. 205; AFSPACECOM Regultion 23-50, "9 Missile Warning Squadron," September 2, 1986; "Space Command Completes Acquisition of Pave Paws Warning Radar Installations," *Aviation Week and Space Technology*, May 18, 1987, pp. 128–29; Office of Legislative Liaison, Office of the Secretary of the Air Force, *Systems Information Briefs for Members of Congress*, (Washington, D.C.: Department of the Air Force, 1987), p. 80.

70.   "AN/FPS-85," *Jane's Weapons Systems 1982–1983*, pp. 505–6; "The Arms Race in Space," pp. 114–24 at p. 116; John Hambre, et al., *Strategic Command, Control and Communications: Alternate Approaches for Modernization* (Washington, D.C.: Congressional Budget Office, 1981), p. 10.

71.   Owen Wilkes, *Spacetracking and Spacewarfare* (Oslo: International Peace Research Institute, 1978), p. 27.

72.   Ibid.

73.   "AN/FPS-85"; Wilkes, *Spacetracking and Spacewarfare*, p. 27; Philip J. Klass, "FPS-85 Radar Expands to Cover SLBMs," *Aviation Week and Space Technology*, February 19, 1973, pp. 61–67.

74.   Stares, *Space and National Security*, p. 205; AFSPACECOM Regulation 23-46, "10th Missile Warning Squadron (MWS)," June 12, 1987.

75. AFSPACECOM Regulation 23-33, "16 Surveillance Squadron (16 SURS)," June 30, 1986; AFSPACECOM Regulation 23-35, "19 Surveillance Squadron (19 SURS)," June 30, 1986; "SAC Fact Sheet"; "The Arms Race in Space"; Stares, *Space and National Security*, p. 205.

76. Stares, *Space and National Security*, p. 205.

77. "SAC Fact Sheet"; Defense Marketing Survey, *Codename Handbook 1981* (Greenwich, Conn.: DMS, 1981), p. 168; Stares, *Space and National Security*, p. 205; U.S. Congress, House Committee on Appropriations, *Department of Defense Appropriations for 1981, Part 8*, p. 241.

78. Stares, *Space and National Security*, p. 205; "SAC Fact Sheet."

79. The United States has not yet ratified the Threshold Test Ban Treaty. Both the United States and the Soviet Union have said they would abide by its provisions. See Walter Pincus, "White House Reassesses Opposition to Ratifying Nuclear Test Treaty," *Washington Post*, June 25, 1983, p. A14.

80. U.S. Congress, Senate Committee on Appropriations, *Department of Defense Appropriations for Fiscal Year 1972, Part 1* (Washington, D.C.: U.S. Government Printing Office, 1971), p. 672.

81. "Forum: The Explosion of October 16," *Bulletin of the Atomic Scientists* (February 1965).

82. See Jeffrey Richelson, "PD-59, NSDD-13 and the Reagan Strategic Modernization Program," *Journal of Strategic Studies* 6, no. 2 (1983): 125–46.

83. Desmond Ball, *A Suitable Base for Debate: The U.S. Satellite Station at Nurrungar* (Sydney: Allen & Unwin Australia, 1987), pp. 20–21.

84. Ibid., p. 17.

85. U.S. Congress, Senate Committee on Armed Services, *Department of Defense Authorization for Appropriations for FY 1981, Part 6* (Washington, D.C.: U.S. Government Printing Office, 1980), p. 3449.

86. Ball, *A Suitable Base for Debate*, p. 4.

87. Ibid., pp. 47–49.

88. Ibid., p. 50; Arkin and Fieldhouse, *Nuclear Battlefields*, p. 181.

89. U.S. Congress, General Accounting Office, *Satellite Acquisition: Global Positioning System Acquisition Changes After Challenger's Accident* (Washington, D.C.: GAO, 1987), pp. 8, 29.

90. Ibid., p. 29.

91. U.S. Congress, House Committee on Appropriations, *Department of Defense Appropriations for 1983, Part 5*, p. 16; U.S. Congress, House Committee on Appropriations, *Department of Defense Appropriations for 1984, Part 8*, p. 337; U.S. Congress, House Committee on Armed Services, *Department of Energy National Security and Military Applications of Nuclear Energy Authorization Act of 1984* (Washington, D.C.: U.S. Government Printing Office, 1983), pp. 383–84; Stares, *Space and National Security*, p. 29; Charles A. Zraket, "Strategic Command, Control, Communications and Intelligence," *Science*, June 22, 1984, p. 1309; "Navstar Bloc 2 Satellites to Have Crosslinks, Radiation Hardening," *Defense Electronics* (July 1983): 16; Department of the Air Force, *Supporting Data for Fiscal Year 1985*, pp. 394–95.

92. U.S. Congress, House Committee on Armed Services, *Department of Energy National Security and Military Applications of Nuclear Energy Authorization Act*

of 1984, pp. 383–84, 392; RCA Astro-Electronics Briefing Slides, "Defense Meteorological Satellite Program," n.d.

93. Air Technical Applications Center, CENR 55-3, "Aerial Sampling Operations," October 22, 1982, p. 2-7.

94. Henry R. Myers, "Extending the Nuclear Test Ban," *Scientific American*, (January 1972): 13–23; Lynn R. Sykes and Jack F. Evernden, "The Verification of a Comprehensive Nuclear Test Ban," *Scientific American* (October 1982): 47–55; "The Comprehensive Test Ban," in *SIPRI Yearbook 1978 World Armaments and Disarmament* (New York: Crane, Russak, 1978), pp. 317–359 at p. 335.

95. "The Comprehensive Test Ban," p. 335.

96. Ibid., p. 340.

97. 3400 Technical Training Wing, *Introduction to Detection Systems* (Lowry AFB, Colo.: 3400 TTW, October 18, 1984), p. 17.

98. Ibid.

99. Ibid.

100. Ibid.

101. Ibid., p. 18.

102. "Soviet Test Monitors," *Bulletin of the Atomic Scientists*, p. 63; Private information.

103. Desmond Ball, *A Suitable Piece of Real Estate: American Installations in Australia* (Sydney, Australia: Hale & Iremonger, 1980), pp. 84–85.

104. Ibid.

105. Private information.

106. U.S. Congress, House Committee on Appropriations, *Military Construction Appropriations for 1987, Part 3* (Washington, D.C.: U.S. Government Printing Office, 1986), p. 1097.

107. U.S. Congress, Senate Committee on Appropriations, *Energy and Water Development Appropriations FY 1986, Part 2* (Washington, D.C.: U.S. Government Printing Office, 1985), pp. 1360–61.

108. *Introduction to Detection Systems*, p. 18.

109. Ibid.

10 HUMAN SOURCES

The increasing capability to collect intelligence via technical means has reduced reliance on human sources; however, human sources are not inconsequential. Much valuable information, particularly documents, are accessible only through human sources. Such sources can be used to fill gaps—in some cases important gaps—left by technical collection systems. Sometimes gaps will result because of the inherent limitations of technical systems—with proper security, many discussions will be immune to interception; also, technical systems cannot photograph planning or policy documents locked in a vault. Additionally, technical systems are expensive and can be employed against a limited number of targets. Thus, information on lower priority targets may be desired, but only if it can be acquired without introducing a new or enhanced technical collection system or diverting an operating system away from higher priority targets. Human sources can also serve to determine targets for technical collection systems. Thus, it may have been a human source who first alerted U.S. intelligence to the existence of a new radar system at Krasnoyarsk.

A high priority for U.S. intelligence is to understand the decision processes involved in foreign, military, and economic policymaking in the Soviet Union. This includes the processes of the Politburo, the Defense Council, the entire military command (most especially that involved in military R & D), the GOSPLAN, the KGB, and the theater command structure.[1] An understanding of both the processes and people involved can lead to a more accurate estimation of the likely course of action in a given circumstance. Some data on such matters may be obtained by technical means, but there will be gaps that may be filled only by other sources.

A further objective of human intelligence activities is the acquisition of planning documents, technical manuals, contingency plans, and weapons systems blueprints.

As Amrom Katz has noted, "the analysts . . . want the designer's plan, notebooks, tests on components, tests of materials, conversation between designer and the customer."[2] Although in most cases the analyst must settle for images and electronic data concerning test activities, it is often the designer's documentation that constitutes the "best evidence."

Certain stages of military R & D are simply not available for technical monitoring. Once plans have reached the testing stage, a variety of U.S. technical collection systems can be employed. But when the weapon is being designed, and its characteristics debated, technical collection can be of very limited utility—particularly if communications security is stringent. It is desirable to know about the characteristics of weapons systems when they have reached the testing stage, but it is also important to know whatever possible about activity in the design bureaus. It is always possible that by the time some weapon reaches the testing stage it will be too late to develop a counter weapon prior to its becoming operational.

In addition to the secrets of Soviet military R & D, there are numerous other types of Soviet documents that the United States desires—the minutes of Politburo, Military-Industrial Commission, Defense Council meetings, war planning documents, and secret treaties—that can only be acquired, if at all, via human agents.

In some countries, both Allied and Third World, U.S. intelligence requirements may focus primarily on domestic political conflict and economic activity. The information desired may concern the activities of a nation's Communist or Socialist Party or the country's economic prospects in the short term. In such cases, the information might be best acquired by penetrations of the Communist Party or Ministries of Commerce and Trade.

Or, in the case of Libya's Colonel Qaddafi, a terrorist group, or underground political party, information about planned actions may only be available through infiltration of an agent. Such an agent might be able to cast light on a situation discovered by overhead photography—for example, the massing of Libyan troops near Chad's border.

OFFICERS

Human sources include officers, agents, and attachés as well as defectors, emigres, and travelers. The core of U.S. human intelligence operations are the intelligence officers of the CIA's Directorate of Operations. These officers are U.S. citizens who almost always operate under the cover of U.S. embassies and consulates. While business or other forms of "deep cover" may be used on occasion, only official diplomatic establishments provide the CIA officer abroad with secure communications (within the embassy and with other locations), protected files, and diplomatic immunity.

CIA stations in foreign countries are headed by the Chief of Station (COS) and vary substantially in size, from just a few officers, to over 150—as in the Philippines. The COS and officers operate under a variety of cover positions which vary from embassy to embassy and include political counselor, second secretary, and economic attaché. They also operate under the cover of a variety of cover offices in the embassy. Thus, in the late 1970s, the CIA station in London, the agency's largest liaison station, was staffed by some forty CIA officers, who worked out of five offices—the Political Liaison Section; the Area Telecommunications Office, with a staff between nine and thirteen at any one time; the Joint Reports and Research Unit, with a staff of about thirty; the Foreign Broadcast Information Service; and the Office of the Special U.S. Liaison Officer, with mostly NSA but some CIA officers. The station is generally headed by a very senior CIA officer. (The present Deputy Director for Operations, Richard F. Stolz, was Chief of Station in the late 1970s).[3]

In France, the Regional Reports Office, the Regional Administrative Support, and American Liaison Section served as CIA cover offices in the late 1970s. In Italy, the Embassy Political Section and United States Army Europe Southern Projects Unit performed that function, while the Office of the Coordinator and Adviser, Research Office, Records Office, and Liaison Office performed that function in West Germany. The CIA also makes great use in Germany of the United States Army Europe (USAREUR) for cover. Among the units it has used for cover are the: U.S. Army Field Systems Office, U.S. Army General Research Detachment, U.S. Army Scientific and Technical Programming Detachment (Provisional), U.S. Army Scientific Projects Group and U.S. Army Security Evaluation Group.[4]

The attachés who operate as part of the Defense Attaché system also constitute a second group of intelligence officers. The function of Defense Attachés include:

- identifying and gaining cooperation of human sources believed to possess the ability to furnish intelligence information;
- identifying and capturing collection opportunities presented by trade fairs, military demonstrations, parades, symposia, convocations, conferences, meetings, etc.;
- traveling to identified geographic target areas to observe and report information specifically needed by consumers/users;
- identifying and establishing contact, and maintaining liaison with foreign military officers who by virtue of their rank, position or assignment, can furnish potential intelligence information or are considered to be future leaders;
- gaining and maintaining area reality to observe and report political, sociological, psychological, and economic developments of potential value in gauging the military plans, capabilities, and intentions of foreign governments, their military forces and their stability; and
- identifying and gaining access to assist in the acquisition and exploitation of foreign military equipment and material.[5]

In addition to cultivating sources and collecting open source material, CIA officers and defense attaches may also engage in clandestine collection on their own. In 1985, the Polish government claimed to have stopped a car in a restricted military zone near the town of Makow Mazowiecki, sixty-five miles north of Warsaw.

According to the Polish story, the passengers, U.S. Defense Attaché Colonel Frederick Myer, Jr. and his wife, covered themselves with blankets and exposed six roles of film. Police were said to have found two cameras with telephoto lens and detailed maps of the area that had been produced by the Defense Mapping Agency. Subsequently, Albert Mueller, then Second Secretary in the U.S. Embassy's Political Section, was arrested for allegedly attempting to photograph an army radar and Soviet helicopters, in addition to passing on espionage equipment, orders, ciphers, and money to a Polish citizen. The Polish government supported its charges with videotape.[6]

In early 1987, Colonel Marc B. Powe, the attaché at the U.S. Embassy in Baghdad was declared *persona non grata* and given two weeks to leave Iraq after he was accused of spying on and photographing truck loads of tanks and other military equipment in Kuwait in early December. Powe, who was also responsible for Kuwait, discovered a convoy of Soviet military equipment in Kuwait en route to Baghdad. He was spotted by Kuwaiti authorities taking photographs of the convoy and taking notes.[7]

In May 1986, the Nicaraguan government charged that two military officers, including the U.S. Embassy's military attaché, were discovered traveling without permits in a restricted war zone and suggested they were involved in espionage activity. The two were found traveling near the town of Siuna, a remote area in north central Nicaragua that had been a focus of combat between the Sandinista army and guerilla forces.[8]

As noted in Chapter 4, various military intelligence services—INSCOM, Task Force 168, and the Air Force Special Activities Center—also conduct human intelligence activities, including the recruitment and running of agents.

Army groups involved in HUMINT activities are the 470th Military Intelligence Group (Ft. Clayton, Panama); the 501st Military Intelligence Group (Seoul, Korea); the 500th Military Intelligence Group (Camp Zama, Japan); and the 66th Military Intelligence Group (Munich). In West Germany INSCOM clandestine collection activities that are coordinated by the 66th Military Intelligence Group are actually run by the case officers of the 430th Military Intelligence Detachment. The Detachment has four operational bases within West Germany—at Frankfurt, Berlin, Munich, and Bremerhaven—from which intelligence collection operations are administered for Soviet and East European targets in East and West Germany, Czechoslovakia, and other Warsaw Pact countries (excluding the Soviet Union). The agents run are never Americans or Germans—rather, a British or Turkish businessman living in Germany who travels to Eastern Europe may be recruited as an agent.[9]

Specific responsibilities of these units include:

- debriefing of emigres, defectors, detainees, and internees;
- tasking and/or debriefing Army personnel whose placement or travel provides access to information of Army interest;
- acquiring and exploiting foreign documents;

Table 10–1. Location of Task Force 168 Units.

Group	Unit	Location
168.0		Suitland, Md.
	168.0.1	New Orleans, La.
	168.0.3	San Diego, Calif.
	168.0.5	Norfolk, Va.
	168.0.7	New York, N.Y.
	168.0.9	Miami, Fla.
	168.0.10	Pearl Harbor, Haw.
	168.0.11	San Francisco, Calif.
	168.0.12	Newport, Rhode Island
168.1 (PACFAST)		Pearl Harbor, Ha./Norfolk, Va.
	168.1.1	Kamiseya, Japan
	168.1.2	Subic Bay, Philippines
	168.1.3	San Diego, Calif.
168.3		Naples, Italy
168.4		Munich, Germany
	168.4.1	West Berlin, Germany
	168.4.2	Naples, Italy
	168.4.3	London, United Kingdom
168.5		Yokosuka, Japan
	168.5.1	Singapore
	168.5.2	Subic Bay, Philippines
168.6		Rodman Naval Station, Panama

- acquiring foreign materiel;
- strategic clandestine human source collection;
- liaison with foreign intelligence agencies;
- combined activities with Allied Army HUMINT activities;
- joint collection activities with other U.S. government intelligence agencies; and
- debriefing Army personnel who evade capture, escape, or are released from enemy control.[10]

As noted in Chapter 4, Task Force 168 is responsible for a variety of intelligence collection activities, including identifying Soviet ships carrying nuclear weapons. As indicated by Table 10–1, its officers are stationed in the United States, Panama, Europe, and Asia.

An additional set of U.S. employees involved in human intelligence operations are the members of the U.S. Military Liaison Mission (MLM) to East Germany. The Mission is a fourteen-person unit that operates in teams of four that "prowl East Germany conducting what amounts to legal espionage."[11]

The teams travel in sedans packed with telescopes, infrared cameras, and listening devices. By listening in on radio communications, counting and photographing tanks and aircraft, and monitoring troop movements, the Mission has been able to glean highly detailed information on the capabilities and firepower of the Soviet forces in East Germany. The MLM teams have also been able to develop good personality profiles of Soviet soldiers stationed there.[12] The early warning value of the MLM was expressed by a senior intelligence officer who stated that "There is no other place on earth where you can watch 20 Russian divisions and see if the Soviet Army is planning to go to war."[13]

In an effort to limit effectiveness of their activities, East German military vehicles commonly tail USMLM automobiles. The mission's cars are sometimes bumped and bracketed by trucks to keep them from probing in sensitive areas. In July 1985, a Soviet Army truck rammed into a Land Rover carrying three members of the U.S. Military Liaison Mission. To avoid such incidents the teams would, at times, "go in at 90 miles per hour between 11 at night and 1 in the morning to try to keep the Russians from seeing where we were going."[14]

In March 1985 the stakes increased, when Major Arthur Nicholson was shot and killed on a mission in Ludwigslust, East Germany, during which he was photographing the inside of a Soviet military building through a window. The area in which the building was located had been off limits to Americans until the previous month. In an earlier mission Nicholson had sneaked into a Soviet tank and photographed the interior.[15]

AGENTS

Agents are foreign nationals recruited by U.S. intelligence officers to collect information, either in their home country or a third nation. Obviously, the identities of present U.S. agents are not known publicly. However, revelations in recent years indicates the nature of those agents who have been recruited by CIA officers, many of whom were operating until quite recently.

As with technical collection, the agents' primary target is the Soviet Union. Despite the closed nature of Soviet society and the size of the KGB's counterintelligence operation, the United States has had some notable successes in recruiting Soviet citizens to provide valuable information. The most significant success remains GRU Colonel Oleg Penkovskiy. In the 1961–62 period, Penkovskiy passed great quantities of material to the CIA and British Secret Intelligence Service, including information on Soviet strategic capabilities and nuclear targeting policy. Additionally, he provided a copy of the official Soviet MRBM (medium range ballistic missile) manual—which was of crucial importance at the time of the Cuban Missile Crisis.[16]

More recent recruits were Anatoli Filatov and Alexsandr Dmitrevich Ogorodnik. During the mid-1970s, Algiers-based GRU Colonel Anatoli Nikolaevich Filatov approached the CIA with a proposal to pass information to the United States. Over the next fourteen months, Filatov provided the United States with a variety of Soviet intelligence and military secrets, including details of Soviet links with national liberation movements. After being reassigned to GRU headquarters in Moscow,

Filatov continued to provide the CIA with information. This continued for about a year—at which time he was detected filing a "dead drop," which the KGB had probably located from routine surveillance on known CIA officers.[17]

Filatov's was only one of three penetrations that shook the Soviet establishment in the 1970s. The second also began abroad—this time in Bogota, Colombia, where Alexsandr Dmitrevich Ogorodnik was serving as a secretary in the Soviet Embassy. According to one account, Ogorodnik was an official "who changed from an idealistic Communist to a passionate anti-Communist," while another account described him as the victim of a "sexual blackmail" operation.[18]

Whatever his motivation, Ogorodnik became a CIA agent in 1974 and was assigned the code name TRIGON. By the time his tour ended in 1975, he had been thoroughly trained in the espionage trade. Upon his return to Moscow he managed to get a position in the Foreign Ministry's (MFA) Global Affairs Department, "one of the few MFA sections the KGB trusts with sensitive intelligence" and "the repository of other exceedingly secret and revealing data."[19]

The Department would receive the year-end comprehensive report of each Soviet ambassador analyzing the political situation, likely developments, and the Soviet standing in the country where an ambassador is stationed. The KGB residency is required to assist by contributing information and judgements based on the reports of its agents. In cases where the chief resident and ambassador are on good terms, the chief resident often will make available virtually all the information obtained from his agent network. Examination of such reports could reveal Soviet views of the world and Soviet strengths and weaknesses in specific countries, allow inferences about Soviet intentions, and in some cases permit an estimation of the nature and extent of KGB penetrations.[20]

Exactly how long TRIGON escaped Soviet detection has been the subject of dispute. According to John Barron's account, over the twenty months following Ogorodnik's transfer back to Moscow, he provided the CIA with microfilm of hundreds of secret Soviet documents, including ambassadorial reports. Soviet defector Arkady Shevchenko's account states that the KGB had begun to suspect the loyalty of a secretary in a Soviet Embassy in Latin America, so what appeared to be a routine transfer back to Moscow was arranged. Whatever the case, it is clear that before fall 1977 Ogorodnik had been detected by the KGB, possibly as a result of a tip from a Czech agent in the CIA. Ogorodnik apparently committed suicide shortly after his arrest by swallowing a cyanide pill.[21]

Another U.S. recruit—a Colonel attached to the General Staff, provided information in the mid-1970s on the Soviet Five Year Defense Plan. The Colonel reported that the Soviets were planning to build five SS-20 (PIONEER) IRBMs for each SS-20 launcher—a piece of information that was relied on in U.S. intelligence estimates for many subsequent years.[22]

The most recent, known penetration of the Soviet national security establishment involved a civilian employee of the Moscow Aviation Institute. *Pravda* reported on September 22, 1985 that

The USSR State Security Committee has uncovered and arrested an agent of the U.S. secret service—A.G. Tolkachev, a staff member of one of Moscow's research institutes. The spy was caught in the act during an attempt to pass on secret defense materials to Paul M. Stombaugh, an officer of the U.S. CIA, who acted under the cover of the second secretary of the U.S. Embassy in Moscow.[23]

An electronics expert at the Moscow Aviation Institute, Tolkachev was, according to one source, "one of our most lucrative agents," who "saved us billions of dollars in development costs" by telling the United States about the nature of Soviet military aviation efforts. The information made it significantly easier for the United States to develop systems to counter Soviet advances in this area.[24]

Over a period of years, Tolkachev passed on information concerning Soviet research efforts in electronics guidance and countermeasures, advanced radar, and "stealth," or radar avoidance technologies. In addition, Tolkachev may have been the key to U.S. discovery of the large phased-array radar being built at Krasnoyarsk in violation of the ABM Treaty.[25] U.S. satellite photography of the area was obtained, according to one expert, only after "we were told where to look."

Tolkachev was arrested in July 1985 (and subsequently executed) but announcement of his arrest was withheld until after CIA officer Edward L. Howard, who apparently told the KGB of Tolkachev's role as an American spy, had been exposed and fled the United States. Howard had been trained to become Tolkachev's case officer but had been discharged by the agency when a routine polygraph indicated drug use and petty theft.[26]

The information Howard provided to the Soviets apparently led to the arrest and execution of at least six Soviets working for the CIA—effectively ending some of the United States' most productive intelligence operations in the Soviet Union. According to one U.S. official, "it will take us at least ten years to recover from this." However, CIA Director William Webster has claimed that the CIA is presently having success in recruiting "assets" in the Soviet Union.[27]

HUMINT activities in the Soviet Union and Eastern Europe were a particular priority under William Casey's tenure as DCI. Three years into his tenure, the CIA had more than twenty-five regularly reporting sources within the Soviet Union and Eastern Europe, nearly all of whom had been developed since 1981.[28]

Among the sources in Eastern Europe was Colonel Wladyslaw Kuklinski, a longtime CIA asset. Kuklinski was a senior staff officer involved in planning the martial law crackdown conducted by Poland's General Wojciech Jaruzelski. By the time General Jaruzelski sent his tanks and troops into the streets, the CIA had a complete copy of his operations plan for a full month. Kuklinski was not, however, able to provide the exact date of the crackdown.[29]

In the Fall of 1980, when labor unrest in Poland first aroused fear of a Soviet invasion, Colonel Kuklinski reported that the Polish army had no intention of initiating or joining an operation that might end in violence and bloodshed. According to one U.S. official, "It was precisely because of this guy that we knew that Poles weren't going to act in December." Without Polish help, the Soviet invasion would have needed forty divisions. Having only twenty-seven divisions ready for action, the Soviets could not seriously consider invasion as an option.[30]

Subsequently, in late March and early April 1981, the Colonel reported that the KGB had instigated disturbances in the Polish industrial city of Bydgoszcz. The Colonel had reported further that Jaruzelski had refused the KGB's gambit and declined to ask for Soviet aid, deciding instead to wait for guidance of the Polish Communist Party Congress in July. The Colonel also reported Jaruzelski's hardening attitude and growing confidence among both the Polish and Soviet military that Polish security forces could handle the situation on their own.[31]

HUMINT operations in Latin America have involved Cuba, El Salvador, Nicaragua, and Argentina. The operations in Cuba highlighted the potential dangers in HUMINT operations. In 1987, Cuban television showed films of apparent CIA officers operating in Cuba picking up and leaving material at dead drops. The programs claimed that since September 1977, thirty-eight of sixty-nine diplomats permanently accredited to the U.S. Diplomatic Mission in Havana have been CIA officers. Apparently a significant number of Cubans had been operating as double agents, feeding information to CIA officers under the provision of Cuban security officers. The Cubans decided to reveal the operation as a result of the defection of a senior intelligence officer.[32]

In Central America the head of El Salvador's Treasury Police, Nicolas Carranza, was an informant of the CIA from the late 1970s, having received more than $90,000 a year from the CIA for at least six years. In Nicaragua, General Reynaldo Perez Vega, the second-ranking officer in the national guard under Somoza, was a CIA asset.[33]

Another high Central American official who has been on the CIA payroll is General Manuel Antonio Noriega of Panama. Noriega is alleged to have worked for the CIA while at military college in Peru, supplying information on suspected leftists among his fellow cadets. When he became head of the intelligence (G-2) section of the National Guard, he worked for both the CIA and the DIA, being paid for particular deals. Subsequently, he received a regular stipend from the CIA in exchange for his providing information on Cuban activities and Panamanian politics.[34]

Allegations of CIA clandestine collection activities in Nicaragua came with the arrest, in March 1986, of three Nicaraguans accused of working to infiltrate the Interior Ministry. One of the three was José Edwards Trejas Silva, a sublieutenant in the Interior Ministry, allegedly recruited by the CIA while he was outside Nicaragua in November 1983. He had been tasked to provide information on connections between the Sandinistas and leftist guerillas in Colombia and El Salvador.[35]

Evidence of U.S. operations in the Middle East and Africa have emerged with respect to Israel, Egypt, the PLO, Iraq, Ethiopia, and Ghana. According to the *Jerusalem Post*, between 1982 and 1984 the United States ran a high-level spy in the Israeli military, an operation personally authorized by DCI William Casey. The Egyptian government has apparently been penetrated extensively by the CIA. The CIA also has had a variety of sources in the PLO that provided operational details of PLO attacks in Israel.[36]

In Ethiopia, the CIA has had a senior official on its payroll; in Ghana, 1985 saw several individuals who pleaded guilty to or were convicted of spying for the CIA. Felix Peasah, a security officer at the U.S. Embassy in Accra, and Theodore Atiedu, a police inspector with Ghana's Bureau of National Investigation, pleaded guilty. Convicted were Stephen Balfour Ofusu, a former chief superintendent of police, who gave government secrets to the CIA and arranged taps on the telephones of diplomatic missions and high-level government officials, and Robert Yaw Appiah, a technician with the Post and Telecommunications Corporation who gave a CIA officer copies of keys to manhole covers.[37]

In Asia India, China, Japan and the Philippines are among the CIA's target countries. In India in 1977, six individuals were arrested for spying for the United States. The kingpin of the operation was P.E. Mehta, who apparently confessed to selling information to U.S. Embassy officials between 1962 and 1977. Also arrested were K.K. Sareen, a former Director at the Planning Commission who had also worked for the Soviet Union; E.L. Choudhuri of the State Trading Corporation; R.P. Varshney of the Planning Commission; Mahabir Prasid, personal Secretary to Y.B. Chaven when he was External Affairs Minister; and C.S. Balakrishanan, a clerk in the office of the Minister for Defense Production. Mehta received secret reports of the external affairs, chemical and petroleum ministries, as well as information about India's main aircraft design and production center, plus drawings of Soviet-made guns, missiles, and radar.[38]

The CIA also has had an Indian cabinet official on its payroll in the past, specifically during the war between Pakistan and India over Bangladesh in 1971.[39]

At least one CIA penetration of the Chinese establishment has involved someone with access to information concerning Chinese nuclear relations with Pakistan. That source reported on:

- China's nuclear exports to Argentina and South Africa
- Chinese technicians helping at a suspected Pakistani bomb development site
- Chinese scientific delegations who were spending a substantial amount of time at a centrifuge plant in Kahuta where Pakistani scientists were attempting to produce enriched uranium, which can be used to trigger a nuclear detonation
- Pakistani scientists from a secret facility at Wah showing a nuclear weapon design to some Chinese physicists in late 1982 or early 1983 and who sought Chinese evaluation of whether the design would yield a nuclear blast
- The triggering mechanism for the Pakistani bomb design that appeared to be very similar to one used by China in its fourth nuclear test.[40]

Information about the Taiwanese nuclear program was also provided by an informant. The informant, Colonel Chang Hsien-Yi, worked in a Taiwanese research institute. The information provided indicated the Taiwanese were in the process of building a secret installation that could have been used to obtain plutonium. Construction of the installation would violate Taiwanese commitments to the United

States not to undertake nuclear weapons research. U.S. pressure forced the Taiwanese to stop work on the secret installation, as well as shut down its largest civilian reactor, which the United States felt had military potential.[41]

Operations against Japan involved CIA authorization of a payment of $55,000 in bribes to obtain a blueprint of the secret technology used in Japan's high-speed surface transport (HSST).[42]

CIA assets in the Phillippines have provided important information at crucial times. On September 17, 1972, a CIA asset in the Philippines informed the CIA station that Ferdinand Marcos would proclaim martial law. Another asset provided a list of the individuals Marcos planned to arrest and imprison. In 1982 a CIA officer was able to locate a Philippine immigration official who was willing to provide the names of two doctors who visited the Philippines to treat Marcos, giving the agency a clue to the nature of Marcos' problems.[43]

At any given time the United States may have developed a wide array of agents in a particular society. Table 10–2 lists some of the agents the United States had in Iran before the fall of the Shah.

DEFECTORS AND EMIGRES

Human sources also involve defectors and emigres. The United States attaches major importance to the intelligence information that can be obtained via defectors. Thus, it has a coordinated Defector Program managed by the CIA-led Interagency Defector Committee (IDC) with an IDC within every American embassy.[44] Whatever country the embassy may be located in, the primary targets will be the officials of the Soviet Bloc and Cuban embassies.

In some cases, the defectors might be high-level Soviet Bloc officials such as scientists, diplomats, or intelligence officers. In the aftermath of the declaration of martial law in Poland, several Polish ambassadors defected to the West, bringing with them their knowledge of personalities, procedures, policies, and relations with the Soviet Union.

A defector may be able to settle disputes concerning matters of data acquired via technical collections systems. Thus, one defector was asked to

> look at an elaborate anlaysis of something our cameras detected by chance when there was an abnormal opening in clouds that normally covered a particular region.

> Learned men had spent vast amounts of time trying to figure out what it was and concluded that it was something quite sinister, an Air Force officer said "Viktor took one look at it and convincingly explained why what we thought was so ominous was in fact comically innocuous.[45]

Recent defectors from Cuba and Nicaragua include Rafael Del Pino Diaz and Roger Miranda Bengoechea. Diaz apparently held important aviation posts in the 1960s, including head of Cuban Airlines and the Cuban Aviation Agency. Diaz

Table 10–2. CIA Iranian Assets Circa 1979.

Codename	Comments
SD/BEEP-1	———
SD/BETTLE	———
SD/BLADE	———
SD/CARAWAY	———
SD/DAZE	———
SD/ENORMOUS-1	———
SD/FACE-1	Iranian informant in London
SD/FICKLE	Member of Democratic Party of Kurdistan of Iran. Contacted the CIA in 1976 and passed on information to the CIA, for which was paid monthly fee. In May-June 1979 was meeting with Soviets as CIA double agent.
SD/FORWARD-1	———
SD/FORGIVE-1	———
SD/JANUS-13	SAVAK employee
SD/JANUS-20	SAVAK employee
SD/JANUS-38	SAVAK employee
SD/JULEP-1	Journalist
SD/MARKET	———
SD/PECAN	———
SD/PEPPER-11	Iranian exile living in Washington, former Chief of Iranian Embassy Secretariat in Washington.
SD/PLOD	———
SD/PRAWN	———
SD/PRETEXT	———
SD/PROB	———
SD/PUTTY	———
SD/RAP	Iranian exile living in New Jersey, wanted to lead exile movement.
SD/RIGHT	———
SD/ROOF-1	Close friend and relative of Lt. General Siavouch Behzradi
SD/ROTTER-4	———
SD/SLIPPERY	Lebanese businessman in Paris
SD/STAY	Liaison with Khomeini during Bakhtiar premiership.
SD/THROB-1	Worked for SAVAK as Kurdish expert before the revolution.
SD/TRAMP-1	Provided complete list of PLO delegation to Iran, October 1979.
SD/ULTIMATE	———
SD/UPBEAT-1	Iranian military attaché in Paris, broke with government around September 1979.
SD/URN-1	———
SD/VALID	———

Source: Volumes published by Students Following the Line of the Iman.

claimed to be the Cuban Air Forces Deputy Chief of Staff, while the Cuban government claimed he had been relegated to organizing a museum about the history of the Cuban Air Force.[46]

Roger Miranda Bengoechea, a senior military officer, was chief contact for all military advisers in Nicaragua—which probably gave him knowledge concerning the Cuban presence in that country. He had toured all Sandinista military bases the week prior to his defection. Miranda, who made frequent trips to Mexico for medical reasons, may have been passing information to the CIA before his defection. According to the Nicaraguan defense minister, Miranda made copies of air force plans, artillery brigades and other Managua installations.[47]

Emigres—those legally allowed to leave the Soviet Union or other country—may also provide useful information. Many of these emigres, some of whom move to the United States or Israel, have held positions in scientific research institutes or social science institutes such as the USA and Canada Institute or IMEMO (the Institute of World Economy and International Affairs). The former group can offer information concerning research in their specific fields while the latter group can offer information and insights into both the Soviet policymaking apparatus and the perceptions and personalities of the leadership. Thus, several emigres have produced analyses concerning the formation of Soviet defense, arms control, and foreign policy.[48]

Neither defectors nor emigres need be high-level officials to provide valuable strategic or tactical information. A workman at a military base may be able to provide information concerning the functions of structures identified by satellite photography—whether a structure is a command and control bunker or a repair facility will have important implications for targeting. Thus

> although a comparatively low-level Soviet defector . . . would seem to have a small potential for providing useful intelligence, the CIA . . . had so little success in penetrating the Soviet military that the lieutenant underwent months of questioning. Through him, agency analysts were able to learn much about how Soviet armor units and the ground forces in general, are organized, their training and tactical procedures, and the mechanics of their participation in the build-up that preceded the invasion of Czechoslovakia.[49]

Emigres who were ordinary citizens can provide information concerning local events of international interest. Initial reports of the 1979 anthrax incident at Sverdlovsk circulated internally among dissidents and were carried abroad by emigres.[50]

Processing of defectors and emigres is anything but an *ad hoc* procedure. The CIA and the Air Force Intelligence Service's Special Activities Center maintain extensive facilities in the United States and abroad for such processing activities. The CIA's defector reception center at Camp King near Frankfurt, West Germany handles escapees from the Soviet Union and Eastern Europe. At Lindsey Air Station in Wiesbaden, Germany, the Air Force 7113th Special Activities Squadron maintains a computerized list of questions they ask individuals who come across the border.[51]

TRAVELERS

Travelers, who are not necessarily intelligence officers, may often be able to provide information. At one time, before the United States developed satellites to penetrate the Soviet interior, travelers played a more significant role in intelligence activities.[52]

Among present traveler collection programs is CREEK GRAB, a USAFE program. USAFE Regulation 200-6 states that:

> During peacetime, USAFE military and DAF [Department of the Air Force] civilian personnel, other U.S. employees, and contractors may occasionally have opportunities to acquire information of intelligence value either while performing their normal duites or by pure chance . . . USAFE intelligence personnel must be able to respond effectively to unexpected opportunities for foreign intelligence collection in peacetime as well as wartime.[53]

Among those considered potential intelligence contributors are amateur radio operators, persons in contact with foreign friends and relatives, and foreign (primarily Communist-controlled) aircraft that land or crash nearby. Regulation 200-6 also specifies procedures for photographing aircraft, specifying that photography should be obtained of:

a. cockpit interior
b. weapons system controls, panel instruments
c. seat(s)
d. weaponry
e. electronics gear (avionics, radar, black boxes, etc.)
f. propulsion system (air intake, variable geometry, fuel parts, and fuel tankage)
g. documents and maintenance records.[54]

The CIA's National Collection Division (NCD) seeks to interview businessmen, tourists, and professionals, either because of specific contacts they may have had during their foreign travels or because of the sites of their travel—for example, Cuba and North Korea. The information sought may include the health and attitudes of a national leader or the military activities in a particular region. In some instances, the NCD, upon hearing that a particular person plans to visit a particular location, will ask the traveler in advance to seek out information on certain targets. However, the NCD has been reluctant to assign specific missions. Since the travelers are not professional agents, they might be arrested as a result of taking their espionage roles too seriously.[55]

NOTES TO CHAPTER 10

1. Roy Godson, "Clandestine Collection: An Introduction," and "Collection Against the Soviet Union and Denied Areas," in Roy Godson, ed., *Intelligence Requirements for the 1980s: Clandestine Collection* (New Brunswick, N.J.: Transaction, 1982), pp. 1–14 at p. 3, pp. 15–31 at p. 27.

2. Amrom Katz, "Technical Collection Requirements for the 1980s," in Roy Godson, ed., *Intelligence Requirements for the 1980s: Clandestine Collection*, pp. 101–117 at pp. 106–7.

3. Philip Agee and Louis Wolf, ed., *Dirty work: The CIA in Western Europe* (Secaucus, N.J.: Lyle Stuart, 1978), pp. 131–32.

4. Ibid., pp. 721–22, 726; Private information.

5. Private information.

6. "Poland Expelling Army Attache," *New York Times*, February 26, 1985, p. A3; Bradley Graham, "Poland Expelling U.S. Attache as Spy," *Washington Post*, February 26, 1985, pp. A1, A10; "A Colonel with a Camera," *Newsweek*, March 11, 1985, p. 47; "Poland Claims U.S. Envoy Snared While Spying," *Washington Times*, April 23, 1987, p. 8A; Michael T. Kaufman, "Warsaw Accuses U.S. Aide of Spying," *New York Times*, April 23, 1987, p. A9.

7. Richard Mackenzie, "A Gulf War Intrigue: The Tale of the Colonel's Camera," *Washington Times*, April 20, 1987, p. 9A.

8. Nancy Nusser, "U.S. Officials Cited as Spies by Managua," *Washington Post*, May 10, 1986, p. A14.

9. Private information.

10. Private information.

11. James M. Markham, "On the Prowl in East Germany: Team of G.I. Spies," *New York Times*, April 21, 1984, p. 2.

12. Ibid., William Drozdiak, "Soldiers Living 'in a Cage'," *Washington Post*, May 19, 1985, pp. A1, A22.

13. David Alpern, et al., "The Rules of the Game," *Newsweek*, April 8, 1985, p. 22.

14. "On the Prowl in East Germany"; "U.S. Vehicle is Hit in East Germany," *New York Times*, July 17, 1985, p. A10; George C. Wilson and James R. Dickenson, "Slain Officer Described as Talented Specialist," *Washington Post*, March 26, 1985, p. A12.

15. Bernard Gwertzman, "U.S. Says Slain Major Had Photographed Military Site," *New York Times*, March 28, 1985, p. A3; James M. Markham, "Slain U.S. Major Had One Exploit," *New York Times*, April 24, 1985, p. A7.

16. See Jeffrey T. Richelson, *American Espionage and the Soviet Target* (New York: William Morrow, 1987), pp. 56–65.

17. John Barron, *The KGB Today: The Hidden Hand* (New York: Reader's Digest Press, 1983), p. 428.

18. Ibid.; Ernest Volkman, *Warriors of the Night: Spies, Soldiers and American Intelligence* (New York: Morrow, 1985), p. 224.

19. Barron, *The KGB Today*, p. 428.

20. Ibid., pp. 428–9.

21. Ibid., pp. 429; Arkady Shevchenko, *Breaking with Moscow* (New York: Knopf, 1985), p. 314; Volkman, *Warriors of the Night*, pp. 224–25; David Martin, "A CIA Spy in the Kremlin," *Newsweek*, July 21, 1980, pp. 69–70; Ronald Kessler, "Moscow's Mole in the CIA," *Washington Post*, April 17, 1988, pp. C1, C4.

22. Peter Samuel, "1977 Spy Data on SS-20s Cast Shadow Over INF Talks," *New York City Tribune*, November 17, 1987, p. 1; Walter Pincus, "U.S. May Have Miscounted Some Soviet Missiles," *Washington Post*, December 16, 1987, p. A6.

23. Foreign Broadcast Information Service, "PRAVDA: KGB Arrests CIA-Controlled Moscow Spy," *Daily Report: Soviet Union*, September 24, 1985, p. A1.

24.   William Kucewicz, "KGB Defector Confirms Intelligence Fiasco," *Wall Street Journal*, October 17, 1985, p. 28.

25.   Ibid.

26.   Patrick E. Tyler, "Soviet Seized as U.S. Spy Exposed by Howard," *Washington Post*, October 18, 1985, p. A10; Stephen Engelberg, "U.S. Indicates Ex-CIA Officer Helped Soviet Capture a Russian," *New York Times*, October 18, 1985, p. A18.

27.   Michael Wines and Ronald J. Ostrow, "Deaths of U.S. Agents Blamed On Marine Link," *Los Angeles Times*, April 12, 1987, pp. 1–20; Michael Wines and Ronald J. Ostrow, "Soviet Execution of Six Informers for U.S. Reported," *Los Angeles Times*, April 11, 1987, pp. 1, 24; Jack Nelson, "Scandal Fails to Stem CIA Recruiting Webster Says," *Los Angeles Times*, October 6, 1987, pp. 1, 10.

28.   Bob Woodward, *Veil: The Secret Wars of the CIA 1981–1987* (New York: Simon & Schuster, 1987), p. 306.

29.   Bob Woodward and Michael Dobbs, "CIA Had Secret Agent on Polish General Staff," *Washington Post*, June 4, 1986, pp. A1, A31; "A Polish Agent in Place," *Newsweek*, December 20, 1982, p. 49.

30.   "A Polish Agent in Place."

31.   Ibid.

32.   "Cuban TV Purports to Show U.S. Spies," *Washington Times*, July 8, 1987, p. A8; Lewis H. Diuguid, "Spy Charges Strain U.S.-Cuban Ties," *Washington Post*, July 25, 1987, p. A17; Michael Wines and Ronald J. Ostrow, "U.S. Duped by Cuban Agents, Defector Says," *Los Angeles Times*, August 12, 1987, pp. 1, 14.

33.   Philip Taubman, "Top Salvador Police Official Said to Be CIA Informant," *New York Times*, March 22, 1984, pp. A1, A4; Stephen Kinzer, "Sandinistas Tap Heroine as Envoy, But Some in U.S. Oppose Her," *New York Times*, March 22, 1984, pp. A1, A4.

34.   "Drugs, Money, and Death," *Newsweek*, February 15, 1988, pp.32–38.

35.   Stephen Kinzer, "Nicaragua Says It Has Cracked CIA Spy Ring," *New York Times*, March 15, 1986, p. 3.

36.   Wolf Blitzer, "U.S. Changed Rules of the Spy Game," *Jerusalem Post International Edition*, March 28, 1987, pp. 1, 2; Woodward, *Veil*, pp. 87, 161.

37.   Philip Smith, "Events Spark Speculation that Spy Swap is Imminent," *Washington Post*, November 21, 1985, p. A16; "2 More Convicted in Ghana of Spying for CIA," *Washington Post*, November 23, 1985, p. A8; Woodward, *Veil*, p. 167.

38.   Sanjoy Hazarika, "In Secret Trial, India Sentences 6 For Spying for U.S.," *New York Times*, October 30, 1986, p. A5.

39.   Thomas Powers, *The Man Who Kept the Secrets: Richard Helms and the CIA* (New York: Alfred A. Knopf, 1979), p. 206.

40.   Jack Anderson and Dale Van Atta, "Nuclear Exports to China?," *Washington Post*, November 3, 1985, p. C7; Patrick E. Tyler and Joanne Omang, "China-Iran Nuclear Link is Reported," *Washington Post*, October 23, 1985; pp. A1, A19; Joanne Omang, "Nuclear Pact with China Wins Senate Approval," *Washington Post*, November 22, 1985, p. A3; Patrick E. Tyler, "A Few Spoken Words Sealed China Atom Pact," *Washington Post*, January 12, 1986, pp. A1, A20–1.

41.   Stephen Engelberg and Michael R. Gordon, "Taipei Halts Work on Secret Plant to Make Nuclear Bomb Ingredient," *New York Times*, March 23, 1988, pp. A1, A15.

42. Jack Anderson, "CIA Linked Firm Spied on Japan," *Washington Post*, October 16, 1984, p. B11.
43. Raymond Bonner, *Waltzing with a Dictator*, (New York: Times Books, 1977), pp. 3, 5, 340.
44. E. Howard Hunt, *Undercover: Memoirs of an American Secret Agent* (New York: Berkley, 1974), p. 80.
45. John Barron, *MIG Pilot* (New York: Avon, 1981), p. 186.
46. John M. Goshko and Julia Preston, "Defector Arrives for Debriefing; Cuba Plays Down Military Role," *Washington Post*, May 30, 1987, p. A3.
47. Glenn Garvin and John McCaslin, "Key Nicaraguan Aide Dubs Military Defector U.S. Spy," *Washington Times*, November 4, 1987, p. A10.
48. See, for example, Vladimir Petrov, "The Formation of Soviet Foreign Policy," *Orbis* (Fall 1973): 819–50.
49. Victor Marchetti and John Marks, *The CIA and the Cult of Intelligence*, p. 185.
50. Roy Godson, "Collection Against the Soviet Union and Denied Areas," in Roy Godson, ed., *Intelligence Requirements for the 1980s: Clandestine Collection*, p. 28.
51. Marchetti and Marks, *The CIA and the Cult of Intelligence*, p. 185; Private information.
52. See Richelson, *American Espionage and the Soviet Target*, pp. 52–55.
53. USAFE Regulation 200-6, "CREEK GRAB," May 31, 1986, p. 2.
54. Ibid., p. 15.
55. Marchetti and Marks, *The CIA and the Cult of Intelligence*, pp. 236–37.

11 OPEN SOURCES, TECHNICAL SURVEILLANCE AND MAIL OPENING, MATERIEL EXPLOITATION

Significant intelligence concerning the political, military, and economic affairs of other nations can be obtained through means other than clandestine technical and human source collection—included are open sources, technical surveillance and mail opening, and materiel exploitation.

Open source collection includes the acquisition of any verbal, written, or electronically transmitted material that can be legally acquired. Thus, open source collection includes the acquisition of newspapers, magazines, and unclassified journals as well as the monitoring of public radio and television.

An important part of the intelligence activities conducted by the Central Intelligence Agency and other intelligence units is acquired by electronic surveillance and mail openings. The electronic surveillance usually takes the form of bugging or phone tapping. Although strictly a "technical collection" activity, bugging and phone tapping are so distinct from satellite, aircraft, or ground station interception as to merit separate consideration. Further, such operations are conducted as an adjunct to CIA and military service human intelligence activities.

Another significant aspect of intelligence collection revolves around "materiel exploitation"—the acquisition and analysis of foreign weapons, communications, and other systems. Such acquisition and analysis yields information on weapons systems such as firearms that cannot be acquired by overhead photography and more detailed information on systems such as tanks—information that can be used to design countermeasures.

OPEN SOURCES

Open source collection involves one of three activities: collection of legally available documents; open observation of foreign political, military, or economic activity;

and the monitoring and recording of public radio and television broadcasts. In more open societies, a variety of open source data concerning political, military, and economic affairs is available through newspapers, magazines, trade journals, academic journals, and government publications. These published sources may yield intelligence concerning the internal disputes plaguing a West European political party, French nuclear strategy, Japanese willingness to restrict exports, or scientific advances in West Germany.

The statement of Roscoe Hillenkoeter, the Director of Central Intelligence in 1948, that "80 percent of intelligence is derived from such prosaic sources as foreign books, magazines, technical and scientific surveys, photographs, commercial analysis, newspapers and radio broadcasts, and general information from people with a knowledge of affairs abroad" remains true today.[1]

Of course, in a closed society, much less information will be available. Most particularly, direct reporting on internal political and military affairs will be absent. Further, all reporting will be conducted under the direction of government propaganda guidelines. However, even in a closed society, there is a significant amount of intelligence that can be gleaned from legally obtainable documents.

The obtainable documents will include newspapers, magazines, collected speeches, academic journals, and even official documents on military affairs. In the Soviet Union, these latter documents, while generally devoid of information concerning specific weapon systems, do discuss details of Soviet views concerning operational tactics and grand strategy.

The Soviets publish eleven major military journals and newspapers—including *Communist of the Armed Forces*, *Military-Historical Journal*, *Soviet Military Review*, and the *Military Herald*. Additionally, there are a significant number of minor and more specialized publications, and as many as 500 books on military affairs published each year in the Soviet Union.[2]

The most important military newspaper is *Krasnaya Zvezda (Red Star)*, published by the Main Political Administration of the Soviet Army and Navy (MPA). The MPA is responsible for ensuring the ideological conformity of Soviet military personnel and is outside the normal military chain of command; thus *Krasnaya Zvezda* is somewhat more open about military shortcomings such as incompetence and corruption. It can also provide information on Soviet military operations. For example, an early 1983 article by Lt. Colonel Artemko entitled "An Assault Landing Force Capturing Its Objective" discussed a particular Soviet operation in Afghanistan.[3]

Civilian newspapers and collected speeches can provide a variety of information. According to Kohler, et al.:

> The members of the ruling hierarchy provide through their public utterances a substantially accurate picture of what they are up to and why, at least in a strategic sense. This is due to the requirement for uniformity that is so vital to the Soviet political system. Not only must those at the top speak with a single voice, but the entire hierarchy must echo that voice.

Words are a critical factor in holding the system together . . . The only way in which the regime can carry forward a program or effect a change in direction without creating confusion and uncertainty is to talk about it.[4]

The uniformity of which Kohler et al. speak applies to overall Soviet strategy, and on many occasions the tactics for implementing that strategy. Yet at times there are differences, particularly with regard to tactics. Such differences can often be detected by material, usually speeches, that appear in the press. The signs are more obscure than in Western society, but they do exist. There is a Soviet "language of conflict" indicating both ideological and practical disputes. The subject of these disputes might involve agricultural or economic policy, military strategy, or foreign policy. The signs of conflict might be a dropped signature, a pruned speech, or more direct indications. Thus

In the fall of 1969, just as the talks were beginning in Helsinki, *Pravda*, the official organ of the Communist Party, reported a speech by the Foreign Minister, Andrei Gromyko, in which he had mentioned that "some people" were not convinced of the correctness of undertaking such negotiations. In the spring of 1973, Defense Minister Grechko had been promoted to the ruling Politburo at the same time as Gromyko, who had been prominently associated with the SALT I treaty signed in 1972, and Brezhnev's ally, Yuri Andropov. In January 1974, *Pravda* began publishing extracts of Grechko's speeches rather than full versions, something that does not happen to members of the Politburo who are in good standing with the inner leadership.

In 1974 the dispute erupted into what, by Soviet standards, was a public slanging match. A frequently expressed precept of Soviet military doctrine had been that the best way to keep the peace was to prepare for war. In June 1974 *Pravda* reported a remark by Brezhnev that the best way to preserve peace was by "waging peace"—meaning detente, SALT negotiations, and so forth. Shortly after, *Kranaya Zvezda* featured articles by both Grechko and Kulikov rejecting this concept and reaffirming the concept of military preparedness as the best way of preventing war.[5]

Additionally, the relative power of members of the ruling elite in Soviet society can be detected by following Soviet reporting. Hence, the first indication of Yuri Andropov's accession to the post of General Secretary was the public announcement that he had been designated to head the funeral procession for Leonid Brezhnev.

In some situations, local newspapers can reveal useful data concerning local conditions, transfers of individuals, and, in wartime, casualty rates. In World War II, the Office of Strategic Services went to great trouble to obtain local newspapers because "there was a fairly constant ration of enlisted men to officers killed. By underground means we obtained small-town newspapers. We read them carefully. By 1943 we were able to make an estimate of the strength of the German army that turned out to be curiously exact."[6] Even in peacetime newspaper obituaries may be of value, as they might indicate where someone worked as well as his/her position.

Academic journals can also be quite revealing. Journals of the social science research institutes—the USA and Canada Institute, for example—might indicate the subjects of particular concern to the Soviet leadership; that is, those about which it is considered most important to influence opinion. Technical journals are of more importance. Although the areas that are considered to be secret military research are much broader in the Soviet Union than in the West, there is still much material available. For one thing, Soviet researchers, as those elsewhere, are interested in publishing their results—even if the results are in watered-down form. Such publication is also a necessary part of scientific communication, which allows cumulative work in any field of research. Hence some indication of the work being done at research institutes with military functions can be determined by examining the articles appearing in technical journals and the author's names and affiliations.

In any case, examination of journals in fields such as chemistry, physics, biology, optics, or mathematics can indicate the state of Soviet knowledge in particular fields, ones that either have a military application or, at the very least, affect Soviet economic capability. Noting the authors and their affiliations will indicate which ones may also be working at nearby research institutes involved in military projects.

In addition, charting the frequency with which researchers publish may yield insights into the formation of new research groups, new weapons systems, and new directions of research. Thus, the first indication to Soviet intelligence that the United States was producing an atomic bomb was the noted absence of publications by top U.S. nuclear physicists such as Hans Bethe, Eugene Wigner, and Edward Teller. Recently, it has been noted that the Soviet Union once had a large number of research groups that published extensively on the theory of X-ray lasers until 1977. The sudden end to the published reports has led to speculation that the program has moved into direct military applications.[7]

Examination of the technical literature might also provide clues to the occurrence of events of interest to the intelligence community. Thus, on the basis of articles in Soviet technical journals, historian Zhores Medvedev has concluded that a serious nuclear accident took place in the Soviet Union in the late 1950s.[8] In 1979, an anthrax outbreak in Sverdlovsk was attributed by some to biological warfare experiments performed in violation of Soviet treaty commitments. It is certain that U.S. intelligence analysts have examined both local newspapers and Soviet biological and chemical journals to detect information that would cast light on what actually happened.

The utility of open source information in producing intelligence estimates concerning the Soviet Union was the subject of the following exchange between a member of the U.S. Congress, House Permanent Select Committee on Intelligence (Representative Anderson) and two Soviet experts (Richard Pipes and Raymond Garthoff):

> Mr. Anderson: If I may, I would like to return to this question of how you use open sources in the NIEs. How big a volume of material is there? How many journals and newspapers are we talking about?
>
> Mr. Pipes: It is a very large immense body of literature but a trained person can scan it quite rapidly, because so much of it is unimportant. This applies not only to strategic weapons. I am speaking in general terms. For example, a few years ago I did a sort

of study of Soviet policy *vis-à-vis* the Third World. I had to wade through many articles, but they began to fall into sentences as to what the policy will be, or the controversies, such as they were. When the volume is extremely large, you can develop analysts who go through it quickly, and then if they are well trained, their eyes will alight on what are the critical things. They can look at an article and say, now this is something new, and they can study the text more closely, whereas much of the text is repetitious.

Mr. Anderson: But it would be fair to describe it as a full-time job for more than one person.

Mr. Pipes: Oh, heavens yes. This is a full-time job for many people.

Mr. Garthoff: But with one or two exceptions, there are about a dozen serious Soviet military journals which are available on subscription . . . there are a number of people working with these materials. As we were both saying earlier, the main problem is in the attention to be given to and in the thorough use of the material. The basic job of acquiring and of going through these materials and translating many of them is being done on a regular basis, and there are many people in the government and a few outside who do follow these things fairly closely. So it is more a question of the weight to be given to it and the utilization of it—it is not a matter of ignoring it totally in the process.

Mr. Pipes: In London there is a small outfit called the Central Asian Research Center, which publishes a periodical called "The Soviet Union and China in the Third World." This is an invaluable source because they go through all the Soviet and Chinese literature dealing with the Third World. Now, this operation is carried on by a handful of people. It is a marvelous source of information on Soviet intentions, because you can tell a great deal about what the Russians intend to do from their pronouncements, from the quantity of aid they give to a country, and so on.

Take a methodological example. You trace over the years the amount of economic aid given by the Soviet Union to various countries, divide it by the number of its inhabitants, and you get a pecking order of its importance to the Soviet Union. Afghanistan and Yemen have the highest ratings. You could almost have predicted the Soviet involvement in Afghanistan on that basis. . . . Of course, this is more difficult in the military field than in the political one, but in the political field you have an enormous volume of material available which, if intelligently used, gives you a very good idea of their intentions, and then, if you superimpose or add it to the military information you have from intelligence sources, you obtain a very good picture of what the Russians are up to.[9]

Simple observation can also be of intelligence value. Noting the public appearances of Soviet leaders can indicate their relative positions at any given moment—either by their order of appearance or their absence. In December 1983, Western embassies monitored the passage of a high-speed motorcade that moved to and from the Kremlin during the morning and evening rush hours along the route from the city center to a special Kremlin hospital, in an attempt to determine if Soviet General Secretary Yuri Andropov had returned to work. The first signs of Andropov's death came on February 9, 1984 from a variety of public signs: changes in the programming of the state radio and television (from jazz to classical music), as well as scores of lit windows (rather than the normal three or four) in the offices in the headquarters of the KGB, Soviet general staff, and Ministry of Defense.

Half the lights on the sixth and eighth floors of the KGB were visible, as were those on three full floors of the Ministry of Defense. Additionally, there was an unusual amount of movement by cars belonging to the KGB.[10]

Chinese journals can also be exploited to produce intelligence. The journal *Knowledge of Ships* which is considered to provide naval data that is generally low quality and unreliable occasionally does contain useful information. One article, "The Role of Guided Missile Speedboat in Engagement" stated that "planners" were considering assigning an antiaircraft mission to one or two of the six boats in a typical OSA or KOMAR squadron.[11]

The Journal of Shipbuilding in China focuses on research topics in marine engineering in considerable detail and demonstrates that the Chinese are actively exploiting American, British, Soviet, Japanese, and German work in the field. Examination of the *Journal* also demonstrates that the instruments being employed by China for test purposes are of German, Japanese, and Chinese manufacture and that the Chinese experiments generally pick up where the exploited source stopped—either advancing the testing process a step further or seeking empirical verification of a theory propounded by the source.[12]

According to one analyst: "from the technical intelligence perspective the publication can be valuable in providing new information about the marine engineering topics of interest to China, an appreciation of the foreign sources being exploited by the Chinese and the results of their experiments in the field." This information, when combined with other intelligence "offers a reasonably accurate assessment of where China stands in this area of technology.[13]

Also of interest to intelligence analysts is a publication entitled *Contemporary Military Affairs*, in which the Pacific and Indian Ocean theaters receive good coverage.[14]

As shown in the case of Andropov's death, monitoring radio and television broadcasts can also be a valuable source of information. Through the Foreign Broadcast Information Service (FBIS) and its partner, the BBC Monitoring Service, the United States obtains a vast amount of information concerning political, military, and economic events throughout the world. This monitoring also allows the United States to assess the impact of its own propaganda efforts.

FBIS monitoring stations are located at: Abidjan, Ivory Coast; Amman, Jordan; Asuncion, Paraguay; Athens, Greece; Bangkok, Thailand; Chiva Chiva, Panama; Hong Kong; Key West, Florida; London; Nicosia, Cyprus; Okinawa; Seoul; Tel Aviv; Vienna; and Washington, D.C.[15] The station in Key West targets Cuban radio and television; of particular interest is any information on Cuban military exercises.

TECHNICAL SURVEILLANCE AND MAIL OPENING

An important aspect of political intelligence gathering is the technical surveillance and mail-opening operations conducted by the CIA and other intelligence units. Such operations can provide information in addition to, or a substitute for, information provided by human sources. Technical penetration of a presidential residence offers twenty-four-hour coverage and can capture the exact conversations that occur. Technical penetration of foreign embassies can provide information on plans, policies, and the activities of diplomats and intelligence agents.

Two prominent forms of technical surveillance are "bugs" and telephone taps. A bug or audio device, which will transmit all conversations in a room, is planted by experts from the Office of Technical Services of the Directorate of Science and Technology. Planting such a device is a complex operation involving surveillance of the site, acquisition of building and floor plans, and determination of the color of the interior and texture of the walls. Activity in the room as well as the movements of security patrols are noted. When the information is acquired and processed, it will be employed to determine the time of surreptitious entry and the materials needed to install the device in such a way as to minimize the probability of its discovery.[16]

During the early 1970s one target of CIA audio devices was Nguyen Van Thieu, President of South Vietnam. Presents given to Thieu by the CIA—television sets and furniture—came equipped with audio devices, allowing the agency to monitor his personal conversations. The CIA also attempted to install devices in the office and living quarters of the South Vietnamese observer at the Paris Peace Talks.[17]

Another Asian ally that has been subject to CIA and NSA technical penetration is South Korea. A substantial part of the evidence against Tongsun Park concerning his alleged attempt to bribe America congressmen came from tape recordings of incriminating conversations inside the South Korean presidential mansion.[18]

An area in which audio devices have, at least in the past, produced much of the CIA's intelligence is Latin America. A report on clandestine collection activities in Latin America during the 1960s revealed that the CIA had managed to place audio devices in the homes of many key personnel, including cabinet ministers.[19]

Telephone taps also provided much of the CIA's intelligence, according to the report. During E. Howard Hunt's tenure in Mexico City, the CIA bugged or tapped several Iron Curtain embassies. During Hunt's tenure in Uruguay, the CIA station conducted technical penetrations of embassies and the living quarters of key personnel. During Philip Agee's time in Uruguay seven telephone lines were being monitored, including telephones of the Soviet and Cuban embassies, consulates, and commercial offices.[20]

In 1982 or 1983, a unit of INSCOM, then known as the Quick Reaction Team (QRT) and subsequently as the Technical Analysis Unit, placed an electronic listening device in a Panama apartment belonging to General Manuel Antonio Noriega. Paying bribes to the maids who cleaned and to the guards who protected the apartment, a QRT agent was able to place a listening device in Noriega's conference room. The six ninety-minute tapes that resulted did not produce any substantial intelligence information.[21]

QRT agents also bugged the apartment of a Cuban diplomat in Panama. When the diplomat was away, agents slipped into his apartment and wired it with microtransmitters; again, the result was of little value.[22]

In 1983, the QRT targeted Soviet representatives on several occasions during a visit to the United States. Soviet officials who traveled to Livermore, California, home of the Lawrence Livermore Laboratory, had their rooms bugged by QRT agents. The bugging was repeated when the Soviets moved on to Denver. This time the results were more useful—sensitive discussions were recorded and leads obtained on possible Soviet agents in the United States.[23]

Technical surveillance operations may also employ lasers. A laser beam can be directed at a closed window from outside and used to detect the vibrations of the sound waves resulting from a conversation inside the room. The vibrations can be transformed back into the spoken words. Such a device was successfully tested in West Africa but never seemed to function properly elsewhere except in the United States.[24]

For many years, until forced to stop by fear of public revelations, both the CIA and FBI conducted mail openings on a widespread basis in the United States. Between 1952 and 1972, the CIA ran a mail-opening program, called HTLINGUAL, targeted against mail being sent to and from the Soviet Union. The operation, which took place mainly at La Guardia and Kennedy International Airports in New York, involved over 215,000 letters. The CIA maintained a watch list that singled out certain groups for special attention, including many with no intelligence connections.[25]

Although domestic mail opening in the absence of a warrant may have ceased, a special Army unit, the Army Special Operations Field Office in Berlin, is involved in opening mail flowing between East and West Europe. The exact extent of the Office's activities is not clear, including the extent, if any, to which the mail of U.S. citizens is being opened.[26]

The Office was the subject of an early Carter Administration Presidential Directive, PD/NSC-9, of March 30, 1977, the contents of which are considered top secret. PD/NSC-9 is listed as one of the references for Department of Defense Directives 5240.1, 5240.1-R, and 5240.1-TS, all titled "Procedures Governing the Activities of DOD Intelligence Components that Affect U.S. Persons."

DOD 5240.1-R of December 1982 specifies that

> DOD intelligence components are authorized to open mail to or from a United States person that is found outside United States postal channels only pursuant to the approval of the Attorney General.

> Heads of DOD intelligence components may authorize the opening of mail outside U.S. postal channels when both the sender and intended recipient are other than United States persons if such search are otherwise lawful and consistent with any Status of Forces Agreement that may be in effect.[27]

In addition to its mail-opening operations, the Special Operations Field Office is also involved in wiretap operations.[28]

MATERIEL EXPLOITATION AND
RECOVERY OPERATIONS

An important source of information comes from the acquisition of new or used foreign weapon systems, communications, and other devices of military significance. In many cases information on small systems cannot be obtained by overhead reconnaissance or signals intelligence. In any case, possession of the actual system adds significant new information to whatever is already possessed. The acquisition and analysis—materiel exploitation—of such systems, a function of all the military scientific and technical intelligence units, allows scientists to determine not only the capabilities of the system but how such capabilities are achieved. Such knowledge can then be exploited to improve U.S. systems as well as to develop countermeasures.

According to Army Regulation 381-26, materiel exploitation allows

- production of scientific and technical intelligence in support of force, combat, and materiel development;
- assessment of foreign technology, design features, and scientific developments for infusion into U.S. developmental efforts;
- support of U.S. systems and developmental testing/operational testing by providing adversary systems for use in evaluating U.S. systems capabilities; and
- development of simulator systems in support of simulation of foreign systems.[29]

Acquisition of systems is a high-priority intelligence objective and attained by a variety of methods. In Indonesia in the 1960s, the CIA conducted an operation known as HABRINK. In one phase of the operation, CIA operatives entered a warehouse holding SAM-2 missiles, removed the guidance system from one missile, and took it with them. The acquisition allowed U.S. Air Force scientists to equip B-52s with appropriate countermeasures. HABRINK also obtained the designs and workings of numerous Soviet weapons—the surface-to-surface Styx naval missile, W-class submarine, Komar guided-missile patrol boats, a RIGA-class destroyer, a Sverdlov cruiser TU-16 (BADGER) bomber, and a KENNEL air-to-surface missile.[30]

In a more recent version of HABRINK, the CIA purchased, from retired officers of the Indian Army and Air Force, details on weapons furnished to India by the Soviet Union. The Indian officers involved included an Army Major General and Lt. Colonel and an Air Vice Marshal.[31]

In 1979, the CIA and the DIA planned Operation GRAY PAN, which was to involve the theft of a Soviet-made antiaircraft gun and armored personnel carrier that the Soviets had sold to the Iranian Army in 1978.[32]

The most significant ground forces equipment obtained by the CIA has been a Soviet T-72 tank; only the T-80 is newer. In 1981 the Intelligence Support Activity, in an operation code-named GREAT FALCON, attempted to obtain a T-72 and other equipment (including a MiG-25) from Iraq in exchange for U.S. 175-mm.

cannons. Ultimately, Iraqi officials vetoed the deal. Another ISA attempt to acquire a T-72 at the behest of Lt. Colonel Oliver North involved the attempted delivery of U.S.-made machine guns to Iran in October 1986 in exchange for a T-72 captured from Iraq. Apparently, by March 1987, the CIA had acquired several T-72 tanks.[33]

The United States can acquire advanced Soviet aircraft from the defection of pilots or by purchasing the aircraft from third parties. Once obtained, the aircraft is examined thoroughly by Foreign Technology Division officers and scientists. Thus, when a MiG-25 pilot defected from the Soviet Union in 1976 with his plane, landing in Japan, a high priority of U.S. intelligence and the FTD was the examination of the airplane. Before being returned to the Soviet Union, the entire MiG-25 was disassembled at Hyakuri Air Base in Japan. The engines, radar, computer, electronic countermeasures, automatic pilot, and communications equipment were placed on blocks and stands for mechanical, metallurgical, and photographic analysis.[34]

Examination of the plane, as well as debriefing of the pilot, sharply altered Western understanding of the plane and its missions. Among the discoveries was a radar more powerful than one ever installed in any interceptor or fighter and the use of vacuum tubes rather than transistors.[35] (Vacuum tubes, although they represent a more primitive technology than transistors, are resistant to the electromagnetic pulse (EMP) created by nuclear detonations.)

The MiG-25 was far from the first MiG obtained for purposes of exploitation. In early 1951 the Allied Air Force Commander in Korea was asked to make every effort to obtain a complete MiG-15 for analysis. As a result of the request, a MiG that was shot down and crashed off Korea was retrieved within a short time. Portions of another MiG were recovered by helicopter. In 1953, a defecting North Korean pilot flew an intact MiG-15 to South Korea.[36]

Aircraft may be purchased, on occasion, from former Soviet client states. The United States has apparently purchased at least one MiG-23 from Egypt. And in the fall of 1983, Vought Aero Products offered to sell twenty-four MiG-21 fighters to the Navy. Since the fighters were to be new and the only MiG-21s available on the international arms market were used, Vought's source would seem to be China—the only nation still making MiG-21s.[37]

The offered MiG-21s and the purchased MiG-23 provide an example of another exploitation of such weapons systems: use in mock combat. The United States maintains OpFors (Opposition Forces) detachments to engage in such combat and allow U.S. forces to determine how they would perform against Soviet equipment, as well as to gain an internal view of the operations of the equipment. Thus, at Nellis Air Force Base, MiG aircraft are tested against U.S. fighters. In addition, U.S. fighters are tested against Soviet air defense radars and electronic warfare equipment.[38]

Most recently, the CIA has acquired several advanced Soviet military helicopter gunships, specifically Mi-24 Hinds, from both Pakistan and Chad. The helicopters were obtained by Pakistan and Chad as a result of the defection of a Soviet pilot from Afghanistan and Chad's victory over Libya in their border war. It has been reported that as a result of acquiring the helicopters the U.S. has determined how to penetrate its electronic defense systems with Stinger surface-to-air missiles.[39]

In some instances, materiel exploitation follows from the completion of a recovery operation in which a crashed plane or sunken ship is retrieved. In 1970 the United States recovered a nuclear weapon from a Soviet aircraft that crashed in the Sea of Japan; in 1971 the Navy recovered electronic eavesdropping equipment from a sunken trawler; and in 1972 a joint U.S.-British operation recovered electronic gear from a Soviet plane that had crashed earlier that year into the North Sea. In 1975, in Project JENNIFER, the CIA recovered half of a Golf-II submarine that had sunk northwest of Hawaii.[40]

A continuous recovery operation was Operation SAND DOLLAR. SAND DOLLAR involved the recovery of Soviet test warheads that landed in the ocean. By international agreement, the Soviet Union is required to specify the impact areas for such tests. U.S. radars tracked the warheads to determine their precise impact point. What appeared to be civilian drilling ships were sent to the Pacific test range after the tests had been completed to recover nosecones whose self-destruct devices did not detonate. Ships were guided to the proper location by computers coordinated with U.S. satellites, and the objects were located by sonar and magnetometer devices. Scientists at the FTD who analyzed the captured nosecones learned how the Soviets designed and constructed each part.[41]

Materiel exploitation represents far more than the result of chance defections and intelligence collection opportunities. Rather, it is a major and coordinated part of CIA, Army, Navy, and Air Force intelligence activities, the military services having a particular stake in the development of countermeasures to Soviet weapons systems.

Proposals for Naval foreign materiel exploitation projects are submitted to the Chairman of the Navy Foreign Materiel Program (NFMP) Committee. The proposal identifies and describes as completely as possible the foreign equipment/materiel involved and its location, as well as the objectives of the exploitation project and the anticipated technical gain to the U.S. Navy as a result. The proposal then must describe the work effort to be performed, resources required, planned timetable for completion, and the estimated total cost of the exploitation. An example of an NFMP proposal is shown in Figure 11-1.

Figure 11–1. Navy FMEP Proposal.

CLASSIFICATION   UNCLASSIFIED

MANAGEMENT PLAN—PROJECT: CLUSTER BILL (fictitious)

| PROJ./PROG. MGR./COORDINATOR: Mr. D. L. Jones CODE 342B.   EXT. 123 –4567 | PROGRAM: Foreign Material Exploitation ELEMENT No.: 64761N   BUDGET ACT. ____ | Date 7 September 72 |

DESCRIPTION: CLUSTER BILL — The exploitation of the BIRDLEGS RADAR which is installed in the Soviet BIG BIRD bomber and provides acquisition and guidance data to the AS –O air-to-surface anti-shipping missile.

No.		FY 72 J A S O N D J F M A M J	FY 73 J A S O N D J F M A M J	FY 1 2 3 4	FY 1 2 3 4	FY 1 2 3 4	FY 1 2 3 4
1	Photos/Sketches/ schematics	$4K					
2	Markings data coverage	$6K	$0.5K				
3	Initial evaluation	$34K					
4	Repairs/Parts Procurement		$78K				
5	Test Operations/Analysis		$7K				
6	Teardown Inspection		$28K				
7	Systems Evaluation		$36K				
8	Vulnerabilities Analysis		$15K				
9	Reports		108K				
	(Items may be broken down into subelements as appropriate)						
Funds	RDT&E P R I O R	100.5K	108K				
Total – 208.5K							

KEY:

Remarks: (Use additional pages as required; continue remarks on plain sheets)   (For progress reports, shade areas to indicate progress)

Source: Naval Material Command Instruction C3882.1A, "Prosecution of the Navy Foreign Material Program (NFMP) in the NMC (U)," February 1, 1977.

NOTES TO CHAPTER 11

1. Roscoe H Hillenkoeter, "Using the World's Information Sources," *Army Information Digest*, November 1948, pp. 3–6.
2. Andrew Cockburn, *The Threat: Inside the Soviet Military Machine* (New York: Random House, 1983), p. 22; Jonathan Samuel Lockwood, *The Soviet View of U.S. Strategic Doctrine* (New Brunswick, N.J.: Transaction, 1983), p. 5.
3. Cockburn, *The Threat*, p. 22; Philip Jacobson, "The Red Army Finally Gets a Chance to Test Its Stuff," *Washington Post*, February 13, 1983, pp. C1, C4.
4. F.D. Kohler, et al., *Soviet Strategy for the Seventies: From Cold War to Peaceful Coexistence* (Coral Gables, Fla.: Center for Advanced International Studies, 1973), p. 5, cited in Lockwood, *The Soviet View of Soviet Strategic Doctrine*, at p. 3.
5. Cockburn, *The Threat*, p. 67.
6. Richard Dunlop, *Donovan: America's Master Spy* (Chicago: Rand McNally, 1982). p. 366.
7. David Holloway, "Entering the Nuclear Arms Race: The Soviet Decision to Build the Atomic Bomb, 1939–1945," *Wilson Center International Security Studies Program, Working Paper* No. 9, (Washington, D.C.: Wilson Center, 1979), William J. Broad, "X-Ray Laser Weapon Gains Favor," *New York Times*, November 15, 1983, pp. C1–C2.
8. Zhores Medvedev, *Nuclear Disaster in the Urals*, (New York: Vintage, 1980).
9. U.S. Congress, House Permanent Select Committee on Intelligence, *Soviet Strategic Forces*, (Washington, D.C.: U.S. Government Printing Office, 1980), pp. 30–32.
10. John F. Burns, "2 Moscow Meetings May Lift the Veil on Andropov," *New York Times*, December 24, 1983, p. 2; Dusko Doder, "Unusual Activity in Moscow," *Washington Post*, February 10, 1984, pp. A1, A27.
11. Carl B. Crawley, "On the Intelligence Exploitation of Open Source Chinese Documents," *Naval Intelligence Quarterly* 2, No. 4 (1981): 7–9.
12. Ibid.
13. Ibid.
14. Ibid.
15. Military Communications Electronics Board, *Joint Department of Defense Plain Language Address Directory* (Washington, D.C.: Department of Defense, August 9, 1982), p. II-15.
16. Victor Marchetti and John Marks, *The CIA and the Cult of Intelligence*, (New York: Knopf, 1974), p. 89.
17. John Stockwell, *In Search of Enemies: A CIA Story* (New York: Norton, 1978), p. 107; Thomas Powers, *The Man Who Kept the Secrets: Richard Helms and the CIA* (New York: Knopf, 1979), p. 198.
18. Steve Weissman and Herbert Krosney, *The Islamic Bomb*, (New York: Times Books, 1981), p. 151.
19. Marchetti and Marks, *The CIA and the Cult of Intelligence*, p. 189.
20. E. Howard Hunt, *Undercover: Memoirs of an American Secret Agent*, (New York: Berkeley, 1974), pp. 80, 126; Philip Agee, *Inside the Company: A CIA Diary* (New York: Stonehill, 1975, pp. 346–347.
21. Steve Emerson, *Secret Warriors: Inside the Covert Military Operations of the Reagan Era* (New York: Putnam's, 1988), p. 111.
22. Ibid., p. 112.

23. Ibid., p. 116.
24. Marchetti and Marks, *The CIA and the Cult of Intelligence* pp. 190–91.
25. Morton Halperin, Jerry J. Berman, Robert L. Borosage, and Christine M. Marwick, *The Lawless State* (New York: Penguin, 1976), pp. 140–42.
26. Private information.
27. DOD 5240.1-R, "Procedures Governing the Activities of DOD Intelligence Components that Affect United States Persons," December 1982, p. 8-2.
28. Defense Audit Service, *Report on the Review of Accounting Systems for Wiretap and Eavesdrop Equipment* (Washington, D.C.: Defense Audit Service, September 29, 1980), p. 7.
29. Army Regulation 381-26, "Army Foreign Materiel Exploitation Program," March 6, 1987, p. 3.
30. John Barron, *The KGB Today: The Hidden Hand*, (New York: Reader's Digest, 1983), pp. 233–34; Statement of Facts, *United States of America v. David Henry Barnett*, K 80-0390, United States District Court, Maryland, 1980.
31. William J. Eaton, "CIA Reportedly Caught Buying India Military Secrets," *Los Angeles Times*, December 15, 1983, p. 4.
32. "What the U.S. Lost in Iran," *Newsweek*, December 28, 1981, pp. 33–34.
33. Emerson, *Secret Warriors*, p. 185; Michael Wines and Richard E. Meyer, "North Apparently Tried a Swap for Soviet Tank," *Washington Post*, January 22, 1987, p. A37; Richard Halloran, "U.S. Has Acquired Soviet T-72 Tanks," *New York Times*, March 13, 1987, p. A12.
34. John Barron, *MIG Pilot* (New York: Avon, 1981), pp. 172–73.
35. Ibid.
36. Foreign Technology Division, *FTD 1917–1967* (Dayton, Ohio: FTD, 1967), p. 24.
37. "Washington Roundup," *Aviation Week and Space Technology*, May 14, 1984, p. 17; "Periscope," *Newsweek*, May 21, 1984, p. 17.
38. Wayne Biddle, "General Killed in Nevada Crash Flew Soviet Jet," *New York Times*, May 3, 1984, pp. 1, 22; "Washington Roundup," *Aviation Week and Space Technology*, May 7, 1984, p. 13.
39. James Bruce, "CIA Acquires Soviet MI-24 and T-72," *Jane's Defence Weekly*, March 28, 1987, p. 535; James Brooke, "Chad, With Victories, Is Awash in War Booty," *New York Times*, August 17, 1986, p. A4.
40. Clyde W. Burleson, *The Jennifer Project*, (Englewood Cliffs, N.J.: Prentice-Hall, 1977), p. 47; "The Great Submarine Snatch," *Time*, March 31, 1975, pp. 20–27.
41. Roy Varner and Wayne Collier, *A Matter of Risk* (New York: Random House, 1977), p. 26.

12 EXCHANGE AND LIAISON ARRANGEMENTS

Despite its huge investment in technical and human intelligence activities, the United States relies for a significant portion of its intelligence on exchange and liaison arrangements with a variety of foreign nations. Some arrangements are long standing, highly formalized, and involve the most sensitive forms of intelligence collection. Others are less wide ranging and reflect very limited common interests between the United States and other nations.

The most important arrangements are the multilateral arrangements with the United Kingdom, Australia, Canada, and until recently, New Zealand, concerning the collection and distribution of signals intelligence and ocean surveillance data. The United States also maintains bilateral arrangements with each of those nations. Also of major importance are the arrangements with Israel, Japan, Norway, and China. Among the other nations with which the United States has exchange and liaison agreements are Italy, Finland, and South Korea.

UKUSA

The U.S.-British military alliance in World War II necessitated a high degree of cooperation with respect to intelligence activities. It was imperative that the United States and Britain, as the main Allied combatants in the European and Pacific theaters, establish a coordinated effort in the acquisition of worldwide intelligence and its evaluation and distribution. Of all the areas of intelligence collaboration, it was in the area of signals intelligence that the most important and vital cooperation took place.

Cooperation began in the spring of 1941 when four representatives (two from the Navy and two from the Army) delivered a model of the Japanese PURPLE machine—used by Japan to encipher diplomatic communications to British code-breakers at Bletchley Park. In return, the British gave the U.S. representatives an assortment of advanced cryptological equipment, including the Marconi-Adcock high-frequency direction finder.[1]

Further cooperation involved both the exchange of personnel and a division of labor. A small U.S. mission was sent to the Combined Bureau at Singapore for the purpose of cooperation in signals intelligence, and a British naval officer trained in Japanese and experienced in cryptanalysis was introduced into the U.S. signals intelligence station on Corregidor in the Philippines. A secret channel of communication was established between Corregidor and Singapore for the direct exchange of cryptanalytical material. Meanwhile, it was agreed that the British would break Tokyo-London traffic while the Americans broke Tokyo-Washington traffic. The results of the U.S. codebreaking effort that were considered useful to Britain in its war with Germany were passed to London via the British ambassador in Washington.[2]

U.S. entry into the war expanded the scope of the U.S.-British signals intelligence cooperation. Both U.S. and British commanders in the field (whether directing U.S. forces, British forces, or joint forces) required the most up-to-date intelligence available on the enemy order of battle and plan of action—exactly the type of information that could best be provided by intercepts of military wireless traffic. Thus, in addition to the intercepts of diplomatic traffic being widely exchanged, it was necessary to broaden the exchange of intercepted military traffic and make arrangements for a coordinated attack on such traffic. Britain's production of such intelligence was labeled ULTRA.[3]

Although ULTRA information was made available to U.S. and British military commanders via Special Liaison Units, the exact nature of its acquisition was initially obscured. It was not until April 1943 that the British revealed to U.S. military intelligence officials the secret—that Britain's codebreaking organization could break the ciphers produced by the German ENIGMA machine used for much of German military communications.[4]

During the same visit to Bletchley Park at which British officials revealed the ULTRA secret to the United States, a formal agreement of cooperation, the BRUSA Agreement, was concluded between Britain and the United States. The Agreement established high-level cooperation on SIGINT matters and covered the exchange of personnel, joint regulations for the handling of ULTRA material, and procedures for its distribution. The joint regulations included strict security provisions that applied to all British and U.S. recipients of ULTRA material.[5]

Along with the increased cooperation between Britain and the United States, there was increased involvement by the Anglo-Saxon members of the British Commonwealth—Canada, Australia, and New Zealand—in a wide variety of intelligence activities. U.S.-Canadian cooperation began in October 1941, when the Canadians offered the Federal Communications Commission free access to the product of

Canadian monitoring activities. In return, the United States provided Canada with technical direction-finding data that were "invaluable for pinpointing the location of a transmitter."[6]

Canadian DF stations subsequently made significant contributions to the Allied North Atlantic SIGINT/ocean surveillance network. The Canadian codebreaking agency was also successful in intercepting and decoding German espionage control messages to and from agents in South America, Canada, Hamburg and Lisbon. In addition, messages to and from the Vichy delegation in Ottawa were intercepted and decoded. Further, the peculiarities of radio wave propagation resulted in Canadian monitoring facilities being able to intercept military transmissions originating in Europe that were inaccessible to equipment based in Britain.[7]

It was with respect to Japan, however, that SIGINT cooperation among all five nations reached its highest level. Monitoring stations in Canada, particularly the major one at Halifax, gathered large quantities of coded Japanese transmissions. In April 1942, a combined Allied signals intelligence agency for the Pacific, the Central Bureau of the Allied Intelligence Bureau, was activated in Melbourne with a U.S. Chief and an Australian Deputy Chief.[8]

The extent of cooperation is particularly highlighted in the case of Australian intercept stations. There was an Australian Air Force intercept station at Darwin, a U.S. Army radio intercept station in Townsville, a Royal Australian Navy monitoring station at Darwin, and a British post in Brisbane for the interception and distribution of Japanese radio communications. Additionally, a Canadian Special Wireless Group arrived in Australia on May 18, 1945 to take over the task of intercepting and analyzing Japanese military Morse code signals.[9]

The intelligence relationship among Australia, Britain, Canada, New Zealand, and the United States that was forged during World War II did not end with the war. Rather, it became formalized and grew stronger. In 1946, William Friedman, America's premier cryptographer, visited the British cryptographers to work out methods of postwar consultation and cooperation. A U.S. Liaison Office was set up in London, and schemes were derived for avoiding the duplication of effort. It was agreed that solved material was to be exchanged between the two agencies. In addition, an exchange program was started under which personnel from each agency would work two or three years at the other.[10]

Nineteen forty-seven saw an event that set the stage for post-World War II signals intelligence cooperation: the formulation and acceptance of the UKUSA Agreement, also known as the UK-USA Security Agreement or the "Secret Treaty." The primary aspect of the agreement was the division of SIGINT collection responsibilities among the First Party (the United States) and the Second Parties (Australia, Britain, Canada, and New Zealand). The specific agencies now involved are the U.S. National Security Agency, the Australian Defence Signals Directorate (DSD), the British Government Communications Headquarters (GCHQ), the Canadian Communications Security Establishment (CSE) and until 1986, the New Zealand Government Communications Security Bureau (GCSB).[11]

Under the present division of responsibilities the United States is responsible for Latin America, most of Asia, Asiatic Russia and northern China. Australia's area of responsibility includes its neighbors (such as Indonesia), southern China, and the nations of Indochina. Britain is responsible for the Soviet Union (west of the Urals) and Africa. The polar regions of the Soviet Union are Canada's responsibility, New Zealand's area of responsibility was the western Pacific. Specific tasking assignments are specified in the SIGINT Combined Operating List (SCOL).[12]

Britain's geographical position gives it a significant capability for long-range SIGINT collection against certain targets in the Soviet Union. Britain's historical role in Africa led to its assumption of SIGINT responsibility for that area. Canada's responsibility for the northern Soviet Union stems from its geographical position, which gives it "unique access to communications in the northern Soviet Union." The areas of responsibility of Australia and New Zealand clearly result from their geographical location.[13]

The UKUSA relationship (and its SIGINT aspect) is more than an agreement to coordinate separately conducted intelligence activities and share the intelligence collected. Rather, the relationship is cemented by the presence of U.S. facilities on British, Canadian, and Australian territory; by joint operations (U.S.-U.K., Australian-U.S., U.K.-Australian) within and outside UKUSA territory and, in the case of Australia, of U.K. and U.S. staff at all DSD facilities.[14]

In addition to specifying SIGINT collection responsibilities, the Agreement also concerns access to the collected intelligence and security arrangements for the handling of data. Standardized code words (e.g., UMBRA for signals intelligence), security agreements that all employees of the respective SIGINT agencies must sign, and procedures for storing and disseminating code word material are all part of the implementation of the Agreement.[15] Thus, in a memo concerning the Agreement, dated October 8, 1948, the U.S. Army Office of the Adjutant General advised the recipients of the memo that

> the United States Chiefs of Staff will make every effort to insure that the United States will maintain the military security classifications established by the United Kingdom authorities with respect to military information of UK origin and the military security classifications established by the UK-US Agreement with respect to military information of joint UK-US origin.[16]

Similarly, in 1967, the "COMINT Indoctrination" declaration, which all British-cleared personnel had to sign, included in the first paragraph the statement,

> I declare that I fully understand the information relating to the manner and extent of the interception of communications of foreign powers by H.M. Government and *other cooperating Governments*, and intelligence produced by such interception known as Communications Intelligence (COMINT) is information covered by Section 2 of the Official Secrets Act 1911 (as amended).[17]

These requirements for standardized code words (see Chapter 18), security arrangements, and procedures for the handling and dissemination of SIGINT material are apparently detailed in a series of "International Regulations on SIGINT" (IRSIG), which was in its third edition as of 1967.

Despite numerous references to the Agreement in print, officials of some of the participating countries have refused to confirm not only the details of the Agreement but even its existence. Thus, on March 9, 1977, the Australian Opposition Defense Spokesman asked the Prime Minister:

1. Is Australia a signatory to the UKUSA Agreement?
2. Is it a fact that under this agreement NSA operates electronic intercept stations in Australia?
3. Does any other form of station operate in Australia under the Agreement; if so, is it operated by an Australian or overseas authority, or is it operated under some sort of joint authority?
4. Will he [the Prime Minister] identify the participating country or countries in any such Agreement?

The Prime Minister refused to answer and referred to a previous response wherein he said the government would not confirm or deny speculation in that area. And the Australian D Notice, "Ciphering and Monitoring Activities," requests the media to refrain from publishing material on Australian collaboration with other countries concerning monitoring activities.[18]

Similarly, a 1982 Freedom of Information Act request to the NSA asking for "all documents from 1947 outlining United States–United Kingdom–Australian–Canadian–New Zealand cooperation in Signals Intelligence" was responded to with the statement: "We have determined that the fact of the existence or non-existence of the materials you request is in itself a currently and properly classified matter."[19]

Cooperation exists on a similar level in the area of ocean surveillance, with British and Australian stations feeding into the U.S. Ocean Surveillance Information System (OSIS). A station at Hong Kong, jointly operated by the United Kingdom and Australia was, until the mid-1970s, directed almost entirely against the People's Republic of China. Presently, however, it is involved in monitoring Soviet naval movements down the coast of Asia from major Soviet naval bases at Vladivostok and Petropavlovsk-Kamchatka to Cam Ranh Bay in Vietnam. Likewise, an Australian–New Zealand unit, the Australian–New Zealand Military Intelligence Service (ANZMIS), located in Singapore, monitors (along with Task Force 168) Soviet naval activities in the region. The information collected, including intercepts and photographs, is distributed to the United States, Britain, Singapore, and Malaysia.[20]

Several Australian-operated stations also contribute significantly to the Ocean Surveillance Information System. These stations are located at Pearce, Western Australia; Cabarlah, Queensland; and Shoal Bay, New Territories. The Pearce station primarily monitors naval and air traffic over the Indian Ocean. In the early 1980s a Pusher antenna was installed for the interception, monitoring, direction finding, and analysis of radio signals in a portion of the HF band.[21]

The Cabarlah station on the east coast of Australia is operated by the DSD. Its main purpose is to monitor radio transmissions throughout the Southwest Pacific. Thus, the Cabarlah system was used to monitor Soviet intelligence-gathering trawlers that were watching the Kangaroo II naval exercises of October 1976.[22]

The most important station for monitoring the Southeast Asian area is the DSD station at Darwin (Shoal Bay), which originally had a very limited direction-finding capability. However, contracts signed in 1981 provided for the procurement of modern DF equipment to enable the station to "participate fully in the OSIS."[23]

Contributions to monitoring of the European-Atlantic ocean areas is made by Canadian stations at Halifax and a joint U.S.-British station on Ascension Island (which monitors naval traffic in South Atlantic).[24]

The U.S. Armed Forces Medical Intelligence Center (AFMIC) has also been involved in medical intelligence exchange with Australia, Canada, and the United Kingdom. The AFMIC is a member of the Quadripartite Medical Intelligence Committee; other members include the Canadian and UK medical liaison offices and the Australian scientific attache.[25]

In addition to collection activities, the UKUSA nations are also involved in cooperative arrangements concerning defense intelligence analysis, and hold periodic conferences dealing with a wide range of scientific and defense intelligence matters. Thus, in 1974, the United States participated in the Annual Land Warfare Intelligence Conference, the International Scientific Intelligence Exchange, the Quadripartite Intelligence Working Party on Chinese Guided Missiles, and the Tripartite Defense Intelligence Estimates Conference. Held in London in May 1974, the Annual Land Warfare Intelligence Conference involved British, Canadian and Australian defense intelligence organizations, whose members gathered to discuss the armaments used by Communist armies.[26]

The Third International Scientific Exchange, involving U.S., British, New Zealand, and Australian defense intelligence organizations, was held in Canberra from June 18–27, 1974. Initially established to discuss Chinese scientific developments, particularly with respect to nuclear weapons, the 1974 meeting also focused on technical developments in India and Japan, nuclear proliferation in Asia, development and military applications of lasers, and application of peaceful nuclear explosives.[27]

The Quadripartite Intelligence Working Party on Chinese Guided Missiles met in London in 1974. The panel, consisting of representatives from the U.S., British, Australian, and Canadian defense intelligence organizations, focused on Chinese guided missiles and satellite launch vehicles. The United States, New Zealand, and Australia constituted the participants in the Tripartite Defense Intelligence Estimates Conference. This 1974 conference, held in Wellington, New Zealand, involved "the exchange of military estimates and assessments among the countries."[28]

As a result of New Zealand's policy of prohibiting nuclear vessels, the United States has decreased the access of New Zealand to signals intelligence gathered by U.S. sources, although the extent of this reduction is unclear. According to the New Zealand Ministry of Defense:

It is of particular concern that the Maritime Defence Commander (NZ) now has an incomplete picture of movements of ships within his area of responsibility, NZ has also lost access to communication/electronic information. . . .

Although NZ Defence has continued to provide intelligence to the United States without change since 15 Feb 85, intelligence information from US Defense Intelligence Agencies has virtually ceased, except for selected maritime information. Exchange officers have been withdrawn and New Zealand participation in all intelligence conferences attended by US agencies has been denied. However, NZ Defence (DDI) continues to receive some unprocessed intelligence from US sources but the continued flow is less than 20% of that received before the last election.[29]

However, New Zealand Prime Minister David Lange called the Ministry's claim of a greater than 80% cutoff "totally and absolutely wrong."[30] Additionally, the Chairman of the New Zealand Intelligence Committee said the loss of United States intelligence had no significant effect on New Zealand's knowledge of events in the South Pacific. Defence officials disputed the Chairman's statement, suggesting that information on military movements and changes and assessments of the related implications had been reduced and that the Chairman had been referring to mainly economic and political intelligence.[31]

AUSTRALIA

Although there are formal arrangements among the UKUSA countries with respect to signals intelligence, ocean surveillance, and radio monitoring, no such agreement exists with respect to human intelligence activities. However, there is significant cooperation between the United States and Australia in this area.[32]

Both the British Secret Intelligence Service (SIS) and the CIA have sought Australian cooperation in areas where deployment and operations have been easier for the Australian Secret Intelligence Service (ASIS). The ASIS has provided significant assistance in Chile, Thailand, Indonesia, and Cambodia. Thus, in 1975, William Colby, then Director of the CIA, stated that

ASIS reporting has naturally been of most value in areas where our own coverage is limited, including the following:

(a)   reporting on Portuguese Timor and North Vietnam
(b)   reporting from Indonesian sources
(c)   operations and reporting on Chile; and
(d)   unique operations and reporting on Cambodia. . .

During the period we were not present in Chile the service was of great help in assisting us to maintain coverage of that country's internal developments. For example, two of our Santiago Station assets were turned over to ASIS for handling and produced 58 disseminated reports during the period January, 1972 through July 1973. The effective and professional handling of these assets by ASIS made possible continued receipt of this very useful information. The same basic comments apply to the case of Cambodia.[33]

An ASIS station in Phnom Penh was approved by the Department of Foreign Affairs on February 5, 1965 and opened later in the year with one officer and one operational assistant. A second officer slot was added in 1970 but eliminated in 1972. The opening of the second station coincided, approximately, with the withdrawal of the United States Mission in Cambodia.[34]

The CIA had strongly supported the ASIS proposal to open a new station and, upon U.S. withdrawal, turned a network of agents over to the ASIS. Some agents were still operating when Australia withdrew from Cambodia in 1974, following the fall of the government. Information collected by the ASIS-CIA network was made available to the CIA.[35]

The presence of the Australian Secret Intelligence Service in Chile can be traced back to a CIA request for ASIS support in early November 1970. It appeared to the U.S. government that the Allende government might sever diplomatic relations with the United States. The CIA, in anticipation of such a move, sought the opening of at least a limited ASIS network. The proposal was supported by the Secretary of the Department of Foreign Affairs and approved by the Foreign Affairs Minister. The justification was not in terms of the ability of a Santiago station being able to produce intelligence important to Australia, but rather as reciprocation for the large amount of intelligence the United States made available to Australia.[36]

Actual agent-running operations did not begin until early 1972, after a five-month period during which embassy cover was established, the operational climate was assessed, and sufficient language fluency obtained. Details concerning three agents were passed to the ASIS by the CIA for approval. After the ASIS was satisfied that the agents were trustworthy, approval was given to begin operations. In March 1973, the Minister requested a review of the Chilean station and in April decided that it should be closed down. This decision was communicated to the CIA, active operations were halted on May 1, 1973, and the agents were returned to the CIA. For cover purposes, the ASIS officer remained in Santiago until July, and the operational assistant until October 1973.[37]

According to the findings of the Hope Report, ASIS activities in support of the CIA in Cambodia and Chile were strictly confined to intelligence gathering and did not involve covert action (destabilization) activities. Thus, according to an Australian Royal Commission report, "at no time was ASIS approached by CIA, nor made aware of any plans that may have been prepared to affect the internal political situation in Chile. The ASIS station in Santiago; was concerned only with intelligence gathering via the agents handed over to it."[38]

In return for such help, the ASIS has received CIA human intelligence reports concerning areas of the world where the ASIS is represented, although little or nothing concerning areas without ASIS representation. The reports the ASIS has received were described in an official study of the ASIS as being large in quantity and high in quality. Those reports, code-named REMARKABLE, numbered 588 in 1974 and 794 in 1975, and focused mainly on China and Southeast Asia—ranging "from high-grade political and scientific intelligence to relatively humdrum, but intensely detailed, reporting on insurgency in Southeast Asia and sociological conditions within China."[39]

CANADA

Canada also has a variety of bilateral intelligence agreements with the United States. Joint U.S.-Canadian estimates produced in the late 1950s focused on Soviet capabilities and likely actions in the event of a major Soviet attack on North America. Thus, the document *Soviet Capabilities and Probable Courses of Action Against North America in a Major War during the Period 1 January 1958 to 31 December 1958*, as well as a similarly titled document for the period 1 July 1958 to 30 June 1958, prepared by the Canadian-U.S. Joint Intelligence Committee, assessed the Soviet threat to North America. Factors considered included Communist Bloc political stability and economic support; the internal threat to North America; Soviet nuclear, radiological, biological, and chemical weapons; aircraft, including bombers, transport aircraft, and tanker aircraft; guided missiles; naval weapons; electronics; ground, naval, and surface strength and combat effectiveness; Soviet worldwide strategy; and capabilities to conduct air and airborne missile, naval, amphibious, and internal operations against North America. Preparation of such estimates continue on a yearly basis under the title *Canadian-United States Intelligence Estimate of the Military Threat to North America.*[40]

In addition to its UKUSA participation, Canada's SIGINT relationship to the United States is defined by the CANUS agreement. On September 15, 1950, Canada and the United States exchanged letters formally recognizing the "Security Agreement between Canada and the United States of America" (which was followed exactly two months later by the "Arrangement for Exchange of Information between the U.S., U.K. and Canada").[41]

Negotiations for the CANUS Agreement had been taking place since at least 1948. There was some concern on the part of the U.S. intelligence officials that original drafts of the Agreement provided for too much exchange. Thus, a 1948 memorandum by the Acting Director of Intelligence of the U.S. Air Force noted that Paragraph 6a of the proposed agreement was

> not sufficiently restrictive. In effect, it provides for the complete exchange of information. Not only is it considered that the Canadians will reap all the benefits of complete exchange but wider dissemination of the information would jeopardize the security of the information. It is believed that the exchange should be related to mutually agreed COMINT activities on a 'need to know' basis.[42]

A more recent agreement is the "Canadian–United States Communications Instructions for Reporting Vital Intelligence Sightings" (CIRVIS/MERINT), signed in March 1966. This Agreement specifies the type of information to be reported by airborne or land-based observers—that is, information concerning:

- hostile or unidentified single aircraft or formations of aircraft which appear to be directed against the United States or Canada or their forces.
- missiles

- unidentified flying objects
- hostile or unidentified submarines
- hostile or unidentified groups of military vessels
- individual surface vessels, submarines, or aircraft of unconventional design, or those engaged in suspicious activity or observed in a location or on a course which may be interpreted as constituting a threat to the United States, Canada or their forces
- any unexplained or unusual activity which may indicate a possible attack against or through Canada or the United States, including the presence of any unidentified or other suspicious ground parties in the Polar Region or other remote or sparsely populated areas.[43]

The agreement also specifies eleven types of information that should be provided in any report, among them a description of the object(s) sighted (of which nine aspects are specified), a description of the course of the object and the manner of observation, and information on weather and wind conditions.[44]

The agreement further specifies that reports (known as MERINT reports) are to be forwarded by seaborne vessels concerning:

- movement of Warsaw Pact/unidentified aircraft (single or in formation)
- missile firings
- movement of Warsaw Pact/unidentified submarines
- movement of Warsaw Pact/unidentified group or groups of surface combatants
- any airborne, seaborne, ballistic or orbiting object which the observer feels may constitute a military threat against the United States or Canada, or may be of interest to military and civilian government officials
- individual surface ships, submarines or aircraft of unconventional design, or those engaged in suspicious activities or observed in unusual locations
- any unexplained or unusual activity which may indicate possible attack against or through the United States or Canada, including the presence of any unidentified or other suspicious ground parties in the Polar Region or other remote or sparsely populated areas.[45]

UNITED KINGDOM

Bilateral intelligence relations between the United States and the United Kingdom include human intelligence, signals intelligence, and radio and television broadcast monitoring. The British-U.S. Communications Intelligence Agreement of 1943 is still in force and regulates the bilateral part of the British-U.S. SIGINT relationship.

A second highly formalized arrangement consists of an agreement to divide up, geographically, the responsibility for monitoring public radio and television broadcasts—mainly news and public affairs broadcasts. The specific organizations involved are the British Broadcasting Corporation (BBC) Monitoring Service and the CIA's Foreign Broadcast Information Service (FBIS). Together, those two organizations monitor most of the world's most significant news and other broadcasts. As noted, both the BBC Monitoring Service and the FBIS have a network of overseas stations, operated with varying degrees of secrecy to gather their raw material.[46]

Cooperation between the BBC Monitoring Service and the FBIS began in 1948 as an openly acknowledged arrangement. Thus, the BBC Annual Report for 1948–49 noted

> There [is] close cooperation between the BBC's Monitoring Service and its American counterpart, the Foreign Broadcast Information Branch of the United States Central Intelligence Agency, and each of the two services maintained liaison units at each other's stations for the purpose of a full exchange of information.[47]

The area of responsibility for the Monitoring Service is roughly equivalent to the GCHQ's area of responsibility for SIGINT collection—Europe, Africa, and western Russia. Thus, the Monitoring Service maintains a remotely controlled listening post on the rooftop of the Vienna embassy to monitor VHF radio and television broadcasts originating in Hungary and Czechoslovakia. It also maintains listening posts in Accra, Ghana, and Abidjan in the Ivory Coast. In 1976–77, the Monitoring Service turned over responsibility for monitoring Far East broadcasts to the FBIS. To compensate, it had to step up its reporting of events in Portugal and Spain to meet CIA requirements.[48]

ISRAEL

One of the strongest Western intelligence links is that between the United States and Israel. These arrangements involve the Mossad, AMAN (military intelligence) and a variety of U.S. intelligence agencies—the CIA, the FBI, Defense Intelligence Agency, National Security Agency, Foreign Technology Division, and the Foreign Science and Technology Center.

The intelligence liaison between the United States and Israel dates back to the early 1960s, when

> the governments of Israel and the United States had agreed to exchange intelligence secrets. . . . Most important of all as far as the Israelis were concerned, the Central Intelligence Agency along with the Federal Bureau of Investigation, had undertaken to supply the Israelis with some top secret equipment, including the most advanced computers for cryptanalysis, as well as to train selected Israeli officers in their use.[49]

The centerpiece of CIA-Mossad cooperation, until 1975, was the CIA's Chief of Counterintelligence, James Jesus Angleton. Angleton had developed extensive contacts with future Israeli intelligence officials during his World War II activities in Europe with the Office of Strategic Services. In 1957 Angleton set up a liaison unit to deal with the Mossad, and the unit was made responsible for producing Middle East intelligence for both services. In addition, the CIA received intelligence from Mossad networks in the Soviet Union.[50]

After Angleton's dismissal from the CIA in 1975, the liaison unit was abolished, and the Israeli account was moved to the appropriate Directorate of Operations regional division of the CIA. The CIA also began to operate more independently of the Mossad; in the late 1970s the agency began operating on the West Bank.[51]

Among the present arrangements between the two countries is Israeli provision of information concerning Soviet weapons systems, particularly those captured in various battles. This exchange has given the United States access not only to the captured weapons systems but also data concerning their performance.

Such exchanges took place after the 1967 and 1973 Arab-Israeli Wars. Israel furnished the United States with captured air-to-ground and ground-to-air missiles and with Soviet antitank weapons. Also furnished were Soviet 122- and 130-mm. artillery pieces, along with ammunition for evaluation and testing. After the 1973 war, the furnished material included a Soviet T-72 tank. Upon examination, it was discovered that the T-72 was equipped with a special type of air filter to defend against germ warfare. Additionally, extensive joint analyses were done after the 1973 war: eight volumes of between 200 and 300 pages apiece were produced. These analyses influenced subsequent developments in U.S. weapons tactics and military budgets.[52]

In early 1983 the Israeli government offered to share military intelligence gained during the war in Lebanon. The offer included details of an "Israeli invention" that was alleged by Prime Minister Menachem Begin to be the key to Israel's ability to destroy Syria's Soviet-made surface-to-air missiles during the war. However, Secretary of Defense Caspar Weinberger rejected a proposed agreement for sharing that information, feeling it would have trapped the United States into long-range commitments to Israel that he wanted to avoid. Administration officials argued that the information had already been learned through normal military contacts.[53]

As a condition for sharing the information, Israel insisted on sending Israeli experts to the United States with captured weapons and receiving whatever analysis came from U.S. research. Israel also insisted on the right to veto the transfer of information and analysis to third parties, including members of NATO, and on measures to ensure that sensitive data remained secret. According to diplomats, the Israelis expressed fears that Soviet intelligence agents who had penetrated Western European governments would find out what Israel had learned and would then pass that information along to the Soviets' Arab allies. Subsequently, an agreement was reached that continued the flow of information.[54]

A late 1983 reassessment of U.S. policy in the Middle East, following the deteriorating situation in Lebanon and continued Syrian intransigence, resulted in National Security Decision Directive 111, which specified a "tilt" toward Israel and expanded U.S.-Israeli strategic cooperation.[55]

This expanded cooperation reportedly involved a higher degree of sharing of reconnaissance satellite data, including such data on Saudi Arabia and Jordan. William J. Casey, in his first three years as CIA Director (1981–1984), provided Israeli intelligence with access to sensitive photographs and other reconnaissance information that the Israelis had been denied under the Carter Administration. The head of AMAN from 1979 to 1983, Major General Yehoshua Saguy, said in early 1984 that the CIA was providing Israel with access to data from reconnaissance satellites, and "not only the information but the photos themselves." Under the Carter Administration, DCI Stansfield Turner refused to provide the satellite imagery that had been furnished when George Bush was DCI in 1976 and 1977.[56]

Upon becoming the DCI in 1981, William Casey decided to resume supplying Israel with actual photographs. Inside the Israeli intelligence community, the satellite photos were often referred to as "Casey's gift" and were considered invaluable. After Israel used some of those photos to aid in targeting Iraq's Osirak reactor, however, Casey restricted Israeli access to only those photographs which could be used for "defensive" purposes relating to Arab states directly on or near the Israeli border.[57]

Another aspect of the expanded cooperation was reported to be greater Israeli access to the "take" of Cyprus-based SR-71 flights. The United States had been sharing such data with Israel, Egypt, and Syria on a "highly selective basis" as a result of an agreement signed in 1974 after the war of October 1973. The information previously transmitted to Israel primarily concerned Egyptian or Syrian military developments but was now to be expanded to cover a "broader range."[58]

Israel did not, however, receive everything it wanted. Among the items it did not receive were a dedicated satellite and a system of ground stations that would "directly access" the KH-11 as it passed over the Middle East.[59]

Another area of expanded U.S.-Israeli cooperation involves the emigres who arrive in Israel from the Soviet Union each year. Information obtained by interviews conducted by the Mossad is reportedly passed on to the CIA.[60] Although it is unlikely that any startling revelations are produced, the collective data can be quite valuable.

Israel has supplied the United States with intelligence on the Middle East—both reports from agents and finished intelligence analyses. Some U.S. officials have not been impressed by the political intelligence, however. One CIA official said that he was "appalled at the lack of quality, of the political intelligence on the Arab world. . . . Their tactical military intelligence was first rate. But they didn't know their enemy. I saw this political intelligence and it was lousy, laughably bad. . . . It was gossip stuff mostly."[61]

Both the United States and Israel have received intelligence from the other in crises situations. During the 1973 war Israel received data obtained by the RHYO-LITE satellite. In 1976 the United States supplied Israel with both aerial and satellite reconnaissance photographs of Entebbe Airport to supplement the information obtained by Israeli agents in preparation for the Israeli hostage rescue mission. During the 1985 hijacking of the *Achille Lauro*, Israel provided the United States with the location of the ship on several occasions, the location of the ship's hijackers when they were in Egypt, and the identification number and call signs of the plane carrying the hijackers seconds after it took off from Egypt.[62]

NORWAY

To the northwest of the Soviet Union, Norway also provides a home for several interception and nuclear detection stations targeted on the Soviet Union and the surrounding ocean area. The SIGINT stations are operated by personnel of Norwegian Military Intelligence but were erected by the NSA and operated for them. Further, according to former U.S. intelligence official Victor Marchetti, CIA and NSA personnel were regularly on assignment at those stations. Although no U.S. personnel are assigned there now, Norway does pass the information acquired to the United States.[63]

One of the stations is at Vadso, a small fjord town in Norway's Arctic region, close to the Soviet border. Somewhere between several hundred and 1,500 of the town's 5,000 residents are said to work at the intercept station. There are four interception locations at Vadso. The principal high-frequency (HF) listening equipment is a 492-foot diameter array of monopole antennas, within which is a further array of monopoles. About two miles to the southeast is a smaller circular antenna array with an outer ring, eighty-two feet in diameter and consisting of twelve dipoles, while the inner ring consists of six dipoles. There is a hut in the center of the array. The array's location, apart from the main HF site, may mean that they are used for transmission rather than reception. The location of the antenna arrays on the northern shore of Varangerfjord gives them uninterrupted overseas propagation paths all the way to the Soviet Union.[64]

In addition to the circular arrays there are two VHF-UHF interception sites in the Vadso area. The main site is at the summit of a 397-foot hill. The site is the home of a variety of VHF-UHF antennas known as Yagis, log-periodic arrays (LPAs), vertical wire dipoles, and broadband dipoles. Four of the antennas are pointed in the direction of Murmansk and the associated complex of naval and air facilities—one toward Wickel; two to the coast; and one northeast, towards the Barents Sea. The antennas at the smaller site also point toward the Soviet Union. It has been suggested that the Yagi antennas at the main site are intercepting emissions from a Soviet troposcatter communications system similar to the NATO Ace High system. It has also been reported that Vadso has the capability to intercept voice communications from Soviet pilots to their ground controllers.[65]

Also, in the very north of Norway, are Viksjofell and Vardo. At Viksjofell, on a 1,476-foot-high hill only three miles from the Soviet border, is a concrete tower with a geodesic radome. On the side of the tower facing toward the Soviet border is a semi-cylindrical extension apparently made of the same material as the radome and surmounted by a VHF log-periodic antenna. The dome itself is surmounted by a VHF Adcock direction-finding antenna. The Viksjofell facility appears to be a very sophisticated VHF installation, and it might be presumed that the dome contains a movable dish antenna that can either be constantly rotated in a scanning or tracking mode. Installations of this type are capable of monitoring all kinds of VHF-SHF frequencies, including ground-based and air-based radars, communications, and missile command and control links.[66]

At Vardo there is a tower identical to the one at Viksjofell except that the external direction-finding and log-periodic antennas are absent. Vardo can intercept signals from Plesetsk, a major Soviet missile testing and space center. It has also been suggested that another likely target is the telemetry from Soviet SLBM tests in the Barents Sea. The Viksjofell station apparently was established in 1972, and the Vardo station in 1971, at the same time that an earlier submarine-launched missile, the SS-N-8, became operational.[67]

At Skage (in Namdalen) and Randaberg (near Stavanger, on Norway's western coast) there are arrays similar to the smaller of the Vadso arrays. These arrays probably are used mainly to intercept HF communications from Soviet ships, submarines, and long-range marine reconnaissance aircraft in the Norwegian Sea. The two stations are operated probably as paired units to allow triangulation of emitter locations.[68]

Norway also serves as the home of nuclear detonation detection stations. Until 1975 a detachment of the Air Force Technical Applications Center was located in the Lappish community of Karasjok. A still-operational system, the NORSAR (Norwegian Seismic Array), is run under a cooperative arrangement between the United States and Norway. The array is in southeastern Norway, north of Oslo and near the town of Hamar. The NORSAR's location places it on the same continental plate as the Kazakh Soviet Socialist Republic, home of the Semipalatinsk nuclear weapons testing area. The result is an uncomplicated vibration travel path from Semipalatinsk, over 2,500 miles away, to the NORSAR—a prime requirement for producing high-confidence estimates of the yield of a nuclear explosion. The NORSAR is only 1,500 miles from Novaya Zemlya, a large island in the Barents Sea that is also used by the Soviets for nuclear weapons testing.[69]

Since 1970, when it began operation, the NORSAR has detected about 100,000 earthquakes and more than 500 presumed nuclear explosions. A teleseismic array, the NORSAR's optimum performance occurs when the seismic event takes place 1,860 to 6,200 miles away. Thus the NORSAR is also able to effectively detect U.S. nuclear tests in Nevada. The array itself is made up of twenty-two subarrays, seven of which are operational. Each subarray is approximately six miles in diameter and consists of one long-period and six short-period seismometers, all placed in vaults or shallow boreholes with depths ranging from ten to forty-nine feet. The long-period seismometers measure ground motion in the vertical, horizontal north-south, and horizontal east-west directions, while the short-period seismometer senses vertical ground motion. The recorded earth motions are transmitted via trenched cables to a central terminal vault at the subarray center and then to the NORSAR Data Processing Center at Kjeller, just north of Oslo, for analysis. The data also can be transmitted by satellite back to the United States.[70]

A newer facility, the Norwegian Seismic Array, (NORESS), opened in June 1985. Located about sixty miles northeast of Oslo, NORESS was designed and constructed on a cooperative basis by the U.S. and Norwegian governments. Data from each of the twenty-five sensors in the array's four concentric rings are sent via fiber optics transmission to a hub. The data are collected at the hub and then retransmitted to four receiving stations. The hub is connected by telephone link to the Norwegian analysis center in Kjeller. The same information is sent via satellite to U.S. sites in Virginia, California, and New Mexico. NORESS's capabilities were demonstrated in July 1985, when the array detected a Soviet test of a 0.25-kiloton device at Semipalatinsk.[71]

The United States also receives the results of Norwegian Air Force photography of Soviet aircraft taken over the Baltic. Among such photographs are those taken of a MiG-31 taken from below and the left-rear, which shows AA-9 antiaircraft missiles. Another photograph showed the SU-27 Flanker carrying AA-10 Alamo radar homing missiles, and two AA-10 Alamo IR homing missiles.[72]

PEOPLE'S REPUBLIC OF CHINA

The PRC's intelligence relationship with the United States began with the late 1970's visit to China of Morton Abramowitz, Deputy Assistant Secretary of Defense for International Security Affairs. In a meeting with a senior Chinese defense official, Abramowitz gave him a highly classified briefing on the deployment of Soviet forces along the Chinese border, and pulled out satellite photographs of Soviet military installations and armor that were facing China. China has apparently continued to receive such photography. According to one U.S. official, the Chinese reconnaissance satellite's footprint "is very small, and they want mapping support, especially of the Soviet Union" in addition to photographs of Soviet forces deployed along their border.[73]

The Abramowitz meeting led to the most important aspect of U.S.-PRC intelligence cooperation—the establishment of two SIGINT stations in western China located at Qitai and Korla in the Xinjiang Uighur Autonomous Region. The United States initially suggested setting up such posts in 1978, prior to the establishment of diplomatic relations between the countries. At first the Chinese, apparently concerned about cooperating too closely with the United States, were reluctant to agree. The issue was raised again after the overthrow of the Shah of Iran in January 1979. In an April 1979 meeting with a visiting U.S. Senate delegation, PRC Vice Premier Deng Xiao Ping indicated that China was willing to use U.S. equipment "to monitor Soviet compliance with a proposed new arms limitation treaty." Deng also indicated that the monitoring stations would have to be run by Chinese and that the data would have to be shared with the PRC.[74]

The United States and the PRC reached a basic agreement in January 1980. Actual intelligence operations began in the fall of 1980. The stations were constructed by the CIA's Office of SIGINT Operations, whose personnel trained the Chinese technicians and now periodically visit the stations to advise them and to service the equipment as required.[75] The initial set of equipment allowed for the interception of telemetry from Soviet missile test and space shots conducted from two major Soviet launch sites—at Tyuratam near the Aral Sea and at Sary Shagan near Lake Balkash. While somewhat farther from Tyuratam than the Iranian sites, the Chinese sites are closer to the Sary Shagan ABM test site.

Another aspect of U.S.-Chinese intelligence cooperation involves a joint project to set up nine monitoring stations in China, primarily to study and predict earthquakes. These U.S. seismic devices will also monitor Soviet nuclear tests. One device is located in Urumqi in Xinjiang province, and is approximately 600 miles from the Soviet nuclear test site at Semipalatinsk in Central Asia. A second device, in Manchuria, will help U.S. analysts learn more about the geology of the Soviet Union, which in turn will increase the accuracy of intelligence estimates of Soviet test explosions.[76]

A third aspect of cooperation lies in the covert action area. The International Liaison Department (ILD) and the CIA have both been active in conducting coordinated operations against Soviet-backed forces in Angola, Cambodia, and Afghanistan. Some camps in Pakistan to train Mujahdeen guerillas operate under the joint direction of the CIA and ILD.[77]

JAPAN

Japan has an extensive intelligence exchange relationship with the United States. One aspect of that relationship is the sharing of signals intelligence, as indicated by the Japanese sharing of Soviet communications intercepted by a unit on Wakkanai on the night the Soviets shot down Korean Airlines Flight 007. SIGINT sharing is based on mutual interests and intended as partial payment by the United States to Japan for the SIGINT facilities the United States maintains on Japanese territory.[78] The Japan-U.S. SIGINT relationship is a formal one, with Japan being one of ten third parties to the UKUSA Agreement.

Japan has also received satellite photographs from U.S. authorities. In 1982 Secretary of Defense Caspar Weinberger presented the Chief of the Japanese Defense Agency with satellite photographs "showing a Japanese-made floating dock being used in the repair of the Soviet aircraft carrier *Minsk*."[79] That revelation was made to convince the Japanese that technology made available to the Soviets for nonmilitary purposes was being misused.

In addition, it is likely that the Japanese Defense Agency receives satellite photographs or information derived from those photos on a regular basis. Such information would concern Soviet naval capabilities and movements in the vicinity of Japan, Soviet air activity in Siberia, and the deployment of Soviet troops and weapons systems (particularly the SS-20) in the vicinity of Japan.

But the most extensive exchange undoubtedly occurs with respect to ocean surveillance information, particularly regarding Soviet naval movements. One aspect of such cooperation is the CINCPACFLT [U.S. Commander in Chief Pacific Fleet]— JMSDF [Japanese Maritime Self-Defense Forces] Intelligence Exchange Conference. Likewise, a responsibility of the Intelligence Liaison and Production Section of the Intelligence Division, U.S. Naval Forces, Japan is to "coordinate Commander in Chief, U.S. Pacific Fleet and Commander U.S. Naval Forces, Japan intelligence exchange with the Chief of the Intelligence Division, Maritime Staff Office and the Intelligence Officer, CINCSDFLT [Commander in Chief Self-Defense Fleet].[80]

Information derived from U.S. worldwide ocean surveillance assets—especially from WHITE CLOUD satellites and the SOSUS network—can substantially increase the effectiveness of Japan's surface and submarine detection efforts. Among much of the information likely to be passed on to Japan is that information coming into the Fleet Ocean Surveillance Information Center at Kamiseya, Japan. At the same time, the Japanese share information obtained by their sonar arrays and P-3Cs. According to the staff manual for U.S. Naval Forces, Japan, the Operations Special Projects Officer of the Operations Division, U.S. Naval Forces Japan, conducts liaison with cognizant Japanese officials with respect to Operations Special Projects 6100, 6200, and 6300 Oceanographic Station Detachments.[81]

SOUTH AFRICA

The United States has, at times, maintained a SIGINT exchange relationship with the Republic of South Africa's Directorate of Military Intelligence. The arrangement began in the 1960s and initially concerned Soviet shipping and submarine movements in the South Atlantic and Indian Oceans.[82] Since that time the scope of the arrangement has changed with changing political and military events.

By the early 1970s, NSA personnel were stationed at the South African Silvermine facility and reports on Soviet shipping routinely flowed from South Africa to the NSA. South Africa's intelligence installations were vastly expanded in the mid-1970s, as the Soviet Union and Cuba became directly involved in Angola along with the CIA and South Africa. Vast quantities of electronic equipment, including antennas and sophisticated interception receivers, were secretly shipped from Britain and West Germany to South Africa to enable South Africa to build more listening posts. American-made computer chips and other electronic components were involved in the shipments, although under Presidential directive, they could have been banned. In the Carter Administration, Richard M. Moose, Assistant Secretary of State for African Affairs, ordered an end to all collaboration on COMINT between the United States and South Africa. The liaison was continued by the Navy anyway, and South Africa continued to report on Soviet submarine and shipping activity.[83]

With the advent of the Reagan Administration, cooperation included information on the activities of the African National Congress (ANC), including information obtained from the interception of communications between ANC headquarters in Lusaka, Zambia, its guerilla training camps in Angola, and its offices in Africa and Western Europe. Such cooperation was presaged by a 1980 conference at Cheltenham between GCHQ, NSA, and South African Directorate of Military Intelligence representatives. The South African representatives requested

- political, military, and diplomatic intelligence about Zambia, Botswana, Tanzania, Angola, and Mozambique;
- intelligence about the ANC's Oliver Tambo and ten members of his ANC high-command staff;
- information on any flights Tambo took abroad on Soviet and Cuban airlines; and
- special attention by the NSA (and the GCHQ) to the ANC communications.[84]

To make fulfillment of their first request easier, South Africa provided the GCHQ with information about the radio frequencies used by the various nations. In return, the NSA (and the GCHQ) asked South Africa for

- continued monitoring of Soviet and Cuban activities in Angola and Mozambique;
- weekly reports on Soviet submarines and shipping activity around the Cape of Good Hope; and
- reports on Soviet commercial and economic activity in sub-Saharan Africa with special emphasis on support for rebel activity.[85]

In the early 1980s, the information that the United States received from South Africa was apparently passed through the GCHQ without specific indication as to its South African origin.

OTHER ARRANGEMENTS

Other intelligence exchange arrangements include:

UKUSA Third Parties: Countries with which the United States has formal SIGINT sharing relationships with and are "Third Party" signatories of the UKUSA Agreement are: Thailand, Japan, South Korea, Norway, Denmark, West Germany, Italy, Greece, and Turkey.

Pakistan: Pakistan acts as a pipeline for the hundreds of millions of dollars in CIA covert assistance that is provided to the Afghan rebels. Pakistan also cooperates with U.S. intelligence agencies in electronic intelligence gathering near the Soviet Union (at Peshawar) and in southeast Asia.[86]

Finland: The NSA purchases radar intelligence concerning the Soviet Union collected by the Finnish VKL (Communications Experience Facility).[87]

Mexico: The CIA is reported to cooperate closely with the Federal Directorate of Security, which is said to tap telephone calls by some Soviet-Bloc embassy staff and send the transcripts to the CIA.[88]

In 1986 it was reported that the United States had been receiving valuable information about Cuba and Nicaragua from Panamanian "double agents" who, in turn, provide information to those nations about U.S. activities. According to Norman Bailey, a former NSC staff member, Panama's role as an intelligence asset is a principal reason the United States muted (until 1988) its public criticism of General Noriega's drug-trafficking activities and dictatorial control over Panama.[89]

NOTES TO CHAPTER 12

1. James Bamford, *The Puzzle Palace: A Report on NSA, America's Most Secret Agency* (Boston: Houghton Mifflin, 1982), p. 312.
2. Ronald Lewin, *The American Magic: Codes, Ciphers and the Defeat of Japan* (New York: Farrar, Strauss and Giroux, 1982), p. 46.
3. Ibid., p. 47.
4. Bamford, *The Puzzle Palace*, p. 314.
5. Ibid.
6. Bob Elliot, *Scarlet to Green: Canadian Army Intelligence 1903-1963* (Toronto: Canadian Military Intelligence Association, 1982), p. 461.
7. F.H. Hinsley, E.E. Thomas, C.F.G. Ransom, and R.C. Knight, *British Intelligence in the Second World War Volume 2* (New York: Cambridge University Press, 1981), p. 55ln; See p. xv of David Kahn's "Introduction" to Herbert O. Yardley, *The American Black Chamber* (New York: Ballantine, 1981); Robert Sheppard, "Lack of Quick Action Upset Gouzenko, Papers Say," *Toronto Globe and Mail*, October 17, 1981, p. 5; Elliot, *Scarlet to Green*, p. 401.
8. U.S. Congress, Joint Committee on the Investigation of the Pearl Harbor Attack *Pearl Harbor Attack, Part 2* (Washington, D.C.: U.S. Government Printing Office, 1946), p. 947; D.M. Horner, "Special Intelligence in the South-West Pacific Area in World War II," *Australian Outlook* 32, no. 4 (1978): 310–27.
9. Desmond Ball, "Allied Intelligence Cooperation Involving Australia During World War II," *Australian Outlook* 32, no 4 (1978): 299–309; Elliot, *Scarlet to Green*, pp. 384–85.
10. Ronald Clark, *The Man Who Broke Purple* (Boston: Little Brown, 1977), p. 208.
11. Ball, "Allied Intelligence Cooperation"; Duncan Campbell, "The Threat of the Electronic Spies," *New Statesman*, February 2, 1979, pp. 140–44; John Sawatsky, *Men in the Shadows: the RCMP Security Service* (New York: Doubleday, 1980), p. 9n; Transcript of "The Fifth Estate—The Espionage Establishment," broadcast by the Canadian Broadcasting Company, 1974.
12. Private information; Seymour Hersh, *"The Target is Destroyed": What Really Happened to Flight 007 and What America Knew About It* (New York: Random House, 1986), p. 48n.
13. Chapman Pincher, *Inside Story: A Documentary of the Pursuit of Power* (New York: Stein & Day, 1979), p. 157; Sawatsky, *Men in the Shadows*, p. 9n.
14. Desmond Ball, *A Suitable Peace of Real Estate: American Installations in Australia* (Sydney: Hale & Iremonger, 1980), p. 40.
15. Campbell, "Threat of the Electronic Spies."
16. Department of the Army, Office of the Adjutant General, "United States–United Kingdom Security Agreement," October 8, 1948.
17. See Jeffrey T. Richelson and Desmond Ball, *The Ties that Bind: Intelligence Cooperation Between the UKUSA Countries* (London: Allen & Unwin, 1985), pp. 148–49.
18. Paul Kelly, "NSA, The Biggest Secret Spy Network in Australia," *The National Times*, May 23–28, 1977.
19. Letter to the author from Eugene Y. Yeates, Director of Policy, National Security Agency, December 7, 1982.

20. Desmond Ball, "The U.S. Naval Ocean Surveillance Information (NOSIS)—Australia's Role," *Pacific Defence Reporter* (June 1982): 40–49; Michael Richardson, "Australia and NZ Use Singapore Base to Spy on Soviet Ships for CIA," *The Age*, April 12, 1984, p. 1.

21. Ball, "The U.S. Naval Ocean Surveillance Information System."

22. Ibid.

23. Ibid.

24. "Britania Scorns to Yield," *Newsweek*, April 19, 1982, pp. 41–6.

25. Armed Forces Medical Intelligence Center, *Organization and Functions of the Armed Medical Intelligence Center*, April 1, 1986, p. vii.

26. Joint Intelligence Organization, *Fourth Annual Report, 1974* (Canberra: JIO, 1974), pp. F1–F2.

27. Ibid., pp. 36, F1–F2.

28. Ibid., p. F2.

29. Answer from the Ministry of Defense to a Parliamentary question.

30. Kevin O'Connor, "Defence Heads Shy from PM Clashes," *Dominion*, October 8, 1986.

31. Ibid.

32. Justice Hope, *The Fifth Report of the Royal Commission on Intelligence and Security* (Canberra: Australian Government Printer, 1977), Appendix 5-E, para. 19.

33. Ibid., n. 5-38.

34. Ibid., para. 142–44.

35. Ibid., para. 143.

36. Ibid., para. 179–80.

37. Ibid., para. 181.

38. Ibid., para. 184.

39. Ibid., para. 236, 239; Appendix 5-E, para. 21.

40. Canadian-U.S. Joint Intelligence Committee, *Soviet Capabilities and Probable Course of Action Against North America in a Major War Commencing During the Period 1 January 1958 to 31 December 1958* (Washington, D.C.: Central Intelligence Agency, March 1, 1957) in *Declassified Documents Reference System 1981-169A*; U.S. Congress, Senate Committee on Armed Services, *Department of Defense Authorization for Appropriations Fiscal Year 1984, Part 5* (Washington, D.C.: U.S. Government Printing Office, 1983), p. 2708.

41. *Canada-U.S. Arrangements in Regard to Defence, Defence Production, Defence Sharing* (Washington, D.C.: Institute for Policy Studies, 1985), p. 31.

42. Walter Agee, Acting Deputy Director of Intelligence, "Memorandum for the Coordinator of Joint Operations: Proposed U.S.-Canadian Agreement," Modern Military Branch, National Archives, R 341, Entry 214, File Nos. 2-1900 through 2-1999.

43. Joint Chiefs of Staff, *Canadian–United States Communications Instructions for Reporting Vital Intelligence Sightings (CERVIS/MERINT)* (Washington, D.C.: JCS, March 1966), p. 2-1.

44. Ibid., pp. 2-4 to 2-6.

45. Ibid., p. 3-1.

46. Duncan Campbell and Clive Thomas, "BBC's Trade Secrets," *New Statesman*, July 4, 1980, pp. 13–14.

47. Ibid., p. 14.

48. Ibid., pp. 13–14.

49. Stewart Steven, *The Spymasters of Israel* (New York: Doubleday, 1979), p. 27.
50. Judith Perera, "Cracks in the Special Relationship," *The Middle East* (March 1983): 12–18.
51. Ibid.
52. Stanley A. Blumberg and Gwinn Owens, *The Survival Factor* (New York: Putnam, 1981), p. 272; Richard Halloran, "U.S. Offers Israel Plan on War Data," *New York Times*, March 13, 1983, pp. 1, 13.
53. Edmund Walsh, "Begin Offers to Give War Intelligence to U.S.," *Washington Post*, October 15, 1982, p. A18; Richard Halloran, "U.S. Said to Bar Deal with Israel," *New York Times*, February 10, 1983, pp. A1, A7.
54. Halloran, "U.S. Said to Bar Deal with Israel"; Bernard Gwertzman, "Israelis to Share Lessons of War with Pentagon," *New York Times*, March 22, 1983, pp. 1, 12.
55. Bernard Gwertzman, "Reagan Turns to Israel," *New York Times Magazine*, November 27, 1983, pp. 62ff.
56. Bob Woodward, "CIA Sought 3rd Country Contra Aid," *Washington Post*, May 19, 1984, pp. A1, A13.
57. Bob Woodward, "Probes of Iran Deals Extend to Roles of CIA Director," *Washington Post*, November 28, 1986, pp. A1, A33.
58. "U.S. to Share More Recon Data, Tighten Air Links with Israel," *Aerospace Daily*, December 8, 1983, pp. 193–94.
59. Ibid.
60. "Is the CIA Hobbled?" *Newsweek*, March 5, 1979, pp. 18–20.
61. Charles Babcock, "Israel Uses Special Relationship to Get Secrets," *Washington Post*, June 15, 1986, p. A1.
62. "How the Israelis Pulled it Off," *Newsweek*, July 19, 1976, pp. 42–47; David Halevy and Neil C. Livingstone, "The Ollie We Knew," *The Washingtonian*, July, 1987, pp. 77ff.
63. F.G. Samia, "The Norwegian Connection: Norway (Un)willing Spy for the U.S.," *Covert Action Information Bulletin* (June 1980): 4–9.
64. Ibid.; R.W. Apple, Jr., "Norwegians, Ardent Neutralists, Also Want their Defense Strong," *New York Times*, August 5, 1978, p. 2; Owen Wilkes and Nils Petter Gleditsch, *Intelligence Installations in Norway: Their Number, Location, Function and Legality* (Oslo, Norway: Peace Research Institute Oslo, 1979), pp. 17–20.
65. Wilkes and Gleditsch, *Intelligence Installations in Norway*, pp. 24–26; Seymour Hersh, *"The Target is Destroyed,"* p. 42.
66. Wilkes and Gleditsch, *Intelligence Installations in Norway*, p. 32.
67. Ibid., p. 35; Hersh, *"The Target is Destroyed,"* p. 42.
68. Wilkes and Gleditsch, *Intelligence Installations in Norway*, p. 20.
69. Ibid., p. 52.
70. Ibid., pp. 52–56; Svein Mykkeltveit, "Seismological Facilities in Norway," in *Workshop on Seismological Verification of a Comprehensive Nuclear Test Ban* (Oslo, Norway: Norwegian Ministry of Foreign Affairs, 1985), pp. 2–5.
71. Glenn Zorpette, "Monitoring the Tests," *IEEE Spectrum* (July 1986): 57–66.
72. "AA-10 Alamo Missile in Close-Up," *Jane's Defence Weekly*, July 25, 1987, pp. 145–46; "Norwegian Air Force Intercepts MiG-31 Foxhound," *Aviation Week and Space Technology*, February 17, 1986, p. 30.

73. Nayan Chandra, *Brother Enemy: The War After War* (New York: Harcourt, Brace and Jovanovich, 1983), p. 280; "Washington Round-Up," *Aviation Week and Space Technology*, March 19, 1984, p. 15; Daniel Southerland, "U.S. Navy Call at Chinese Port Symbolizes Growing Military Relationhship," *Washington Post*, November 5, 1986, pp. A23, A29.

74. Philip Taubman, "U.S. and Peking Jointly Monitor Russian Missiles," *New York Times*, June 18, 1971, pp. 1, 14; Murrey Marder, "Monitoring Not So-Secret-Secret," *Washington Post*, June 19, 1981, p. 10.

75. Robert C. Toth, "U.S., China Jointly Track Firings of Soviet Missiles," *Los Angeles Times*, June 18, 1981, pp. 1, 9; David Bonavia, "Radar Post Leak May Be Warning to Soviet Union," *London Times*, June 19, 1981, p. 5; Taubman, "U.S. and Peking Jointly Monitor Russian Missiles."

76. Michael R. Gordon, "U.S. Uses Seismic Devices in China to Estimate Size of Soviet A-Tests," *New York Times*, April 4, 1987, pp, 1, 4.

77. Roger Faligot and Remi Kauffer, *Kang Sheng et les Services Secret Chinois*, (Paris: Robert Laffont, 1987), p. 505.

78. Hersh, *"The Target is Destroyed,"* pp. 63–72.

79. "U.S. Warns Japan Not to Increase Soviet Military Power," Xinhau General Overseas News Service, March 30, 1982.

80. U.S. Naval Forces Japan, COMNAVFORJAPAN Staff Instruction 5450.1G, *Staff Organization Manual*, May 13, 1983, p. V-5.

81. Ibid., p. VI-8.

82. Seymour M. Hersh, "U.S. is Said to Have Given Praetoria Intelligence on Rebel Organization," *New York Times*, July 23, 1986, pp. A1, A10.

83. Ibid.

84. Ibid.; Duncan Campbell and Patrick Forbes, "UK's Listening Link to Apartheid," *New Statesman*, August 1, 1986, pp. 10–11.

85. Hersh, "U.S. is Said to Have Given Praetoria Intelligence on Rebel Organization"; Campbell and Forbes, "UK's Listening Link with Apartheid."

86. Bob Woodward, "Pakistan Reported Near Atom Arms Production," *Washington Post*, November 4, 1986, pp. A1, A16.

87. Jukka Rislakki, "Suomi Kuuntelee Kaikiin Ilmansuuntiin," *HSKK-Inte*, December 1987, pp. 32–35.

88. "The CIA and Mexico," *Foreign Report*, July 31, 1986, pp. 1, 2.

89. "Panamanians Spying on, for U.S.," *Washington Post*, September 20, 1986, p. A2.

13 ANALYSIS AND ESTIMATES

The U.S. intelligence community produces a vast amount of numerous varieties of intelligence. National intelligence is produced for national decisionmakers and comes in several forms: current intelligence, estimates, analysis, and reports. Current intelligence focuses on a situation of immediate concern. Estimates both summarize a present state of affairs and project those affairs into the future. Other reports may be concerned solely with summarizing a particular situation, whether political, military, or economic.

Similar intelligence is produced by various agencies in support of national intelligence production or for departmental officials—distinguishable both on substantive and on current/estimate/report dimensions. As shown in Chapters 2 through 6, there are numerous analytical units throughout the U.S. government.

This chapter examines the intelligence product of the intelligence community as a whole (i.e., national intelligence) as well as intelligence of a variety of significant analytical units—those of the Central Intelligence Agency, Defense Intelligence Agency, Bureau of Intelligence and Research, the Drug Enforcement Administration, the military service scientific and technical intelligence units, and those units belonging to selected unified and specified commands.

NATIONAL INTELLIGENCE

National intelligence produced by the U.S. intelligence community comes in several forms. These include the *President's Daily Brief*, the *National Intelligence Daily*, the *Weekly Watch Report*, the *National Intelligence Situation Report*, National Intelligence Estimates, Special National Intelligence Estimates, National Intelligence Analytical Memorandums, and Interagency Intelligence Memorandums.

The *President's Daily Brief* (PDB) is delivered to the President every morning. The PDB, with a circulation limited to the President and a select number of his principal advisors (the Vice President, Secretaries of State and Defense, and the Assistant to the President for National Security Affairs in the Carter Administration) and contains information from the more sensitive U.S. sources. It is designed to be read in ten to fifteen minutes at the beginning of the day.[1] It provides whatever significant information has been acquired during the previous day and commentary as to its significance. According to Cord Meyer, a former CIA official, in the hands of the CIA Director, the PDB

> is a powerful tool for focusing the attention of the President on potential crisis areas and for alerting him to situations that may require rapid policy adjustment. Occasionally, when fresh intelligence sheds new light on a complex problem an annex is attached to the PDB to give the President more extensive background for the decisions he has to make.[2]

Under Gerald Ford the PDB was rather lengthy, but was reduced to a maximum of about fifteen pages under Jimmy Carter, although DCI Stansfield Turner occasionally appended longer "trend pieces" at the end of the PDB. Carter would often write in the margins of the PDB, requesting more information.[3]

The second daily national current intelligence publication is the *National Intelligence Daily* (NID). The NID was the idea of former CIA Director William Colby, who had repeatedly recommended during the mid-1960s that the CIA's daily intelligence report, then known as the *National Intelligence Digest*, be issued in newspaper format to emphasize the more important items and to offer its readers a choice between a headline summary and in-depth reading. Colby's interest was sufficient to lead him to join, on every evening possible, the editorial conference that determined subjects carried in the next day's edition. Subsequently, the newspaper format was judged to be too inflexible and the publication reverted to a magazine format.[4]

The NID is somewhat longer than the PDB and serves a somewhat larger audience—about 200 top-level foreign policy officials in Washington plus a limited number of U.S. Ambassadors and CIA Station Chiefs. For security reasons, it does not contain some of the more sensitive items in the PDB.[5]

Despite deletion of such items, the *Daily* may be classified TOP SECRET RUFF UMBRA, indicating the presence of intelligence derived from satellite photography as well as signals intelligence, as in the issue of November 12, 1975. That issue contained the following front-page headlines: "Motion to Impeach President Gaining Support in Argentina." "Disorders Seen in Aftermath of Whitlam Firing," "Military Leader Warns Turkey on Violence," "Morocco, Spain Discuss Sahara," and "Israel is Exaggerating Gravity of Deteriorating Trade Situation."[6] In the article on the Whitlam firing it was stated that

Australia may be entering a period of unprecedented disorder in the wake of Governor General Kerr's sacking of former Prime Minister Whitlam. Inflammatory remarks by Whitlam could turn scattered demonstrations and work stoppages supporting him to a nationwide general strike, despite calls for restraint by some trade union leaders.[7]

A more recent NID, of May 9, 1985, contained a review of Libya on the First anniversary of an attempted coup on May 8, 1984, in which Qaddafi's barracks had been attacked. According to the NID, Libyan dissident and exile groups, led by the National Front for the Salvation of Libya, were planning to blow up a military installation in Libya to demonstrate their ability to attack Qaddafi on Libyan soil.[8]

During the early years of the Reagan Administration, Director of Central Intelligence (DCI) William Casey initiated publication of the *Weekly Watch Report* (WWR).[9] The WWR apparently is restricted to items concerning "front-burner" situations.

A fourth current intelligence product is the *National Intelligence Situation Report* (NISR). NISRs are issued only in the midst of a crisis. During a major crisis, the NISRs are issued at frequent intervals and are prepared by a community task force, usually under the DCI or a National Intelligence Officer. This coordination attempts to provide crisis managers with a single "authoritative" report that summarizes all important developments during the reporting period, preventing the White House and other authorities from being inundated with redundant, conflicting reports from different agencies.[10]

The best-known national intelligence products are the National Intelligence Estimates (NIEs) and Special National Intelligence Estimates (SNIEs). As their name implies, these documents attempt to project, into the future, existing military, political, and economic trends and to estimate for policymakers the likely implications of these trends. According to the House Committee on Foreign Affairs, A NIE is "a thorough assessment of a situation in the foreign environment which is relevant to the formulation of foreign, economic, and national security policy, and which projects probable future courses of action and developments."[11]

The NIEs cover a wide variety of topics, both geographic and functional. In 1961 there was a World Wide Series (00), Communist State Series (10), Western and Southern Europe Series (20), Middle East Series (30), Far East Series (40), Southeast Asia Series (50), North and West Africa Series (60), South and East African Series (70), Caribbean Area Series (80), and American States Series (90).[12]

Thus, NIEs issued in the 1960–62 period were NIE 100-2-60, *Sino-Indian Relations*; NIE 10-61, *Authority and Control in the Communist Movement*; NIE 24-61, *The Outlook for Italy*; NIE 36-61, *Nasser and the Future of Arab Nationalism*; NIE 41-61, *Prospects for Japan*; NIE 51-62, *The Prospects for Burma*; NIE 60-62, *Guinea and Mali*; NIE 76-60, *Probable Trends in the Horn of Africa*; NIE 85-62, *The Situation and Prospects in Cuba*; and NIE 99-61, *Trends in Canadian Foreign Policy*.[13]

Some of the NIEs—for example, those concerning the Soviet Union and China—are issued on an annual or biannual basis; others—for example, *The Prospects*

Table 13–1.   NIE-11 Series, 1960–1962.

NIE Number	Title
11-1-62	Soviet Space Programs
11-2-61	The Soviet Atomic Energy Program
11-3-61	Sino-Soviet Air Defense Capabilities through mid-1966
11-4-60	Soviet Policy and Courses of Action
11-4-61	Main Trends in Soviet Capabilities and Policies 1961–66
11-5-61	Soviet Technical Capabilities in Guided Missiles and Space Vehicles
11-6-60	Strength of the Armed Forces of the USSR
11-7-60	Soviet Capabilities and Intentions With Respect to the Clandestine Introduction of Weapons of Mass Destruction in the United States
11-8-61	Soviet Capabilities for Long-Range Attack
11-8-62	Soviet Capabilities for Long-Range Attack
11-9-62	Trends in the Soviet Foreign Policy
11-11-62	Trends in the Soviet Economy
11-12-62	Soviet Policy Toward Africa

Source: National Security Council Information Liaison, "National Intelligence Estimates," May 25, 1962, LBJ Library, Vice Presidential Security File, Box 5, Folder: NSC Records of NSC Actions, 1962.

for Burma—are issued less frequently. The NIEs concerning the Soviet Union are, or course, the most significant ones and constitute the NIE-11 series.

In the 1960–62 period at least fourteen NIEs were issued in the 11 Series; their titles are given in Table 13–1. Included were NIEs on the Soviet space program, air defense, offensive capabilities, foreign policy, and the economy.

Among the NIEs now declassified is NIE 11-4-57, *Main Trends in Soviet Capabilities and Policies 1957–1962*. This sixty-one page estimate consists of six chapters on internal political developments, and trends in the Soviet economy, Soviet science and technology, Soviet military posture, Soviet relations with Other Communist states, and Soviet foreign policy.[14]

Subsequently, the NIE-11 series has undergone some revision from its 1961 structure. As of the mid-1970s, the 11 Series consisted of twelve estimates—including ones on Soviet general purpose forces, military R & D, the economy, political-military operations outside the Soviet Union and the Warsaw Pact, Soviet space programs, and Soviet foreign policy. The two major estimates were 11-3, *Soviet Strategic Defensive Forces* and 11-8, *Soviet Capabilities for Strategic Nuclear Conflict*.[15] Today, the two subjects are covered in a single estimate, 11-3/8, *Soviet Strategic Forces, Offense and Defense*. The first volume, a summary volume of about 125 pages, reads as a systematic, blow-by-blow description of Soviet weapons and military doctrine. Each chapter deals with a different category of Soviet weaponry. For instance, one chapter might deal with long-range missiles, another with bombers, and another with defensive radars and antiaircraft missiles. Along with the description of current Soviet forces, parts of the text also summarize the intelligence community's projection for future Soviet force levels in a given year and the time at which the Soviets are expected to be able to deploy a weapon incorporating a certain type of technology. The second volume contains supporting documents.[16]

In addition to NIE 11-3/8, the present NIE series included 11-1 (*Space Operations*), 11-11 (*Intelligence Denial and Deception in Soviet Strategic Military Programs: Implications for U.S. Security*), 11-15 (*Soviet Naval Strategy*), and 11-17 (*Chemical Warfare*). Within the Chinese series there is also a combined estimate of Chinese offensive and defensive strategic forces, NIE 13-3/8.[17]

The importance and frequency of the NIEs have varied from administration to administration. In 1961 there were more than twenty-five issued. The yearly total rose to fifty in the late 1960s before falling to eleven to twelve a year during the final years of the Carter Administration. The decline was largely due to CIA Director Stansfield Turner's view that "national intelligence estimates are [not] a very efficient of way of preparing finished intelligence."[18]

Under the Reagan Administration, and then CIA Director William Casey, the number of NIEs rose to thirty-eight in 1981 and sixty in 1982. The 1981 NIEs included estimates on: the balance of power in the Middle East, Soviet strategic offensive and defensive capabilities, the strategic implications of Soviet economic problems, Soviet dependence on Western technology and trade for its military buildup, the likely impact and effectiveness of allied trade sanctions against the USSR, the European peace movement, the Mexican financial crisis, the Iran-Iraq war, international terrorism, Soviet and Cuban involvement in Central America, prospects for free elections in El Salvador, involvement of external powers in the Salvadoran conflict, and the prospects for conflict in South Africa.[19]

Subsequent NIEs have included 1983 NIEs on the "Security of North America" and on "Nicaragua: The Outlook for the Insurgency"; four 1985 NIEs on Nicaragua—on the Sandinista military buildup, on efforts to consolidate authority within Nicaragua, on outside support from the Soviet Union and Cuba, and on the Nicaraguan export of revolution; and 1985 NIEs on narcotics trafficking, *State-Sponsored Terrorism* and *Terrorist Use of Chemical and Biological Warfare*.[20]

In addition to the regularly scheduled NIEs, the President and members of the National Security Council may call for production of SNIEs when some unforeseen development requires production of an additional estimate. Thus, as indicated in Tables 13-2 and 13-3, at least six SNIEs were written during the 1961 Berlin crisis and seven or more during the period 1960–62 concerning Southeast Asia. During the Cuban missile crisis of 1962, at least two SNIEs were prepared: SNIE 85-3-62, *The Military Buildup in Cuba* and SNIE 11-19-62, *Major Consequences of Certain U.S. Courses of Action on Cuba*. SNIE 11-19-62 thus covered the status of the Soviet buildup (with regard to MRBMs, aircraft, antiaircraft sites, cruise missile sites, and cruise missile patrol boats); the purpose of the buildup; and the likely effects and Soviet actions in response to U.S. acquiescence, warning, a naval blockade, or use of military force.[21]

More recent SNIEs include SNIE 85-79, *The Cuban Foreign Policy*; the 1981 SNIEs entitled *Soviet Support for International Terrorism and Revolutionary Violence*

Table 13–2. SNIEs Concerning the 1961 Berlin Crisis.

Number and Date	Title
SNIE 2-61, June 13	Soviet and Other Reactions to Various Courses of Action Regarding Berlin
SNIE 2-2-61, July 11	Soviet and Other Reactions to Possible U.S. Courses of Action With Respect to Berlin
SNIE 2-3-61, July 18	Probable Soviet Reactions to a Western Embargo
SNIE 2-4-61, August 31	Reaction to Certain U.S. Measures in the Berlin Crisis
SNIE 2-5-61, September 14	Soviet Reactions to Certain U.S. Courses of Action
SNIE 2-6-61, October 19	Probable Soviet and Other Reactions to Certain U.S. Military Measures in the Berlin Crisis

Source: National Security Council Information, "National Intelligence Estimates," May 25, 1962, LBJ Library, Vice Presidential Security Files, Box 5, Folder: NSC Records of NSC Actions, 1962.

Table 13–3. SNIEs 1960–1962 on Southeast Asia.

Number and Date	Title
SNIE 10-61, February 21, 1962	Communist Objectives, Capabilities, and Intentions in Southeast Asia
SNIE 13-3-61, November 30, 1961	Chinese Communist Capabilities and Intentions in the Far East
SNIE 10-2-61, June 27, 1961	Likelihood of Minor Communist Military Intervention in Mainland Southeast Asia
SNIE 58-62, January 11, 1962	Relative Military Capabilities of Opposing Forces in Laos
SNIE 58/1-1962, January 31, 1962	Same title as 58-62
SHIE 10-3-61, October 10, 1961	Probable Communist Reaction to Certain SEATO Undertakings in South Vietnam
SNIE 58-2-61, November 19, 1961	Bloc Support of the Communist Effort against the Government of Vietnam
SNIE 10-4-61, October 5, 1961	Probable Communist Reaction to Certain U.S. Actions in South Vietnam
SNIE 52-61, December 13, 1961	Thailand's Security Problems and Prospects

Source: National Security Council Information Liaison, "National Intelligence Estimates," May 25, 1962, LBJ Library, Vice Presidential Security Files, Box 5, Folder: NSC Records of NSC Actions, 1962.

and *Libya: Aims and Vulnerabilities*; the 1982 SNIE on the *Likelihood of Attempted Acquisition of Nuclear Weapons or Materials by Foreign Terrorist Groups for Use Against the United States*; SNIE 34-84 on *Iran: The Post-Khomeini Era*; the 1985 SNIEs entitled *Libya's Qaddafi: The Challenge to the United States and Western Interests* and *Iran: Prospects for Near Term Instability*; and a 1986 SNIE on the Soviet threat to Iran, which concluded that the Soviets were less likely to attack Iran or have influence in a post-Khomeini regime than had previously been believed.[22]

A more recently instituted form of national intelligence product is the Interagency Intelligence Memorandum (IIM), coordinated like an NIE but designed to provide basic information rather than projections. The IIM was promoted while James Schlesinger was DCI to deal in depth with highly technical issues such as Soviet civil defense and defense spending. The IIMs include NI-IIM 10025 of December 1981, "INF Support: Theater Nuclear Forces," and NI-IIM 10002 of March 1981, "SALT Support: European Theater Nuclear Forces."[23]

A fourth type of noncurrent, national intelligence product is the National Intelligence Analytical Memorandum (NIAM). One NIAM was NIAM 11-20-75, "Soviet Policy Toward Selected Countries of Southern Europe."[24] The NIAMs include more detailed analyses of political, military, or economic situations than do the IIMs.

CENTRAL INTELLIGENCE AGENCY

In addition to providing much of the analytical capability for the production of national intelligence products, the CIA also produces a wide variety of studies on political, economic, social, and military matters.

The primary focus of the CIA's analyses and reports is, of course, the Soviet Union. It is particularly with regard to the Soviet Union that CIA reports touch all aspects of a nation's activities. CIA reports on the Soviet Union show particular concern about both civilian and military decisionmaking. Thus, the CIA's Directorate of Intelligence has produced code word-level reports entitled *The Soviet Defense Council and Military Policy Making* (April 1972), *The Soviet Decision Making Process for the Selection of Weapons Systems* (June 1973), and *The Politburo and Soviet Decisionmaking* (April 1972).

The CIA is also concerned with the key individuals who make and implement decisions, as well as with many lesser individuals. Thus, the April 1977 *Biographic Handbook, USSR, Supplement IV*, includes profiles on twenty-one officials, listed in Table 13-4. The biography of Eduard Shevardnadze, then a Georgian party official and now Foreign Minister, is shown in Figure 13-1. With regard to Soviet military activities, one area of CIA concern has been the amount of money spent on defense—a concern resulting in *Soviet and U.S. Defense Activities: A Dollar Cost Comparison 1971-80* (1980), *Estimated Soviet Defense Spending in Rubles 1970-1975* (May 1976), and *Soviet and U.S. Investment in Intercontinental Attack Forces, 1960-1980 and Outlook for the Future* (August 1981).[25]

Other reports on Soviet military matters have focused on Soviet manpower issues (*Soviet Military Manpower Issues in the Eighties*, May 1980); political control of the Soviet armed forces (*Political Control of the Soviet Armed Forces*, July 1980); attack submarine threats (*The Soviet Attack Submarine Force and Western Lines of Communications*, April 1979); and topics that would be more suited to the DIA or service intelligence units—for example, *Soviet Military Aircraft Maintenance* (October 1979), and *Soviet Naval Mine Counter-Countermeasures* (June 1980).[26]

Figure 13–1. Biography of Eduard Shevardnadze

USSR   **Eduard Amvrosiyevich SHEVARDNADZE**
First Secretary, Central Committee, Communist Party of Georgia

One of the youngest regional Party leaders in the Soviet Union, Eduard Shevardnadze (pronounced shevardNAHDzeh) became first secretary of the Georgian Communist Party in September 1972, at the age of 43. He was a newcomer to the Georgian Party hierarchy, having served in the government for the previous 7 years as republic minister of internal affairs, charged with the preservation of law and order. The chief factor in Shevardnadze's promotion was his experience as a police administrator.

In the Soviet Union, Georgia has long been known as an enclave of high living and fast runners. Its most important economic activity, wine production, is one of the oldest and the best loved branches of Georgian agriculture. Georgians are freedom loving and individualistic; they have always lived by looser rules than other Soviet nationalities, first because former Premier Josif Stalin (himself a Georgian by birth) indulged them, and later, apparently, because the pattern had been established.

Disciplinarian in a Loose Republic

Former police official Shevardnadze, who has nurtured an image as a firm, austere disciplinarian (the Georgians refer to him as the "boss"), has tried since 1972 to overturn the habits of generations regarding easy virtue, political corruption, underground capitalism and heavy drinking. The Georgians are not giving in easily. Shevardnadze's cleanup campaign met with early and continued foot dragging, and during his first years as Georgian Party leader he encountered considerable bureaucratic opposition. Speakers at an August 1973 Party Plenum hinted at disorders among the public at large, and rumors of anonymous threats against Shevardnadze and his family were prevalent throughout 1973.

Several recent developments indicate that Shevardnadze's cleanup campaign in Georgia has been intense, broad and continuous. An underground Soviet publication that appeared in 1975 claimed that nearly 25,000 persons had been arrested in Georgia in the past 2 years. (A Soviet who visited Georgia in late 1974 reported that 13,000 Party and Komsomol members had been arrested.) In addition, the republic's second secretary, Al'bert Churkin, was dismissed in April 1975 for gross errors and shortcomings.

During 1976 there was a series of bomb and arson attacks in the republic as Shevardnadze continued his all-out campaign against corruption, nationalism and ideological deviation in Georgia. The attacks may have been intended to blacken Shevardnadze's reputation by showing his inability to control the Georgian situation; there were rumors that the first secretary was on the way out because of the disorders. A long hard-hitting report delivered by Shevardnadze in July 1976 seemed to indicate that despite the disturbances he was still in control. His repeated allusions to approval of his campaign by the central authorities in Moscow, however, betrayed a certain unease about his authority in the republic.

Views on Agriculture

In 1975, when Georgia was suffering from the Soviet Union's general harvest failure, Shevardnadze set forth several new ideas on agriculture. In a report delivered to a local Party meeting, he attacked the existing program for construction of large mechanized livestock facilities—a pet project of top Soviet agricultural officials—and proposed instead to divert a part of the material and money to help expand the feed base. Shevardnadze also made several proposals designed to strengthen the position of individual farmers. For example,

Figure 13–1. continued

he asked that the feed allotment be ensured for livestock owned by individuals; that unwanted land (swamp lands or rocky areas) be turned over to the population, with technical assistance and fertilizer provided by the state; and that individual farmers form cooperative associations. Little has been heard of these proposals since 1975, but they are indicative of Shevardnadze's surprisingly pragmatic leadership style, which may serve him well in the face of continuing political problems in his republic.

Early Life and Career

A native Georgian, Eduard Amvrosiyevich Shevardnadze was born on 25 January 1928. He was the son of a teacher and was educated as a historian at a pedagogical intitute, but he began his career as a Komsomol functionary in 1946. He rose through the ranks to become first secretary of the Georgian Komsomol Central Committee in December 1957. Shevard-nadze was elected a nonvoting member of the Bureau of the Georgian Party Central Committee, his first Party post, in 1958; and 3 years later he advanced from nonvoting to voting membership on the Bureau of the All-Union Komsomol Central Committee.

Political Eclipse and Recovery

In 1961 Shevardnadze was released without explanation as Komsomol chief and removed from his position on the Party Bureau. His career in eclipse, he served for 3 years in minor Party posts in Tbilisi, the Georgian capital. He began his political comeback in 1965, when he was appointed Georgian minister for the protection of public order, a title later changed to minister of internal affairs. His career may have benefited at this stage from an association with Aleksandr Shelepin, at that time a member of the Communist Party of the Soviet Union (CPSU) Politburo: When Shevardnadze became Georgian Komsomol chief, Shelepin was first secretary of the All-Union Komsomol, and when he was named minister, Shelepin's influence in Moscow was at its peak.

In July 1972 Shevardnadze was elected a voting member of the republic's Party Bureau and first secretary of the Tbilisi City Party Committee. Shevardnadze did not serve as first secretary for long—2 months later he became Georgian Party chief. He has been a Deputy to the USSR Supreme Soviet since 1974.

Travel

While he was Komsomol first secretary, Shevardnadze made several trips abroad to attend youth conferences, visiting Belgium, Tunisia and France. Since becoming republic first secretary, he has increased his contacts with foreign officials through travel and attendance at official functions. During 1974 he headed a CPSU delegation to the Austrian Communist Party Congress, attended a dinner in Moscow given by CPSU General Secretary Leonid Brezhnev for the President of France, met with Senator Edward Kennedy in Georgia, and traveled with Politburo member Nikolay Podgorny to Sofia. He accompanied Brezhnev to the Hungarian Party Congress in March 1975.

Shevardnadze has a brother, Ippokrat, who has been active in the Georgian Party apparatus. No further personal information on Shevardnadze is currently available.

CIA/DDI/OCR
JZebatto
                                                                1 April 1977

Table 13–4. Biographies of Soviet Officials in Biographic Handbook, USSR, Supplement IV

Viktor Grigor'yevich Afanas'yev, Chief Editor, Pravda
Andrey Mikhaylovich Aleksandrov-Agentov, Aide to CPSU General Secretary Brezhnev
Vladimir Sergeyevich Alkhimov, Chairman of the Board, State Bank
Aleksey Konstantinovich Antonov, Minister of the Electrical Equipment Industry
Eduard Asaturovich Aykazan, Chief, USA Section, Foreign Relations Administration, State Committee for Science and Technology
Ivan Ivanovich Bodyul, First Secretary, Central Committee, Communist Party of Moldavia
Konstantin Ustinovich Chernenko, Secretary, CPSU Central Committee, General Department, CPSU Central Committee
Nikolay Timofeyevich Glushkov, Chairman, State Committe for Prices
Aleksandr Akimovich Ishkov, Minister of the Fish Industry
Leonid Vital'yevich Kantorovich, Head, Problems Laboratory of Economic-Mathematical Models and Operations Research, Institute of Management of the National Economy
Mikhail Stepanovich Kapitsa, Chief, First Far Eastern Department, Ministry of Foreign Affairs
Georgiy Arkad'yevich Karavayev, Minister of Construction
Georgiy Markovich Korniyenko, Deputy Minister of Foreign Affairs
Aleksey Nikolayevich Manzhulo, Deputy Minster of Foreign Trade
Igor Dmitriyevich Morokhov, First Deputy Chairman, State Committee for the Utilization of Atomic Energy
Viktor Nikolayevich Polyakov, Minister of the Automotive Industry
Yaklov Petrovich Ryabov, Secretary, CPSU Central Committee
Eduard Amvrosiyevich Shervardnadze, First Secretary, Central Committee, Communist Party of Georgia
Kiril Stepanovich Simonov, Chief, Transport and Communications Department, CPSU Central Committee
Nikolay Ivanov Smirnov, First Deputy Commander in Chief of the Navy
Semen Kuz'mich Tsvigun, First Deputy Chairman, Committee for State Security

---

Scientific intelligence reports on the Soviet Union have included *Soviet Research on Excimer Lasers, Soviet and East European Parapsychology Research* (April 1977), and *New Soviet Large-Scale Scientific Computer* (April 1979). Both broad trends in the Soviet economy and the situation in particular industries are the subjects of Intelligence Directorate studies, for example, *The Soviet Economy in 1976–1977 and Outlook for 1978* (1978), *Soviet Long Range Energy Forecasts* (1978), *Outlook for Soviet Oil and Gas* (1976), and *The Soviet Tin Industry: Recent Developments and Prospects Through 1980* (1977).[27]

Soviet grain production, with its impact on the country's internal and external developments, has been the subject of numerous reports. Included among them are *Biological and Environmental Factors Affecting Soviet Grain Quality* (1978), *USSR: The Long-Term Outlook for Grain Imports*, and *USSR: The Impact of Recent Climate Change on Grain Production* (1976). Likewise demographic shifts among the multiple Soviet nationalities—especially declines in the proportion of Great Russians and White Russians—might have a major impact on Soviet military and economic policy. Thus, the Intelligence Directorate has produced reports such as *USSR: Some Implications of Demographic Trends for Economic Policies*.[28]

The basic thrust of CIA research with regard to the Soviet Union is duplicated with respect to the People's Republic of China. Its reports on the PRC include *Defense Modernization in China* (October 1980), *China's First Nuclear-Powered Ballistic Missile Submarine* (April 1981), *China: Agricultural Performance* (1975), *China: Internatinal Trade 1976–1977* (1978), and *China: Gross Value of Industrial Output 1965–1977* (1978).[29]

While the Soviet Union and the PRC are the subjects of a significant portion of the CIA's analytical attention, a substantial amount of CIA effort is devoted to other areas of the world. Political, economic, military, social, agricultural, and demographic trends are examined. Reports on Allied and Third World countries have included *France: Nuclear Non-Proliferation Policy* (1982), *French Nuclear Reactor Fuel Reprocessing Program* (1984), *Korea: The Economic Race Between the North and South*, *Kampuchea: A Demographic Catastrophe*, *The Refugee Resettlement Problem in Thailand*, *Pakistan: The Ethnic Equation*, and *Elites and the Distribution of Power in Iran* (1976).

Other analyses focus not on individual nations but on regional or international issues or problems such as international energy levels, markets, or regional politics. Reports produced since 1977 in these areas include *Central America: Short-Term Prospects for Insurgency*, *World Shipbuilding: Facing Up to Oversupply*, *World Steel Market: Continued Trouble Ahead*, and *The International Energy Situation: Outlook to 1985*.[30]

In addition, CIA offices produce a variety of current intelligence items. These reports have included the *Scientific Intelligence Weekly Review*, *Middle East and South Asia Review*, *Military Weekly Review*, *Weapons Intelligence Summary*, and others.[31]

Articles in the *Scientific Intelligence Weekly Review* included "Haiti: Nationwide Spread and African Swine Fever Disastrous for Agricultural Economy" (June 15, 1979), and "Dominican Republic: First Occurrence of Sugar Cane Rot in Western Hemisphere" (December 11, 1978). Articles in the *Middle East and South Asia Review* have included "Iran: the Prospects for Responsible Government" (October 20, 1978) and "The Tudeh Party: the Lazarus of Iranian Politics" (October 20, 1978). An article in the February 2, 1979 *Military Weekly Review* was entitled "Iran: Navy Expansion Program Endangered."[32] There has probably been a restructuring of this current intelligence product in accord with the 1981 reorganization of the Directorate of Intelligence.

DEFENSE INTELLIGENCE AGENCY

As with the CIA, the DIA produces a wide variety of intelligence products—current intelligence, estimates, general intelligence, and scientific and technical intelligence. The DIA also coordinates the counterintelligence products of the military services.

One of the DIA's reports is intended specifically for the President—the *Defense Intelligence Weekly for the President*.[33]

Paralleling the NIEs and the SNIEs are the Defense Intelligence Estimates (DIEs) and Special Defense Intelligence Estimates (SDIEs). These estimates often cover topics similar to those covered by the NIEs and SNIEs; the defense estimates however, have more of a military slant. Being departmental estimates, they are produced without interdepartmental coordination. The DIEs in the 1970s included *Military Significance of Soviet Developed Facilities in Somalia* (1976), *Prospects for Soviet Naval Aviation* (1976), and *PRC Strategic Nuclear Forces: How Much is Enough?* (1977). Recent DIEs include *The U.S. Central Command Area of Operations: Challenge for US Security Interests Abroad* (March 1986), and *The Eastern Caribbean: Prospects for the Regional Security System* (April 1986). Recent SDIEs include *Vietnam's China Problem* (May 1986), *Indochina: Embers of Resistance Through 1990* (February 1986), and *Future Soviet Threat to US Airbreathing Reconnaissance Platforms* (April 1986).[34]

Current intelligence products include the *Weekly Intelligence Summary* (WIS), which contains items on foreign defense personnel as well as military hardware. The July 4, 1975 WIS contained a SECRET NOFORN item entitled "New Australian Defense Minister is Whitlam's Man," which called the Minister, William L. Morrison, "an articulate, if sometimes blustery, opposition spokesman on foreign affairs" and noted that he had "routine access to sensitive U.S. and Australian intelligence, including information on U.S. military facilities." It also noted that "Morrison may have an unsettling impact on the top management of the Defense Department in view of his long-standing enmity with Defense Permanent Secretary Sir Arthur Tange."[35]

A more recent issue of the WIS, July 23, 1982, had articles entitled "New Philippine Defense Attaché Team is Assigned" and "Tracked Multiple Rocket Launchers Noted in Beijing Military Region." The first article, classified SECRET NOFORN, noted that the attachés would undoubtedly report on, and possibly operate against, anti-Marcos Philippine activists in the United States. The second reported that "eighteen tracked MRLs [Multiple Rocket Launchers] were sighted with the 359th Artillery Regiment of the 79th Infantry Division, 27th Army, at Xingtai, Hebei on 18 May. This is the second infantry division noted with tracked MRLs." Included was a SECRET/WNINTEL/NOFORN satellite photograph of the MRLs. A third article, also with a classified title, concerned the testing of a possible Soviet chemical weapon launcher and included satellite photography of the test area.[36]

Altogether the July 23, 1982 issue of the WIS contained twenty-one articles on five different regions of the world: the Soviet Union/Eastern Europe, Asia, Western Europe, Africa, and Latin America. The table of contents for the issue is shown as Table 13–5. Other WIS articles have included "Soviet Space and Missile Wrapup" (December 15, 1978), "Chinese Navy Adopts New Training Practices," "Flexibility of Soviet Air Defense Forces Increased" (March 5, 1982), and "Chinese IRBM Training Activity" (January 18, 1980).[37]

Table 13–5. Table of Contents for WIS 29-82.

SECRET   23 JULY 1982
CONTENTS

A second current intelligence product is the *Defense Intelligence Commentaries*, a newsletter-like publication containing articles on several subjects. These are more analytical and more personal then those appearing in the WIS. Articles in recent *Defense Intelligence Commentaries* have included: "Soviets Have SS-20 Reload and Refire Capability" (December 2, 1982), "Israeli Press Claims of Lebanese Army Atrocities May Be Effort to Direct Attention from Inquiry on Phalange" (December 2, 1982), "Interest in Commercial Ties with US Points to Iraq Desire for Improved Relations" (November 9, 1982), and "Cubans Are Worried About Sandinista Regime's Problems" (October 22, 1982).[38]

Other DIA current intelligence products include the *Defense Intelligence Notice* (DIN), the *Spot Intelligence Report* (SPIREP), the *Daily Intelligence Summary* (DISUM), and the *Periodic Intelligence Summary.* Normally, each DIN addresses a single development, situation, event, or activity that is felt to have a possible impact on future planning and operations. The primary objective of the DIN is to report an event, to explain why it occurred, and to make an assessment of its impact on the United States.[39]

The Spot Intelligence Report is intended to inform the Joint Chiefs of Staff, the unified and specified commands, the military services, and selected agencies of particular events of importance. The events that are the subject of a SPIREP, however, are required to have an immediate and significant effect on current planning and operations. The report is intended to answer four questions: (a) what is the nature of the event?, (b) when did the event occur?, (c) where did the event occur?, (d) and what is the source of the information?.[40]

The DISUM provides the JCS, the National Military Intelligence Center, the unified and specified commands, the military services, and selected agencies with a daily analysis of an actual or simulated crisis situation and a summary of related intelligence of significance produced during the preceding twenty-four-hour period. The SPIREP is intended to provide the same entities with timely intelligence regarding events that could have an immediate and significant effect on current planning and operations. Each DISUM is expected to include, at a minimum, information in four areas; general hostile situation, hostile operations during the period, other intelligence factors, and counterintelligence situations.[41]

The *Periodic Intelligence Summary* is intended to provide the JCS, military services, and worldwide military commanders with periodic intelligence concerning actual or training exercises that could have an immediate, actual (or simulated) effect on U.S. plans and operations. Information, if applicable, is included in the following format:

1. Situation summary/highlights
2. Political developments
3. Military activity
    a. air
    b. ground
    c. navy
    d. missile
    e. other
4. Outlook[42]

Other DIA products include the Defense Intelligence Projections for Planning (DIPPs) that summarize the state of the Soviet and Chinese armed forces and project future trends and force levels. Each set consists of seven volumes. Volume I examines Ballistic Missile Forces. Volume II of the DIPP on the PRC is concerned with Strategic Bomber Forces and in the Soviet DIPP with Long Range Aviation. In both DIPPs, Volume III is devoted to Aerospace Defense Forces. Volume III contains at least four sections—IIIC is concerned with Surface-to-Air Missile Forces, and IIID with Ballistic Missile Defenses. Volume IV on General Purpose Forces has at least five sections, including A—Ground Forces, B—General Purpose Naval Forces, D—Military Transport Aviation, and E—Military Helicopter Aviation, Volume V is entitled *Space Systems for the Support of Military Operations*, and Volume VII bears the title *Military Manpower Implications.*[43]

Other future projections may be done on either a regular or occasional basis. Some of these are *Projected Space Programs—USSR* (1982), *ASW Weapons and Decoys (Current and Projected)—ECC* (1976), and *Combat Vehicle Systems (Current and Projected)—European Communist Countries* (1976).[44]

Within the general intelligence category the DIA publishes a variety of products. These include: Area Handbooks, Order of Battle Studies, Military Intelligence Summaries, Defense Intelligence Studies, Targeting/Installation Documents, Lines of Communication Studies, and Tactical Commanders' Terrain Analysis Studies. Examples of such products include *Soviet Strategic Surface-to-Surface Missile Order of Battle* (September 1978), *Defense Intelligence Electronic Order of Battle Volume I: USSR and Mongolia* (March 1982), *Ground Order of Battle: PRC* (January 1980), *Military Intelligence Summary: Volume VII, People's Republic of China and Eastern Asia* (January 1980), *Naval Forces Intelligence Study: People's Republic of China* (March 1981), *Handbook on the Chinese Armed Forces* (July 1976), and *Soviet Kola Peninsula Missile Submarine Base: Two Decades in the Making* (August 1978).[45]

All such studies are intended to form an extensive data base relevant to assessing foreign military capabilities in general or for specific matters (e.g., seizure of the Falklands or the Iran-Iraq war) and for use in U.S. military operations. Order of Battle Studies specify in as much detail as possible the organization and armaments of a nation's military establishment or component thereof. Targeting/Installation Documents will be used by operations planners to assess the requirements for destroying or damaging an airfield, port facility, or missile base. Lines of Communications Studies describe the means by which military forces are supported and supplied and thus are used in designing plans to sever those lines.

In addition, the DIA produces thousands of reports on military and military-related scientific and technical matters that are not part of the series mentioned above. The subjects of these reports include strategy, politico-military relations, scientific and technical matters, weapons systems, intelligence, geopolitics, C^3 and R & D.

DIA reports on strategy include *Luring Deep: China's Land Defense Strategy* (September 1980) and *Detente in Soviet Strategy* (September 1975). Political-military subjects were the focus of *China's Urban Militia: Military Arm or Political Tool?* (June 1974) and *USSR: The Unity and Integration of Soviet Political, Military and Defense Industry Leadership* (March 1977).[46]

Scientific and technical reports concern general assessments, computer technology, microelectronics, and medical activities. Included among such reports are

Long-Range Scientific and Technical Assessment: The People's Republic of China (October 1973) and *Psychopharmacological Enhancement of Human Performance— USSR.*[47]

As might be expected, reports on specific weapons systems constitute the bulk of DIA reports. The reports vary from a focus on an entire class of weapons to reports of more than 100 pages on a single weapons system. Such reports include *Ballistic Missile Payloads (Current and Projected)—USSR and China, Antisatellite System—USSR* (November 1979), *Over the Horizon Radars for Air Defense* (December 1979), *Typhoon/Oscar—A Special Report, Soviet ALFA Class SSN Study* (December 1979), *Backfire Weapon System* (July 1980), and *SS-17 ICBM System* (March 1982.)[48]

Reports concerning C^3 have focused on Warsaw Pact and Soviet C^3 capabilities as a whole, as well as on the command structures for particular military regions. Reports have included *Warsaw Pact Forces Command, Control and Communications* (August 1980); *New Military Command Structure of Soviet Forces Opposite China*; and *Soviet Command, Control and Communications Capabilities.*[49]

Another major area of DIA analysis is in R & D weapons acquisition. The concern is with the decisionmaking acquisition process, the role of design bureaus, and design and testing philosophy. Among the DIA studies dealing with the subjects is the 1972 study entitled *Soviet Military Research and Development—An Overview*, and the five-volume 1980 study on *U.S. and Soviet Weapon System Design Practice.*[50]

BUREAU OF INTELLIGENCE AND RESEARCH

As noted in Chapter 5, the State Department's INR contributes to national intelligence production and provides the Secretary of State and the rest of the State Department with intelligence support. In the latter role it provides both current and long-term intelligence.

Daily current intelligence is contained in the *Morning Summary*, intended to inform the Secretary and principal deputies of current events and intelligence and provide concise commentaries concerning their significance. The first part of the *Summary* consists of short "list and comment" reports based on newly available information. The second part usually consists of four one-page essays drafted by INR analysts.[51]

Also, within the current intelligence category is a series of regional and functional summaries published up to six times a week. These include *Arab-Israeli Highlights* (six times); *Afghanistan Situation Report* (twice); *African Trends, East Asia and Pacific Weekly Highlights*, and *Inter-American Highlights* (all once a week); and *Central American Highlights, Global Issues Review, Politico-Military Analyses, Science and Technology*, and *Soviet Weekly*. These publications consist of short essays or brief analyses, usually followed by summaries of significant intelligence reports.[52]

Single-subject reports are published under three titles: *Current Analyses, Assessments and Research*, and *Policy Assessments*. *Current Analyses* are papers that analyze recent or ongoing events and assess prospects and implications in the next six months. Analyses have included "El Salvador: Brighter Prospects for Land Reform" (1983), "Soviet Exercise 'ZAPAD-81': Implications for CBMs" (September 28, 1981), "Soviets Seek Restraints on Use of Space Shuttle" (May 7, 1981), and "Moscow's Response to NATO Defends Soviet TNF Position" (May 20, 1981).[53]

Assessment and Research (AR) papers are studies that either assess past trends or project the course of events more than six months into the future. They are reports in which the analyst has done substantial background or in-depth research. AR papers have included "Central Issues in Soviet Nuclear Strategy" (January 12, 1981), "Soviet Activities in Africa in the 1980s" (May 21, 1982), "The Japanese Market: Obstacles and Opportunities" (1983), and "Chile: Political Revival and Party Realignment" (1983). *Policy Assessments* are papers that analyze the context or results of past policies or assess comparative policies or policy options.[54]

The focus of *Current Analyses, Assessment and Research*, and *Policy Assessments* papers is not exclusively, or even predominantly, the Soviet Union. Non-Soviet Bloc economic intelligence is the primary responsibility of the INR. Economic intelligence reports have concerned natural resources, trade within and among various Blocs, prospects for various commodity markets, and the economic/agricultural situation within specific ountries. Thus, the INR has produced reports entitled "The Majors' Declining Share of Oil Distribution" (February 26, 1980), "The Revised Outlook for Oil Demand" (September 22, 1981), "The International Sugar Agreement Besieged" (March 5, 1981), "Dim Prospects for Coffee Exporters" (September 14, 1981), "Trade Patterns of the West" (July 17, 1980), "Trade of NATO Countries with the Communist Countries 1976–1979" (December 1, 1980), and "Energy Food/Population Balances in the Maghreb Countries" (July 21, 1982).[55]

DRUG ENFORCEMENT ADMINISTRATION

In addition to participating in the production of an annual NIE on narcotics trafficking, the DEA produces a variety of intelligence reports. Its primary, recurring reports are the *Monthly Digest of Drug Intelligence* and *Quarterly Intelligence Trends*. It also publishes the annual *Narcotics Intelligence Estimate* and a compendium of worldwide production, smuggling, and trafficking trends and projections. In 1985 it also produced the 135-page *Worldwide Narcotics Threat Assessment* to provide specifics on the quantities and types of narcotics, conveyances and routes used by international narcotic traffickers to introduce narcotics into the United States. Another report dealt with the illicit drug traffic from the Mideast to and through Bulgaria.[56]

MILITARY SERVICE SCIENTIFIC AND TECHNICAL INTELLIGENCE CENTERS

As noted in Chapter 4, each military service has at least one scientific and technical (S & T) intelligence organization. Included in this category are the Air Force System Command's Foreign Technology Division and the Naval Intelligence Command's Naval Intelligence Support Center. Not to be outdone, the Army has two such organizations—the Foreign Science and Technology Center, and the Army Missile and Space Intelligence Center.

Among the publications of the FTD are regular reports that include the *FTD Monthly All-Source Soviet and PRC Missile Launch Data Reports*, the *FTD Weekly Aerospace System Report*, and the *FTD Core Team Intelligence Summaries*.[57]

Additionally, the FTD publishes, weekly, the *Foreign Technology Bulletin*, a classified magazine with articles of a current intelligence nature. Among the articles that have appeared in the *Bulletin* are: "SS-17 Accelerometer Quality Assessment" (August 17, 1979), "Further Data on the Soviet 270-Liter Cold Cathode Electric Discharge Laser" (August 31, 1976), "PRC S & T Intelligence Organization Identified" (June 28, 1977), "Soviet Tactical and Strategic Photoreconnaissance and Aerial Film Technology" (June 29, 1976), and "Chinese CSSC-2 (Silkworm) Coastal Defense Missile" (July 31, 1980).[58]

In-depth studies by the FTD include studies of Soviet space activities (*Soviet Space Program*, October 1974); electromagnetic combat (*Electromagnetic Combat Threat Environment Description*, four volumes, 1981); the use of lasers for air defense (*Soviet Laser Tactical Air Defense Design Study*, November 1981); Soviet aircraft (*Backfire-B*, June 1979; *The MiG-19*, June 1972); design and acquisition procedures (*Soviet Aircraft Design and Acquisition*); and exploitation reports (*Gram Troy Exploitation Report*, December 27, 1977).[59]

The NISC produces a variety of regular reports which are divided into four echelons. First-echelon reports provide initial notification to consumers of new developments. Second-echelon publications generally provide succinct, comprehensive updates of threat characteristics. Third-echelon publications provide dissemination of navy assessments and technical observations. Fourth-echelon publications are comprehensive reference documents.[60]

First-echelon publications include the *Weekly Wire (Part I)* and the *Acoustic Intelligence Newsletter*. Part I of the *Weekly Wire* provides a summary of significant NISC intelligence findings and preliminary analyses prior to their inclusion in finished intelligence documents. Parts II and III provide information on the Status of Products and Current Contract Data, respectively. Second-echelon publications include the *CNO Intelligence Point Papers*, the *Naval Science and Technical Intelligence Review* (NAVSTIR) and the *Missile Matrix*. CNO Intelligence Papers are quarterly updates of nineteen naval warfare papers on topics ranging from ASW to aircraft carriers. The NAVSTIR is a monthly periodical covering scientific and technical developments which affect the combat potential of foreign navies, their support facilities, and their R & D communities.[61]

Third-echelon publications include *Naval Intelligence Technical Assessments* (NITAs), *Naval Intelligence Technical Summary* (NITS), *Foreign Materiel Evaluation Reports* (FMERs) and *Basic Imagery Interpretation Reports* (BIIRs). NITAs disseminate intelligence on "significant issues of high importance" while NITAs are informal means of "disseminating discrete analyses or bodies of technical data." FMERs represent the analysis of foreign materiel obtained by U.S. intelligence, while BIIRs are detailed, imagery-derived reports on foreign submarines, surface ships, sensors, and air and weapons platforms as well as construction yards and major operational facilities. Fourth-echelon publications include *Naval Warfare Publications* such as NWP 12-6-1, *Threat Emitter Evaluation Guide*; NWP 12-7-1, *Recognition Guide to Major Combatants*; NWP 12-7-2, *Recognition Guide to Aircraft*; and NWP 12-7-8, *Threat Intelligence Summary–Naval Air Forces.*[62]

The FSTC publishes several current intelligence products—the *Biweekly Intelligence Summary* (BSTIS), the *Army Scientific and Technical Intelligence Bulletin* (ASTIB), the *Scientific and Technical Analysis Bulletin*, and the *Weekly Wire.* Among the articles in the September 1981 ASTIB was "Recent Developments in Soviet Artillery."[63]

Studies by the FSTC have focused on subjects directly and indirectly related to the Army mission. These studies have included: *Microelectronics Technology and Applications—Eurasian Communist Countries and Japan* (December 1974), *Chinese Land Defense Forces* (June 1973), *Soviet Twin 57-mm Self-Propelled Antiaircraft Gun ZSU-522-2* (June 1976), *Soviet Large Helicopter Mil Mi-12* (June 1972), *USSR Ground Forces R & D Overview 1975* (June 1975), *An Outstanding Weapons System for Soviet Air Defense Troops* (1972), and *Chemical Warfare Capabilities— Warsaw Pact* (October 31, 1979).[64]

UNIFIED AND SPECIFIED COMMANDS

Among the major functions of the intelligence components of the unified and specified commands is the preparation of current and other intelligence specifically geared to the needs of the command and its Commander in Chief. In many cases the publications they prepare are derived from already existing CIA and DIA publications.

Among the regular publications of the Strategic Air Command (SAC) intelligence component is the *SAC Intelligence Quarterly.* As with the FTD's *Foreign Technology Bulletin*, the *SAC Intelligence Quarterly* is a classified journal containing articles of current intelligence interest. Issues of the *Quarterly* have included articles on Soviet tactical and strategic aircraft ("Comparison Between Soviet and USAF Tactical Fighter Training," (July 1978) and "Backfire Development Status" (April 1978)); Soviet strategic rocket forces ("Modernization of the Soviet Strategic Rocket Forces" (July 1978)); SAC reconnaissance ("SAC Reconnaissance and the

SA-5" (April 1978)); Soviet civil defense ("Soviet Civil Defense, Personnel Shelters" (October 1978)); and Soviet surface-to-air missiles ("SA-10 Missile System" July 1981)).[65]

The PACOM's Intelligence Center, Pacific (IPAC), in addition to its current intelligence product, has produced reports on the surveillance of PRC naval activities (*Clipper Troop West (CTW) Surveillance Operations Against PRC Broad Ocean Area Task Group*, March 1981); the Chinese-Vietnamese conflict (*PRC SRV Conflict*, July 1979); Soviet Far Eastern military capabilities and activities (*Soviet Far East Logistics*, September 1978, and *Soviet Far East Sea and Airborne Landing Capabilities*, 1979); and nuclear targeting issues (*Targeting Potential Soviet Attack Corridors*, 1981).[66]

The LANTCOM's Fleet Intelligence Center, Europe and Atlantic (FICEURLANT) produces a *Monthly Intelligence Digest* with articles such as "Update of Soviet Development and Use of Facilities at Berbera, Somalia" (December 1976); and "SA-8 Missile System Review" (November 1976). Longer studies have included *Soviet Naval Air Long Range Reconnaissance* and *U.S. Sixth Fleet Missile Threat Guide*.[67]

The EUCOM's European Defense Analysis Center (EUDAC) is, as noted earlier, the electronics intelligence analysis center for the European Command. In addition to its current intelligence product, its reports have included *Badger AS-5 Kelt Operations in the Forward Area* (1979); *Analysis of AN-12/CUB ECM Capabilities Against the NATO Air Defense System* (February 1975); *Detection Ranges for Soviet Ground Based Radar in the Forward Areas* (May 1, 1980); and *Fencer Aircraft in the Forward Area* (July 1, 1979).[68]

Table 13–6 summarizes the general intelligence production responsibilities of a variety of unified, specified, and theater commands.

Table 13–6. General Intelligence Production Responsibilities.

Unit	Military Capabilities				Military Geography and Transportation	Targets
	Ground	Air	Navy	Missiles		
DIA[a]	All strategic including space OB.				NIS data base. Assists Commands as resources permit.	National data base BE, TDI, CPFL, physical vulnerability studies. Evaluation of target lists.
SAC	Produces intelligence on communist countries, world wide. Maintains EOB data base on USSR and Mongolia.					SIOP-NSTL targets weapons applications. Field AIF inputs.
USEUCOM	Monitors theater military capabilities. Performs timely analysis of all-source intelligence to determine foreign military, political, psychosocial and economic capabilities and vulnerabilities and to provide imminence of hostilities intelligence. Insures production of counterintelligence to satisfy operational command requirements. Produces intelligence in support of operational planning requirements. Monitors support of the DoD OB System. Produces ELINT of both tactical and technical significance and fuses ELINT with all-source inteligence in support of electronic warfare operations. Produces EOB on Albania, Bulgaria, Czechoslovakia, East Germany, Hungary, Poland, Romania, Yugoslavia, Western Europe, Africa and the Middle East (less India and Pakistan). Arranges for production of required intelligence by supporting CONUS production agencies.				Assures production of studies to support JCS-approved contingency plans as required to supplement national intelligence products, and monitors theater MGID production in support of NATO.	Field AIF inputs into DIA Data Base. Verification of targets selected from DIA data base for inclusion in theater OPLANS. Monitors and insures production of target intelligence and target materials in support of USCINCEUR/SACEUR.
USAREUR	Monitors theater ground military capabilities. Produces ground intelligence to support operational planning requirements. Performs timely analysis of all-source intelligence to determine foreign military, political, psychosocial and economic capabilities and vulnerabilities and to provide imminence of hostilities intelligence. Produces GOB, including technical information on Albania, Bulgaria, Czechoslovakia, East Germany, Hungary, Poland, Romania, Yugoslavia and the Soviet Group of Forces in Eastern Europe. Monitors and is responsive to current and general intelligence requirements of ground forces in North Africa and the Middle East. Monitors GOB on Western Military Districts of the USSR and technical intelli-				Produces Military Geographic Information and Documentation (MGID) in conformance with NATO Standardization Agreements (STANAGs).	Field AIF inputs into DIA data base. Produces tactical target intelligence in support of USCINSEUR/SACEUR.

	gence on the USSR for military equipment and weapons in the hands of the troops. Produces AAAOB on Czechoslovakia, East Germany and Poland. Produces MOB (including Tactical Missile/Rocket OB) on Czechoslovakia, East Germany, Hungary and Poland.		
USNAVEUR	Monitors theater naval capabilities. Produces naval intelligence in support of operational planning requirements. Performs timely analysis of all-source intelligence to determine foreign military, political, psychosocial and economic capabilities and vulnerabilities and to provide imminence of hostilities intelligence. Produces European, Middle East and African NOB. Produces installations, biographic and OB digitized data bases (including AOB, GOB, EOB, AAOB and Aerospace OB) for the USEUCOM area in support of the Naval Intelligence Processing System (NIPS).	Produces port, urban amphibious, weather and country intelligence studies for approved plans.	Field AIF inputs into DIA data base. Produces target intelligence and target materials and performs mission planning in support of USCINCEUR/SACEUR.
USAFE	Monitors theater aerospace capabilities. Performs timely analysis of all-source intelligence to determine foreign military, political, psychosocial and economic capabilities and vulnerabilities and to provide imminence of hostilities intelligence in support of operational planning requirements. Directs the multisensor exploitation activities of the European Special Activities Facility. Produces AOB on Eastern European Communist countries. Provides NATO with AOB to 75 degrees East. Produces NATO releasable MOB (including SAGMOB) on Albania, Bulgaria, Czechoslovakia, East Germany, Hungary, Poland, Romania and Yugoslavia.	Evasion and Escape for approved plans.	Field AIF inputs into DIA data base. Provides weapons application data, target intelligence and target materials in support of USCINCEUR/SACEUR.
PACOM	Managers theater military capabilities production.		Manages PACOM targets materials program. Monitors production of target intelligence by IPAC.

DIA: Defense Intelligence Agency
SAC: Strategic Air Command
USEUCOM: European Command
USAREUR: U.S. Army, Europe
USNAVEUR: U.S. Naval Forces, Europe
USAFE: U.S. Air Forces, Europe
PACOM: Pacific Command

Table 13-6. continued

Unit	Military Capabilities				Military Geography and Transportation	Targets
	Ground	Air	Navy	Missiles		
IPAC	Produces EOB on PACOM area. Produces Theater Intelligence. Supports DoD GOB Inputs to S. Vietnam, Cambodia, and Laos GOB.			Air defense analyses; Support DoD AOB; produces SEA AAAOB.	Detailed studies in support of JCS-approved contingency plans as required to supplement DIA finished intelligence. Studies include terrain, urban area, transportation, and cross-country movement.	Field AIF inputs into DIA data base; verification of targets selected from DIA data base for inclusion in theater OPlans; development of intelligence on CINCPAC OPlan and on DIA data base (AIF) installations in PACOM.
PACAF			Produces theater air intelligence.		Evasion and escape for approved plans.	Confirmation of targets assigned by PACAF. Field AIF inputs.
PACFLT			Monitors theater naval intelligence.		Port, amphibious, POL, weather and country studies for approved plans.	Confirmation of targets assigned to PACFLT.
ALCOM	Monitor Soviet strategic and general purpose forces East of 100°E longitude.		Monitors and reports on Soviet Fishing Fleet Activity in Alaskan Waters north of 45°N and east of 170°E.			
USARAL	Monitors theater Soviet Far East ground.					
Alaskan Air Command		Monitors theater Soviet Far East air.				
SOUTHCOM	Manages theater military capability production.				Detailed studies to support JCS-approved contingency plans as required to supplement DIA finished intelligence.	

LANTCOM		Manages theater military capabilities production. Supports DoD OB system. Maintains EOB in Latin America and Caribbean. Inputs to specific Caribbean GOB; to specific Caribbean, Latin American and Africa NOB.	Detailed studies to support JCS-approved contingency plans as required to supplement DIA finished intelligence.	Field AIF inputs. Confirmation of de-emph targets selected from DIA data base for inclusion in theater OPS plans.
LANTFLT		Supports DoD NOB with inputs as above.	Port, amphibious, weather, and country intelligence studies for approved plans.	
ARLANT		Produces Caribbean GOB	Lines of communication studies, terrain, urban areas, telecom, drop zones, and TacCTAs to support contingency plans.	Field AIF inputs.
AFLANT	AOB, Caribbean	MOB, Caribbean		
CONAD	Supports DoD OB system. Supports production on LRA activity.	Monitors and supports production on ICBM's. (Supports production on Foreign Space Objects).		
MIL	Certain SIGINT products.	Maritime Shipping	Oceanographic.	Field AIF inputs.

a. DIA has sole responsibility for the production of intelligence on the topics of military economics, military material production, and telecommunications.
b. Navy makes inputs to DoD NOB on certain East European countries.
IPAC: Intelligence Center, Pacific
PACAF: Pacific Air Forces
PACFLT: Pacific Fleet
ALCOM: Alaskan Command
USARAL: U.S. Army Alaska
SOUTHCOM: Southern Command
LANTCOM: Atlantic Command
LANTFLT: Atlantic Fleet
ARLANT: U.S. Army, Atlantic
AFLANT: U.S. Air Force, Atlantic

NOTES TO CHAPTER 13

1. Cord Meyer, *Facing Reality: From World Federalism to the CIA*, (New York: Harper and Row, 1980), p. 352; Zbigniew Brzezinski, *Power and Principle: Memoirs of the National Security Adviser 1977–1981* (New York: Farrar, Straus & Giroux, 1983), p. 224.
2. Meyer, *Facing Reality*, p. 352.
3. Loch K. Johnson, "Making the Intelligence "Cycle" Work," *International Journal of Intelligence and Counterintelligence*, 1, no. 4 (1987); 1–23.
4. William Colby with Peter Forbath, *Honorable Men: My Life in the CIA* (New York: Simon & Schuster, 1978), p. 354; Letter, Arthur S. Hulnick, CIA Office of Public Affairs to author, April 7, 1988.
5. Meyer, *Facing Reality*, pp. 352–54.
6. Brian Toohey and Dale Van Atta, "How the CIA Saw the 1975 Crisis," *National Times*, March 28–April 3, 1982, pp. 16ff.
7. Ibid.
8. Bob Woodward, *Veil: The Secret Wars of the CIA 1981–1987* (New York: Simon & Schuster, 1987), pp. 410–11.
9. "America's Secret Warriors," *Newsweek*, October 10, 1983, pp. 38ff.
10. Meyer, *Facing Reality*, p. 357.
11. U.S. Congress, House Committee on Foreign Affairs, *The Role of Intelligence in the Foreign Policy Process* (Washington, D.C.: U.S. Government Printing Office, 1980), p. 235.
12. National Security Council Information Liaison, "National Intelligence Estimates," May 25, 1962, LBJ Library, Vice Presidential Security File, Box 5, Folder: NSC Records of NSC Actions, 1962.
13. Ibid.
14. NIE 11-4-57, *Main Trends in Soviet Capabilities and Policies 1957–1962*, in *Declassified Documents Reference System 1979-128A*.
15. Lawrence Freedman, *U.S. Intelligence and the Soviet Strategic Threat* (London: MacMillan, 1977), pp. 34–35; *Office of Naval Intelligence Command History 1985, Annex D* (Washington, D.C.: ONI, 1987), p. 6.
16. Bruce Berkowitz, "Intelligence in the Organizational Context," *Orbis* (Fall 1985); 571–76; Victoria S. Price, *The DCI's Role in Producing Strategic Intelligence Estimates* (Newport, R.I.: Naval War College, 1980), p. 37.
17. *Office of Naval Intelligence Command History 1985, Annex D*, p. 6. Navy Operational Intelligence Center, *Navy Operational Intelligence Center Command History 1986* (Washington, D.C.: NOIC, 1986), p. 8; Diane T. Putney, *History of the Air Force Intelligence Service 1 January–31 December 1984, Volume 1, Narrative and Appendices* (Ft. Belvoir, Va.: AFIS, n.d.), p. 349.
18. Philip Taubman, "Casey and His CIA on the Rebound," *New York Times Magazine*, January 16, 1983, pp. 20ff.
19. Ibid.; Robert C. Toth, "Casey Shapes Up CIA, Survives as Top Spy," *Los Angeles Times*, January 3, 1983, pp. 1, 18.

20. Private information; Peter Kornbluh, *Nicaragua: The Price of Intervention* (Washington, D.C.: Institute for Policy Studies, 1987), p. 243 n. 22; Bob Woodward, *Veil*, p. 400; Brian Barger and Robert Parry, "Nicaraguan Rebels Linked to Drug Trafficking," *Washington Post*, December 27, 1985, p. A22; *Office of Naval Intelligence Command History 1985, Annex C*, p. 4.

21. *Declasified Documents Reference System 1975-48E, 1976-15B*.

22. Woodward, *Veil*, pp. 94, 409; *The Tower Commission Report* (New York: Times Books, 1987), pp. 114–15; Bob Woodward and Dan Morgan, "Soviet Threat Toward Iran Overstated, Casey Concluded," *Washington Post*, January 13, 1987, pp. A1, A8; U.S. Congress, House Permanent Select Committee on Intelligence, *U.S. Intelligence Performance on Central America: Achievements and Selected Instances of Concern* (Washington, D.C.: U.S. Government Printing Office, 1982), p. 7.

23. U.S. Congress, Senate Committee on Armed Services, *Department of Defense Authorization for Appropriations FY 1983, Part 7*, (Washington, D.C.: U.S. Government Printing Office, 1982), p. 4393; Price, *The DCI's Role in Producing Strategic Intelligence Estimates*, p. 44.

24. AR 381-19, "Military Intelligence: Intelligence Support," July 19, 1981, p. 2-5; *History of the Assistant Chief of Staff, Intelligence United States Army 1 January–30 January 1975*, (Washington, D.C.: OACSI, 1975), p. 7.

25. Air University Special Bibliography No. 205, *Soviet Military Capabilities* (Maxwell AFB, Ala.: Air University, February 1977), p. 9; Air University Special Bibliography No. 205, Supplement 2, *Soviet Military Capabilities, Part 1* (Maxwell AFB, Ala.: Air University, March 1982), p. 7.

26. Air University Special Bibliography No. 205, Supplement 2, *Soviet Military Capabilities, Part 1*, pp. 11, 33, 38.

27. Ibid., pp. 70, 72, 86.

28. Myron Smith, ed., *The Secret War: Intelligence, Espionage and Covert Operations* (Santa Barbara, Calif.: ABC-Clio, 1980), p. 122; *Documents from the U.S. Espionage Den 50: U.S.S.R. The Aggressive East, Section 2* (Teheran: Muslim Students Following the Line of the Iman, n.d.), p. 3.

29. Air University Special Bibliography No. 207, Supplement 1, *Communist China: Military Capabilities* (Maxwell AFB, Ala.: Air University, August 1981), p. 9.

30. Smith, *The Secret War*, p. 122.

31. United States of America v. Lee Eugene Madsen, Criminal No. 79-130F, District Court for Eastern District of Virginia; U.S. Congress, Senate Select Committee on Intelligence, *National Security Secrets and the Administration of Justice*, (Washington, D.C.: U.S. Government Printing Office, 1978), p. 4.

32. Private information.

33. Defense Intelligence Agency, *Organization, Mission and Key Personnel* (Washington, D.C.: DIA, April 1984), p. 31.

34. Air University Special Bibliography No. 205, *Soviet Military Capabilities*, p. 43; Air University Special Bibliography No. 207, *Communist China: Military Capabilities* (Maxwell AFB, Ala.: Air University, September 1977), p. 28; Titles pages of recent DIEs and SDIEs obtained under the FOIA.

35. "New Defense Minister is Whitlam's Man," *Weekly Intelligence Summary*, July 4, 1975, pp. 10–11.

36. *Weekly Intelligence Summary* 29–82, July 23, 1982.

37. Ibid.
38. Titles provided by Defense Intelligence Agency.
39. Joint Chiefs of Staff, *Joint Reporting Structure (JRS) Volume II-Joint Reports, Part 10—Intelligence* (Washington, D.C.: JCS, March 15, 1985), pp. 10-1-1 to 10-1-2.
40. Ibid., pp. 10-2-1 to 10-2-2.
41. Ibid., pp. 10-3-1 to 10-3-3.
42. Ibid., pp. 10-4-1 to 10-4-3.
43. Air University Special Bibliography No. 205, *Soviet Military Capabilities*, pp. 19, 33, 62; Air University Special Bibliography No. 207, *Communist China: Military Capabilities*, pp. 17, 22, 24, 28, 33; Air University Special Bibliography No. 205, Supplement 1, *Soviet Military Capabilities* (Maxwell AFB, Ala.: Air University, July 1979), pp. 23, 34, 43, 68; Air University Special Bibliography No. 205, Supplement 2, *Soviet Military Capabilities, Part I*, pp. 18, 26, 28, 31; Air University Special Bibliography No. 207, Supplement 1, *Communist China: Military Capabilities*, pp. 5, 13; Air University Special Bibliography No. 204, Supplement 6, *Strategic Triad* (Maxwell AFB, Ala.: Air University, January 1983), p. 57.
44. Air University Special Bibliography No. 205, Supplement 2, *Soviet Military Capabilities*, p. 88; Air University Special Bibliography No. 205, *Soviet Military Capabilities*, p. 42.
45. Air University Special Bibliography No. 207, *Communist China: Military Capabilities*, pp. 5, 12; Air University Special Bibliography No. 205, Supplement 1, *Soviet Military Capabilities*, p. 35; Air University Special Bibliography No. 204, Supplement 2, *Strategic Triad* (Maxwell AFB, Ala.: Air University, March 1978), p. 52; Air University Special Bibliography No. 205, Supplement 2, *Soviet Military Capabilities, Part I*, p. 13; Air University Special Bibliography No. 207, Supplement 1, *Communist China: Military Capabilities*, p. 5.
46. Air University Special Bibliography No. 207, Supplement 1, *Communist China: Military Capabilities*, pp. 9, 11; Air University Special Bibliography No. 205, Supplement 1, *Soviet Military Capabilities*, p. 7; Air University Special Bibliography No. 207, *Communist China: Military Capabilities*, p. 12.
47. Air University Special Bibliography No. 207, *Communist China: Military Capabilities*, p. 12; Air University Special Bibliography No. 205, Supplement 2, *Soviet Military Capabilities, Part I*, p. 72.
48. Air University Special Bibliography No. 205, Supplement 2, *Soviet Military Capabilities, Part I*, pp. 16, 26, 38, 52, 55; Air University Special Bibliography No. 204, Supplement 6, *Strategic Triad*, p. 57.
49. Air University Special Bibliography No. 205, Supplement 1, *Soviet Military Capabilities*, p. 41; Air University Special Bibliography No. 205, Supplement 2, *Soviet Military Capabilities, Part I*, p. 74.
50. Air University Special Bibliography No. 205, Supplement 2, *Soviet Military Capabilities, Part I*, p. 55.
51. *INR: Intelligence and Research in the Department of State* (Washington, D.C.: Department of State, 1983), p. 6.
52. Ibid.
53. Air University Special Bibliography No. 205, Supplement 2, *Soviet Military Capabilities, Part I*, pp. 5, 58, 84; INR, "Biannual Summary of Intelligence Reports, January 1–June 30, 1983," p. 17.

54.   *INR*, p. 7; Air University Special Bibliography No. 205, Supplement 2, *Soviet Military Capabilities, Part II*, (Maxwell AFB, Ala.: Air University, August 1982), pp. 6, 12, 20; Bureau of Intelligence and Research, "Biannual Summary of Intelligence Reports," pp. 14, 32.

55.   Bureau of Intelligence and Research, "Available Reports 1980 to Present," (Mimeo: Department of State, 1981).

56.   U.S. Congress, House Committee on Appropriations, *Departments of Commerce, Justice and State, the Judiciary and Related Agencies Appropriations for 1986, Part 7: Department of Justice* (Washington, D.C.: U.S. Government Printing Office, 1985), p. 492.

57.   Foreign Technology Division, FTD Pamphlet 23-4, *FTD: Mission, Organization and Key Personnel* (Wright-Patterson AFB, Ohio: FTD, December 1986), p. 17.

58.   Air University Special Bibliography No. 205, *Soviet Military Capabilities*, pp. 56, 79; Air University Special Bibliography No. 207, *Communist China: Military Capabilities*, p. 34; Air University Special Bibliography No. 205, Supplement 2, *Soviet Military Capabilities, Part I*, p. 51.

59.   Air University Special Bibliography No. 205, *Soviet Military Capabilities*, pp. 60, 86; Air University Special Bibliography No. 205, Supplement 2, *Soviet Military Capabilities, Part I*, pp. 30, 60.

60.   NISC Instruction 3120.1A, *NISC Organization and Regulations Manual*, November 15, 1985, p. 4-1.

61.   Ibid., pp. 4-2, 4-3, 4-8.

62.   Ibid., pp. 4-10 to 4-12, 4-16.

63.   *U.S. Army Foreign Science and Technology Center* (Charlottesville, Va.: FSTC, n.d.), p. 19.

64.   Air University Special Bibliography No. 207, *Communist China: Military Capabilities*, pp. 11, 14; Air University Special Bibliography No. 205, *Soviet Military Capabilities*, pp. 30, 61.

65.   Air University Special Bibliography No. 205, Supplement 1, *Soviet Military Capabilities*, pp. 21, 50, 56, 80; Air University Special Bibliography No. 205, Supplement 2, *Soviet Military Capabilities, Part I*, p. 52.

66.   Air University Special Bibliography No. 207, Supplement 1, *Communist China: Military Capabilities*, p. 6; Air University Special Bibliography No. 205, Supplement 2, *Soviet Military Capabilities, Part I*, pp. 5, 77; Air University Special Bibliography No. 205, Supplement 2, *Soviet Military Capabilities, Part II*, p. 9.

67.   Air University Special Bibliography No. 205, *Soviet Military Capabilities*, pp. 45, 56.

68.   Ibid.; Air University Special Bibliography No. 205, Supplement 2, *Soviet Military Capabilities, Part I*, pp. 18, 22, 24.

14 COUNTERINTELLIGENCE

Counterintelligence is a term often associated with catching spies. In fact, it is necessary to distinguish between offensive and defensive counterintelligence. It is not a perfect distinction but it is valid. Defensive counterintelligence, or counter-espionage, is basically concerned with detecting and apprehending agents and intelligence officers involved in espionage operations. Offensive counterintelligence is a more involved activity.

Counterintelligence was defined by President Reagan's Executive Order 12333 as both "information gathered" and "activities conducted," the purpose of which is "to protect against espionage, other intelligence activities, sabotage or assassination conducted on behalf of foreign powers, organizations or persons, or international terrorist activities but not including personnel, physical, documents or communications security."[1] Thus, as defined by this Executive Order, counterintelligence incorporates a wide range of activities not strictly in the counterintelligence tradition. The definition above essentially stresses the "counter" aspect and lets the term "intelligence" represent activities below the conventional military level. Some would also consider counterdeception and counterillicit technology transfer to be counterintelligence subcatagories.[2] Such a view essentially mixes traditional counterintelligence with positive intelligence designed to counter any form of hostile activity short of conventional military operations (e.g., terrorist attacks, illegal acquisition of advanced technology, sabotage) with a framework of analysis (counterdeception) for the analysis of positive intelligence.

The traditional notion of counterintelligence, the one that will be used here, focuses on counterintelligence as being information gathered and activities conducted with the purpose of disrupting and neutralizing the activities of hostile intelligence services. In this view there are four basic functions of counterintelligence activity:

- collection of information on foreign intelligence and security services through open and clandestine sources
- the evaluation of defectors
- research and analysis concerning the structure, personnel, and operations of foreign intelligence and security services
- disrupting and neutralizing the activities of hostile intelligence and security services.

COLLECTION

The information obtained concerning the activities of foreign intelligence and security services comes from a variety of sources.

Open sources provide information concerning friendly and hostile services. The open sources may include official government documents (e.g., telephone directories, yearly reports, parliamentary hearings, reports of commissions of inquiry), books, and articles in magazines and newspapers. Clearly, in the case of Soviet Bloc countries, open source material is limited—but analysts may get some useful insights into high-ranking personnel or some aspects of internal operations from the occasional government-approved account of security service operations.

Information about friendly services may also come from liaison and training arrangements. Thus, Dominic Perrone of the U.S. Military Liaison Office, U.S. Embassy Rome, was able, in 1978, to gather inside information on the effectiveness of the newly established Italian intelligence and security services (SISMI and SISDE) from several sources in the Italian government. As a result, Perrone was able to prepare a 4,000-word report for the DIA which indicated that the resources devoted to the SISDE's antiterrorist activities were making effective counterespionage impossible, that the Commander of SISDE was not qualified for the job, and that both the SISDE and the SISMI were performing poorly.[3]

Liaison with friendly services also provides information about the activities of hostile services, such as when the French Directorate for Surveillance of the Territory (DST) provided the CIA with information about its agent (FAREWELL) in Directorate T of the KGB. Beginning in 1981, FAREWELL provided the DST with more than 4,000 documents on Soviet scientific and technical espionage, including Soviet plans to steal Western technological secrets and Soviet assessments of the value of its covert, technology acquisition activities. Specifically, FAREWELL reportedly provided: (1) the complete, detailed list of all organizations involved in scientific and technical intelligence; (2) the plans, accomplishments, and savings every year in all branches of the military industry due to the illegal acquisition of foreign technology; (3) the list of all KGB officers, throughout the world, involved in scientific and technical espionage; and (4) the identity of principal agents recruited by the officers of "line X" in ten western nations, including the United States, West Germany, and France. At the July 1981 economic summit in Ottawa, President Mitterrand informed President Reagan about FAREWELL and provided a sample of intelligence material. Several weeks later, the head of the DST at the time, Marcel Chalet, visited Vice President Bush in Washington to discuss FAREWELL.[4]

Two types of human sources may provide useful counterintelligence information. On occasion, penetration of a hostile service may be attained. Penetration—having an agent inside a service—may be accomplished via a mole (someone recruited prior to their entry into the service) or a "defector in place" (someone who agrees to provide information after having attained an intelligence or security position). An individual may agree to provide information for ideological or financial reasons or as the result of coercion. Coercion or blackmail might be based on evidence of misbehavior (sexual or financial).

The United States has had some success in penetrating the Soviet military organization, the Chief Intelligence Directorate of the General Staff (GRU). In the late 1950s and early 1960s, Peter Popov and Oleg Penkovskiy, both Colonels in the GRU, volunteered their services to the CIA. In addition to providing detailed information concerning the structure of the GRU, they provided information on its physical layout and the identities and personalities of GRU agents. As noted in Chapter 10, GRU Colonel Anatoli Filatov also provided the CIA with information in the mid-1970s.

The CIA also apparently penetrated the Indian Research and Analysis Wing (RAW). In 1987, a senior RAW man, K.V. Unnikrishnan, was arrested and charged with spying for the CIA. Unnikrishnan, was reported to have been stationed in Madras, where he was responsible for coordinating Tamil insurgency activities. He was reportedly blackmailed with compromising photographs of himself and a "stewardess."[5]

A second type of human intelligence source is the defector. Defectors provide information concerning various aspects of an intelligence or security services structure, operations, and leadership. The CIA certainly reaped an intelligence bonanza when Major Bolanos Hunter of the Nicarguan Directorate General of State Security (Direccion General de Seguridad del Estado, DGSE) defected in 1983. For almost all of the period between January 1980 and May 7, 1983, Hunter had special responsibility for surveillance of the U.S. Embassy and CIA activities in Nicaragua. Hunter provided information on the structure of the DGSE, the numbers of Nicaraguans in the DGSE (2,000 to 3,000), the presence of foreign advisers to the DGSE (70 Soviets, 400 Cubans, 40 to 50 East Germans, 20 to 25 Bulgarians), and the Soviet provision of sophisticated bugging devices.[6]

Similarly, the defections of senior Cuban and Chinese intelligence officers have provided the United States with new information on those nations' intelligence and counterintelligence operations. In June 1987, Major Florentino Apillaga Lombard defected to the United States from the Cuban DGI (General Directorate of Intelligence) and proceeded to inform the CIA that the great majority of their "assets" in Cuba were actually double agents working for the Cuban government. In 1986 Yu Zhensan, the former head of the Foreign Affairs Bureau of the PRC's Ministry

Table 14–1. Soviet Intelligence Defectors.

Year	Defector	Employer
1945	Igor Gouzenko	GRU
1946	Anatoly Granovsky	NKVD
1954	Petr Deriabin	MGB
1954	Evdokia Petrov	MVD
1954	Vladimir Petrov	MVD
1954	Nikolai Kholokov	MGB
1957	Reino Hayhanen	KGB
1961	Bodgan Stashinsky	KGB
1962	Anatoli Golitsyn	KGB
1962	Yuri Nosenko	KGB
1968	Yvgeny Runge	KGB
1971	Oleg Lyalin	KGB
1971	Vladimir Sakharov	KGB
1972	Artush Hovanesian	KGB
1974	Aleksey Myagkov	KGB
1975	K.G. Nadirashvili	KGB
1978	Vladimir Rezun	GRU
1979	Stanislav Levchenko	KGB
1980	Ilya Dzhirkvelov	KGB
1982	Vladimir Kuzichkin	KGB
1984	Vadim Ivanov	KGB
1985	Sergei Bokhane	GRU
1985	Oleg Gordievsky	GRU
1985	Vitaly Yurchenko	KGB
1985	Viktor Gudarev	KGB
1986	Oleg Argraniants	KGB
n.a.	Rupert Sigl	KGB
n.a.	Alexsandr Sakharov	KGB
n.a.	Kaarlo Tuomi	KGB

Sources: Vladislov Krasnov, *Soviet Defectors: The KGB Wanted List* (Stanford, Ca.: Hoover Institution Press, 1986), pp. 178–199; assorted articles.

of State Security defected, and provided the United States with extensive information about Chinese intelligence operations abroad, including the names of Chinese agents and suspected agents from other nations working in China. Before defecting, he apparently provided the United States with information leading to the arrest of Larry Wu-Tai Chin, an employee of the CIA's Foreign Broadcast Information Service, and a long-term Chinese mole.[7]

Known defectors from the KGB and GRU are listed in Table 14–1, which indicates the substantial number of such defections since 1946. This large number of defectors has substantially aided the CIA in developing a comprehensive picture of those organizations' structures and activities.

Before his redefection, KGB official Vitaly Yurchenko provided the CIA with information concerning several penetrations of the U.S. intelligence community—a former CIA officer (Edward Lee Howard) and a former NSA employee (Ronald Pelton). He also stated that Pelton and naval spy John Walker were the KGB's most prized assets in the United States.[8]

In January 1986, it was reported that another KGB officer defected in 1985 and may have been the most valuable defector from the Soviet Bloc in recent years—providing far more information than provided by Yurchenko. The defector allegedly escaped from East Germany via helicopter in the spring of 1985. His reported expertise was in the area of KGB organization and procedures rather than ongoing operations. The existence of the alleged defector was adamantly denied by the White House and the CIA.[9]

In June 1986 it was reported that the head of KGB operations in North Africa and KGB liaison to the Palestine Liberation Organization, Oleg Agraniants, had defected to the United States. Agraniants, who may have been working for the CIA for the three years prior to his defection, apparently gave the United States the names of KGB agents in Tunisia, Algeria, Morocco, and Libya.[10]

EVALUATION OF DEFECTORS

The evaluation and debriefing of defectors is another important aspect of counterintelligence operations. The United States has provided political asylum to officials from the Soviet Union, China, Nicaragua, Cuba, and a number of East European countries. When the defector is not an intelligence officer debriefers will seek information on the policies and leaders of whatever government component employed the defector. In addition to eliciting information the debriefers also seek to determine the reliability of the information offered.

When the defector has been employed by a foreign intelligence service the debriefers will attempt to extract the maximum information on the structure, functions, agents, operations, procedures, and leaders of the defector's intelligence community, as well as to determine the defector's reliability. Debriefers will attempt to obtain as much information as soon as possible to allow action before the hostile intelligence service realizes its officer/agent has defected. A particular problem with defectors from hostile intelligence services is to determine where their knowledge ends and exaggeration or fabrication in the face of depleted information begins. Complicating the debriefers' task is the practice of many defectors of holding back information as insurance for continued protection.[11]

The inability of the CIA's Counterintelligence Staff to determine conclusively the bona fides of several important defectors was a vital factor in much of the conflict that divided the U.S. intelligence community for fifteen years. In addition to the problems of defector exaggeration and fabrication, there is the possibility that the defector is a plant—a hostile counterintelligence operator directed at the

CIA. A false defector might allege, for example, the existence of a highly placed mole. Thus, a high official of the British Security Service and its subsequent Director-General was at one point the subject of a KGB disinformation campaign, alleging that he was a Soviet agent. Such an allegation can lead to huge expenditures of resources spent chasing false leads. It can also damage the careers and reputations of effective intelligence officers, and cause a decline in the morale of the allegedly penetrated service.[12]

This was the case in the controversy that stemmed from the defection in 1962 of Anatoli Golitsin. Golitsin defected to the CIA from Helsinki, Finland. He identified himself as a Major in the First Chief Directorate of the KGB, working primarily against targets in the NATO alliance. Given the code-name AE/LADLE and the cover name John Stone by the United States (he was KAGO to the British and MARTEL to the French), Golitsin caused a sensation. According to Golitsin, the KGB had planted an agent within the highest echelons of U.S. intelligence. The penetration agent would be assisted by "outside" men—other Soviet-controlled agents masking as defectors or double agents—who would supply pieces of disinformation designed to bolster an "inside" man's credibility. The inside agent, in turn, would be in a position to help confirm the authenticity of the outside agent.[13]

During his debriefing sessions with Angleton in 1962, Stone had called particular attention to a trip made by V.M. Kovshuk to the United States in 1957. Kovshuk traveled under diplomatic cover, using the alias Komarov. Stone identified Kovshuk as the then-reigning head of the all-important American Embassy section of the KGB, and stressed that only an extremely important mission would account for his leaving his post in Moscow to come to the United States. He suggested that Kovshuk's mission might have involved contacting or activating a high-level Soviet penetration agent within the CIA who had been recruited years before in Moscow.[14]

Golitsin further cautioned that the KGB, realizing he knew about Kovshuk's mission, would almost certainly attempt to discredit or deflect the CIA from the information he was providing. Golitsin warned Angleton that Sovet disinformation agents could be expected to make contact with the CIA for this purpose. Six months later, Yuri Nosenko defected to the CIA. Nosenko's information ran counter to that of Golitsin in many instances, and tended to downplay the possibility of a Soviet penetration of the CIA. The explanation Nosenko gave concerning Soviet detection of Peter Popov stressed Soviet security measures. There were, however, several problems with Nosenko's story and bona fides that made him and his explanations suspect. Indeed, the extent of doubt about Nosenko led to his being incarcerated by the CIA for a period of three years until he was freed by Director Richard Helms.[15]

From the very beginning, Nosenko's story was confirmed by an FBI source code-named FEDORA. FEDORA was a Soviet intelligence agent working under diplomatic cover at the United Nations; he had contacted FBI officials in March 1962 with information about Soviet intelligence operations, just weeks after Golitsin's defection. FEDORA claimed to be an officer of the KGB's First Chief Directorate who was disaffected with the Soviets, and offered to supply the FBI with secret information on Soviet missile capability and nuclear development plans.[16]

FEDORA also confirmed that Nosenko was indeed a Lt. Colonel in the KGB (a point of dispute), with access to extraordinarily valuable information, and had indeed received a recall telegram from Moscow ordering him back on February 4 (Nosenko's claimed reason for defecting). FEDORA also apparently told the FBI that Daniel Ellsberg had delivered a copy of the Pentagon Papers to the Soviet Embassy.[17]

FEDORA's veracity eventually came to be doubted by the FBI. Nosenko admitted that he was not a Lt. Colonel but a Captain. In addition the NSA was not able to detect any indication of the telegram that Nosenko and FEDORA claimed to have prompted his defection. In addition, Daniel Ellsberg never delivered a copy of the Pentagon Papers to the Soviet Embassy. The acid test in the view of the FBI was what FEDORA would do when his retirement came in 1981. His return to the Soviet Union seemed to confirm that he had been under Soviet control all along.[18]

In the case of Vitaly Yurchenko, the CIA Conterintelligence Staff was faced with assessing whether he was a legitimate defector who changed his mind or a plant who intended to redefect from the beginning. Yurchenko, a KGB staff officer with twenty-five years of service, requested political asylum in the United States at the American Embassy in Rome on August 1, 1985.[19]

In 1960, Yurchenko was transferred from the Soviet Navy to the KGB's Third Chief Directorate; from 1961 to 1965 and from August 1967 until December 1968 he worked as an operations officer and the Deputy Chief in the KGB Special Department for the Black Sea Fleet. From December 1968 to May 1972 he was assigned to the KGB residency in Egypt as a Soviet adviser to the staff of the Egyptian fleet in Alexandria. From May 1972 to May 1975 he was Deputy Chief of the Third (Intelligence) Department of the Third Chief Directorate, responsible—among other things—for the recruitment of foreigners using the resources of Soviet military counterintelligence, as well as the insertion of agents into Western intelligence services.[20]

From August 1975 to August 1980, Yurchenko was the security officer at the Soviet Embassy in Washington. He was responsible for ensuring the security of Soviet establishments and citizens in Washington, protecting classified information, and handling foreign visitors. In September 1980 he was transferred to the First Chief Directorate. From that date until March 1985 he was Chief of the Fifth Department of Directorate K, responsible for the investigation of suspected espionage incidents involving KGB staff personnel, investigation of information leaks concerning the First Chief Directorate, and other security functions. From April to July 1985 he was Deputy Chief of the First Department, whose operations are directed against the United States and Canada.[21]

Three months after his defection, Yurchenko appeared at a press conference at the Soviet Embassy in Washington, claiming to have been kidnapped, drugged, and kept in isolation at a CIA safe house in Fredricksburg, Virginia. His "escape," according to Yurchenko, was due to a "momentary lapse" by his captors. (In fact, he walked out of a Georgetown restaurant without opposition from his CIA escort). Two days later, Yurchenko, after a visit by U.S. officials to determine he was acting of his own free will, took off for Moscow. Back in Moscow, he held a two-hour press conference at which he and other Soviet officials accused the United States of "state terrorism." Subsequent reports that he had been executed were proved incorrect when he was discovered walking on a Moscow street.[22]

Yurchenko's redefection resulted in questions being raised concerning the CIA's handling of defectors, as well as whether Yurchenko was in fact a defector who changed his mind or a plant who was going to redefect from the beginning. Motives for such an operation were alleged to run from gathering information on CIA treatment and debriefing of defectors, to a desire to embarrass the CIA and discourage CIA acceptance of defectors. Among those suggesting that Yurchenko was a plant were President Reagan, Senator Patrick Leahy (then Vice-Chairman of the Senate Select Committee on Intelligence) and other officials who considered Yurchenko's information to be largely "historical."[23]

Explanations for his actual change of heart involve his rejection by the wife of a Soviet official stationed in Canada with whom Yurchenko had had a relationship and visited almost immediately after his arrival in the United States, the great publicity generated by his defection, a general homesickness for "Mother Russia" often experienced by Soviet defectors, and a specific longing to be reunited with his family—especially his sixteen-year old son. Among those doubting a staged defection was FBI Chief William H. Webster, who said that Yurchenko provided the United States with valuable information concerning Soviet espionage activities—including the roles of Edward Lee Howard and Ronald Pelton.[24]

RESEARCH AND ANALYSIS

It is fundamental to both intelligence and counterintelligence missions that there exists a store of knowledge concerning the personalities, past operations, structure, and activities of other nations' intelligence and security services. Only with such knowledge can positive intelligence collection operations be planned and conducted effectively. Likewise, only with such knowledge can effective penetration and disruption, and neutralization activities be conducted.

The most significant research and analysis on foreign intelligence services conducted within the U.S. intelligence community are those prepared by the CIA's Counterintelligence Staff (CIS). The CIS prepares reports ranging from 50 to 100 pages on all intelligence communities of interest—hostile and friendly. Until recently at least, each report bore the name of the country and the subtitle "Foreign Intelligence and Security Services." The reports detailed the origins of the intelligence services, their structure, function, and mode of operation, and the arrangements for control by higher authority.

Thus, the forty-seven page study *Israel: Foreign Intelligence and Security Services*, published in March 1979, focused in its first section on the background and development of the Israeli services, objectives and structure, the relationship between the government and the services, and professional standards. The second, third, and fourth sections each focused on one of the three major Israeli intelligence and security units—the MOSSAD, Shin Bet, and Military Intelligence. In each case, the report examined the function, organization, administrative practice (including training), and methods of operation of the services. Additionally, liaison with other Israeli and foreign services was considered. The final four sections examined the Foreign Ministry's Research and Political Planning Center, the National Police, key officials, and comments on principal sources. The contents of the study are shown as Table 14–2.

A 1984 CIA study, titled *Soviet Intelligence: KGB and GRU*, discussed the background and development of the Soviet services, national intelligence objectives and structure, the relationship between the Communist Party/government and the services, internal security and counterintelligence operations of the KGB and the foreign clandestine operations of the KGB and GRU.

Likewise, the Air Force Office of Special Investigations (AFOSI) prepares studies on a variety of nations' intelligence services (listed in Table 14–3) as well as selected aspects of hostile intelligence operations. The April 1977 AFOSI report on "The Czecholslovak Intelligence Services" discusses the political aspects, headquarters structure and functions, targets and modus operandi, staff training, liaison and staffing abroad and includes a case history. A January 1975 AFOSI study on "Soviet Overt Intelligence Collections in the United States" discusses the role of Soviet official residents, exchange programs, commercial representatives, tourists in the overt collection of intelligence, and the type of material collected.[25]

In addition to focusing on the intelligence communities of particular countries, other AFOSI reports focus on the hostile intelligence establishments in foreign countries. Thus, the "Hostile Intelligence Establishment in Japan" discusses the threat to the U.S. military, the hostile establishments and Japanese internal security, the Soviet, Cuban, PRC and other hostile establishments, personnel, targets, modus operandi, and a case study—"Foyo Kyodo: A Case of Soviet Commercial Cover."[26] Table 14–4 lists some *AFOSI Hostile Intelligence Establishment Reports.*

Counterintelligence studies are also prepared by the Defense Intelligence Agency and the Army's Intelligence and Threat Analysis Center. The DIA prepared a November 15, 1978 study entitled *Italy: Reorganization of Intelligence and Security Services,* which discussed the background, present intelligence and security service structure, key intelligence and security service personalities, intelligence reforms, and the outlook for the future. The studies prepared by the ITAC include: *Italy: A Counterintelligence Assessment* (April 1984), which reviewed the various intelligence and security services of the Italian government and various types of threats including terrorism, wartime sabotage, and espionage; *The DST: An Organization in Flux* (September 1986); *France: A Counterintelligence Assessment* (June 1981); and *Israel's Shin Bet Scandal* (June 1986).[27]

Table 14–2. Table of Contents for Israel: Foreign Intelligence and Security Services.

SECRET
NOFORN/NOCONTRACT/ORCORN

TABLE OF CONTENTS

Table 14–2. continued

Table 14–3. AFOSI Special Reports on Foreign Intelligence and Security Services.

The Czechoslovak Intelligence Services	April 1977
The Polish Intelligence Services	December 1976
Hungarian Intelligence Services	June 1975
East German Intelligence Services	June 1975
Romanian Intelligence Services	June 1975
The North Korean Intelligence Services: A Case Study	August 1977
Bulgarian Intelligence Services	June 1975
The Soviet Intelligence Services	September 1978
The NKIS: Mission and Structure	April 1974

Sources: Documents obtained under the Freedom of Information Act; Fleet Marine Force Pacific Order 3850.1B, "Counterintelligence Contingency Materials," March 14, 1983.

Table 14–4. Air Force OSI Hostile Intelligence Establishment Reports.

The Hostile Intelligence Establishment in Italy, January 1975.
The Hostile Intelligence Establishment in the Federal Republic of Germany, April 1975.
The Hostile Intelligence Establishment in France, November 1975.
The Hostile Intelligence Establishment in Japan, August 1977.
The Hostile Intelligence Establishment in the United Kingdom, November 1977.

NEUTRALIZATION

The neutralization of the activities of hostile intelligence services can be accomplished by various means. Penetrations of a hostile service can be used not only to gather information but to damage the service's operations.

In 1980, the Polish civilian intelligence and security service, the SB, began receiving classified information from James D. Harper, a Silicon Valley engineer. Harper, via his wife, who worked for a southern California defense contractor, obtained copies of well over 100 pounds of classified reports—which he sold to the SB for over $250,000. Most of the documents pertained to the U.S. Minuteman missile and ballistic missile defense programs and were classified Confidential or Secret. Documents sold to the SB included the 1978 *Minuteman Defense Study (Final Report)*, the 1981 *Report on the Task Force on U.S. Ballistic Missile Defense*, and a 1978 Martin-Marietta Corporation study entitled *Endoatmospheric Nonnuclear Kill Technology Requirements and Definition Study*. Harper was detected by a CIA penetration of the SB. When arrested he was preparing to deliver an additional 150 to 200 pounds of documents.[28]

A second means of neutralization is the passing of information to a third country which leads it to take action against the officers and agents of a hostile service. In many cases the CIA's passing of such information will be a natural result of liaison with a friendly security service—such as when the CIA provides the British Security Service with information on East German intelligence operations in the United Kingdom. When GRU officer Sergei Bokhane, who had been stationed in Greece, defected, he provided information on at least three Greeks involved in spying for the Soviet Union. Included was Michael Megalokonomos, who when picked up was in possession of a code book, microfilm reading device, radio (for picking up special frequencies) and instructions on how to work a radio transmitter. Also named by Bokhane was Nikos Pipitsoulis, who sold an electrical device to Soviet officials for $43,000. In addition, a Lt. Commander working in the data processing unit at Greece's defense headquarters was also involved in passing information to the Soviet Union. The information provided to the CIA by Bokhane was passed on to Greek security authorities, leading to the arrest of the three agents.[29]

On other occasions the recipient of the information may itself be a hostile nation. In the spring of 1983, when the Iranian Communist (Tudeh) Party had been closed down, the CIA provided a list of Soviet agents and collaborators operating in Iran to the Khomeini regime and its security service (SAVAMA). The result was 18 Soviet diplomats expelled, 200 suspects executed, and the imprisonment of Tudeh Party leaders.[30]

Another means of neutralization is through the running of double agents. One CIA double agent operation that came to light is one that backfired.

In 1959, Captain Nikolai Federovich Artamanov, the youngest commanding officer of a destroyer in Soviet naval history, defected to Sweden. Information about Armanatov was transferred to the United States by the CIA Station Chief in Sweden.[31]

Artamanov was subsequently recruited by the Office of Naval Intelligence (ONI) to come to the United States. In his debriefing he provided the ONI with information on Soviet use of AGIs (intelligence trawlers), Soviet nuclear strategy, and Soviet destroyer tactics against submarines. Subsequent to the debriefing, he was given a new name, Nicholas Shadrin, and a position as a translator in the Naval Scientific and Technical Intelligence Center (now the Naval Intelligence Support Center). In 1966 two events of importance occurred. Shadrin went to work for the Defense Intelligence Agency, and was also approached by a Soviet intelligence officer who tried to recruit him. Shadrin did not close the door on the officer but reported it to the FBI. After initial hesitation, Shadrin was persuaded to become a double agent, to "accept" the Soviet offer and feed the KGB CIA-doctored disinformation.[32]

Among the reasons for U.S. pressure on Shadrin to accept the double agent role is that his recruiter, "Igor," was believed to be a Soviet defector-in-place whose assigned mission was the recruitment of Shadrin. Successful completion of his mission, said Igor, would propel him to the Chief of the KGB's American Department.[33]

After several years of working for the KGB, Shadrin began to make trips abroad to meet his controller. He never returned from a December 20, 1975 meeting in Vienna. According to temporary defector Vitaly Yurchenko, Shadrin was, by accident, fatally chloroformed while struggling in the back seat of a sedan with Soviet agents who were trying to spirit him out of Austria.[34]

The military, particularly the Army, also runs double agent operations. According to U.S. Army Regulation 381-47, offensive counterintelligence operations, such as double agent operations

> . . . may require engagement in unorthodox operations and activities. These unorthodox activities may be at variance with recognized standards or methods normally associated with the military Service. They will be undertaken only when authorized by the commander of a counterintelligence unit or higher authority.[35]

Double agent operations are often initiated after a U.S. serviceman reports an approach made by a foreign intelligence officer. In 1984 there were 481 incidents of soldiers being approached by people suspected of being Soviet Bloc intelligence officers or sympathizers.[36]

Under the direction of counterintelligence authorities, the servicemen will maintain contact with a foreign intelligence officer, providing a combination of factual low-level and false high-level information provided by INSCOM, the Naval Investigative and Security Command, or the Air Force Office of Special Investigations. Such operations yield information on the intelligence targets of hostile services; allow identification of the intelligence officers and agents of hostile services; tie up hostile service resources; and permit the transmission of disinformation concerning the plans and capabilities of U.S. military forces. The INSCOM agents involved in such operations bear code names such as ROYAL MITER, LANCER FLAG, HOLE PUNCH, LARIAT TOSS, CANARY DANE, and LANDSCAPE BREEZE.[37]

One operation involved Chief Warrant Officer Janos Szmolka, who had left Hungary to become an American citizen. Szmolka eventually joined the Army and was stationed in West Germany, from where he went on authorized leaves to Budapest to visit his mother in 1978 and 1979. On his third trip he was approached by a man described as a Hungarian intelligence officer who offered to insure that Szmolka's family had better living conditions in exchange for information.[38]

Szmolka returned to West Germany and reported the offer to his superiors. For the next four years, under the direction of Army counterintelligence officers, he was in contact with Hungarian agents in Europe and in the United States, where he was transferred in 1980 under normal rotation procedures. In 1982 the Army desired to uncover the Hungarian intelligence network in the United States, and Szmolka was instructed to inform the Hungarians, through coded letters, that he had valuable information to turn over. On April 17, 1982, he went to the Confederate monument in Augusta, Georgia, near his post at Ft. Gordon, to meet a Hungarian agent. Federal agents arrested Otto A. Gilbert, an expatriate Hungarian and naturalized U.S. citizen, and charged him with espionage. Gilbert received a reduced sentence in exchange for information about Hungarian intelligence.[39]

Neutralization may also involve prevention of the bugging of U.S. facilities. An operation code-named GUNMAN involved "rolling up [the] KGB...operation that had planted sophisticated bugs in the typewriters of the U.S. Embassy in Moscow."[40]

NOTES TO CHAPTER 14

1. Ronald Reagan, "Executive Order 12333, United States Intelligence Activities," *Federal Register 46*, no. 235 (December 8, 1981); 59941-55 at 59953.
2. For example, see William Harris, "Counterintelligence Jurisdiction and the Double Cross System by National Technical Means," in Roy Godson, ed., *Intelligence Requirements for 1980s: Counterintelligence* (New Brunswick, N.J.: Transactions, 1980), pp. 53-82.
3. Dominic Perrone, "I&SS, Status of SISDE/SISMI Anti-Terrorist Orientation," *Covert Action Information Bulletin* (April-May 1979) pp. 6-9.
4. Thierry Wolton, *Le KGB en France* (Paris: Bernard Grasset, 1986), pp. 248-49.
5. Inderjit Badhwar, "Spy-Catching," *India Today*, September 20, 1987, p. 33.
6. Don Oberdorfer and Joanne Omang, "Nicaraguan Bares Plan to Discredit Foes," *Washington Post*, June 19, 1983, pp. 1, 4.
7. Jack Anderson and Dale Van Atta, "Cuban Defector Impeaches CIA Spies," *Washington Post*, March 21, 1988, p. B15; Jack Anderson and Dale Van Atta, "CIA Recruits Were Castro's Agents," *Washington Post*, March 23, 1988, p. D11; Jack Anderson and Dale Van Atta, "CIA, Cubans in Looking-Glass War," *Washington Post*, March 25, 1988, p. E5; "Chinese Official Said Exposer of CIA Turncoat," *Washington Post*, September 5, 1986, p. A18; Michael Wines, "Spy Reportedly Unmasked by China Defector," *Los Angeles Times*, September 5, 1986, pp. 1, 12; Daniel Southerland, "China Silent on Reported Defection of Intelligence Official," *Washington Post*, September 4, 1986, p. A30.

8. "Did Yurchenko Fool the CIA?," *Newsweek*, November 18, 1985, pp. 34–39.

9. Philip Shenon, "High K.G.B. Officer is Said to Defect," *New York Times*, January 26, 1986, pp. A1, A18; Lou Cannon and Patrick Tyler, "KGB Defector Report Flatly Denied," *Washington Post*, January 28, 1986, p. A10.

10. "High-Ranking KGB Agent Defects," *Washington Post*, June 20, 1986, p. A5.

11. Ralph Blumenthal, "Moscow Moves Rapidly In Defections to the U.S.," *New York Times*, November 7, 1985, p. A12.

12. For details of the Soviet campaign against Michael Hanley, see Nigel West, *Molehunt: The Full Story of the Soviet Spy in MI5* (London: Weidenfeld and Nicolson, 1987), p. 45.

13. Edward Jay Epstein, *Legend: The Secret World of Lee Harvey Oswald* (New York: McGraw-Hill, 1978), p. 27.

14. Ibid., pp. 46–47; 264–65; David C. Martin, *Wilderness of Mirrors* (New York: Harper & Row, 1980), p. 110.

15. Thomas Powers, *The Man Who Kept the Secrets: Richard Helms and the CIA* (New York: Knopf, 1979), p. 284.

16. Epstein, *Legend*, p. 20.

17. "Tale of a Double Agent," *Newsweek*, September 14, 1981, p. 25.

18. Ibid.

19. Central Intelligence Agency, "Vitaly Sergeyevich Yurchenko," November 8, 1985, p. 1.

20. Ibid., pp. 1–2.

21. Ibid., pp. 2–3.

22. "Did Yurchenko Fool the CIA?;" Celestine Bohlen, "Yurchenko Regales Moscow Audience," *Washington Post*, November 15, 1985, p. A33; "How Yurchenko Bade C.I.A. Adieu," *New York Times*, November 7, 1985, p. A12; Stephen Engelberg, "U.S. Is Convinced that K.G.B. Agent Wants to Go Home," *New York Times*, November 6, 1985, pp. A1, A12.

23. "Did Yurchenko Fool the CIA?;" Stephen Engelberg, "President Sees a Soviet 'Ploy' in 3 Defections," *New York Times*, November 7, 1985, pp. A1, A12; Stephen Engelberg, "Washington Ponders Yurchenko: A Troubled Spy or Actor?," *New York Times*, November 10, 1985, p. 20; Bob Woodward, "CIA Takes Serious Look at Theory that Yurchenko Was Double Agent," *Washington Post*, November 20, 1985, p. A35; Stephen Engelberg, "U.S. Aides Split on Yurchenko's Authenticity," *New York Times*, November 8, 1985, p. A10.

24. John Mintz, "FBI Chief Doubts Defection of Yurchenko Was Staged," *Washington Post*, December 2, 1985, pp. A1, A14; Joel Brinkley, "Publicity Said to Have Upset Defector," *New York Times*, November 14, 1985, p. A12; Christopher S. Wren, "K.G.B. Man Reportedly Met with Envoy's Wife," *New York Times*, November 9, 1985, p. 4; Arkady N. Shevchenko, "A Lesson of the Yurchenko Affair," *New York Times*, November 12, 1985, p. 35; Dale Russakof, "In Yurchenko Case, Truth Remains a Covert Factor," *Washington Post*, November 10, 1985, pp. A1, A40–41.

25. Documents obtained under the Freedom of Information Act.

26. Air Force Office of Special Investigations, "The Hostile Intelligence Establishment in Japan," August 1977, p. 1.

27. Documents obtained under the Freedom of Information Act.

28.   "Partners in Espionage," *Security Awareness Bulletin* (August 1984): 1–8; Linda Melvern, David Hebditch, and Nick Anning, *Techno-Bandits: How the Soviets Are Stealing America's High Tech Future* (Boston: Houghton Mifflin, 1984), p. 242; Affidavit of Allen M. Power, Federal Bureau of Investigation, submitted to State and Northern District of California, City and County of San Francisco, October 16, 1983, pp. 1–2; "For Love of Money and Adventure," *Time*, October 31, 1983, pp. 39–40; Howard Kurtz, "California Man Charged with Spying," *Washington Post*, October 18, 1983, pp. A1, A4; David Wise, "How Our Spy Spied Their Spy," *Los Angeles Times*, October 23, 1983, pp. 1–6.

29.   "Greece Charges Three As Spies After U.S. Tip," *Washington Post*, September 17, 1985, p. A29.

30.   Bob Woodward and Dan Morgan, "Soviet Threat Toward Iran Overstated, Casey Concluded," *Washington Post*, January 13, 1987, pp. A1, A8.

31.   Henry Hurt, *Shadrin: The Spy who Never Came Back* (New York: McGraw-Hill, 1981), p. 52.

32.   Ibid., pp. 52–82; 140–51.

33.   Ibid., pp. 120–51.

34.   Ibid., p. 206; Patrick E. Tyler, "Missing U.S. Agent Dead," *Washington Post*, October 30, 1985, p. A9.

35.   AR 381-47, "U.S. Army Offensive Counterintelligence Operations," May 15, 1982, p. 7.

36.   Richard Halloran, "Overtures to Soldiers to Spy for Soviet Bloc Said to Rise," *New York Times*, June 29, 1985, pp. A1, B5.

37.   "Former Counterspy for Army is Indicted on Subversion Charges," *New York Times*, April 10, 1984, p. A20.

38.   Halloran, "Overtures to Soldiers to Spy for Soviet Bloc Said to Rise."

39.   Ibid.

40.   Robert E. Lamb, "Embassy Espionage: New Awareness of an Old Problem," *American Politics* (July 1987): 23, 32.

15 COVERT ACTION

Traditionally, covert action, which has often been the most visible aspect of U.S. intelligence activity, involves activities designed to influence foreign governments, events, organizations, or persons in support of U.S. foreign policy in such a way that the involvement of the U.S. government is not apparent. In recent years the notion of the "overt covert operation" has emerged—the clear example being U.S. aid to those seeking to overthrow the Sandinista government in Nicaragua.

U.S. covert actions have taken place in all major (and many minor) areas of the world: Europe and the Soviet Union, Africa, the Middle East, Asia, and Latin America. The operations have included: (1) political advice and counsel; (2) subsidies to an individual; (3) financial support and technical assistance to political parties; (4) support to private organizations, including labor unions and business firms; (5) covert propaganda; (6) training of individuals; (7) economic operations; (8) paramilitary or political action operations designed to overthrow or support a regime; and (9) attempted assassination.[1]

Many of these operations, such as paramilitary or political action operations, have had high visibility and have been designed to achieve a specific objective, for example, the overthrow of a regime or defeat of an insurgent force. Many behind-the-scenes political support and propaganda activities were also designed to achieve a specific objective, the electoral defeat or victory of a political candidate or party. Such low-visibility operations were conducted for an extended period of time in Italy. Other low-visibility operations involving propaganda or aid to individuals or organizations were less directed towards achieving a specific objective than to the long-term enhancement of U.S. objectives and the provision of a counter to similar Soviet activities. A high-visibility operation might also be conducted without expectation of "success." When the United States began aiding the Afghan rebels, there was no expectation of actually inducing Soviet withdrawal, only of draining Soviet resources and keeping international attention focused on the Soviet role in the country.

HISTORY

The initial U.S. covert actions taken in Europe were low-visibilty operations with a specific goal—prevention of a Communist victory in Italy. On December 20, 1947, a special procedures group was set up to organize propaganda in Italy, and it continued to initiate projects until its functions were taken over by the newly created Office of Policy Coordination (OPC). Ten million dollars was secretly taken from the economic stabilization fund and used to pay for local election campaigns, anti-Communist propaganda, and bribes. The covert operation was coupled with Italian-American lobbying and dire threats by President Truman about reductions in aid if the Communists won. In the 1948 election the Christian Democrats gained an overall majority of forty seats.[2]

In France, CIA covert action had two objectives: the reduction of Communist party influence, especially in the unions, and the influencing of French opinion behind the European Defense Community. The CIA assisted in the moderate Force Ouvriere's splitting away from the Communist-dominated CGT labor union. Aid was also given to the Catholic CFTC labor union and several other non-Communist groups.[3]

In Eastern Europe and the Soviet Union, CIA-supported resistance groups committed sabotage and assisted in developing escape and evasion networks. The earliest operation involved the establishment of guerrilla networks in countries surrounding the Soviet Union in case of a Soviet invasion. Additionally, the OPC supported Polish resistance groups operating south of Warsaw, while pumping money and arms into Lithuania and the Ukraine to assist resistance groups. These operations ended by the mid-1950s. The Polish resistance organization turned out to have been under the control of Polish security forces, while the Soviet forces demolished the Ukranian resistance by 1953.[4]

The CIA has been involved in numerous covert actions in Latin America, frequently of the high-visibility variety and with a specific objective in mind—a change in government or the death of a leader. The earliest major operation was targeted against the leftist government of Guatemala. The United States created, trained, funded, and directed a paramilitary force that succeeded, in 1954, in overthrowing the leftist government of Jacobo Arbenz. The regime was alleged to be Communist-dominated and had alienated the powerful United Fruit Compay with its social welfare legislation, including minimum wage rates, strict tax laws, and land redistribution.[5]

Cuba was the target of an intense covert action campaign, beginning shortly after Castro's rise to power in 1959. Before the Eisenhower Administration had left office it had trained Cuban exiles and developed plans for an invasion of Cuba. Those efforts culminated in the Kennedy Administration's first foreign policy disaster, the Bay of Pigs landing of April 17, 1961.[6]

The assassination of Castro was timed to coincide with the Bay of Pigs landing. At the behest of the CIA, Robert Maheu, an official of Howard Hughes' Summa Corporation, recruited mobster Johnny Rosselli to kill Castro. Several other attempts followed. A former employee of the Cuban Treasury Ministry was brought to Florida, trained to make the "hit," and then infiltrated back into Cuba. On September 24, 1961, the Cuban government announced that it had discovered the plot. In September 1963 Major Roland Cubela, a Castro official, offered to kill Castro for the CIA. Cubela was meeting CIA officials in Paris at the very time John Kennedy was assassinated.[7]

After the Bay of Pigs, a new set of Cuban operations were undertaken. On November 30, 1961, a memorandum instructed that the program "use our available assets...to help overthrow the Communist regime." The operations were to be part of Operation MONGOOSE. The first planned mission, the demolition of a railroad yard and a bridge on Cuba's north coast, was aborted when the boat carrying the saboteurs was spotted. Other operations involved pressuring European shippers to turn down Cuban consignments, persuading a German ball bearing manufacturer to send off-center bearings to Cuba, and sabotaging Leyland buses Cuba had ordered that were on the London docks.[8]

Operation MONGOOSE was terminated in January 1963, only to be followed by a new set of operations. On June 19, 1963 President Kennedy authorized an escalated program of sabotage in Cuba. Targets included petroleum facilities, railroad and highway transportation, and electric power communication facilities. The anti-Castro Movement for the Recovery of the Revolution (MRR) was revived and soon received $250,000 a month to launch a campaign, known as Second Naval Guerrilla. The purpose of this operation was to attack Cuban shipping and mount commando raids on shore installations. The CIA would supply the funding, logistical support, intelligence data, and guidance. The MRR would function "independently" of the CIA but submit each proposed operation to the CIA for approval.[9]

In addition to the high-visibility operations, with both specific and nonspecific objectives, low-visibility operations were also conducted. Forgeries of various kinds were employed. The Cuban Consul in Buenos Aires resigned unexpectedly after having held his post through previous Cuban administrations. He took eighty-two documents from the Cuban Embassy safe and turned them over to the Cuban Revolutionary Council (CRC) in Miami. The documents detailed a master plan, allegedly devised in Cuba, for the overthrow of Argentina's Frondizi government via infiltrating business and politics and training guerillas.[10]

The CRC held onto the documents so it could use them to maximum advantage during the Argentine President's state visit to the United States. The week before the Argentinian chief of state left, however, *La Nacion* of Buenos Aires ran a long article that was accompanied by photocopies of the documents and resulted in a clamorous protest against Cuba. The Cubans claimed that the documents had been forged by Cuban exiles working in collusion with the CIA, which was true. The forgery was the beginning of a campaign aimed at "documenting" that Castro was exporting revolution by subverting nations in the Organization of American States (OAS), so Cuba would be ousted from the OAS.[11]

Prior to the Reagan Administration, the most dramatic recent instance of CIA covert action in Latin America occurred in Chile. The 1973 coup against Salvador Allende ended a long series of covert action operations that sought to prevent Allende from coming to power or remove him once he assumed power. The CIA worked secretly in 1958 and 1964 to block Allende's election to the presidency. In 1964, the CIA spent over $2.6 million in support of Chile's Christian Democratic party. The candidate, Eduardo Frei, was victorious, with 56 percent of the total vote.[12]

In the next presidential election, Allende was again a candidate, competing with a Christian Democrat and a right-wing candidate, and the CIA was again involved in attempting to prevent his election. Despite a variety of media and propaganda operations as well as continued support for the Christian candidate, Allende emerged as the plurality winner with 36 percent of the vote. Since Allende failed to obtain an absolute majority, the final choice had to be determined by a joint vote of the 50 Senators and 100 members of the Chamber of Deputies. Traditionally, Chile's Congress confirmed the plurality winner as President.

In the wake of Allende's victory, the U.S. government explored a variety of options to block his accession to power. On September 15, 1970, President Nixon informed CIA Director Richard Helms that an Allende regime was unacceptable to the United States, and instructed the CIA to play a role in organizing a military coup that would prevent Allende from ever taking office. The subsequent campaign proceeded on two tracks. Under Track I (which was approved by the interagency 40 Committee, which was responsible for supervising covert operations), the CIA employed a variety of covert political, economic, and propaganda tactics to manipulate the political scene. This Track included the allocation of $25,000 to bribe members of the Chilean Congress, money that was never spent. Other CIA funds were spent in a strident propaganda campaign. In addition, efforts were made to create financial and political panic sufficient to produce a military coup. Helms's instructions from Nixon had been to "make the economy scream," and multinationals were approached to take such actions as cutting off aid to Chile, stopping the shipments of spare parts and causing runs on financial institutions.[13]

Track II involved direct efforts to produce a military coup; neither the State Department nor the 40 Committee was informed about such activities. Helms was told that at least $10 million would be available to do the job. The CIA proceeded to make twenty-one contacts in two weeks with key Chilean military personnel to assure them that the United States would support a coup d'etat. The main obstacle to such a coup was Chief of Staff General Rene Schneider, a strong supporter of the Chilean military's tradition of non-intervention in political affairs. Fearing the weight Schneider's dissent would carry, the CIA passed three submachine guns and ammunition to Chilean officers planning to abduct the General. In the third kidnap attempt, on October 22, 1970, General Schneider was mortally wounded. The Senate's Church Committee later found that the guns used in the abortive kidnapping were probably not those supplied by the CIA.[14]

Allende was confirmed as President on October 24, 1970. Track II, however continued. The CIA was instructed to "stay alert and to do what we could to contribute to the objectives and purposes of Track II." In the aftermath of Allende's inauguration, the CIA operated in several key areas. It spent an additional $1.5 million in support of the opposition newsletter *El Mercurio*. Financial support was given to labor unions and trade associations with the intention of encouraging economic, and thus political, disorder. It has been suggested that the economically crippling truckers' strikes of 1972 and 1973 were supported by the CIA.[15]

Probably the most successful CIA covert action, in the short term, was Operation AJAX. AJAX was the U.S.-British response to the 1951 nationalization of the Anglo-Iranian Oil Company by Prime Minister Mossadegh. AJAX—the plan for toppling Mossadegh—was first proposed to the British government by the Anglo-Iranian Oil Company nine months after the nationalization.[16]

The British Secret Intelligence Service (SIS) then approached the CIA with the plan in November 1952. The plan ultimately involved the organization of pro-Shah gangs with clubs, knives, and occasionally a rifle or pistol. CIA representative Kermit Roosevelt was approached by the Anglo-Iranian Oil Company and met the SIS spokesman for AJAX, Deputy Director General John Sinclair. It was explained to Roosevelt that AJAX involved the overthrow of Mossadegh and that the British desired to begin the operation immediately.[17]

SIS officials traveled to Washington in December 1952 and February 1953. The first meeting involved purely operational discussions; the February 1953 delegation attended a series of formal planning meetings at which CIA Director Allen Dulles was also present. At these meetings the British briefed the CIA on the capabilities of their principal agents and gave their assessment of the Army and the loyalty of the population. Dulles gave his support to AJAX, and plans were developed to attain the AJAX objective with the British government and the SIS as the "driving force."[18]

While the SIS was the driving force, Kermit Roosevelt was selected as overall commander of the operation, at British suggestion. In conducting the operation Roosevelt relied on both U.S. and British agents the SIS turned over to Roosevelt. At Roosevelt's instruction the Shah fired Mossadegh, named General Fazollah Zahedi premier and let the CIA do the rest. Up to 6,000 pro-Shah rioters were turned out by the CIA, and full-scale rioting broke out on August 18–19, 1953, followed by an attack by pro-Shah tank units on Mossadegh's residence.[19]

Two African nations that have been the subjects of intensive covert action operations have been Zaire and Angola. Covert action in Zaire resulted from the June 30, 1960 grant of independence to the Belgian Congo under a democratic coalition government headed by "militant nationalist" Patrice Lumumba. Shortly after independence, the Congolese army mutinied; Belgian troops reoccupied part of the country and helped to organize the secession of Katanga province. The Prime

Minister, Lumumba. and Chief of State Joseph Kasavubu called in U.N. forces to help reorganize the army and remove the Belgians. The United Nations, with U.S. approval, delayed and secessionist pressures against the Lumumba government began to mount.[20]

U.S. policymakers viewed with alarm Lumumba's threats to expel the U.N. force (except for African left-nationalist contingents) and to invade Katanga with Afro-Asian and Soviet military assistance. On August 18 the Station Chief in the Congo cabled CIA headquarters that

> Embassy and Station believe Congo experiencing classic Communist takeover government. . .Whether or not Lumumba is actually Commie or just playing Commie games to assist in his solidifying power, anti-west forces rapidly increasing power Congo and there may be little time left in which to take action to avoid another Cuba.[21]

In light of those reports, President Eisenhower approved an agenda of covert action measures, possibly including assassination. The CIA station began covert operations through labor groups and attempted to arrange a no confidence vote against Lumumba in the Congolese Senate. On August 25, the Special Group (then in charge of supervising covert action) decided that "planning for the Congo would not necessarily rule out consideration of any particular kind of activity which might contribute to getting rid of Lumumba," and a series of assassination plots were encouraged and developed. Ultimately, Lumumba was captured by troops loyal to opponent Joseph Mobutu, and transferred to Katanga province, where he was murdered.[22]

Subsequently, the CIA became heavily involved in the Angolan Civil War. In January 1975, Portugal set up a transitional tripartite coalition in Angola. The parties were Holden Roberto's National Front for the Liberation of Angola (FNLA) (backed by the People's Republic of China and Zaire), the Soviet-backed Popular Movement for the Liberation of Angola (MPLA), and Joseph Savimbi's National Union for the Total Independence of Angola (UNITA). In late January a CIA proposal to bolster the FNLA with $300,000 in political action funds was approved by the 40 Committee and President Gerald Ford.[23]

On July 17, 1975, the 40 Committee approved a $14 million, two-stage program of arms, communications gear, and other aid to Roberto and Savimbi, with an additional 10.7 million being approved in early September. The covert action program apparently had three objectives: to avoid a precedent of "Soviet expansion," to work with the "moderate" anti-Communist leaders of Zaire and Zambia, and to prevent Soviet- and MPLA-assisted black extremists from making gains in Namibia, Rhodesia, and the rest of southern Africa.[24]

Among the CIA's lower-visibility operations are the propaganda and media operations activities. At its peak the CIA's Propaganda Assets Inventory contained over 800 news and public information organizations and individuals. Among these propaganda assets were the well-known "Radio Free Europe" and "Radio Liberty" as well as the lesser known "Radio Free Asia," which began broadcasting to mainland China from Manila in 1951. Radio Free Asia went off the air in 1965. "Free

Cuba Radio" did not have its own station but purchased airtime on Florida and Louisiana stations.[25]

CIA propaganda operations have also included the subsidization of anti-Castro publications in the United States: *Advance, El Mundo, El Prensa, Libre, Bohemia*, and *El Diario de las Americas.* In addition, AIP, a radio news agency in Miami, produced programs that were sent free to more than 100 small stations in Central and Latin America.[26]

The CIA also subsidized numerous social democratic magazines in Europe and elsewhere, simply to project the center-left alternative. Thus, CIA conduits provided support to *Prevves* (France), *Der Monat* (West Germany), *El Mundo Nuevo* (Latin America), *Quiet* and *Thought* (India), and *Argumenten* (Sweden).[27]

The CIA has also been active in regards to book publishing. Nearly a dozen publishing houses have printed at least twenty of the more than 200 English-language books financed or produced by the CIA since the early 1950s. Altogether, over 1,000 volumes were produced or subsidized in some way by the CIA by the late 1970s. Some publishers were unaware of any CIA connection with the books they published. Some published books they knew to be CIA produced or subsidized. Some, like Allied Pacific Printing of Bombay and the Asia Research Center in Hong Kong, were simply CIA proprietaries.[28]

THE CARTER YEARS

At the beginning of the Carter Administration, in the wake of the Church Committee, covert action represented a smaller than usual proportion of U.S. intelligence activities. Over the course of time this proportion grew steadily. By 1981 the CIA was conducting a substantial number of propaganda operations.[29]

Most of the covert operations undertaken were propaganda and media support operations. One program, strongly advocated by National Security Adviser Zbignew Brzezinski, involved smuggling thousands of books and other written material into Eastern Europe and the Soviet Union. Another operation took place in Western Europe and concerned the intended deployment of the neutron bomb. In the face of unfavorable reactions in the West Europe press, and from the West European population, and a massive Soviet propaganda campaign to block deployment of the enhanced radiation weapon, a covert action campaign was initiated. Its objective was to place favorable articles in the West European press. In particular, it was desired to have articles compare the dangers of the newly deployed Soviet SS-20 versus the neutron bomb. Beginning in February and March 1978 the SS-20/neutron bomb comparison began appearing frequently. Newspapers, including the *Dusseldorf Rheinische Post, Die Welt, Bonn General Anzeiger, Freiburg Badische Zeitung, Sudduetsche Zeitung, Koblenz Rhein-Zeitung*, the *London Times, London Daily Telegraph*, and *The Economist*, began either to contrast the dangers of the SS-20 versus the neutron bomb or ridicule the Soviet propaganda campaign against the bomb.[30]

Additionally, within six months of the Sandinista takeover, President Carter had signed a top-secret finding authorizing the CIA to provide political support to opponents of the Sandinista regime. The support would take the form of money and backing to encourage and embolden the opposition, pay for newsprint, and funds to keep the newspaper *La Prensa* alive.[31]

At least two paramilitary operations were initiated in the Carter Administration. One involved limited paramilitary support to undermine the Soviet-supported state of South Yemen. Several small teams of Yemenis were trained to blow up bridges and sabotage other targets. Second, prior to Soviet invasion of Afghanistan the United States supplied, to those opposing the Marxist regime, medical supplies, communications equipment, and technical advice as to where arms could be acquired. In the hours after the Soviets crossed the border, President Carter told a NSC meeting that the United States had a moral obligation to help arm the resistance. According to then Egyptian President Anwar Sadat: "The first moment that the Afghan incident took place, the U.S. contacted me. . .and the transport of armaments to the Afghan rebels started from Cairo on U.S. planes."[32]

THE REAGAN YEARS

The Reagan Administration has considerably expanded activities in the covert action area. Covert action has been seen as a fundamental part of foreign policy and a means of overthrowing Marxist regimes outside of the Warsaw Pact. While continuing its general propaganda and media operations, the Administration has undertaken covert actions directed against the governments of Afghanistan, Angola, Cambodia, Ethiopia, Iran, Libya, and Nicaragua. It has undertaken covert actions in support of the governments of El Salvador and the Philippines.

Afghanistan

The Reagan Administration's covert action in support of the Afghan resistance (which revolves around six major political groups and a variety of tribal bands, with 90,000 to 100,000 active insurgents at any one time) continued and expanded the program begun by the Carter Administration immediately after the Soviet invasion in late 1979. By the fall 1981 the United States was involved with China, Pakistan, Egypt, and Saudi Arabia in a covert aid program. Saudi Arabia provided money, Egypt provided training, China provided weapons, and the United States provided Kalashnikov rifles, antitank missiles, and other weapons from U.S. and Egyptian stocks. Copies of Soviet weapons were produced by CIA-controlled factories in Egypt and the United States. In addition, some weapons such as SAM-7 antiaircraft missiles were upgraded.[33]

Weapons would arrive by air in Pakistan, aboard planes whose markings were constantly changed. Under agreement with Pakistani ruler Zia-ul Huq, the arms were then placed under the jurisdiction of Pakistan's Inter-Services Intelligence Directorate (ISID). The Directorate was responsible for overseeing their transfer by a Pakistani army unit, the National Logistics Cell, to mujaheddin leaders. Among the arms were surface-to-air missiles, which resulted in the downing of at least sixty helicopters in the first year.[34]

In December 1982, President Ronald Reagan instructed the CIA to again increase the quality and quantity of weapons being sent to the resistance. For the first time, some heavier weapons, including bazookas, mortars, grenade launchers, mines, and recoilless rifles were supplied and reported entering Afghanistan in increasing numbers by late January 1983. Also sighted were U.S.-supplied communications equipment, range-finders for rocket launchers, silencers, and other equipment.[35]

A large increase in funding began in the fall of 1983 with a secret amendment to the defense appropriations bill, authored by Representative Charles Wilson, which rechanneled $40 million of DOD money to the CIA for the Afghan operation. Part of the money was for new, foreign-made, heavy antiaircraft cannons. Another $50 million for more supplies and weapons was reprogrammed at Wilson's initiative in July 1984.[36]

By Fiscal Year 1985, expenditures for support of the resistance had reached $250 million per year. The money was primarily used to purchase Soviet-made arms and ammunition from countries such as China, Egypt, and Israel. The arms would then be delivered to Pakistani ports and airfields, at which point the ISID would take control and deliver the weapons (or at least a portion of them) to the mujaheddin leaders who lived in Peshawar. In addition to weapons, U.S. dollars bought medical supplies, food, and clothing for an estimated 200,000 to 300,000 full or part-time insurgents.[37]

Support was further increased in the last part of 1985. In October 1985 Congress secretly appropriated $470 million for Fiscal Year 1986. Part of the funding was used for ammunition and small weapons. More significantly, part of those millions went for the purchase of advanced Stinger missiles. The decision to provide Stingers was made in March 1986. By summer, the initial shipment of 150 missiles was being distributed to some of the insurgents.[38]

U.S. instructors trained rebels in a camp in Pakistan after the guerrillas had initial difficulties in handling the weapon. Once the Afghan resistance began effectively employing the Stingers, Soviet pilots were forced to fly higher, reducing the effectiveness of air power against the guerrillas. On the first day of their use in Afghanistan, the Stingers resulted in three Soviet helicopters being shot down. At least 270 Soviet aircraft have been shot down since.[39]

The success of the initial shipment led to a more widespread program. By March 1987 more than 300 missiles had been delivered, with hundreds (maybe 600) more in the pipeline. In addition, the Stingers, including some of a more accurate later model, were being widely distributed among the resistance groups. When the program began in 1986 each four-man rebel unit, after a six to eight week course, was given just one launcher and one missile at a time. Before another missile was released the unit had to show that it still had the launcher. By mid-1987 more than one missile was handed out at a time.[40]

The initial proposal to supply Stingers was opposed by the CIA, at least partially on the grounds that the missiles were too easy to trace. It was only in March 1986 that the decision was made to send the missiles. Before, when the resistance was using SA-7 Strela SAMs, the Soviets were "able to operate with virtual impunity in the air, which given the fact that perhaps 80 percent of Soviet combat and logistics operations depend on air, virtually preclude[d] any significance and lasting Mujaheddin military gains."[41]

Estimates of the ratio of targets hit to missiles ranged from four of ten to eight of ten. Whatever the case, the Stingers clearly have had an effect beyond the simple destruction of Soviet planes—Soviet and Afghan warplanes were forced to drop bombs from an altitude of 10,000 feet rather than a previous 2,000 to 4,000 feet, which greatly reduced their accuracy.[42]

In the later half of 1987 the Reagan Administration decided to provide the guerrillas with long-range 120-mm mortars and mine-clearing equipment to help them attack Soviet and Afghan military bases. The insurgents had been pressing for such material so they could more effectively attack eight major Soviet airbases and approximately thirty smaller Soviet or Afghan garrisons with airstrips scattered around Afghanistan. The long-range mortars allowed attacks from a greater distance, while the mine-clearing equipment would allow insurgents to penetrate isolated bases.[43]

Six weeks before the Soviet Union was to begin withdrawal from the country on May 15, 1988, weapons were pouring into Afghanistan for the resistance fighers. Included were TOW antitank missiles, 120-mm Spanish mortars, and advanced antitank cannons. Giant U.S. C5A transports were being met by scores of trucks belonging to Pakistan's government-run trucking line. Despite the Soviet withdrawal the United States will continue to supply the mujaheddin. After initial resistance the Soviet Union accepted the U.S. position that the United States would reserve the right to continue to aid the resistance as long as Soviets continued to aid the present Afghan government.[44]

Beyond the countermeasures taken by the Soviets and Afghan governments the resistance has been hampered by a persistent leakage problem. According to one report, at least $340 million worth of weapons—and perhaps more—intended for the insurgents never reached them. In January 1985 the CIA withdrew $50 million from a Swiss bank account to buy forty Oerlikon antiaircraft guns—only eleven made it to the guerrillas. The reasons for disappearing weapons range from expediency to personal profit. Those siphoning off the weapons include Pakistani forces, Afghan political parties based in Pakistan, rebel commanders (who stole AA guns, rocket-propelled grenades, AK-47 rifles, and other weapons for personal use or sale on the black market), and individual guerrillas. Islamic fundamentalists among the resistance have been stockpiling weapons in preparation for a power struggle after the Soviet withdrawal. Others who have acquired the weapons have included

Iranian revolutionaries (who bought or stole twelve Stingers from Afghan rebels in the summer of 1987) and drug traffickers in Afghanistan and Pakistan.[45]

In addition to supplying the resistance with weapons, the CIA also provided at least $2 billion in counterfeit Afghan currrency. The counterfeit currency has allowed the resistance to pay the exorbitant fees of mule drivers and truckers hauling supplies inside Afghanistan, in addition to allowing outright bribery.[46]

Angola

The Reagan Administration's military aid to the rebels fighting the Marxist government of Angola did not begin until the later half of 1985. It was in June 1985 that the Senate, by a 63 to 34 vote, approved an amendment to the State Department authorization bill that reversed the 1976 Hughes-Ryan amendment, which prohibited military assistance. Whereas in 1981 the Senate took similar action, that amendment died in a conference committee with a strongly opposed House of Representatives. In 1985, however, the House concurred.[47]

Both the Department of Defense and the CIA urged the White House to approve a large covert military operation to aid the Joseph Savimbi-led UNITA forces, estimated to number between 200,000 and 300,000. In early 1986 the Reagan Administration informed Congress that it decided to provide UNITA forces with antiaircraft and antitank missiles at a cost of approximately $15 million.[48]

Weapons are apparently first shipped to Kinshasa, Zaire and then to a small abandoned formerly Belgian air base at Kamina in Zaire. On three occasions in 1986, C-141 aircraft flown by "Santa Lucia Airways" arrived at Kamina from Kinshasa, loaded with arms. From there a light blue C-130 cargo plane shuttles the weapons to areas in Angola. In 1987 a new $15 million package was sent to the UNITA forces. In addition to Stingers, the UNITA forces were to receive some variety of antitank missile to counter a new shipment of Soviet tanks to the Angolan government.[49]

Cambodia

Since 1982 the Reagan Administration has been providing millions of dollars for non-military purposes to non-Communist Cambodian resistance groups. The CIA's aid has been funneled through Thailand, with the objective of strengthening those resistance groups' position in their loose coalition with the Communist Khmer Rouge. Apparently, CIA officers in Thailand work closely with the Thai military to advise the insurgents and to insure that none of the covert aid gets to the Khmer Rouge.[50]

El Salvador

The CIA has undertaken a number of operations to support the government of Christian Democratic leader Jose Napolean Duarte. One operation, phased out in 1985, involved organizing special Salvadoran Army anti-guerrilla units to track leftist rebels attempting to overthrow the government.[51]

In 1982, the CIA supplied invisible ink to stamp the wrists of Salvadoran voters to indicate that they had voted as well as ultraviolet light devices that illuminated the ink. Polling officials could thus determine if a prospective voter had already voted, while rebels would be unable to detect the ink and implement their threat to retaliate against those who voted.[52]

Another operation was directed toward avoiding the election of right-wing Arena (National Republican Alliance) party leader Roberto D'Aubuisson. Between 1982 and 1984 the CIA gave $960,000 to Duarte's Christian Democratic Party and $437,000 to the National Conciliation Party to provide its candidate, Francisco Jose Guerrero with advertising and media assistance. An additional $700,000 was spent to bolster the electoral process and to discredit D'Aubuisson. The CIA covertly subsidized visits to El Salvador by unwitting European and Latin journalists, and provided them with derogatory information about Mr. D'Aubuisson. The first group of journalists visited in early October 1983; a group of European television journalists on December 6–9, 1983 and the final group, several Venezuelans and a Colombian journalist, during the last weekend in February 1984.[53]

Another part of the operation involved a "non-partisan" effort to streamline election logistics, and provide media advice and technical assistance to ease the financial burden on interest groups such as trade unions and peasant cooperatives. In addition, the CIA helped in computerizing voting lists.[54]

Ethiopia

In 1981, President Reagan signed a Presidential Finding authorizing the CIA to conduct a "nonlethal campaign" to support the resistance to the Marxist regime. As a result, the CIA set aside $500,000 to help the Ethiopian People's Democratic Alliance conduct a small propaganda campaign. The campaign included a CIA contract with a Washington consultant, who wrote material criticizing the regime's internal policies. The written material, along with audio and video tapes of anti-regime speeches by leading exiles in the United States and Europe, have been shipped to Addis Ababa in diplomatic pouches, where it is given to dissident "cells" for distribution thoughout the country.[55]

The CIA rejected a $546,000 request from an Alliance splinter group, which in October 1982 presented the CIA with a twenty-eight page memorandum that spelled out the expenditure of the requested funds for training an initial group of 350 Ethiopian guerrillas to enter western Ethiopa to organize and spread the resistance already underway.[56]

Iran

In addition to the NSC-directed covert operation that ended in the Iran-Contra affair, other covert operations, directed by the CIA, have been directed at aiding Iranian paramilitary and political exile groups. The operations, underway by 1982, were designed to counter Soviet influence in Iran and give the United States a role of its own in the event that the Khomeini regime fell. The immediate goal was to knit together a coalition of exile groups and their supporters still in Iran, so if the opportunity arose they could become a significant factor in shaping the future of Iran.[57]

The covert action included providing several million dollars to units composed largely of Iranian exiles in eastern Turkey. The larger of the paramilitary groups had 6,000 to 8,000 men under the command of former Rear Admiral Ahmad Madani, who was the Commander of the Iranian Navy under the Shah and court-martialed for "being against the government." Madani was the first Defence Minister in the Khomeini regime. The second unit, of less than 2,000 men, was commanded by General Bahram Aryana, Chief of Staff of the Iranian Army under the Shah. The paramilitary groups were intended to perform two functions. In the event of a Soviet invasion of Iran they could harass the flanks of the Soviet armed forces. In the event of a civil war or domestic upheaval, they would be able to enter Iran to protect and bolster any centrist forces.[58]

The CIA was also reported to be financing Iranian exile groups said to be situated principally in France and Egypt. Support was made available to groups on the left (up to but not including Bani-Sadr) and to groups on the right (up to but not including the monarchist factions).[59]

The CIA also established and financed a radio station in Egypt to broadcast anit-Khomeini information. In 1987, regular features included reports on long food lines, pockets of opposition and small uprisings against the clergy and revolutionary guards, reports of torture and killings by the government, and charges that Iranian Communists and agents of the Soviet Union were gaining control of Iran. In September 1986 the Agency provided a miniaturized television transmitter and technical assistance for an eleven-minute clandestine broadcast to Iran by the Shah's son. The broadcast disrupted two channels of Iranian television for eleven minutes at 9 p.m. on September 5.[60]

Another aspect of CIA covert action directed against Iran was supplying information to Iraq to aid it in its war with Iran. The CIA secretly supplied Iraq with detailed intelligence to assist Iraqi bombing raids on Iran's oil terminals and power plants. In 1984, when some feared that Iran might overrun Iraq, the United States began supplying Iraq with some intelligence, which Iraq reportedly used to calibrate mustard gas attacks on Iranian ground troops.[61]

In early 1985, Iraq began receiving regular satellite information, which was supplied through Washington channels as needed by the Iraqis, particularly after an Iraqi bombing raid. It is not clear, at that point, whether the Iraqis received actual photos as opposed to information derived from the photos.[62]

In August 1986 the CIA established a direct top secret Washington-Baghdad link to provide the Iraqis with better and more timely satellite information. The Iraqis thus would receive information from satellite photos "several hours" after a bombing raid in order to assess damage and plan the next attack. By December 1986 the Iraqis were receiving selected portions of the actual photos taken by KH-11 and SR-71 overhead platforms. According to one account, some of the information or images provided were incomplete or doctored—inflating the size of the Soviet troop strength on the Iranian border—in order to further the Reagan Administration's goals.[63]

Libya

In addition to authorizing an NSC disinformation operation, Ronald Reagan authorized a CIA covert operation to undermine the Libyan regime. The plan involved CIA assistance to other countries in North Africa and the Middle East that opposed Qaddafi. Authorized in a fall 1985 Presidential Finding, its first objective was to disrupt, preempt, and frustrate Qaddafi's subversive and terrorist plans. Beyond that, it might lure him into some foreign adventure or terrorist exploit that would give a growing number of Qaddafi opponents in the Libyan military a chance to seize power or justify a military response by Algeria or Egypt.[64]

Another CIA operation, code-named TULIP, involved support for anti-Qaddafi exile movements, including the National Front for the Salvation of Libya and the efforts of other countries such as Egypt.[65]

Nicaragua

In March of 1981 President Reagan transmitted his first "Presidential Finding on Central America" to congress. The finding authorized CIA operations in Nicaragua—specifically, continued funding to "moderate" opponents of the Sandinistas' and a covert "arms interdiction program" with the stated aim of halting any flow of weapons from Nicaragua to guerrillas in El Salvador, Honduras, and Guatemala. The CIA then proceeded to funnel money indirectly to Miami-based exiles and to 300 former National Guardsmen, the latter group being known as the "15th of September Legion."[66]

In August 1981 the main guerrilla force took shape when the 15th of September Legion and Nicaragua Democratic Union joined with other anti-Sandinista forces to form the Nicaraguan Democratic Force, with 4,000 to 5,000 soldiers. Subsequently, the National Liberation Army joined the Force.[67]

In late 1981 President Reagan signed National Security Decision Directive 17 on preventing "Cuba-model" states, and on November 23 the President gave the CIA authority to create a paramilitary squad of exiles, and to work with foreign governments (i.e., Honduras and Argentina) as "appropriate." Envisioned was a 500-man U.S.-trained paramilitary force, with another 1,000 being trained by Argentina. On December 1, DCI William Casey presented the second Presidential Finding to Congress and depicted the program as being limited to attacks against the Cuban presence and Cuban/Sandinista support of the infrastructure in Nicaragua. The cost was estimated at $19.9 million.[68]

Shortly after Casey's appearance before congress, new U.S. intelligence operatives began to arrive in Honduras, with the size of the CIA station in Tegucigalpa doubling. After the initial phase of CIA training in weapon uses, tactics, and communications in Honduras, the contras began, in January and February 1982, raiding small outposts in villages in northern Nicaragua. On March 14, CIA-equipped sabo-teurs blew up two major bridges in the Chinandega and Nueva Segovia provinces. According to the July 16, 1982 *DIA Weekly Intelligence Summary*, between March 14 and June 21, 106 insurgent incidents occurred. Included was sabotage of highway bridges and attempted destruction of fuel tanks, sniper fire and attacks against small military patrols, attacks by small guerrilla units on individual Sandinista soldiers, and several incidents of arson. The targets were a customs warehouse, buildings belonging to the Ministry of Construction, and crops. The contras also targeted civilian personnel involved in Nicaraguan social service programs.[69]

In July 1983 the CIA began aiding another anti-Sandinista group, supplying Eden Pastora's Revolutionary Democratic Alliance (ARDE) with 500 Soviet AK-47 assault rifles, shipped from Israel to Venezuela and delivered to his ARDE at Tortuguero, a Costa Rican fishing lodge near the Nicaraguan border.[70]

In addition to supporting the contras, the CIA initiated its own campaign against the Sandinistas. To supplement activities of its own agents, it recruited a group of specially trained "unilaterally controlled Latino assets" (UCLAs)—Spanish-speaking operatives recruited from El Salvador, Honduras, Chile, Argentina, Ecuador, and Bolivia. Between September 1983 and April 1984, it carried out twenty-two or more attacks on vital Nicaraguan installations. The attacks apparently resulted from a CIA judgment that attacks on industrial and transportation targets in Nicaragua would be a quicker and more effective way of hurting the Sandinistas than previous efforts. The first U.S. attack occurred on September 8, 1983. Speed-boats manned by the UCLAs and launched from a mother ship, anchored twelve miles offshore, hit Puerto Sandino. Five weeks later they returned to sabotage an underwater oil pipeline. On October 10, the port of Corinto, Nicaragua's largest commercial port, was hit. The CIA's Latin commandos positioned their speedboats behind a South Korean ship and then fired mortars and grenades at five large oil and gasoline storage tanks, igniting 3.4 million gallons of fuel. According to the Nicaraguan government, over 100 people were injured in the attack, and 25,000 inhabitants of the city had to be evacuated while a fire raged out of control for two days.[71]

Beginning in January 1984, the CIA's assets and contra guerrillas, operating from a mother ship, used speedboats to begin depositing mines in the shipping channels of Nicaragua's major Atlantic and Pacific coast ports—Corinto, Puerto Sandino, and El Bluff. The mines were large metal cylinders stuffed with 300 pounds of C-4 plastic explosives, sufficient to sink small boats and damage larger vessels. They were placed two to three feet below the surface of the water, anchored into the bottom, in all channels of the three ports. The mine casings were produced by the CIA Weapons Group from sewer pipes, and packed with explosives. The fuses were apparently provided by the Mines Division of the Naval Surface Weapons Center in Maryland.[72]

By the first week of April 1984, ten commercial vessels had hit the CIA mines—four Nicaraguan and six non-Nicaraguan (registered to Japan, the Netherlands, Liberia, Panama, and the Soviet Union). At least eight merchant marine vessels turned back from Nicaraguan ports to find safer waters, including a Mexican oil tanker carrying 75,000 barrels of much needed fuel. The mining operation cost the Nicaraguans over $10 million—cotton and coffee piled up on the docks, and imports and exports had to be trucked to and from ports in neighboring Central American countries.[73]

Two further CIA operations involved the production of two guidebooks or manuals. One was a comic book-style manual produced by the CIA, urging Nicaraguans to call in sick to work, pour sand into engines, hurl firebombs, and engage in various acts of sabotage. The introduction to the sixteen-page *Freedom Fighers Manual* calls the book "a practical guide to liberate Nicaragua from oppression and misery by paralyzing the military-industrial complex of the traitorous Marxist state without having to use special tools and with minimal risk for the combatant." Its captioned drawings illustrated thirty-eight ways to sabotage or undermine the Nicaraguan government. It urged Nicaraguans to report late to work and take it easy on the job, leave the lights and water on, damage books and office equipment, smash windows, clog up toilets, cut telephone lines, call in false alarms, slash tires, spread rumors, make false hotel and plane reservations, short circuit electrical systems, paint anti-government slogans, damage truck engines, fell trees, release farm animals, steal government food supplies, set fires, and throw firebombs at police officers and fuel depots.[74]

The second manual, *Psychological Operations in Guerrilla Warfare*, was prepared by a CIA contract employee, allegedly in response to his learning of corruption and abuses in contra operations. The manual, of which 2,000 copies were printed, covers various aspects of the guerrilla operation. It suggests that in order to conduct "armed propaganda" in an effective manner, the rebels, when occupying a town, should

- destroy the military or police installations and remove the survivors to a "public place"
- cut all the outside lines of communications: cables, radio, messengers
- set up ambushes in order to delay the reinforcements in all possible entry routes
- kidnap all officials or agents of the Sandinista government and replace them in "public places" with military or civilian persons of trust.[75]

The manual also suggested that if it were necessary for one of the advanced posts to fire on an individual attempting to leave the town or city in which the guerrillas are carrying out armed propaganda or political proselytism, the rebels should

- explain that if that citizen had managed to escape he would have alerted the enemy that is near the town or city and they would carry out acts of reprisal such as rapes, pillage, destruction
- make the town see that he was an enemy of the people, and they shot him because the guerrillas recognized as their first duty the protection of their citizens.[76]

Several controversial recommendations led to a public outcry and internal inquiry and disciplinary action at the CIA. At one point the manual suggests that "it is possible to *neutralize* carefully selected and planned targets, such as court judges, *mesta* judges, police and State Security officials, CDS [Committee for Defense of Sandinismo] chiefs etc." (emphasis added). It also suggests that "the notification of the police, denouncing a target who does not want to join the guerrillas, can be carried out easily, when it becomes necessary, through a letter with false statements of citizens who are not implicated in the movement." The manual also suggests creation of martyrs by "taking the demonstrators to a confrontation with the authorities in order to bring about uprisings or shootings, which will cause the death of one or more persons, who would become the martyrs, a situation that should be made use of immediately. . . in order to create greater conflicts."[77]

A limited number (less than 100) manuals were distributed by attaching them to balloons and floating them from Honduras into Nicaragua. The CIA's apparent purpose was to create the perception that the U.S.-backed insurgency was more serious than it was; a shortage of funds curtailed the program.[78]

The CIA's direct entry into the conflict added to the actions being taken by the contras. In early September 1984 the contras used three rocket-equipped Cessna 02A observation planes to conduct a raid on a Nicaraguan military school near the Honduran border. Two Americans were killed when the accompanying helicopter they were flying in was shot down. The planes had been obtained from the CIA.[79]

Another CIA-funded contra operation involved bribing journalists. Rebel leaders, under CIA instructions and using CIA funds, bribed nearly two dozen Honduran and Costa Rican journalists to write favorable stories about rebel activities, paying each of them $50 to $100 a month.[80]

Between October 1984, when Congress adopted the second Boland amendment and October 1986, no funds were authorized by Congress for lethal assistance (although as is well known, NSC/"private" supply efforts took up some of the slack). In October 1986 Congress voted $70 million for lethal aid. As a result Nicaraguan rebels, estimated by then to number 11,000 began receiving military training in Florida. By January 1987 they had returned to Central America and a second group was in training.[81]

The CIA resumed providing the contras with precise information on dams, bridges, electrical substations, port facilities, and other targets inside Nicaragua that the rebels had targeted. Many of those installations were built by the Army Corps of Engineers and other U.S. agencies in the 1960 and 1970s. The CIA found and turned over detailed maps, blueprints and floor plans to the contras.[82]

On February 16, 1987, a new wave of contra sabotage attacks began when contra commandos blasted a power station near the town of La Trinidad, blacking out three northern provinces for four days. On March 16, commando groups hit a high-tension tower on the outskirts of Managua, but it did not fall. Altogether, in the last weeks of March, contra saboteurs struck ten times along Nicaragua's Pacific coast, toppling electric towers and putting out lights in towns on Nicaragua's northern and southern borders. Destruction of undefended telephone-relay stations, electrical switching stations, and bridges would disrupt the daily lives of many Nicaraguans and would presumably demonstrate that the Sandinistas could not maintain control over the areas involved.[83]

The CIA was also to supply the contras with weapons outside the aid package, by retaining legal title to materials it would turn over to the contras. The material included new planes, hundreds of .50 caliber machine guns, Redeye surface-to-air missiles, LAW anti-armor rockets, and C-4 plastic explosives.[84]

In late 1987, the CIA followed up the defection of a top aide to Nicaraguan Defense Minister Humberto Ortega by producing a videotape for distribution throughout Central America. In a forty-five minute statement, broadcast on San Salvador television and circulated in Honduras and Nicaragua, Major Roger Miranda Bengoechea embraced the "heroic struggle" of the contras and painted the Sandinistas as a privileged class who betrayed the goals of the revolution. Miranda also claimed that Humberto Ortega had maintained sexual relationships with the wives of at least three leading Sandinistas.[85]

U.S lethal aid to the contras was not continued by Congress in the aftermath of the 1987 ceasefire between the Contras and the Sandinistas.

Philippines

In attempting to bring about the ouster of Ferdinand Marcos, the CIA secretly funded a group of Philippine military officers who formed, in March 1985, the Reform the Armed Forces Now Movement (RAM). RAM leaders were brought to the United States to meet with members of Congress and other opinion makers, as proof of the possibility of reform in the Philippines.[86]

Subsequent to the fall of Marcos and the collapse of negotiations between the Aquino government and the Communist insurgents, the CIA launched a $10 million operation against the insurgents. The plan called for the CIA to gather intelligence—including by airborne reconnaissance—map insurgent controlled areas, train soldiers, and launch undercover political activities.[87]

South Yemen

In March 1982 a thirteen-man team of Yemenis sponsored by the CIA and Saudi intelligence had been sent into South Yemen to conduct a sabotage. The team was captured and a second team, already inserted in South Yemen, had to be withdrawn.[88]

NOTES TO CHAPTER 15

1. "The Bissell Philosophy," Appendix to Victor Marchetti and John Marks, *The CIA and the Cult of Intelligence* (New York: Knopf, 1974) at p. 387; U.S. Congress, Senate Select Committee to Study Governmental Operations with Respect to Intelligence Activities, *Alleged Assassination Plots Involving Foreign Leaders* (Washington, D.C.: U.S. Government Printing Office, 1976).

2. Trevor Barnes, "The Secret Cold War: The CIA and American Foreign Policy in Europe, 1946–1956, Part II," *Historical Journal* 25, no. 3 (1982): 399–415.

3.   Ibid.
4.   John Prados, *President's Secret Wars: CIA and Pentagon Covert Operations from World War II Through Iranscam* (New York: Quill, 1988), pp. 30–44.
5.   See Stephen Schlesinger and Stephen Kinzer, *Bitter Fruit* (Garden City, N.Y.: Doubleday, 1982); Richard H. Immerman, *CIA in Guatemala: The Foreign Policy of Intervention* (Austin: University of Texas Press, 1982).
6.   For an account of the Bay of Pigs episode see Peter Wyden, *Bay of Pigs: The Untold Story* (New York: Simon & Schuster, 1979).
7.   Warren Hinckle and William Turner, *The Fish is Red: The Story of the Secret War Against Castro* (New York: Harper & Row, 1981), pp. 101, 108, 191, 219.
8.   Hinckle and Turner, *The Fish is Red*, pp. 121, 122, 143.
9.   Hinckle and Turner, *The Fish is Red*, p. 148.
10. Ibid., pp. 129–30.
11. Ibid.
12. U.S. Congress, Senate Select Committee to Study Governmental Operations with Respect to Intelligence Activities, *Covert Action in Chile* (Washington, D.C.: U.S. Government Printing Office, 1976), pp. 1, 9.
13. Ibid., pp. 23–25.
14. Ibid., pp. 25–26; U.S. Congress, Senate Select Committee to Study Governmental Operations with Respect to Intelligence Activities, *Alleged Assassination Plots Involving Foreign Leaders*, p. 226.
15. U.S. Congress, Senate Select Committee to Study Governmental Operations with Respect to Intelligence Activities, *Alleged Assassination Plots Involving Foreign Leaders*, p. 254; U.S. Congress, Senate Select Committee to Study Governmental Operations with Respect to Intelligence Activities, *Covert Action*, pp. 29–31.
16. M. Richard Shaw, "British Intelligence and Iran," *Counter Spy* (May–June 1982): 31–33.
17. Ibid.; Kermit Roosevelt, *Countercoup: The Struggle for Control of Iran* (New York: McGraw-Hill, 1979), pp. 3, 107, 119.
18. Shaw, "British Intelligence and Iran"; Roosevelt, *Countercoup*, pp. 119, 121.
19. Prados, *President's Secret Wars*, pp. 96–97.
20. Stephen R. Weissman, "CIA Covert Action in Zaire and Angola: Patterns and Consequences," *Political Science Quarterly* 94, no. 2 (1979): 263–86.
21. Ibid., at p. 266.
22. Ibid., at pp. 267, 269.
23. Ibid., p. 282.
24. Ibid., pp. 282–83.
25. John Crewdson, "Worldwide Propaganda Network Built by the CIA," *New York Times*, December 26, 1977, pp. 1, 37.
26. Ibid.
27. Ibid.
28. Ibid.
29. Stansfield Turner, *Secrecy and Democracy: The CIA in Transition* (Boston: Houghton Mifflin, 1985), pp. 88–89.
30. David Whitman, *The Press and the Neutron Bomb* (Cambridge, Mass.: Kennedy School of Government, 1984), pp. 96–97; Bob Woodward, *Veil: The Secret Wars of the CIA 1981–1987* (New York: Simon & Schuster, 1987), p. 78.

31. Woodward, *Veil*, p. 113.
32. Jay Peterzell, *Reagan's Secret Wars* (Washington, D.C.: Center for National Security Studies, 1984), p. 9.
33. Carl Bernstein, "CIA's Secret Arms Aid to Afghanistan," *Chicago Sun-Times*, September 6, 1981, p. 1; Tim Weiner, "The CIA's Leaking Pipeline," *Philadelphia Inquirer*, February 28, 1988, pp. 1-A, 12-A; Peterzell, *Reagan's Secret Wars*, pp. 9, 10, 13; Prados, *President's Secret Wars*, p. 359.
34. Bernstein, "CIA's Secret Arms Aid to Afghanistan."
35. Peterzell, *Reagan's Secret Wars*, p. 11.
36. Robert Pear, "Arming the Afghan Guerrillas: A Huge Effort Led by U.S.," *New York Times*, April 18, 1988, pp. A1, A11; Bob Woodward and Charles R. Babcock, "U.S. Covert Aid to Afghans on the Rise," *Washington Post*, January 13, 1985, pp. A1, A30.
37. Leslie H. Gelb, "U.S. Aides Put '85 Arms Supplies to Afghan Rebels at $280 Million," *New York Times*, November 28, 1984, pp. A1, A9; Woodward and Babcock, "U.S. Covert Aid to Afghans on the Rise."
38. Joanne Omang, "Secret Votes Give Afghans $300 Million," *Washington Post*, October 10, 1985, p. A16; "Leaks in the Pipeline," *Time*, December 9, 1985, pp. 50–51; David B. Ottaway, "Afghan Rebels to Get More Missiles;" *Washington Post*, February 8, 1987, pp. A1, A28.
39. Bernard Gwertzman, "Stingers Aiding Afghans' Fight, U.S. Aides Say," *New York Times*, December 13, 1986, pp. 1, 9; Ottaway, "Afghan Rebels to Get More Missiles;" "Afghan Transport Plane Downed by Guerrilla Force with a Missile," *New York Times*, February 10, 1987, pp. A1, A5; Pear, "Arming the Afghan Guerrillas: A Huge Effort Led by U.S."
40. David B. Ottaway, "Afghan Rebels Due More Arms," *Washington Post*, April 5, 1987, pp. A1, A19; James M. Dorsey, "Afghan Rebels Receive Hundreds of Stingers," *Washington Times*, March 25, 1987, p. 9A.
41. "U.S. Aides Put '85 Arms Supplies to Afghan Rebels at $280 Million"; Woodward and Babcock, "U.S. Covert Aid to Afghans on the Rise."
42. David B. Ottaway, "U.S. Missiles Alter War in Afghanistan," *Washington Post*, July 19, 1987, p. A16.
43. David B. Ottaway, "U.S. Widens Arms Shipments to Bolster Afghan Guerrillas," *Washington Post*, September 21, 1987, pp. A1, A7.
44. Richard M. Weintraub, "New Arms Reaching Afghans," *Washington Post*, April 5, 1988, pp. A1, A19.
45. Weiner, "The CIA's Leaking Pipeline."
46. Tim Weiner, "U.S. Used Secret Global Network to Arm Afghans," *Philadelphia Inquirer*, February 29, 1988, pp. 1-A, 8-A.
47. David B. Ottaway, "Senate Votes to End Ban on Aiding Angola Rebels," *Washington Post*, June 12, 1985, p. A6.
48. David B. Ottaway, "Angola Rebel Aid is Pushed," *Washington Post*, November 1, 1985, pp. A1, A14; Bernard Gwertzman, "Reagan Decides to Send Weapons to Angola Rebels," *New York Times*, February 19, 1986, pp. A1, A3; David B. Ottaway and Patrick E. Tyler, "Superpowers Raise Ante as Fighting Intensifies," *Washington Post*, July 27, 1986, pp. A1, A21.

49. James Brooke, "CIA Said to Send Rebels in Angola Weapons via Zaire," *New York Times*, February 1, 1987, pp. 1, 2; Neil A. Lewis, "Administration Decides that Aid to Angola Rebels will Continue," *New York Times*, June 11, 1987, pp. A1, A9; James Brooke, "U.S. Arms Airlift to Angola Rebels is Said to Go On," *New York Times*, July 27, 1987, pp. A1, A2.

50. Charles R. Babcock and Bob Woodward, "CIA Covertly Aiding Pro-West Cambodians," *Washington Post*, July 8, 1985, pp. A1, A18.

51. Doyle McManus, "Inquiry Discloses CIA Officers' Aid to Salvador Army," *Los Angeles Times*, July 9, 1987, pp. 1, 22.

52. Philip Taubman, "C.I.A. Chief Tells of Attempt to Aid Salvador Vote," *New York Times*, July 30, 1982, p. 2.

53. Philip Tabuman, "CIA Said to Have Given Money to 2 Salvador Parties," *New York Times*, May 12, 1984, p. 6.

54. Joanne Omang, "CIA Channeled $2 Million Into Salvador Voting," *Washington Post*, May 11, 1984, p. A24.

55. Patrick E. Tyler and David B. Ottaway, "Ethiopian Security Police Seized, Tortured CIA Agent," *Washington Post*, April 25, 1986, pp. A1, A16.

56. Ibid.; James Brooke, "In Ethiopia, Rulers Seem to Be Widely Resented," *New York Times*, March 15, 1987, p. 14; David B. Ottaway and Joanne Omang, "U.S. Course Uncharted on Aid to Insurgencies," *Washington Post*, May 21, 1985, pp. A1, A23.

57. Leslie H. Gelb, "U.S. Said to Aid Iranian Exiles in Combat and Political Units," *New York Times*, March 7, 1982, pp. 1, 12.

58. Ibid.

59. Ibid.

60. Ibid.; Bob Woodward, "CIA Curried Favor With Khomeini Exiles," *Washington Post*, November 19, 1986, pp. A1, A28.

61. Bob Woodward, "CIA Aiding Iraq in Gulf War," *Washington Post*, December 15, 1986, pp. A1, A18–A19.

62. Woodward, "CIA Aiding Iraq in Gulf War."

63. Woodward, "CIA Aiding Iraq in Gulf War"; Stephen Engelberg, "Iran and Iraq Got 'Doctored' Data U.S. Officials Say," *New York Times*, January 12, 1987, pp. A1, A16.

64. Bob Woodward, "CIA Anti-Qaddafi Plan Backed," *Washington Post*, November 3, 1985, pp. A1, A19.

65. Woodward, *Veil*, p. 411.

66. Peter Kornbluh, *Nicaragua: The Price of Intervention, Reagan's War Against the Sandinistas* (Washington, D.C.: Institute for Policy Studies, 1987), pp. 18–20.

67. James LeMoyne, "The Secret War Boils Over," *Newsweek*, April 11, 1983, pp. 46–50; Joanne Omang, "A Historical Background to the CIA's Nicaraguan Manual," in *Psychological Operations in Guerrilla Warfare* (New York: Vintage, 1985), pp. 15, 22.

68. "A Secret War for Nicaragua," *Newsweek*, November 8, 1982, pp. 42–53; Kornbluh, *Nicaragua*, pp. 22–23; Robert C. Toth, "CIA Covert Action Punishes Nicaragua for Salvador Aid," *Los Angeles Times*, December 20, 1982, p. 11.

69. LeMoyne, "The Secret War Boils Over"; Kornbluh, *Nicaragua*, pp. 23, 24, 40.

70. "The CIA Blows an Asset," *Newsweek*, September 3, 1984, pp. 48–49.

71. Kornbluh, *Nicaragua*, p. 48; Philip Taubman, "U.S. Officials Say C.I.A. Helped Nicaraguan Rebels Plan Attacks," *New York Times*, October 16, 1984, pp. 1, 22; "Oct. 10 Assault on Nicaraguans Is Laid to C.I.A.," *New York Times*, April 18, 1984, pp. A1, A12.

72.   Kornbluh, *Nicaragua*, pp. 48–50; Hedrick Smith, "Britain Criticizes Mining of Harbors Around Nicaragua," *New York Times*, April 7, 1984, pp. 1, 4; Fred Hiatt and Joanne Omang, "CIA Helped to Mine Ports in Nicaragua," *Washington Post*, April 7, 1984, p. 1; Philip Taubman, "Americans on Ship Said to Supervise Nicaragua Mining," *New York Times*, April 8, 1984, pp. 1, 12; Leslie H. Gelb, "Officials Say CIA Made Mines with Navy Help," *New York Times*, June 1, 1984, p. A4.

73.   Kornbluh, *Nicaragua*, pp. 48–50; Smith, "Britain Criticizes Mining of Harbors Around Nicaragua"; Taubman, "Americans on Ship Said to Supervise Nicaragua Mining."

74.   "CIA-Produced Comics Inspire Revolutionaries with Rebellious Antics," *Toronto Globe and Mail*, June 30, 1984, p. 11.

75.   *Psychological Operations in Guerrilla Warfare*, (New York: Vintage, 1985), p. 52.

76.   Ibid., p. 56.

77.   *Psychological Operations in Guerrilla Warfare*, pp. 57, 74, 85.

78.   "Balloons Took CIA Manuals to Nicaragua," *Washington Post*, December 7, 1984, p. A44.

79.   Blaine Harden and Joe Pichirallo, "CIA is Said to Supply Planes to Nicaraguan Rebels," *Washington Post*, September 15, 1984, pp. A1, A24–A25.

80.   Joel Brinkley, "Nicaraguan Rebel Tells of Killings as Devices for Forced Recruitment," *New York Times*, September 12, 1985, p. A10.

81.   Joe Pichirallo and Molly Moore, "70 Contras Said to Be Training in U.S.," *Washington Post*, November 20, 1986, pp. A1, A34; James LeMoyne, "First Group of the Contras Completes Florida Training," *New York Times*, January 9, 1987, p. A10; "Turning Points in the Contra War," *Newsweek*, March 28, 1988, p. 38.

82.   Joel Brinkley, "C.I.A. Gives Contras Detailed Profiles of Civil Targets," *New York Times*, March 19, 1987, pp. A1, A10.

83.   Julia Preston, "Nicaraguan Rebels Increase Pace of Sabotage Attacks," *Washington Post*, April 3, 1987, pp. A29–A30.

84.   Kornbluh, *Nicaragua*, p. 211.

85.   Douglas Farah, "Videotape of Defector Circulated," *Washington Post*, December 17, 1987, pp. A41, A43.

86.   Raymond Bonner, *Waltzing with a Dictator: The Marcoses and the Making of American Policy* (New York: Times Books, 1987), p. 368.

87.   "Covert Help for Cory Aquino," *Newsweek*, March 23, 1987, p. 7; Nayan Chanda, "Here Comes the Spies," *Far Eastern Economic Review*, April 9, 1987, p. 19.

88.   Woodward, *Veil*, p. 215.

KH-11 Photo of Soviet Nuclear-Powered Aircraft Carrier Under Construction.

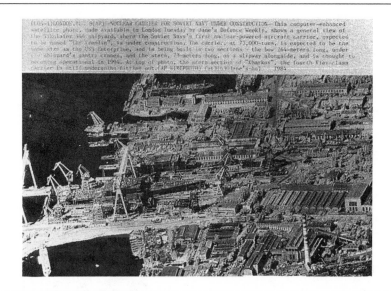

Photo Credit: AP/Wide World Photos.

Defense Communications Electronics Evaluation and Testing Activity at Fort Belvoir, Virginia, the Receiving Station for KH-11 Imagery.

SR-71 Reconnaissance Plane. The SR-71 Can Fly at Over 2,100 mph.

Photo Credit: Lockheed.

SR-71 Photograph of Libya's Benina Airfield After U.S Raid of April 15, 1986.

Photo Credit: U.S. Department of Defense.

P-3C Ocean Surveillance/Antisubmarine-Warfare Aircraft.

Photo Credit: Lockheed.

An Artist's Conception of the Defense Support Program Satellite, Which Performs Early Warning and Nuclear Detonation Detection Missions.

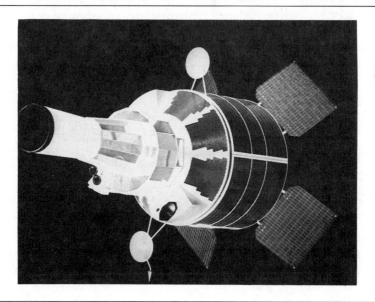

Photo Credit: U.S. Air Force.

COBRA DANE, Phased Array Radar, Shemya Island. COBRA DANE is Used to Track Soviet Missile Warheads as They Descend to Earth During Tests.

Photo Credit: Raytheon.

Chicksands Listening Post. Manned by Air Force Electronic Security Command Personnel, Chicksands Monitors, Among Other Things, Soviet Air Defense Communications.

Photo Credit: Duncan Campbell.

U.S. Ocean Surveillance Facility at Edzell, Scotland.

Photo Credit: Duncan Campbell.

Menwith Hill, England. A Ground-Station for SIGINT satellites, Menwith Hill is Also the Site of Projects SILKWORTH and MOONPENNY.

Photo Credit: Duncan Campbell.

Joint Defense Space Research Facility at Alice Springs, Australia (Pine Gap), the Ground Control Station for RHYOLITE and MAGNUM.

Photo Credit: Desmond Ball.

COBRA JUDY, Phased Array Radar on USNS.

Photo Credit: Raytheon.

Kiev Communication Tower. A Target of NSA's Intercept.

Photo Credit: Bob Windrem.

An Exterior View of the Ground-Based Electro-Optical Deep Space Surveillance Experimental Test Site.

Photo Credit: U.S. Air Force.

A U.S.S. Sturgeon (SSN-637) Submarine. Sturgeon Submarines are Used in the Special Navy Control Program.

Soviet T-72 Tanks. After Several Attempts, U.S. Intelligence Acquired One for Analysis.

Photo Credit: Department of Defense.

Contras in Honduras in 1983.

Photo Credit: Edgar Chamorro.

The Contra Leadership with Ronald Reagan.

Photo Credit: White House, courtesy of Peter Kornbluh.

Vitaly Yurchenko, A temporary defector from the KGB.

Photo Credit: AP/Wide World Photos.

Mujaheddin Preparing 14.5mm Ammunition and Recoilless Rifle.

Photo Credit: David Stewart-Smith, Courtesy Philadelphia Inquirer.

16 MANAGEMENT AND DIRECTION

Given the number of intelligence agencies, services, and offices; the conflicting and diverse supervisory executive departments; and the wide range of intelligence activities; it is clear that the U.S. intelligence community requires coordination and control to guide its work. Furthermore, the highly sensitive nature of some of these activities requires their approval by high-level officials. Thus it is not surprising that over the last thirty years an elaborate system of directives, committees, offices, plans, and programs has been established.

This system can be divided into three basic categories. Executive Orders, Presidential directives and agency or departmental regulations establish the basic missions and structure of the intelligence community. Individuals, committees and offices implement and formulate directives, seek to resolve conflicts, provide advice and counsel, and establish collection and analysis priorities. Finally, there are the plans, programs, and requirements documents that establish objectives or specify resource allocation to attain specific collection or analysis goals.

ORDERS, DIRECTIVES, AND REGULATIONS

The orders, directives, and regulations that guide the activities of the intelligence community all stem from presidential Orders and directives. Presidential Orders and directives represent the apex of the system and come in two varieties—unclassified Executive Orders and (often classified) Presidential directives. The title of the second type of document changes with each administration. Thus, Ronald Reagan's National Security Decision Directives (NSDDs) were Presidential Directives (PDs) in the Carter Administration, National Security Decision Memoranda

365

(NSDM) in the Nixon-Ford Administration, and National Security Action Memoranda (NSAM) in the Kennedy-Johnson Administration.

Executive Orders governing the intelligence community are reissued with each new administration, although they often overlap in content. President Reagan's Executive Order 12333, "United States Intelligence Activities" of December 4, 1981, is divided into three parts: Goals, Direction, Duties, and Responsibilities with Respect to the National Intelligence Effort; The Conduct of Intelligence Activities; and General Provisions.[1] Part 1 authorizes the establishment of National Foreign Intelligence Advisory Groups, specifies the agencies and offices that constitute the intelligence community, defines their general functions, and lists the duties and responsibilities of the senior officials of the community.

Part 2, on the conduct of intelligence activities, establishes procedures concerning and restrictions on the collection of information abroad and in the United States concerning U.S. persons. It also establishes (or continues) procedures concerning assistance to law enforcement authorities, human experimentation, and prohibits assassinations. Part 3 deals with congressional oversight, implementation, and definitions.

Changes in the contents of the Executive Orders governing the intelligence community over the last twelve years have been the product of three factors: different modes of National Security Council (NSC) organization, revelations concerning abuses by the intelligence community, and differing attitudes concerning domestic intelligence activities. Thus, Gerald Ford's Executive Order "United States Foreign Intelligence Activities" of February 18, 1976, imposed restrictions on physical and electronic surveillance activities, experimentation, and assistance to law enforcement authorities, in response to the 1974–1975 revelations concerning various CIA, FBI and NSA activities. It also specified, for the first time, that "no employee of the United States Government shall engage in, or conspire to engage in, political assassination."[2]

The Carter Executive Order, "United States Intelligence Activities," was primarily concerned with restrictions and oversight.[3] The Reagan Executive Order loosened some of those restrictions, allowing the collection of "significant foreign intelligence" within the United States by the CIA so long as the collection effort is not undertaken for the purpose of acquiring information concerning the domestic activities of U.S. persons.

In addition to an Executive Order governing the intelligence community, each President has also issued an order concerning national security information. These orders deal with classification levels and classification authority, downgrading and declassification, safeguarding classified information, and implementation of the provisions. The most recent of these orders is Executive Order 12356 of April 2, 1982. This order reversed trends that began in the Nixon Administration towards the lowering of classification levels and reducing the absolute quantity of classified material. The 1982 order no longer required a balancing of national security considerations with the public interest in access to information, and allows "reclassification" of previously declassified material if such material is considered "reasonably recoverable."[4]

The usually classified Presidential directives that deal with intelligence matters tend to deal with more specific areas of intelligence operations—intelligence community organization and procedures, covert operations, and space reconnaissance. Carter Administration PDs concerning intelligence included PD-9 of March 30, 1977, "Army Special Operations Field Office Berlin"; PD-17 of August 4, 1977, "Reorganization of the Intelligence Community"; PD-19 of August 25, 1977, "Intelligence Structure and Mission (Electronic Surveillance Abroad and Physical Searches for Foreign Intelligence Purposes)"; and PD-55 of January 10, 1980, "Intelligence Special Access Programs: Establishment of the APEX Program." Additionally, PD-37 of May 11, 1978, "National Space Policy," apparently contained substantial portions concerning employment of reconnaissance satellites.[5]

At least eight Reagan NSDDs have concerned intelligence matters. NSDD-17 deals with covert operations in Central America. NSDD-19 of January 12, 1982 is entitled "Protection of Classified National Security Council and Intelligence Information" and NSDD-22 of January 29, 1982 concerns the "Designation of Intelligence Officials Authorized to Request FBI Collection of Foreign Intelligence." NSDD-42 of July 4, 1982, "National Space Policy," dealt in part with space reconnaissance. NSDD-84 of March 11, 1983, "Safeguarding National Security Information," specified new security requirements for individuals to obtain access to code word information. NSDD-159 of January 18, 1985 specified "Covert Action Policy Approval and Coordination Procedures" and NSDD-196 of November 1, 1985 concerned the "Counterintelligence/Countermeasure Implementation Task Force." NSDD-202 concerned the impact of a new methodology for assessing the yields of Soviet nuclear weapon tests and NSDD-286 dealt with covert action procedures.[6]

Both Executive Orders and Presidential directives deal with subjects in fairly general terms. Implementation requires more detailed directives. The directives that emanate from the Presidential level are of two basic types: (1) National Security Council Intelligence Directives (NSCIDs) and their descendents and (2) departmental directives and their descendents.

NSCIDs offer guidance to the entire intelligence community, and the Director of Central Intelligence (DCI) in particular, concerning specific aspects of U.S. intelligence operations. The NSCID numbering system is unlike that for NSDMs, PDs, or NSDDs, which are temporally numbered. In general, a NSCID number is assigned to a particular topic, and subsequent revisions of the NSCID bear the same number. At the same time, the topic assigned to a particular number may change over time, one topic being subsumed under another.

NSCIDs were first issued in 1947 and have been updated numerous times since then. Sometimes revisions have been of selected documents; other times the entire group has been revised. As of 1981 the last major revision appears to have been completed on February 17, 1972. Many of those NSCIDs may still be in effect. The number and names of those NSCIDs are listed in Table 16-1.

NSCID No. 1, "Basic Duties and Responsibilities," was first issued in 1947 with subsequent updates in 1952, 1958, 1961, 1964, and 1972. NSCID No. 1 of February 17, 1972 assigned four major responsibilities to the DCI:

Table 16–1. NSCIDs Issued on February 17, 1972.

Number	Title
1	Basic Duties and Responsibilities
2	Coordination of Overt Activities
3	Coordination of Intelligence Production
4	The Defector Program
5	U.S. Espionage and Counterintelligence Activities Abroad
6	Signals Intelligence
7	Unknown
8	Photographic Interpretation
9	Unknown
10	Unknown

1. planning, reviewing, and evaluating all intelligence activities and the allocation of all intelligence resources;
2. producing national intelligence required by the President and national consumers;
3. chairing and staffing all intelligence advisory boards; and
4. establishing and reconciling intelligence requirements and priorities with budgetary constraints.[7]

NSCID No. 1 also (1) instructs the DCI to prepare and submit to the Office of Management and Budget (OMB) a consolidated budget, (2) authorizes the issuance of Director of Central Intelligence Directives as a means of implementing the NSCIDs, and (3) instructs the DCI to protect sources and methods.[8]

NSCID No. 2 of February 17, 1972, makes the DCI responsible for planning the utilization of collection and reporting capabilities of the various government departments and the CIA responsible for conducting, as a service of common concern, radio broadcast monitoring. The Department of State is charged with overt collection of political, sociological, economic, scientific, and technical information; militarily pertinent scientific and technical intelligence; and economic intelligence.[9]

The 1972 version of NSCID No. 3 makes the Department of State responsible for the production of political and sociological intelligence on all countries and for economic intelligence on countries of the "Free World." It makes the Department of Defense (DOD) responsible for the production of military intelligence and scientific and technical intelligence pertinent to the missions of DOD components. The CIA is given responsibility for economic, scientific, and technical intelligence plus "any other intelligence required by the DCI."[10] In practice, this has meant that the CIA is heavily involved in the production of political and military intelligence, especially strategic intelligence. In addition, atomic energy intelligence is decreed, by NSCID No. 3 to be the responsibility of all National Foreign Intelligence Board (NFIB) agencies.[11]

Originally, NSCID No. 4 concerned Priority National Intelligence Objectives (PNIOs)—a system for prioritizing collections efforts. The system of PNIOs has been eliminated; hence, NSCID No. 4 no longer concerns that system. NSCID No. 4 bears the title "The Defector Program" and presumably concerns the inducement of defections and the responsibility of the CIA and other agencies in the program.[12]

NSCID No. 5 of February 17, 1972 is entitled "U.S. Espionage and Counterintelligence Activities Abroad." That version is the successor to versions issued in 1947, 1951, 1958, and 1961. The directives authorize the DCI to "establish the procedures necessary to achieve such direction and coordination, including the assessment of risk incident upon such operations as compared to the value of the activity, and to ensure that sensitive operations are reviewed pursuant to applicable direction."[13]

NSCID No. 6, "Signals Intelligence," serves as the charter for the NSA. The February 17, 1972 version was still in effect as of the Reagan transition. NSCID No. 6 defines the nature of SIGINT activities and directs the Director of the NSA (DIRNSA) to produce intelligence "in accordance with objectives, requirements and priorities established by the Director of Central Intelligence and the United States Intelligence Board." It further authorizes the DIRNSA "to issue direct to any operating elements engaged in SIGINT operations such instructions and assignments as are required. All instructions issued by the Director under the authority provided in this paragraph shall be mandatory, subject only to appeal to the Secretary of Defense."[14]

The most recent available version of NSCID No. 7 was issued in 1948. Thus, NSCID No. 7 of February 12, 1948, "Domestic Exploitation," stated that "the Central Intelligence Agency shall be responsible for the exploitation on a highly selective basis within the U.S. of business concerns, non-governmental organizations and individuals as sources of foreign intelligence information."[15] Subsequent guidance on the subject of domestic exploitation has been contained in NSCID No. 2, the topic of NSCID No. 7 being changed. The most recent information suggests that NSCID No. 7 concerns "critical information."[16] It might deal with the classification system as well as with conditions and procedures for information distribution among U.S. and foreign organizations.

The original NSCID No. 8 was issued on May 25, 1948 and was entitled "Biographical Data on Foreign Scientific and Technological Personalities;" by 1961 it dealt, instead, with "Photographic Interpretation." NSCID No. 8 of February 17, 1972 continues the National Photographic Interpretation Center as a service of common concern to be provided by the DCI. Additionally, it specifies that the Director of the NPIC is to be selected by the DCI with the concurrence of the Secretary of Defense.[17]

The NSCIDs state, in general terms, the responsibilities of the DCI and other components of the intelligence community. One provision of NSCID No. 1 authorizes the DCI to issue more detailed directives—The Director of Central Intelligence

Directives (DCIDs)—in pursuit of the implementation of the various NSCIDs. DCIDs are keyed to the NSCIDs from which they follow by the NSCID numbering system. Thus, DCID 1/3 is the third DCID issued pursuant to NSCID No. 1.

DCIDs in the DCID 1/ series include 1/2, 1/3, 1/5, 1/7, 1/8, 1/10, 1/13, 1/14, 1/16, 1/18, 1/19, and 1/20.

DCID 1/2 of January 21, 1972 specified "U.S. Intelligence Requirements Categories and Priorities" that served to guide for planning and programming for the subsequent five years. It identified intelligence targets in terms of the information needed "to enable the U.S. intelligence community to provide effective support for decisionmaking, planning and operational activities of the Unites States government."[18] DCID 1/3 of May 18, 1986, entitled "Committees of the Director of Central Intelligence," outlines the basic composition and organization of the committees and authorizes the DCI to designate their chairmen. DCID 1/5 of May 1976 dealt with "Data Standardization for the Intelligence Community." DCID 1/7 of May 4, 1981, "Control of Dissemination of Intelligence Information," imposes restrictions on the dissemination of intelligence to immigrant aliens and foreign governments. DCID 1/8 of May 6, 1976, "The National Foreign Intelligence Board," established the Board as the successor to the United States Intelligence Board. A more recent version of DCID 1/8 was issued on January 28, 1982.[19]

DCID 1/10 of January 18, 1982, is entitled "Security Policy Guidance on Liaison Relationships with Foreign Intelligence Organizations and Foreign Security Services." DCID 1/11 of July 15, 1982, spelled out the mission, functions, and composition of the now defunct Security Committee, while DCID 1/17 of May 18, 1976, does the same for the Human Resources Committee. Another NFIB committee, the Committee on Imagery Requirements and Exploitation (COMIREX) is the main subject of DCID 1/13, "Coordination of the Collection and Exploitation of Imagery Intelligence."[20]

Security standards are the subject of DCIDs 1/14, 1/16, 1/19, and 1/20. DCIDs 1/14 and 1/19 are concerned with the protection of Sensitive Compartmented Information. DCID 1/14 of April 14, 1986, is entitled, "Minimum Personnel Security Standards and Procedures Governing Eligibility for Access to Sensitive Compartmented Information." The directive focuses on personnel security standards, investigative requirements, the implications of various outside activities on security, the determination of access eligibility, continuing security programs, and security violations. DCID 1/19, "Uniform Procedures for Administrative Handling and Accountability of Sensitive Compartmented Information (SCI)," focuses on physical security requirements, while DCID 1/20 concerns "Security Policy Concerning Travel and Assignment of Personnel with Access to Sensitive Compartmented Information." DCID 1/16 of June 6, 1978, deals with the " Security of Foreign Intelligence in Automated Data Processing Systems and Networks."[21]

DCID 1/18 of May 18, 1976, concerned "Recognition of Exceptional Service to the U.S. Intelligence Community" and established criteria for the award of the National Intelligence Distinguished Service Medal, National Intelligence Medal of Achievement, and Intelligence Community Certificate of Distinction.

DCID 2/1 of March 8, 1960, concerned the "Coordination of Overt Collection Abroad." Today's version of 2/1 apparently deals with the same subject and would thus cover the procurement of foreign publications and the acquisition of intelligence information from non-government organizations and individuals (such as businesses and travelers).[22]

DCIDs in the 3/ series have involved implementation of NSCID No. 3, "Coordination of Intelligence Production." These directives have dealt with the production of National Intelligence Estimates as well as the establishment of numerous NFIB committees to facilitate production of intelligence in specific areas. Early versions of DCID 3/1 (July 8, 1948), 3/2 (September 13, 1948), and 3/5 (September 1, 1953) were entitled, respectively, "Standard Operating Procedures for Departmental Participation in the Production and Coordination of National Intelligence"; "Policy Governing Departmental Concurrences in National Intelligence Reports and Estimates."; and "Production of National Intelligence Estimates."[23]

Later DCIDs in the 3/ series have defined the mission and functions of the Economic Intelligence Committee (3/1), the Joint Atomic Energy Intelligence Committee (3/3), the Guided Missile and Astronautics Intelligence Committee (3/4), the Scientific and Technical Intelligence Committee (3/5), the Human Resources Committee (3/7 of October 12, 1982), the Critical Intelligence Problems Committee (3/8 of April 6, 1983), the Technology Transfer Intelligence Committee (3/13 of December 3, 1981), the Information Handling Committee (3/14 of May 4, 1982) and the Foreign Language Committee (3/15 of March 5, 1982).[24]

DCIDs 4/1 and 4/2 of May 1976 concern the "Interagency Defector Committee" and "The Defector Program Abroad." DCID 5/1 of May 1976 is entitled "Coordination of U.S. Clandestine Foreign Intelligence Activities Abroad"; DCID 5/2, also of May 1976, is entitled "U.S. Clandestine Foreign Intelligence and Counterintelligence Liaison." DCID 6/1 of May 12, 1982 focuses on the functions, composition, and mission of the SIGINT Committee. DCID 7/1 of August 1976 is entitled "Handling of Critical Information."[25]

DCIDs for which numbers are not available include the March 30, 1983 DCID, "Intelligence Producers Council;" the DCID of May 25, 1983, on "Intelligence Disclosure Policy;" and the DCID of January 28, 1983, on the "Establishment of the National Foreign Intelligence Council."[26]

Both the DCI and the Director of the NSA are authorized to issue directives concerning aspects of the signals intelligence effort. The DCI issues Communications Intelligence Supplementary Regulations while the NSA Director issues U.S. Signals Intelligence Directives.[27]

The most important departmental regulations and directives on intelligence matters are DOD Directives, which concern both intelligence policies and the operations of specific units. Hence, DOD Directive 3310.1, "International Intelligence Agreements," specifies that:

1. The Deputy Undersecretary of Defense (Policy). . . is the principal within the Department of Defense responsible for oversight, coordination, and policy review of intelligence matters relating to agreements with foreign parties.

2. The Director, Defense Intelligence Agency (DIA), shall exercise, for the Department of Defense, approval authority (which may not be further delegated) to negotiate and conclude non-SIGINT intelligence agreements. . . .[28]

A related DOD Directive, C-5230.23 of November 18, 1983, on "Intelligence Disclosure Policy," specifies the functions of various DOD officials in the disclosure process. Thus, the Director of the DIA is to "coordinate within and for the Department of Defense, proposed disclosures of classified U.S. intelligence to senior foreign officials" while the Deputy Undersecretary for Policy is to resolve conflicts among DOD components relating to disclosure of classified U.S. intelligence to senior foreign officials.[29]

Other DOD Directives with respect to intelligence policy include "Signals Intelligence" (S-3115.7, January 25, 1983); "Implementation of National Security Council Intelligence Directive No. 7." (S-5100.19, March 19, 1959); "Human Resources Intelligence Activities" (S-5105.29, December 7, 1984); "The Security, Use and Dissemination of Communications Intelligence (COMINT)" (S-5200.17, January 26, 1965); "Coordination and Reporting of Foreign Intelligence Related Contacts and Arrangements" (S-3315.1 of March 23, 1984); "Foreign Materiel Program" (S-3325.1, September 18, 1986); and "Protection of Classified National Security Council and Intelligence Information" (5230.21, March 15, 1982).[30]

These directives may represent initial DOD implementation of an NSCID, DCID or NSDD. Thus, S-5100.19 represents initial implementation of NSCID No. 7; 3310.1 represents implementation of DCID 1/10; and 5230.21 represents implementation of NSDD-19.

Other DOD Directives specify the mission and functions of the National Security Agency and Central Security Service (S-5100.20, December 23, 1971); the Defense Intelligence Agency (5105.21, May 19, 1977); the Defense Special Missile and Astronautics Center (S-5100.43, April 27, 1964); the Defense Mapping Agency (5125.40, April 23, 1986); and the Armed Forces Medical Intelligence Center (6240.1, December 9, 1982; 6240.1-R, April 1986).[31]

Directive 6240.1 specified that

The Director, Armed Forces Medical Intelligence Center, shall:

1. have sole responsibility within the Department of Defense for the production of required medical scientific and technical intelligence (S & TI) and general medical intelligence (GMI);
2. provide timely medical intelligence support to the following:
    (1) DOD components
    (2) national-level intelligence production agencies;
    (3) other federal agencies as required;
3. organize and execute all medical aspects of the DOD Foreign Materiel Exploitation Program (FMEP);
4. exploit foreign medical materiel obtained in support of the DOD-FMEP;
5. plan, coordinate, and provide intelligence studies in accordance with the DOD S & TI production policies and procedures;

6. prepare medical intelligence under DIA technical direction for submission to the DOD-GDIP [General Defense Intelligence Program];
7. manage the medical intelligence data base and the medical portion of the DOD S & TI data base;
8. provide quick response capability in medical intelligence for the DOD and other government agencies as required;
9. assist in debriefing personnel on matters related to medical intelligence;
10. sponsor medical intelligence training for selected reserve military units and individual mobilization designees;
11. maintain coordination and liaison with members of the intelligence community on matters involving medical intelligence;
12. provide the medical intelligence adviser to the military services;
13. comply with medical intelligence collection management and production tasking policies and procedures established by the DIA and the Executive Agent;
14. provide coordinated collection requirements for medical intelligence in accordance with DOD Directive 5000.11...for the DOD intelligence community; and
15. administer contracts funded outside the GDIP when there is a technical or administrative advantage in doing so.[32]

Military service and command regulations also state intelligence policies as well as define the mission and functions of service intelligence units. Among Air Force Regulations (AFRs) governing intelligence policy are those listed in Table 16-2. AFRs governing the activities of specific intelligence units include AFR 23-30 of August 13, 1982, "Electronic Security Command," as well as those dealing with the Air Force Technical Applications Center (AFR 23-44, May 18, 1983) and the Air Force Intelligence Service (AFR 23-45, June 10, 1974).[33]

The Foreign Technology Division's activities are governed by Air Force Systems Command Regulation 23-2, with AFSC being the subject of AFR 23-8 of June 4, 1979.[34] Similar Army Regulations (ARs) governing intelligence units and activities are listed in Table 16-3.

The most detailed regulations and directives are those issued by the intelligence units themselves. These directives seek to implement the broader DOD and military service directives by adopting the guidelines, restrictions, and procedures mandated by those broader directives and by specifying the internal structure and organization of the unit and the functions of its components.

Among the eighty-eight INSCOM Regulations is INSCOM Regulation 10-2, "Organization and Functions, UNITED STATES ARMY INTELLIGENCE AND SECURITY COMMAND," of April 1, 1982. It is 131 pages long and enumerates the functions of each of the Deputy Chiefs of Staff and the divisions, branches, and offices that make up the organization. Likewise, the Air Force Technical Application Center (AFTAC) publication index lists hundreds of regulations covering administrative practices, organization and mission, personnel operations, equipment maintenance, R & D, security, and supply. Among the regulations are R55-3, "Aerial Sampling Operations," and numerous regulations specifying requirements

Table 16–2. Selected Air Force Regulations (AFRs) Concerning Intelligence Policy.

AFR	Title	Date
200-1	Air Force Intelligence Mission and Responsibilities	June 1984
200-3	The Medical Intelligence Program	Sept. 1985
200-5	Air Force Intelligence Support of the Defense Attache System	July 1985
200-7	Sensitive Compartmented Information (SCI)	April 1987
200-11	Air Force Space Intelligence Mission and Responsibilities	Nov. 1983
200-12	Foreign Materiel Program	Jan. 1983
200-15	Air Force Intelligence Functional Doctrine	Sept. 1974
200-19	Conduct of Intelligence Activities	Oct. 1983
200-25	International Intelligence Agreements	Jan. 1984

Source: Air Force Regulation 0-2, "Numerical Index of Standard and Recurring Air Force Publications," July 1, 1987, pp. 83, 84.

Table 16–3. Selected Army Regulations (ARs) Concerning Intelligence.

AR	Title	Date
10-61	U.S. Army Intelligence Operations Detachment	March 1, 1983
10-86	U.S. Army Intelligence Agency	Feb. 27, 1986
10-53	U.S. Army Intelligence and Security Command	June 15, 1978
381-1	Control of Dissemination of Intelligence Information	Nov. 15, 1982
381-3	Signals Intelligence	Jan. 15, 1982
381-10	U.S. Army Intelligence Activities	July 1, 1984
381-15	Foreign Military Intelligence Collection Activities Program	Jan. 1, 1979
381-19	Intelligence Support	July 15, 1981
381-20	U.S. Army Counterintelligence Activities	Sept. 26, 1986
381-26	Army Foreign Materiel Exploitation Program	Nov. 15, 1980
381-47	U.S. Army Offensive Counterintelligence Operations	May 15, 1981
381-100	Army Human Intelligence Collection	Aug. 1, 1981
381-155	Foreign Officer Contact Program	Nov. 8, 1985

Source: Department of the Army Pamphlet 310-1, *Consolidated Index of Army Publications and Blank Forms,* September 1, 1986.

for specific AFTAC detachments. Similarly, the 1982 *DIA Index of Administrative Publications* covered thirty-eight categories in thirty-four pages that list administrative, intelligence collection and production, and counterintelligence regulations.[35]

INDIVIDUALS, COMMITTEES, AND OFFICES

No matter how thorough the documents and directives described above or the plans described below are in stating the responsibilities and subjects for collection and analysis, they will, for several reasons, be insufficient as complete guides. First, every document leaves some room for interpretation. Second, attainment of the objectives specified will require coordination and cooperation on a regular basis. Hence, it is necessary to maintain a structure that facilitates such coordination and cooperation. Third, it is necessary to see that the components of the intelligence community are performing their activities within the restrictions imposed on them—that activities planned to attain specified objectives are acceptable to a higher authority. Fourth, some management structure is needed to generate the directives, plans, and programs under which the intelligence community operates. Finally, changing circumstances will require alterations in preconceived plans and priorities.

At the top of the individual, committee, and office control systems is the President and National Security Council committees charged with the supervision of intelligence activities. Under the Carter Administration there were two such committees: the Special Coordination Committee (SCC) and the Policy Review Committee (PRC). The SCC had jurisdiction over covert operations and counterintelligence matters, while two components of the PRC were concerned with positive intelligence. PRC—Intelligence (PRC-I) was concerned with the preparation of a consolidated national intelligence budget and resource allocation for the entire intelligence community. PRC-Space probably had some role in space reconnaissance decisions.[36]

The SCC and the Policy Review Committee were two more in a long line of NSC committees responsible for supervising intelligence activities. Until the Nixon Administration, such committees were exclusively concerned with covert operations. The first of these committees was established in 1948 by NSC 10/2 and known as the 10/2 Panel. In subsequent years, as it was re-created and its membership and functions altered or maintained, it was renamed the 10/5 Panel (NSC 10/5, October 23, 1951), the Operations Coordinating Board (NSC 5412, NSC 5412/1 of March 12–15, 1954), the 5412 Group or Special Group (NSC 5412/2 of December 28, 1955) and the 303 Committee (NSAM 303 of June 2, 1964). In 1959 the Special Group became responsible for the approval of sensitive air and naval reconnaissance missions conducted on the Soviet periphery.[37]

With the signing of National Security Decision Memorandum 40, "Responsibility for the Conduct, Supervision and Coordination of Covert Action Operations," on February 17, 1970, it was required that "the Director of Central Intelligence shall obtain policy approval for all major and/or politically sensitive covert action operations through the 40 Committee." The Memorandum also called for an annual review of all covert action programs previously approved.[38]

In addition to the 40 Committee, the Nixon Administration created a second committee, the National Security Council Intelligence Committee (NSCIC), for the supervision of the intelligence activities not under the purview of the 40 Committee. Creation of the NSCIC acknowledged that there were intelligence issues of importance in addition to covert action and sensitive reconnaissance operations. These issues included the need to make the intelligence community more responsive to policymakers, the establishment of intelligence priorities, and the allocation of resources.[39]

The basic two-committee system was continued by the Ford Administration and, as already noted, the Carter Administration. In Executive Order 11905, President Ford established the Committee on Foreign Intelligence (CFI) and the Operations Advisory Group (OAG). The CFI was chaired by the DCI, with the Deputy Secretary of Defense for Intelligence and the Deputy Assistant to the President for National Security Affairs as members. The CFI was given control over budget preparation and resource allocation for the National Foreign Intelligence Program (NFIP). Supervision of covert operations was the responsibility of the Operations Advisory Group, which consisted of the Assistant to the President for National Security Affairs, the Secretary of State, the Secretary of Defense, the Chairman of the Joint Chiefs of Staff, and the DCI—with the Chairman being determined by the President.[40] The membership of the OAG represented an upgrading in the status of the covert action supervision mechanism. Previously, membership on such committees involved officials at the under secretary and deputy secretary levels.

The upgrading was maintained in the Carter Executive Order 12036 and extended to both committees. The SCC consisted of the Assistant to the President for National Security Affairs as Chairman, the Secretary of State, the Secretary of Defense, the DCI, the Chairman of the JCS, the Attorney General, and the Director of the OMB. The PRC consisted of the same group except that the Vice-President and Secretary of the Treasury were members instead of the Attorney General and Director of the OMB.[41]

Ronald Reagan established Senior Interagency Groups (SIGs), including the Senior Interagency Group—Intelligence (SIG-I). The SIG-I was given the responsibility of advising and assisting the NSC with respect to intelligence policy and intelligence matters. The SIG-I is chaired by the DCI, and its members include the Assistant to the President for National Security Affairs, the Deputy Secretary of State, the Deputy Secretary of Defense, and the Chairman of the JCS. In addition to the statutory members, provision is made for attendance by representatives of departments and agencies with a direct interest in the activities under consideration. When meeting to consider counterintelligence activities referred by the DCI, the membership of the group is augmented by the FBI Director and the NSA Director. When meeting to consider sensitive intelligence collection activities referred by the DCI, the SIG-I's membership is augmented, as required, by the head of each organization within the intelligence community directly involved in the activity in question.[42]

The functions of SIG-I require it to:

1. establish requirements and priorities for national foreign intelligence;
2. review such National Foreign Intelligence Program and budget proposals and other matters as referred to it by the Director of Central Intelligence;
3. review proposals for sensitive foreign intelligence collection operations referred by the Director of Central Intelligence;
4. develop standards and doctrine for the counterintelligence activities of the United States; resolve interagency differences concerning the implementation

of counterintelligence policy; and develop and monitor guidelines, consistent with applicable law and Executive Orders, for the maintenance of central counterintelligence records;

5. consider and approve any counterintelligence activity referred to the Group by the head of any organization in the intelligence community;

6. submit to the NSC an overall annual assessment of the relative threat to U.S. interests from intelligence and security services of foreign powers and from international terrorist activities; including an assessment of the effectiveness of U.S. counterintelligence activities;

7. conduct an annual review of ongoing sensitive national foreign intelligence collection operations and sensitive counterintelligence activities and report thereon to the NSC; and

8. carry out such additional coordination review and approval of intelligence activities as the President may direct.[43]

Subordinate to the SIG-I are several Interagency Groups, including the Interagency Group for Counterintelligence (IG-CI) and two Interagency Groups for Countermeasures (IG-CM). The IG-CI is chaired by the Director of the FBI and includes representatives of the Secretary of State, Secretary of Defense, the DCI, Assistant to the President for National Security Affairs, Chairman of the JCS, and the NSA, as well as representatives of any other intelligence community organization directly involved in the activities to be discussed. The IG-CI is responsible for developing policy and recommendations for counterintelligence and counter-hostile covert action activities.[44]

The Interagency Group for Countermeasures (Technical) (IG-CM (T)) is headed by the Assistant Secretary of Defense for C^{3}I and serves as a bridge between the SIG-I and the National Telecommunications and Information System Security Committee. Non-technical matters, including security policy, are handled by the Interagency Group for Countermeasures (P). The National Operations Security Advisory Committee of the IG-CM (P) was asked in 1987 to review the security aspects of civilian imaging satellite operations. The single IG-CM originally established under the SIG-I was split in two at the same time the NFIB Security Committee (SECOM) was abolished. The two IG-CMs will handle many of the functions previously performed by the SECOM.[45]

Subsequent to the initial establishment of the NSC's SIGs, a SIG-Space was established. As with the PRC-Space, this committee may have some role in space reconnaissance decisions.

The structure of the NSC committee system and the names of the committees will undoubtedly change with the succession of the Reagan administration.

Responsibility for management of the intelligence community emanates in two different but not totally distinct directions from the President and the NSC. One direction is toward the DCI, the other toward the Secretary of Defense.

The DCI is the statutory head of the intelligence community. Executive Order 12333 instructs him to:

1. act as the primary adviser to the President and the NSC on national foreign intelligence;

2. develop such objectives and guidance for the Intelligence Community as will enhance capabilities for responding to expected future needs for national foreign intelligence;

3. promote the development and maintenance of service of common concern by designated intelligence organizations on behalf of the Intelligence Community;

4. ensure implementation of special activities;

5. ...coordinate foreign intelligence and counterintelligence relationships between agencies of the Intelligence Community and the intelligence or internal security services of foreign governments;

6. ensure the establishment by the Intelligence Community of common security and access standards for managing and handling foreign intelligence systems, information, and products;

7. ensure that programs are developed which protect intelligence sources, methods, and analytical procedures;

8. establish uniform criteria for the determination of relative priorities for the transmission of critical national foreign intelligence, and advise the Secretary of Defense concerning the communications requirements of the Intelligence Community for the transmission of such intelligence;

9. establish appropriate staffs, committees, or other advisory groups to assist in the execution of the Director's responsibilities;

10. have full responsibility for production and dissemination of national foreign intelligence, and authority to levy analytical tasks on departmental intelligence production organizations, in consultation with those organizations' policymakers;

11. ensure the timely exploitation and dissemination of data gathered by national foreign intelligence collection means;

12. establish mechanisms which translate national foreign intelligence objectives and priorities approved by the NSC into specific guidance for the Intelligence Community, resolve conflicts in tasking priority...and provide for the development of plans and arrangements for transfer of required collection tasking authority to the Secretary of Defense when directed by the President;

13. develop, with the advice of the program managers and departments and agencies concerned, the consolidated National Foreign Intelligence Program budget;

14. monitor National Foreign Intelligence Program implementation, and, as necessary, conduct program and performance audits and evaluation and;

15. together with the Secretary of Defense, ensure that there is no unnecessary overlap between national foreign intelligence programs and Department of Defense intelligence programs consistent with the requirement to develop competitive analysis, and provide to and obtain from the Secretary of Defense all information necessary for this purpose.[46]

The responsibilities of the DCI, as stated in Executive Order 12333, previous Executive Orders, and the National Security Act of 1947, have not been matched by the power to fulfill these responsibilities. As Richard Helms noted in 1969, while the DCI was theoretically responsible for 100 percent of U.S. intelligence activities, he controlled less than 15 percent of the intelligence community's assets, while almost 85 percent were controlled by the Secretary of Defense and the JCS. And, until the signing of PD-17 in the Carter Administration, the DCI had neither budgetary or day-to-day management control. Management control of the National Reconnaissance Office and National Security Agency remained with the Secretary of Defense. The DCI did receive full and exclusive authority to approve the National Foreign Intelligence Program (NFIP) budget—which includes the Department of Defense portion, comprising the General Defense Intelligence Program, the National Reconnaissance Program (Air Force Special Reconnaissance Activities), Navy Special Reconnaissance Activities, the Consolidated Cryptologic Program, and the Defense Foreign Counterintelligence Program.[47]

Four organizations established to help the DCI fulfill responsibilities are the Intelligence Community Staff (ICS), the National Intelligence Council (NIC), the National Foreign Intelligence Council (NFIC), and the National Foreign Intelligence Board (NFIB). The present ICS is the descendant of the National Intelligence Programs Evaluation Staff created in 1963 as well as the more recent Resource Management Staff. The ICS, with a full-time staff of approximately 230, is the principal support element of the DCI on matters relating to the NFIP budget prior to its presentation to the President, for budget presentation to Congress, and for reprogramming NFIP funds and monitoring the implementation of the programs.

As part of its review function, the ICS set up a Community Counterintelligence Staff drawn from the FBI, the CIA, the Department of Defense to make regular overall assessments of intelligence threats and U.S. countermeasures.[48] It has also reviewed technical collection programs to evaluate their efficiency and provide data for resource allocation decisions. It has conducted studies to evaluate the utility of imaging, signals, and other intelligence collection systems in producing high-level intelligence.

The ICS took over some of the collection tasking work performed in the Carter Administration by the National Intelligence Tasking Center (NITC) via its Collection Tasking Staff.[49]

The present organization of the Intelligence Community Staff is shown as Figure 16–1. As indicated, the ICS contains several staffs for budget, review, and other purposes. The Program and Budget Staff develops and justifies before Congress the budget for the National Foreign Intelligence Program. The Policy and Planning Staff is responsible for promoting long-range planning throughout the intelligence community. The Legislative Liaison Staff is a primary conduit for community matters to Congressional intelligence committees. The Secretariat Staff provides secretariat services to the NFIB, the SIG-I and other senior level groups. It also serves as home for the support elements for six NFIB committees.[50]

Figure 16–1. Intelligence Community Staff.

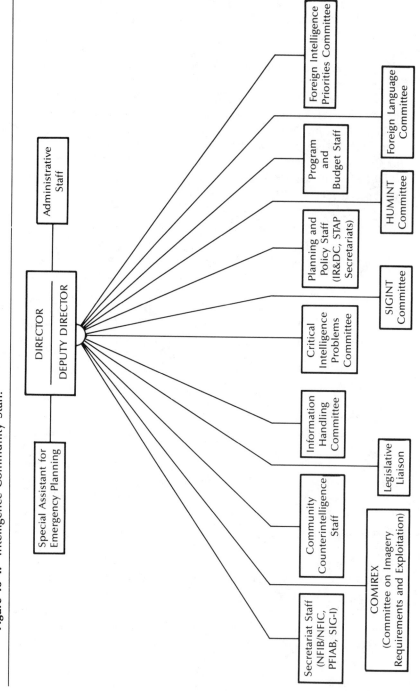

The National Intelligence Council is the DCI's principal means of producing National Intelligence Estimates, Special National Intelligence Estimates and Interagency Intelligence Memoranda. The Council consists of a chairman, seventeen National Intelligence Officers responsible for specific geographic or substantive areas, and an Analytic Group consisting of approximately fifteen analysts.[51]

While the ICS and National Intelligence Council are subordinate to the DCI, the NFIB and the NFIC provide "advice and counsel" to the DCI and are the DCI's principal means of coordinating intelligence community activities and attaining consensus on major issues.

The NFIB is the successor to the U.S. Intelligence Board (USIB), which had been formed in 1958 by the merger of the Intelligence Advisory Committee and the Communications Intelligence Board. The functions of the NFIB, as defined in DCID 1/8 of May 6, 1976, are:

- review and coordination of national intelligence products;
- maintenance of effective interface between intelligence producers and consumers and the development of procedures for continuing identification of consumer needs for intelligence;
- the establishment of appropriate objectives, requirements and priorities for substantive intelligence;
- the review of requirements coordination and operational guidance for intelligence collection systems;
- the production of sensitive intelligence sources and methods and sensitive intelligence information;
- the development, as appropriate, of policies regarding arrangements with foreign governments on intelligence matters; and
- such other matters as the Director of Central Intelligence may refer to the Board for advice.[52]

The DCI serves as Chairman of the NFIB, whose other members include the Directors of the NRO, the NSA, and the Bureau of Intelligence Research, and representatives of the FBI, Department of Energy, and Department of the Treasury as well as the Deputy Director of the CIA. The Assistant Chief of Staff, Intelligence of the Air Force, the Deputy Chief of Staff for Intelligence of the Army, the Director of Naval Intelligence, and the Director of Intelligence for the Marine Corps sit on the Board as observers.[53]

Subordinate to the NFIB is an elaborate committee structure. It is through these committees that the NFIB

lists the targets for American intelligence and the priority attached to each one, coordinates within the intelligence community the estimates of future events and enemy strengths, controls the classification and security systems for most of the U.S. government, directs research in the various fields of technical intelligence, and decides what classified information will be passed on to foreign friends and allies.[54]

The committees also serve as a means of informing the members of the intelligence community on particular matters (e.g., weapons and space systems) and providing support to agencies outside the intelligence community.

Present committees include the SIGINT Committee, the Technology Transfer Intelligence Committee, Economic Intelligence Committee, Human Resource Committee, Critical Intelligence Problems Committee, Scientific and Technical Intelligence Committee, Information Handling Committee, Joint Atomic Energy Intelligence Committee, the Weapons and Space System Intelligence Committee, the Foreign Language Committee, and the Committee on Imagery Requirements and Exploitation.[55]

There are additional NFIB committees whose existence is classified. Among the classified committees may be a Watch Committee—whose function, when first established, was to evaluate intelligence with respect to possible indications of an attack on the United States, U.S. troops, or U.S. allies. The Committee had been disestablished many years before the advent of the Reagan Administration but reestablished at the direction of William Casey. Another of the classified committees may be the Denial and Deception Analysis Committee, which is concerned with attempts by foreign nations to deny or decrease information acquired by U.S. intelligence collection systems, whether human or technical.[56]

The SIGINT Committee was formed in 1962 by the merger of the COMINT and ELINT Committees. It reviews and validates all proposed requirements before they are levied on the NSA. The Technology Transfer Intelligence Committee (TTIC) was created in 1981 to deal with what was perceived to be a growing hemmorhage of critical technology to the Soviet Union. The TTIC, which operates through two subcommittees (the Subcommittee on Exchanges and the Subcommittee on Export Control), draws on scientific and technical analysts throughout the military technical intelligence centers and elsewhere in the intelligence community.[57]

The TTIC's functions are to:

- advise the DCI on the effectiveness of the Intelligence Community's role in support of U.S. Government policy on technology transfer issues;
- as directed, prepare coordinated intelligence assessments on the significance of technology transfer and, as appropriate, their implications for national security;
- advise appropriate U.S. government departments and agencies of the technology transfer implications and foreign intelligence equities involved in exchange programs and commercial contacts with nationals from designated foreign countries and recommend changes as appropriate;
- provide foreign intelligence support on export control issues to appropriate U.S. Government agencies;
- monitor all technology transfer intelligence concerning foreign efforts to acquire U.S. and Western technology and provide appropriate analyses to U.S. Government organizations concerned with protection and countermeasures, including counterintelligence organizations;
- provide priority guidance to collection systems on technology transfer issues; and

- establish an exchange of information with all departments and agencies concerned with the technology transfer program to ensure that utility of the Intelligence Community's activities is maintained.[58]

The Economic Intelligence Committee (EIC) was established in 1948 as a subsidiary of the Intelligence Advisory Committee and has continued as a subsidiary of the USIB and NFIB. The Subcommittee on Requirements and Coordination of the EIC produces the Economic Alert List (EAL) which highlights the current economic information needs of all agencies participating in the Combined Economic Reporting Program (CERP). The EIC is chaired by the head of the Office of Global Issues of the CIA's Directorate of Intelligence.[59]

The Joint Atomic Energy Intelligence Committee, chaired by the chief of the CIA's Office of Scientific and Weapons Research, was created to "foster, develop and maintain a coordinated community approach to the problems in the field of atomic energy intelligence, to promote interagency liaison, and to give added impetus and community support to the efforts of individual agencies."[60]

The Critical Intelligence Problems Committee (CIPC) was created in 1958—as the Critical Collection Problems Committee (CCPC)—to examine, as its name suggests, particularly difficult collection problems regardless of the techniques involved. In 1971, one subject considered by the CCPC was narcotics intelligence. In 1985 the CIPC sponsored a conference on Combat Intelligence Analysis and produced at least three studies—on combat intelligence analysis, cruise missile collection, and Strategic Defense Initiative intelligence. Among its components is the CIPC Narcotics Working Group.[61]

According to a DCID of April 6, 1983, the Committee is to identify:

- the specific intelligence requirements and shortfalls associated with the critical intelligence problem under review;
- current and programmed collection, processing, and production resources directed against the critical intelligence problem;
- options for adjustments in collection, processing and production efforts which could be accomplished within existing resources, and the associated impact such adjustments would have on the Intelligence Community's ability to respond to other priority intelligence needs; and
- recommendations for new initiatives which could increase collection, processing, and production efforts against the critical intelligence problem, noting which options would require reprogramming of supplemental funding actions.[62]

The Scientific and Technical Intelligence Committee (STIC), also chaired by the head of the OSWR (Office of Scientific and Weapons Research), serves as the supervisory committee over all civilian/military scientific and technical intelligence production and the necessary intelligence acquisition. Subordinate to the STIC are a number of groups, panels, and subcommittees, which apparently include the Life Sciences Group, Radar and Optical Steering Group, Radar Subcommittee, Multispectral High Energy Laser Panel, Scientific and Technical Information

Support Program Committee, the Scientific and Technical Thermal Applications Group, and the Multispectral/Laser Applications Group.[63]

The Information Handling Committee is responsible for all aspects of information handling—supervising research and development of information-handling systems, developing rules and procedures for the exchange of information between agencies, and establishing education and training programs in information science. Among its components is the Geographic Information Systems Subcommittee (with a similarly titled working group).[64]

The Weapons and Space System Intelligence Committee, chaired by the head of the OSWR, was created, as the Guided Missile Intelligence Committee, in 1956. In addition to producing analyses of the technical characteristics of Soviet and other foreign missile systems it assigns designators and code names for such systems. It also serves as a means for disseminating weapons and space system intelligence to the rest of the intelligence community, and promoting liaison among intelligence units on weapons and space system matters. Among its subordinate elements are the Ballistic Missile Systems Subcommittee, the Telemetry and Beacon Analysis Subcommittee, and the PVO Strany Subcommittee (with a C^3 Working Group).[65]

The Foreign Language Committee's three basic responsibilities are to:

- appraise the effectiveness of programs to recruit, train, and retain personnel with adequate foreign language competence for elements of the Intelligence Community;
- recommend to the DCI new initiatives to be undertaken to ensure the continuing availability within the Intelligence Community of requisite foreign language competence;
- coordinate replies to all queries from Congressional committees concerning the Community's overall foreign language competence.[66]

The NFIC was a Reagan Administration creation. The Council evolved out of the NFIB and deals with priorities and budgets. As with the NFIB, the DCI is chairman, and the Deputy DCI is designated vice-chairman and represents the CIA. Membership includes those agencies represented on the NFIB as well as the intelligence chiefs of the military services and senior representatives of the Secretary of Defense, the Attorney General, the Secretary of Commerce, and the Assistant to the President for National Security Affairs.[67]

Another Reagan Administration initiative is the Intelligence Producers Council (IPC), created by a DCID on March 30, 1983. In addition to the Chairman of the Council, IPC members include senior representatives of the CIA, the DIA, INR, and the NSA, with senior representatives of the military intelligence services attending, on some occasions, as observers. The functions of the IPC include monitoring the intelligence producer's needs for intelligence information, participating in assessments and evaluations of present and proposed intelligence community collection and processing systems and activities, and identifying means to improve intelligence production programs.[68]

The Secretary of Defense exerts control over intelligence matters through several channels: two executive committees, two under secretaries and the JCS.

The executive committees responsible to the Secretary are both concerned with reconnaissance matters. The National Reconnaissance Executive Committee (NREC) makes basic decisions concerning the operation of the NRO—overall budget and allocation of funds to different projects. It is chaired by the DCI and also includes the Assistant to the President for National Security Affairs and a DOD representative as members. A second executive committee, probably called the National Executive Committee for Special Navy Activities, supervises sensitive underseas intelligence programs. As with the NREC, it is chaired by the DCI and reports to the Secretary of Defense.[69]

Decisions made by the NREC then go to the Secretary of Defense for approval. If the DCI disagrees with the decision of the Secretary of Defense, he may appeal to the President. In 1975, the Committee, with the concurrence of DCI William Colby, approved development and deployment of a SIGINT satellite code named ARGUS. ARGUS was intended as a follow-up to the RHYOLITE satellite. Secretary of Defense James Schlesinger ruled the system unnecessary, apparently preferring to maintain a peak level of photo reconnaissance coverage. Colby appealed to President Ford, who ordered the National Security Council to examine the issue. On the basis of that review, Ford sided with Colby. However, funding for the satellite was deleted by the Congressional supervisory committee.[70]

Subordinate to the Deputy Under Secretary of Defense for Policy (DUSD (P)) are several offices with the responsibility of establishing policies for and supervising intelligence activities. These include the Special Advisory Staff, and the Office of Counterintelligence and Investigative Programs.[71]

Particularly interesting is the Special Advisory Staff, the Director of which is

responsible for serving as the principal assistant to the DUSD (Policy) for all matters relating to the conduct of sensitive intelligence, intelligence—related and reconnaissance activities. In this regard, the Director, Special Advisory Staff will formulate policy positions that will strongly influence the deployment of U.S. reconnaissance assets, the movement of personnel in support of special operations, and the allocations of DOD fiscal and physical resources to operations within and outside DOD.[72]

Subordinate to the Under Secretary of Defense Acquisition is the Assistant Secretary of Defense (C³I), whose Deputy Assistant Secretary of Defense (Intelligence) supervises the Director of National Intelligence Systems, the Director of Intelligence Resources, and the Director of Tactical Intelligence Systems. The agencies that fall under the purview of the Deputy Assistant Secretary include the NSA, the DIA and the DMA.[73]

Under the authority of the JCS, and ultimately the Secretary of Defense, management and control of some intelligence activities is conducted through the JCS. The JCS runs the Joint Reconnaissance Center (JRC), which approves and monitors air and sea reconnaissance missions.

JCS management responsibilities are also fulfilled by the Director of the DIA. In addition to the management role exercised through the DIA's internal organization, the DDIA also chairs the Military Intelligence Board. In addition to the Director, DIA, the board includes the Assistant Chief of Staff, Intelligence, Air Force; the Deputy Chief of Staff, Intelligence, Army; the Director of Naval Intelligence, and the Director of Intelligence, Marine Corps. The Board serves to provide a forum for the defense intelligence community to discuss coordination and cooperation in a variety of areas.

Within the individual services, most management responsibility is exercised through the offices just mentioned. The Navy did maintain a two-person (one military officer, one civilian assistant) Naval Reconnaissance Center. The Center provided information and guidance to Fleet Commanders with regard to the conduct of reconnaissance missions in accordance with JCS guidance, as well as participated in the planning of reconnaissance and surveillance operations "in satisfaction of Navy and National requirements." Through liaison with the JRC, it monitored worldwide reconnaissance activity each day.[74]

Subordinate to the Under Secretary of the Air Force is the Defense Support Project Office (DSPO), which is responsible for providing central management for the Defense Reconnaissance Support Program (DRSP). This program is directed at providing space reconnaissance data in support of operational military forces. Subordinate to the Director and Deputy Director of the DSPO is the DSPO Staff Director, who supervises a small staff of Army, Navy, and Air Force personnel divided into offices for Program Management, Operations and Plans, and Program Control.[75]

The Army Space Program Office, is the Army point of contact to the Tactical Exploitation of National Space Capabilities (TENCAP) program.[76]

PROGRAMS, PLANS, AND REQUIREMENTS DOCUMENTS

In any given year there must be a specific allocation of resources (collection systems) to targets in order to produce the intelligence required by decisionmakers and other government officials. Two programs govern the allocation of resources: the NFIP and the Tactical Intelligence and Related Activities (TIARA) program.

The NFIP encompasses all national foreign intelligence activity. One component of the NFIP is the Central Intelligence Agency Program. There are five DOD components: the Consolidated Cryptologic Program (CCP), the General Defense Intelligence Program (GDIP), Navy Special Reconnaissance Activities, Air Force Special Reconnaissance Activities, and the Defense Foreign Counterintelligence Program.[77]

The CCP is managed by the NSA and includes all SIGINT resources in the NFIP. The GDIP includes all non-SIGINT, non-reconnaissance programs. Specifically, the GDIP includes eight activities:

1. General military production
2. Imagery collection and processing
3. HUMINT
4. Nuclear monitoring
5. R & D and procurement
6. Field support
7. General support
8. Scientific and technical intelligence production.

The Navy Special Reconnaissance Activities Program specifies the allocation of attack submarines and other craft for the performance of intelligence gathering in the Arctic and near (or in) Soviet territorial waters. The Air Force Special Reconnaissance Activities Program is also known as the National Reconnaissance Program, the program that dictates the spending and procurement activities of the NRO.

The TIARA program is composed of three programs: Tactical Intelligence, Reconnaissance, Surveillance, and Target Acquisition; the DRSP; and the Tactical Cryptologic Program.[78]

The number of individual programs that constitute a military service's portion of the TIARA may be quite large. As of 1983, the Navy's portion of the TIARA consisted of the following thirty-three programs: AN/SKR-7, Battle Group Passive Horizon System, BEARTRAP, Classic Wizard, Combat Direction Finding, Combat Underwater Exploitation System, Cryptologic Direct Support, Cryptologic Training, Defense Meteorological Satellite Program (DMSP), Fleet Intelligence Support Center (Western Pacific), Guardian Bear, Integrated Tactical Surveillance System (ITSS), Intelligence Engineering, Intelligence Staff Support, Joint Tactical Fusion Program, Naval Intelligence Processing System, Naval Space Surveillance System, Ocean Surveillance Information System, Outboard, Over the Horizon Targeting, Photo Reconnaissance Squadrons—Tactical Air Reconnaissance Pod System, Prairie Wagon Augmentation, Rapidly Deployable Surveillance System (RDSS), Reserve Intelligence Program, Tactical Air Reconnaissance System (RF/A18), Shore-Based Electronic Warfare Squadrons (VQ), Fixed Underseas Surveillance System (SOSUS), Surface Towed Array Surveillance System (SURTASS), Tactical Intelligence Support, Tactical Cryptologic Shore Support, Tactical Cryptologic Technical Development, Training, and TENCAP.[79]

Based on such national plans, plans are established at lower levels to specify the allocation of resources to targets/activities and objectives. Thus, the Air Force established the Air Force Intelligence Plan with three subsidiary plans: the Signals Intelligence Baseline Plan, the Imagery Architecture Plan, and the Air Force Intelligence Communication Plan.[80]

Prior to the allocation of resources to collection tasks, there needs to be (at least in theory) appropriate guidance that tells intelligence officials which items or subjects are of greatest priority to their customers. Guidance documents are of varying levels of specificity, and several guidance documents might emerge from the same source.

One document used to guide COMINT collection is the "Intelligence Guidance for COMINT Production."[81]

In the Ford Administration the DCI alone had a *Directive* (a matrix of 120 countries against eighty-three topics, with numerical priorities assigned from one to seven for each country); *Perspectives*, defining the major problems that policymakers would face over the next five years; *Objectives*, detailing resources management; and Key Intelligence Questions (KIQs), identifying topics of particular interest to national policymakers.[82]

The KIQs were introduced by William Colby during his tenure as DCI. They were designed to get all of the intelligence agencies to respond to policymakers' needs rather than just their own operational requirements. They also were designed "to replace an enormous paper exercise called the requirements process with a simple set of general questions about the key problems we should concentrate on."[83]

As the process was described by Colby,

> once each KIQ was formulated, the various agencies discussed what each would do to answer the question. This was followed by a statement of the resources that each agency would apply, so that an initial judgement would be made as to whether too many or too few were involved in the resolution of each KIQ.[84]

In Fiscal Year 1975 there were sixty-nine KIQs covering military, political, and economic topics. KIQ 57 asked: "What are the principal objectives of the major economic powers (especially France, West Germany, Japan, the U.K., Italy, Canada and Brazil) in forthcoming multi-lateral trade (GATT) and financial negotiations (IMF)?" KIQ 59 asked: "What are the policies, negotiating positions and vulnerabilities of the major petroleum exporters with respect to the production and marketing of oil, and how are their policies affected by the prospects for development of non-OPEC energy sources?"[85]

The KIQs apparently never had the desired effect of directing the intelligence collection units toward collection in response to the concerns of national leaders. Thus, the Church Committee concluded that the "DIA and DDO invoked the KIQs to justify their operations and budgets, however they did not appear to be shaping the programs to meet KIQ objectives."[86]

Under the Carter and Reagan Administrations the KIQs have been replaced by the National Intelligence Topics (NITs). These documents were first issued by the NSC Policy Review Committee and were intended to "articulate National level policymakers' intelligence requirements which are reflective of current national policy."[87]

Along with "U.S. Foreign Intelligence Requirements Categories and Priorities," a basic requirements document that is reissued annually and periodically updated, the NITs are intended to "provide all elements of the intelligence community with guidance for the conduct of collection, analysis, and production management activities."[88]

NOTES TO CHAPTER 16

1. Ronald Reagan, "Executive Order 12333: United States Intelligence Activities," *Federal Register*, 46, no. 236 (December 8, 1981): 59941-54.

2. Gerald Ford, "Executive Order 11905: United States Intelligence Activities," *Weekly Compilation of Presidential Documents* 12, no. 8 (1976): 234-43.

3. Jimmy Carter, "Executive Order 12036: United States Intelligence Activities," *Federal Register*, 43, no. 18 (January 24, 1978): 3675-98.

4. Ronald Reagan, "Executive Order 12356: National Security Information," *Federal Register*, 47, no. 66 (April 6, 1982): 14874-84.

5. Lawrence J. Korb, "National Security Organization and Process in the Carter Administration," in Sam C. Sarkesian, ed., *Defense Policy and the Presidency: Carter's First Years* (Boulder, Col.: Westview, 1979), pp. 111-37; PDs 37 and 55 were obtained from the National Archives and under the Freedom of Information Act, respectively.

6. On NSDD-17 see Raymond Bonner, "President Approved Policy of Preventing 'Cuba-Model' States," *New York Times*, April 7, 1983, pp. 1, 16. On NSDD-42 see U.S. Congress, House Committee on Science and Technology, *National Space Policy* (Washington, D.C.: U.S. Government Printing Office, 1982), p. 13; NSDDs 19, 22, 84, and 196 were obtained, in whole or in part, under the Freedom of Information Act. NSDD-159 was released during the Iran-Contra hearings. On NSDD-202 see U.S. Congress, Senate Committee on Armed Services, *Department of Defense Authorization for Appropriations for Fiscal Years 1988 and 1989, Part 4* (Washington, D.C.: U.S. Government Printing Office, 1987), pp. 1783-84; NSDD-286 is discussed in David C. Morison, "An Eye on the CIA," *National Journal*, April 16, 1988, pp. 1009-1013.

7. NSCID No. 1, "Basic Duties and Responsibilities," February 17, 1972, *Declassified Documents Reference System 1976-167G*.

8. Ibid.

9. NSCID No. 2, "Coordination of Overt Collection Activities," February 17, 1972, *Declassified Documents Reference System 1976-253D*.

10. NSCID No. 3, "Coordination of Intelligence Production," February 17, 1972, *Declassified Documents Reference System 1976-253E*.

11. Ibid.

12. U.S. Congress, House Permanent Select Committee on Intelligence, *Annual Report* (Washington, D.C.: U.S. Government Printing Office, 1978), p. 70.

13. NSCID No. 5, "U.S. Espionage and Counterintelligence Activities Abroad," February 17, 1972, *Declassified Documents Reference System 1976-253F*.

14. Department of Justice, *Report on Inquiry into CIA–Related Electronic Surveillance Activities* (Washington, D.C.: Department of Justice, 1976), pp. 77–8.

15. NSCID No. 7, "Domestic Exploitation," February 12, 1948, Declassified Documents Reference System 1976-166A.

16. U.S. Congress, House Permanent Select Committee on Intelligence, *Annual Report*, p. 71.

17. NSCID No. 8, "Photographic Interpretation," February 17, 1972, Declassified Documents Reference System 1976-253G.

18. Department of Justice, *Report on Inquiry into CIA-Related Electronic Surveillance Activities* (Washington, D.C.: Department of Justice, 1976), p. 100.

19. DCID 1/3, "Committees of the Director of Central Intelligence," May 18, 1976; DCID 1/4, "Intelligence Information Handling Committee," May 18, 1976; U.S. Congress, House Permanent Select Committee on Intelligence, *Annual Report*, p. 70; Enclosure 1 of DOD Instruction 5230.22, "Control of Dissemination of Intelligence Information," April 1, 1982; DCID 1/8, "The National Foreign Intelligence Board," May 6, 1976; HQ USAF, ACS, I, INOI 11-3, "Intelligence Community Boards, Councils and Committees," December 30, 1983.

20. Reference (d) to DOD Directive 3310.1, "International Intelligence Agreements," October 22, 1982; DCID 1/11, "Security Committee," July 15, 1982; DCID 1/17, "Human Resources Committee," May 18, 1976; DCID 1/13, "Coordination of the Collection and Exploitation of Imagery Intelligence," February 2, 1973, *Declassified Documents Reference System 1980-132D.*

21. U.S. Congress, House Permanent Select Committee on Intelligence, *Security Clearance Procedures in the Intelligence Agencies* (Washington, D.C.: U.S. Government Printing Office, 1979), pp. 25–29; U.S. Congress, House Permanent Select Committee on Intelligence, *Espionage Laws and Leaks* (Washington, D.C.: U.S. Government Printing Office, 1979), p. 276; Working Group on Computer Security, *Computer and Telecommunications Policy* (Washington, D.C.: National Communications Security Committee, July 1981), p. 158; DCID 1/14, "Minimum Personnel Security Standards and Procedures Governing Eligibility for Access to Sensitive Compartmented Information," April 14, 1986; Department of Energy Order 5636.2, "Security Requirements for Classified Automatic Data Processing Systems," January 10, 1980.

22. DCID 2/1, "Coordination of Overt Collection Abroad," March 8, 1960, *Declassified Documents Reference System 1980-131B.*

23. John Prados, *The Soviet Estimate: U.S. Intelligence Analysis and Russian Military Strength* (New York: Dial, 1982), pp. 306–307.

24. U.S. Congress, House Permanent Select Committee on Intelligence, *Annual Report*, pp. 35, 49; DCID 3/3, "Production of Atomic Energy Intelligence," April 23, 1965, *Declassified Documents Reference System 1980-131G*; DCID 3/4, "Production of Guided Missile and Astronautics Intelligence," April 23, 1965, *Delcassified Documents Reference System 1980-132A.*

25. U.S. Congress, House Permanent Select Committee on Intelligence, *Annual Report*, pp. 42, 70–71; DCID 6/1, "SIGINT Committee," May 12, 1982.

26. HQ USAF, ACS, I INOI 11-3, "Intelligence Community Boards, Councils and Committees."

27. U.S. Congress, House Permanent Select Committee on Intelligence, *Security Clearance Procedures*, p. 29.

28. DOD Directive 3310.1, "International Intelligence Agreements," October 22, 1982.

29. DOD Directive C-5230.23, "Intelligence Disclosure Policy," November 18, 1983.

30. DOD 5025.1-I, *DOD Directives System Annual Index*, (Washington, D.C.: DOD, January 1987), pp. 17, 19, 34, 36, 42.

31. Ibid., pp. 34, 35, 37.

32. DOD Directive 6240.1, "Armed Forces Medical Intelligence Center," December 9, 1982.

33. AF Regulation 0-2, "Numerical Index of Standard and Recurring Air Force Publications," July 1, 1987, pp. 83–84.

34. AFSC Regulation 23-2, "Foreign Technology Division—Organization and Mission-Field," June 4, 1979.

35. INSCOM Pamphlet 310-1, "Index of Administrative Publications," July 31, 1986; AFTAC Center Regulation 0-2, "Numerical Index of Center Publications," November 1986; DIA Regulation 0-2, "Index of DIA Administration Publications," December 10, 1982.

36. Korb, "National Security Organization and Process in the Carter Administration."

37. Emmanuel Adler, "Executive Command and Control in Foreign Policy: The CIA's Covert Activities," *Orbis* 23 (Fall 1979): 671-96; U.S. Congress, Senate Select Committee to Study Governmental Operations with Respect to Intelligence Activities, *Foreign and Military Intelligence, (Final Report: Book I)* (Washington, D.C.: U.S. Government Printing Office, 1976), p. 53.

38. National Security Decision Memorandum 40, "Responsibility for the Conduct, Supervision and Coordination of Covert Action Operations." *Declassified Documents Reference System 1976-297A.*

39. U.S. Congress, Senate Select Committee to Study Governmental Operations with Respect to Intelligence Activities, *Foreign and Military Intelligence, (Final Report: Book I)*, p. 61.

40. Gerald Ford, "Executive Order 11905: United States Intelligence Activities."

41. Jimmy Carter, "Executive Order 12036: United States Intelligence Activities."

42. NSDD-2, "National Security Council Structure," January 12, 1982; National Defense University, *Publication 5—Intelligence For Joint Forces* (Norfolk, Va.: Armed Forces Staff College, August 1985), pp. 2-1 to 2-2.

43. NSDD-2, "National Security Council Structure," January 12, 1982.

44. U.S. Congress, Senate Select Committee on Intelligence, *Report, January 1, 1981 to December 31, 1982* (Washington, D.C.: U.S. Government Printing Office, 1983), p. 23.

45. U.S. Congress, Senate Select Committee on Intelligence, *Meeting the Espionage Challenge: A Review of United States Counterintelligence and Security Programs* (Washington, D.C.: U.S. Government Printing Office, 1986), pp. 60–61.

46. Ronald Reagan, "Executive Order 12333: United States Intelligence Activities," pp. 59943-44.

47. Victor Marchetti and John Marks, *The CIA and the Cult of Intelligence* (New York: Knopf, 1974), pp. 98–99; Caspar Weinberger, *FY 1983 Report of Secretary of Defense Caspar Weinberger* (Washington, D.C.: U.S. Government Printing Office, 1982), p. III-88.

48. U.S. Congress, Senate Select Committee on Intelligence, *Report, January 1, 1981 to December 31, 1982*, p. 23.

49. Stephen J. Flanagan, "The Coordination of National Intelligence," in Duncan Clarke, ed., *Public Policy and Political Institutions: United States Defense and Foreign Policy—Policy Coordination and Integration* (Greenwich, Conn.: JAI Press, 1987), p. 178.

50. Vice Admiral E.A. Burkhalter, Jr., "The Role of the Intelligence Community Staff," *Signal* (September 1984): 33–35.

51. Ibid.; U.S. Congress, House Permanent Select Committee on Intelligence, *The Role of Intelligence in the Foreign Policy Process* (Washington, D.C.: U.S. Government Printing Office, 1980), pp. 73, 135.

52. DCID 1/8, "National Foreign Intelligence Board," May 6, 1976.

53. DIA Regulation 50-17, "Release of Classified DOD Intelligence to Non-NFIB U.S. Government Agencies," July 26, 1978.

54. Marchetti and Marks, *The CIA and the Cult of Intelligence,* pp. 81, 84.

55. Letter to the author from Lee S. Strickland, CIA Information and Privacy Coordinator, June 5, 1987.

56. Ibid.; "Shifting CIA Production from a Topical to a Geographical Base," CIA memo, April 1982; Diane T. Putney, *History of the Air Force Intelligence Service 1 January—31 December 1984, Volume 1—Narrative and Appendices*, (Fort Belvoir, Va.: AFIS, n.d.), p. 31.

57. National Academy of Sciences, *Scientific Communication and National Security* (Washington, D.C.: National Academy Press, 1983), pp. 72, 141–412.

58. DCID 3/13, "Technology Transfer Intelligence Committee," December 3, 1981.

59. Konrad Ege, "CIA Targets African Economies," *Counter-Spy* (July–August 1982): 30–38; "Shifting CIA Production from a Topical to a Geographic Base."

60. DCID 3/3, "Production of Atomic Energy Intelligence"; "Shifting CIA Production from Topical to a Geographic Base."

61. Department of Justice, *Report on Inquiry into CIA-Related Electronic Surveillance Activities*, pp. 72–73; Office of Naval Intelligence, *Office of Naval Intelligence (ONI) Annual History, 1985* (Washington, D.C.: ONI, 1987), pp. 5, 9.

62. DCID 3/8, "Critical Intelligence Problems Committee," April 6, 1983.

63. Diane T. Putney, *History of the Air Force Intelligence Service, 1 January—31 December 1984*, pp. 335–36; Department of the Air Force, *Headquarters Publication 21-1*, pp. 6–23; "Shifting Production from a Topical to a Geographic Base"; Diane T. Putney, *History of the Air Force Intelligence Service, 1 January—31 December 1983 Volume 1—Narrative and Appendices* (Fort Belvoir, Va.: AFIS, n.d.), p. 340.

64. DCID 3/14, "Information Handling Committee," May 4, 1982; Diane T. Putney, *History of the Air Force Intelligence Service, 1 January—31 December 1983*, p. 95.

65. Prados, *The Soviet Estimate*, pp. 59–61; U.S. Congress, House Committee on Appropriations, *Department of Defense Appropriations for 1978, Part 1* (Washington, D.C.: U.S. Government Printing Office, 1977), p. 224; Frederick C. Engelman, Jr., *Trends in the Modernization of U.S.S.R. Strategic Air Defense Command and Control* (Maxwell AFB, Ala.: Air Command and Staff College, 1979), p. 3; NISC Instruction 3120.1A, "Organization and Regulations Manual," November 15, 1985, pp. 2-27, 2-33.

66. DCID 3/15, "Foreign Language Committee," March 5, 1982.

67. National Defense University, *Publication 5—Intelligence for Joint Forces*, pp. 2-4 to 2-5.

68. DCID, "The Intelligence Producers Council," March 30, 1983.

69. U.S. Congress, Senate Select Committee to Study Governmental Operations with Respect to Intelligence Activities, *Final Report Book IV: Supplementary Detailed Staff Reports* (Washington, D.C.: U.S. Government Printing Office, 1976), p. 75; U.S. Congress, Senate Select Committee to Study Governmental Operations with Respect to Intelligence Activities, *Final Report, Book I: Foreign and Military Intelligence*, p. 335.

70. Philip Klass, "U.S. Monitoring Capability Impaired," *Aviation Week and Space Technology*, May 14, 1979, p. 18; Robert Lindsey, *The Falcon and the Snowman: A True Story of Friendship and Espionage* (New York: Simon & Schuster, 1979), p. 347.

71. *Department of Defense Telephone Directory* (Washington, D.C.: U.S. Government Printing Office, December 1987), p. O-4.

72. Senior Executive Service Vacancy Announcement No. SES 3-83.

73. *Department of Defense Telephone Directory* p. O-3; "OSD Reorganization," *Signal* (February 1985): 6.

74. Officer Billet Description/Requisition, Head, Naval Reconnaissance Center.

75. Office of the Secretary of the Air Force, "Defense Support Program Office (DSPO)," undated.

76. Robert D. Hammond and Frank B. Bragg, Jr., "An Army Space Program Update," *Signal* (June 1987): 45–48.

77. Weinberger, *FY 1983 Report of Secretary of Defense*, p. III-88.

78. Ibid.

79. "Navy's Portion of TIARA Consists of 23 [sic] Programs," *Aerospace Daily*, April 8, 1983, p. 231.

80. William E. Parson, "Improving Intelligence Communications Programming," *Signal* (January 1983): 74–75.

81. DIA, DIAM 56-3, *Defense Intelligence Organization: Operations and Management* (Washington, D.C.: DIA, 1979), p. 54.

82. Richard Betts, "American Strategic Intelligence Politics, Priorities and Direction," in Robert L. Pfaltzgraff, Jr., Uri Ra'anan, and Warren Milberg, eds., *Intelligence Policy and National Security* (Hamden Conn.: Archon, 1981), pp. 245–67 at p. 251.

83. Ibid.; William Colby with Peter Forbath, *Honorable Men: My Life in the CIA* (New York: Simon & Schuster, 1978), p. 361.

84. Colby with Forbath, *Honorable Men*, p. 361.

85. Philip Agee and Henry Kissinger, "What Uncle Sam Wants to Know About You: The KIQs," in Philip Agee and Louis Wolf, eds., *Dirty Work: The CIA in Western Europe* (Seacaucus, N.J.: Lyle Stuart, 1978), pp. 111–26.

86. U.S. Congress, Senate Select Committee to Study Governmental Operations with Respect to Intelligence Activities, *Final Report, Book I: Foreign and Military Intelligence*, p. 91.

87. U.S. Congress, House Committee on Foreign Affairs, *The Role of Intelligence in Foreign Policy*, p. 112.

88. Flanagan, "The Coordination of National Intelligence," p. 163.

17 MANAGING INTELLIGENCE COLLECTION AND COVERT ACTION

Management of the three different types of intelligence collection—imagery, SIGINT, and HUMINT—reflects the commonality and diversity of the operations and collection systems employed by the intelligence community. Both imagery and SIGINT are collected by satellites and systems (e.g., aircraft) that can be involved in international incidents. At the same time, SIGINT is collected by land stations, ships, and submarines—which are not employed, to a significant extent, for the acquisition of imagery. And, of course, human collection is a quite different method of collection.

Managing covert action is another aspect of the intelligence management task. Inadequate management can result not only in an inefficient use of resources but in political disaster.

MANAGING SATELLITE IMAGING

Basic decisions concerning satellite imaging activities are the responsibility of the National Foreign Intelligence Board, one of its committees, and the National Reconnaissance Executive Committee (NREC). While the Board and its committees are concerned with collection priorities and their implementation, the NREC focuses on a different set of issues.

As noted in Chapter 16, NREC is chaired by the Director of Central Intelligence and reports to the Secretary of Defense. If the DCI objects to a decision made by the Secretary, he may appeal directly to the President. When initially formed, the Committee consisted of the President's Science Adviser and an Assistant Secretary of Defense in addition to the DCI. Subsequently, the Assistant to the President for National Security Affairs replaced the Science Adviser.[1] The position of the DOD representative has changed as the upper echelons of the Department have been reorganized. In the Reagan Administration the DOD representative was probably the Assistant Deputy Under Secretary of Defense (Intelligence).

According to one account, formation of the NREC was the product of several years (1962–1965) of conflict between the Air Force and DCI John McCone. The original agreement concerning the National Reconnaissance Office gave the Air Force responsibility for the launchers, bases, and recovery capability for reconnaissance systems but gave the CIA responsibility for R & D as well as contracting and security. The arrangement, as the Air Force saw it, left the CIA in control of the overhead reconnaissance program. Others have portrayed the conflict as an initial rivalry over reconnaissance systems, with Air Force attempts to unilaterally conduct the program producing a CIA counterattack. The fiercest battles were those fought from 1962 to 1965 between Albert Wheelon, CIA Director for Science and Technology, and NRO Director Brockaway McMillan.[2]

Air Force sensitivity was heightened by two other developments unrelated to intelligence. One was the introduction of the ICBM and the consequent downgrading of the Air Force's main weapon system, the strategic bomber. Second was the creation in 1958 of the civilian-controlled National Aeronautics and Space Administration (NASA), which denied the Air Force complete control of the U.S. aerospace effort. The Air Force and Strategic Air Command thus viewed any CIA control of reconnaissance R & D to be another intrusion on Air Force "turf."[3]

More was at stake, however, than the Air Force's collective ego. Control of R & D meant control of the type of systems that would be produced. The Air Force and the military in general had a greater interest in tactical intelligence and detailed technical intelligence than did the CIA, with its national intelligence mission. The Air Force, for example, would be far more interested in obtaining every detail possible concerning Soviet aircraft—details that would aid them in specifying or estimating the aircraft's performance and in designing countermeasures. Such requirements place a higher value on high-resolution photography than do requirements concerned primarily with the number or general type of aircraft.

In 1965 an agreement was reached creating the NREC, chaired by the DCI but reporting to the Secretary of Defense, who had final authority subject only to the DCI's appeal to the President. The Committee was given responsibility over NRO's budget, structure, and R & D.[4]

The choice by the NREC and the Secretary of Defense of one satellite system over another obviously has significant implications regarding the type of targets on which information is acquired and the detail of the information. Clearly, choice of a SIGINT system over a photo reconnaissance system, or a higher-resolution system over a lower-resolution area surveillance system automatically constrains coverage in one direction and enhances it in another.

But even without such sharp choices, there will be a wide range of options—a large number of targets from which to choose. Overall responsibility for approval of imaging and SIGINT satellite collection requirments is the responsibility of the National Foreign Intelligence Board. Thus, in 1970, the Air Force requested permission from the Board—then the U.S. Intelligence Board—to alter the targeting of a "very sophisticated satellite." This apparently involved maneuvering the satellite, and the Board—citing the great cost of the satellite and the possibility that maneuvering might lead to a malfunction—denied the request. Ten years later, a KH-11 that was maneuvered to increase coverage of the Iran-Iraq war malfunctioned.[5]

The actual job of translating general imagery collection priorities into the targeting of systems against installations is the responsibility of the NFIB's Committee on Imagery Requirements and Exploitation (COMIREX). The COMIREX was established on July 1, 1967 by Director of Central Intelligence Directive 1/13 as the successor to the Committee on Overhead Reconnaissance (COMOR). The COMOR's responsibilities included coordination of collection requirements for the development and operation of all imaging satellites. As these programs grew, the number of photographs substantially increased, resulting in serious duplication of imagery exploitation activities. One proposed and implemented solution was the replacement of the COMOR by the COMIREX. As presently constituted, the membership of the COMIREX consists of representatives from all NFIB agencies, plus the Deputy Chief of Staff for Intelligence, Army; the Director of Naval Intelligence; and the Assistant Chief of Staff, Intelligence of the Air Force. The Committee is staffed with personnel from the CIA and the DIA.[6]

The functions of the COMIREX have been summarized by former chairman Roland S. Inlow:

COMIREX performs the interagency coordination and management functions needed to direct photographic satellite reconnaissance, including the process of deciding what targets should be photographed and what agencies should get which photos to analyze. It also evaluates the needs for, and the results from, photographic reconnaissance, and oversees security controls that are designed to protect photography and information derived from photography from unauthorized disclosure.[7]

The COMIREX is faced with three basic questions with regard to the establishment of targets and priorities:

1. What installations/areas are to be imaged?
2. What systems will be targeted on specific installations/areas?
3. What will be the frequency of coverage?

During the period in which the United States operated a single type of satellite imaging system (the KH-11), the COMIREX's decision problem on Question 2 was eased, but as the KH-12 and LACROSSE join the KH-11 launched in 1987 the decision will become more complicated. In any case, there will be significant areas of contention among consumers over priorities and targeting.

The main conflict over satellite imagery targeting and priorities is between those consumers with national intelligence responsibilities (e.g., the CIA) and the parts of the military more concerned with tactical intelligence. The military, with its mission of being able to fight a war, wants as much warning as possible, as well as the most up-to-date and detailed coverage concerning Warsaw Pact capabilities. Day-to-day coverage is thus seen as valuable on the tactical level, in revealing movements of troops or weapons and small changes in capabilities; at the national level, in the absence of a crisis, it is of little interest. The COMIREX serves as a means to prioritize claims of the CIA, the DIA, the military services, and other consumers, attempting to distribute a strictly limited resource so as to at least minimally satisfy the legitimate requests of several competitive bureaucracies.

In the area of imagery exploitation, the COMIREX allocates imagery interpretation tasks among the National Photographic Interpretation Center, the CIA's Office of Imagery Analysis, and the imagery exploitation components of the DIA, ITAC, NISC, AMSIC, FSTC, and FTD. The basic division of labor is spelled out in the COMIREX's National Tasking Plan for Imagery Processing and Exploitation.[8]

In carrying out its responsibilities, the COMIREX functions through a network of subcommittees and working groups. Among these components are the Imagery Collection Requirements Subcommittee, Operations Subcommittee, the Exploitation Research and Development Subcommittee (EXRAND), Imagery Interpretation Keys Subcommittee (KEYSCOM), Current and Standing Requirments Working Group, COMIREX Automated Management System (CAMS) Task Force, the MC&G [Mapping, Charting and Geodesy] Working Group, and the TK Modification Working Group.[9]

MANAGING SIGINT

Management of the U.S. Signals Intelligence System (USSS) is vested in the Director of the NSA by National Security Council Intelligence Directive No. 6. The most recently available version of NSCID 6, that of February 17, 1972, was still "in force" as of early 1981.[10] In addition to defining the components of SIGINT—COMINT and ELINT—the Directive states:

> The Secretary of Defense is designated as Executive Agent of the Government for the conduct of SIGINT activities in accordance with the provisions of this directive and for the direction, supervision, funding, maintenance, and operation of the National Security Agency. The Director of the National Security Agency shall report to the Secretary of Defense, the Director of Central Intelligence, and the Joint Chiefs of Staff. The Secretary of Defense may delegate in whole or part authority over the Director of the National Security Agency within the Office of the Secretary of Defense...

> It shall be the duty of the Director of the National Security Agency to provide for the SIGINT mission of the United States, to establish an effective unified organization and control of all SIGINT collection and processing activities of the United States, and to

produce SIGINT in accordance with the objectives, requirements and priorities established by the Director of Central Intelligence Board. No other organization shall engage in SIGINT activities except as provided for in this directive.

Except as provided in paragraphs 5 and 6 of this directive (re unique responsibilities of CIA and FBI) the Director of the National Security Agency shall exercise full control over all SIGINT collection and processing activities. . . .The Director of the National Security Agency is authorized to issue direct to any operating elements engaged in SIGINT operations such instructions and assignments as are required. All instructions issued by the Director under the authority provided in the paragraph shall be mandatory subject only to appeal to the Secretary of Defense. . . .The Armed Forces and other departments and agencies often require timely and effective SIGINT. The Director of the National Security Agency shall provide such SIGINT. . . .

The intelligence components of the individual departments and agencies may continue to conduct direct liaison with the National Security Agency in the interpretation and amplification of requirements and priorities within the framework of objectives, requirements and priorities established by the Director of Central Intelligence.[11] (Emphasis in original).

One means of managing the SIGINT system is via the U.S. Signals Intelligence Directives (USSIDs), issued by the Director, NSA. USSIDs include USSID 1, "SIGINT Operating Policy," (June 1987); USSID 3, "SIGINT Security" (August 1972); USSID 4, "SIGINT Support to Military Commanders" (July 1, 1974); USSID 18, "Limitations and Procedures in Signals Intelligence Operations of the U.S.S.S." (May 18, 1976); USSID 40, "ELINT Operating Policy" (October 1970); USSID 300, "SIGINT Reporting;" USSID 302, "SIGINT Alert Systems;" USSID 701, "Sanitizing and Declassifying ADP Storage Devices" (September 30, 1976); USSID 702, "Automatic Data Processing Systems Security" (September 1980); and USSID 1045, "SIGINT Tasking for USM-45, Misawa" (January 16, 1980).[12]

As indicated in the previous extract from NSCID 6, although the Secretary of Defense is the executive agent and the Director of NSA is the program manager, requirements and priorities are to be established by the SIGINT Committee of the NFIB. The SIGINT Committee is the successor to a series of predecessors. As of 1950, prior to the creation of the NSA, the work was divided between the Armed Forces Security Agency Council's Intelligence Requirements Committee (AFSAC/IRC) and the U.S. Communications Intelligence Board's Intelligence Committee (USCIB/IC). The AFSAC/IRC consisted of representatives from the Office of Naval Intelligence, Army Intelligence, Air Force Intelligence, and the AFSA, and was responsible primarily for targeting and setting priorities for military traffic intercepts. The USCIB/IC was primarily concerned with nonmilitary traffic.[13]

Following the creation of the NSA, NSCID No.9 of December 9, 1952, reconstituted the USCIB to operate under the Special Committee of the NSC for COMINT, which consisted of the Secretary of State, Secretary of Defense, and Attorney General and was assisted by the DCI. In 1958, when the USCIB and the Intelligence Advisory Committee were merged into the USIB, two committees were created: the COMINT Committee (by DCID 6/1 on October 21) and the ELINT Committee (by DCID 6/2 also on October 21). The SIGINT Committee was formed by DCID 6/1 on May 31, 1962, which merged the ELINT and COMINT committees.[14]

The responsibilities of the SIGINT Committee are extensive, as indicated by the May 12, 1982 DCID, reprinted as Figure 17-1. Those responsibilities include specification of SIGINT collection requirements, the responsiveness of U.S. and cooperating foreign SIGINT agencies, the development of policies for the conduct of SIGINT liaison, and the security of information obtained through SIGINT.

Prior to the Middle East war in 1973, the USIB SIGINT Committee recommended that the Middle East become a priority target for intelligence collection if hostilities erupted. The NSA was asked to evaluate the intelligence collected and to determine appropriate targets. Upon the outbreak of war, the NSA implemented the SIGINT Committee's guidance. Later that week, the Committee discussed and approved the DIA's recommendation to change the primary target of one collector.[15]

As with other NFIB committees, an elaborate subcommittee/working group structure handles the tasks assigned to the committee. Among the subcommittees and groups are the SIGINT Requirements Validation and Evaluation Subcommittee (SIRVES), Special Reconnaissance Group, PROFORM Steering Committee, Joint Proforma Coordinating Group, and the Measurement and Signature Intelligence Subcommittee.[16]

While the SIRVES may validate and evaluate SIGINT general requirements another SIGINT Committee component, SORS (with SORS possibly being the Space Operational Requirements Subcommittee) may be responsible for tasking SIGINT satellites. According to one document the SORS is "responsible for receipt, approval, and subsequent generation of intelligence guidance in response to tasks to be levied on national resources [a standard euphemism for space systems]" and "continually monitors requirements and provides collection and processing guidance for both long and short term needs."[17]

A second NFIB committee that might on occasion have input on the subject of SIGINT requirements is the Critical Intelligence Problems Committee (CIPC). Thus, on January 31, 1972, the DCI requested the CIPC—then the Critical Collection Problems Committee (CCPC)—to conduct a review of intelligence efforts against narcotics. In October 1972 the CCPC report noted in a section entitled "SIGINT Information on Narcotics and Dangerous Drugs" that

1. No SIGINT resources are dedicated solely to the intercept of narcotics information. The SIGINT which is now being produced on the international narcotics problem is a by-product of SIGINT reporting on other national requirements. . . .
5. The effective use of SIGINT information in support of ongoing operations while at the same time protecting the source has been a problem.
6. Successful usage of the SIGINT product is largely contingent upon close collaboration between the SIGINT producers and the appropriate customer agencies.

The CCPC therefore recommended that the "NSA, in conjunction with the interested customers, particularly BNDD and Customs, make appropriate determination

Figure 17–1.   DCID 6/1, The SIGINT Committee

SECRET
NOFORN

DIRECTOR OF CENTRAL INTELLIGENCE DIRECTIVE[1]
SIGINT Committee
(Effective 12 May 1982)

Pursuant to the provisions of Section 102, the National Security Act of 1947, and Executive Order 12333, there is established a Signals Intelligence (SIGINT) Committee.

1. Mission

The mission of the SIGINT Committee is to advise and assist the Director of Central Intelligence (DCI) and the Director, National Security Agency (DIRNSA) in the discharge of their duties and responsibilities with respect to Signals Intelligence as specified in Executive Order 12333, to monitor and assist in coordinating within the Intelligence Community the accomplishment of objectives established by the DCI, and to promote the effective use of Intelligence Community SIGINT resources.

2. Functions:

Under the general guidance of the Deputy Director of Central Intelligence, the SIGINT Committee shall:

    a. advise the DCI on the establishment of SIGINT requirements, priorities, and objectives;

    b. develop statements, based on the DCI's objectives and priorities, of collection and exploitation requirements for COMINT, ELINT, foreign instrumentation signals, nonimagery infrared, coherent light, and nonnuclear electromagnetic pulse (EMP) sources. (These statements will provide guidance for resource programming, mission planning, and reporting. Each statement should take into account practical limitations, costs, and risk factors.)

    c. monitor and evaluate the responsiveness of present and programmed United States and cooperating foreign SIGINT resources to United States needs for intelligence information;

    d. monitor the impact on SIGINT programs of information needs levied by intelligence comsumers;

    e. advise and make recommendations on the dissemination and sanitization of SIGINT or information derived therefrom and the release of disclosure of SIGINT or derived information to foreign governments or international organizations in which the United States Government participates;

    f. develop and recommend to the DCI policies, directives, and guidance for the conduct of SIGINT arrangements with foreign governments;

    g. assess and report to the DCI on the potential impact on current and future United States SIGINT capabilities of providing cryptographic assistance to foreign governments; and

---

[1]This directive supersedes DCID No. 6/1, 18 May 1976.

SECRET

Classified by: DCI
Declassify on: OADR

Figure 17-1. continued

SECRET
NOFORN

h. review, develop, and recommend to the DCI policies for the protection, through classification and compartmentation, of COMINT, ELINT, and other SIGINT or of information about them or derived from them and procedures enabling United States Government entities outside of the Intelligence Community to receive and use SIGINT.

3. Intelligence Community Responsibilities

Upon request of the Committee Chairman, Intelligence Community elements shall provide information pertinent to the Committee's mission and functions within DCI-approved security safeguards.

4. Composition and Organization

The Committee Chairman will be appointed by the Director of Central Intelligence.

The members of the committee will be representatives designated by Intelligence Community principals.

The Chairman will establish subcommittees or task forces as required.

With the approval of the DCI, the Committee Chairman may invite representatives of relevant United States Government entities to participate as appropriate.

The Committee will be supported by an Executive Secretariat.

William J. Casey
Director of Central Intelligence

of what COMINT support is required on the narcotics problem and that the requisite priorities be established through the SIGINT Committee."[18]

During 1975, the NFIB approved a new National SIGINT Requirements System which requires the NFIB to initiate a formal community review and approval of each requirement before its validation and placement on the National SIGINT Requirements List (NSRL). The NSRL is today the basic guidance document for the NSA and specifies SIGINT targets according to well-defined priorities, including cross-references to the DCI and other national requirements documents. The system does not, however, prevent the Director, NSA from determining which specific signals to intercept in fulfillment of requirements. Nor does it prevent the Secretaries of State and Defense or military commanders from directly tasking the NSA in a crisis, informing the DCI and SIGINT Committee afterward.[19]

The yearly statements of objectives, requirements, and priorities are stated in the yearly Consolidated Cryptologic Program (CCP) and Tactical Cryptologic Program (TCP), as noted in Chapter 16. The majority of U.S. signals intelligence activities is funded through the CCP. The TCP "was established in 1979 to correct the problem of disparate requirements competing for limited available funding within the NFIP which resulted in inadequate treatment of Service tactical support needs."[20]

MANAGING SENSITIVE
RECONNAISSANCE MISSIONS

Reconnaissance conducted by satellite is relatively nonintrusive, not requiring actual violation of a target nation's airspace. Further, with the exception of the Soviet Union, no nation possesses the means for destroying U.S. satellites. And, short of war, the costs to the Soviet Union of interfering in an obvious way with such satellites is likely to be far greater than the potential benefits.

When airborne overflights or air and sea missions close to a nation's borders are involved, the potential for an international incident is much greater. The early U.S. aircraft reconnaissance missions directed at the Soviet Union involved this risk—approaching or penetrating the margins of Soviet and East European territory to collect a variety of intelligence, including the signatures and operating frequencies of air defense systems.[21]

When the U-2 program was approved, it was clear that the projected series of overflights for the Soviet Union, China and other locations further heightened the risk of an international incident.

The risk was very apparent to President Eisenhower. At a meeting of the NSC on February 12, 1959, he expressed reservations concerning extensive continuation of the program, noting that nothing would make him request authority to declare war more quickly than a Soviet violation of U.S. airspace. In a meeting of the NSC on February 8, 1960, he noted that if a U-2 were lost "when we are engaged in apparently sincere deliberations," it could be put on display in Moscow and ruin the President's effectiveness.[22] The President's alarm was validated a few months later with shooting down of Francis Gary Powers's U-2.

In subsequent years, numerous other incidents occurred involving air and sea missions, some of which have been mentioned earlier. In 1962, during the Cuban missile crisis, one U-2 strayed into Soviet territory while another was shot down during a flight over Cuba. In 1967 the Israeli Air Force bombed the *U.S.S. Liberty* while it was collecting signals intelligence in the midst of the Six Day War. In 1968, the *U.S.S. Pueblo* was seized by North Korea during a SIGINT mission off the North Korean coast, and in 1969 an EC-121 SIGINT aircraft was shot down by North Korean forces while it patrolled off the same coast. The North Koreans have also made hundreds of attempts to shoot down overflying SR-71s.[23]

The potential still exists for such incidents. U-2s and SR-71s conduct overflights of Cuba, North Korea, Vietnam, and a variety of Third World countries (e.g., Libya) and missions on the periphery of the Soviet Bloc. RF-4C Phantoms fly close to the East German border, while EC-130s are used to collect intelligence (code-named CREEK MISTY and CREEK FLUSH) while on transport missions through the Berlin Corridor. Surface ships of various types are employed for SIGINT purposes—off the coasts of Libya, Nicaragua, and the Soviet Union. Submarines still come close to and sometimes enter Soviet territorial waters.

The U.S. system for management of these missions reflects many considerations. Many of the missions are conducted in support of and proposed by the unified and specified commands. Others are clearly designed to provide national intelligence. In either case, such missions represent the possible cause of an international incident; thus, they require national-level approval.

As noted in Chapter 16, the special Navy reconnaissance programs are the initial responsibility of the National Executive Committee for Special Navy Activities, chaired by the DCI and reporting to the Secretary of Defense. Missions originating from the Commanders in Chief of the unified commands go through a chain of supervisory offices and divisions, beginning with the Joint Reconnaissance Center of the JCS.

The JRC acts as an intial approval authority for reconnaissance plans developed by unified, specified, and theater commands; develops a Joint Reconnaissance Schedule (JRS), which is "always several inches thick and filled with hundreds of pages of highly technical data and maps"; monitors the progress of the missions; and provides the National Military Command Center with real-time information regarding the status and disposition of forces, mission activity, and other reconnaissance-related information.[24]

The JRC operates through three branches: the Reconnaissance Programs Branch, the Reconnaissance Plans Branch, and the Reconnaissance Operations Branch. The Reconnaissance Programs Branch receives, reviews, evaluates, and submits for approval to the JCS the reconnaissance plans, programs, and schedules originated by the commanders of the unified and specified commands, the military services, and other governmental agencies. It also prepares the planning guidance for the execution of reconnaissance operations of special significance or sensitivity.[25]

The Reconnaissance Plans Branch participates in the review of intelligence support plans and prepares policy guidance, planning, analysis, and review of reconnaissance related activities which support trans- and post-SIOP nuclear operations.[26]

The Reconnaissance Operations Branch is responsible for performing the mission monitoring functions of the JRC. It performs flight-following functions on reconnaissance missions and is responsible for insuring that all incidents and significant activities are promptly brought to the attention of appropriate authorities. It is also responsible for displaying, on a current basis, all peacetime military reconnaissance and some other sensitive operations.[27] Thus, on any given day, the Branch may be monitoring on a real-time basis the flights of all RC-135, SR-71, U-2 aircraft, the journeys of a variety of surface ships, and the exploits of submarines performing Special Navy Control Program missions.

MANAGING HUMAN COLLECTION

Managing human source collection involves managing the collection of information from foreign service officers, clandestine agents, and defectors, as well as nongovernment individuals. These diverse sources are reflected in the management arrangements for human source collection.

The titles of NSCID No. 4 of February 4, 1972, "The Defector Program," and two DCIDs—4/1, "The Interagency Defector Committee," and 4/2, "Defector Program Abroad"—suggest the importance of defectors to U.S. security. In addition to defining a variety of terms (defectors, inducement, potential defector, disaffected person, walk-in, refugee, and escapee), Directive 4/2 also states that "[d]efection, particularly from the USSR, should be encouraged and induced, employing both conventional and unconventional means, whenever there is a net advantage to U.S. interests" and that the United States should:

1. encourage and induce the defection of the maximum number of persons from the USSR and of Soviet nationals outside the USSR; and
2. continue, and if possible expand, efforts to encourage and induce the defection of key members of elite groups of countries other than the USSR who may qualify as defectors.

In addition, DCID 4/2 also suggests that before any U.S. department or agency takes any action to induce defection, the possible value of recruitment in place will be considered carefully. When an individual does defect the first priority is to determine if the defector possesses any information indicating the imminence of hostilities.[28]

NSCID No. 5, "U.S. Espionage and Counterintelligence Abroad," of February 17, 1972, gives the DCI primary responsibility for coordination of clandestine collection activities. Paragraphs 2a and 2b authorize the DCI to:

establish the procedures necessary to achieve such direction and coordination, including the assessment of risk incident upon such operations as compared to the value of the activity, and to ensure that sensitive operations are reviewed pursuant to applicable directives [and to] coordinate all clandestine activities authorized herein and conducted outside the United States and its possessions, including liaison that concerns clandestine activities or that involves foreign clandestine services.[29]

At the NFIB committee level, these responsibilities belong to the Human Resources Committee. The Committee was first proposed in 1970 by General Donald Bennett, Director of the DIA, as a means of providing a national-level forum to coordinate both overt and clandestine human source collection. Immediate formation of such a committee was prevented by objections from the CIA's Directorate of Plans. In addition to the bureaucratic "territorial imperative," the Directorate also sought to minimize the number of individuals with access to information concerning clandestine sources. DCI Richard Helms established an *ad hoc* task force to study the problem of human source collection. After a year of study the task force recommended the establishment of a USIB committee on a one-year trial basis—a suggestion endorsed by the President's Foreign Intelligence Advisory Board (PFIAB) in a separate study. In June 1974 it attained permanent status as the Human Sources Committee and in 1975 its name was changed to the Human Resources Committee.[30]

The Committee's functions, specified by DCID 3/7 of October 12, 1982, are

1. to examine problems and consider possible improvements in collection and procedures for dissemination of intelligence obtained by human resources and to provide recommendation to the DCI related thereto; and
2. to encourage and promote collection activities and coordination among human resources collection agencies concerning the allocation of effort and responsibility for the satisfaction of foreign intelligence needs.[31]

The Committee, through its Assessments Subcommittee, has conducted community-wide assessments of human source reporting in individual countries. It has not defined a national system for establishing formal collection requirements for the agencies that employee human sources.[32]

The Committee, when established, was specifically not given responsibility for reviewing the operational details or internal management of the individual departments or agencies. Departments and agencies were authorized to withhold "sensitive" information from the Committee and report directly to the DCI.[33]

As of 1975, the Committee had "only just begun to expand community influence over human collection," issuing a general guidance document called the Current Intelligence Reporting List (CIRL). The military made some use of the document but the CIA's Directorate of Operations instructed CIA stations that the list was provided only for reference and did not constitute collection requirements for CIA operations.[34]

During 1977 the Committee provided the U.S. Ambassador to Iran, William Sullivan, with a short prioritized list of items of national intelligence interest. The list was developed by the Committee with advice of the National Intelligence Officer for the Near East and South Asia. The Chairman of the Human Resources Committee, in his cover letter, expressed his hope that the list would "be of some use...as a coordinated interagency expression of the most important information Washington needs."[35]

In addition to the HRC, the Intelligence Community Staff has played a role in HUMINT tasking. During the 1970s it began to issue the National Human Intelligence Collection Plan. The Plan includes an advisory for HUMINT collectors such as foreign service officers, who are outside the National Foreign Intelligence Program (NFIP). The Plan's effect has been limited by being only one of several guidance documents levied on human source collectors.[36]

DCID 2/3 of July 25, 1963, entitled "Domestic Exploitation of Nongovernmental Organizations and Individuals," vests in the CIA responsibility for managing the domestic exploitation program. The CIA is instructed to determine the foreign intelligence potential of nongovernmental organizations and individuals, serve as coordinator for other government agencies, and disseminate to intelligence departments and agencies all foreign intelligence information obtained through the program.[37]

HUMINT guidance may also be issued by the military services. Thus, in 1985 the Commander, Naval Intelligence Command issued the Navy HUMINT Plan.[38]

MANAGING COVERT ACTION

Management of U.S. covert action programs involves procedures and review groups within the CIA and the NSC. To initiate a covert action, a Presidential Finding is required by the Hughes-Ryan Amendment to the Foreign Assistance Act of 1961. The Finding must state that the President has determined that the "operation in a foreign country...is important to the national security of the United States" and then go on to describe the scope (the country or countries that are the target) and a description of what the operation involves. Present Findings also specify whether significant foreseeable DOD support will be required.[39] Figure 17–2 shows one of the Findings, signed in pursuit of the attempt to establish contact with Iranian "moderates."

Findings are initially prepared within the CIA's Directorate of Operations, either as a result of Directorate initiative or in response to requirements from the DCI, who in turn may be responding to a Presidential request.[40]

Before a proposed finding leaves the Directorate of Operations, it is reviewed by the Covert Action Planning Group (CAPG), which is composed of the Associate Deputy Director for Operations, senior staff chiefs, and those individuals who have a substantive responsibility for the Finding and its eventual implementation. If approved by the CAPG, the Finding is sent on to the top echelon of CIA management for review and recommendations and then to the DCI.[41]

Figure 17–2. Presidential Finding on Iran.

Finding Pursuant to Section 662 of

The Foreign Assistance Act of 1961

As Amended, Concerning Operations

Undertaken by the Central Intelligence

Agency in Foreign Countries, Other Than

Those Intended Solely for the Purpose

of Intelligence Collection

I hereby find that the following operation in a foreign country (including all support necessary to such operation) is important to the national security of the United States, and due to its extreme sensitivity and security risks, I determine it is essential to limit prior notice, and direct the Director of Central Intelligence to refrain from reporting this Finding to the Congress as provided in Section 501 of the National Security Act of 1947, as amended, until I otherwise direct.

SCOPE   DESCRIPTION

Iran   Assist selected friendly foreign liaison services, third countries and third
                    parties which have established relationships with Iranian elements,
                    groups, and individuals sympathetic to U.S. Government interests and
                    which do not conduct or support terrorist actions directed against U.S.
                    persons, property or interests, for the purpose of: (1) establishing a
                    more moderate government in Iran, (2) obtaining from them significant
                    intelligence not otherwise obtainable, to determine the current Iranian
                    Government's intentions with respect to its neighbors and with respect
                    to terrorist acts, and (3) furthering the release of the American hostages
                    held in Beirut and preventing additional terrorist acts by these groups.
                    Provide funds, intelligence, counter-intelligence, training, guidance and
                    communications and other necessary assistance to these elements,
                    groups, individuals, liaison services and third countries in support of
                    these activities.

                    The USG will act to facilitate efforts by third parties and third countries
                    to establish contact with moderate elements within and outside the
                    Government of Iran by providing these elements with arms, equipment
                    and related materiel in order to enhance the credibility of these
                    elements in their effort to achieve a more pro-U.S. government in Iran
                    by demonstrating their ability to obtain requisite resources to defend
                    their country against Iraq and intervention by the Soviet Union. This
                    support will be discontinued if the U.S. Government learns that these
                    elements have abandoned their goals of moderating their government
                    and appropriated the material for purposes other than that provided by
                    this finding.

The White House
Washington, D.C.
Date January 17, 1986

If the proposed finding is approved by the DCI it then goes to the Planning and Coordination Group (PCG) of the NSC, which consists of senior representatives of the State Department, Defense Department, and the NSC. If the PCG supports the Finding, it is then sent with a favorable recommendation to the National Security Planning Group (NSPG). Approval by the NSPG then results in a Presidential Finding. NSDD 159, of January 18, 1985, "Covert Action Policy Approval and Coordination Procedures," specified that all intelligence findings are written and circulated among the eight senior members of the NSPG before being put into effect.[42]

NOTES TO CHAPTER 17

1. U.S. Congress, Senate Select Committee to Study Governmental Operations with Respect to Intelligence Activities, *Foreign and Military Intelligence, (Book IV)*, (Washington, D.C.: U.S. Government Printing Office, 1976), p. 75; Victor Marchetti and John Marks, *The CIA and the Cult of Intelligence* (New York: Knopf, 1974), p. 206.

2. U.S. Congress, Senate Select Committee to Study Governmental Operations with Respect to Intelligence Activities, *Foreign and Military Intelligence, (Book IV)*, p. 74; Jeffrey Richelson, "The Keyhole Satellite Program," *Journal of Strategic Studies* 7, no. 2 (1984): 121–53.

3. U.S. Congress, Senate Select Committee to Study Governmental Operations with Respect to Intelligence Activities, *Foreign and Military Intelligence, (Book IV)*, p. 74.

4. Ibid., p. 75; James Bamford, *The Puzzle Palace: A Report on NSA, America's Most Secret Agency* (Boston: Houghton Mifflin, 1982), p. 189.

5. Marchetti and Marks, *The CIA and the Cult of Intelligence*, pp. 85–86; Philip Taubman, "Gulf War Said to Reveal U.S. Intelligence Lapses," *New York Times*, September 27, 1980, p. 3.

6. DCID 1/13, "Coordination of the Collection and Exploitation of Imagery Intelligence," February 2, 1973, *Declassified Documents Reference System 1980-132D;* DCID 1/13, "Committee on Imagery Requirements and Exploitation," July 1, 1967, *Declassified Documents Reference System 1980-132B;* U.S. Congress, Senate Select Committee to Study Governmental Operations with Respect to Intelligence Activities, *Foreign and Military Intelligence, Book I*, (Washington, D.C.: U.S. Government Printing Office, 1976), p. 85.

7. Roland S. Inlow, "An Appraisal of the Morison Espionage Trial," *First Principles* 11, no. 4 (May 1986): 1, 2–5.

8. CINCPACFLT Instruction S 3822.1E, "PACOM Imagery Reconnaissance Procedures and Responsibilities," July 5, 1983, p. 1; HQ EUCOM Directive No. 40-4, "Exploitation and Dissemination of Time Sensitive Imagery," November 4, 1983, p. 1.

9. CINCPACFLT Instruction S 3822.1E, "PACOM Imagery Reconnaissance Procedures and Responsibilities"; Department of the Air Force, *Headquarters Publication 21-1*, March 1, 1986, p. 6–23; U.S. Congress, House Permanent Select Committee on Intelligence *Annual Report* (Washington, D.C.: U.S. Government Printing Office, 1978), p. 54.

10. National Security Agency, *NSA Transition Briefing Book* (Ft. Meade, Md.: NSA, 1980) n.p.

11. Department of Justice, *Report on CIA-Related Electronic Surveillance Activities* (Washington, D.C.: Department of Justice, 1976), pp. 77–79.

12. U.S. Congress, House Permanent Select Committee on Intelligence, *Annual Report*, pp. 70, 72; Working Group on Computer Security, *Computer and Telecommunications Security* (Washington, D.C.: National Communications Security Committee, July 1981), pp. 110, 157; Defense Intelligence College, *Instructional Management Plan: Advanced Methods of Intelligence Collection*, March 1984; Private information.

13. George A. Brownell, *The Origins and Development of the National Security Agency* (Laguna Hills, Calif.: Aegean Park Press 1981), p. 3.

14. Bamford, *The Puzzle Palace*, p. 50; Department of Justice, *Report on CIA-Related Electronic Surveillance Activities*, p. 91; DCID 6/1, "Communications Intelligence Committee," October 21, 1958 *Declassified Documents Reference System, 1980-130C*; DCID 6/2, "Electronics Intelligence Committee," October 21, 1958 *Declassified Documents Reference System 1980-130D*; DCID 6/1, "SIGINT Committee," May 1, 1962 *Declassified Documents Reference System 1980-131D*.

15. U.S. Congress, Senate Select Committee to Study Governmental Operations with Respect to Intelligence Activities, *Foreign and Military Intelligence, Book I*, p. 85.

16. Department of the Air Force, *Headquarters Publication 21-1*, p. 6–23.

17. Department of the Army, Office of the Assistant Chief of Staff, Intelligence, *Annual Historical Review, 1 October 1984–30 September 1985*, (Washington, D.C.: OACS, I, 1986) p. 2–30.

18. Department of Justice, *Report on CIA-Related Electronic Surveillance Activities*, pp. 101–103.

19. U.S. Congress, Senate Select Committee to Study Governmental Operations with Respect to Intelligence Activities, *Foreign and Military Intelligence, Book I*, pp. 85–86; U.S. Congress, House Permanent Select Committee on Intelligence, *Annual Report*, p. 55; Stephen J. Flanagan, "The Coordination of National Intelligence," in Duncan Clarke, ed., *Public Policy and Political Institutions: United States Defense and Foreign Policy—Policy Coordination and Integration* (Greenwich, Conn.: JAI, 1985) p. 177.

20. National Security Agency, *NSA Transition Briefing Book*, n.p.

21. See Jeffrey Richelson, *American Espionage and the Soviet Target* (New York: Morrow, 1987), pp. 120–126.

22. John Eisenhower, "Memorandum for the Record," February 12, 1959, in *Declassified Documents Reference System 1981-622B*.

23. Bamford, *The Puzzle Palace*, pp. 184–185, 216–31; U.S. Congress, House Committee on Armed Services, *Inquiry into the U.S.S. Pueblo and EC-121 Plane Incidents* (Washington, D.C.: U.S. Government Printing Office, 1969); "Radar Detector Aboard SR-71 Alerted Plane Missile Attack," *New York Times*, August 29, 1983, p. 3.

24. Joint Chiefs of Staff, JCS Publication 4, *Organization and Functions of the Joint Chiefs of Staff* (Washington, D.C.: JCS 1985), p. III-3-73; Marchetti and Marks, *The CIA and the Cult of Intelligence*, p. 332.

25. Joint Chiefs of Staff, JCS Publication 4, *Organization and Functions of the Joint Chiefs of Staff*, p. III-3-28; *Department of Defense Telephone Directory* (Washington, D.C.: U.S. Government Printing Office, December 1987), p. O-12.

26. Joint Chiefs of Staff, JCS Publication 4, *Organization and Functions of the Joint Chiefs of Staff*, p. III-3-28.

27. Ibid., p. III-3-29.

28. DCID 4/2, "The Defector Program Abroad," June 26, 1959 in *Documents from the Espionage Den (53). U.S.S.R., The Aggressive East, Section 4.* (Tehran: Muslim Students Following the Line of the Imam, n.d.) pp. 4–11; U.S. Congress, House Permanent Select Committee on Intelligence *Annual Report*, p. 70.

29. NSCID No. 5, "U.S. Espionage and Counterintelligence Activities Abroad," February 17, 1972, *Declassified Documents Reference System 1976-253F.*

30. U.S. Congress, Senate Select Committee to Study Governmental Operations with Respect to Intelligence Activities, *Foreign and Military Intelligence, Book I*, p. 85, n. 42.

31. DCIS 3/7, "Human Resources Committee," October 12, 1982.

32. U.S. Congress, Senate Select Committee to Study Governmental Operations with Respect to Intelligence Activities, *Foreign and Military Intelligence, Book I*, pp. 86–87.

33. Ibid., p. 86.

34. Ibid.

35. Scott Armstrong, "Intelligence Experts Had Early Doubts About Shah's Stability," *Washington Post*, February 2, 1982, pp. 1, 9.

36. Flanagan, "The Coordination of National Intelligence," p. 177.

37. DCID 2/3, "Domestic Exploitation of Nongovernmental Organizations and Individuals," July 25, 1963, *Declassification Documents Reference System 1980-131E.*

38. Office of Naval Intelligence, *ONI Command History CY 1985* (Washington, D.C.: ONI, 1987), Annex A, p. 7.

39. U.S. Congress, House Select Committee to Investigate Covert Arms Transactions with Iran and Senate Select Committee on Secret Military Assistance to Iran and the Nicaraguan Opposition, *Report of the Congressional Committees Investigating the Iran–Contra Affair with Supplemental, Minority, and Additional Views* (Washington, D.C.: U.S. Government Printing Office, 1987), pp. 376–77; Caspar Weinberger, "Memorandum to the Secretary of the Army. Subject: DOD Support [to CIA Special] Activities," June 13, 1983, p. 1.

40. Wilhelm G. Hinsleigh, "Covert Action: An Update," *Studies in Intelligence* (Spring 1986).

41. Ibid.

42. Ibid; NSDD 159, "Covert Action Policy Approval and Coordination Procedures," January 18, 1985; NSDD 266, "Implementation of the Recommendations of the President's Special Review Board," March 31, 1987, p. 7.

18 MANAGING INFORMATION ACCESS AND ANALYSIS

The U.S. intelligence collection effort produces an enormous volume of information, particularly from the variety of technical collection systems. The National Security Agency alone generates several tons of paper on a daily basis.

Collection, however, is only an intermediary step in the intelligence process between the statement of requirements and the production of finished intelligence. Thus, the information collected must be chanelled to those who are responsible for processing and analysis—the National Photographic Interpretation Center, the Defense Intelligence Agency, the State Department's INR, the CIA's Directorate of Intelligence, and the intelligence analysis components of the military services. The same information, either in its raw or processed/analyzed form must also be made available to a wide variety of individuals—policymakers, policy implementers, strategists, contractors, and consultants—who need the information to perform their jobs. At the same time, much of the information needs to be protected, since its disclosure might reveal nonobvious targets of collection and collection capabilities—disclosures that could lead to effective countermeasures and precautions and the denial of such information in the future. Much information is also made available to U.S. allies under treaty or other arrangements for intelligence sharing. Hence, it is necessary to establish guidelines for the classification and distribution of, as well as access to intelligence information, with respect to both U.S. citizens and foreign governments.

Although the numerous analytical intelligence units have substantially distinct functions, it is still necessary to manage the analytical process on a community-wide basis. Aside from the avoidance of undesired duplication where the potential for such duplication exists, it is necessary to ensure that intelligence production is responsive to the requirements of national and departmental leaders. It is also necessary to have mechanisms to deal with analytical problems and ensure that there is an adequate degree of cooperation on a day-to-day basis among agencies working on similar problems. Further, it is necessary to coordinate the production of national estimates—a delicate process involving several agencies with differing perspectives.

MANAGING THE ACCESS TO INFORMATION

The basic means for managing or controlling access to intelligence information is the classification system, which defines different levels of sensitivity and restricts access to those who have been cleared at that level and have a "need to know." The best-known classifications are those used to restrict access to a wide range of national security information: Confidential, Secret, and Top Secret.

Confidential information is defined as information "the unauthorized disclosure of which reasonably could be expected to cause damage to the national security." Secret information differs from confidential information in that the expected damage would be "serious." In the case of the Top Secret information, the damage would be "exceptionally grave."[1]

In theory, at least, access for an individual with clearance at a certain level is further restricted on a need-to-know basis to the information needed to perform his or her job. In some cases the need-to-know principle is implemented by compartmentalizing certain sets of data, such as that concerning specific types of operations or individuals. Thus, the Army Intelligence and Security Command's offensive counterintelligence operations are designated by a special code word used to restrict access to information about those operations. Similar operations conducted by the Air Force Office of Special Investigations have had the designation SEVEN DOORS. Information about sensitive or clandestine attache collection activities involving non-U.S. sources or foreign materiel acquisition projects is sent via the DOD RODCA channel.[2]

The CIA's Directorate of Operations maintains several dozen compartments for the transmission of human source reports. The compartments are informally designated "blue border" or "blue stripe" material because of the blue stripes on the border of the cover sheet to any document containing such material. The CIA's Soviet Bloc Division has used compartments such as REDWOOD, REDCOAT, and RYBAT. Among the documents classified SECRET RYBAT was a January 9, 1973 message from the Chief, Soviet Bloc Division (of CIA) to Chiefs of Station and Base on "Turning Around REDTOP [Soviet Bloc] Walk-ins."[3]

In addition to the traditional Confidential, Secret, and Top Secret classifications, additional sets of classifications are employed for information that fall into the Sensitive Compartmented Information (SCI) category. According to a 1984 report by the NFIB Security Committee,

Sensitive Compartmented Information is data about sophisticated technical systems for collecting intelligence and information collected by those systems. The characteristics of the systems that necessitated the development of SCI programs are (a) that compared to conventional intelligence activities employing human sources, many more people normally must know sensitive information in order to develop, build and operate the systems and to analyze the material they collect; (b) that they generally produce large quantities of accurate, detailed intelligence, which is needed and relied upon by senior planners and policymakers, and which, by its nature, is extremely fragile, in that it reveals the characteristics of the systems that collect it; and (c) that they are extremely vulnerable to adversary countermeasures, i.e. denial or deception.[4]

The systems that generate SCI information are imaging and signals intelligence satellites; aircraft such as the SR-71, U-2, and RC-135; submarines involved in Special Navy Control Program missions; and ground stations involved in the interception of foreign signals. Information about imaging and signals intelligence satellites also falls in the SCI category.

A more stringent background investigation is required to gain access to SCI information than to Top Secret information. In addition, whereas denial of a Top Secret clearance requires the presence of a well-defined character or personality defect that poses a threat to national security, "no risk is tolerable where SCI is involved, and individuals who have been granted Top Secret clearances may be denied approval for access to SCI." In addition, the physical security measures used to protect SCI are more extensive than those used to protect Top Secret information—particularly the holding of SCI information in vault areas from which it is not permitted to be removed.[5]

The first public hint of the existence of such a security category occurred during the Senate hearing on the Gulf of Tonkin Resolution in 1964, when Senate Committee Chairman William Fulbright inquired into the source of a report that North Vietnamese patrol boats were about to attack the Turner Joy on the night of August 4, 1964. Defense Secretary Robert McNamara, Fulbright, and Senators Frank Lausche and Albert Gore engaged in the following colloquy:

McNamara: We have some problems because the [committee] staff has not been cleared for certain intelligence.

Lausche: I do not understand that. The members of our staff are not cleared?

Fulbright: All of those who have worked on this matter, but he is talking of a special classification of intelligence communications. . .

Gore: Mr. Chairman, could we know what particular classification that is? I had not heard of this particular super classification.

McNamara: . . .Clearance is *above* Top Secret for the particular information on the situation. (Emphasis added).[6]

The "above Top Secret" category dealt with communications or signals intelligence (rather than intelligence communications), and McNamara revealed that it was called Special Intelligence, or SI.[7] SI is one of several categories of SCI.

The institutionalization of such categories and clearances, particularly SI, can be traced to the successful interception and decryption of Japanese, German, and Italian signals during World War II by the United States and Great Britain. The machine by which the United States was able to decode the Japanese diplomatic messages was known as PURPLE, and the intelligence provided by the decryption activity was known as MAGIC. Distribution of MAGIC material was sharply restricted by George Marshall, who drew up a "Top List" of those authorized to have access. The list was restricted to President Roosevelt; the Secretaries of State, War, and the Navy; and the Directors of Military and Naval Intelligence. Among those not on the list was the Commander of U.S. Naval Forces at Pearl Harbor, Admiral Husband Kimmel.[8]

The British also instituted a code word system to guard the fact that they were able to decrypt German and Italian military and intelligence communications. The most sensitive military material was originally designated PEARL, ZYMOTIC, SWELL, and SIDAR. Later, the British settled on three code words—ULTRA, PEARL, and THUMB—to indicate material of special sensitivity. Eventually, PEARL and THUMB were combined into a single code word—PINUP. Intercepts of German intelligence communications by the British Radio Security Service were given the labels ISOS and ISK, depending on whether they were intercepts of ENIGMA-generated or hand-generated cipher systems. This information, when passed to the United States, became ICE and PAIR.[9]

In addition to intercepting Japanese diplomatic communications, the United States also spent considerable effort in intercepting and trying the decipher Japanese military communications. The United States employed several code names to represent the product of such activity. DEXTER was the code word used for intercepts of the highest level traffic—for example, Admiral Yamomoto's travel plans. CORRAL indicated less sensitive intercepts. RABID was used to indicate Traffic Analysis intelligence. With the signing of BRUSA Communications Intelligence Agreement in 1943, which standardized SIGINT procedures between the United States and Britain, ULTRA was made a prefix to each classification so that they became ULTRA DEXTER, ULTRA CORRAL, and ULTRA RABID.[10]

Although the outbreak of World War II required a significant expansion of those with a need to know concerning ULTRA, extraordinary security procedures were maintained and distribution restricted as much as possible. Thus, the British maintained a system of Special Liaison Units to facilitate the transmission of ULTRA from the Government Code and Cypher School in Bletchley to military commanders. It was required that those with knowledge of ULTRA remain outside of battle areas to avoid any chance of capture. On occasions where exceptions were made and ULTRA-cleared personnel did risk capture, they carried cyanide pills to allow them to commit suicide to avoid interrogation.[11]

The restricted distribution of ULTRA by the United States is indicated by the fact that in 1943 there were only sixty-one individuals in China-Burma-India theater, outside of the personnel in the Signals Intelligence Service and Radio Intelligence Units, who were cleared for ULTRA. It was required that "requests for. . .additions [to the list] . . . be kept by each headquarters to the absolute minimum necessary for the efficient handling of the material."[12]

The restricted nature of the material was clearly indicated by the same directive, which stated:

> The Assistant Chief of Staff, G-2, War Department, requires that all ULTRA DEXTER material be classified TOP SECRET and so marked in addition to the prescribed code words. This classification will in no way be interpreted as releasing ULTRA DEXTER from the requirements defined herein or authorizing TOP SECRET control officers or other personnel to handle, see, or discuss ULTRA DEXTER in any form, unless they are also on the list of authorized ULTRA DEXTER recipients.[13]

Within the SCI category are several sets of clearances—the three best known being Special Intelligence (SI), Talent-Keyhole (TK), and BYEMAN (B).

As McNamara indicated, the SI category concerns signals intelligence. Just as there were different ULTRA levels (for the United States) there are different compartments of the SI category which corresponds to different levels of sensitivity. UMBRA is the successor to DINAR and TRINE as the compartment with the most sensitive SI material. Less sensitive is the SPOKE compartment, which might contain information from intercepts of PLO communications. Least sensitive is the information in the MORAY compartment.[14]

To express these differing levels of sensitivity, a page containing only UMBRA SCI will be stamped TOP SECRET UMBRA; a page containing only SPOKE SCI will be stamped SECRET SPOKE. The view that the use of the Top Secret, Secret, and Confidential prefixes implies that UMBRA, SPOKE, and MORAY are simply "need-to-know" compartments of those conventional classifications is inconsistent with, among other things, the fact that greater physical security measures are taken to protect a SECRET SPOKE document than a plain TOP SECRET document.[15]

Within the UMBRA category there are further designators employed by the NSA for especially sensitive UMBRA. GAMMA is a designator that at one time was reserved exclusively for intercepts of Soviet communications, until the NSA received orders in 1969 to use the same methods and procedures to monitor the communications of U.S. antiwar leaders. At one point, there were at least twenty GAMMA designations, including GILT, GOAT, GULT, GANT, GUPY, GABE, GYRO, and GOUT, each of which referred to a specific operation or method. As discussed previously, GAMMA GUPY referred to the interception of radio-telephone conversations being conducted by Soviet leaders as they were driven around Moscow in their limousines; GAMMA GOUT referred to the material obtained by interception of South Vietnamese government communications.[16] Thus, a document might bear the classification TOP SECRET UMBRA GAMMA GYRO.

At one time, there was a DELTA compartment of UMBRA which referred to intercepts relating to Soviet military operations, such as the locations of Soviet submarines or Russian aircraft operations. DELTA categories included DACE, DICE, and DENT.[17]

In addition to compartments within SCI categories, documents might bear designators which provide further information as to the source of the information. TOP SECRET UMBRA documents might also bear a fourth word indicating that the SIGINT was obtained from a third party to the UKUSA agreement. DRUID designates a third-party intercept. Other designations indicate the specific nations involved: ISHTAR (Japan), SETEE (Korea), DYNAMO (Denmark), RICHTER (West Germany), and DIKTER (Norway).[18]

The TK, or TALENT-KEYHOLE clearance, restricts access to information concerning the product of certain overhead collection systems—satellites, the U-2, and the SR-71. Compartments within the TK system include RUFF, ZARF, and CHESS. RUFF pertains to information produced by imaging (KEYHOLE) satellites. ZARF may indicate SIGINT obtained by satellite while CHESS designates SR-71 or U-2 photography. Thus, the December 1986 final report of the DCI Mobile Missile Task Force Intelligence Requirements and Analysis Working Group is classified TOP SECRET RUFF ZARF UMBRA.[19]

In some cases, it is felt that certain code word information needs to or should be made available to a larger audience than the code word system permits. Secret or Top Secret documents, when authorized to contain such information, bear the additional designator WNINTEL: Warning Notice—Intelligence Sources and Methods Involved.

In practice, SI and TK clearances, representing the product of technical collection systems, are almost always awarded jointly. Hence, the term "SI-TK clearance" is more common than the terms "SI clearance" or "TK clearance." SI-TK clearance give individuals access to the product of sensitive intelligence systems; they do not grant access to information concerning the systems themselves. Information about the type of system, its location, name, orbit, or capabilities, is not accessible to an individual simply on the basis of an SI-TK clearance. Clearances for such information are granted on a system-by-system basis, each system having a specific code word. These code words represent the compartments of the BYEMAN system. RHYOLITE, AQUACADE, CHALET, VORTEX, JUMPSEAT, and MAGNUM represent the BYEMAN compartments pertaining to SIGINT satellites, while KENNAN, LACROSSE, GAMBIT, HEXAGON, and CORONA represent the BYEMAN compartments of present, future, and past imaging satellites.[20]

Additional CIA, NSA, and Navy SCI systems include CS, PM, VER, SNCP, and M.[21] VER is probably the designation for the NSA "Very Restricted Knowledge" SCI system. Different levels of that system involve access to varying types of SCI, for example, satellite imagery. SNCP refers to the Special Navy Control Program—the use of submarines to collect intelligence in or near the territorial waters of the Soviet Union, as discussed in Chapter 8. M also represents a Navy SCI system—MEDITATE—which concerns information about IVY BELLS-type operations.

The classification system just described, as well as personnel and security standards for access to and handling of intelligence information, is defined by a series of Executive Orders, National Security Decision Directives (NSDDs), National

Security Council Intelligence Directives (NSCIDs), Director of Central Intelligence Directives (DCIDs), and DOD Directives. Additionally, several NSC committees are concerned with the security of information acquired, as well as the security of sources and methods.

As noted earlier, since the Eisenhower Administration, every administration has issued an Executive Order on National Security Information, the latest three being Executive Order 11652 of March 10, 1972, "Classification and Declassification of National Security Information and Material," with amendments during the Ford Administration; Executive Order 12065 of June 28, 1978, "National Security Information"; and Executive Order 12356 of April 2, 1982, "National Security Information."[22]

Part 1 of Executive Order 12356 defines classification levels (Top Secret, Secret, and Confidential) and specifies the officials (by position) who can classify (at different levels) or delegate authority to classify information, as well as the identifications and markings that are to be shown on the face of all documents and basic rules concerning the duration of the classification.

In addition, Part 1 defines the types of information that shall be considered for classifications as well as establishing limitations on classification. Information may be considered for classification if it concerns:

1. military plans, weapons, or operations;
2. the vulnerabilities or capabilities of systems, installations, projects, or plans relating to the national security;
3. foreign government information;
4. intelligence activities (including special activities), or intelligence sources or methods;
5. foreign relations or foreign activities of the United States;
6. scientific, technological, or economic matters relating to the national security;
7. U.S. government programs for safeguarding nuclear materials or facilities;
8. cryptology;
9. a confidential source; or
10. other categories of information that are related to national security and that require protection against unauthorized disclosure as determined by the President or by agency heads or other officials who have been delegated original classification authority by the President.[23]

Section 1.6, which deals with limitations on classification, forbids classification meant to conceal violations of law, inefficiency, or administrative error as well as classifications made to prevent embarrassment to a person, organization or agency. It also prohibits classification of basic scientific research information "not clearly related to national security." However, in a sharp reversal from such past orders, Part 1 of Executive Order 12356 contains the provision that

The President or an agency head or official designated under Section 1.2 (a) (1), 1.2 (b) or 1.2 (c) (1) may reclassify information previously declassified and disclosed if it is determined in writing that (1) the information requires protection in the interest of national security; and (2) the information may reasonably be recovered.[24]

The remaining parts of the Order deal with derivative classification, declassification and downgrading, safeguarding and implementation, and review. Part 4, "Safeguarding," includes Section 4.2, "Special Access Programs," which states that

agency heads designated pursuant to Section 1.2(a) may create special access programs to control access, distribution and protection of particularly sensitive information classified pursuant to this order or predecessor orders. Such programs may be created or continued only at the written direction of these agency heads. For special access programs pertaining to intelligence activities (including special activities but not including military operational, strategic and tactical programs), or intelligence sources or methods, this function will be exercised by the Director of Central Intelligence.[25]

This section has been used as the justification for the creation of military special access programs as well as intelligence special access programs.

The Reagan Administration issued two NSDDs concerning the control of intelligence information: NSDD-19 of January 12, 1982, "Protection of Classified National Security Council and Intelligence Information," and NSDD-84 of March 11, 1983, "Safeguarding National Security Information."[26]

NSDD-19 requires that all contacts with any element of the news media in which classified National Security Council (NSC) or classified intelligence information is to be discussed receive advance approval by a senior official; that the number of officials with access to documents relating to NSC matters be kept to the minimum essential; and that in the event of unauthorized disclosure of such information, government employees who have had access to that information will be subject to investigation that will include the use of all legal methods.[27]

NSDD-19 has led to the requirement that those granted access to classified NSC information sign a cover sheet acknowledging access and agreeing to "cooperate fully with any lawful investigation by the United States Government into any unauthorized disclosure of classified information contained therein."[28]

NSDD-84 specified that all government officials and employees with access to SCI must sign a nondisclosure agreement that provides for prepublication review of any writings or speeches that deal with subjects relating to SCI—for example, START verification. Beginning in 1981, individuals with access to SCI were required to sign Form 4193, shown as Figure 18–1, providing for lifetime prepublication review of all writings "including works of fiction, which contain or purport to contain SCI or that I have reason to believe are derived from SCI." As a result of the promulgation of NSDD-84 a new form replaced 4193, as shown in Figure 18–2. The prepublication review provision of the new form was suspended by President Reagan in response to Congressional criticism. However, employees are still required to sign the prior version of Form 4193 before being granted access to SCI.[29]

NSCID No. 1 of February 17, 1972, "Basic Duties and Responsibilities," specifies that the Director of Central Intelligence is authorized to

disseminate national intelligence and interdepartmental intelligence on a strictly controlled basis to foreign governments and international bodies upon his determination after consultation with the United States [now National Foreign] Intelligence Board, that such action would substantially promote the security of the United States, provided that such dissemination is consistent with existing statutes and Presidential policy, including that reflected in international agreements.[30]

NSCID No. 1 also makes the DCI responsible for the development of policies and procedures for the protection of intelligence and of intelligence sources and methods from unauthorized disclosure—including personnel and physical security policies.

In carrying out the responsibilities stated in NSCID No. 1, the DCI has issued several DCIDs concerning the dissemination of intelligence information to foreign governments and personnel, and physical security policies.

DCID 1/7, "Control of Dissemination of Intelligence Information," contains several provisions concerning the release of intelligence information to foreign governments. Release of intelligence to foreign governments *in original form* requires originator approval. Any information contained in classified intelligence documents originated by another component may be released if it bears no restrictive markings prohibiting such transfer and

1. no reference is made to the source documents upon which the release product is based;
2. the information is extracted or paraphrased to ensure that the source or manner of acquisition of the intelligence cannot be deduced or revealed in any manner; and
3. foreign release is made through established foreign disclosure channels and procedures.[31]

The Directive also authorizes control markings in addition to the classification levels. ORCON is an abbreviation used to indicate that dissemination and extraction of information is controlled by the originator and is employed "when unique source sensitivity factors, known to the originator, require strict compliance with third agency rule procedures, in addition to continuing knowledge and supervision on the part of the originator as to the extent to which the original document and information therein disseminated." NOCONTRACT indicates the document is not available to contractors or consultants, *regardless of their level of clearance.* PROPIN is short for "CAUTION—PROPRIETARY INFORMATION INVOLVED." It is used in conjunction with foreign intelligence obtained from various sources in the U.S. private business sector, and indicates that a source has a proprietary interest in the information or that the information could be used to the source's detriment.[32]

The most significant control marking with respect to foreign release is the NOFORN marking, which is short for "SPECIAL HANDLING REQUIRED—

Figure 18–1. Form 4193.

Sensitive Compartmented Information Nondisclosure Agreement

An Agreement Between _____ and the United States

(Name—Printed or Typed)

1. Intending to be legally bound, I hereby accept the obligations contained in this Agreement in consideration of my being granted access to information protected within Special Access Programs, hereinafter referred to in this Agreement as Sensitive Compartmented Information (SCI). I have been advised that SCI involves or derives from intelligence sources or methods and is classified or classifiable under the standards of Executive Order 12065 or other Executive order or statute. I understand and accept that by being granted access to SCI, special confidence and trust shall be placed in me by the United States Government.

2. I hereby acknowledge that I have received a security indoctrination concerning the nature and protection of SCI, including the procedures to be followed in ascertaining whether other persons to whom I contemplate disclosing this information have been approved for access to it, and I understand these procedures. I understand that I may be required to sign subsequent agreements upon being granted access to different categories of SCI. I further understand that all my obligations under this Agreement continue to exist whether or not I am required to sign such subsequent agreements.

3. I have been advised that direct or indirect unauthorized disclosure, unauthorized retention, or negligent handling of SCI by me could cause irreparable injury to the United States or be used to advantage by a foreign nation. I hereby agree that I will never divulge such information to anyone who is not authorized to receive it without prior written authorization from the United States Government department or agency (hereinafter Department or Agency) that last authorized my access to SCI. I further understand that I am obligated by law and regulation not to disclose any classified information in an unauthorized fashion.

4. In consideration of being granted access to SCI and of being assigned or retained in a position of special confidence and trust requiring access to SCI, I hereby agree to submit for security review by the Department or Agency that last authorized my access to such information, all information or materials, including works of fiction, which contain or purport to contain any SCI or description of activities that produce or relate to SCI or that I have reason to believe are derived from SCI, that I contemplate disclosing to any person not authorized to have access to SCI or that I have prepared for public disclosure. I understand and agree that my obligation to submit such information and materials for review applies during the course of my access to SCI and thereafter, and I agree to make any required submissions prior to discussing the information or materials with, or showing them to, anyone who is not authorized to have access to SCI. I further agree that I will not disclose such information or materials to any person not authorized to have access to SCI until I have received written authorization from the Department or Agency that last authorized my access to SCI that such disclosure is permitted.

5. I understand that the purpose of the review described in paragraph 4 is to give the United States a reasonable opportunity to determine whether the information or materials submitted pursuant to paragraph 4 set forth any SCI. I further understand that the Department or Agency to which I have submitted materials will act upon them, coordinating within the Intelligence Community when appropriate, and make a response to me within a reasonable time, not to exceed 30 working days from date of receipt.

6. I have been advised that any breach of this Agreement may result in the termination of my access to SCI and retention in a position of special confidence and trust requiring such access, as well as the termination of my employment or other relationships with any Department or Agency that provides me with access to SCI. In addition, I have been advised that any unauthorized disclosure of SCI by me may constitute violations of United States criminal laws, including the provisions of Sections 793, 794, 798, and 952, Title 18, United States Code, and of Section 783(b), Title 50, United States Code. Nothing in this Agreement constitutes a waiver by the United States of the right to prosecute me for any statutory violation.

7. I understand that the United States Government may seek any remedy available to it to enforce this Agreement including, but not limited to, application for a court order prohibiting disclosure of information in breach of this Agreement. I have been advised that the action can be brought against me in any of the several appropriate United States District Courts where the United States Government may elect to file the action. Court costs and reasonable attorneys fees incurred by the United States Government may be assessed against me if I lose such action.

8. I understand that all information to which I may obtain access by signing this Agreement is now and will forever remain the property of the United States Government. I do not now, nor will I ever, possess any right, interest, title, or claim whatsoever to such information. I agree that I shall return all materials, which may have come into my possession or for which I am responsible because of such access, upon demand by an authorized representative of the United States Government or upon the conclusion of my employment or other relationship with the United States Government entity providing me access to such materials. If I do not return such materials upon request, I understand this may be a violation of Section 793, Title 18, United States Code, a United States criminal law.

9. Unless and until I am released in writing by an authorized representative of the Department or Agency that last provided me with access to SCI, I understand that all conditions and obligations imposed upon me by this Agreement apply during the time I am granted access to SCI, and at all times thereafter.

10. Each provision of this Agreement is severable. If a court should find any provision of this Agreement to be unenforceable, all other provisions of this Agreement shall remain in full force and effect. This Agreement concerns SCI and does not set forth such other conditions and obligations not related to SCI as may now or hereafter pertain to my employment by or assignment or relationship with the Department or Agency.

11. I have read this Agreement carefully and my questions, if any, have been answered to my satisfaction. I acknowledge that the briefing officer has made available Sections 793, 794, 798, and 952 of Title 18, United States Code, and Section 783(b) of Title 50, United States Code, and Executive Order 12065, as amended, so that I may read them at this time, if I so choose.

12. I hereby assign to the United States Government all rights, title and interest, and all royalties, remunerations, and emoluments that have resulted, will result, or may result from any disclosure, publication, or revelation not consistent with the terms of this Agreement.

13. I make this Agreement without any mental reservation or purpose of evasion.

(12)

Figure 18–1. continued.

13. I make this Agreement without any mental reservation or purpose of evasion.

SIGNATURE _____ DATE _____

The execution of this Agreement was witnessed by the undersigned who accepted it on behalf of the United States Government as a prior condition of access to Sensitive Compartmented Information.

WITNESS and ACCEPTANCE:

SIGNATURE _____ DATE _____

SECURITY BRIEFING ACKNOWLEDGEMENT

I hereby acknowledge that I was briefed on the following SCI Special Access Program(s):

_____

(Special Access Programs by Initials Only)

Signature of Individual Briefed _____ Date Briefed _____

Printed or Typed Name _____

Social Security Number (See Notice Below) _____ Organization (Name and Address) _____

I certify that the above SCI access(es) were approved in accordance with relevant SCI procedures and that the briefing presented by me on the above date was also in accordance therewith.

Signature of Briefing Officer _____

Printed or Typed Name _____ Organization (Name and Address) _____

Social Security Number (See Notice Below) _____

★   ★   ★   ★   ★   ★

SECURITY BRIEFING ACKNOWLEDGEMENT

Having been reminded of my continuing obligation to comply with the terms of this Agreement, I hereby acknowledge that I was debriefed on the following SCI Special Access Program(s):

_____
(Special Access Programs by Initials Only)

_____   _____
Signature of Individual Debriefed   Date Debriefed

_____
Printed or Typed Name

_____   _____
Social Security Number (See Notice Below)   Organization (Name and Address)

I certify that the debriefing by me on the above date was in accordance with relevant SCI procedures.

_____
Signature of Debriefing Officer

_____   _____
Printed or Typed Name   Organization (Name and Address)

_____
Social Security Number (See Notice Below)

NOTICE: The Privacy Act, 5 U.S.C. 522a, requires that federal agencies inform individuals, at the time information is solicited from them, whether the disclosure is mandatory or voluntary, by what authority such information is solicited, and what uses will be made of the information. You are hereby advised that authority for soliciting your Social Security Account Number (SSN) is Executive Order 9397. Your SSN will be used to identify you precisely when it is necessary to 1) certify that you have access to the information indicated above, 2) determine that your access to the information indicated has terminated, or 3) certify that you have witnessed a briefing or debriefing. Although disclosure of your SSN is not mandatory, your failure to do so may impede such certifications or determinations.

Figure 18–2. Revised Form 4193

SENSITIVE COMPARTMENTED INFORMATION NONDISCLOSURE AGREEMENT

An Agreement Between _____ and the United States
(Name-Printed or Typed)

1.   1. Intending to be legally bound, I hereby accept the obligations
2   contained in this Agreement in consideration of my being granted
3   access to information known as Sensitive Compartmented Information
4   (SCI). I have been advised and am aware that SCI involves or
5   derives from intelligence sources or methods and is classified or
6   classifiable under the standards of Executive Order 12356 or under
7   other Executive order or statute. I understand and accept that by
8   being granted access to SCI, special confidence and trust shall be
9   placed in me by the United States Government.

1   2. I hereby acknowledge that I have received a security indoctrination
2   concerning the nature and protection of SCI, including the procedures
3   to be followed in ascertaining whether other persons to whom I
4   contemplate disclosing this information have been approved for
5   access to it, and that I understand these procedures. I understand that
6   I may be required to sign subsequent agreements as a condition of
7   being granted access to different categories of SCI. I further
8   understand that all my obligations under this Agreement continue to
9   exist whether or not I am required to sign such subsequent agreements.

1   3. I have been advised and am aware that direct or indirect unauthorized
2   disclosure, unauthorized retention, or negligent handling of SCI by
3   me could cause irreparable injury to the United States or could be
4   used to advantage by a foreign nation. I hereby agree that I will
5   never divulge such information unless I have officially verified
6   that the recipient has been properly authorized by the United States
7   Government to receive it or I have been given prior written notice of
8   authorization from the United States Government Department or Agency
9   (hereinafter Department or Agency) last granting me either a security
10   clearance or an SCI access approval that such disclosure is permitted.

1   4. I further understand that I am obligated to comply with laws and
2   regulations that prohibit the unauthorized disclosure of classified
3   information. As used in this Agreement, classified information is
4   information that is classified under the standards of E.O. 12356, or
5   under any other Executive order or statute that prohibits the
6   unauthorized disclosure of information in the interest of national
7   security.

1   5. In consideration of being granted access to SCI and of being
2   assigned or retained in a position of special confidence and trust
3   requiring access to SCI and other classified information, I hereby
4   agree to submit for security review by the Department or Agency
5   last granting me either a security clearance or an SCI access
6   approval all materials, including works of fiction, that I contemplate
7   disclosing to any person not authorized to have such information,
8   or that I have prepared for public disclosure, which contain or
9   purport to contain:

Figure 18–2. continued

10   (a) any SCI, any description of activities that produce or
11   relate to SCI, or any information derived from SCI;
12   (b) any classified information from intelligence reports
13   or estimates; or
14   (c) any information concerning intelligence activities,
15   sources or methods.

16   I understand and agree that my obligation to submit such information
17   and materials for review applies during the course of my access to
18   SCI and at all times thereafter. However, I am not required to
19   submit for review any such materials that exclusively contain
20   information lawfully obtained by me at a time when I have no employment,
21   contract or other relationship with the United States Government,
22   and which are to be published at such time.

1   6. I agree to make the submissions described in paragraph 5 prior
2   to discussing the information or materials with, or showing them to
3   anyone who is not authorized to have access to such information. I
4   further agree that I will not disclose such information or materials
5   unless I have officially verified that the recipient has been
6   properly authorized by the United States Government to receive it or
7   I have been given written authorization from the Department or
8   Agency last granting me either a security clearance or an SCI
9   access approval that such disclosure is permitted.

1   7. I understand that the purpose of the review described in paragraph 5
2   is to give the United States a reasonable opportunity to determine
3   whether the information or materials submitted pursuant to paragraph 5
4   set forth any SCI or other information that is subject to classification
5   under E.O. 12356 or under any other Executive order or statute that
6   prohibits the unauthorized disclosure of information in the interest
7   of national security. I further understand that the Department or
8   Agency to which I have submitted materials will act upon them,
9   coordinating with the Intelligence Community or other agencies when
10   appropriate, and substantively respond to me within 30 working days
11   from date of receipt.

1   8. I have been advised and am aware that any breach of this Agreement
2   may result in the termination of any security clearances and SCI
3   access approvals that I may hold; removal from a position of
4   special confidence and trust requiring such clearances or access
5   approvals; and the termination of my employment or other relationships
6   with the Departments or Agencies that granted my security clearances
7   or SCI access approvals. In addition, I have been advised and am
8   aware that any unauthorized disclosure of SCI or other classified
9   information by me may constitute a violation or violations of United
10   States criminal laws, including the provisions of Sections 641, 793,
11   794, 798, and 952, Title 18, United States Code, the provisions
12   of Section 783(b), Title 50, United States Code, and the provisions
13   of the Intelligence Identities Protection Act of 1982. I recognize
14   that nothing in this Agreement constitutes a waiver by the United
15   States of the right to prosecute me for any statutory violation.

Figure 18–2. continued

1   9. I hereby assign to the United States Government all royalties,
2   remunerations, and emoluments that have resulted, will result, or
3   may result from any disclosure, publication, or revelation not
4   consistent with the terms of this Agreement.

1   10. I understand that the United States Government may seek any
2   remedy available to it to enforce this Agreement including, but not
3   limited to, application for a court order prohibiting disclosure of
4   information in breach of this Agreement.

1   11. I understand that all information to which I may obtain access
2   by signing this Agreement is now and will forever remain the property
3   of the United States Government. I do not now, nor will I ever,
4   possess any right, interest, title, or claim whatsoever to such
5   information. I agree that I shall return all materials which have
6   or may come into my possession of for which I am responsible
7   because of such access, upon demand by an authorized representative
8   of the United States Government or upon the conclusion of my employment
9   or other relationship with the Department or Agency that last
10   granted me either a security clearance or an SCI access approval.
11   If I do not return such materials upon request, I understand that
12   this may be a violation of Section 793, Title 18, United States
13   Code, a United States criminal law.

1   12. Unless and until I am released in writing by an authorized
2   representative of the United States Government, I understand that
3   all conditions and obligations imposed upon me by this Agreement
4   apply during the time I am granted access to SCI and at all times
5   thereafter.

1   13. Each provision of this Agreement is severable. If a court should
2   find any provision of this Agreement to be unenforceable, all other
3   provisions of this Agreement shall remain in full force and effect.

1   14. I have read this Agreement carefully and my questions, if any,
2   have been answered to my satisfaction. I acknowledge that the
3   briefing officer has made available to me Sections 641, 793, 794,
4   798, and 952 of Title 18, United States Code, Section 783(b) of
5   Title 50, United States Code, the Intelligence Identities Protection
6   Act of 1982, and Executive Order 12356 so that I may read them at
7   this time, if I so choose.

1   15. I make this Agreement without mental reservation or purpose of
2   evasion.

SIGNATURE   DATE

SOCIAL SECURITY NUMBER   ORGANIZATION
(SEE NOTICE BELOW)

Figure 18–2. continued

1 The execution of this Agreement was witnessed by the undersigned,
2 who, on behalf of the United States Government, agreed to its terms
3 and accepted it as a prior condition of authorizing access to
4 Sensitive Compartmented Information.

WITNESS and ACCEPTANCE:

_____   _____

SIGNATURE   DATE

_____

ORGANIZATION

SECURITY BRIEFING ACKNOWLEDGEMENT

I hereby acknowledge that I was briefed on the following SCI Special
Access Program(s):

_____

(Special Access Programs by Initials Only)

_____   _____

Signature of Individual Briefed   Date Briefed

_____   _____

Printed or Typed Name

_____   _____

Social Security Number (See Notice   Organization (Name and Address)
Below)

I certify that the above SCI access(es) were approved in accordance
with relevant SCI procedures and that the briefing presented by me on the
above date was also in accordance therewith.

_____   _____

Signature of Briefing Officer

_____   _____

Printed or Typed Name   Organization (Name and Address)

_____   _____

Social Security Number (See Notice
Below)

Figure 18–2. continued

SECURITY DEBRIEFING ACKNOWLEDGEMENT

Having been reminded of my continuing obligation to comply with the terms of this Agreement, I hereby acknowledge that I was debriefed on the following SCI Special Access Program(s):

(Special Access Programs by Initials Only)

Signature of Individual Debriefed   Date Debriefed

Printed or Typed Name

Social Security Number (See Notice   Organization (Name and Address)
Below)

I certify that the debriefing presented by me on the above date was in accordance with relevant SCI procedures.

Signature of Debriefing Officer

Printed or Typed Name   Organization (Name and Address)

Social Security Number (See Notice
Below)

1   NOTICE: The Privacy Act, 5 U.S.C. 552a, requires that federal
2   agencies inform individuals, at the time information is solicited
3   from them, whether the disclosure is mandatory or voluntary, by
4   what authority such information is solicited, and what uses will
5   be made of the information. You are hereby advised that authority
6   for soliciting your Social Security Account Number (SSN) is Executive
7   Order 9397. Your SSN will be used to identify you precisely when
8   it is necessary to 1) certify that you have access to the information
9   indicated above, 2) determine that your access to the information
10   indicated has terminated, or 3) certify that you have witnessed
11   a briefing or debriefing. Although disclosure of your SSN is not
12   mandatory, your failure to do so may impede the processing of such
13   certifications or determinations.

(391557)

NOT RELEASABLE TO FOREIGN NATIONALS." According to DCID 1/7, examples of when the control marking may be used include: "(1) the possible compromise of the status of relations with collaborating foreign governments or officials [and] (2) jeopardizing the continuing viability of vital technical collection programs."[33]

One document labeled SECRET NOFORN ORCON PROPIN is the previously mentioned 1977 CIA study entitled *Israel: Foreign Intelligence and Security Services.* Its NOFORN control marking was assigned for a variety of reasons including (1) above. When the study became public, due to its being removed from the U.S. Embassy in Tehran in 1979, it caused acute embarrassment to both governments, as it alleged that Israeli intelligence agencies blackmailed, bugged, wiretapped, and offered bribes to U.S. government employees in an effort to gain sensitive information. Israeli spokesman denounced such allegations as "ridiculous."[34]

As its title indicates, DCID 1/10 of January 18, 1982, "Security Policy Guidelines on Liaison Relationships with Foreign Intelligence Organizations and Foreign Security Services," established procedures concerning liaison relationships with foreign organizations, including the exchange of information.

Personnel and physical security are the subject of DCID 1/14 of April 14, 1986, "Minimum Personnel Security Standards and Procedures Governing Eligibility for Access to Sensitive Compartmented Information"; DCID 1/19, "Uniform Procedures for Administrative Handling and Accountability of Sensitive Compartmented Information"; and DCID 1/20, "Security Policy Concerning Travel and Assignment of Personnel with Access to Sensitive Compartmented Information."

Under DCID 1/14

the granting of access to SCI shall be controlled under the strictest application of the 'need-to-know' principle and all individuals who are given access are required, as a condition of gaining access, to sign an agreement that they will not disclose that information to persons not authorized to receive it.

The Directive also specifies that, except under special circumstances (which include liaison arrangements), individuals to be given SCI access and their families must be U.S. citizens. It also requires that intended recipients undergo a Special Background Investigation (SBI) before being awarded SCI access—an investigation that is more extensive than the Background Investigation required for Secret or Top Secret clearances. After the initial SBI, a periodic reinvestigation every five years (or less) is required. Additionally, DCID 1/14 requires all departments with personnel who have SCI access to institute security programs that involve security education, security supervision, and security review. As of 1979, 115,000 individuals had SCI clearances, including 13,000 contract employees.[35]

According to DCID 1/14, items to be considered in determining eligibility for access to SCI include: loyalty, close relatives and associates, sexual considerations, cohabitation, undesirable character traits, financial irresponsibility, alcohol abuse, use of illegal drugs and drug abuse, emotional and mental disorders, record of law violations, security violations, and involvement in outside activities.[36]

DCID 1/19 concerns physical security issues such as the establishment of vault facilities for holding SCI information; and intrusion detection systems, communications, computer and data-processing security relating to the transmission of SCI information; other physical security systems; and the location of vault facilities in exposed or combat areas. Thus, DCID 1/19 requires that "all electronic equipment which is used to process or transmit Sensitive Compartmented Information (SCI) shall meet national standards for TEMPEST."[37]

On the basis of the Executive Orders, NSDDs, NSCIDs, and DCIDs, the Departments of Defense, State, Treasury, and others produce directives and manuals to implement the directives—hence, DOD Instruction 5230.22, "Control of Dissemination of Foreign Intelligence"; DIA Regulation 50-10, "Control of Dissemination of Foreign Intelligence"; and DIA Manual 50-3, *Physical Security Standards for Sensitive Compartmented Information Facilities*.[38]

Abolition of the Security Committee left two NFIB committees concerned, in part, with security issues. The COMIREX's security function pertains to the security of information about and derived from satellite imaging systems. The Information Handling Committee was established by DCID 1/4 of May 18, 1976, but is now governed by DCID 3/14 of May 4, 1982. Among the responsibilities of the Committee, in coordination with the DCI SCI Forum, is to ensure that the "security aspects of information handling systems are given appropriate consideration."[39]

MANAGING THE ANALYTIC PROCESS

Management of the analytic process has two basic aspects. The most visible aspect is the management of the production of national intelligence—specifically, the National Intelligence Estimates (NIEs) and Special National Intelligence Estimates (SNIEs).

In addition to the NIEs, SNIEs, and Interagency Intelligence Memorandums (IIMs), the U.S. intelligence community, as is clear from Chapter 13, produces a vast amount of finished intelligence—military, economic, political, and scientific and technical. Although much of this intelligence is not "national" in the sense of being produced for national policymakers, it is important to the attainment of national security objectives.

Extensive intelligence production on atomic energy problems; space and weapons systems; and economic, social, and political matters is necessary as input to national estimates, as well as to inform officials to various departments who need detailed intelligence. Thus, it is necessary to ensure that departmental intelligence production is consistent with national priorities.

As with other types of intelligence activities, management of the analytical process is handled through NSCIDs, DCIDs, various committees, and requirements documents. NSCIDs No. 1 and 3 are the general guidance documents for all aspects of intelligence production.

Section 6 of NSCID No. 1 defines national intelligence as intelligence required for the formulation of national security policy, concerning more than one department or agency, and transcending the exclusive competence of a single department or agency. It authorizes the DCI to produce national intelligence and disseminate it to the President, the NSC, and other appropriate U.S. government components. Section 6 also stipulates that national intelligence will carry a statement of abstention or dissent of any NFIB member or intelligence chief of a military department.[40]

NSCID No. 3 of February 17, 1972, "Coordination of Intelligence Production," distinguishes between different types of intelligence—basic intelligence, current intelligence, departmental intelligence, interdepartmental intelligence, and national intelligence—and assigns responsibilities for the production of basic and current intelligence to the CIA and a variety of other agencies.

This Directive also specifies that:

1. The Department of State shall produce political and sociological intelligence on all countries and economic intelligence on countries of the Free World.
2. The Department of Defense shall produce military intelligence. This production shall include scientific, technical and economic intelligence directly pertinent to the mission of the various components of the Department of Defense.
3. The Central Intelligence Agency shall produce economic, scientific and technical intelligence. Further, the Central Intelligence Agency may produce such other intelligence as may be necessary to discharge the statutory responsibilities of the Director of Central Intelligence.

This Directive assigns to all NFIB members charged with the production of finished intelligence the responsibility of producing atomic energy intelligence. In addition, when an intelligence requirement is established for which there is no existing production capability, the DCI, in consultation with the NFIB, is responsible for determining which departments or agencies of the intelligence community can "best undertake the primary responsibility as a service for common concern."[41]

On the basis of NSCIDs No. 1 and No. 3, the DCI issues DCIDs in the 1/ and 3/ series to further implement the NSCIDs. The original DCIDs governing the national intelligence process were issued in July and September 1948. DCID 3/1 of July 8, 1948, "Standard Operating Procedures for Departmental Participation in the Production and Coordination of National Intelligence," required, except under exceptional circumstances, that upon initiation of a report or estimate the CIA inform departmental intelligence organizations of

1. the problem under consideration;
2. the nature and scope of the report or estimate involved;
3. the scheduled date of issuance of the first draft;
4. the requirements for departmental contributions...; and
5. the date upon which such departmental action should be completed.[42]

Under normal procedures the CIA was to prepare an initial draft and then furnish copies to departmental intelligence organizations with a request for their review and preparation. If the comments received indicated differences of opinion, the CIA was instructed to arrange for an informal discussion with departmental personnel. The CIA was then to prepare a final draft and distribute it to departmental intelligence organizations for concurrence or statements of substantial dissent which would be incorporated in the final paper.

DCID 3/2 of September 13, 1948, complemented 3/1. Entitled "Policy Governing Departmental Concurrences in National Intelligence Reports and Estimates," the Directive specified three options for departmental intelligence organizations: concur, concur with comment, or dissent. The Directive further stated the considerations that should be involved in choosing among the options.[43]

Subsequently, DCIDs 3/1 and 3/2 were superseded by DCID 3/5 of September 1, 1953, entitled "Production of National Intelligence Estimates." The Directive reflected the changes that occurred in the intervening years—particularly the establishment of the Board of National Estimates (BNE) and the Intelligence Advisory Committee (IAC). It was required that by January 1 the BNE present to the IAC a production program for NIEs and SNIEs.[44]

In 1950 an Office of National Estimates (ONE) was established within the CIA's Directorate of Intelligence with the responsibility for drafting national and specific national estimates. The Office consisted of a Board of National Estimates and its staff. The Board consisted of between seven and twelve senior officials with expertise in particular areas who were responsible for managing the production of national estimates. Members of the Board were initially drawn from academia and subsequently from the CIA.[45]

The Board was serviced initially by fifty professional analysts, subsequently by thirty. In theory, the Board reacted to specific requests from the NSC. In emergencies this was often the case. Thus, as noted, several SNIEs were commissioned during the Cuban missile crisis. However, the subject of NIEs became routine, on the basis of the Board's judgement as to the requirements of policymakers.[46]

The process for drafting NIEs was initially established by DCID 3/1: initial drafting by BNE/ONE, interagency review, revision, and submission to the USIB with dissenting footnotes, if any. During the process, the BNE operated in collegial fashion, taking collective responsibility for the estimates produced and exercising collective judgement in approving it.[47]

The ONE suffered a decline of prestige and influence during the Nixon Administration for a variety of reasons, including Henry Kissinger's unhappiness with its product. In June 1973, John Huizenga, the BNE Chairman, retired on an involuntary basis. DCI William Colby decided not to replace him and abolished ONE.[48] Colby gave two reasons for his decision:

> One, I had some concern with the tendency to compromise differences and put out a document which was less sharp than perhaps was needed in certain situations. Second, I believed that I needed the advantage of some individuals who could specialize in some of the major problems not just as estimative problems but as broad intelligence problems.

They could sit in my chair, so to speak, and look at the full range of an intelligence problem: Are we collecting enough? Are we processing the raw data properly? Are we spending too much money on it? Are we organized right to do the jobs?[49]

Colby created the National Intelligence Officer (NIO) system in which specific individuals were held solely responsible for producing a particular estimate. NIOs are recruited mainly, but not exclusively, from the CIA and are specialists in a specific functional or geographical area. The number of NIOs have varied from thirteen, to eight, to the present seventeen.

In addition to three at-large NIOs there are NIOs for Africa, East Asia, Europe, the Near East and South Asia, Latin America, the USSR, Counter-Terrorism, Science and Technology, Economics, General Purpose Forces, Strategic Programs, Warning, Foreign Denial and Intelligence Activities, and Narcotics. The NIO for Warning serves as the focal point for the receipt of all Indications and Warning intelligence and for its evaluation. The responsibilities of the NIO for Foreign Denial were summarized by one former holder of that position:

> The responsibilities for the National Intelligence Officer for Foreign Denial and Intelligence Activities focuses on the question and issue of what are foreign governments doing to deny us the capabilities of collecting certain intelligence, to analyze the degree to which that has been done, to make recommendations as to how that might be alleviated. The intelligence activities aspect of it is related to that, but also includes such items as foreign disinformation programs, what are people doing to make it difficult for us to get at the truth.[50]

Initially, NIOs were purposely not given a staff but were expected to draw on the resources of the CIA, the DIA, the INR, and other analytical units to produce the required estimates. Subsequently, the NIO process was further revised on January 1, 1980, when the National Intelligence Council (NIC) was established, giving the NIOs a collective existence.[51] The NIOs are specifically tasked with

1. becoming knowledgeable of what substantive intelligence questions policymakers want addressed;
2. drawing up the concept papers and terms of references for the NIE;
3. participating in the drafting and draft review of the NIE;
4. chairing coordinating sessions and making judgements on substantive questions in debate; and
5. ensuring that the final text accurately reflect the substantive judgement of the DCI.[52]

In addition to the NIEs, the NIOs are responsible for the SNIEs and the IIMs.

Besides giving the NIOs a collective identity, creation of the NIC also provided the NIOs with a staff—the NIC Analytical Group, providing the Council with control over production resources.[53]

When created, the BNE/ONE was firmly a part of the CIA. Under DCI John McCone the BNE was attached to the DCI's office, responsible to him alone. Under the Carter Administration the NIOs became part of the National Foreign Assessment Center (NFAC) and hence under the direct control of the CIA's Deputy Director for National Foreign Assessment.[54]

As noted earlier, one of the Reagan Administration's earliest actions concerning intelligence was the downgrading of the NFAC to its previous identity: the Directorate of Intelligence. With that change the NIOs were once again placed under the control of the DCI. According to the Director of NFAC at the time, John McMahon, that was a decision that

> the Director and I debated long and hard because at the time that happened I was in charge of national foreign assessments, and I did not want it to happen out of the symmetry of management. The Director wanted to have it because he felt that intelligence was so vital, so important that it should not be left to one person to manage and control. And so by having the NIOs separate and under himself, he could insure that he could get a balanced view coming out of the agency on one hand and the rest of intelligence community and NIOs on the other. And it was just his way of assuring that all alternative views bubble to the top.[55]

Similar to the NIO system is the Defense Intelligence Officer (DIO) system, with DIOs for: European and Soviet Political/Military Affairs, General Purpose Forces and MBFR, Middle East and South Asia, Africa, East Asia and Pacific, Strategic Programs/R & D, Latin America, and Global Affairs. DIOs serve as senior advisers to the Director and Deputy Director of DIA and prepare specialized intelligence reports on issues that cut across the assigned responsibilities of more than one element of the DIA.[56]

In addition to the NIC, several NFIB committees—the Economic Intelligence Committee, the Joint Atomic Energy Intelligence Committee, the Scientific and Technical Intelligence Committee, the Weapons and Space Systems Intelligence Committee, and the Intelligence Producers Council—play a significant role in managing the intelligence production effort.

DCID 3/3, "Production of Atomic Energy Intelligence," governs the responsibilities of the Joint Atomic Energy Intelligence Committee. The Directive, pursuant to NSCID No. 3, notes that atomic energy intelligence is the responsibility of all NFIB committees and further declares that

> the mission of the Joint Atomic Energy Intelligence Committee (JAEIC) shall be to foster, develop and maintain a coordinated community approach to the problems in the field of atomic energy intelligence, to promote interagency liaison and to give imeptus and community support to the efforts of individual agencies.[57]

The JAEIC's specific responsibilities are classified, but certainly must include assessing the adequacy of the U.S. nuclear monitoring program; evaluating the methodology used in estimating the yield of foreign nuclear detonations; assessing major developments in the nuclear weapons development of the nuclear powers; considering the possible impact of atomic power programs on proliferation in countries not yet possessing nuclear weapons; providing national decisionmakers with advice on the possible authorization of U.S. foreign sales in the nuclear energy area; providing warning of a country "going nuclear"; and assessing the regional impact of such an event.

The Weapons and Space Systems Intelligence Committee (WSSIC) was created in 1956 as the Guided Missile Intelligence Committee and subsequently became the Guided Missile and Astronautics Intelligence Committee (GMAIC). According to DCID 3/4, "Production of Guided Missile and Astronautics Intelligence," the Committee's membership consists of representatives of all NFIB agencies plus Army, Navy, and Air Force representatives. Its Chairman is named by the DCI with approval of the NFIB. The CIA was made responsible for providing secretarial support. In addition to coordinating the guided missile and astronautics intelligence activities of the intelligence community, the WSSIC has performed technical studies on Soviet missiles as *inputs* to the NIEs. These papers have been coordinated in the same manner as NIEs but have been directed at informing the intelligence community.[58]

At one time, the functions of the Economic Intelligence Committee were governed by DCID 15/1, "Production and Coordination of Foreign Economic Intelligence." The Directive allocated primary production responsibilities for economic intelligence among the Department of State (INR) and the CIA, the former responsible for economic intelligence for all non-Soviet Bloc countries, the latter with Soviet Bloc economic intelligence. The Economic Intelligence Committee was assigned responsibility for periodic review of the allocations and interpreting the provisions of the Directive in areas of common or overlapping interest.[59]

The present Committee plays a significant role in establishing economic reporting requirements. It also probably plays a similar role in coordinating the production of economic intelligence, especially since the relative importance of such intelligence (relative to military and political intelligence) has increased in recent years.

Management of intelligence production is also partially a function of the requirements documents discussed in Chapter 13, documents such as the National Intelligence Topics.

NOTES TO CHAPTER 18

1. Ronald Reagan, "Executive Order 12356, National Security Information," *Federal Register 47, no. 66* (April 6, 1982): 14874–84 at pp. 14874–75.
2. *Documents from the U.S. Espionage Den (52), U.S.S.R.: The Aggressive East, Section 3-2* (Tehran: Muslim Students Following the Line of the Iman, n.d.), pp. 46–94; Army Regulation 381-47, "U.S. Army Offensive Counterintelligence Operations," May 15, 1982, p. B-1.
3. Philip Agee, *Inside the Company: CIA Diary* (New York: Stonehill, 1975), p. 68; *Documents from the U.S. Espionage Den (52), U.S.S.R.: The Aggressive East, Section 4* (Tehran: Muslim Students Following the Line of the Imnam, n.d.), p. 28.
4. NFIB Security Committee, "Sensitive Compartmented Information: Characteristics and Security Requirements," June 1984, p. 1.

5. Ibid., p. 3.

6. Quoted in David Wise, *The Politics of Lying: Government Deception, Secrecy and Power* (New York: Vintage, 1973), p. 86.

7. Ibid.

8. Ronald Lewin, *The American Magic: Codes, Ciphers and the Defeat of Japan* (New York: Farrar, Straus & Giroux, 1982), p. 17; Anthony Cave-Brown, *The Last Hero* (New York: Times Books, 1982), p. 193.

9. James Bamford, *The Puzzle Palace: A Report on NSA, America's Most Secret Agency* (Boston: Houghton Mifflin, 1982), p. 314; Nigel West, *MI6: British Secret Intelligence Service Operations 1909–1945* (London: Weidenfeld & Nicolson, 1983), p. 163; Cave-Brown, *The Last Hero*, p. 182; David Martin, *Wilderness of Mirrors* (New York: Harper & Row, 1980), p. 15.

10. Bamford, *The Puzzle Palace*, p. 314.

11. F.W. Winterbotham, *The Ultra Secret* (New York: Harper & Row, 1974), pp. 88–89.

12. *Procedures for Handling ULTRA DEXTER Intelligence in the CBI* (Rear Echelon, HQ U.S. Army Forces, China, Burma, India Theater, March 22, 1944) SRH-046, RG 457, Modern Military Branch, U.S. National Archives.

13. Ibid.

14. Wise, *The Politics of Lying*, p. 83; Jack Anderson, "Syrians Strive to Oust Arafat as PLO Chief," *Washington Post*, November 10, 1982, p. D-22; Bob Woodward, "ACDA Aid Faulted on Security," *Washington Post*, November 4, 1986, pp. A1, A16.

15. Bamford, *The Puzzle Palace*, p. 120.

16. Bob Woodward, "Messages of Activists Intercepted," *Washington Post*, October 13, 1975, pp. 1, 14; Seymour Hersh, *The Price of Power: Kissinger in the Nixon White House* (New York: Summit, 1983), p. 183.

17. Woodward, "Messages of Activists Intercepted."

18. Seymour Hersh, *"The Target is Destroyed": What Really Happened to Flight 007 and What America Knew About It* (New York: Random House, 1986), p. 4; Private information.

19. James Ott, "Espionage Trial Highlights CIA Problems," *Aviation Week and Space Technology*, November 27, 1978, pp. 21–22; Gregory A. Fossedal, "U.S. Said to Be Unable to Verify Missile Ban," *Washington Times*, November 18, 1987, p. A6; Dale Van Atta, "The Death of the State Secret," *New Republic*, February 18, 1985, pp. 20–23.

20. William Burrows, *Deep Black: Space Espionage and National Security* (New York: Random House, 1987), p. 23; Bob Woodward, *Veil: The Secret Wars of the CIA 1981–1987* (New York: Simon & Schuster, 1987), pp. 221–24, 402–03.

21. HQ USAF, ACSI, INOI 205-4, "Designation of Special Security Officer (SSO), TK Control Officer (TCO), Gamma Control Officer (GCO), and Bravo Control Officer (BCO)," March 15, 1985, p. 2.

22. Richard Nixon, "Executive Order 11652, Classification and Declassification of National Security Information and Material," *Federal Register 37, no. 48* (March 10, 1972): 5209–18; Jimmy Carter, "Executive Order 12065, National Security Information," *Federal Register 43, no. 128* (July 3, 1978): 28950–61; Reagan, "Executive Order 12356, National Security Information."

23. Reagan, "Executive Order 12356, National Security Information," p. 14876.

24. Ibid., pp. 14877–78.

25. Ibid., p. 14881.

26. DOD Instruction 5230.21, "Protection of Classified National Security Council and Intelligence Information," March 15, 1982; NSDD-84, "Safeguarding National Security Information," March 11, 1983.

27. NSDD-19, "Protection of Classified National Security Council and Intelligence Information," January 12, 1982.

28. Ibid.; William Clark, "Implementation of NSDD-19 on Protection of Classified National Security Council and Intelligence Information," (Washington, D.C.: Office of the Assistant to the President for National Security Affairs, February 2, 1982).

29. U.S. Comptroller General, General Accounting Office, *Information and Personnel Security: Data on Employees Affected by Federal Security Programs* (Washington, D.C.: GAO, 1986), p. 2.

30. NSCID No. 1, "Basic Duties and Responsibilities," February 17, 1972, *Declassification Documents Reference System 1976-167G.*

31. DCID 1/7, "Control of Dissemination of Intelligence Information," May 4, 1981 enclosure to DOD Directive 5230.22, "Control of Dissemination of Intelligence Information, April 1, 1982, pp. 2-3.

32. Ibid., pp. 3-4.

33. Ibid., p. 4.

34. Scott Armstrong, "Israelis Have Spied on U.S. Secret Papers Show," *Washington Post*, February 1, 1982, pp. A1, A18; "Israel Calls Report of CIA Findings Ridiculous," *Washington Post*, February 3, 1982, p. 10.

35. DCID 1/14, "Minimum Personnel Security Standards and Procedures Governing Eligibility for Access to Sensitive Compartmented Information," April 4, 1986, Annex A.

36. Ibid., p. 7.

37. Defense Intelligence Agency, *Physical Security Standards for Sensitive Compartmented Information Facilities* (DIAM 50-3), (Washington, D.C.: DIA, 1980), p. i.

38. Ibid., entire text; Department of Defense Instruction 5230.22, "Control of Dissemination of Intelligence Information"; Defense Intelligence Agency Regulation 50-10, "Control of Dissemination of Foreign Intelligence," May 11, 1977.

39. DCID 1/4, "Intelligence Information Handling Committee," May 18, 1976; DCID 3/14, "Intelligence Information Handling Committee," May 14, 1982, updated January 1987.

40. NSCID No. 1, "Basic Duties and Responsibilities."

41. NSCID No. 3, "Coordination of Intelligence Production," February 17, 1972, *Declassified Documents Reference System 1976-253E.*

42. DCID 3/1, "Standard Operating Procedures for Departmental Participation in the Production and Coordination of National Intelligence," July 8, 1948.

43. DCID 3/2, "Policy Governing Departmental Concurrences in National Intelligence Reports and Estimates," September 13, 1948.

44. DCID 3/5, "Production of National Intelligence Estimates," September 1, 1953.

45. Lawrence Freedman, *U.S. Intelligence and the Soviet Strategic Threat* (Princeton, N.J.: Princeton University Press, 1986), p. 31

46. Ibid.

47. DCID 3/1, "Standard Operating Procedures for Departmental Participation in the Production and Coordination of National Intelligence."

48. Freedman, *U.S. Intelligence and the Soviet Strategic Threat*, p. 54.

49. Ibid.

50. Private information; Transcript of the trial of Samuel L. Morrison, U.S. District Court, Baltimore, October 8–16, 1985, p. 1025.

51. U.S. Congress, House Select Committee on Intelligence, *U.S. Intelligence Agencies and Activities: Fiscal Costs and Procedures, Part I* (Washington, D.C.: U.S. Government Printing Office, 1975), p. 389; U.S. Congress, House Committee on Foreign Affairs, *The Role of Intelligence in the Foreign Policy Process* (Washington D.C.: U.S. Government Printing Office, 1980), p. 135.

52. U.S. Congress, House Committee on Foreign Affairs, *The Role of Intelligence in the Foreign Policy Process*, p. 230.

53. Ibid., p. 73.

54. Freedman, *U.S. Intelligence and the Soviet Strategic Threat*, p. 31.

55. U.S. Congress, Senate Select Committee on Intelligence, *Nomination of John N. McMahon* (Washington D.C.: U.S. Government Printing Office, 1982), pp. 48–49.

56. DIA, *Organization, Mission and Key Personnel* (Washington D.C.: DIA, September 1986), p. 31.

57. DCID 3/4, "Production of Atomic Energy Intelligence," April 23, 1965, *Declassified Documents Reference System 1980-131G.*

58. DCID 3/4, "Production of Guided Missile and Astronautics Intelligence," April 23, 1965, *Declassified Documents Reference System 1980-132A;* Prados, *The Soviet Estimate*, p. 202.

59. DCID 15/1, "Production and Coordination of Foreign Economic Intelligence," September 14, 1954, *Declassified Documents Reference System 1980-129E.*

19 ISSUES

During the mid-1970s, the U.S. intelligence community was placed under prolonged scrutiny by both Senate and House investigating committees. Both committees concerned themselves with more than simple questions of improper activity and went further than a mere historical replay of events. Since that time there have been numerous changes within the intelligence community and on the international scene, but most of the issues raised then remain today.

Among the issues of present relevance are the role and powers of the Director of Central Intelligence, the organization of the intelligence community, the priorities for collection and analysis, covert action, secrecy, and oversight.

THE ROLE OF THE DCI

From its very creation, the role of the DCI has been a subject of controversy, being seen as a threat to the power and independence of the other intelligence agencies. In addition, the desire of Secretaries of Defense and military chiefs to be able to direct "their" intelligence assets has placed the DCI up against formidable opposition in exerting control over the intelligence community.

When he took office in 1951, DCI Walter Bedell Smith was viewed, by the heads of other intelligence agencies who served on the Intelligence Advisory Committee, as acting at their direction. One of Smith's innovations was to put the IAC in an advisory rather than supervisory role.

Smith's action was only a small first step in exerting control over the community, since the DCI still had no control over the assets of the other intelligence agencies. Smith was succeeded by Allen Dulles, brother of Secretary of State John Foster

Dulles, in 1953. Dulles, despite his long tenure as DCI (1953–61) and unique level of influence, did little to enhance the powers of the DCI, despite repeated urgings by Presidential consultants.

Thus, it was not surprising that in 1956, three years after Dulles's appointment as DCI, the President's Board of Consultants on Foreign Intelligence Activities (PBCFIA) stated:

> Despite his title, the Director of Central Intelligence neither by law, directive nor otherwise, is the central director of the total intelligence effort of the government. Actually, his control of intelligence *operations* is restricted to those of the Central Intelligence Agency. On the other hand, he does have a broad responsibility for the correlation, evaluation and dissemination of intelligence related to national security.
>
> But the dominant responsibility for the production of "Departmental" intelligence ("subject to refinement through a continuous process of coordination by the Director of Central Intelligence") rests with the head of each of the separate Departments and Agencies represented in the Intelligence Community. In our judgement this arrangement, with its division of responsibility and despite the elaborate intelligence committee coordinating mechanism which exists, is not any longer adequate. Wherever their Department needs are judged by them to be paramount the separate elements of the Intelligence Community are inclined to operate independently. This has resulted in an undue amount of built-in duplication in our national intelligence effort. It has also generated competition and frictions, some long standing, which have impeded the real integration of intelligence activities.[1]

One means the PBCFIA suggested of enhancing the DCI's control was the creation of a Chief of Staff or Executive Director to relieve Dulles of his management responsibilities. By 1958 the recommendation had been made several times to the President and DCI without Dulles accepting the recommendation. Thus, President Eisenhower noted on December 16, 1958, "that there had already transpired considerable discussion but said he would talk to him once again."[2]

The issue still persisted near the end of Eisenhower's term in office when it finally became clear that Dulles would not accept such a recommendation. Thus, in a conference with members of the PBCFIA, the President noted the

> recommendation that the Board had made once concerning an Administrative Deputy to Mr. Allen Dulles. He said it became clear that he would have to make a choice either to keep Mr. Dulles without such a deputy or relieve him in order to carry out the reorganization. He thought that Mr. Dulles's value was such that he should not take the latter course.[3]

Dulles quite possibly missed a unique opportunity to gain the DCI a more central role in the intelligence process. This failure has been noted by a former PBCFIA head, James Killian. In his memoirs, Killian wrote:

> I do feel that Eisenhower failed to recognize the administrative inadequacies of Allen Dulles. ...At least he failed to take remedial measures...I several times questioned Dulles' administrative competence, while recognizing his charismatic, even legendary, gifts as an intelligence expert. Each time Eisenhower responded by asking me: "Whom

could I get as a replacement whose competence would approach that of Dulles as an intelligence officer?" I now think the Board was at fault in accepting Eisenhower's answer without explaining insistently our concern about Dulles's handling of his broader responsibilities. Some of the fissure that later showed up in the CIA might well have resulted from loose administration.[4]

Advances in the administration of the community that did occur during Dulles's tenure tended to stem from the PBCFIA. The 1958 merger of the IAC and the U.S. Communications Intelligence Board (USCIB) into the U.S. Intelligence Board (USIB), giving the DCI greater control over the SIGINT activities of the armed services, was the result of the PBCFIA's recommendations.[5]

It was not until Dulles's successor, John McCone, became DCI that significant management reforms were attempted. Both the Kennedy Administration's desire for greater central organization and coordination of national security activities (particularly after the Bay of Pigs fiasco), and McCone's personal attitudes toward the role of DCI contributed to those attempted reforms.

On January 16, 1962, President Kennedy sent a letter to McCone defining his role as DCI. It read in part:

> In carrying out your newly-assigned duties as DCI, it is my wish that you serve as the government's principal foreign intelligence officer, and as such that you undertake as part of your responsibility, the coordination and effective guidance of the total U.S. foreign intelligence effort. As the government's principal intelligence officer, you will assure proper coordination, correlation and evaluation of intelligence from all sources and its prompt dissemination to me and to other recipients as appropriate. In fulfillment of these tasks, I shall expect you to work closely with the heads of all departments and agencies having responsibilities in the foreign intelligence field.[6]

Further, with the Dulles experience in mind, the letter went on to say:

> As head of the CIA, while you will continue to have overall responsibility for the Agency, I shall expect you to delegate to your principal deputy, as may deem necessary, as much of the direction of the detailed operation of the Agency as may be required to permit you to carry out your primary task as DCI.[7]

Even with the support of Kennedy's letter, McCone could only make a marginal dent in the established situation, for nothing in the letter required the military intelligence units to treat McCone as their director. Thus, institutions established by McCone, such as the National Intelligence Program Evaluation (NIPE) Staff, had only a small impact in rationalizing the national intelligence effort.

The years subsequent to McCone's tenure saw further efforts to enhance the role of the Director; such efforts were often consummated only on paper. Under Richard Helms the National Intelligence Resources Board was established, followed in 1971 by the Nixon-mandated National Security Council Intelligence Commitee (NSCIC) and the Intelligence Resources Advisory Committee (IRAC)—the latter to advise in the allocation and use of intelligence resources and the formulation of the DCI's recommendation on the NFIP.[8]

However, the NSCIC had only a single meeting and Helms was more inclined to rubber-stamp requests rather than risk conflicts. Thus, in 1969, he noted that although the "DCI is theoretically responsible for 100 percent of the nation's intelligence activities, he in fact controlled less than 15 percent of the community's assets and most of the other 85 percent belonged to the Secretary of Defense and the Joint Chiefs of Staff."[9]

Subsequent to Helms's dismissal in 1973, both of his successors, James Schlesinger and William Colby, began management reforms. However, neither held office long enough to make a significant impact. President Carter's DCI, Stansfield Turner, sought day-to-day as well as budgetary control of the National Reconnaissance Office and National Security Agency. This was an essential part of a program to give the DCI and his staff the power to fully direct the activities of the entire intelligence community.

Turner argued that economic and other non-military information might be more important to the President and national decisionmaking than is tactical military intelligence. Turner was opposed by Secretary of Defense Harold Brown, who argued that without control of the NSA and the NRO the military would not be able to properly advise the President on military matters.[10]

Turner attained only a portion of his goals. When President Carter signed Presidential Directive-17, he assigned Turner responsibility for approving the budgets (but not daily control) of the NRO and the NSA. In addition, Turner established a National Intelligence Tasking Center (NITC), headed by a Deputy to the DCI and responsible for tasking the entire intelligence community. Offices under the NITC included those for photo, signals intelligence, and human source tasking. The objective was two-fold: (1) to provide stronger direction than was coming, in Turner's eyes, from NFIB collection committees such as the COMIREX and the SIGINT committee; and (2) to create an organization that could rationalize the overall assignment of different collection systems to the entire target set. In 1970, James Schlesinger had noted the failure of any mechanism for making trade-offs between different collection techniques.[11]

The NITC's fate during the Carter Administration was an example of a major paper reform that resulted in only a marginal actual change. Actual activities were still directed by the DOD and the individual service components, which largely ignored the NITC, as did the CIA's Directorate of Operations. At the beginning of the Reagan Administration, the NITC was disestablished with no formal successor created.

The underlying issues that made the powers of the DCI a subject of contention at the beginning and end of the Carter Administration still exist. Satellite and other forms of technical collection are valuable methods for both strategic and tactical intelligence consumers and thus create competing demands. Thus, Marchetti and Marks note that "an American commander in Germany may desire data on the enemy forces that would oppose his troops if hostilities broke out, but the day-to-day movements of Soviet troops along the East German border are of little interest to high officials back in Washington."[12]

This problem, known in the community as the "national-tactical interface," is likely to become an even more acute problem. As U.S. real-time imagery and SIGINT capabilities have increased with the development of systems such as the KH-11 and a variety of real-time SIGINT systems, tactical users, such as theater commanders, can see a greater value to a constant flow of intelligence data reporting on the movements of opposing forces. The establishment of a variety of programs and installations—the Tactical Exploitation of National Space Capabilities (TENCAP), the National Intelligence Systems to Support Tactical Requirements (NISSTR), the Defense Reconnaissance Support Program (DRSP), the Joint Tactical Fusion Program, Fleet Imagery Support Terminals, and the Tactical Fusion Center at Boerfink—to provide and receive such data is a reflection of this value. As real-time capabilities expand and programs grow, tactical users will be in greater competition with strategic and non-military users than ever before—a competition that will manifest itself in regard to both tasking and the nature of new technical collection systems.

A related issue of importance is the ability of the DCI to establish collection and analysis priorities. This overlaps in part with the issue of allocating and developing collection assets for national versus tactical purposes. But within the national intelligence category there are many choices to be made as a variety of different types of intelligence fall in that category—military, political, economic, scientific, and even sociological. The choice of collection and analysis can have a significant impact on how senior decisionmakers will deal with a variety of situations—whether they will have the background knowledge necessary to deal with a crisis situation (military or political) or whether they initiate policies that bring about positive changes in different areas of the world.

Two additional subsidiary issues concern the NSA and the control of information. The NSA's power to act independently of the DCI—not simply in regard to the micro-management of the SIGINT effort, but in distributing the product of that effort after it has been "analyzed" by NSA but not by the agencies with formal analysis functions—manifested itself most clearly in the Carter Administration. In view of some, including former DCI Turner, it was premature release of NSA analysis of SIGINT data that precipitated the Cuban brigade crisis in 1979. Turner argues that the DCI needs sufficient authority to curb such NSA independence—an independence he argues stems from the NSA's subordination to the Secretary of Defense.[13]

Control of information in the area of intelligence can appear to be all-important to an organization, for it is the intelligence they provide that determines their stature and power. In addition, organizations often come to feel that only *they* can properly protect information they have developed through their sensitive sources, whether human or technical. On the other hand, some would contend that the DCI must be able to determine how intelligence information should be distributed based on the establishment of analysis priorities.

ORGANIZATION AND STRUCTURE

The immense size of the U.S. intelligence community may make it seem like a Rube Goldberg device and cause observers to wonder if there is any method in the apparent madness. Over the years there have been numerous suggestions for reorganization of various parts of the community. Suggestions have included creating a Director of National Intelligence separate from the head of the CIA with an office in the White House; separating the analytical and clandestine operations sides of the CIA; creating a separate covert action agency; establishing a central collection agency (to handle both technical and human collection); abolition of the military service intelligence units and the transferring of their functions to the DIA.[14]

The notion of separating the head of the intelligence community from direct control of the CIA has been advocated by numerous observers and professional intelligence officers. It was also included as a provision of the National Intelligence Act of 1980. Its advocates see such a separation as a means of placing the head of intelligence closer to the President (both physically and personally), of allowing the Director of National Intelligence to focus on the major intelligence issues, and inducing the heads of intelligence agencies other than the CIA to view the Director of National Intelligence as an impartial arbiter of intelligence decisions.

However, for a variety of reasons, such a step would probably be a setback for centralized direction of the intelligence community. The likely outcome of a separation of the role of head of intelligence from the CIA would be a Director of National Intelligence with far less actual power than the present DCI—for the result would be a Director with no resources trying to establish control over the CIA, the NSA, and the DIA—all of which would have far more resources and influence than the Director. It was acknowledged by the 1975 Murphy Commission that

> to function as the President's intelligence adviser, it is essential that the DCI have immediate access to and control over the CIA facilities necessary to assemble, evaluate and reach conclusions about intelligence in all functional fields including political, economic, military and scientific subjects.[15]

It is of some significance that during the Cuban missile crisis DCI John McCone abandoned use of his Washington office to remain at the Langley headquarters.

The President's intelligence director also needs to have significant control over the development of technical collection systems and the other aspects of CIA activities (counterintelligence, HUMINT, covert action). In addition, separation of the DCI from the CIA will also retard the flow of information through the intelligence community—adding the Director of the CIA to the head of the NSA and the DNI as guardians of "their" information. Finally, by creating a position of Director of National Intelligence, the position of Director of the CIA will be sharply lowered in prestige and further exacerbate rivalries among the CIA, the DIA, and the NSA as each fights to place itself at the top of the intelligence hierarchy.

A related issue is the structure of the CIA. From the previous remarks it follows that any significant change in the structure of the CIA would be counterproductive, since it would weaken the power of the DCI.

Proposals to strengthen the DIA by eliminating the military service intelligence units have been based in part on the argument that the existence of the service intelligence units inhibits the DIA from fulfilling its intended role—to eliminate the parochial interests of military services from dictating the content of intelligence analysis. In addition, it is argued that career advancement pressures dictate that the best analysts stay in the military services rather than work in the DIA.[16]

Some drawbacks of such a proposal can be easily imagined. As an OSD study team noted, such a proposal may not be politically feasible. One can imagine an intense and unified opposition by the JCS to an attempt to strip the military services of their intelligence capabilities. The study team also suggested that such a course would produce few efficiencies and many problems.[17] Among the problems would presumably be the need to disestablish units at several locations and consolidate all personnel under the DIA. Second, there is some rationale for having intelligence units responsive to those who most need the information. Thus, while there is reason to fear that letting the Navy estimate Soviet naval capabilities will bias the estimate, it is also understandable that a Chief of Naval Operations with responsibility for managing the U.S. naval effort and recommending naval policies would want to have some control over intelligence production concerning naval affairs. Further, DIA does have some present control over the S & T intelligence centers of the military services that do the bulk of the services intelligence analysis. The DIA tasks and validates the work of the FTD, the FSTC, the MSIC, and the NISC.

A more moderate proposal is that of the OSD study team—that the DIA should retain its present mission with added authority and resources. This would allow the DIA to more closely control the work of the S & T intelligence centers. Additionally, some further rationalization of intelligence functions within the military services might be reasonable. The Army has taken a step in this direction by removing control of the major intelligence analysis—FSTC, MSIC—units from non-intelligence commands and placing them under the authority of the Army Intelligence Agency, a field operating agency of the Deputy Chief of Staff for Intelligence. In the Navy and Air Force, past attempts to establish operating agencies subordinate to the offices of the DNI and the ACSI respectively seem to have produced more command echelons than necessary. Thus, some consideration should be given to a merger between the Office of Naval Intelligence and the Naval Intelligence Command and the Air Force Assistant Chief of Staff, Intelligence and the Air Force Intelligence Agency.

Finally, consideration should be given to the disestablishment of the NRO and creation of a Reconnaissance Support Activity, subordinate to the Air Force Space Command to handle day-to-day support functions—launches, turning satellites on and off, turning them away from the sun, issuing new instructions for targeting purposes. Such an action would give the DCI, through the CIA, relatively complete control of the satellite reconnaissance research and development effort, which, given the CIA's dominant role in developing advanced systems such as the KH-8, KH-9, KH-11, RHYOLITE and others, would not be likely to damage U.S. capabilities in the future. It would also sharply decrease the undue influence of the Air Force and military in satellite reconnaissance decisions.

PRIORITIES

One of the most important issues that faces the U.S. intelligence community and its supervisors is the question of priorities. Despite the huge investment in technical collection systems, worldwide human sources, and elaborate exchange arrangements, the United States cannot begin to collect complete information on all aspects of world affairs of relevance to national decisionmakers. In addition, limitations on processing and analytical capabilities means that only part of the information collected can be analyzed.

Decisions on priorities can be of immense importance in determining future policy. Failure to collect in-depth information on a subject can mean an inadequate understanding of a particular problem or area of the world, or an inability to deal with crises or combat situations when they arise.

A basic decision that has to be made is the extent to which information primarily relevant to war fighting (conventional or nuclear) is to be collected. Some would argue that such information is the key to deterrence and that identifying and tracking "relocatable targets" (i.e., mobile ICBMs and mobile command posts) must be an extremely high priority for U.S. intelligence.[18]

Others, including the author, would argue that war with the Soviet Union is extraordinarily unlikely, partially because the probable costs of a conflict are too large to risk. Rather, it could be argued that the primary objective of U.S. intelligence collection and analysis should be to permit the United States to conduct policies aimed at further reducing tensions with the Soviet Union and encouraging further liberalization within the Soviet Bloc; to understand the internal situations in a variety of non-European nations (including Brazil, Mexico, the Phillipines, Argentina, Indonesia, and others) so as to be able to encourage the development (or further development) of prosperous democratic societies; and to determine the likely course of international economic events on the United States and to assess the threat to the United States from such problems as drugs, terrorism, and nuclear proliferation.[19]

Thus, in the case of the Soviet Bloc, prime questions for collection and analysis would include internal opposition to Gorbachev, implications of economic and other events for the stability of Gorbachev's rule, the ethnic situation in the Soviet republics, the impact of the "yellowing" of the Soviet armed forces on military policy (as opposed to simply how to exploit the "yellowing" in wartime), and developments in Eastern Europe.

COVERT ACTION

One of the most contentious issues in the area of intelligence activities has been U.S. use of covert action to advance U.S. foreign policy goals. This issue is of particular importance given the covert action operations undertaken during the Reagan Administration and the apparent success of the Afghanistan operation. The questions concerning covert action are both practical and ethical.

Several U.S. presidents have proclaimed the right of the United States to conduct a variety of covert actions. President Ford argued that such activities are acceptable international conduct, defending U.S. funding of political parties in Italy as well as destabilization activities in Chile—even offering the comment that the Chilean people were better off as a result. More recently, President Reagan said he believed in "the right of a country when it believes its interests are best served to conduct covert activity."[20]

An absolutist position against covert action would hold that no such action was permissible, since it represents a violation of national sovereignty. However, "respecting" national sovereignty could imply taking no action while one group in a foreign nation proceeds to oppress and murder another. Thus,

> it can be argued that there are occasions, or there may be occasions, when political action of a clandestine nature may be the only feasible way to produce a desirable circumstance beneficial not only to the instigating country, but to a larger portion of the world's peoples. One can imagine, for example, such operations, mounted in South Africa, that might have positive consequences throughout the southern part of the continent.[21]

Many would also argue that U.S. covert actions in democratic societies such as Italy and France—in the form of aid to political parties and individuals—helped to establish relatively stable democratic societies free of Communist control, and that such future interventions should not automatically be ruled out. Others would argue that unless the possible election outcome will result in a direct physical threat to U.S. territory or installations, the United States should let democracy take its course.

While one can create many theoretical scenarios in which U.S. covert action is appropriate, the reality is less encouraging. Covert action, particularly when it involves paramilitary operations and support of attempts to unseat a government, cannot be fine-tuned—both because it can be difficult or impossible to control completely the actions of those the U.S. chooses to support, and because of the dynamics of conflict (affected by the actions of those the U.S. is trying to unseat).

The history of U.S. covert action is replete with examples of operations which have produced disastrous results for the people of the targeted country. Subsequent to the U.S.-inspired overthrow of the Guatemalan government of Jacobo Arbenz in 1954, Guatemala has been subjected to over thirty years of brutal right-wing dictators, complete with death squads. (Included was one ruler who referred to Jimmy Carter as "Jimmy Castro.") Similarly, the installation of the Shah of Iran both brought the repression of the Shah and helped set the stage for the madness of the Khomeini regime. In Chile, U.S. covert action certainly contributed to the replacement of the democratically elected regime of Salvador Allende with the brutality of Augusto Pinochet. While U.S. decisionmakers may have preferred different outcomes—democratic regimes firmly tied to the U.S. and free enterprise—these were not the outcomes that resulted.

On the secondary issue (which is usually considered the primary issue)—whether U.S. interests were enhanced—it can be argued that in the long-term such operations tend to damage U.S. standing. Certainly, the long-term outcome in Iran has cost the United States that nation as an ally and created a foe that does not hesitate to attack U.S. vessels and undertake terrorist attacks. It is a result that may well be repeated elsewhere.

Further, the nature of the groups supported by the United States leaves much to be desired. If any other President than Ronald Reagan were to refer to the groups supported by the United States as "freedom fighters" one would assume it was simply a cynical ploy that the President believed was required to gain support for his policies. In Ronald Reagan's case, he may actually believe his rhetoric.

But the reality is that while these groups may seek to overthrow leftist governments or attain independence from the Soviet Union, their commitment to a society that respects individual rights is questionable. Thus, in 1984, the Council on Hemispheric Affairs labeled the contras one of the "worst human rights violators" in Central America and noted that over 880 non-combatants had been killed by the contras after capture and hundreds more died as a result of contra attacks, with a grand total of 5,000 Nicaraguans having died as a result of Contra activities. According to the Council "the contras have killed, tortured, raped, mutilated and abducted hundreds of civilians they suspect of sympathizing with the Sandinistas."[22] In 1987 the contras were still kidnapping young men to augment volunteers. In February 1988, a contra fighter apparently hurled a hand grenade at a Sandinista street march, killing nine Nicaraguans and injuring thirty-two while another nineteen, including five children, were killed in a neighboring town when uniformed men believed to be contras blasted a civilian passenger bus with a rifle.[23]

Among the Afghan resistance groups, the four most powerful groups are those who want to establish an "Islamic State." The leader of one of those parties, Gulbuddin Hekmatyar, has expressed his approval of a society in which Islamic punishments—corporal punishment, amputation of limbs and the stoning of women—are commonplace. The more moderate elements have charged that the fundamentalists would introduce religious zealotry, the total isolation of women from education and public life, and an economy based on the limitations specified in the Koran.[24]

SECRECY

The U.S. intelligence community is the most open intelligence community in the world. Aside from the large amount of information the Freedom of Information Act mandates that it release in response to requests—information that in many other nations is classified—the community also voluntarily releases more information than those of other nations. Indeed, many democratic societies, such as Britain, Norway, Sweden, and Israel, maintain almost total silence concerning intelligence activities and the organizations that conduct them.

However, the openness of the U.S. intelligence community is relative, because absolute secrecy concerning intelligence operations has been so uncritically accepted in many countries.

Clearly, intelligence operations require secrecy in a variety of respects. Generally speaking, secrecy is mandatory when revelation of a piece of information would allow a target of intelligence collection to take countermeasures to deny the U.S. information or give that target the ability to conduct effective deception operations. From that general proscription it follows that one can enumerate some areas where secrecy is required:

- the identities of human sources
- aspects of tradecraft that would allow hostile security services to identify and track human sources
- foreign security failures that allow intelligence penetrations
- knowledge of penetrations by hostile intelligence services
- beyond state-of-the-art aspects of technical collection systems.

Unfortunately, rather than restricting secrecy to areas where it is imperative, the intelligence community has, either by design or inadvertence, sought to protect legitimate secrets with a buffer of trivial secrets. This logic was exemplified in 1972 when Secretary of Defense Elliot Richardson opposed revealing the budgets of the intelligence agencies because "then pressure will rise to provide an ever more detailed breakdown."[25]

Thus, basic documents such as the NSCIDs were released only in the midst of the Church Committee hearings. No information is available on those issued after 1972, or even whether the 1972 NSCIDs are still in effect—although clearly the content of many of the NSCIDs is rather mundane. Likewise, while keeping in mind that many of the DCIDs are available, the content of DCID 6/1 shown in Chapter 17 indicates that there are probably many classified DCIDs that could be made public with absolutely no damage to U.S. intelligence operations.

The most pervasive area of secrecy concerns technical collection systems, particularly satellite systems. Beyond President Carter's acknowledgement of photo reconnaissance satellites, the United States provides no information on its space reconnaissance program—unless forced to by trial requirements. Nor does it even acknowledge the existence of the National Reconnaissance Office.

The original motivation for the secrecy of the NRO and the entire satellite reconnaissance program was plausible, although disputed by some. In the face of the Soviets' destruction of the U-2 and threats to shoot down space reconnaissance systems anything the United States could do to avoid embarrassing the Soviets would increase the chances that U.S. systems would be allowed to operate unmolested.

But by 1963, the Soviets had accepted the principle of space reconnaissance and ceased their diplomatic campaigns against the U.S. program. Twenty-five years later the rationale no longer exists.

In the area of signals intelligence operations from space, one could argue that up until the mid-1970s there were grounds for maintaining strict secrecy concerning the space COMINT program—specifically, that the Soviet Union was unaware of this capability and therefore not protecting communications and signals in the heart of the Soviet Union, such as at the ABM test center at Sary Shagan, which could not be intercepted by external monitoring stations. But with the sale of information about RHYOLITE to the KGB and the further public exposure of the program, the basic secret is out—COMINT operations from space are feasible. As a result, the strong case for not even acknowledging such operations no longer exists.

Of course, in the case of both photographic and signals intelligence satellites, there are clearly aspects of present operations which justify secrecy. With regard to imagery satellites, exotic, beyond the state-of-the-art, means of producing imagery, might justifiably be kept secret. In the case of SIGINT satellites the ability to pick up low-powered signals would be one area of legitimate secrecy. In the case of both satellites the vulnerabilities to attack and protective measures would be legitimate secrets.

It has been argued by Richard Lehman, former head of the National Intelligence Council, that:

> ... in 1947 the tradition of secrecy that the creators of CIA sought to maintain was primarily that of espionage. A break meant the loss of an agent or a net ... the existence of the agent and the system that supports him must be totally concealed if he is to survive; the "fact of" is a crucial consideration. Technical systems, however, usually cannot be and therefore need not be concealed; only the degree of success must in all cases be kept secret ... it has become apparent that the requirements for security for human and technical collection are radically different.[26]

A third area where more information needs to be made available is with respect to the estimates and reports produced by the intelligence community. While it is clear from Chapter 13 that a great deal of information can be accumulated concerning these reports and estimates, information is lacking to allow truly informed debate on the priorities being devoted to different areas. What is needed is statistical information about the distribution of effort in each year—in number of staff hours devoted to different areas of study, as well as the number of reports produced concerning different nations or subjects.

In addition, budgetary data broken down by agency should be made available, as recommended by a Special Senate Committee in 1973.[27]

Forty years after the creation of the CIA it is time to make intelligence policy and activities part of the national security debate. A failure to do so could ultimately be disasterous. As Richard Lehman wrote:

the elite accepted the tradition of total secrecy characteristic of other national systems, notably the British, as appropriate for an American system . . .

In hindsight, this appears to have been a mistake, because it prevented the education of the public and all but a few Congressmen in the realities of intelligence, and because it protected intelligence itself from the oversight that could have required a greater sensitivity to public interests.[28]

OVERSIGHT

Since the establishment of the Church and Pike Committees in the mid-1970s to investigate a variety of charges concerning U.S. intelligence activities, the relationship between the intelligence community and Congressional oversight committees has become much less adversarial.

This relationship received several jolts during the tenure of William Casey—most notably as a result of the CIA mining of Nicaraguan harbors and the belief of Committee members that they had not been adequately informed. It is likely however, that with the advent of a new administration the relationship will resume a more placid course.

The Committees have been able to influence a variety of intelligence activities. Objections from the Committees have killed some proposed covert action programs—an economic destabilization program targeted on Grenada in 1981, and a plan to overthrow the leader of Suriname in 1983.[29]

The Committees have also played a major role in monitoring the development of technical collection systems. In early 1988 they pushed for a $6 to 12 billion commitment to the production of sufficient LACROSSE satellites to permit adequate verification of INF and START treaties.[30]

The Committees have also investigated questions concerning the adequacy of intelligence analysis, counterintelligence, and intelligence legislation. The Senate Intelligence Committee was instrumental in getting the DCI to develop a forty-page national intelligence strategy that spells out intelligence community priorities and strategy for a ten-year period.[31]

There is one area where there has been a clear failure by the Committees—they have done little to provide the public with a coherent view of U.S. intelligence activities. While over the course of their existence they have issued a significant number of reports, these reports represent only small looks into selected subjects. The Committees have been willing partners with the intelligence community in perpetuating the unnecessary secrecy that covers much U.S. intelligence activity. Thus, on such an important issue as the verification of the INF, the Committees judgements as to what is required and how much it costs has been expressed to the President and not to the public.

Rather than acting as if they were simply executive branch review committees, the Committees should seek to force the intelligence community to declassify the many aspects of its operations that can reasonably be made public. In addition it should prepare a yearly report to the public on all aspects of U.S. intelligence activity—providing the maximum reasonable degree of information as well as its judgements about strengths and weaknesses of the community.

NOTES TO CHAPTER 19

1. Letter from the President's Board of Consultants on Foreign Intelligence Activities to the President, December 20, 1956, *Declassified Documents Reference System 1978-204C.*
2. John Eisenhower, "Memorandum of Conference with the President, December 16, 1958," December 22, 1958, *Declassified Documents Reference System 1981-621B.*
3. A.J. Goodpaster, "Memorandum of Conference with the President," February 2, 1960, February 5, 1960, *Declassified Documents Reference System 1981-622B.*
4. James B. Killian, Jr., *Sputniks, Scientists, and Eisenhower: A Memoir of the First Special Assistant to the President for Science and Technology* (Cambridge, Mass.: MIT Press, 1982), p. 222.
5. U.S. Congress, Senate Select Committee to Study Governmental Operations with Respect to Intelligence Activities, *Final Report, Book IV: Supplementary Detailed Staff Reports on Foreign and Military Intelligence* (Washington, D.C.: U.S. Government Printing Office, 1976), pp. 62–63.
6. Ibid., p. 73.
7. Ibid.
8. U.S. Congress, House Select Committee on Intelligence, *U.S. Intelligence Agencies and Activities, Part 1* (Washington, D.C.: U.S. Government Printing Office, 1976), p. 114.
9. Victor Marchetti and John Marks, *The CIA and the Cult of Intelligence* (New York: Knopf, 1974), p. 99.
10. Joseph Fromm, "Inside Story of the Battle to Control Spying," *U.S. News and World Report*, August 8, 1977, p. 27.
11. Central Intelligence Agency, *CIA Fact Book* (Washington, D.C.: CIA, 1978), upaginated; author's interview; James Schlesinger, *A Review of the Intelligence Community* (Washington, D.C.: Office of Management and Budget, 1970), p. 10.
12. Marchetti and Marks, *The CIA and the Cult of Intelligence*, p. 87.
13. Stansfield Turner, "Foreword," to David D. Newsom, *The Soviet Brigade in Cuba: A Study in Political Diplomacy* (Bloomington, In.: Indiana University Press, 1987).
14. J. Patrick Coyne, Memorandum for the President, Subj: Reorganization of Intelligence and Covert Activities, July 14, 1961, *Declassified Documents Reference System 1981-623B*; Peter Szanton and Graham Allison, "Intelligence: Seizing the Opportunity," *Foreign Policy* (Spring 1976): 183–214; Allen E. Goodman, "Reforming U.S. Intelligence," *Foreign Policy* (Summer 1987): 121–36; Allen E. Goodman, "Dateline Langley: Fixing the Intelligence Mess," *Foreign Policy* (Winter 1984–85): 160–79; Stansfield Turner, "The Pentagon's Intelligence Mess," *Washington Post*, January 12, 1986, pp. D1, D2.
15. Commission on the Organization of the Government for the Conduct of Foreign Policy, *Report*, (Washington, D.C.: U.S. Government Printing Office, 1975), p. 98.
16. Turner, "The Pentagon's Intelligence Mess."

17. OSD Study Team, *Reassessment of Defense Agencies and DoD Field Activities*, (Washington, D.C.: Department of Defense, October 1987), p. D-4.

18. Edgar Uslamer, "Moving Targets," *Air Force Magazine*, May 1987, pp. 24–29.

19. See Stansfield Turner, *Secrecy and Democracy: The CIA in Transition* (Boston: Houghton Mifflin, 1985), pp. 272–73.

20. Tom Wicker, "A Policy of Hypocrisy," *New York Times*, October 21, 1983, p. A35.

21. E. Drexel Godfrey, Jr., "Ethics and Intelligence," *Foreign Affairs* 56 (1978): 624–42.

22. "Nicaraguan Contras Hit on Human-Rights Faults," *Washington Post*, December 30, 1984, p. A21.

23. Julia Preston, "28 Deaths, Mostly Civilians Are Said Laid to Contras in Nicaragua: Neighbor Northern Towns Jolted by Explosions," *Washington Post*, February 10, 1988, pp. A1, A30, A31.

24. Henry Kamm, "Afghan Rebel Faction Leader Vows War Beyond Any Pact," *New York Times*, March 19, 1988, p. 14; Henry Kamm, "Afghan Rebels Discord Widens as Pullout Nears," *New York Times*, March 9, 1988.

25. U.S. Congress, Senate Committee on Appropriations, *Department of Defense Appropriations for Fiscal Year 1973, Part 1* (Washington, D.C.: U.S. Government Printing Office, 1972), p. 619.

26. Richard Lehman, Memorandum for [deleted], July 9, 1975.

27. Special Senate Committee on Secret and Confidential Documents, *Report 93-466* (Washington, D.C.: U.S. Government Printing Office, 1973), p. 16.

28. Lehman, Memorandum to [deleted].

29. Patrick E. Tyler, "U.S. Tracks Cuba Aid to Grenada," *Washington Post*, February 27, 1983, pp. 1, 11; "The CIA vs. the Colonel," *Newsweek*, June 13, 1983, p. 31.

30. Susan F. Rasky, "Senators Balking Over Verification," *New York Times*, April 29, 1988, p. A7.

31. "The Senator vs. the Spooks," *Time*, March 3, 1988, pp. 18–19.

INDEX

access to intelligence information and, 420, 421, 432
analysis and estimates and, 291, 433, 435, 436, 437, 445
collection of intelligence and, 444–445
covert action and, 375, 407, 409
exchange and liaison agreements and, 276–277
intelligence community and role of, 377–379, 441–444, 453
management of intelligence activities by, 388, 395–396, 397, 399, 403, 404, 405–406, 433, 446, 448
National Reconnaissance Office (NRO) and, 385, 448
"national-tactical interface" issue and, 444–445
orders and directives and, 367–368, 369–370
organization of, 379–384
Director of Central Intelligence Directives (DCIDs), 369–371, 381, 399, 400, 401–402, 405, 406, 407, 419, 421–432, 433–434, 437, 451
Discovery space shuttle, 173
Disinformation, and covert actions, 3
Dissemination of intelligence, 4
DOD Directives, 371–372, 419
Domestic political activities
Central Intelligence Agency (CIA) and, 12–13, 369, 407
Federal Bureau of Investigation (FBI) and, 137
intelligence and, 7, 234
Double agent operations, 328–330
Dozier, James, 64
Drug Enforcement Administration (DEA), 9, 135–136, 137, 168, 305
Duarte, Jose Napolean, 343, 344
Dulles, Allen, 337, 441–442, 443

Eastern Europe, 240–241, 334, 339, 403, 448
East Germany, 237–238, 404
EA-3B aircraft, 201, 204
EC series aircraft, 179, 404

Economic activities, and intelligence, 168, 234
Economic Alert List (EAL), 383
Economic intelligence, 7, 8–9, 368, 432, 437
Economic Intelligence Committee, 383, 436, 437
Economic operations, and covert actions, 3
Economic policy, and utility of intelligence, 4
Ecuador, 347
Egypt, 9, 168, 241, 277, 340, 345, 346
Eisenhower Administration, 6, 27, 35, 157, 190, 334, 338, 403, 419, 442, 443
Elections, and covert action, 344
Electromagnetic Pulse System (EMP), 221, 222
Electronic Intelligence (ELINT), 167, 168–169, 251
airborne collection in, 176, 177, 178, 180, 186
Atlantic Command and, 107
encipherment system for, 171–172
European Defense Analysis Center (EUDAC) and, 110
frequencies used in, 170–171
management of, 398, 399
method of transmission of, 170
National Security Agency (NSA) and, 22–23, 25
ocean surveillance and, 203, 204, 205
Pacific Command and, 101
submarines and, 190
targets of, 169
Electronic Order of Battle, 110
Electronic Warfare Reprogrammable Library Program, Navy, 107
Electronic Security Command (ESC), Air Force, 76, 82–83, 183, 184, 185, 186, 358, 373
Ellsberg, Daniel, 323
El Salvador, 168, 179, 188, 189, 241, 343–344, 346, 347
Embassies, 134
covert listening posts at, 187–188
Federal Bureau of Investigation (FBI) representation at, 136–137

ABOUT THE AUTHOR

Jeffrey T. Richelson is an author and consultant. He received his M.A. and Ph.D. in political science from the University of Rochester in 1974 and 1975, respectively. He has taught at the University of Texas, Austin and at The American University. He was also a senior fellow at the Center for International and Strategic Affairs, UCLA.

Richelson's publications are in the areas of intelligence, defense, policy, and social choice theory. His articles have appeared in the *Review of Economic Studies*, *Journal of Economic Theory*, *Political Science Quarterly*, *Journal of Strategic Studies*, and *Journal of Conflict Resolution*. He is also the author of *Foreign Intelligence Organizations* (Ballinger, 1988), *Sword and Shield: The Soviet Intelligence and Security Apparatus* (Ballinger, 1985), and *The Soviet Target* (Morrow, 1987).

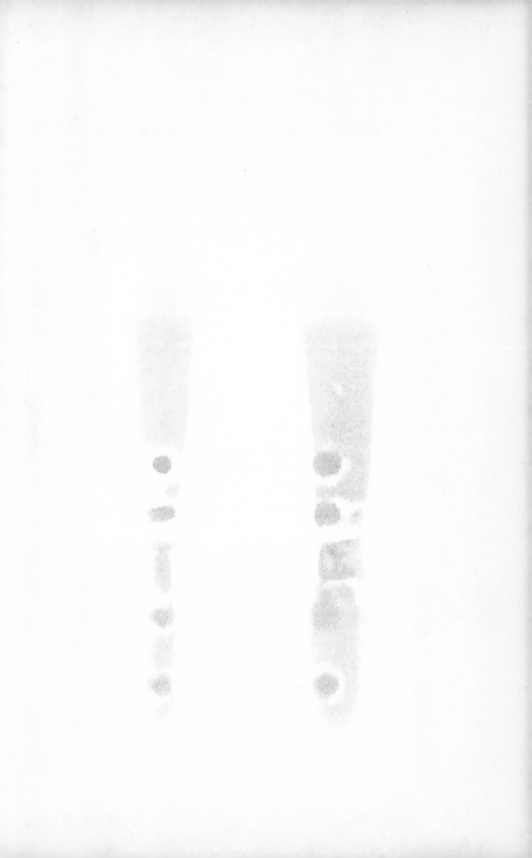

DATE DUE